Freemasonry
in the
Province of Somerset
From 1733

Edited by
Martin Yates

Photography by Paul Mallon

The Provincial Grand Lodge of Somerset

The Provincial Grand Lodge of Somerset
Church Street
Wedmore
Somerset
BS28 4AB

Tel: 01934 713115
e-mail: pglsomerset@btconnect.com
www.pglsomerset.org.uk

First Published in Great Britain in 2010 by The Provincial Grand Lodge of Somerset

A catalogue record of this book is available from the British Library
ISBN: 978-0-9565484-0-5

Printed in Great Britain by Butler Tanner & Dennis, Frome, Somerset

Contents

His Royal Highness The Duke of Kent KG
The Most Worshipful Grand Master
United Grand Lodge of England

I congratulate the Province of Somerset on the production of this historical review in celebration of 275 years of Freemasonry in the county. It forms a fitting tribute to the many thousands of Brethren who have served the Craft and the Province of Somerset with distinction and pride for nearly three centuries.

There is much to interest all Freemasons, their families and friends within its pages. These contain the historical development of Provincial Masonry, richly illustrated by pictorial coverage of Lodges and their treasures.

I wish the Province continued good fortune and prosperity.

HRH The Duke of Kent, KG
Grand Master

Right Worshipful Brother David Lloyd Jenkins

Foreword

The celebration of the 275th Anniversary of the Royal Cumberland Lodge, Bath, held in 2008 triggered the thought that led to the production of this book. The two extant books recording historical events in the Province of Somerset were written in the 20th century: History of the Provincial Grand Lodge of Somerset by W.Bro Wilfred Fisher in 1962, and Freemasonry in the Province of Somerset 1735-1987 by W.Bro Ron Walker GM in 1988. Both were narrative based format and lacked the pictorial element necessary to bring the rich diversity of Masonic Buildings, Lodges and their treasures to life. Technology has moved so fast in the past two decades, thus enabling this book to give us a colourful insight into our rich heritage through the wonders of modern photographic technology.

While 1733 was the officially recorded start of organised Masonry in the County, the book will show that meetings took place in Bath before that time. It is not a history, per se, but rather a record of known development and activity which led to the creation of 88 Lodges meeting in 27 centres and with some 4000 members. The intention in producing this book was to create a good reference document that would enable Masons and non-Masons alike who browse through it to get a feel for the rich Masonic life it captures. It will not answer every question but will hopefully leave the reader with a much enhanced knowledge of Freemasonry in Somerset and, for those who have not had the opportunity to visit many Masonic Halls, a real appreciation of what they represent and the joy they have provided for the Lodges that meet in them.

None of this would have been possible without the sheer dedication and immense amount of work put in by the Editor, W.Bro Martin Yates, supported by a splendid team. W.Bro Malcolm Shearer's knowledge of Masonic artefacts and his enquiring mind have helped in 'digging out' many rare and interesting treasures from around the Province, and some that Lodges didn't know they possessed. W.Bro Paul Mallon's superb photography has provided a tapestry of colour, form and depth of magical proportions, and the late Bro Keith Gardner's initial preparatory work created a good foundation upon which to build this superb tome. W.Bro Stuart Hadler, W.Bro Pat Morrisey, W.Bro Charles Cornish and Bro Malcolm Toogood have provided input in many other ways, and to them all go our thanks for a job well done.

I hope everyone who has the pleasure of thumbing the pages of this book, Mason and non-Mason alike, will appreciate the historical relevance of Freemasonry in the life of Somerset. The characters that formed what we now have and enjoy, the history of Lodges, and the beauty of rare artefacts that have provided such pleasure for their owners over nearly three hundred years will, I hope, reflect the importance of the Craft and the joy and inspiration it has provide for countless thousands of like-minded men.

David Jenkins
Provincial Grand Master
May 2010

Acknowledgements

from the Editor W.Bro Martin Yates

The basic historical research for this work was carried out by W.Bro Wilfred Fisher, Past Grand Standard Bearer of England, whose resulting paper was published by the Provincial Grand Lodge of Somerset in 1962. Bearing in mind the paucity of easily available material it was a magnificent effort, and indeed formed the basis of W.Bro Ronald Walker's update in 1988 who added the passing of a further quarter of a century. Now, after another twenty years, a team formed by the Provincial Grand Master has not only produced an historical review of Freemasonry in Somerset, but one which looks at the present and indeed at the future of this Antient Brotherhood.

The Team consisted of the PGM as Chairman, myself as Project Manager and Editor, Bro Keith Gardner, a retired historian, author and publisher, W.Bro Malcolm Shearer, knowledgeable in Masonic antiques and artefacts, and W.Bro Pat Morissey, Editor of the Compass Magazine.

In January 2008 the project was dealt a bitter blow with the sudden death of Bro Keith. His great knowledge, ability, guidance, his '*joie de vivre*' and perhaps, most of all, his friendship, were irreplaceable; the project faltered for a while. The content of the early sections of this book are almost entirely based on his work.

As source material was assembled, it became clear that we needed to have greater consistency in the quality of the photography, and the Team welcomed on board W.Bro Paul Mallon who, amongst his many other talents, is a professional photographer. Many readers will have seen him scrambling around every Masonic Hall in the Province taking the wonderful photographs that adorn the pages of this book.

Approaching the publication phase a huge amount of work was put in by W.Bro Stuart Hadler and Bro Malcolm Toogood, both of whom were instrumental in getting this book to the printers, and finally into your hands.

For all their incredibly hard work, support and encouragement, I thank everyone on the Team.

In addition, I would like to thank the Secretaries of all of the Lodges and the Managers of the Province's Masonic Halls for their assistance. Likewise the Librarian of the Somerset Local Studies Library, Mr David Bromwich, and the staff of the Somerset Records Office. Last, but by no means least, I thank the Rulers of the Other Masonic Orders for their help and contributions to the text.

The Lodge histories have, in the main, been written by members of those Lodges. They are far too numerous to mention individually, but their contributions have been invaluable. It is the eclectic style of these contributions which adds to the uniqueness of this book and hopefully to the enjoyment gained from its reading.

Finally, my heartfelt thanks go to my family. To my son Rick who sat up until all hours teaching me how to convert the manuscript and images into the publishing format, and to my lovely and long suffering wife Di, without whose unfailing patience and understanding over more than three years and who, incidentally, retyped most of this book, I would have failed miserably.

I promise I will not do it again!

Martin Yates

Part One

INTRODUCTION

What is Freemasonry?

A Brief Introduction

Modern Freemasonry has been described as an organized system of morality, based on a belief in a supreme entity, yet forbidding any doctrinal or political differences. It is therefore a society that seeks to encourage its members to act according to the 'Golden Rule' which runs through virtually all the great religions; it is the summary statement of basic requirement for all human behaviour.

The Christian principle 'Do unto others what you would have them do unto you' (Matthew 7:12) is by no means the unique property of the Bible. 'What is hateful to you do not do unto others' is a main Jewish principle. This is paralleled by Muhammad 'None of you is a believer until you love for your neighbour what you love for yourself'. The Mahabharata teaches Hindus 'This is the sum of all duty – do nothing to others which, if it were done to you, would cause you pain.' The Buddha phrases it 'Do not hurt others with that which hurts yourself' and Confucius really did say 'What you do not want done unto you, do not do unto others'.

Thus in reality one can sit in Lodge and break bread with all; the Catholic with the Protestant, the Muslim with the Jew, the Sikh with the Hindu. But these principles are not only to be applied to one's Brethren in Lodge but to the wide world at large. We seek to benefit society wherever we can.

Charity therefore is high on the Agenda; education for the young, sheltered homes for the aged, treatment for the sick, help for the destitute. Masonic Charities exist for all these good purposes, but not only for Masons alone. Cancer and Heart research, Hospices, Lifeboats, Air Ambulances, earthquake disasters, wherever funding is needed Freemasonry is there; our purse is not bottomless but our funds are constantly augmented from every Lodge meeting and social event in the country.

The organization of Freemasonry is widely spread throughout the world. In particular, but by no means exclusively, it is to be found in the old Empire, or to be more politically correct, the English-speaking world. It was on a Masonic 'Volume of the Sacred Law' that the first President of the United States took his oath; it was in full regalia that he laid the cornerstone of the Capitol in Washington DC.

W.Bro General George Washington;
President of the United States of America
Reproduced by kind permission of
United Grand Lodge of England

In these days of Nuclear Physics and walking on the Moon, we tend to disregard the imagination, skills, and indeed the social esteem, of those men who designed the great Abbeys, and the impregnable Castles, of our Medieval Churchmen and Kings. Theirs was a long and noble tradition emanating from the construction of the great Acropolis, the massive Temples at Luxor and indeed the Temple of Solomon at Jerusalem. These craftsmen and designers followed wherever work might take them, they were of varying skills, from apprentices, through working craftsmen to master masons. Indeed a medieval Pope is said to have sent Italian masons far and wide across Europe to spread and teach their skills.

Their proof of position in the great order of things was not entrusted to fragile parchment bonds but to signs, tokens and words. By these indestructible symbols would they be known to strangers seeking to employ these skills. Not only do we find their work in great Castles and Abbeys but of course in any English country Parish Church. In the yards of today's Cathedrals you will still find masons working quietly away, preparing replacement stones for the restoration of time ravaged gargoyles and sheelagh-na-gigs. In many remote corners of our Cathedrals may be found the tracing floors on which the master templates were inscribed for the craftsmen to work from, and in Somerset we are fortunate to have a surviving example in that most beautiful Church of the Cathedra Episcopi at Wells.

The admiration in which Royalty, Bishops and the gentry at large held the Craft was probably the reason behind the eventual establishment of 'the Craft' as a non-operative but 'speculative' vehicle for the instruction and practice of high moral virtues.

As to origins, there are what are referred to as "The Old Charges"; medieval documents laying down rules, the earliest dating from the late 14th and early 15th centuries. These may well have been applicable to Operative Masons only. In 1583, however, there appeared a manuscript known as Grand Lodge No. 1, and this possibly marks the beginning of Speculative Masonry. Certainly the diaries of Elias Ashmole, after whom the famous Oxford Museum, the Ashmolean, was named, bear references to his attending such Lodges in 1646 and 1682.

Elias Ashmole
Portrait after John Riley reproduced by kind permission of
The National Portrait Gallery, London

Initially these lodges would have been few and far between, but as London has always been the centre of all things both novel and elite it appears that with Freemasonry too it flourished in the great metropolis. As numbers of Lodges and Masons increased it became apparent that some overseeing body was required to set and supervise standards. Thus Grand Lodge was established in 1717 with one Anthony Sayer as Grand Master. Sadly, well within the decade, dissent and defiance were in the air. A second Grand Lodge was formed in London and another short-lived one at York.

By the mid-18th century one appeared dedicated to the rituals of "the Old Institutions", which was regarded by the "Premier" Grand Lodge as an "Insult on our Grand Master." The Ancient Lodges were ordered to be erased and their members refused admission to 'regular' Lodges. The Antients reciprocated with similar edicts. For many decades this internecine squabble progressed, with brotherly love being replaced by fraternal bitterness until eventually two blood-brothers became Grand Masters of each, the Dukes of Kent, (Antients) and Sussex (Moderns), Kent the father and Sussex the uncle of Queen Victoria.

They were able to bring together the warring factions and under their control the Act of Union came into effect in 1813, with the Duke of Kent bowing out in favour of his brother as Grand Master. Thus the United Grand Lodge of England came into being, and eventually under it the Provinces and indeed the Districts developed into the world encompassing system that they are today. This did not spring up overnight however, the administration in the days of the quill rather than of the computer must have made things very slow if not difficult, particularly in the days before the 'Penny Black'

For administrative convenience, much of English speaking Freemasonry is still headed by the United Grand Lodge of England, based in London. Scotland and Ireland have their own Grand Lodges but within England and Wales Provincial Grand Lodges operate on a County basis, with one or more lodges in each town. Interchange relationships exist with other Grand Lodges across the world, and although this book relates to the history of male Freemasonry, the ladies too have their own Orders around the globe.

Excerpt from The London Calendar 1729
showing the City of Bath Lodge No. 28
Reproduced by kind permission of
United Grand Lodge of England

Freemasonry and the Learned Societies

The Hidden Mysteries of Nature & Science

The emergence of speculative or allegorical Masonry as opposed to Operative Masonry should really be viewed against the historic background of the period.

The Renaissance was understood as a historical age in Europe which followed the Middle Ages, and preceded the Reformation, spanning roughly the 14th through to the 16th century. The Renaissance saw the development of the Arts, including Architecture, and such names as Raphael, Michaelangelo and Leonardo da Vinci are prominent. Much work was of Religious subjects, the Ceiling of the Sistine Chapel for example. It was a period driven by Religious divides, and by the associated development of Science, which was often regarded as being Anti-Christ, whilst Alchemy was the temptation of the Devil! These were the days of the 'Da Vinci Code'!

It should be remembered that Da Vinci, (1452-1519) famous for his paintings, 'The Adoration of the Magi', 'the Mona Lisa' etc, was also an engineer and a scientist. He had the foresight to design futuristic engines of war, flying machines, submarines and even tanks. Long after Da Vinci was dead, Galileo (1564-1642) was lucky to escape being burned at the stake for heresy, for daring to tell the Pope that the earth was not flat but spherical and that it went around the sun rather than being the centre of the Universe. He died the year after the first known Speculative Mason was initiated in England

In the beginning of the Speculative Fraternity under the Grand Lodge system, Freemasons avowed their devotion to the Sciences boldly, for early Freemasons were responsible for the foundation of many of our Learned Societies,

and indeed vice versa. The post Civil War period saw the dawning of the 'Age of Enlightenment'. The 'hidden mysteries of nature and science' were to be explored.

The Royal Society 1660

The first of the great learned societies was the 'Royal Society of London for Improving Natural Knowledge', founded in 1660. It was, in the British public's mind synonymous with Science, and for more than a century it, and its offshoots, were the only exponents and practitioners of Science in Britain. It began in 1660 and took its first organized form at a meeting of scholars in Gresham College who had assembled to hear a lecture by the King's Architect W.Bro. Sir

W.Bro Sir Christopher Wren
Reproduced by kind permission of
United Grand Lodge of England

Christopher Wren, Master of Original Lodge No. 1 (now Lodge of Antiquity No 2), both an Operative and a Speculative Mason.

W.Bro Sir Robert Moray was elected the first President of the Royal Society, on March 6th, 1661. He had been made a Freemason at Newcastle-on-Tyne twenty years before on May 20th, 1641, the first known initiate into the Craft of Freemasonry on English soil.

"At Neucastell the 20th day off May, 1641. The quilk day ane serten number off Mesters and others being lafule conveined, doeth admit Mr the Rt. Hon. Robert Moray, General Quarter Master to the Armie of Scotland, and the same being aproven be the hell Mester off the Mesone of the Log off Edenroth, quherto they heave set to ther handes or markes. A. Hamilton, R. Moray, Johne Mylln. James Hamilton"

Elias Ashmole, another great intellectual of the age, after whom the Ashmolean Museum in Oxford is named, is often presented as the first English Speculative Freemason as he refers in his Diaries to being initiated in his father's Lodge (Warrington Lancs) in 1646 and visiting in 1682, but Moray is the first recorded Installation. Ashmole too, was an antiquarian and a Fellow of the Royal Society.

M.W.Bro Dr. Jean Theophilus Desaguliers LL.D., FRS, became secretary of the Royal Society for a long period of years, and was also the "father of the Grand Lodge System." He was born in Rochelle, France, the son of a Huguenot clergyman, and a protestant refugee in England. He was educated at Christ Church, Oxford and his reputation as a lecturer on experimental philosophy obtained for him his Fellowship in the Royal Society. Desaguliers was one of Sir Isaac Newton's closest friends. Sir Isaac (1642-1727), a genius in mathematics and physics, was one of the foremost scientific intellects of all time. There are now several lodges named after him, including one in Somerset.

Elected the third Grand Master of England in 1719, Desaguliers was a zealous collector of early Masonic manuscripts. Although attributed to Dr. James Anderson, the General Regulations found in the first edition of the Constitutions were compiled under his supervision. He it was who brought a number of scientists to Bath to best witness an eclipse of the Sun and stayed to Initiate Beau Nash and others. This association of the Royal Society with the City of Bath Lodge No. 28 continued, with no less than six Fellows becoming Members of the Lodge by 1725

A Masonic Lodge, largely composed of Royal Society members, met in a room belonging to the Royal Society Club in London. At a time when Priests preached against these scientists, newspapers thundered against them, street crowds hooted at them, and neither Oxford nor Cambridge would admit Science courses, Masonic Lodges invited Royal Society members in to give lectures, many of which were accompanied by scientific 'demonstrations'.

W.Bro Rev. Dr. William Stukeley FRS FSA
Reproduced by kind permission of
United Grand Lodge of England

The Antiquaries 1707

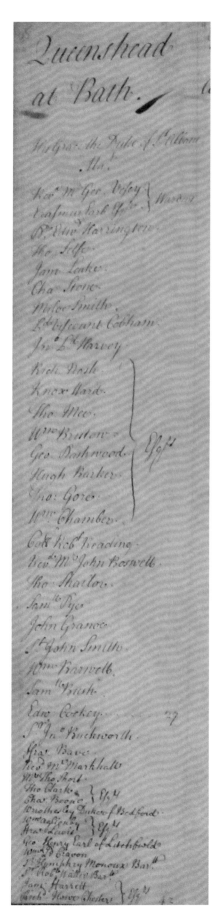

1707 saw the inauguration of the oldest of the 'Courtyard Societies', the 'Society of Antiquaries of London', into which Fellows are still elected by black-ball ballot and admitted under a quasi-Masonic ceremony. A number of Masonic Fellows of the Royal Society were involved in its official foundation.

The first minutes of the Society record that, on Friday, 5th December 1707, a meeting was held at the Bear Tavern in the Strand. The following January the Society agreed to meet in the Young Devil Tavern. The first President was W.Bro Peter Le Neve, Norroy King of Arms, and it was agreed that the business of the Society should be the subject of antiquities, particularly as they related to the history of Great Britain. The period of study was that which pre-dated the reign of James I.

The Society encountered a few problems before it became firmly established, the bankruptcy of the owner of the Young Devil being one, as well as matters of a more complex political, Jacobite nature. However, from 1717 the Society was established in the Mitre Tavern, Fleet Street, and there is a continuous series of minutes from then until the present day. The minute books of the Ordinary Meetings are still composed in manuscript. W.Bro. Rev. Dr. William Stukeley FRS, initiated at the Salutation Tavern Lodge, in Tavistock St., on 6th January 1721, was the first Secretary of the Antiquaries and ostensibly, the 'father of British Archaeology'

Other early Masonic Antiquarians included Bro. The Duke of Montague FSA, Grand Master, Bro. Henry Hare FSA Grand Master and Martin Folkes FSA Deputy GM.

In the 19th century the 4th Earl of Carnarvon, Pro Grand Master of England, was also Provincial Grand Master for Somerset and President of the Antiquaries.

Left: The 1725 Return of Members of the Queens Head Lodge at Bath.
Six members of the Royal Society were also members of the Lodge at various times. They were: Charles Beauclerk, 1st Duke of St Albans (Master), John Russell, 4th Duke of Bedford, Dr Edward Harrington, William Bristow, Joseph Andrews and William Beckett.
Reproduced by kind permission of United Grand Lodge of England

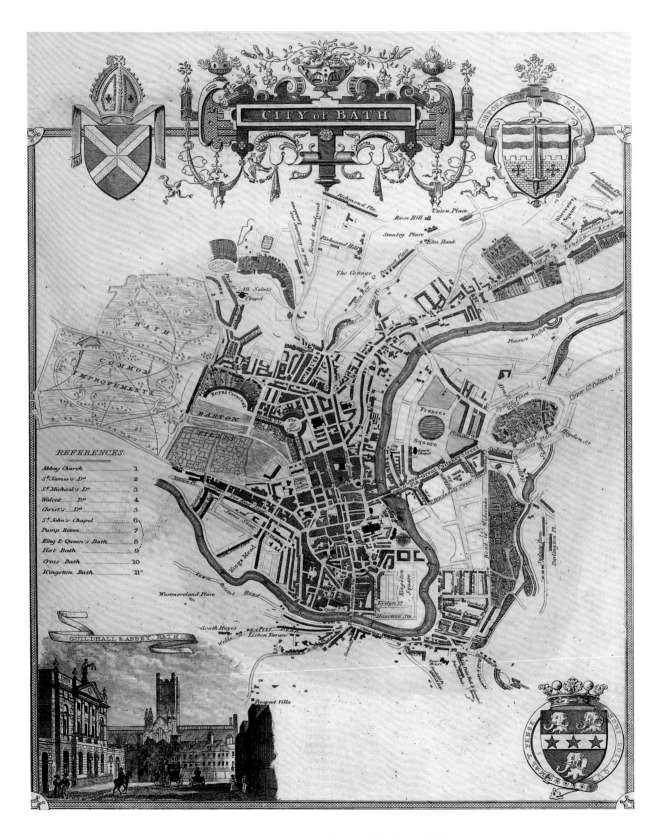

Thomas Moule's "The City of Bath." 1837
Reproduced by kind permission of Bath in Time/Bath Central Library Collection

Freemasonry in Somerset 1725-1768

Setting the Scene

Although Ashmole's diaries indicate that there were speculative Masonic Lodges in the mid-17th century, it would seem likely that Freemasonry was not brought to Somerset until the early 18th century. It is most likely to have been introduced by some of the many visitors to Bath from London who came to the Spa for the season.

The first record of a Lodge meeting in Somerset is a list of members of a Lodge which met at the Queen's Head, Bath, shown as Lodge No. 28 on the Grand Lodge list of 1725. Although this was erased in 1736 it can be considered as probably the first Lodge in the Provinces constituted by the new Grand Lodge, all the previous ones having been in London.

Richard 'Beau' Nash 1674-1762.
Welsh Dandy, sometime Scholar, Lawyer, Gambler and Impresario of fashionable Bath. Received into Freemasonry at the Queens Head, Bath 11th May 1724
Reproduced by kind permission of
Bath in Time/Bath Central Library Collection

Details of this Lodge are somewhat scanty but the Duke of St Albans, a son of Charles II, was stated to be Master with a number of other titled persons on the list of members, including the Duke of Bedford, Viscount Cobham, the Earl of Lichfield, Earl Craven, Earl Darnley, Lord Hervey, Sir Humphrey Morroux Bt. and Sir Robert Walker Bt. The list also included the Mayor of Bath, Miloe Smith, the City's Master of Ceremonies Richard 'Beau' Nash, professional men such as Knox Ward, later to become Clarenceaux King of Arms, Dr Edward Harrington, plus leading and tradesmen such as James Leake, the owner of the City's main Reading Room and Library.

This is not the only example of members of all social classes meeting together in Masonic Lodges at that time, which it must be remembered was only 40 years after the Battle of Sedgemoor with all that implied for the West Country, and also twenty years before the second Jacobite rebellion.

The Lodge, although not erased until 1736, is likely to have ceased regular activity not long after the Duke's death in 1726, having probably only met when called by him during his periodic visits to Bath Spa. Masonry did not, however, die in Bath with the end of the first Lodge, as another had started in late 1732 at the Bear Inn, although a Deputation was not issued until May 1733. This Lodge contained no ennobled Brethren, but from the list of members seemed to consist of professional men and tradesmen with a firmer and more permanent local attachment.

The Lodge at the Bear merged in 1786 with a newly formed Bath Lodge, and the united Lodge is still in existence as the Royal Cumberland Lodge No. 41.

One of the more intriguing minutes of the Bear Lodge refers to a meeting held on the 28th October 1735 when certain brethren were made 'Scots Master Masons'. There is unfortunately no further information about this, and it may refer to a ceremony introduced by a visitor to Bath or possibly to the holding of a Royal Arch Chapter.

In 'Le Parfait Macon', a French exposure of 1744, there is a reference to ECOSSAIS (Scots) Masons who claimed that they were concerned with rebuilding Solomon's Temple and forming the fourth grade.

At this time membership of the Royal Arch was restricted to those brethren who had 'passed the chair', the procedure for which is amplified in the minutes of the Lodge of Perpetual Friendship, Bridgwater, which had been founded in 1757.

It is recorded that the actual Master resigned and closed the Lodge after the candidate(s) for passing the chair had been elected. The newly elected Master then opened and closed the Lodge and paid a fee of a bottle of wine to the regular Master, and one shilling to the Tyler. The former Master was then re-elected and returned to the chair.

The first Masonic record, in Lodge minutes, of a Somerset Lodge being visited by a Grand Master (or rather a former Grand Master) was when Dr J.T. Desaguliers, a French philosopher, presided as Master of the Lodge which met at the Bear Inn, Bath, on the 28th September 1737.

However, a report in a London newspaper in May 1724 stated that Dr Desaguliers was to receive into Masonry Viscount Cobham, Lord Hervey, Richard Nash and others, on the 11th May 1724 at the Queen's Head in Bath. There are no minutes to confirm this, but the names mentioned are among those appearing as members of the Lodge, on the list submitted to Grand Lodge in November 1725.

Dr John Theophilus Desaguliers
Reproduced by kind permission of
United Grand Lodge of England

Dr Desaguliers was a frequent visitor to Bath, and as he was an enthusiastic propagator of Masonry it is probable that he had paid previous visits to the Lodge prior to 1737.

A further Somerset Lodge was formed on 12th December 1737, this being the Lodge at 'Shipton' Mallet (sic) which met at the Angel Inn. It did not have a very long life and was erased in 1768, although it had really ceased to exist long before, as had the Angel Inn itself. Very little is known about this Lodge or why Shepton Mallet should have been the second town in Somerset to have a Lodge. Shepton Mallet lies only twenty miles from Bath, but in those times twenty miles was a considerable journey.

It is, however, possible that because of the extensive woollen and knit stockings industry which flourished in Shepton Mallet during the 18th Century, there were close business associations with the tailors of Bath, who catered

The 1733 Deputation of the Bear Inn Lodge, Bath

Other early Somerset Lodges which formed the basis of the Provincial Grand Lodge included that formed in Bridgwater in 1757 at the Swan Inn (this was subsequently called the Lodge of Perpetual Friendship), one in Bath in 1758 which for a time was called the Lodge of Perfect Friendship but in 1817 was renamed the Royal York Lodge of Perfect Friendship, and a third at the Fountain Inn, Taunton, in 1764. The minutes of this latter Lodge, St. George's, which was erased in 1783, provide confirmation that, whilst it was the custom for Antients' Lodges to appoint Deacons. The Moderns' Lodges called St George's was in the habit of appointing a Master's Steward and a Warden's Steward each St John's Day.

It would seem reasonable that these three lodges, together with the original which met at the Bear Inn, Bath, were the four that formed the Province of Somerset when the first Provincial Grand Master, John Smith of Combe Hay near Bath, was appointed in 1768. He continued in office until his death in 1775, after which the position seems to have remained vacant until 1784, when the ubiquitous Thomas Dunckerley added Somerset to his belt.

for the sartorial tastes of their fashionable customers when visiting the town from London. Whether or not the Lodge did originate because of business connections cannot now be determined, but like many lodges in those days it did not last long.

Re-enactment of 18th century ceremony

The Province of Somerset from 1768

A Short Summary

As one might have gathered from the foregoing pages, the names chosen by lodges; "Unanimity & Sincerity", "Peace and Harmony" and so forth, were moral targets which seemed beyond the reach of the squabbling Grand Lodges of the 18th century. Even into the 19th century, after the Act of Union, matters still left something to be desired

The first Provincial Grand Master for Somerset was a 'Modern', John Smith MP for Bath, but after his death no attempt appears to have been made by Grand Lodge to replace him and the Provincial 'Throne' lay vacant for three years. Some years later, Gloucestershire got themselves into trouble for protesting about the same apparent lack of activity. Eventually the ubiquitous Thomas Dunckerley added Somerset to his string of Provinces and on his demise Col. John Smith-Leigh, the son of the MP and first PGM, succeeded him, conveniently dying in 1813, the year which saw the Union of the warring Grand Lodges.

Another four years were to pass before, in 1817, Grand Lodge appointed Arthur Chichester to the Chair of a Province that saw 'the science of Masonry wrecked, forlorn and forsaken'. His answer, to put the Province on an even keel, was to raise funds by mandatory fees, punitive fines for absence and by charging lodges for Provincial regalia. This was, to say the least, a series of unpopular proposals, and the enthusiasm with which his appointment was greeted turned so sour that he resigned after three years, in 1820. The state of Masonry in Somerset was now perilous, and Grand Lodge were not slow, for once, in appointing Col. Charles Kemeys Kemeys Tynte, MP for Bridgwater, to the Chair.

His was a great stabilizing factor and although he had to fight off scurrilous and untrue accusations before Grand Lodge, he served the Province well for 40 years. On his death the Province proposed to Grand Lodge that the 4th Earl of Carnarvon be appointed in his stead. The plea was ignored and for four years the Province was effectively overseen by the Grand Registrar. Following this Col. Alexander William Adair occupied the Chair from 1864 until his resignation in 1868. He was respected as PGM but resigned due to pressure of his military duties.

It was at this stage that the Earl of Carnarvon, a peer of the realm and a high-ranking Grand Lodge officer, began his twenty year rule. He became Pro-Grand Master under The Prince of Wales, and was scrupulously conscientious in his duties to this Province. It may probably be said that it was he who really laid the firm foundation and standards on which the Province rests today. He was followed by Viscount Dungarvan, heir to the Irish peer the Earl of Cork & Orrery, who held estates in Somerset. His appointment by Grand Lodge caused some concern, as he had not held any rank in Somerset and joined Unanimity & Sincerity 261 before he was eventually Installed as PGM. On his inheriting the Earldom he sold his Somerset estates, and retired to Ireland as Earl of Cork.

The next in line had no such problem, in fact he was the only Deputy PGM ever to ascend to the Chair of the Province. The much respected, and indeed loved, Col William Long was born in Bath, retired from the Indian Army and became a member of the Lodge of Agriculture in Yatton. He was followed by the Venerable Archdeacon Walter Farrer; 'humility and kindliness', and 'dignified and revered' were used to sum him up , he ran the Province as a kind Christian soul.

Back to the Army for the next two successive PGMs who were both retired Brigadiers, Norman and Cazenove. Each had distinguished public careers, were well regarded, and Masonry flourished under them with no particular problems. Col Harry Owen Hughes came out of the east, the mystic east, as Past District Grand Master of Hong Kong & South China. He settled at Compton Dundon and after some years of retirement, ascended to the Provincial Chair. He was however the last of the 'men of rank', if one can say that without being discourteous to his successors. He was a Colonial Colonel, and when he said 'jump' the only question was 'how high?'

Since 1768 all Provincial Grand Masters for Somerset had been Landed Gentry, Peers of the Realm, high-ranking Army Officers and one, just one, a Venerable servant of the Church. With less than 40 Lodges, without telephones and the combustion engine in many cases, with High offices to attend to, MPs, ADC, Army careers etc, the Province saw little and required

less of their leader than is the case today. Times however were changing and Freemasonry had to change too.

As the Province grew in numbers of Lodges so too did the Provincial Team. Initially the Provincial Grand Master was aided in the administration by a Deputy, a Secretary and a Treasurer, as well as those officers who worked the Ritual when the Province actually met as a Lodge. It was not until 1950 that the role of Assistant PGM was established and only when the Province numbered 80 Lodges was a second Assistant added to the list. The minute books of Provincial Grand Lodge show little other than polite records written to a formula, once a year. Decision-making was the autocratic prerogative of the PGM and his Deputy. There was a distinct 'them & us' atmosphere abroad.

On Hughes' retirement the Colonial Colonel was replaced by an ironmonger. Somerset businessman, Kenneth Caswell Kinnersley was from Midsomer Norton. Ironically he looked every inch the Colonel but where there was steel in the eye of Harry Owen Hughes there was a genial twinkle in Kenneth Kinnersley's. His was perhaps a half-way house in the necessary modernisation of attitude. He and his team still ruled in the old ways but they were at least approachable.

Grand Lodge was becoming aware that twenty years in office for a PGM was perhaps counter-productive, and at least was not compatible with the fast changing standards of society. They set age limits and time limits and in 1991 Kenneth Kinnersley retired. His replacement was a Somerset farmer, Stanley Hopkins, a Past Asst. PGM from the mid 1980s, who in fact had retired from office and was in Australia. He was as surprised as the rest of the Province to receive the summons, but it transpired that some wise head somewhere had seen the necessary traits in his personality that were needed. He dragged Somerset into the 20th century, before the 21st was upon it. He shared his reign with an Executive, he was a leader the rank and file could identify with, and his impact upon the Province was as effective as it was necessary.

R.W.Bro David Lloyd Jenkins was one of the two Assistant PGMs, and in April 2002 he succeeded to the Provincial Chair. The other, J.

Peter Layzell became Deputy PGM and together they carried on the good work for which Stanley Hopkins had prepared the ground.

We have today, we like to think, a Province whose attitudes are not anachronistic, that is compatible with the 21st century, and which has a long and doubtless interesting future.

The Pilgrim's Porch at Wells Cathedral recently restored with the support of Somerset Freemasons.
Insets, the Provincial Emblems engraved into the Threshold Stone

Freemasonry and Charity

*Chevalier Ruspini, one of the founders of the first school
leading the pupils into Grand Lodge in the presence of
HRH George, Prince of Wales. Circa 1802*

Concern for others is one of the fundamental principles of Freemasonry. For nearly 300 years every Freemason has affirmed his willingness to give generously to charity, according to his means, and over a similar period Freemasonry has made charitable donations to the needy, both within and outside of the fraternity. Indeed nowadays Freemasonry is the second largest provider of charitable grants in the UK.

Before anyone becomes a Freemason he is advised that one of the principles of Freemasonry is the support and relief of those who are in need of assistance. Every Freemason is expected to contribute, as his means allow, to both the work of the central Masonic charities and to the support of local good causes. This charitable work is funded through the contributions of members, and their families.

Freemasonry is not in any sense, however, a benefit society. The central Masonic charities are solely for those who, having been in good circumstances, have been overtaken by misfortune or adversity. Neither a Freemason, his wife nor his children or other dependants have any claim upon them. In other words no member or dependant has a right to assistance.

Masonic Charities

Throughout Masonic history the structure of the Masonic charities has varied, reflecting the changing needs and provisions in society, but the current structure of four main charities dates from the early 1980s. Throughout their history, Somerset brethren have given generously to the charities they support and those in need have derived benefit and support from them. The Charities are:-

The Freemasons' Grand Charity
Providing financial support within the Craft and the wider community

The Grand Charity was established in 1981 and is the successor to various committees and boards established by Grand Lodge over the years, the earliest of which was established in 1727. The Grand Charity is a grant-making charity that supports Freemasons, and their dependents who are in financial need; national charities serving England and Wales; worldwide emergency relief work and other Masonic charities

Help provided to Freemasons and their dependants provides support with daily living costs and for the provision of mobility equipment. Applicants are means tested. Grants of over £15m have been made in the last five years alone.

Grants to non-Masonic national charities are made to organisations working in the areas of medical research, vulnerable people and youth opportunities. In addition annual grants are made to hospices and Air Ambulance services in England and Wales. The Grand Charity is one of the first to make emergency grants for disaster relief worldwide. In total some £3m is donated to these causes each year.

Royal Masonic Trust for Girls & Boys
Relieving poverty & providing education

Since the late 18th Century, the Royal Masonic Institution for Girls and the Royal Masonic Institution for Boys have helped relieve poverty and advance the education of the children of deceased and distressed Freemasons and, when funds permit, support other children in need. This function and other wider terms of reference, were taken up by the Trust when in 1986, it took over the running of the former charities. At the time of the amalgamation, the Trust had 749 beneficiaries. The numbers have risen and in 2008 the Trust supported over 1700 girls and boys.

Assistance is provided in every practical way, including Maintenance Grants to help poor families support a child, grants for books clothing, accommodation, fees, and travel, topping up LEA grants with scholarships, educational holidays, and educational/career counselling. Support is often long term and can be for a child's entire time in education. Annual grants have averaged £8m in recent years.

Masonic Samaritan Fund
Providing support for medical treatment

The Masonic Samaritan Fund, established in 1990, makes grants to cover all or part of the cost of private medical treatment for eligible Freemasons and their dependents who have a medical need, a long wait for, or no access to, NHS treatment and cannot afford to fund their own private medical treatment without undue hardship. The Fund will also support applications to fund the provision of Respite

Care so that the carer can take a well-earned rest confident that their loved one is being looked after in a safe and caring environment.

Royal Masonic Benevolent Institution
Providing accommodation for the elderly and infirm

The RMBI has been caring for older Freemasons and their dependents for over 160 years. It operates 17 care homes across England and Wales offering a range of high quality care. The nearest home to Somerset, Cadogan Court in Exeter, is actively supported by Somerset Freemasons jointly with the Provinces of Devon and Cornwall. The Association of Friends raises funds for the welfare and development of amenities for residents. In recent years the Province has organised a 'Somerset Produce' stall at the Summer Fayre which has raised thousands of pounds for the benefit of the residents.

Masonic Charity Festivals

One might wonder how funds raised by Members are channelled to the central Masonic Charities. Every year there are four Masonic Festivals throughout the English and Welsh Provinces, each being in favour of one of the four Masonic charities and each the responsibility of a Province. The Festival system spreads the load evenly over the 47 Provinces in England and Wales. This ensures an annual income for each of the charities but also allows those Provinces not currently in a Festival period to alternatively donate to other causes of their own choice.

Members of the Province are encouraged to support the appeal over a six or seven year period and which traditionally culminates in a Festival dinner at which the final total raised is announced. The Festivals undertaken by Somerset and the amounts raised are shown in the table below:

Year	Charity	Total raised £	Total raised from Somerset £
1869	Royal Masonic Benevolent Institution	2,219	
1878	Royal Masonic Institute for Girls	8,351	
1895	Royal Masonic Benevolent Institution	14,690	1,657
1899	Royal Masonic Institute for Girls	21,045	2,191
1905	Royal Masonic Institute for Boys	25,504	3,010
1913	Royal Masonic Benevolent Institution	31,167	4,340
1929	Royal Masonic Institute for Boys	83,091	15,139
1943	Royal Masonic Institute for Girls	88,271	26,673
1953	Royal Masonic Benevolent Institution	129,106	49,972
1963	Royal Masonic Institute for Boys	184,966	98,193
1973	Royal Masonic Institute for Girls	336,674	219,739
1983	Royal Masonic Benevolent Institution	1,145,251	760,197
1993	Masonic Trust for Girls and Boys	2,071,000	1,571,000
2007	Royal Masonic Benevolent Institution	3,566,171	2,666,866

The total raised usually includes additional money given to the Charity, but not specifically as a result of the host Province's fund-raising efforts. This is because all other money received by the Charity in the final year is simply added on. By way of example, for the 2007 Festival the RMBI announced figure of £3,566,171, includes £897,298 from other sources, so Somerset's real result that year was £2,666,866

Local support for Good Causes in Somerset

Apart from support for the four central Masonic charities, Somerset members have a long tradition of generous support for a wide range of local charities and good causes. Much of this support comes direct from individual lodges as will be illustrated in the succeeding chapters of this book. It is estimated that each year the amount given in this way averages £100,000.

The Provincial Benevolent Fund was established in the 1980s. The Fund has an important role in that it is able to respond to appeals that fall between national charities, supported by the Freemason's Grand Charity and the valuable support given by many individual lodges to the needs in their own locality.

Donations from the Benevolent Fund made in recent years are shown in the table on the right.

Year	Total amount donated to local charities and good causes £
1996	1,350
1997	1,700
1998	2,250
1999	6,895
2000	3,268
2001	37,650
2002	8,280
2003	3,050
2004	5,015
2005	9,450
2006	54,785
2007	2,500
2008	53,750
2009	15,570

The amounts include:
In 2001:
£20,000 for St. Margaret's Hospice and £13,500 for the Farmer's Appeal.
In 2006:
£50,000 for Children's Hospice, South West.
In 2008:
£50,000 for the Wells Cathedral Appeal.
In 2009:
A further £10,000 for the Wells Cathedral Appeal.

Part Two

PROVINCIAL GRAND MASTERS

The Provincial Grand Masters for Somerset

John Smith MP	1768 - 1775
Vacant	1775 - 1784
Thomas Dunckerley	1784 - 1795
Lt. Col. John Smith-Leigh	1796 - 1813
Vacant	1813 - 1817
Arthur Chichester	1817 - 1820
Col. Charles Kemeys Kemeys Tynte	1820 - 1860
Under the control of the Grand Registrar	1860 - 1864
Col. Alexander William Adair	1864 - 1868
The Earl of Carnarvon	1869 - 1890
Viscount Dungarvan	1891 - 1909
Col. William Long	1909 - 1926
The Ven. Archdeacon William Farrer	1926 - 1934
Brig. Gen. Claude Lumsden Norman	1935 - 1960
Brig. Arnold de Lerisson Cazenove	1961 - 1969
Lt. Col. Harry Owen Hughes,	1969 - 1980
Kenneth Caswell Kinnersley	1981 - 1991
Stanley Herbert Ambrose Frank. Hopkins	1991 - 2002
David Lloyd Jenkins	2002 - date

The Deputy Provincial Grand Masters

Richard Roberts	1768
Benedict Masters	1773
Benedict Masters	1784
Thomas West	1785
John Dunning	1792
Charles Phillott	1799
William Meyler	1803
George Percival	1811
Dr Henry Sully	1817
John Bawden	1820
Capt. Charles Maddison	1832
James Randolph	1843
Capt. Henry Bridges	1861
Richard Charles Else	1875
Col. William Long	1902
Col. Alfred Thrale Perkins	1909
Rowland Armstrong Hughes	1926
Frederick Edward Nutt	1936
Henry Frampton	1949
Herbert Ernest Dyke	1973
Gilbert Arthur Parrott	1983
Thomas Albert Hughes	1991
Roger Duckett Clark	1998
Vernon Richard. Harding	2000
Jeremiah Peter Layzell	2001
Clarence Alfred Stuart Hadler	2010

The Assistant Provincial Grand Masters

Geoffrey Herbert Harrison	1950	V.R. Harding & Roger Duckett Clark	1995
Herbert Ernest Dyke	1958	V.R. Harding & Arthur H.P. Forse	1997
Kenneth Caswell Kinnersley	1973	V.R. Harding & David L. Jenkins	1999
David Bernie Durie	1981	David L. Jenkins & J. Peter Layzell	2000
Stanley H.A.F. Hopkins	1983	David L. Jenkins & Raymond Guthrie	2001
Thomas A Hughes	1989	Raymond Guthrie & Terence E. Hart	2002
Vernon R Harding	1994	David J. Medlock & C.A. Stuart Hadler	2006
		David J. Medlock & John W. Winston	2010

Secretaries and Treasurers

The Provincial Grand Secretaries

William Smith	1768
William Meyler	1784
Charles Mines	1792
H.J. Leigh	1817
W. East *(see below)	1818
B. Waldron (pro tem)	1818
R. Beadon,(pro tem)	1819 - 1821
T.W. Inman	1821 - 1842
Capt. C.M. Maher	1842 - 1853
A. P. Browne	1853 - 1858
C. Babbage	1858 - 1861
R. Smith	1861 - 1865
R.C. Else	1865 - 1871
F.R. Prideaux	1871 - 1872
R.C. Else	1872 – 1875
F.R. Prideaux	1875 - 1875
J.C. Hunt	1879 - 1899
E. Fry Wade	1899 – 1904
A'Deane G. Wood	1904 - 1910
C.C. Gill	1910 - 1937
Major G.T. Biggs	1937 - 1950
Lt. Col. H.L. Petavel	1950 - 1966
R.V. Showering	1966 - 1969
D.B.M. Durie	1969 - 1978
G.A. Parrott	1978 - 1982
R.D. Clark	1982 - 1987
K.J.L. Wilkinson	1987 - 1988
D.C. Smith	1988 - 1997
T.E. Hart	1997 - 2002
G.J. Bowerman	2002 - 2007
B.E. Kenna	2007 - 2010
R.C. Pring	2010 - date

Note:

W. East was invested as Secretary in 1818, but although present at other meetings in that year and in 1819 he did not carry out his duties.

The Provincial Grand Treasurers

George Percival	1792
John Pinchard	1810 - 1818
J.L. Freeman	1819 - 1819
F. Townsend	1819 - 1820
Capt. J. Barton	1820 - 1821
Col . J. Brown	1821 - 1825
E. Browne	1825 - 1827
R.G. Ayersh	1827 - 1829
W. Stradling	1829 - 1854
J. Eales White	1854 - 1855
R.W. Falconer	1855 - 1860
E.T. Payne	1860 - 1885
C.L. Fry Edwards	1885 - 1924
R.T.A. Hughes	1924 - 1926
E. Brake	1926 - 1932
W.N. Wake	1932 - 1941
P.E. Russell	1941 - 1948
A.E. Philpott	1948 - 1969
S.T.H. Tarr	1969 - 1980
J.H.P. Forte	1980 - 1986
S.E.P. Eydmann	1986 - 1988
D. Hartley	1988 - 1995
J.A.G. Norman	1995 - 2009
M.F. Webb	2009 - date

John Smith MP

1st Provincial Grand Master for Somerset 1768-1775

Extant Lodges Inherited

1733 Pre-Provincial - Royal Cumberland No. 41 in Bath
1764 Pre-Provincial - Perpetual Friendship No. 135 in Bridgwater

John Smith was the son of Dr Robert Smith of Combe Hay near Bath, whose residence was described by Rev. John Collinson (1791) as "elegant and beautifully aided by art and nature." It is certainly a most beautiful house in a most beautiful location. Now designated a Grade One listed building, the house was built in two phases for Robert Smith and his son, John. The first, western, part dates from 1728 to 1730 and is believed to have been built by John Strahan of Bristol. The later eastern and southern elevations were built around 1770 to 1775 and are believed to be the work of James Wyatt or George Steuart

The Smiths belonged to a branch of the Smyth family of Ashton Court, near Bristol. The surname of the latter was spelt "Smith" until an heiress Florence married Jarrit (afterwards Sir Jarrit) Smyth. Coincidentally, Collinson, who wrote an excellent History of Somerset, was Vicar of Long Ashton, appointed to the living by the Smiths and so presumably knew the family well.

In July 1766 the Marquis of Rockingham, the Whig Prime Minister, was dismissed, and William Pitt the Elder, MP for Bath, was entrusted by the King with the task of forming a government entirely on his own conditions. Pitt chose for himself the office of Lord Privy Seal, which necessitated his removal to the House of Lords and in August he became Earl of Chatham and Viscount Pitt. It was John Smith who followed Pitt as the new MP for Bath; a role that he held for eleven years, from 1766 to 1775.

These were the High Georgian days spanned politically by Walpole, Pitt and Fox, of Whigs and Tories, of Clive of India, of General Wolfe and of one W.Bro General George Washington, WM of the Alexandria Lodge No. 22 in the Commonwealth of Virginia .

For much of the time Smith doubled as the first Provincial Grand Master for Somerset but his effectiveness as an MP was somewhat suspect. He beat his opponent for his Bath seat by one vote in 1766 and the only vote credited to him in that Parliament was with the Opposition!

The Duke of Newcastle (Lord Privy Seal before Pitt) classed him as 'doubtful', an assessment his subsequent record proved apt. His record as PGM for Somerset may also well be described in similar terms

He had not been a Mason for very long prior to his appointment as Provincial Grand Master. He was, in fact, initiated into the Lodge which met at the Bear at Bath in October 1766 and his was certainly not a regular presence at their meetings. He was appointed Provincial Grand Master in 1768 and he continued in office until his death in 1775

It is unfortunate that, generally speaking, minutes in the 18th Century were often cryptic and much less comprehensive than they are today. Consequently, whilst it is very tempting to speculate as to what was meant, it is only too easy to reach entirely the wrong conclusion. This lack of detail is certainly true in the case of the Lodge which met at the Bear for some 35 years. On the 1st December, 1767, the Lodge "about Eight o'Clock in the Evening removed from thence with the Jewels, Tools and other Implements in Masonry to the White Hart in Bath where the Lodge was then held."

On the 15th of that month, among those recorded as being present were John Vining Reed, DP Master (for John Smith MP). It has been suggested that this means that John Smith was Master of the Lodge, although he was only a Fellowcraft, since the minutes record that he was not made a Master Mason until the 28th December, which was also the date of the Installation Meeting. It could be that preparatory to being made Provincial Grand Master, he had been elected Master of the Lodge but could not actually occupy the chair until he had become a Master Mason and then, on the night this event occurred, he immediately occupied the Master's chair. But this is of course pure speculation, the dangers of which have already been mentioned.

It was some four months after this, in April 1768, that the minutes of the Lodge first refer to him as Provincial Grand Master, although there is no record of his appointment in the minutes of Grand Lodge, but in a letter dated 12th June 1769 the Grand Secretary referred to the appointment of John Smith as Provincial Grand Master.

There is likewise no record of his ever having called a Provincial Grand Lodge as such, but this is not surprising as it was quite in accordance with the custom of those days, with only some half dozen Lodges in a Province, for the Lodge of which the Provincial Grand Master was a member, in this case the Lodge meeting at the Bear, to consider itself as the Provincial Grand Lodge.

The four Lodges that formed the Province of Somerset when the first Provincial Grand Master was appointed were The Lodge at the Bear Inn, Bath (later Royal Cumberland Lodge), the Lodge of Perpetual Friendship, Bridgwater, St. George's Lodge, Taunton and the Lodge of Perfect Friendship, Bath.

John Smith's last recorded appearance was in June 1768. In 1774, the year before he died, he paid his outstanding dues, covering nearly six years, to the Lodge. His death was announced in the Bath Chronicle on 16th November 1775 as follows: 'Sunday died, at his home in Berry Street, St James's, John Smith Esq., one of the representatives for this city. His death was occasioned by the bursting of a blood vessel in a violent fit of coughing

Below: The Manor House, Combe Hay
"elegant, and beautifully aided by art and nature"

Thomas Dunckerley

2nd Provincial Grand Master for Somerset 1784-1795

Extant Lodges Consecrated

1788 - Unanimity and Sincerity No 261 in Taunton
1792 - Love and Honour No. 285 in North Wootton
1793 - Rural Philanthropic No 291 in Burnham-on-Sea

Thomas Dunckerley
Portrait by Thomas Beach
Now in Loyal Lodge 251 Barnstaple

Thomas Dunckerley, 1723-95, was brought up in humble circumstances, though well educated. He ran away from school to join the Royal Navy in which, by the age of 22, he had Warrant Officer rank as a "gunner and school-master". After 26 years as a sailor he retired to study law at the Middle Temple and was called to the Bar in 1774. In view of the threat of a French invasion, he then became a soldier with a commission in the South Hampshire Militia, serving with distinction for several years. In his middle-age he was given the right to bear the Royal Arms and a pension, as an acknowledged natural son of King George II.

When in Quebec with HMS Vanguard in 1760 he installed the Provincial Grand Master of Canada, having been "possessed with a power from the Grand Lodge of England to inspect into the state of the Craft wherever he might go". Dunckerley was made a Mason at Portsmouth in 1754 and was promoted rapidly in the Craft. After retiring from the sea he was appointed Provincial Grand Master for Hampshire in 1767, and from then until his death nearly thirty years later, he devoted his life, with missionary zeal, to the Craft.

He played a very important part in the development of Freemasonry in England at that crucial period in its history, influencing the future structure of its organisation, helping in the reconciliation with the Antients and the building of Freemasons' Hall. He also became Provincial Grand Master for eight other Counties, and was Grand Superintendent in and over eighteen Counties. In 1784 Dunckerley's royal nephew, the Duke of Cumberland, by then, Grand Master, appointed him Provincial Grand Master for Bristol and Gloucestershire as a single Province.

Within a few months he succeeded in re-establishing Freemasonry in these Provinces after its long lapse and before the year was out he was appointed Provincial Grand Master for Somerset. He did not waste much time before starting to organise Somerset Province, as only three months after his appointment he called the first of his Provincial Grand Lodges in the County. It was held at the White Hart Inn, Stall

Street, Bath, on the 19th August 1784, and a report which appeared in the Bristol Journal stated that 'The attendance was very numerous and respectable and the entertainment plentiful and elegant. The day was spent with that social harmony which has ever characterised the brotherhood, and was indeed "The feast of reason and the flow of soul".'

Later Grand Lodges were held at Wells in October 1785, June 1786 and August 1789. One was also held at Bridgwater on the 12th August 1789. In the Bath Journal of 12th June 1786 the following report appears:

'On Monday last in honour of His Majesty's birthday Thomas Dunckerley Esq. held a Provincial Grand Lodge for this county at the Assembly Room at Wells. The appearance of the fraternity on this occasion was most numerous and respectable indeed. The procession to St Cuthbert's Church, preceded by a band of wind music, was regular and splendid; the officers of the different Lodges with their jewels, the Grand Officers and standards in their appropriate clothing, and several Reverend brothers dressed in their canonicals, made one of the grandest spectacles that have ever perhaps been seen in that part of the country.

Lt. Col. John Smith-Leigh

3rd Provincial Grand Master for Somerset 1796-1813

Extant Lodges Consecrated

1801 - Marine No. 232 in Portishead and Nailsea
1812 - Royal Sussex No. 53 in Bath
1810 - Brotherly Love No. 329 in Yeovil

This John Smith was the son of the earlier John Smith of Combe Hay, MP for Bath and the Hon. Anne Tracy, third daughter of Thomas Charles, 5th Viscount Tracy. He was probably born in 1759 and it is intriguing whether he was the John Smith who in that year was entered an Ensign ('subject to his Majesty's approval') in the 1st Somerset Militia. It was not unknown in those days for infants to be granted commissions even in the Regular Army. His father being MP for Bath would scarcely require the approval of his Majesty to become an Ensign in a Militia Regiment, and he would not normally be appointed to the rank of Ensign anyway, so it is most probably Smith junior.

John Smith Junior, who became Lt. Col. John Smith-Leigh, was appointed a Captain in the 1st Somerset Regiment of Militia, 23rd May, 1787, promoted Major 13th August, 1795 and Lieutenant Colonel, 23rd November, 1797.

John Smith was made a Mason in the Royal Cumberland Lodge on 5th January 1788, having been proposed at the previous meeting by William Anderdon, Mayor of Bath in 1786, and his Seconder was Charles Phillott. The minute was as follows :

"This night John Smith, Esq. was balloted for to be made a Mason and unanimously chosen, after which he received the First and Second Degrees of Masonry and was proposed to be a member of the Lodge." On the 5th February following he was raised to the Degree of Master Mason.

He seems to have frequently attended Lodge meetings but it is not always possible to identify him from yet another John Smith, of Bath, a wine merchant. On the 24th June 1791, he was elected WM of the Lodge and was re-elected for a further six months in the following December.

In this second period he attended only two or three meetings. This may have been due to the considerable unrest in the country partly due to the French Revolution.

The Militia were kept on the alert and at the end of the year a Royal Proclamation was made for them to be embodied. John Smith's Regiment, the first Somerset Militia, was under the command of the Earl of Corke, who had been made a Mason in the Royal Cumberland Lodge on 6th November, 1787.

In January 1793 his Militia Regiment was assembled at Wells, when three Companies were sent to be stationed at Falmouth. The following resolutions from the Records of the Falmouth Corporation are of special interest. John Smith was a Captain at the time.

"18th May, 1793. At a Meeting of the Mayor and Corporation, Merchants and principal inhabitants of Falmouth held at the Guildhall. Resolved that the thanks of this Meeting be given to John Smith esq. Commanding the First Somerset Militia, and to the Officers, Non-Commissioned Officers and Privates for their readiness and alacrity in defence of this Town and neighbourhood in the late insurrection of

the Tinners. That a subscription be opened for making a Present to the Privates and that these Resolutions be signed by the Town Clerk and presented to the Commanding Officer."

In 1796 John Smith was appointed Provincial Grand Master for the Province of Somerset. His military service must have prevented him from carrying out most of his Masonic duties, and the state of war under which the people lived was not helpful in any attempt to make any progress in Freemasonry.

The minutes of Royal Cumberland Lodge paint a picture of the times. Time and time again it is recorded that on the regular Lodge night only one or two brethren attended, they were usually Thomas West and Charles Phillott; consequently no business was transacted.

The Regiment was demobilised at Bridgwater on 24th April 1802. Freedom from military service was, however, of short duration for the Regiment was again assembled at Bridgwater on 28th March, 1803. It was about this time that he changed his name to John Smith-Leigh by Royal Licence.

He was related on his mother's side to the Leighs of Stoneleigh Abbey, Warwickshire, represented in 1803 by the Hon. Mary Leigh, who had named John Smith's grandfather, Thomas Charles, 5th Viscount Tracy, and two of his brothers, as her heirs failing her nearer relatives. Her will was made in 1786 and all the relatives mentioned in her will were probably dead; the last Viscount Tracy died in 1797, so that John Smith may have been her heir. The Hon. Mary Leigh died on 2nd July, 1806, possessed of considerable property.

The only Provincial Grand Lodge over which he presided, of which we have any information, was held in Taunton in April 1810 for the purpose of laying the foundation stone of the Taunton and Somerset Hospital.

The officers appointed on that occasion are recorded elsewhere. It is said that George IV was his friend and, when Prince of Wales stayed with him at Combe Hay.

He died at Clifton on the 1st August, 1813, at the age of 53 years. The following obituary notice in the Bath Chronicle of 5th August, 1813, gives a good account of his outstanding merits :

"Sunday, died, aged 53, John Smith-Leigh, esq. of Combe Hay, Provincial Grand Master of the Lodges of Freemasons in this county, and formerly Lieut. Col. of the 1st Regt. of Somerset Militia.

To speak of Mr. Leigh as his talents and his virtues deserve, would require a larger space than the columns of a journal can afford : beneficence, hospitality, a generous warmth of feeling, an abhorrence of injustice and oppression, an amiable and engaging politeness of manners, were united to an understanding vigorous by nature, and enlightened by free intercourse with mankind and a diligent application to the best sources of classical and modern literature.

Invaluable in his stations as a Country Gentleman, and long and universally beloved and respected in this City and its neighbourhood, the death of Mr. Leigh will make a void in Society, which will neither be speedily forgotten or replaced."

Arthur Chichester

4th Provincial Grand Master for Somerset 1817-1820

Extant Lodges Consecrated - *Nil*

Exactly why there was such a delay in appointing a new Provincial Grand Master is not clear, but doubtless the merging of the Antients & Moderns proved an administrative nightmare. Reference in the archives is made to Chichester having found "the Science of Masonry wrecked, forlorn and forsaken", and having raised it to 'its present exalted state.'

According to the Registers of Grand Lodge, Arthur Chichester was born about 1781 as they contain the following entry under the Royal Sussex Lodge of Hospitality, No. 248, now 187. "Arthur Chichester, aged 32 years, date of initiation 6th January 1813, Gentleman, resident at Brislington." He married Margaretta Caroline, daughter of Charles Hill, of Wick House, Brislington. However, in the 1861 Census he appears as living at Stokelake, Hennock in Devon, where he gives his age as 77.

He gives his place of birth as Shirwell (North) Devon and his occupation that of Justice of the Peace. In 1851 he was at the same address, a Magistrate, age 65. He died in 1869 aged 85, so he was born circa 1784.

At his Installation R.W.Bro. Chichester appointed a Charles Hill as PGDC This was probably Bro Chas. Hill of the Lodge of Virtue, Bath, who was about the same age as Arthur Chichester and may have been his brother-in-law.

On the 1st April, 1817, he was elected a Joining Member of the Lodge of Perpetual Friendship, Bridgwater. He was living at Walford House (which is situated nearer to Taunton than Bridgwater), when the Lodge of Perfect Friendship sent its list of members to Dr. Sully in 1818.

Very soon after his appointment as Provincial Grand Master, he paid a visit to most of the Lodges in the Province and impressed every one with his sincerity and enthusiasm. On the 25th May 1817 he met the members of the three Lodges in Bath at the Kingston Rooms where he was received with great ceremony. ".... he returned thanks to the Bath Masons for their brotherly exertions in procuring his election; and professed the urgent hope that by the combined talents of the Craft in Somersetshire cordially enjoined with his own strenuous and zealous endeavours, the divine sun of Masonry might shine forth resplendently in this county and continue the brightest luminary in the Masonic hemisphere".

On the 2nd June, 1817, he visited the Bridgwater Lodge and there he initiated three candidates, Edward Stradling, surgeon, Henry Stradling, attorney, and Morley Chubb, merchant, all of Bridgwater. He visited the Loyal Vacation Lodge on 23rd July, when he initiated seven candidates. In September he announced the appointment of Dr. Henry Sully, of Wiveliscombe, as his Deputy, and of Henry James Leigh, of Lodge of Unanimity and Sincerity, as Provincial Grand Secretary.

On the 15th October, he visited the Lodge of Unanimity and Sincerity "attended by his Deputy Grand Master and Secretary, when Sir T. B. Lethbridge, Bart., T. M. Chanter, W. Elton, W.P. Prichard, J. Ambrose (R.N.), H.C. Standart, A. Schalch (R. Artillery) and R. Beadon, were initiated by the Grand Master into the mysteries of Masonry." After all the initiation ceremonies he delivered an interesting lecture "explanatory of the use and signification of the Masonic jewels and describing in the most luminous manner the moral purpose of the implements of working and symbolical furniture of a Masonic Lodge".

Unfortunately, but perhaps understandably bearing in mind the low state of the Province,

he tried to introduce financial income by new rules that were regarded by many as draconian. Mandatory fees were to be paid to Province, punitive fines were to be paid in respect of absence from Provincial Grand Lodge and Lodges were to pay for Provincial regalia.

The minutes of the meeting of Provincial Grand Lodge held in December 1819, reveal a devastating vote of no confidence. Almost immediately Arthur Chichester wrote to HRH The Duke of Sussex, Grand Master, resigning from the office of Provincial Grand Master, which he had accepted with so much enthusiasm.

He was still living at Walford House in 1823, but he probably left very soon afterwards and settled at Stokelake, Devon, where he died in 1869.

The Chichester Minute Book

Handsomely produced in leather with brass hasps. To be used, optimistically for posterity, in recording the Proceedings of the restoration of a Province, then 'wrecked, forlorn and forsaken'. Now lies sadly neglected with only three Meetings recorded and those showing the Lodges' deep opposition to Chichester's plans to put the Province on an even economic keel.

Col. Charles Kemeys Kemeys Tynte MP

5th Provincial Grand Master of Somerset 1820-1860

Extant Lodges Consecrated

1825 - Honour No. 379 in Bath
1836 - Science No. 437 in Wincanton
1837 - Benevolent No. 446 in Wells
1859 - Pilgrims No. 772 in Glastonbury

Col. Charles Kemeys-Kemeys Tynte

The 1851 Census records Col Tynte as aged 72 and born at St George's Hanover Square, London and thus born circa 1789. He gives his occupation as Magistrate.

When Colonel Charles Kemeys Kemeys. Tynte, MP for Bridgwater, became Provincial Grand Master for Somerset, Freemasonry in the Province was in considerable danger. R.W.Bro Arthur Chichester's attempts to place the affairs of the Province on a sound financial basis had been defeated. There were one or two brethren who obviously desired to use Freemasonry for their own ends and only a firm hand and steady principles could keep it on an even keel. It was fortunate for the Province that Charles K.K. Tynte possessed these qualities in full measure.

One of his 14th century forbears was in Wraxall and a descendant married a Gorge of Chelvey combining the estates. The insignia of Wraxall Lodge 9011 is the 'whirlpool' of the Gorges and of course the Tynte's name is enshrined in the National Trust property at Tyntesfield.

He was initiated in the Lodge of Perpetual Friendship, Bridgwater, on 27th September, 1817, 'passed' on 6th October and 'raised' 2nd November. He assisted R.W.Bro. Arthur Chichester to initiate his son C.J.K. Tynte on 20th November 1817.

On the 13th April, 1818 he, with other members of the Lodge, 'passed the Chair'. Almost immediately after his initiation he became a Joining Member of the Lodge of Unanimity and Sincerity and in 1818 was elected WM of that Lodge.

In the following year he was elected WM of his mother Lodge. On the resignation of Bro. Arthur Chichester he was appointed Provincial Grand Master. One of his very first duties, armed only with a Patent of Appointment, appears to have been to go, with the full Provincial team, to Devon and there Invest their new Provincial Grand Master, Hugh, 2nd Viscount Ebrington, Master of the Staghounds on 4th Dec 1819.

He was an 'Original Member' of the Lodge of Honour, Bath, which was formed in 1825 by members of the Royal York Lodge of Perpetual Friendship which had been erased towards the end of 1824. According to the Bye-laws of the Lodge of Honour an 'Original Member' was one who, not being a Petitioner, became a member before the first Monday in April, 1825. He presented the Lodge of Honour with a Chair for the use of the WM

The Royal York Lodge of Perfect Friendship was erased by Grand Lodge in consequence of irregularities and mismanagement for which Thomas Whitney, PPGSW, was largely responsible. He had made bitter and unworthy accusations against Col. Tynte. When his case was being heard by Grand Lodge he claimed that he had the support of the Provincial Grand Lodge for Bristol. As soon as certain members of that Provincial Grand Lodge heard this they wrote the following letter to the PGM for Bristol:

"To the Right Worshipful John H. Moggridge, Esq. Provincial Grand Master for Bristol.

Rt. W. Sir and Brother,

"Having been credibly informed by a Brother of this Province, who was present in the Grand Lodge of England, on Wednesday, the 22nd December last, when the appeal of Bro. Thomas Whitney, of Bath, was heard against the decision of the Board of General Purposes upon the charges preferred against him by Col. Tynte, PGM for Somersetshire, and that Bro. Whitney stated in his address to the M.W. GM, His Royal Highness the Duke of Sussex, and the Grand Lodge of England, that his conduct towards Col. Tynte, was approved and upheld by all the Brethren in this Province.

We the undersigned, feeling anxious to vindicate our Characters from so foul a slander and desirous at the same time, to testify to

Col. Tynte the high sense we entertain of his dignified, zealous and truly correct conduct, in his office of Provincial Grand Master, and his amiable deportment in general Society, have determined to be present at the White Lion Inn, Bath, on Tuesday, the 1st of February next being the first Provincial Grand Lodge convened since the decision on that appeal and as we are quite assured that your feelings of attachment to the PGM for Somersetshire are in unison with our own, we beg to solicit the favour of you, as PGM of this Province, to accompany us on that occasion".

We are,
Rt. Worshipful Sir,
Yours fraternally,
F.C. Husenbath, PDPGM, et al

The Provincial Grand Master for Bristol attended the meeting on 1st February, 1825, in person with members of his Provincial Grand Lodge and read the letter as an expression of his own feelings in the matter. The whole dispute was deplorable and must be attributed to a defect in the character of Bro. Whitney. In the early years of his Masonic career he seems to have been a zealous and hard-working Mason. He did much for his Lodge and for Freemasonry generally. When his personal vendetta against Col. Tynte began in 1821, his Lodge had a membership of 102, far more than any other Lodge in the Province. By the end of 1823 it had dropped to 47 and within twelve months it had practically ceased to exist. These figures indicate that he received very little, if any, support from the members of his own Lodge. Two of them, Bros. John Ashley and Charles Maddison, attended the meeting of Grand Lodge and gave evidence against him.

During the 40 years he was Provincial Grand Master a great many changes took place in the administration and practice of Masonry. The union of the two Grand Lodges was consolidated and the universal character of Freemasonry was established. Such changes can only be effected smoothly and without rancour by the exercise of great tact and a tolerant understanding. After the first few years of his reign disputes are rarely mentioned in the minutes of the Provincial Grand Lodge.

Time and time again the minutes record the respect and affection of the Freemasons of Somerset. Such expressions as "the beloved Chief under whom the Masons of Somerset enjoyed the privilege of acting", or "our revered Prov. G. Master" are not used by Secretaries unless they are generally accepted. At the meeting of Provincial Grand Lodge held on 13th October, 1835, the following resolution was adopted "That measures be immediately taken by the fraternity to present the Rt. Wor. Provincial Grand Master with some substantial mark of their respect."

Col. Tynte died at Bridgwater in 1860. On his demise the Province proposed to Grand Lodge that the 4th Earl of Carnarvon be appointed in his stead. The plea was ignored, possibly because of an ongoing row between Carnarvon, who was Deputy Grand Master, and the Grand Master the Earl of Zetland and for four years the Province was effectively overseen by the Grand Registrar, with a Deputy resident in the Province.

Grand Lodge Patent appointing
Charles Kemeys-Kemeys Tynte
as Provincial Grand Master for Somerset

The Grand Registrar

1860-1864

Extant Lodges Consecrated

1860 - Parrett & Axe No. 814 in Crewkerne
1862 - Royal Albert Edward No. 906 in Bath
1863 - Royal Somerset No. 973 in Frome
1863 - Royal Clarence No. 976 in Bruton

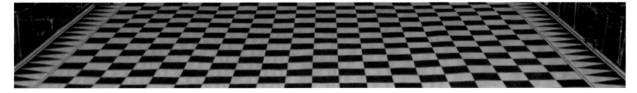

Col. Alexander William Adair JP

6th Provincial Grand Master of Somerset 1864-1868

Extant Lodges Consecrated

1867 - Nyanza No. 1197 in Ilminster
1867 - Agriculture No. 1199 in Yatton
1868 - St. Kew No. 1222 in Weston-super-Mare

Col. Alexander William Adair
Reproduced by kind permission of
United Grand Lodge of England

He was born in 1829 and was never really intended for a military career but in 1852 he was appointed to a Captaincy in the 1st Somerset Regiment of Militia. It was the usual thing for one destined to live the life of a country gentleman to do.

On the outbreak of the Crimean War he felt that something more than service in the Militia was required of him and he obtained a commission in the Coldstream Guards in February 1855. He was present at the Battle of Inkerman and at the Siege of Sebastopol. Either during or after the Crimea he was a Captain in the 52nd Foot, which became the 2nd Bn. of the Oxfordshire Light Infantry. On the 4th May, 1864, he was re-appointed Captain in the 1st Somerset Regt. of Militia. This Regiment became the 4th Bn. Somerset Light Infantry, of which, at the time of his death, he was Lieut. Col. Commandant, having been appointed to that rank on 12th. September 1870. Two of his Captains were William Long, PGM 1908-1926 and Alfred Thrale Perkins, Deputy PGM 1908-1926. In August 1888, Col. Adair was appointed Brigadier General of the new Western Brigade but died of congestion of the lungs within twelve months.

His patent as Provincial Grand Master was dated 15th December, 1863, and he was installed at the Assembly Rooms, at Bath, on 23rd May 1864 by his uncle, R.W.Bro Colonel Robert Alexander Shafto Adair, PGM, Suffolk. The Installing Grand Master succeeded as the 2nd Baronet in, 1869. They both belonged to a family which was more recently represented by the late Assistant Grand Master, R.W.Bro Major-General Sir Allan Adair, Bart. After he had re-appointed Henry Bridges as his Deputy the whole of the assembled brethren proceeded in full regalia to the Bath United Hospital, where the newly installed Provincial Grand Master laid the foundation stone of the Albert Wing, so named in memory of the late Consort of Queen Victoria.

His Initiation had been in the Apollo University Lodge, Oxford, and he subsequently joined the Unanimity and Sincerity Lodge, Taunton, of which he was Master, not only in 1860 but also in their centenary year 1888. He also joined the Lodge of Honour, Bath, in 1854 and although appointed Senior Warden of that Lodge the next year he was not installed as Master until 1857 due to his absence in the Crimean War.

Col. Adair's tenure of Office as Provincial Grand Master was a short one, from the date of his installation, 23rd May, 1864, to 12th January, 1869, when his successor was installed. During that time he attended every meeting of Provincial Grand Lodge. He resigned towards the end of 1868 on account of his military duties.

Until his death he continued to take an active interest in Masonic affairs in the Province and was Grand Superintendent of the Royal Arch, 1880-1889. On one or two occasions he presided over Prov. Grand Lodge and one of the last Masonic Ceremonies which he performed was the laying of the Foundation Stone of the Church at Rockwell Green, near Wellington on 10th September, 1888.

Col. Adair died suddenly at Bath on 16th May, 1889, described as "personally and officially greatly respected and beloved. He was a grand looking man. As PGM Col. Adair was most popular. His noble manners, high bred courtesy, and his kind and fraternal heartiness, won for him the cordial respect and love of all his Brethren."

Henry Howard Molyneux Herbert PC DL FRS FSA
The 4th Earl of Carnarvon

7th Provincial Grand Master for Somerset 1869-1890

Extant Lodges Consecrated

1869 - Vale of Brislington No. 1296 in Keynsham
1878 - Coleridge No. 1750 in Clevedon
1878 - Eldon No. 1755 in Clevedon
1879 - St. Keyna No. 1833 in Keynsham
1881 - Prudence & Industry No. 1953 in Chard
1882 - Fidelity & Sincerity No. 1966 in Wellington
1884 - Portcullis No. 2038 in Langport

The 4th Earl of Carnarvon
Reproduced by kind permission of
United Grand Lodge of England

the Bath Lodges had recommended the Earl as replacement, but this received a letter of reprimand from the Grand Secretary. It appears that there was difference between Carnarvon and the Earl of Zetland, The Grand Master. Carnarvon had the last laugh however for not only did he eventually become Provincial Grand Master for Somerset, but Albert Edward, Prince of Wales, who succeeded the Earl Grey of Ripon as Grand Master when the latter became a Catholic, required, as Prince of the Royal Blood, a Pro Grand Master. He wisely chose the Earl of Carnarvon.

Henry Howard Molyneux Herbert became the Earl of Carnarvon on the death of his father, also Henry, in 1849. After taking his degree at Oxford, he began to play a prominent role in the House of Lords. In 1858, he was Under Secretary for the Colonies, and in 1866 Secretary of State. In 1867 he introduced the British North America Act, which conferred self-government on Canada. Later that year, he resigned over Benjamin Disraeli's Reform Bill, along with Lord Cranborne. Resuming office in 1874, he endeavoured to confer self-government on South Africa as he had on Canada, but the timing was not right. In 1878 he resigned in opposition to Lord Beaconsfield's policy on the Eastern Question, but on his party's return to

The Earl of Carnarvon was an English politician and a leading member of the Conservative Party. On the death of Col. Tynte in 1860,

power in 1885 he became Lord Lieutenant of Ireland. His short period of office, memorable for a conflict on a question of personal veracity between himself and Charles Stewart Parnell as to his negotiations with the latter in respect of Home Rule, was terminated by another premature resignation. He never returned to office.

The first Earl of Carnarvon was the son of Major-General the Hon. William Herbert who was a member of a Lodge meeting at The Rummers at Charing Cross, which seems to have ceased working soon after 1727. The title should not be confused with the Marquisate of Carnarvon which was one of the many titles of the Dukes of Chandos, one of whose seats was Keynsham Abbey.

The 4th Earl was one of the most distinguished of Somerset Freemasons. He was born 24th June, 1831 and was Deputy Grand Master of England, 1870-74 and Pro Grand Master, 1874-1890. He was educated at Eton and entered Christ Church, Oxford, where he matriculated, as Viscount Porchester, 17th October, 1849, and obtained a first class in classics, BA 1852. After leaving Oxford he was appointed to high public offices and received many distinctions, both political and academic:

1854 Constable of Carnarvon Castle.
1858-59 Under Secretary of State for the Colonies
1859 High Steward of the University of Oxford
1866-67 Secretary of State for the Colonies, and again in 1874 - 1878
1866 Appointed to Privy Council
1884 High Steward of Newbery
1885-86 Lord Lieutenant of Ireland.
1887-90 Lord Lieutenant of Hampshire.

As a statesman his career was marred by extreme sensitiveness; but he was beloved as a man of worth and admired as a man of culture. He was High Steward of Oxford University,

and President of the Society of Antiquaries. It was his son, the 5th Earl, who worked with and financed Howard Carter in his discovery of the tomb of Tutankhamun in the 1920s

He was initiated in the Westminster and Keystone Lodge, No. 10, in 1856, and was installed WM of that Lodge in the following year, before a most distinguished company of Freemasons, which included the Grand Master and Deputy Grand Master of England. He was a speaker of great force and eloquence and in the same year that he was initiated he addressed Grand Lodge on the persecution of Freemasons by the Roman Catholic Church. The motion moved by him was not adopted by Grand Lodge, but he championed a cause which touched the sensibilities of many Freemasons.

Lord Carnarvon's initiation into Freemasonry was popular in Somerset where the Herbert family have always been warmly esteemed. He attended, by special invitation from the Royal Cumberland Lodge, the installation of Bro Edmund Lloyd Bagshawe, as WM of that Lodge on 8th January, 1857. He and the Rev. G.W. Portal, Past GSW Eng. were elected Hon. Members of the Lodge on 5th February, 1857. The latter was a member of the Board of General Purposes of Grand Lodge and an ardent supporter of the Canadian Freemasons' desire to be independent under a Grand Lodge of their own. The Canadians had another supporter in the Earl of Carnarvon and he made his views known when he was elected to the Board of General purposes on 3rd June, 1857. He was only 26 years of age. As mentioned, when Col. Tynte died in 1860, everyone hoped that Lord Carnarvon would be appointed Provincial Grand Master for Somerset. He was eventually installed as PGM for Somerset on 12th January, 1869. The Installing Officer on that occasion was W.Bro Wm. Beach, PPSGW of Oxfordshire and Hampshire; not a Grand Lodge Officer, it will be noted.

This was curious, for there were present not only Col. Adair, the retiring PGM, but the PGM for Oxfordshire, his Deputy, the DPGMs of Wiltshire and Bristol as well as two Somerset Freemasons who were Past Grand Chaplains, Bros C.R. Davey and R.J.F. Thomas. Obviously there was some personal reason for Bro Beach's selection for this important ceremony. It may very well be due to the fact that Bro. Beach Initiated him into Freemasonry and also installed him as WM of his Lodge, the Westminster and Keystone Lodge, No. 10.

Then followed a long period of 21 years which are noteworthy in the annals of the Province. In spite of his many public engagements and the high offices he was destined to fill in Freemasonry and elsewhere, he devoted much of his time to the affairs of the Province. The Charity Organisation Committee was formed in 1872, which marked a notable step forward in the organisation of contributions to the Charities and the securing of benefits for those in need.

When the Earl of Zetland resigned in 1870, the Earl de Grey and Ripon (afterwards 1st Marquess of Ripon) was appointed Grand Master and he appointed the Earl of Carnarvon as his Deputy. In 1874 the Marquess astonished Freemasons throughout the world by becoming a Roman Catholic. The Church required him to resign from Freemasonry and the Earl of Carnarvon and Grand Lodge decided to ask Edward, Prince of Wales, to accept the office.

The Prince had been initiated surreptitiously in Sweden by the King of Sweden in 1869. This infuriated his mother and allegedly took UGLE completely by surprise but a recently discovered letter at Windsor shows that he had consulted his shooting friends de Grey & Ripon who saw no problem. The truth was that there was nobody in this country of rank senior enough to initiate him.

A deputation consisting of Lord Carnarvon, Deputy Grand Master, John Havers, Junior Grand Warden and J. McIntyre, were appointed to approach the Prince of Wales. The Prince accepted the office and on 28th April, 1875, he was Installed by the Earl of Carnarvon in the Albert Hall, in the largest assembly of Freemasons ever held in Great Britain. The Prince of Wales immediately afterwards appointed the Earl of Carnarvon as Pro Grand Master and Lord Skelmersdale (afterwards 1st Earl of Lathom) as Deputy Grand Master.

Towards the end of his life, owing to Parliamentary business and the pressure of public affairs, to say nothing of the burden of high office in Grand Lodge, the Province did not see so much of him.

On his death a meeting of Provincial Grand Lodge was held at the Town Hall, Highbridge, to propose a resolution of regret "at the death of the R.W Provincial Grand Master, the Rt. Hon. the Earl of Carnarvon and sympathy with the Hon. the Countess of Carnarvon and family in their affliction".

Speaking in support of the Resolution, Bro Edmund White said:

"I happened to be present at the invitation of the members of the Lodge when Lord Carnarvon was initiated and also when he was installed WM of No. 10. With the interest of an old Mason I have watched Lord Carnarvon's career from the beginning to the end and there is but one opinion that any man can express on the subject, viz., that he was a thoroughly disinterested, a highly enlightened and most liberal member of our Order. He was a man whom to honour was to honour oneself. He was a singularly disinterested man as all who had the slightest knowledge of him must be aware and a more conscientious—a more scrupulously conscientious man it would be impossible to find."

Charles Spencer Canning Boyle DL
Viscount Dungarvan

8th Provincial Grand Master for Somerset 1891-1909

Extant Lodges Consecrated

1891 - Exmoor No. 2390 in Minehead
1899 - Royal Naval (Malta) No. 2761 in Yeovil
1906 - St. George No. 3158 in Taunton
1906 - King Alfred No. 3169 in Weston-super-Mare

Viscount Dungarvan
later the 10th Earl of Cork and Orrery

The appointment of Viscount Dungarvan as Provincial Grand Master seems to have upset the smooth waters into which Somerset Freemasonry had sailed during the Provincial Grand Mastership of the Earl of Carnarvon. An explanation of the troubles was given by Bro. R.C. Else, the Deputy PGM, at the meeting of PGL on 6th November, 1890. The appropriate minute reads as follows :

The V.W.Bro Deputy hereupon explained that the postponement of PGL had been occasioned by the lamented death of the PGM, The Rt. Hon. the Earl of Carnarvon and the appointment of Lord Dungarvan as his successor and said:

"I fear the postponement which has taken place in the Annual Meeting of PGL has occasioned inconvenience to some of the brethren. It has been caused by the important event, altogether beyond my control, which has taken place since we last met, overshadowing our Province with heavy clouds which for a time threatened to destroy that unity, peace, and harmony, which has so long existed amongst us. But I am happy to say that during the last few weeks those clouds have been dispersed. This happy result having been brought about by the mutual concessions of those brethren who whilst fully recognising the prerogative of the M.W Grand Master, were zealous to uphold the honour of the Province and maintain the Landmarks and Constitutions of the Order and of the R.W PGM Designate who has been pleased to respect the feelings of the Province by postponing his Installation until he has taken the position of WM in a Craft Lodge."

He was initiated in the Royal Somerset Lodge, 973 on 2nd October, 1884, and became a Joining Member of the Lodge of Unanimity and Sincerity, 261, Taunton, on 17th December, 1890.

He was installed as Provincial Grand Master at the Assembly Rooms at Bath on 14th May, 1891, in the presence of many distinguished Masons, by the Rt. Hon. Earl Euston, Provincial Grand Master of Northamptonshire and Huntingdonshire.

It was during his term of office as PGM that the practise was adopted of PGMs being appointed to preside at the Annual Festivals of the three Masonic Charities, when their Provinces made an extra effort in collecting subscriptions.

In 1895 Viscount Dungarvan presided at the Festival of the Royal Masonic Benevolent Institution. The subscriptions from Somerset amounted to £1,653. Four years later in 1899 he presided at the Girls' Festival when he contributed £635 towards the total of £2,134 from Somerset.

In 1905 it was the turn of the Boys' Festival, when certain unfortunate happenings may have led to his resignation as Provincial Grand Master in 1908. The Secretary of the Institution thought he would be justified in declaring Somerset's contribution to be £3,010. Actually it amounted to £2,850. This, and the failure of some other contributions from outside the Province to reach their target, resulted in a total deficiency of £242.13s.6d.
Although he had already made a very generous contribution, Lord Dungarvan (now Earl of Cork and Orrery) readily agreed to contribute a further £105. The balance was paid from Provincial Grand Lodge Funds.

Before this however, in 1900, he had to interrupt his duties to proceed to South Africa with his squadron of Imperial Yeomanry, which formed part of the 22nd Imperial Yeomanry. He had been appointed Captain in the North Somerset Yeomanry on 5th June, 1886, of which Regiment his father, the Earl of Cork and Orrery was Lieut.-Colonel Commandant. Viscount Dungarvan later became Lieut.-Colonel and

Hon. Colonel of the North Somerset Yeomanry. His absence on military duty was reported to Prov. Grand Lodge on 29th May, 1901, and on 10th April, 1902, he and Lieut.-Colonel A. Thrale Perkins received the congratulations of Provincial Grand Lodge on their safe return from the Boer War.

He succeeded to the Earldom of Cork and Orrery when his father died on 22nd June, 1904. In 1905 he sold his Somerset estates. The need for this and perhaps the difficulty in keeping up the very generous contributions he made to the Masonic Charities may have led him to resign from the office of Provincial Grand Master of Somerset.

Col. William Long CMG

9th Provincial Grand Master for Somerset 1909-1926

Extant Lodges Consecrated

1912 - Connaught No. 3573 in Midsomer Norton
1915 - Somerset Masters No. 3746 in Bath
1920 - Wessex No. 4093 in Weston-super-Mare
1920 - St. Alphege No. 4095 in Bath
1922 - Severn No. 4399 in Nailsea
1922 - Quantock No. 4446 in Watchet
1922 - Abbey No. 4491 in Keynsham
1922 - Tyntesfield No. 4494 in Nailsea
1923 - Alfred & Guthrum No. 4535 in Wedmore
1924 - Admiral Blake No. 4692 in Bridgwater

Col. William Long

Born in Bath in 1843, he was the son of a Mason, also William Long, a banker and JP, who was initiated into Freemasonry in 1839. William Junior was educated at Eton, and in 1861 (at the age of 18) he received a Commission in the 46th regiment of Foot.

He spent five years in India where, in 1866, he was initiated into Freemasonry in the Morning Star Lodge No. 552 at Lucknow. After completing his commission he was raised to the degree of Master Mason in the Royal Sussex Lodge No. 53, Bath, on 20th January 1866.

He married Anna Hunter in 1867; she was of a family with long military and merchandising connections with India. She died in 1898. They had one son and five daughters (and eight servants according to the 1881 Census). When commissioned in the 4th Battalion of Prince Albert's (2nd) Somerset Regiment of Light Infantry, in 1900 (at the age of 57) he then took the Regiment to South Africa for the Boer War.

Decorated with the CMG (Commander of the Order of St. Michael & St. George) and the Queen's Medal with Clasp and the King's Medal, when the Militia were disbanded in 1903 he was made Honorary Colonel of the Regiment.

His Masonic career flourished on his return to England. At the meeting of Lodge of Agriculture No. 1199 held on 12th October 1868 it is recorded that: "Bro Wm. Long was duly balloted for and accepted".

This simple statement records the admission to the Lodge as a Joining Member, not only one who became its most distinguished member, but one of the greatest figures in Somerset Freemasonry. He occupied the Chair of The Lodge of Agriculture in 1874, 1880 and again in 1918 to mark his fiftieth year as a member of the Lodge. He was also the first WM of Coleridge Lodge No. 1750, Clevedon, and was one of the Founders of the Somerset Masters Lodge.

From the first he took a keen interest in the affairs of Provincial Grand Lodge and in 1869 was appointed Provincial Grand Steward, in 1875 Provincial Grand Sword Bearer and in 1879 Provincial Grand Senior Warden. On 5th June 1902, following his safe return from the Boer War, he was appointed Deputy PGM, and in the same year was honoured by Grand Lodge with the rank of Past Grand Deacon.

Following the resignation in 1908 of the Earl of Cork and Orrery, Col. Long was appointed Provincial Grand Master of Somerset. He was, peculiarly, the only Deputy PGM to ascend to the Chair. He was installed at Bath on 24th April 1909 by the Earl of Radnor, PGM for Wiltshire, whose close family associations with the Long family went back many generations. His first duty as PGM was to welcome the Grand Master, HRH The Duke of Connaught, who was visiting Bath for the Bath Festival. Provincial Grand Lodge met in July, 1909, and received an address from the Duke which is recorded at length in the minutes of PG Lodge.

Colonel Long presided at the Festival of the Benevolent Institution, in 1913, but except for the Great War 1914-18, his long reign of seventeen years was generally uneventful. Provincial Grand Lodge of Somerset had established its well tried traditions over a period of near 150 years and the system, method and plan of its administration caused very little trouble.

His long reign of seventeen years ended with his death on 9th May 1926 after a long illness, which he bore with great fortitude. His successor as PGM, the Venerable Archdeacon Walter Farrer said of him:

"His was a genial personality which expressed itself by his intense kindness of heart and his courtesy, even to the lowest in our ranks. We loved and honoured him, and we respected him. He was truly a Christian and an upright Gentleman in every respect."

Among his many interests was ancient history and, at County level he became President of the Somerset Archaeological & Natural History Society. He and his family lived at a fine country house, 'Woodlands', at Congresbury where this interest in history and the past was catered for by the discovery in the grounds of a Roman Villa and a cemetery in a small cave. He moved later to Newton House, Clevedon where he died in 1926. His remains are interred in St Andrew's Churchyard, Congresbury.

The Ven. Archdeacon Walter Farrer

10th Provincial Grand Master for Somerset 1926-1934

Extant Lodges Consecrated

1927 - Tennyson No. 4947 in Clevedon
1928 - Progressive Science No. 5007 in Yeovil
1930 - Taunton Deane No. 5221 in Taunton
1932 - St Bernard No. 5361 in Minehead

The Venerable Archdeacon Walter Farrer
Reproduced by kind permission of
United Grand Lodge of England

The Rev. Walter Farrer, who had been educated at Eton and Balliol Oxford, was 27 years of age when he became Curate at Wincanton in October 1889. The Rector, the Rev. Colin Grant-Dalton, was a sick man and resigned the living in November 1896; he died less than two years later in January 1898, at the early age of 39 years.

On the 30th November, 1896, the Rev. Walter Farrer wrote to the Parishioners :

"My dear friends", he began, "As I announced in Church last night, the Bishop of Southwark has offered me the living of Wincanton, and after much prayer and thought I have accepted it. During the seven years I have been working here I have always met with the greatest kindness and sympathy.

The Church does not consist of the clergy alone, but of clergy and laity alike, and the efforts of your rector, however earnest he may be, cannot meet with success unless he has the sympathy and active assistance of his parishioners, and no earnestness and activity on the part of rector and people can be of any use unless they have the blessing of God."

There was no arrogance in his make-up and although some found him austere and not easy to approach, the austerity only masked his humility and a kindliness towards his fellow men. He went on to become Vicar of Chard (1907-1916), and of St. Cuthbert's, Wells (1916-1919).

He was initiated into Freemasonry in the Lodge of Science No. 437, Wincanton, on 12th October, 1897, passed in November and raised in December, the same year. He was Worshipful Master of the Lodge in 1906 and Provincial Grand Chaplain in 1906-7. He was appointed Grand Chaplain of England in 1919.

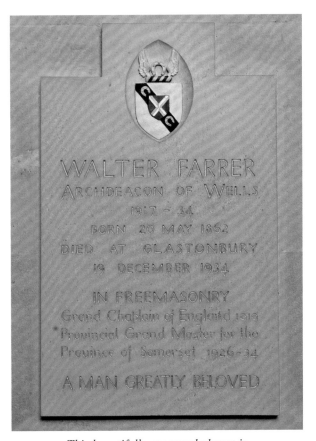

*This beautifully engraved plaque in
Wells Cathedral pays tribute to
R.W.Bro Walter Farrer Archdeacon of Wells
Provincial Grand Master for Somerset, 1926 to 1934*

The eight years during which he was Provincial Grand. Master appear, from the records, remarkably uneventful. He was installed as PGM at the Assembly Rooms, Bath, on 21st October 1926, by Lord Ampthill, the Pro Grand Master. R.W.Bro Farrer's first Masonic duty was to lay the foundation stone of the Queen Alexandra Memorial Hospital, Weston-super-Mare, on 9th November 1926.

He presided at the Boys' Festival in June 1929, when the total contributions from Somerset reached the record sum of £15,138. The grand total was £82,000. The PGM in a letter "to the Freemasons of Somerset" dated 22nd June 1929, wrote:

"I must freely confess that I was a very proud and happy man; proud, because the Masons of Somerset had so splendidly upheld the reputation of the Province and happy, because I believe that you are realising your privileges and responsibilities as Masons, and have confidence in me as your Provincial Grand Master."

W.Bro Farrer was installed as WM of the Somerset Masters' Lodge, No. 3746 on 26th February, 1923. It was not the custom in those early days of the Lodge for the Master to read a paper at his installation.

At the Summer meeting held at Weston-super-Mare on 25th June, he gave an address on "The Volume of the Sacred Law and Freemasonry." It was not printed in the Transactions as, so it was stated, "from the nature of the contents of the paper it is not suitable for publication in a volume which may be read by the outside world".

He passed away very suddenly in the evening on 8th December 1934, at the age of 72, while sitting in his chair at his home St. Michaels, Glastonbury. His health had not been good and he had suffered from a number of heart attacks. He had been feeling better in health however, and just before his death had undertaken to preside at the Girls' Festival in 1943. By his death, Freemasonry in Somerset lost a dignified and revered figure.

Brig. Gen. Claude Lumsden Norman DSO MVO DL

11th Provincial Grand Master for Somerset 1935-1960

Extant Lodges Consecrated

1945 - Loyal Vacation No. 6209 in Wiveliscombe
1946 - Gordano No. 6244 in Yatton
1947 - Winscombe No. 6474 in Yatton
1947 - St. Lukes No. 6540 in Bath
1948 - Southey No. 6650 in Clevedon
1948 - Estune No. 6817 in Nailsea
1949 - Priory No. 6913 in Keynsham
1949 - Whitchurch No. 6942 in Keynsham
1950 - Queen's College No. 6988 in Taunton
1952 - Birnbeck No. 7160 in Weston-super-Mare
1952 - Wellington School No. 7230 in Wellington
1953 - Elizabethan No. 7296 in Bath
1957 - Corinthian Pillar No. 7552 in Yeovil

Brigadier-General Claude Lumsden Norman

He was in East Africa in 1903-4, and in Somaliland. In the Great War in 1914-18 he was mentioned in despatches, awarded the DSO and appointed ADC to the King in 1918. Four years later he retired from the Army and came to live in Somerset. He was then Past District Grand Master of the Punjab.

Initiated in India on the 6th December 1906, Bro Norman became a Joining Member of the Lodge of St. George, No. 3158, Taunton and in 1930 became the first WM of the Taunton Deane Lodge, No. 5221. He was installed as Provincial Grand Master for Somerset at Yeovil on the 23rd May 1935, by the Pro Grand Master, Lord Ampthill who had installed his predecessor, Archdeacon Farrer.

Brig. Gen. Norman was born 19th Feb 1876, the younger son of Field-Marshal Sir H.W. Norman and was educated at Marlborough. He was gazetted a 2nd Lieut. in 1896. He served on the NW Frontier of India in 1897-98, was engaged in operations in the Kurram Valley and Terah.

Throughout his term of Office, not only had there been greater interest shown in the objects and principles of Freemasonry by those who were not Freemasons, but within the Fraternity itself those objects and principles were being observed and practised with greater enthusiasm than ever before. This enthusiasm had been fostered by the example and precept of the

PGM. In his foreword in the Somerset Masonic Reference Book for 1960-61 he said :

"If I have been lucky enough to help anyone to a clearer vision of the tenets and purposes of the Craft, then I have been amply rewarded."

Brig. Gen. Norman always took the greatest interest in the Charities, and he considered it the best work he had been able to do when he divided the Province into two and appointed in each half a Brother to advise and encourage the Lodges in their work for the Charities.

As PGM, he presided at the Girls' Festival on the 13th May 1943, and had the satisfaction of handing to the Girls' School a total sum of £88,271 of which £26,893.6s was contributed by his own Province. This was approximately £11,600 more than the Province contributed for the Boys' Festival in 1929. It must not be forgotten that 1943 was one of the worst years of the War for collecting donations. Few people had much to give. The result, therefore, is all the more to be commended.

He also presided at the Festival of the Royal Masonic Benevolent Institution in 1953. He must have been very gratified to have been able to hand over to the Institution on that occasion a total sum of £129,106 of which no less than £49,972 was provided by the Brethren in the Province of Somerset. (This amount was made up to £50,000 within a few days of the publication of the result.) It was a magnificent combined effort by all the Brethren in the Province, led and guided by the two Charity Representatives who had been appointed for the first time in 1948 by the Provincial Grand Master.

Brig. Gen. Norman was installed as WM of the Somerset Masters' Lodge on 26th February, 1940, the 25th anniversary of its foundation. It is typical of him that he did not attempt to contribute on that occasion a paper on some learned aspect of Masonic History, but drew attention to those fundamental principles the practice of which must be our constant concern:

"We ought to try to encourage our younger brethren to join the Correspondence Circle," he said "and so increase their real knowledge of Freemasonry. Very often too much stress is laid on the outward and visible sign and too little on the inner and more important meaning and spirit of the Brotherhood."

It was, therefore, with profound regret that the Province heard R.W.Bro Norman announce his resignation as Provincial Grand Master for the Province of Somerset, with effect from the 31st of that month, at the meeting of Provincial Grand Lodge, held at the Empire Hall, Taunton, on the 12th May, 1960. He had been a Mason for 54 years, 25 of them PGM for Somerset.

Only once before in a period of nearly 200 years had anyone resigned as Provincial Grand Master in Somerset. However, when the first shock of the announcement began to subside, one realised the level of indebtedness owed to R.W.Bro Norman for the many years of unselfish service he had given to Freemasonry in Somerset.

By way of illustration, Col. Tynte was Provincial Grand Master for 40 years, from 1820 to 1860. During this time only five new Lodges were consecrated, one of which was erased in 1853, as compared with thirteen new Lodges from R.W.Bro Norman's appointment in 1935.

Apparently, one of the reasons why he resigned was to give his successor a chance to prepare for the Festival of the Boys' School in 1963. It was said of him

"Age creeps inexorably upon us, and we cannot admire and praise too much those who recognise that fact and make the path easier for their successors."

Brig. Arnold de Lerisson Cazenove CBE DSO MVO DL

12th Provincial Grand Master for Somerset 1961-1969

Extant Lodges Consecrated

1962 - John de Clivedon No. 7824 in Clevedon
1964 - Backwell No. 7964 in Nailsea
1964 - St. Dunstan's No. 7973 in Glastonbury
1964 - Tynte No. 7994 in Bridgwater
1965 - Forest of Mendip No. 8019 in Blagdon
1968 - Taunton School No. 8215 in Taunton

Brigadier Arnold de Lerisson Cazenove,

At the Quarterly Communication of Grand Lodge, held at Freemason's Hall, Great Queen Street, London, in December, 1960, the M.W the Grand Master proclaimed:

"The other announcement I wish to make is that since the last Quarterly Communication I have appointed W.Bro. Brigadier Arnold de Lerisson Cazenove, PGD, as Provincial Grand Master

for Somerset, to fill the vacancy caused by the resignation of R.W.Bro Brigadier General Norman, who is in his 85th year and has held office for the past 25 years."

R.W.Bro Cazenove resided at Ham Manor, near Shepton Mallet. He was the son of Arthur Philip Cazenove, of the London Stock Exchange and of Isabel, daughter of General Sir Charles Shute, KCB.

Like his predecessor he had a distinguished military career. He was educated at Eton and Sandhurst and joined the Coldstream Guards in 1916. He served over-seas in the First World War and was mentioned in Despatches.

Then followed a period of administrative work in the years between the two World Wars. He was Adjutant of the 2nd Bn. Coldstream Guards between 1922-25; on the General Staff, London District, 1926-29 and Brigade Major of the Brigade of Guards, 1933-36. In the latter year he was appointed a Member of the Victorian Order. From 1937 to 1939 he was Commandant of the Guards Depot

On the outbreak of war in 1939 he was given command of the 1st Bn. Coldstream Guards and in 1940 was awarded the DSO. In 1943 he was also made a Companion of the Order of the British Empire.

After the War he was Deputy Commander of the Aldershot District, 1947-50 and was ADC to King George V, 1949-50. He retired in 1950. Promoted Brevet Lieut. Colonel in 1937 and Lieut. Colonel in 1939, he became Temporary Brigadier in 1940, Colonel in 1942 and Brigadier in 1948.

R.W.Bro Brig. Cazenove was a Freemason for upwards of 41 years. His mother Lodge was Studholme Lodge, No. 1591, in which he was initiated on 28th May, 1920. He was WM of the Lodge in 1938. In that same year he had the unusual experience of being W. Deputy Master of the Household Brigade Lodge, No. 2614, HRH the Duke of Connaught being WM of the Lodge at that time.

This is the Lodge in which King Edward VIII when Prince of Wales, was initiated on 2nd May 1919. R.W.Bro Brig. Cazenove became a Joining Member of that Lodge on 23rd April, 1934. Grand Lodge honoured him with the rank of Senior Grand Deacon of England in 1948.

On his retirement from the Army he came to live at Ham Manor, near Shepton Mallet, and on 17th January, 1951, became a Joining Member of the Lodge of Love and Honour, No. 285, Shepton Mallet and in 1954 was given the rank of PPSGW of Somerset.

In the Royal Arch he was Exalted in the Studholme Chapter on 15th March, 1939, of which he was MEZ in 1953. He was Advanced in the Euston Lodge of Mark MMs on 8th July, 1921, from which he resigned on 31st December, 1931. Apparently the same dates apply to his membership of the Royal Ark Mariners.

He was Perfected in the Eton and Harrow Chapter of the Ancient and Accepted Rite on 8th November, 1949, from which he resigned on 31st December, 1954.

R.W.Bro Brig. Cazenove was duly installed as Provincial Grand Master for Somerset, with the impressive dignity of Grand Lodge ceremonial at a meeting of Provincial Grand Lodge held in the Winter Gardens Pavilion, Weston-super-Mare, on Thursday, 4th May, 1961, by the Most Worshipful the Grand Master, The Earl of Scarborough.

He was assisted and supported by the Assistant Grand Master, R.W.Bro Major-General Sir Allan Adair, Bart, R.W.Bro the Hon. William R.S. Bathurst, FSA, Provincial Grand Master for Gloucestershire; R.W.Bro. Colonel E. Roderick Hill, Provincial Grand Master for Monmouthshire; R.W.Bro The Rev. A.T.A. Naylor, Past Provincial Grand Master for Sussex; V.W.Bro J.W. Stubbs, the Grand Secretary; the R.W.Bro Frank Douglas, The Grand Director of Ceremonies, two Deputy Grand Directors of Ceremonies and a large number of Past Grand Lodge Officers.

He served the Province well and resigned through ill-health in January 1969. His retirement was short, for he died in the April of that year.

Lt. Col. Harry Owen Hughes OBE ED

13th Provincial Grand Master for Somerset 1969-1980

Extant Lodges Consecrated

1973 - Richard Huish No. 8518 in Taunton
1974 - Saltford No. 8633 in Keynsham
1975 - Vivary No. 8654 in Taunton
1977 - Woodspring No. 8791 in Yatton
1980 - Forest of Selwood No 8912 in Frome

Lt. Col. Harry Owen Hughes

R.W.Bro Brig. Cazenove retired from the Provincial Grand Mastership due to ill health in January 1969 and sadly died within three months. His successor was R.W.Bro Lt. Col. Harry Owen Hughes, the Past District Grand Master for Hong Kong & South China (1956-1961).

Initiated in 1924 in the Victoria Lodge in Hong Kong he became its Worshipful Master in 1930. The 1920s were a time of growing internal strife in China coupled with increased resentment of the West. Hong Kong was not excluded from the impact of ideological struggle. The

Seaman's Strike of 1922 and the General Strike of 1925-26 crippled the port and damaged the economy of the Colony. An emergency situation existed, and thus a fresh impetus was given to the Volunteer Corps whose services were again needed for humdrum but essential work. Lt. Col. H. Owen Hughes recalls being called out for six weeks in 1925, and combining office work by day with duty by night patrolling the streets and guarding hospitals and vulnerable points. With the coming of WW2 in the Far East he sent his family home to England, to Somerset, with which he formed the ties which caused him on retirement to settle in Compton Dundon, between Street and Somerton.

In 1964 he was introduced to the Province, giving a lecture on Masonry in the Far East. In 1969 he ascended to the Chair of the Province being installed by R.W.Bro Major-General Sir Allan Adair. His style was that of an ingrained Commanding Officer, already by the 1970s becoming passé.

Many are the apocryphal tales still rumbling around the Province about his autocratic style. A favourite one is how, when visiting an Installation Meeting at Keynsham, where the Lodge in question used Bristol Working, he retained the Gavel when offered to him and ordered that the ceremony be continued in Emulation! R.W.Bro. Hughes died on the 14th April 1984 aged 83, a packed Memorial Service being held in Wells Cathedral in June.

Kenneth Caswell Kinnersley

14th Provincial Grand Master for Somerset 1981-1991

Extant Lodges Consecrated

1981 - Gerard No. 8999 in Keynsham
1980 - Wraxall No. 9011 in Nailsea
1982 - Athelstan No. 9033 in Weston-super-Mare
1982 - Cornucopia No. 9043 in Keynsham
1983 - Somerset Tablers No. 9075 in Ilminster
1983 - Showman's Guild No. 9089 in Clevedon
1985 - Somerset Farmers No. 9180 in Langport
1986 - Sir Thomas de Cheddre No. 9188 in Wedmore
1986 - Somerset Provincial Grand Stewards No. 9189 in Weston-super-Mare
1986 - Kenneth Kinnersley No. 9218 in Midsomer Norton
1987 - Somerset Fairway No. 9251 in Burnham-on-Sea
1988 - Hospitality No. 9299 in Yatton
1989 - St Cecilia No. 9341 in Wedmore
1989 - Emergency Services No. 9391 in Taunton

Kenneth Caswell Kinnersley
Reproduced by kind permission of
Bath in Time/Bath Central Library Collection

R.W.Bro Kinnersley was initiated into Connaught Lodge No. 3573, Midsomer Norton in 1939 and could have had no possible thought of what pleasure, distinction and authority lay ahead of him.

He was educated at Queen's College, Taunton. Following his education he entered the family business until the Second World War called him away for a seven year stint of service in the Somerset Light Infantry following which he was able to take up his civilian occupation again and to resume his Masonic activities.

There now began a lifetime of service to Freemasonry, passing through the offices of Connaught Lodge becoming WM in 1951, and in 1957 received the acting rank of Provincial Junior Grand Warden. In 1966 he was appointed acting Grand Standard Bearer and in 1969 he served as WM of his school Lodge, Queen's College, Taunton No. 6988. In 1970 he became Provincial Grand Charity Representative (North), continuing until 1973 and culminating in the successful Festival for the Royal Masonic Institution for Girls. His appetite for Masonic activity must have been fully satisfied during that year, for in February he was installed WM of Somerset Masters' Lodge No. 3746 and delivered a paper on 'Masonic Fire'.

In May, he was installed as Assistant Provincial Grand Master of Somerset. He was promoted to Past JGD in 1974 and to Past SGD in 1976. The ultimate accolade came in May 1981, when he was installed as the Provincial Grand Master.

Charitable fund-raising was a major feature of R.W.Bro Kinnersley's leadership and included the very successful RMBI Festival in 1983 that raised £1,145,252 and in 1984 over £162,000 was raised and shared between the Royal Masonic Hospital and local hospitals.

Following his retirement he accepted responsibility for the 1993 Festival that raised over £2m for the Masonic Trust for Girls and Boys. Between 1981 and 1990 the number of Lodges rose from 68 to 81 and total membership from 5626 to 6140. These new Lodges included the Kenneth Kinnersley Lodge No. 9218 at Midsomer Norton of which he became first WM in 1986.

An appointment which gave him much pride and pleasure was President (1986-1988) of the Federation of School Lodges, and subsequently a Federation Patron. R.W.Bro Kinnersley's other Masonic interests were widespread. In the Royal Arch he was First Principal of Connaught Chapter No. 3573 in 1956, becoming Provincial Third Grand Principal in 1958, PAGDC in 1966 and Grand Sojourner in 1974.

In the Mark Degree he became the WM of Mendip Lodge 781 in 1960, Provincial Grand Overseer in 1961, PAGDC in 1973 and PGJO in 1981. After serving as Worshipful Commander of Robert Fuller Lodge of Royal Ark Mariners No. 128 in 1985, he was awarded Provincial Grand Rank in 1986.

In the Ancient and Accepted Rite he was M.W Sovereign of Antiquity Chapter, No. 95, in 1974 and rose to the 32nd degree. Finally, in the United Religious Military and Masonic Orders he was Preceptor of Selwood Preceptory of

St. John No. 244 in 1968, Provincial Sub-Prior 1975-1980, Past Great Standard Bearer (Beauceant) in 1976 and 1st Great Constable in 1986.

His personality would be best revealed in the words of a Past Provincial Grand Secretary who served with him as such for five years and was in almost daily contact with him. He wrote:

"He had a warm and friendly manner with no trace of pomposity or self-importance, and was always the same. He was ever ready to listen and often asked for advice. In all his dealings he was scrupulously fair never critical or unkind and always ready to think the best of everyone, whatever their rank and as a result was always popular and good company within and without his Province."

Relaxation and recreation inevitably form an important part of the life of any man as busy as he was, and these things he found in his garden and in his golfing activities. Hence it came about that on the occasion of the 50th anniversary of his Initiation he was presented with a greenhouse and at his retirement party he received a stainless steel spade, together with an electric typewriter. Not long after his retirement he was very pleased to be able to claim that his tomato plants were better than those of the professional gardener next door! So the greenhouse was being fully used.

In all this we remember a lovable personality displaying humility and yet able to carry off the distinguished position to which he had been elevated. Those who had the privilege of knowing him will be grateful for the experience and will remember him with affection and gratitude.

A well attended Memorial Service was held on 23rd November 2002 at St Mary Magdelene Church, Taunton.

Stanley Herbert Ambrose Frank Hopkins

15th Provincial Grand Master for Somerset 1991-2002

Extant Lodges Consecrated

1991 - Tivoli No. 9417 in Weston-super-Mare
1999 - Olympian No. 9703 in Nailsea
2001 - Sylvanus No. 9741 in Yatton

Stanley H.A.F. Hopkins

On the retirement of Kenneth Caswell Kinnersley, a Somerset farmer, Stanley Hopkins, was invited to take the post. He had been Assistant PGM from the mid-1980s and, after five years in office, had resigned. He was actually on the other side of the world, in Australia, when the invitation came to take the Chair.

Initiated in the Lodge of Prudence & Industry at Chard in 1962, he became Worshipful Master ten years later. In 1978 he was given the active rank of PJGW. In 1986 he became Founder WM of a new Lodge very much to his heart, the

Somerset Farmers Lodge No. 9180, meeting in the old medieval chapel over the town gate at Langport. In 1983 he was appointed Assistant PGM to Kenneth Kinnersley, but, being of the view that five years in office was impeding other younger aspirants, he resigned in 1988. In 1990, whilst in Australia, he was to say the least somewhat surprised to receive the invitation to assume the mantle of authority as Provincial Grand Master for Somerset.

As with many of his predecessors much of his life has been devoted to public office, his sporting and other enthusiasms Among his 'out of Province' involvements he was WM of the Somersetshire Lodge No. 2925 in its Centenary year (2002); a large contingent in a (most uncomfortable) double-decker made the journey to Mark Mason's Hall in London to join him in the celebrations.

His membership of Royal Alpha No 16, (the Grand Masters' Lodge) caused a great panic when, Sylvanus being 'on tour' in Devon, someone entered the Hall during the Festive Board and stole the largest and most splendid of the cases. It was Stanley's and contained his Royal Alpha jewel, fortunately it was returned the next day

His popular leadership as Provincial Grand Master has been hinted at in previous paragraphs, and one can do no better to sum up his qualities and achievements than by repeating here the Curriculum cum Laude written by his successor, our present PGM, R.W.Bro David Lloyd

*Still active representing the Province,
PPGM Stanley H.A.F. Hopkins
pictured here in 2009 congratulating
W.Bro K. Goddard on his Installation as
WM of Elizabethan Lodge No. 7296*

Jenkins. He refers to his "sound judgement and firm leadership", to his being "the epitome of loyalty and good humour"- all this and more; with tremendous energy and enthusiasm, he has brought the Province of Somerset to the fore, in modern outlook and progress.

A Tribute to Stanley Hopkins
Provincial Grand Master for Somerset
by David Lloyd Jenkins
Published in 2002

As the time approaches when our Provincial Grand Master will be retiring, I welcome the opportunity, in this the last edition of Compass during his stewardship, to put some thoughts to paper about the Province. This may allow us to reflect on the achievements and progress we have all witnessed over the past twelve years and to consider where the path that leads into the future may take us.

The one thing I positively wish to avoid is making any comment or reflecting thoughts that could in any way be construed as some sort of obituary. Nothing could possibly be further from the aim. I simply wish to pay

tribute to a very special person, and to his equally special and wonderfully supportive wife Sylvia, affectionately known as 'head office', who together have devoted endless time and boundless energy in pursuing, and being involved in, every aspect of Provincial life.

In any good and successful organisation the Chief Executive Officer's principal duty is to assess, determine and implement action considered necessary or prudent to promote performance and progress. While Masonry is not a business, and should never be construed as such, its operations are nevertheless of necessity subject to a number of important parameters often found in a commercial organisation. Without them it would be difficult to see how such an organisation could plan or indeed have cohesive aspirations or objectives.

For this reason of course, each Province has its own management committee to plan, administer, organise and, in the case of a Province like Somerset, accept invitations from Lodges to perform ceremonies and dedications. The strengths and achievements of Freemasonry in Somerset over the past twelve years have been inextricably geared to well defined objectives now being addressed by the Craft as a whole.

Misconceived public conception about the aims of the Craft, its apparent inward looking philosophy and perceived secrecy, has prompted it to be viewed by many as suspicious and undesirable. Regrettably such mistrust has been evident within some Government Departments and elsewhere. Fortunately there is now clear evidence that the situation is changing and more responsible attitudes being adopted by those who have tried to discriminate against Freemasons and have found themselves relentlessly pursued by Grand Lodge.

Under the firm guidance and steadfastness of the Provincial Grand Master, Somerset has been in the forefront of Provinces actively addressing these issues and implementing change and innovation. His close involvement at the highest levels in the Craft including the Grand Master's Council, has enabled him to have an unprecedented insight into the importance and urgency of action needed to protect the long term welfare of the Craft.

His sound judgement and firm leadership have motivated the Province to develop into all sorts of areas that, until his stewardship, had been largely unexplored. Widows Associations, Provincial Team Ceremonies, Provincial Ties, Compass Magazine, the internet, training and education, seminars for Officers and Master Masons, social meetings for new Masons and their wives, Provincial charitable donations to local causes, The Provincial Benevolent Fund, and the Open Days held at major Masonic Centres within the Province are just some of the innovative measures introduced during the past twelve years. There are others on the horizon such as a Provincial Stand at the Royal Bath and West Show.

Openness, perhaps not the choicest of words, and not the choice of all brethren, is not something that Freemasonry was forced to implement. It was introduced because of its unparalleled importance in proving to the world who are not Masons that Masonry has nothing to hide, but on the contrary has much to give to the world.

The generous charitable giving by Masons to non-Masonic causes is well known and widely acknowledged, thus the Freemasonry in the Community initiative scheduled for June 2002 provides a great opportunity for Freemasons together to really demonstrate that 'being happy and communicating happiness' is what we are about. It will hopefully demonstrate that Freemasonry is a way of life open to those prepared to live by its precepts.

R.W.Bro Stanley has been and remains the epitome of loyalty and good humour. He,

above all in this Province, has shown by fine leadership and unswerving dedication that, in spite of the plethora of opportunities available for men to spend their free time, Masonry can offer them great fellowship tempered by good order and self-discipline, confidence in what the Order stands for and self-confidence.

The opportunities provided through the precepts of the Craft to be of service to fellow Freemasons, their families and dependents, as well as underprivileged and less fortunate non-Masons, and the pleasure we derive by helping, may well have prompted that wonderful remark from Delboy, 'everyone's a winner'. The Provincial Grand Master has often said that the future of Freemasonry is in the hands of its members.

This must be right because each Lodge is ultimately responsible for attracting the right calibre of initiate, and carefully nurturing their welfare and progress. The welfare of the Craft however also requires special care and attention, but I'm quite certain that the firm and extensive foundations laid by R.W.Bro Stanley to support the changes we need to continue to make in the coming years, will not only be found to be reliable but eminently satisfactory as we march on into the future.

It is my very great privilege to have been asked to succeed R.W.Bro Stanley in 2002, and I have been honoured to accept in the sure knowledge that he has set the Province on a sound course and manned it with a magnificent crew. I shall do my best when the time comes, but for now extend to Stanley and Sylvia our love and every possible good wish.

We shall as always look forward to the pleasure of their company at all our events in the future, providing of course that they're allowed out of Southern Ireland, take care with the horses, and successfully negotiate pass-out's from the grandchildren!

David Lloyd Jenkins

16th Provincial Grand Master for Somerset

Extant Lodges Consecrated

2005 - Sir Isaac Newton No. 9801

David Lloyd Jenkins

When R.W.Bro Stanley Hopkins retired from Office as Provincial Grand Master on 14th February 2002, R.W.Bro David Jenkins was appointed to succeed him and was installed by R.W.Bro David Williamson, Assistant Grand Master on 4th April 2002 as the 16th Provincial Grand Master for the Province of Somerset.

The Office of Provincial Grand Master needs firm leadership, vision, common sense and above all (these days), the common touch.

R.W.Bro David brought with him those qualities in great abundance

He was born in 1940 and so came to Office at the age of 62. He was educated at Taunton School from 1946 to 1958 and then joined the Dunlop Rubber Company as a management trainee, subsequently working overseas in Lebanon and other areas of the Middle East. From 1971 he spent five years in Nigeria as Marketing Services Manager followed by two years in London.

In 1982 he joined the family business of Sidem UK Ltd as a Director (Military Consultancy and Procurement). David retired from the company in 2006 and was thus able to bring to his new appointment a very considerable commercial experience which is so vital in heading a large, forward looking and growing organisation as our Provincial Grand Lodge.

A devoted family man, David married Pauline (Poo) Austin in 1979 and they in due course produced four sons, all incidentally educated as Taunton School. The wife of the Provincial Grand Master plays a huge part in the running of the Province by giving her active support. Poo has displayed tremendous devotion to the cause and is immensely popular throughout the Province.

It is important for a Provincial Grand Master to possess a wide range of interests other than Freemasonry. Again David brought with him considerable experience in the world of Golf (Past Captain of the Burnham & Berrow Golf Club), Music (a very fine Organist), the

Old Boy's Association of Taunton School, (Past President) and the Church (Sidesman, St. Mary's, Berrow).

R.W.Bro David's Masonic experience is considerable. He was Initiated into Taunton School Lodge No. 8215 in 1979 and became WM in 1989, subsequently becoming a Joining Member of Unanimity and Sincerity, Taunton in 1981 and WM in 1992. Likewise he joined The Old Tauntonian Lodge in 1990, Somerset Master's Lodge in 1993 becoming WM in 2002 and Old Union Lodge No. 46 in 2006.

R.W.Bro David was a founder of the Somerset Fairway Lodge in 1987 and WM in 1989 and was appointed Provincial Almoner in 1994 an Office he held with distinction for four years. He was promoted to PJGD in 1997 and further promoted to PSGD in 1998 on his appointment as Assistant Provincial Grand Master .

David has also been very widely involved in many other Degrees of Masonry. He was Exalted into the Old Tauntonian Chapter No. 5735 in 1984 being a Past Z of the Chapter. A Founder of Taunton Deane Chapter No. 5221 and also a PZ of the Chapter.

He was appointed to Provincial Rank in 1995 and Grand Rank in 2003 with a promotion to Dep. G. Sword Bearer in 2007. He is also a Past Master of the William Long Lodge of Mark Master Masons, a PGSD of Grand Mark Lodge and a member of the William Long RAM No. 191, and is an active member of KT and KT Priests and The Royal Order of Scotland, SW Counties.

Nationally he has served as a council member of the Board of the Grand Charity, Chairman of the Appeals and Donations Committee and a Vice President from 2000 to 2002 He was appointed to the Board of General Purposes in 2003 and a member of the Panel of Clemency in 2007. Under his Presidency of the 2007 Festival for the Royal Masonic Benevolent Institution, the Province produced the remarkable figure of £3,564,167.

This was an outstanding result from a comparatively small Province, a product of his drive and leadership and a triumph for the Brethren and their families of the Province. In addition the new Children's Hospice at Wraxall benefited from our general charity funds, as did many local charities

Part Three

MASONIC CENTRES

Masonic Centres of the Province of Somerset

Masonic Centres in Somerset

Portishead
Clevedon
Nailsea
Yatton
Keynsham Bath
Weston-s-Mare
Blagdon
Midsomer
Norton
Burnham on Sea Wedmore
Wells Shepton
Minehead
Mallet
Frome
Watchet
Glastonbury
Bridgwater
Somerset
Bruton
Wiveliscombe
Wincanton
Taunton
Langport
Wellington
Yeovil
Ilminster
Chard Crewkerne

Introduction

by W.Bro Malcolm Shearer

Treasures come in many shapes and forms, and none more so than those that are Masonic, or are in some way related to Freemasonry. In this sense they can be old and genuinely antique, or much more modern, as a treasure is always measured in the eye of the beholder.

The Province of Somerset is no exception as to the number, richness and beauty of its Masonic artefacts, many of which have been mentioned, described and pictured in the individual Lodge submissions.

These submissions, somewhat inevitably, do not cover everything of worth, and an attempt is made in the following pages to indicate what else is worth describing and where possible illustrated. This has been done by Masonic Hall rather than by Masonic Lodge, the more so to encourage the reader to seek out and expand on those items which excite the most. Indeed, not every Masonic Hall has been mentioned, as several of the Lodge submissions cover those treasures which can be found there.

As one would expect, those Masonic Halls where the Province's older Lodges meet provide the main avenues of discovery and exploration.

Equally inevitable is the need to explain that these descriptions are not and cannot be exhaustive, as in all things one man's meat is another man's poison and Masonic antiques and artefacts are no exception. What is certain is that hidden in back cupboards and out of way drawers in many Masonic Halls there will remain a wealth of Masonic treasures still to be found, and in this sense Somerset will be no different than many other Provinces.

So to all Somerset Masons one must not only express a regret, but also an apology if some object that matters to you, your Lodge, or your Masonic Hall has been missed or wrongly described; this is definitely not intentional. Similarly, there were a small number of important images that we could not photograph, but were subsequently supplied by a Lodge. Because it was necessary to have an image in the book, we have included these even though they are not of the quality of the rest of the book.

As Somerset Freemasonry is at least 275 years old it is perhaps appropriate to commence with Bath, which apart from being the first alphabetically, it is the Province's first known Masonic location.

Bath

The Masonic Hall, Old Orchard Street, Bath BA1 IJU

Lodges Meeting in Bath

Royal Cumberland Lodge No. 41
Royal Sussex Lodge No. 53
Lodge of Honour No. 379
Royal Albert Edward Lodge No. 906
Somerset Masters Lodge No. 3746
St. Alphege Lodge No. 4095
St. Lukes Lodge No. 6540
Elizabethan Lodge No. 7296

Royal Cumberland Chapter 41
Royal Sussex Chapter 53 • St. Lukes Chapter 6540
Royal Cumberland Mark Lodge Tl •,Royal Sussex Mark Lodge No. 177
Bath Lodge of Royal Ark Mariners TI
St. Peter and St. Paul Chapter No. 6 (RC) • Antiquity Chapter No 95 (RC)
Antiquity Encampment No 1(KT) • Bladud Preceptory No 40 (KT)
The Antiquity & Bladud Priory (KH)
King Edgar Tabernacle No 31 (KTP) • Reginald Fitzjocelyn Chapel No. 74 (STA)
Wessex Council 41 (RSM)
Frederick Lace Council No. 55 (AMD)

Where it all began in Cheap Street, Bath. The Bear Inn was the two taller buildings in the centre of this drawing.
The first minuted Meeting was held here in 1732 and it was also the scene of the Initiation of John Smith MP as PGM
The Queens Head, the earlier home of the City of Bath Lodge was the building on the far right
Reproduced by kind permission of Bath in Time/Bath Central Library Collection

It was here that the seeds of Freemasonry in Somerset were first sown, Bath being the first provincial town in England to formally possess a Lodge, The City of Bath Lodge No. 28, which was first formed in 1724, at the Queen's Head Inn in Cheap Street, by Dr John Desaguliers, then Deputy Grand Master of the Order.

Although that Lodge disappeared in 1736, The Masonic Hall, Old Orchard Street, is still the home of the oldest Lodge in the Province, Royal Cumberland Lodge No. 41, which was originally deputised in 1732 as the Bear Inn Lodge; it is also the meeting place of numerous other Lodges and Degrees and had a most interesting history before becoming the Masonic Hall in 1865. But more of that later, as it is actually the second building in Bath to bear the name.

The original Bath Masonic Hall was erected in York Street, by three of the four Lodges then extant in Bath, Royal Cumberland (then No. 55),

The Royal York Lodge of Perfect Friendship No. 243 and Lodge of Virtue No. 311. The latter two both folded during the following few years, for reasons that can all be traced back to the debacle that the enterprise caused. The other Bath Lodge of the time, Royal Sussex No. 53, which was originally formed in 1812 as an Antients Lodge, had decided to take no part in Project. The Hall could not have had a more promising start to its life, for it was officially dedicated in 1819 by the Grand Master of the United Grand Lodge of England, His Royal Highness Prince Augustus Frederick, Duke of Sussex. The ceremony was preceded by a procession through the City where the Grand Master was accompanied by over 1,000 Masons, including representatives of the Grand Lodges of England and Ireland, plus 29 Provincial Grand Lodges, and followed by a Banquet at The Guildhall.

Within three years, the project was in tatters. The three Lodges had overextended themselves financially, and debts amounting to several thousands of pounds had built-up. The Lodges, and their associated Chapters, had each agreed to pay a sum of rent annually, from which this debt would be serviced, but it would appear that no rent had ever been paid by them. The first creditor to become concerned was the landowner, the Duke of Kingston, who was not only entitled to ground rent, but had also advanced a one thousand pound loan to finance part of the building costs. Two senior Masons, W.Bro Geary of Royal Cumberland Lodge, and W.Bro Whitney of Lodge of Virtue, had signed personal guarantees for the loan, so they attempted to resolve the problems through a Tontine, but although there were numerous subscribers willing to take part, including the Duke himself, there were not sufficient of them to raise the entire amount required. It was at this point that Charles Geary, being a wealthy Wine Merchant, paid-off the debt and took over the ownership of the Hall.

As part of that arrangement, the Lodges continued to use the building for another year, but the circumstances surrounding the payment of rent by them, both current and past, appear to have caused continual animosity, and this resulted in the eventual closure of the building by Geary. As part of that move, the Lodge Furniture was locked within the building, and what amounted to a confiscation of the property began a long and acrimonious dispute that lasted nearly twenty years. During that time, many claims and counter-claims were made, and various individuals became embroiled in what became known as The Bath Furniture Incident, of which there have been numerous accounts written. It is difficult to establish what exactly happened over that long period, but whatever actually transpired, the final resolution came in 1842, when the building was sold to The Society of Friends, who still own it to this day, and the Furniture was acquired in its entirety

The Masonic Hall in York Street
Drawn and Engraved by H.S. Storer 1818

by the Loyal Lodge of Barnstaple No. 251. It is still in use in their Lodge Rooms at Trafalgar Lawns in Barnstaple, a building that provides a perfect contemporary period setting for this wonderful Georgian furniture.

The original Master's Chair, Rococo Pillars, Pedestal and Candlestick from the York Street Hall, Now in Loyal Lodge in Barnstaple.

For most of the next twenty years the Bath Lodges, once again numbering three with the creation in 1825 of Lodge of Honour No. 379 from the remnants of the two extinct Lodges, shared rooms rented from the architect Goodridge at the rear of the Corridor, an elegant small shopping arcade he had created opposite the Guildhall. However, with the upsurge in membership from the mid-1850s, a need for larger, and more permanent, accommodation became a necessity. So in 1865, a joint committee was formed to find a suitable location, chaired by one of the City's largest employers, and then Worshipful Master of Royal Sussex Lodge, John Lum Stothert. The result was the acquisition of the original Bath Theatre Royal building in Old Orchard Street.

It was opened in 1750 as Bath's first purpose-built Theatre, by a syndicate headed by John Palmer Senior, a successful Brewer and Tallow-Chandler in the City. Other members of the syndicate included Richard 'Beau' Nash, the City's long-standing Master of Ceremonies, James Quin, a famous London actor who had recently-retired to the City, and John Wood the Elder, the architect responsible for most of Bath's finest buildings, and the landlord for the plot of land it was erected upon.

The original building consisted merely of the room that now forms the Temple. The stage was at the same end as it is now, and there were three galleries along either side. The floor sloped from the rear wall of the building, where the main entrance was situated, to a depth of five feet in front of the stage, forming a pit that accommodated the majority of the audience, which on full houses would number over 500.

Over the next fifteen years, the building was remodelled, and during this period some of the tenement rooms were added along the frontage to Orchard Street to provide lodging and dressing rooms for the actors and staff. A domed roof was added which helped to create an interior that was described in contemporary accounts as 'esteemed, in fancy, elegance, and construction, inferior to none in Europe'.

In 1768, John Palmer Junior took over the management of the Theatre Company from his father, and succeeded in obtaining a Royal Patent, making it the first provincial Theatre Royal, and only the third to hold that honour in England, the other two being Covent Garden and Drury Lane in London. He would go on to also create the Theatre Royal in Bristol, and then to even greater fame as the creator of the Mail Coach system, which brought him the office of Comptroller General of the Post Office. He later became MP for Bath, and was also Mayor of the City twice.

An early photograph of the Lodge Room at Bath c1890

With the additional prestige the Royal title provided, the success of the Company went from strength to strength, and in 1774 major changes and extensions were made which created the building that exists today. A further 25 feet were added at the rear of the building, creating a Crush Room (essentially an entrance foyer) above which were arranged seven grand boxes in a fan-shape, all named after English kings. The stage was raised in height and completely remodelled with the grand Doric and Ionic pillars that still form the backdrop to the Master's Chair today. An orchestra pit was added in front of the stage, and four further boxes were also incorporated at the sides of the stage, one of which still remains on the left hand side. One casualty was the decorous dome, which had not only proved to be a disaster acoustically, but also provided no means of ventilation whatsoever. It was replaced with the current ceiling incorporating a displacement ventilation system supplying fresh air equally diffused across the auditorium, which is still in working order today.

Over the next 30 years, the Theatre Royal Bath would become one of the most prestigious provincial theatres, and would attract to its company some of the most famous actors and actresses of the day. Names like Henderson, Courtney, Incledon, Kemble, Ellison and Dimond would feature regularly on its Playbills, along with probably the finest tragic actress of all time, Sarah Siddons. Mrs Siddons was a member of the Bath Company from 1778 to 1782, where she made her name before moving-on to an international career that would last for over 30 years more. Her name takes pride of place on a bronze plaque commemorating the building's theatre history, erected in 1937

beside the main entrance in Old Orchard Street by Bath Corporation and unveiled by one of her most illustrious successors, Dame Ellen Terry. The theatre company eventually outgrew the facilities and in 1805 moved to its current home in Beauford Square, whereupon the Orchard Street building was closed. In 1809 it was acquired by the Catholic Benedictine Mission to Bath, and converted it into a Chapel. The main changes were the removal of the side galleries and orchestra pit, and to raise and level the floor, creating a series of vaults beneath. An altar was erected in the centre of the stage, with a pulpit to the left; the right-hand stage boxes removed to make room for an organ. Pews were then installed stretching all the way back into the crush room, and the fan-shaped boxes above were retained to provide overall accommodation for around one thousand worshippers.

A few years later, the Mission also acquired the building next door at No.5 Pierrepont Place for use as a lodging house for the priests and other staff, and this allowed them to convert the old dressing rooms at the front of the theatre building into schoolrooms. In 1817, a new Priest came from Ampleforth in Yorkshire to take charge of the Chapel, and he would be responsible for some further changes to the building. His name was Peter Augustine Baines, and he would later become Bishop Baines, the founder of Prior Park College.

Old Orchard Street as a Roman Catholic Chapel

He not only was responsible for Orchard Street, but also for a number of other buildings that the mission had acquired over the previous 50 years since emancipation had begun, all of which he found in a state of dilapidation. He set to work putting the estate in order, and also acquired the building at No.2 Pierrepont Place as his new Presbytery. He struck up a working relationship with the architect Goodridge that would last for many years, the first fruits of which can be seen in Orchard Street. The large windows in the south wall were added by him, but probably the most striking work is in a small private chapel he created in a rear room of No.5 Pierrepont Place, with access from the main chapel behind the stage. This small chapel is now used by the Knights Templar orders that meet at Bath Masonic Hall, and was refurbished in 2010.

The Knights Templar Chapel

Although a lot of the restrictions on Catholic worship had been relaxed by that time, at the time the Chapel was opened it was still illegal to bury Catholics in consecrated ground, a law that would not be fully-repealed until over 30 years later. Therefore, the vaults were used for the interment of parishioners, and more than 300 were buried there between 1809 and 1855. These were all transferred to Perrymead Cemetery when it was opened in 1857, although a number of the memorial tablets were left behind. These were discovered when the vaults were excavated in 2002, and now form part of the display in the Building's Museum.

One of the Vaults

When Royal Sussex Lodge acquired the building on behalf of all of the Lodges in 1865, the chapel itself had been closed two years earlier when the congregation transferred to the newly-built St John's Church on South Parade. The total purchase price was £150, and included the presbytery and lodging houses at numbers 2 and 5 Pierrepont Place.

A further £500 was then expended on converting the main building for use as a Masonic Temple. The lower windows in the south wall were filled in, and the pews were all removed, some of the timber being used to create the two sidescreens. The colonnade between the main auditorium and the crush room was walled-in to create an ante room for changing outside of the Temple. The only other changes that were made were to reconfigure some of the internal accesses to create separate rentable accommodation utilising the various separate entrances to the building. The various rooms at the front of the building, the vaults, and the additional buildings at Nos. 2 and 5 Pierrepont Place were then all leased to tenants to provide income for the upkeep of the Masonic Hall.

The Temple was dedicated by Royal Sussex Lodge on 3rd December 1866, and the other two Lodges, Royal Cumberland and Lodge of Honour, together with their associated side orders, all became tenants, an arrangement that would continue for around 25 years. The next major addition was the Reredos, which was acquired in 1878 from the Chapel of St Mary on the corner of Queen Square, which was demolished in order to widen the road leading to the new Midland Railway station at Green Park. The three paintings of King Solomon, Hiram King of Tyre and Hiram Abiff were added, all of which were painted by John Joseph Barker, a member of the famous Barkers of Bath artist dynasty.

The Reredos

In 1890, the decision was taken to add a Dining Room into the building. To achieve this, the seven boxes over the Ante Room were finally removed, and the dividing wall between the Ante room and the temple extended upwards to the ceiling. The space created on the first floor behind the wall was then fitted-out to provide a kitchen and dining room. The majority of the considerable cost of all of this was borne jointly by Royal Sussex and Royal Cumberland Lodges, but the result was that another Lodge, Royal Albert Edward No. 906, moved from their accommodation in Weston Village to also become tenants. It was at this juncture that it was decided that the maintenance of the building was best financed jointly by all users, and a Trust Committee was formed to do so, with representatives elected from each Lodge to serve upon it.

The next two major additions came from a common source, through the closure of another chapel in the City. The Octagon Chapel had been in Milsom Street for over 150 years, and was famous, among other things, for being the establishment where Sir William Herschel had become the resident organist after moving to the City. So when the contents of the chapel were put up for auction in 1896, the opportunity arose to obtain a replacement for the aged and dilapidated organ that had been inherited from the Catholic Chapel.

Representatives of the Trust Committee attended the auction, and were successful in purchasing the Herschel Organ, a quite magnificent instrument of its time. Unfortunately, when they came to plan for its disassembly and installation at Old Orchard Street, they discovered that it was too large to be accommodated without making major alterations to the Temple. They therefore sought assistance from local organ makers Griffen & Stroud, who were able to dispose of it for them and use the proceeds to acquire and install a Norman Bros & Beard organ purchased from the newly-closed Bath Spa College, previously Vellore House. This is the instrument still installed today and, having been restored in 2009, in regular use for Lodge meetings.

Another item acquired at the same auction was the William Hoare painting of the Pool at Bethesda, which now takes pride of place on the West wall of the Temple, and is the largest of Hoare's works on display in Bath. William Hoare lived and worked in Bath for most of his illustrious career, and was considered by his peers to be the best portrait artist of his day, even above his Bath compatriot and fellow founder

of the Royal Academy, Thomas Gainsborough. He produced the painting in 1768 as one of the altarpieces for the Octagon Chapel. It was purchased at the 1896 auction by W.Bro Charles Radway and subsequently presented to Royal Sussex Lodge by him.

The Bath Organ

In 1923, further major changes were undertaken to accommodate the expanding membership which had resulted in the creation of another Lodge meeting at the Hall, St Alphege No. 4095. The dining room was enlarged to its current capacity of 75 diners, and a new larger kitchen was created in the first floor rooms at the front of the building. An enlarged entrance foyer was also created and a staircase installed that stretches from the foyer right up to the rooms on the other three floors. Two second floor rooms were made into a Stewards' Room and Library, and the rooms on the third floor

The Pool of Bethesda by William Hoare 1768
A painting of national significance

provided for the creation of a Masonic Museum. This was opened in 1925, and named after its first curator, W.Bro George Norman. The remaining rooms on the ground and first floors were converted to create a flat to accommodate the resident caretaker. This room configuration is essentially that of the Hall as used today.

In 1930, the Masonic Hall Trust was presented with an exact replica of the original Master's Chair that had been lost from the York Street Hall. This gift was made by W.Bro A Leonard Fuller, the Provincial Senior Grand Warden for Somerset, to commemorate the 100th anniversary of the Bath Furniture Incident, mentioned previously. The replica was made by the Bath furniture makers Mallet & Son, and it is this chair that takes pride of place in the Temple today. In 1931 a bequest from a member of Royal Albert Edward Lodge enabled the

Trustees to purchase the building next door on the corner of Henry Street, which was also let as flats. This building was lost, however, during the Second World War when it sustained a direct hit during one of the infamous Baedecker Raids on the City and was completely destroyed.

Over a 36-hour period beginning at 10pm on April 25th 1942, three separate raids were mounted on the City by the German Luftwaffe. In that time a total of nearly 5000 bombs were dropped within the City boundaries, ninety percent of which were incendiaries. More than 19,000 buildings were damaged or destroyed and more than 400 civilians lost their lives. One of the damaged buildings was The Masonic Hall in Old Orchard Street. The blast from the direct hit on Henry Street caused damage to the Hall that was so extensive that it was initially included on the Council's demolition list. Once reprieved, a portion of the roof had to be removed and replaced, plus considerable repair work to the stonework and interior. The repairs cost a total of £4,500 (nearly £200,000 at today's values), but it would not be until the early 1950s that the building would be returned to full usage, enabling two further Lodges to be created and take up residence, St Lukes No. 6540 and Elizabethan No. 7296. This work not only preserved the building, but enabled it to be awarded Grade Two Listed Status in 1978.

The biggest loss, however, was to the Museum collection, more than half of which was destroyed in the raid. Nevertheless, the collection was gradually rebuilt during the later years of the last century, primarily by the Museum's longest-serving curator W.Bro Eddie Gaynor, and is now once again a collection of which the organisation can be justly proud.

View of the Museum

In 2002, the Trust embarked on ambitious plans to clear the vaults of the building and create a new dining room and kitchens there, releasing some of the upper rooms within the building for conversion into flats.

Work went ahead, at considerable expense, to remove the tons of rubble that had accumulated over nearly 200 years and, as a result, two of the five vaults were completely cleared, plus two more to half of their depth. It was during this work that the memorial tablets from the Catholic Chapel were unearthed, along with part of what is believed to be the original 16th century hot water drain that led from the King's Bath, out by the Ham Gate and down to the River Avon.

However, planning permission for the final phase of the work failed to be obtained, so the clearance work on the area for the new kitchens could not be commenced and the entire scheme came to a grinding halt. The resultant additional space, however, was put to use as meeting and cloak rooms until the Masonic Museum was relocated from the top of the building into the vaults in 2009, enabling it to be opened to the public as part of the Guided Tours of the building that were also introduced during that year.

Replica WM Chair

Blagdon

The Masonic Hall, Rickford, BS40 7AH

Lodge Meeting in Blagdon

Forest of Mendip Lodge No. 8019

The perfect setting for Blagdon Masonic Hall.

Long before Forest of Mendip Lodge took up residence in what had for many years been a Baptist Chapel, and prior to that the Wills family estate chapel, the old mill pond had been converted to an ornamental lake, and can be easily viewed from the road which runs along Blagdon Coombe. There is also on the site a prominent house which is believed to have been the mill house, as the leat supplying the mill runs behind this building.

Attendance at the first meetings of the Lodge stretched the accommodation to its limits owing to the large number of visiting brethren.

An ingenious plan was hatched to increase the capacity by installing a spiral staircase to the balcony. A few months later such a staircase was obtained by one of the regular visitors, Bro Bill Whalley (now Worshipful Brother) who said it would give him much pleasure to donate it to the Lodge.

It was erected the following September under the guidance of W.Bro Norman Minto. It fitted perfectly and, incidentally, consists of fifteen steps.

The Lodge Room at Blagdon Masonic Hall in Rickford

An ear of corn near to a fall of water

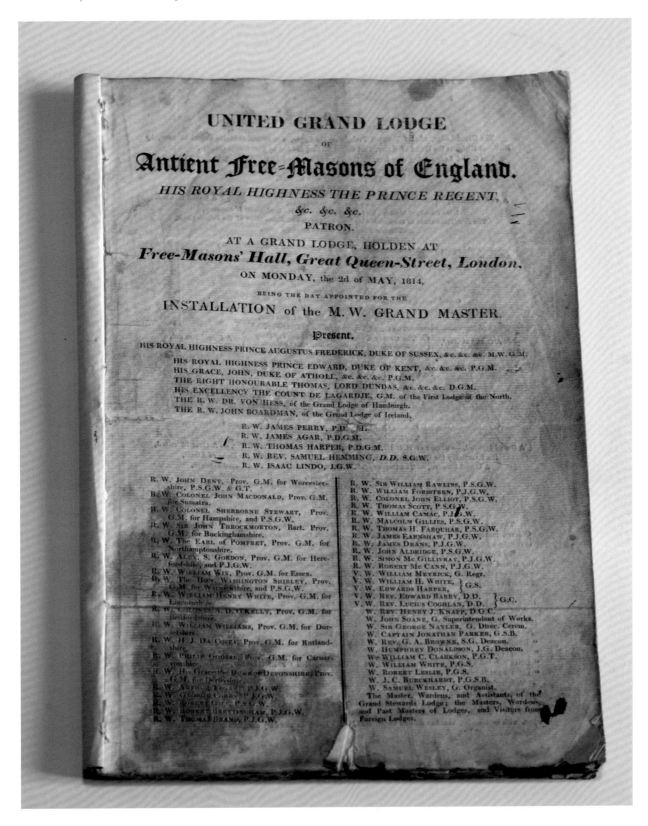

*Summons for the Installation of the First Grand Master of the
United Grand Lodge of Antient Freemasons of England on 2nd May 1814
Archived in the Bridgwater Masonic Hall*

Bridgwater

The Masonic Hall, King Square, Bridgwater, TA6 3DH

Lodges Meeting in Bridgwater

Lodge of Perpetual Friendship No. 135
Admiral Blake Lodge No. 4692
Tynte Lodge No. 7994

Perpetual Friendship Chapter 135 • Somerset First Principals Chapter 3746
Quantock Mark Lodge No. 749
Sedgemoor Chapter No. 966 (RC)

The Bridgwater Masonic Hall, King Square, Bridgwater, is administered by a Committee representing the various Lodges which meet there; these are the Lodge of Perpetual Friendship 135, Admiral Blake Lodge 4692 and Tynte Lodge 7994, together with three Chapters and Mark Lodge.

The Lodge of Perpetual Friendship, which was formed in 1757 although not Warranted until 1764, had met in various licensed premises in Bridgwater before deciding on the provision of a permanent home, but it was not until 1908 that the initial steps were taken to provide a Masonic Hall, and the following year a suitable site in King Square was purchased at a cost of £240.

Fifteen Trustees having been appointed, a building fund was set up which was financed by an increase of two guineas in both initiation and joining fees, and one guinea in the passing and raising fees which were payable in this Lodge, although not necessarily in other Lodges.

Plans were prepared by Bro B. Cottam and tenders sought, the lowest, that submitted by A. Green in the sum of £1188, being accepted together with a further tender from Messrs R. Alger & Sons for Masonic apparel at a cost of £61.10s.0d and work commenced. The new building was dedicated on 11th July 1912, the final cost being £1,427.0s.11d.

The first regular meeting took place later that year, on the 9th September, the minutes of which meeting record a number of gifts of items of equipment from various members of the Lodge.

The Admiral Blake Lodge was Warranted in 1924, and the Tynte Lodge in 1964; both Lodges continue to meet at the Masonic Hall.

From the front in King Square, the building appears single storey and of modest size, which belies the spacious accommodation within. The entrance doors, reached from the street up a short flight of steps, lead directly into the first floor, which contains the Lodge Room and Ante-rooms, whilst an internal staircase leads down to the dining hall, kitchen and bar.

Because of the fall in the land from front to back these latter facilities form the ground floor at the rear and consequently from this elevation it is seen to be a two-storey building.

Early in life Perpetual Friendship Lodge met at the Old Angel and the Swan Inns at Bridgwater, followed by over 50 years at the Royal Clarence Hotel, finally moving in 1912 to the purpose built Masonic Hall in King Square, which remains in use today.

Bruton

The Masonic Hall, High Street, Bruton BA10 0AH

Lodges Meeting in Bruton

Royal Clarence Lodge No. 976

Royal Cyrus Chapter 285

The present meeting place of the Royal Clarence Lodge is one of the oldest buildings in use as a Masonic Hall in the Province. It was originally built as the Bruton Town Hall and bears the date 1642.

The building fronts High Street, although the actual entrance is from Warren Close which is a narrow alley leading off the High Street almost opposite the Post Office.

In 1876 the use of the building changed and it became the Bruton National Infants School and continued as such, with the adjoining school house, until 1932.

In 1932, when this use ceased, it was purchased by the Lodge and the cost of conversion amounted to nearly £1,500. This enabled the school portion to be used as a Lodge Room, whilst the house was let.

One of the oldest buildings in use as a Masonic Hall in the Province

In 1956 when the house became vacant alterations were carried out to provide a dining room for the Lodge on the ground floor, with a flat upstairs, this being that part of the building lying between Warren Close and the Masonic Hall. The former playground, also owned by the Lodge, still exists at the rear and the tubular steel barriers in Warren Close are still in place. The flat was first occupied by the Tyler and his wife, but after the death of his widow it was let on a normal tenancy.

All of the premises occupied by the Lodge are on the ground floor and consist of an entrance from the covered way of Warren Close into the Dining room, which also contains the Bar.

The Dining room leads to an inner lobby and thence on to an ante-room and robing room, through which the Lodge is entered. In recent times consideration has been given to the feasibility of building a new dining room on the former playground, but so far no satisfactory solution has been found which would enable this to be of adequate size to seat the numbers present at an Installation dinner.

Until 1986 there was only one Lodge meeting at the Masonic Hall, Bruton, but in April of that year the Somerset Farmers' Lodge 9180 was consecrated and sponsored by the Royal Clarence Lodge, and it was agreed that this new Lodge should meet at Bruton. However, the anticipated support in Bruton from Dorset Farmer Masons did not materialize and the Somerset Farmers Lodge moved to Langport in September 2003.

Burnham-on-Sea

The Masonic Hall, Burnham-on-Sea, TA8 1NX

Lodges Meeting in Burnham

Rural Philanthropic Lodge No. 291
Somerset Fairway Lodge No. 9251

Vale of Jehoshaphat Chapter 291
William Long Mark Lodge No. 191
William Long RAM Lodge No. 191 • Somerset Commanders RAM Lodge No. 1652
Amulet Conclave No. 457 (RCC)

A Lodge first met at the Highbridge Inn, in the Parish of Huntspill, on Sunday 3rd February 1793 under the name of the "The Rural Lodge of Philanthropy No. 517', and continued to use this name for the first seventeen meetings, when it adopted its present name of the 'The Rural Philanthropic Lodge'. The meetings of the Lodge at first were very frequent, as many as six during the first month. The Lodge continued to meet at the Highbridge Inn until November 1857 when, due to insufficient accommodation, a committee was formed to consider the matter.

It was at first arranged to remove the Lodge to the new hotel being built at Burnham called the Reeds Arms, now the Queens Hotel, but arrangements fell through and the Lodge moved to the Railway Hotel, Highbridge. They continued to meet at the Railway Hotel until 1936, when the brethren became disenchanted with the amenities provided and a sub-committee was formed to investigate the purchase of land at either Highbridge or Burnham to build a Masonic Hall, together with ways and means of financing this proposal. Bro W.J. Pople was

The very fine entrance to the Burnham Lodge Room

asked to prepare plans and specifications for the proposed new building.

In May 1939 negotiations commenced with Bro Bateman, the owner of the Queens Hotel, for the purchase of a site at the rear of the Old Majestic Cinema, and a building appeal fund was launched. The purchase of the land was completed in September 1939 at a cost of £180, but due to the outbreak of war, a start to the actual building was delayed. However, it was not long before Bro Pople had assembled all the necessary materials and work commenced. In October 1939 meetings were transferred to the Queens Hotel, Burnham-on-Sea, until completion of the new Masonic Hall.

The first meeting to be held at the new premises was on the 3rd May 1940, which was followed by an Emergency Meeting on the 6th June when the Temple was dedicated by the Deputy

Provincial Grand Master, W.Bro F.E. Nutt, the Provincial Grand Master being absent on war duties. The Worshipful Master of the Lodge, W.Bro Henry Frampton, who subsequently became Deputy Provincial Grand Master congratulated the Lodge on the building of "this exceedingly nice and commodious Temple, specially arranged for the dignified working of its ceremonies in quietude, free from the noise of hotels or places of public resort".

The cost of the building amounted to £1,358.7s.4d and was built by the local firm of W.J. Pople & Sons Ltd of which Bro Pople was the Managing Director. At the dedication ceremony Bro Pople was presented with a ceremonial key of the building as a memento of the day which saw the crowning glory of his work.

Since the building of the hall there has been a continuous process of improvement to the premises. In 1956 a new dining room and bar were built and in the same year Mrs Minnie

Evans presented the Lodge with a new organ, in memory of her late husband Bro W.S. Evans. The next major addition to the building was in 1974 with the construction of a new kitchen, toilets and Provincial Officers' robing room, thus making the facilities of the Lodge self-contained.

In 1985 the central heating was completely overhauled and converted to gas firing for better efficiency and economy. It is interesting to note that the cost of replacing the boiler in 1985 was more than twice the cost of the original building in 1940.

The origin of the Master's and Wardens' chairs is uncertain but it is thought that they date back to the time of the move to the Railway Hotel in 1857, as the Lodge minutes record that the Lodge furniture at the Highbridge Inn was fitted and not able to be moved.

Most of the Officers' collar jewels are of silver and were presented to the Lodge at various times by the holders of such office. The collar jewels of the Worshipful Master, Senior and Junior Wardens, Secretary and Chief Steward are dated 1814, the two Deacons, 1817, the Chaplain, Director of Ceremonies, Inner Guard and Immediate Past Master 1857, and two additional Director of Ceremonies jewels 1874.

The impressive painting in the Temple depicting the York Union was presented by W.Bro T.W. Rankin in 1858, and the pair of globes were presented by V.W.Bro Captain Henry Bridges in 1860.

Many other items of furniture have been presented at various times including some of the carved chairs in the east, the Secretary's table and the table in the Provincial Officers' robing room. The latest gift is the cabinet made to enclose the Tracing Boards which was presented by W.Bro Cooper in 1980.

Chard

The Masonic Hall, Fore St, Chard, TA20 1PH

Lodges Meeting in Chard

Prudence & Industry Lodge No. 1953

Cerdic Mark Lodge No. 571
Cerdic RAM Lodge No. 571

As at other local Masonic Halls Chard exhibits the names of all Past Masters on shields mounted on the walls;
A pleasing sight, and one that treasures the memories of many worthy Masons who gave great service to their Lodge.

The first Chard Lodge of Prudence and Industry was constituted in March 1799 and continued in existence until the end of 1831, when the Warrant was surrendered to Grand Lodge. Most of the founders and early members appeared to have come from Devon although they were members of a Taunton Lodge, and a number of them were associated with the sea. During its life, the Lodge met at the George Inn, the Red Lion, the Angel Inn and what was called

Freemasons' Hall. This latter was apparently situated at the rear of Mr Cuff's Saddlery Shop, demolished and rebuilt in 1910.

There was a lapse of 50 years after the end of the first Lodge until the present Prudence and Industry Lodge No. 1953 came into existence in 1882, being consecrated in the April of that year. The Lodge met in the George Hotel, Chard, until September 1897, when it moved to a new Lodge room which had been built over some new stables in the yard at the rear of the Hotel.

Not long afterwards, in 1904, a Mark Lodge was formed which also began to use the same premises. The purchase of the two columns took place in 1906 after some twelve months deliberation, and this was followed about a year later by an agreement by the Lodge to accept the tenancy of an extension to the Ante-room for £5.00 a year. The subsequent furnishing cost some £43.00. It was in 1912 that the annual tenancy agreement for the whole Lodge premises, which up till then had been with the landlords of the George Hotel, was altered to become a lease direct with the Brewers.

The Lodge Room was re-carpeted in 1922, the expense being shared with the Mark Lodge which paid one third of the cost, but tradition dies hard in Chard and the brethren continued to resist the installation of electric lighting until 1935.

The Chard Clock with the Lodge Number 598 showing Masonic symbols in place of normal figures.

Further extensions of the premises took place in 1924/5 at the north end, although originally suggested as an enlargement on the west side, but the excessive cost of the necessary land on this side caused the change in the original

Perhaps the oldest possessions are two fine Masonic jugs dating from the period 1799 to 1814. They are both interesting and unusual in terms of the Masonic prints displayed, which are rare, and the colours employed. The original Lodge name and number is prominently shown and for one to have survived is exceptional, for two probably unique.

81

scheme. The cost of the work was borne by the Brewers, Messrs Mitchell, Tom & Co., the Lodge being liable for an additional rent equivalent to 6% of the cost.

By 1964 it had become necessary to negotiate a new lease with Messrs Charringtons who had taken over from the local brewery, as was a quite frequent occurrence at those times. Trustees were appointed to act for the Lodge and internal alterations were made to the building to form a bar. The Prudence and Industry Lodge 1953 continue to meet in its rented premises on the first floor over the former stables block in the yard at the rear of the George Hotel, as it has done for many years, together with the Cerdic Lodge of Mark Master Masons.

Although Masonic history in Chard originated in the late 18th Century, regretfully little now appears to remain of that period.

There is a fine Bible with a well chased cover with the name Prudence and Industry Lodge No. 598, Chard, and a date of 1819. This is complemented by a Bible showing the Lodge name and number 1953, dating it after 1881.

A rare set of miniature Tracing Boards of superb workmanship, most unusual in concept and design.

Clevedon

The Masonic Hall, Albert Road, Clevedon, BS21 7RN

Lodges Meeting in Clevedon

Coleridge Lodge No. 1750
Eldon Lodge No. 1755
Tennyson Lodge No. 4947
Southey Lodge No. 6650
John de Clivedon Lodge No. 7824
Showmen's Guild Lodge No. 9089

Marine Chapter 232 • Adair Chapter 1750 • Eldon Chapter 1755
Hallam Mark Lodge No. 730 • Eldon Mark Lodge No. 807
Thackeray Royal Ark Mariner Lodge 730 •
Clevedon Chapter No. 1167 (RC)

Comfortable, and indeed cosy, are not normally the words to describe a Masonic Lodge Room; in Clevedon's case, however, they are very apt.

The Masonic Hall was built during the mid 1850s as an extension to the Clevedon Public Hall and was used as the meeting room for the Local Board, the body that dealt with local matters before the Council was formed. The rooms were also used for local entertainment, which, in those days, usually consisted of readings.

The first Masonic meeting of Coleridge Lodge 1750 took place in the building on the 14th January 1925. A kitchen was installed in 1926 at a cost of £275 and the Main Entrance was then resited to its present position fronting Albert Road. All the debts that were incurred for the purchase of the building and the extensions were cleared in 1938.

During WW2 the dining room was used by the Hospital Linen League organised locally by Lady Teignmouth, whose husband was a member of Tennyson Lodge.

The Lodge Room originally was equipped with a Harmonium, but following the War it was decided that this should be replaced, and a pipe organ was bought to commemorate those who had died. This organ had originally been the property of a local organist and had been refurbished It was again moved in 2000 to mark the Millennium and was again refurbished at a cost of £10,000.

Coleridge Lodge purchased the wing, which consisted of what are now the Dining Room and the Lodge Room above, in November 1923 for £700. There was no staircase to enable access to the first floor where the Lodge room was situated as the stairs were in the main building and did not form part of the sale. Coleridge Lodge was, however, able to purchase a strip of land roughly the same size at the back of the wing, and it was here that the extension to the original building was erected.

During 1924 alterations were made to make the building suitable for Masonic meetings, which included putting in the present arch ceiling in the Lodge Room. The total costs of the alterations was £1,784, a vast sum considering that Bro Sidney Keen, who owned the local brickyard, donated all of the bricks for the extension on the back of the building to house the staircase, entrance hall, toilets and committee room upstairs.

Again in post WW2 years it was decided to form a Club to serve drinks, and eventually, after a great deal of local opposition, a licence was obtained. Drinks at that time were served on tables erected at the end of the dining room but eventually members of Lodges meeting at Clevedon built a bar. This bar was in use until 1993 when it was moved and reopened by Mrs Sylvia Hopkins, wife of the then Provincial Grand Master.

The final Poets jewel is that of a Past Master of Southey Lodge 6650, again in silver gilt with a superb enamelled coat of arms and motto. This particular jewel was first presented in 1982 and re-issued in 1994.

Clevedon is indeed the Poets town, as amply indicated by the existence of three Lodges, Coleridge, Tennyson and Southey, all of which meet there. Their jewels equally illustrate this Poets connection. The Past Master's breast jewel for Coleridge Lodge 1750 being made of gold, and displaying a fine enamelled coat of arms and motto, and unusually a plumb rule connecting the pendant to the ribbon.

The silver-gilt Past Master's jewel from 1941-42 of the Tennyson Lodge has a particularly fine square and Euclid's theorem. It was probably presented after the 2nd World War as metal was not normally made available for jewels during the war period.

Crewkerne

The Masonic Hall, South St, Crewkerne, TA18 7JU

Lodges Meeting in Crewkerne

Parrett & Axe Lodge No. 814

Parrett & Axe Chapter 814
Harry Franklin Chapter No. 1139 (RC)
Cumba Preceptory No. 476 (KT) • Our Lady of Walsingham Preceptory No. 672 (KT)

The first Lodge to meet in Crewkerne was the Scientific Lodge 203, which was warranted in 1807, and it was stated on the Warrant that this Lodge was to meet at the George Inn, Market Square. Unfortunately the Lodge lapsed in 1827 and some of its furniture passed into the ownership of the Lodge of Unity, Wareham, which had been founded that same year. Some of the founders of the Scientific Lodge subsequently became founders of the Lodge of Brotherly Love at Martock, which Lodge a few years later moved to Yeovil where it still meets.

The next Lodge to be formed in Crewkerne was the Parrett and Axe Lodge, as a result of a petition signed by a number of members of the Lodge of Brotherly Love in July 1859. The Lodge with the number 1116 was consecrated in July 1860, and met at the George Hotel until 1890 when it moved to the Town Hall.

From available records it would seem that this subsequently became part of the Victoria Hall, but this accommodation proved to have its disadvantages because in 1912 the Lodge found it necessary to complain to the Fairs and Markets Committee, their Landlords, regarding noise from the entertainment in the Victoria Hall, below which the Lodge was situated. However, whatever the outcome of the complaint, the Lodge continued to meet there, and on renewal of their lease in 1918 obtained additional accommodation to provide an ante-room.

The present meeting place, the Masonic Hall, South Street, Crewkerne, originally formed part of Henhayes House, which belonged to a Mr Saunders. This property was divided in 1933, and half was purchased by the Lodge for £500. A scheme for conversion into suitable accommodation for Lodge purposes was prepared and a tender accepted in the sum of £630, the architect being Bro D.R. Nicholls. But as is almost invariably the case with conversion works, the actual cost was in excess of the tender although work was not delayed,

The Master's Chair. A striking and attractive design, and beautifully crafted.

Superbly ornate Junior Warden's chair

and in October 1933 application was made for a permanent change of venue to the new Masonic Hall.

The Banner of the Parrett and Axe Lodge incorporates the seal of the Crewkerne School which was founded in 1499. The design represents a castellated monastic abode of the Knights Templars. In a history of the School by the Rev. R. Bartelot it is suggested that the triple tower has reference to the Holy Trinity and summarises its whole history, in that School endowment was first given to the Knights Templars, secondly to the Trinity Chantry and finally to the school.

Although the furniture of the original Crewkerne Lodge has left the town and an attempt to recover at least the chairs in 1910 proved unsuccessful, the Lodge possesses some treasures. In the first

and Treasurer are pictured. Also pictured is the Past Master's breast jewel, which has a large finely enamelled pendant depicting a Knights Templar castle.

floor ante-room there is a Georgian mahogany table inlaid with box and ebony stringing; in the Lodge room itself there are a pair of George III Terrestrial and Celestial Globes by D. Adams of 60 Fleet Street, London, both globes being on appropriate brass and mahogany stands, and in addition to these there are a pair of painted wooden columns just over 7ft high, each with a 10" diameter globe on top, the globes being inscribed by C. Smith and Son.

As at Chard and Ilminster the Crewkerne Masonic Hall is an old building with a particularly fine front doorway, which must have exercised the interest of many non Masons over the years, and as with many Somerset Masonic Halls the interior is a delight to the eye, with a particularly fine Master's chair from Victorian times worthy of close examination.

Among the treasures of the Parrett and Axe Lodge 814 which meets there is a particularly fine set of Victorian collar jewels still worn today by Lodge Officers, and those for the Wardens

Fortunately the original Lodge minutes still exist, with the bye-laws written out in a copperplate hand.

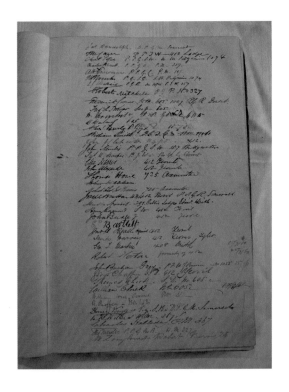

Frome

The Masonic Hall, North Parade, Frome, BA11 1AU

Lodges Meeting in Frome

Royal Somerset Lodge No. 973
Forest of Selwood Lodge No. 8912

Dungarvan Chapter 973
Portal Mark Lodge No. 155 • Portal Royal Ark Mariners Lodge 155
Frome Chapter No. 801 (RC)
Selwood Preceptory of St John No. 244 (KT)
William de Irwin Conclave No. 162 (RCC)

The Royal Somerset Lodge 973, whose Warrant is dated 1863, had to wait nearly 30 years until they were able to build their Masonic Hall in North Parade, Frome. The site was formerly garden ground on the opposite side of the road to the Literary and Scientific Club, and was sold to the Lodge by Bro A.G. Hayman.

The architect for the building was Bro Philip Edinger and all his services were given without cost to the Lodge. The main contractor was Messrs. Hodder & Son of Frome, together with a number of specialist sub-contractors, the cost of building, excluding land, being in the region of £600 which, taking into account the size of the building, gives a figure of 4d per cubic foot

The impressive Masonic Hall at Frome

A token struck to commemorate the election of HRH the Prince of Wales as Grand Master 1790.

The building was dedicated with all pomp and ceremony by the Provincial Grand Master, Viscount Dungarvan, on the 13th October 1891. The original accommodation consisted of, on the ground floor, an entrance hall with a reception room on the left leading to the banqueting hall (now the dining room) and a kitchen at the rear of the entrance hall. The staircase led from the entrance hall to the first floor containing the retiring and Lodge Rooms. The latter was 40ft by 30ft and it is still that size at the present time. The heating installation consisted of gas fires, slow combustion stoves and also hot water pipes to warm the upper part when required. Lighting was by means of gas lamps.

The organ chamber, or recess in the S.E. corner of the Lodge, contained the organ that was paid for by members and their friends. That organ is still in use today, being regularly tuned and maintained each year.

Towards the end of the 1960s, bearing in mind the possible danger to the occupants of the Lodge room in case of fire in the kitchens which were on the ground floor, an iron fire escape

staircase was fitted at the rear of the building. Shortly afterwards an extension to the dining room was carried out to provide a larger bar and additional dining space.

The Lodge is fortunate in that a large area remains at the rear which is let as a car park, together with a separate building used as works accommodation. The ground floor of the Masonic Hall itself is frequently let for Wedding receptions and other local functions.

Above: Just some of the curious objects on display
Their usages are very much open to interpretation
Below: The revolving Tracing Boards

Glastonbury

The Masonic Hall, Hanover Square, Glastonbury, BA6 8BT

Lodges Meeting in Glastonbury

Pilgrims Lodge No. 772
St. Dunstan's Lodge No. 7973

Mendip Mark Lodge No. 781
King Arthur of Avalon Preceptory No. 551 (KT)
Avalon Conclave No. 379 (OSM)

This Masonic Hall became the home of the Pilgrims Lodge in 1929, and is also the meeting place of St. Dunstan's Lodge 7973 which was Consecrated in 1964. Pilgrims Lodge was consecrated on Tuesday 26th July 1859 by the Deputy Provincial Grand Master, W.Bro Randolph, in a room which had been prepared at the Pilgrims Inn, the first Master being Dr Charles Pope and the sponsoring Lodge being

Benevolent Lodge of Wells. There were a mere eight or nine original members, including Bro Baily, the Landlord of the Inn, who probably arranged the use of the room and laid out the furniture, the cost of the furniture having been met by a loan of £50 from Stuckey's Bank. The VSL, a most valuable 'Breeches' Bible, was presented by Bro Cornwall, the original Junior Deacon, in February 1859, five months before the consecration, and the square now used formerly belonged to the first Royal Clarence Lodge of Bruton 360 and is dated 1790.

The first proper inventory of Lodge furniture prepared in 1866 refers to a globe and also to a lantern. The latter was probably used for raisings, but by 1871 there were still no tracing boards. The first actual reference to these was in 1927 when Bro Alves presented a tracing board stand and case, as well as a Glastonbury chair.

In 1883 a meeting of Provincial Grand Lodge was held in the Assembly Rooms at Glastonbury, and the Master of the Lodge at that time appears to have given the first of the Masters' Name Boards. It was also decided that a carpet should be purchased, the one used for the meeting having been borrowed from Benevolent Lodge 446. However, this purchase did not materialise and in 1886 one was bought by W.Bro Bath.

In 1889 the Tyler complained of the heavy work involved in erecting and taking down the wooden partitions at the Pilgrims Inn which was necessary for each meeting, whilst in the same year Bro Hawkins provided a rough ashlar and the Lodge acquired a ballot box.

The meeting place was still causing concern, and in 1894 there were reports of eavesdropping by persons in the yard outside the Lodge room (which was the present dining room at the Pilgrims Inn). It was thus decided to apply to the Town Council for permission to use the Town Hall.

The Council proving uncooperative there was talk of using the Wesleyan Chapel in Lambrook Street, but this was deemed unsuitable as there was no ante-room. Consequently meetings continued at the Inn, even though a new landlord locked the doors on members. In 1909 the Lodge celebrated its 50th anniversary in the Victoria Rooms, with visitors from the Province as well as other Lodges.

The Glastonbury Chair

At last, in 1921, a change in meeting place was achieved when the Lodge moved to the Assembly Rooms, but this was short-lived as later in the same year it moved to the Avalon Hall in Lambrook Street. This was small and inconvenient but had the advantage of allowing the Lodge exclusive use of its own room, which resulted in the Lodge increasing in strength. Ironically the increased number of members exacerbated the problem of the accommodation, which became more and more cramped.

W.Bro Bath purchased the Liberal Club in 1928 and offered it to the Lodge at the purchase price. Four Trustees were appointed and authorised to borrow from the Bank to finance the purchase and necessary alterations, the overdraft being fixed at £500.

W.Bro Alves was the architect and Bro E.D. Wright the builder. Costs escalated, and the overdraft reached £800. In 1931 it was announced that the final cost was £1,387 and an appeal was made to the brethren for money to reduce the debt. The organ, which had previously been lent by W.Bro Eglinton, was now presented by him to the Lodge and continued to be used until the mid-1980s when it was replaced through the generosity of W.Bro C. Webber, Master in 1981

Premises adjoining the Lodge were acquired in 1955, and further premises in 1959, which made it possible to extend and improve the shape of the Lodge Room to become as it is today. Bro J. Smith carried out the entire redecoration of the premises at less than cost price and also supervised the complete rewiring of the building. W.Bro Alves was once again the supervising architect and Bro Grace saw to the re-carpeting.

Thus the Lodge facilities reached the position which the brethren enjoy today. Over the years various presentations were made to the Lodge, a letter 'G' in 1945 by W.Bro Alves, and chairs in 1948 by Bro N James. W.Bro J. Names gave a Glastonbury Chair to mark his year as Master and also provided the necessary timber, at cost, for the reconstruction work.

The very ornate oriental silverware on display at the Glastonbury Masonic Hall

Ilminster

The Masonic Hall, Court Barton, Ilminster, TA19 0DY

Lodges Meeting in Ilminster

Nyanza Lodge No. 1197
Somerset Tablers Lodge No. 9075

The first Lodge to be formed in Ilminster was the Lodge of Unanimity 524 in 1788, but due to lack of support this Lodge moved to Taunton in 1797 where it still exists today as the Lodge of Unanimity and Sincerity 261. It was not until 1867 that another attempt was made to establish a Masonic Lodge in Ilminster, with the formation of the Nyanza Lodge 1197, so named after Lake Victoria Nyanza in Africa, in honour of a local man, Captain J.H. Speke, who had discovered the source of the Nile. For the first year of its existence the Lodge met in the Commercial School premises in Berrymans Lane, which 50 years later was to become the property of and the permanent home for the Lodge.

However, in 1868 the Lodge transferred to the Royal George Assembly Rooms until 1884, when it moved to a room in North Street.

In May 1913 the opportunity arose to purchase the Commercial School premises for £50, the vendor being W.Bro Parrett, and a tender for the necessary alterations from Mr A. Poole was accepted in the sum of £110, the money required being raised by interest free loans from some of the members.

The oak pillars and globes were presented by Bro E.A. Marshalsea on behalf of the junior members of the Lodge to commemorate the end of the 1914-18 war.

January 1968, repairs and replacement of some of the furnishings and fabric were carried out and many donations towards the cost of such work were made, including a new carpet. Throughout the life of the Lodge it has been the custom for brethren to give items of equipment and articles of furniture to the Lodge, and this tradition is still flourishing today.

The Masonic Hall, Ilminster, which for so many years was the home of only one Lodge, Nyanza Lodge 1179, has now acquired another occupant, the Somerset Tablers' Lodge 9075 which was consecrated in 1983 for former members of the Round Table.

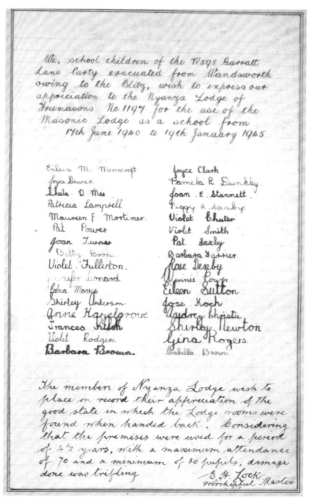

A letter of thanks from the children evacuated from Wandsworth who used the Ilminster Masonic Hall as a school.

During the 1939-45 war the Lodge allowed the premises to be used to house an evacuee school. This meant a great deal of heavy work on meeting nights in removal of furniture to convert from school room to Lodge and back again. At the end of the war the Lodge room was redecorated and remodelled during the summer recess, taking advantage of the time when the brethren reverted to the pre-war months for meetings.

A working party was formed in 1964 to improve the small upstairs room which is now used as a bar and for informal buffet suppers on those Lodge nights when the brethren do not dine formally. The work was soon completed and the room officially declared open in February of that year. In 1967, as part of the centenary celebrations which were due to take place in

Keynsham

The Masonic Hall, Bath Road, Keynsham, BS31 1SR

Lodges Meeting in Keynsham

Vale of Brislington Lodge No. 1296
St. Keyna Lodge No. 1833
Abbey Lodge No. 4491
Uno Corde Lodge No. 5736
Priory Lodge No. 6913
Whitchurch Lodge No. 6942
Saltford Lodge No. 8633
Gerard Lodge No. 8999
Cornucopia Lodge No. 9043

St. Keyna Chapter 1833 • Abbey Chapter 4491
Carnarvon Mark Lodge No. 119 • Somerdale Mark Lodge No. 1608
Irwin Lodge of Royal Ark Mariners No. 119,
Keynsham Chapter No. 678 (RC) • Jubilee Chapter No. 838 (RC)
Keynsham Preceptory of St. Keyna No. 455 (KT)
St. Hugh Conclave No. 115 (OSM)

St. Keyna Lodge for the first 60 years of its existence held its regular meetings at the 'Lamb and Lark' in Keynsham. However, as far back as the years following the First World War there were identified shortcomings in the facilities there.

The roof leaked, and the odour from nearby stables did not improve the 'atmosphere'! However, the main problem was that the membership had increased beyond the capacity of the room. There was a feeling within the Lodge to acquire their own premises.

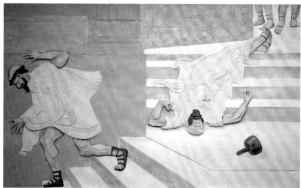

The first seven of the superbly restored friezes that adorn the Temple in Keynsham. These show the story of the fifteen fellowcraft in pictorial form, and are placed around the walls of the Lodge room. The final three are on the next page.

In March 1939 a site on the Bath Road became available and this was purchased for £400. Due to the eminent possibility of war no time could be lost. New plans were prepared and a contract for the building estimated to cost something over £5,000 was given to Bro Sperring, of Saltford, a builder.

Work started on 1st September 1939 and the temple was completed one year later. The building was first used on 26th August 1940 for a Lodge Committee meeting, and the first ceremony took place on the Saturday afternoon, of 14th September 1940. Bros. B.W. Stacey and Gordon Bennett (still a Lodge member in 2007) were the Initiates.

Certainly unique in the Province of Somerset, if not the country, are the magnificent three dimensional plasterwork friezes which surround the Lodge room depicting the slaying of Hiram Abiff and the story of the Fifteen Fellow Craft. These have recently been expertly restored and in their own right make a visit to the Masonic Hall at Keynsham well worthwhile.

The final three friezes in the Temple at Keynsham

Sounding of the magnificent Oriental Dinner Gong ensures that nobody is late for the Festive Board in Keynsham!

Langport

The Masonic Hall, St. Mary's Chapel, The Hill, Langport, TA10 9QF

Lodges Meeting in Langport

Portcullis Lodge No. 2038
Somerset Farmers Lodge No. 9180

Portcullis Mark Lodge No. 1656

In the Victoria History of Somerset we learn that a Chantry of the Blessed Virgin Mary was mentioned in 1344 when nine shillings and eight pence was paid for it from the "Farm of the Windmill" (the windmill was blown down in "the great wind" of 1362 and never rebuilt). It was erected by the Langport Guild Merchants around 1300 and endowed with two Fraternity Priests.

The Building, described as the "Hawning Chapel", was the Town Hall between 1547 and 1600.

In 1596 there is a reference to the "Town Hall commonly called the Hanging Chapel, which the whole town of Langport do use the said Chapel for a place for consultation". A theory that it is called the "Hanging Chapel" after the activities of Judge Jeffreys in the region is incorrect - it 'hangs' over the road

In 1645 the Chapel needed extensive repairs after the Battle of Langport. It became a schoolroom in 1706 (some naughty children scratched their names and dates on the stonework of the east window and they are still clearly visible today) and continued as such until 1790. From 1809 to 1816 it was let to Colonel Pinney for the local militia to use as an arms store, and in 1843 it was let to Mr. E. Queckett as a museum. In 1891 it was let to the present occupants, the Portcullis Lodge of Freemasons.

Above: Size really does matter; the entrance to the Lodge Room can be a tight squeeze for the larger brethren!.
Below: The Smallest Lodge Room in the Province.

In October 1891 it was decided to hold meetings at the Hanging Chapel. Permission was obtained from Provincial Grand Lodge and Grand Lodge. The first meeting was on 12th November 1891 and was (appropriately) an Initiation. The lack of space, such a problem today, was not a consideration when average attendances were around twelve and about 24 at Installations.

In 1915 the stonework, which had blocked the two north facing windows for centuries, was removed four stained glass lights installed in the original hamstone mullions. One window represents the Blessed Virgin and the Angel Gabriel. The other window represents King Alfred the Great, who is said to have fortified Langport, and Lady Margaret Beaufort, the mother of Henry VII, born on 31st May 1443. She was the daughter of John Beaufort, Duke of Somerset, and the great-grand-daughter of John of Gaunt and Catherine Swynford. She was Lady of the Manor and Borough of Langport, and used the Portcullis motif, the badge of the Beauforts that was adopted by Langport town as its Crest. A third internal window also shows the Portcullis motif in one light and the Square and Compasses in the other.

Right: Some of the stained glass, inserted by the brethren, is appropriately designed and connected to both local history and Masonry

Left: The graffiti in the old stonework is a graphic indication that its modern counterpart has a long tradition.

Midsomer Norton

The Masonic Hall, Redfield Road, Midsomer Norton, BA3 2JN

Lodges Meeting in Midsomer Norton

Connaught Lodge No. 3573
Kenneth Kinnersley Lodge No. 9218

Connaught Chapter 3573

The Connaught Lodge 3573, which was consecrated in 1912, meets as it always has at the Masonic Hall, which is 45 metres west of St. John's Church Midsomer Norton.

The provision of a suitable meeting place in the town was one of the first items to be considered by the brethren when in June 1910 the formation of a Lodge was first proposed. The first positive step towards a new Masonic Hall was the purchase of a plot of land described as 'near the church' at a cost of £3 per perch. The site is the one on which the present hall stands, and has a frontage of 38 feet. Plans for the building were prepared by Bro Orchard at half the usual fees, and a tender in the sum of £721.17.7d for the work was accepted from the local firm of F. James & Son. The costs of the heating and electrical installations were in addition to this, making a total of £914, this sum being raised partly by the issue of bonds to the brethren and partly by means of a bank loan.

The consecration was carried out on 11th April 1912 by the Provincial Grand Master, R.W.Bro Col. W. Long, and in order to ensure that the Lodge should be properly furnished for the occasion some of the furniture was borrowed from the Bath Lodges, and it would appear that some of this may still have been in use in 1985 at Midsomer Norton. The Kenneth Kinnersley Lodge was consecrated in 1986 and hold their meetings in the Midsomer Norton Masonic Hall.

In 1939 the ground floor of the Masonic Hall was requisitioned by the War Office, and a company of Welsh Guards was stationed there.

As the years passed and the Hall flourished the absence of kitchen facilities was proving something of a handicap to the proper celebration of the after proceedings, so in the late 1940s a new kitchen was added. This was followed in 1982 by the erection of a new cloakroom including toilet facilities at the rear of the existing building.

The accommodation now includes an entrance hall leading to the dining room which also contains a bar, at the far end of the dining room is the ante-room and cloakroom. The staircase leads from the entrance hall to the first floor where the Lodge Room and a further ante-room are situated. The ground floor dining room, etc,. is often let to certain local organisations to provide some financial income to assist towards the upkeep of the building.

In February 1981 an appeal was launched by the Secretary to open a Building Fund to finance the proposed new cloakroom at the rear of the premises at a cost of £8,000. This resulted in donations from members together with gifts of nearly £4,800, plus interest free loans of £475.

Over the period from 1981 to 1997 a sum of around £34,000 was spent. The Lodge Room was refurbished, a new cloakroom was built, church pews were purchased from a redundant Church at Weston-super-Mare, the roof was leaking badly, and it was necessary to cover the coping stones at the front, the Lodge Room and Hall were decorated throughout, a new concrete floor was installed in the dining room (the wooden floor having collapsed), and new carpet was fitted in the Temple and on the landing. Finally, in 1996, a new roof was installed to the kitchen, and the outside of the building was redecorated.

During these years the Hall was receiving donations annually from the 'Club' of over £1,000, and donations from the Lodge of Instruction, Connaught Chapter, the Ladies' Festival and some income from Hall lettings all helped to fund the work carried out.

This mode of funding has continued to the present day and in 2000 yet more improvements and refurbishments began, including the supply of new Temple Pillars in 2005. From 2000 to 2005 Connaught Lodge spent some £22,000 on the improvement and general upkeep of the Masonic Hall. This has had the effect of reducing the amount that would normally have been available for donations to Charity, particularly the 2007 Festival.

Installation, &c. *on Friday 29th Oct*

The Officers and Brethren of the several Lodges, are to Assemble in the Great Banquetting Room of the Guildhall, at Nine o'Clock in the Morning, and precisely at Eleven, the Lodge will be close tiled.

The Provincial Grand Master for the County of Somerset, will be Installed according to the ancient and accustomed solemnities, by WILLIAM WILLIAMS, Esq. M. P. Provincial Grand Master for Dorsetshire.

The following is the arrangement of the Ceremony :—

After an occasional prelude by a full band of music, the Provincial Grand Lodge will be opened at Eleven o'Clock by the acting Provincial Grand Master, WILLIAM WILLIAMS Esq.

The Lodge being duly formed, the ceremony will commence, by the installation procession, moving forward in the following order :—the band playing a slow march.

PROVINCIAL GRAND TYLER WITH DRAWN SWORD.

Two Provincial Grand Stewards.

The Regalia of the Deputy Provincial Grand Master on a Cushion, borne by a Master Mason.

NINE EXCELLENT MASONS, THREE AND THREE, BEARING THE IMPLEMENTS OF MASONRY.

The first three, those of the Entered Apprentices ; the second three, those of the Fellow Craft ; the last three those of the Master Mason.

A P. G. Steward. { The Gloves and Apron of the Provincial Grand Master on a Cushion, borne by a Master Mason. } { The Collar and Jewel of the Provincial Grand Master on a Cushion, borne by a Master Mason. } A P. G. Steward.

Past P. Grand Treasurer.

PAST P. GRAND SECRETARY, &c.

The Provicial Grand Deacons.

Provincial Grand Superintendant of the Works.—Provincial Grand Director of Ceremonies.

The Provincial Grand Secretary, bearing the Book of Constitutions on a Cushion.

THE PROVINCIAL GRAND REGISTRAR BEARING THE PROVINCIAL GRAND SEAL.

The P. G. Treasurer with his Gold Key.

A Provincial Grand Steward. { The Provincial Grand Chaplain, bearing the Holy Bible, Compass, and Square, on a Cushion. } A Provincial Grand Steward.

PAST PROVINCIAL GRAND WARDENS, TWO AND TWO.

THE PROVINCIAL JUNIOR GRAND WARDEN.

The Senior Provincial Warden.

PAST DEPUTY PROVINCIAL GRAND MASTERS, TWO AND TWO.

Illustrious Visitors two and two.

THE DEPUTY PROVINCIAL GRAND MASTER PRECEDED BY HIS BANNER.

Visiting Provincial Grand Masters and Banners.

THE BANNER OF THE PROVINCIAL GRAND MASTER.

PROVINCIAL GRAND SWORD BEARER.

C. K. K. TYNTE, Esq. M. P. Right Worshipful Provincial Grand Master.

TWO PROVINCIAL GRAND STEWARDS.

Provincial Grand Tyler.

Summons for the Installation of Col. Charles Kemeys Kemeys Tynte as
Provincial Grand Master for the Province of Somerset on 29th September 1820
Displayed in the Minehead Masonic Hall

Minehead

The Masonic Hall, Bancks St, Minehead TA24 5DJ

Lodges Meeting in Minehead

Exmoor Lodge No. 2390
Saint Bernard Lodge No. 5361

Exmoor Chapter 2390
Exmoor Mark Lodge No. 697 • Exmoor Lodge of Royal Ark Mariners 697
St. Decuman & St. Dubricius Chapter No. 784 (RC)
Exmoor Preceptory No. 638 (KT)

Although one of the more isolated Masonic venues, Minehead Masonic Hall is certainly one of the finest in the Province, with a number of interesting features. The front of the building is in true Victorian style and worth more than just a brief look, and the Temple is always a pleasure to visit.

Exmoor Lodge was consecrated on 26th May 1891. It met in the Minehead Public Hall, or Town Hall as it was sometimes called, where the present hospital is located. After a short time friction between the landlord and the Lodge led to Mr Luttrell, who owned most of the town, providing a piece of land in Bancks Street and suggesting the Lodge erect their own building.

*The impressive Victorian frontage of
Minehead Masonic Hall*

The Bancks Street building was opened on 18th June 1893. The money was raised by setting up a limited company and selling shares to the members. This company still exists today and is responsible for the building, but over the years has faced many challenges.

In 1922 the Temple was proving too small and they embarked on a scheme to enlarge the building and construct a new Temple at the rear. This was opened on 20th September 1923.

Building developments have continued over the years, usually financed by generous donations from all the brethren. A few years ago it was discovered that lack of building maintenance meant that the intricate Temple ceiling was in an imminent state of collapse and a major fund raising programme followed. Recent developments to bring the building up to standard have included new fire exits, a chair lift and a new kitchen with quality fittings and more space.

Perhaps the most interesting Masonic item is an original Installation summons for the investiture of Col. Charles Kemeys Kemeys Tynte as Provincial Grand Master at Bath in 1820. This is a rare piece of Provincial history in good condition, and worth studying to realise how well public Masonic events were organised nearly 200 years ago.

The Emblems of Mortality.

A skull and crossbones of real significance are to be seen framed and mounted in the Minehead Masonic Hall, and one can imagine the impact on any Mason confronted with them for the first time. As a symbol of great age they remain a powerful force in this as in earlier Centuries

Nailsea

The Masonic Hall, Nailsea, BS48 1BA

Lodges Meeting in Nailsea

Lodge Marine No. 232
Severn Lodge No. 4399
Tyntesfield Lodge No. 4494
Estune Lodge No. 6817
Backwell Lodge No. 7964
Wraxall Lodge No. 9011
Olympian Lodge No. 9703
Sir Isaac Newton Lodge No. 9801

Tyntesfield Chapter 4494
Nailsea Mark Lodge No. 1548 • Nailsea RAM 1548
Estune Chapter No. 485 (RC) • Cadbury Camp Chapter No. 598 (RC)
Portbury Priory Chapter No. 924 (RC) • Somerset Millennium Chapter No. 1133 (RC)
Estune Command Preceptory No. 354 (KT)
Rose & Lily Conclave No. 387 (RCC) • Nailsea Council No. 249 (RSM)
Morison Meridian Council No. 196 (AMD) • Nailsea Conclave No. 519 (OSM).

The impressive Lodge Room at Nailsea
Those who enter are left in no doubt as to which Lodge established Freemasonry in this building

The Nailsea premises were purchased during 1922. The package included the old Glassworks Manager's House known as The Poplars, a large two storey dwelling with its own approach drive from the Bristol Road, the Volunteer Drill Hall with Model and Display Rooms above, the Drill Hall being an extension to the Manager's House, together with the surrounding land extending to approximately three acres. The conveyance was originally in the names of three Tyntesfield Lodge Founders, the purchase price was £800 and a further £750 was spent on conversions for Masonic use, a goodly sum in those days for a Lodge still to be Consecrated. Little is known regarding the premises role during the 49 years after the Glassworks closed and leading to its Masonic ownership.

The Tyntesfield brethren soon realised that their newly converted Temple and Dining Room was not adequate for their needs, and in 1934/5 extended the rooms to over twice their original size, at a cost exceeding £1500, and that footprint remains unchanged to this day. The description of the extended Temple is best described in the Architect's own words at that time.

"The Brief was to create a Temple to the Glory of the Great Architect of the Universe where Ceremonies could be conducted with due solemnity and dignity. Your attention is drawn to the architectural detail in the East. I'm indebted to C.F. and G.A. Mitchell FRIBAs, who published a series of plates giving typical examples of the five noble orders of architecture from which I selected one giving examples of the Tuscan Order, the panel produced here in our Temple is designated from a portion of an arcade of which no known ancient example is left standing. But the examples referred to probably existed between 600 and 700BC.

So faithfully were the plates detailed and dimensioned that the reproduction is pure Tuscan architecture, and every dimension and proportion is correct. The Cornice around the Temple is of course a continuation of the same. The Ceiling Stars have been placed in position from a chart prepared by Bro Onn, and represent the position of the Constellation as they appeared in the sky on the evening Tyntesfield Lodge was consecrated. I mention that since this time the stars have been removed for maintenance purposes and replaced a few occasions, romantic as this seems the positions can no longer be vouched for. I mention that we have a friendly Spirit at Nailsea that seems to reside in our premises and whose presence has been felt by many over the years. Maybe our current Surveyor should take note with a view to replacing the stars correctly!"

The only changes in the Temple since the time of the mentioned extension is the addition of a perimeter staging, built in seating and a new purpose woven carpet which was specially made and includes a rose in two of the corner panels, a mark of respect to the Rose Croix Chapters that meet on the premises.

In recent years the Temple was designated the Tyntesfield Temple as a mark of respect and appreciation to the early members of that Lodge and their kindness in the 1960s when the premises were entrusted to the new Limited Company which has safeguarded the Masonic Centre to this day.

At the same time the Dining Room was designated the Samuel Bowen Room. Samuel was the Proprietor of the Glass Works in the 1860s who built the Drill Hall and was the Volunteers first Captain; he is also credited for his kindness both to his workers and the village at large and was greatly respected by all. The glazed panels, on display, show his insignia and were recovered from the main entrance door to the old house, now the escape exit in the lounge on the south side. The panels are unique, as are the displayed framed Architectural drawings showing all the available designs.

The Poplars was built by the founder of the Glass Works, John Robert Lucas, as an extension to the Woodview Terrace that was built in 1788, the cellar foundations under the Lounge suggest a previous structure. The terrace was known as the Old Rank and described by Hannah Moore as wretched little habitations. At that time they housed as many as 200 glass workers.

During the 1980s W.Bros Alan Peters of the Backwell Lodge and Charles Cornish of the Estune Lodge became Directors. Alan Peters soon took over the Chairmanship and Charles Cornish the responsibility as Surveyor and Clerk of Works. Since that time little has stood still. A sketch plan prepared by Charles in consultation with Alan was further developed by the whole Board and Professional drawings commissioned.

The improvements were far reaching and included major extensions to the South elevation to provide for a purpose built kitchen and bar store, and the North Elevation to provide for new male toilets and entrance hall with Regalia storage facilities above. What remained of the old house after the demolition of the North wing

in the early 1960s was completely reconfigured to provide a substantial lounge complete with bar and multi-function rooms above. The brickwork to form the bar was achieved using old Nailsea bricks, recovered from the demolitions, which included the remains of a kiln, with a view to maintaining a link with the past. The last phase of the improvements was completed in 2009 with the exception of the exterior cosmetics and landscaping the parking facilities, but no doubt there will be other schemes to follow. W.Bro Alan Peters is still the Chairman, his enthusiasm and commitment show no signs of diminishing.

Although the Centre is steeped in history the interiors are both functional and pleasing, adequately providing for Masonic, social and local needs.

The Foundation Stone for the extension in 1935 was laid on the twenty first of March with Masonic reverence by the then Deputy PGM W.Bro R.T.A. Hughes MA. The inscription on the stone records that it was laid to the Glory of God in memory of R.W.Bro The Venerable Archdeacon Walter Farrar, PGM for Somerset. The building was completed and rededicated by PGM, R.W.Bro Brig. Gen. C.L. Norman DSO, MVO, DL, (PSGD) on 11th December 1935.

Portishead

Royal Hotel 1878-1911 • GWR Pier Station 1911-2006

Lodges that met in Portishead

Lodge Marine No. 232 Calcutta - Moved to Nailsea
Eldon Lodge No. 1755 Portishead - Moved to Clevedon
Severn Lodge No. 4399 Portishead - Moved to Nailsea
Gordano Lodge No. 6244 Portishead - Moved to Yatton

The Pier Hotel, Portishead

There had been a Lodge presence in Portishead since 1878, but due to development of the old Port into the new Marina, one by one the Lodges have moved out to the neighbouring towns of Clevedon, Nailsea and Yatton.

Eldon Lodge No. 1755 was the first Lodge to be established in the town, being consecrated on 3rd September 1878, at the Royal Hotel. The land had been the property of Bristol Corporation which built the hotel in 1831 as accommodation in their attempt to attract the good citizens of Bristol (and elsewhere) to Portishead as a holiday resort.

A pier was later constructed to encourage sea-borne clients, and the GWR ran a line from Bristol to a point at the north end of the High Street, whilst a local line ran from Weston, Clevedon and Portishead (unfortunately abbreviated to W.C.&P.)

An extension of the GWR line about 1865 ran to a ship-berthing pier where there was a new station, but by 1911 this feature became obsolete and was purchased for use as a Masonic Hall. It was not the prettiest of buildings, and was approached via an ill-lit alley of slippery steps.

Shepton Mallet

The Crossways Hotel, North Wootton BA4 4EU

Lodge Meeting in Shepton Mallet
Love & Honour Lodge No. 285

A convenient room adjoining the Hotel

Love & Honour 285 was founded in 1792 and its registered town is Shepton Mallet, where long before, at an even earlier date, in 1737, there was a Lodge meeting at the Angel Inn. Look in vain for their presence in that old town; look in vain too for a quaint olde tavern lying among the cider orchards in the charming country village of North Wootton. The Cross Hands is a Conference Centre/Hotel and the food and the facilities are excellent, but in the words of a professional historian – 't ain't my period'.

Should this sound unkind, two things must be said; firstly that the work put in recently by the brethren of the Lodge in converting the cellars of the Crosshands into a Lodge Room has been tremendous, and secondly, the history of their previous homes is both fascinating and colourful.

There was, as mentioned above, a very early Lodge which met at the Angel Inn at Shepton Mallet (1737-1768), but Love & Honour appears to have been Warranted in 1792 by

Thomas Dunckerley, possibly in the Assembly Rooms at Wells. The minute books record meetings at the Bell Inn at Shepton until 1819 after which they met peripatetically around the town, until in 1912 they began the association with Sales House, eventually purchasing it in 1947.

In 1940 the Lodge bought Highfield House, a large property with outbuildings and 2.5 acres of land for £1,400; the ownership was vested in the Highfield Benevolent Trust which was set up under a legal trust deed. Trustees drawn from members of the Lodge are appointed by the Lodge. Highfield House was never again occupied. After the 1939-45 war it was subject to a compulsory purchase order by the local council. In 1947 the proceeds helped to buy the whole of the Sales House property. The main house had by then been converted into flats by the local authority.

The first record of Sales House being used as a Masonic meeting place was in 1835 when the Provincial Grand Lodge of Somerset met in Shepton Mallet. The normal Lodge meeting room was too small to accommodate them, so they met in a larger room at the former St. Sales Convent, which many years later became the regular meeting place.

The property, St. Sales House, has at various times been known also as The Convent and The Cloisters. Originally developed as a mill complex it was one of many which had grown up during the prosperity of the town at the end of the 18th Century. Its arrangement was typical, consisting of a self-contained compound with mill buildings, workers dwellings and owner's mansion.

The west wing was some 100ft long, and was one of the former mill buildings. The Roman Catholic 'Order of Visitation', which purchased the property in 1810 extensively altered the east wing which had previously consisted of cottages and shops. The Sisters were of a 'closed' order; having been founded in 1617 by Francois de Sales, whence the house derived its name. These alterations included the building of a chapel and also walls to enclose the property; these were latterly not only to keep out intruders but also to prevent the escape of the less dedicated residents.

The old Lodge Room at Sales House

During the 1939-1945 war the premises, apart from the Lodge accommodation, were requisitioned and occupied first by the British and later by the American troops. The main house was subsequently turned into flats by the local authority. This was de-requisitioned in 1957 and returned to the owners, by then the Highfield Benevolent Trust.

As with all old buildings the condition of the property was by the early 1950s already giving cause for concern, and in the summer of 1956 repairs to the roof were carried out, and by 1959 further work to the building was necessary. A considerable amount of work was done to the interior of the Lodge room and ante-room, for which the Lodge was deeply indebted to W.Bro R.V. Showering, Bro F. Showering and Bro K. Showering, all of 'Babycham' fame. An entirely new floor was constructed over the whole area of the Lodge room, with new timber joists and new floor boards. The Lodge Room, being the original Chapel, had a balcony from which the brethren could look down on the proceedings.

In May of 1996 dry rot was discovered in the old chapel and extensive work required to rectify the problem in the walls and on the original oak roof timbers. W.Bro L.M. Smith, WM at that time, at a meeting of the Trustees, recommended work to commence. All this new work meant that some of the walls of the existing nun's cells had to be demolished, this work cost in the region of £41,000, being raised by the brethren and the help of the 'Angel' Lodge, a demonstration team, under the guidance of W.Bro Alastair M. Craig presenting 18th century work. Most of the refurbishment work was carried out on a 'self-help' basis by numerous members of the Lodge, lead by W.Bros M. Frecknall and Len Reakes.

Following the discovering of a further outbreak of 'dry rot' in 2001 the brethren decided that the time for pouring good money after bad into a building which consumed it at an alarming rate, was over. The WM at that time, W.Bro Lenny Baker, together with Bro Paul Davis, was instrumental in pushing forward the decision reached by the trustees that the property had to be sold. A quest now ensued for a new location for the Lodge. Several Lodges in the locality offered the use of their premises for Lodge meetings, for which support the brethren were deeply grateful.

Negotiations with various developers was taking a long time. Fortunately, W.Bro Graham Watts, who resides in North Wootton, during an evening at the Crossways, his 'local', struck up a conversation with the then owner, who was a Freemason in London. It transpired that the hotel had a secure cellar area which was not being used, although in need of decoration and refurbishment. It was suggested that this could be used as a meeting place, and the initial seed to move to that venue was sown.

The last meeting at the Old Convent and Lodge premises in Draycott Road was held on the 15th May 2002. The Ceremony conducted was an Installation, and Bro Paul Davis was Installed into the Chair.

During the summer recess the old building was finally sold and the new venue, the cellar at the 'Crossways Hotel', was secured for a rent from the owners. An enormous amount of effort and work by several of the brethren turned the cellar into an extremely fitting Lodge Room, and it is indeed a credit to their hard work that by the September of that year it was ready to receive the Lodge for their first meeting. The Ceremony was the passing of Bro Andrew Snook conducted by the newly Installed Master W.Bro Paul Davis on 18th September 2002. The meeting was well attended by many distinguished visitors, including W.Bro Raymond Guthrie, Assistant Provincial Grand Master of Somerset.

Despite the recent change with regard to accommodation the Lodge of Love and Honour 285 is a pleasure to visit for the interesting Masonic treasures it exhibits. Having now settled down at North Wootton the Temple displays a number of fascinating Masonic pieces, which vary in form, content and meaning.

Perhaps the most interesting piece is a Hiram's Head dating from 1825, when it was purchased for four guineas. Its actual use appears not to be known, although it may have played some part in the Third degree. It stands ten inches high, carved out of a solid piece of timber and painted and adorned with beard and moustache. Although somewhat the worse for wear it remains a fascinating historical piece, very rare, and possibly unique. It is also unfortunate that this most rare and interesting artifact currently appears to be missing from the Shepton Mallet collection.

Notice also that not only does the Lodge banner display the arms of Grand Lodge, a rarity indeed, with a letter of sanction for its use, but hanging over the Master's chair there is an insignia of the Grand Master, rarely displayed elsewhere and an interesting feature for any visitor.

The Lodge is fortunate to possess two Thomas Harper Past Masters' jewels dating from the early 19th Century. Such jewels are a superb example of those originating from the workshop of Thomas Harper, the premier Masonic jewel

maker of the time and probably ever since. In terms of design they originate from the 18th Century and are particularly interesting to all Masonic jewel collectors.

These two jewels were made from silver and partly goldplated. The hallmark shows them to date from 1817 and that the maker was Thomas Harper, the finest maker of Masonic jewels. This style of jewel was used as a Past Masters Jewel and its design pre-dates the Union of 1813.

Thomas Harper had a lengthy and distinguished career in both the Antients and Modern Lodges, culminating in his participation as Deputy Grand Master for the former in the negotiations leading to the Union and the formation of the United Grand Lodge Of England.
Thomas Harper Lodge no 9612 was named in his memory and encourages its members to research Masonic history with particular regard to the jewels of the Masonic orders.

An intriguing piece is a wooden box with brass ornamentation, probably over 200 years old, which is fastened to a wall and whose original purpose can only be guessed. It is certainly rare, well constructed, with a series of letters stamped on one of the side panels. These letters GRLAGMA represent the seven liberal arts and sciences. It is a fascinating object.

Taunton

The Masonic Hall, The Circus, Taunton, TA1 4EB

Lodges Meeting in Taunton

Lodge of Unanimity and Sincerity No. 261
Lodge of St. George No. 3158
Taunton Deane Lodge No. 5221
Queens College Lodge No. 6988
Old Aluredian Lodge No. 7724
Taunton School Lodge No. 8215
Richard Huish Lodge No. 8518
Vivary Lodge No. 8654
Emergency Services Lodge No. 9391

Chapter of Sincerity 261 • Chapter of St. George 3158 • Taunton Deane Chapter 5221
Fidelity & Unanimity Mark Lodge No. 348 • Langdale Mark Lodge No. 1615
Somerset Installed Mark Master Masons Lodge No. 1652 • Fidelity & Unanimity RAM Lodge 348
Alfred Chapter No. 13 (RC) • Vale of Taunton Chapter No. 826 (RC)
King Ina Preceptory No. 211 (KT) • King Ina Tabernacle No. 4 (KTP)
King Ina Conclave No. 363 (RCC) • Taunton Council No. 164 (RSM)
Taunton Vale Council No. 104 (AMD) • Secundem Artem Conclave No. 314 (OSM)

After Bath, probably the most important Masonic centre in Somerset is Taunton, particularly in relation to its geographical position in the south of the Province, and especially in terms of Masonic history and "treasures". Certainly its Masonic Hall is very fine, both externally and internally, and worthy of a visit if the opportunity avails itself. The Lodge Room is exceptional, as befits a previous life as a Roman Catholic Chapel. There is a fine display of Masonic antiques and artefacts both here and in the 'Sherry Room', and indeed elsewhere.

The Masonic Hall, originally built as a Roman Catholic Chapel, and comprising the Temple, Supper Room, cellars and outbuildings, was acquired in 1878 by the Taunton Masonic Hall Co. Ltd. This company was formed specifically for that purpose by members of Lodge 261, with restriction on transfer of shares only to "Members of the Order of Free & Accepted Masons". Since that date ownership has been vested in or controlled by members of that Lodge.

There was a partial tenancy at the time by Huish's School, subsequently Bishop Fox's School, which only ceased completely in 1905. (Mrs Taylor, wife of the late W.Bro B.U. Taylor and mother of W.Bros T.U. & R.G. Taylor, started her schooling there). Immediately following the acquisition the Company's bankers failed; but the liquidator paid over the balance in 1880.

Various alterations and improvements were made thereafter, and in the years up to 1906 there was intermittent letting of the hall (until then used only by Lodge 261, Royal Arch Chapter 261 and Rose Croix Chapter 13) for dances, parties and municipal elections.

In 1904 there was consideration of alterations to the exits and placing the staircase inside the hall, instead of outside. Preceding 1906 various brethren of 261 transferred their shares to the Lodge as a gift and others bought shares for the same purpose, and the Lodge too purchased shares. In 1909 the Directors of the Company recommended remaining shareholders to accept the scheme of purchase by the Lodge; the Company was wound up and the Masonic Hall property vested in Trustees for the members of Lodge 261; only subscribing members of the Lodge being eligible as Trustees.

Number 20 The Crescent was bought by the Trustees in 1919. The Supper Room was enlarged and central heating installed with the help of donations by the members of Lodges 261 and 3158. Vacant possession was only obtained in 1937 when the major alterations and improvements were made, with re-roofing being carried out at the same time.

In the interim, between 1919 and 1937, the Trustees purchased land at the rear of the Hall; part of which was later sold for the development of the Telephone Exchange, leaving what is now the Hall Car Park. At that time discussions took place for joint ownership of the Hall by the then three Craft Lodges 261, 3158 and 5221, but legal complexities prevented progress. In 1938 however, a Management Committee of elected representatives of all Craft Lodges was formed and took over the day to day management of the Hall which continues to this day.

Masonic chairs frequently hold pride of place among the many Masonic artefacts owned by Lodges, and Taunton Masonic Hall can be very proud of its antique examples. They are superb, varied, in excellent condition, and a testament over 200 years of attention by several caring Masons. That of the Immediate Past Master is the oldest, dating from 1789,and that of the Master from 1807. Both were purchased in 1807. The Wardens Chairs were obtained in 1858

The Warden's Pedestals probably date from 1817 when it was resolved that such be obtained; the "Lesser Lights" were purchased in 1839. The "emblems of mortality" were carved and presented by Bro Strawbridge in 1879 and the Lodge Pillars were made and taken into use in 1881.

The Organ was provided out of the residue of the Estate of the late W.Bro J.G. Vile bequeathed to the Lodge (and placed in position in 1932).

Many more rare artefacts adorn the building. Among them is a very fine pair of free standing globes, terrestrial and celestial, of early 19th Century origin and in good condition given their age. Whilst a late 18th Century piece, now framed for posterity, is a Master's Tracing or Tressall board, used in earlier times by the Master to explain points in the ritual. Very few now exist.

117

Among all the treasures to be found in 'The Sherry Room' of Taunton Masonic Hall, perhaps the most interesting are a pair of old, exceptional and seldom seen Masonic prints, which most unusually portray both a Mason and his wife in a satirical light, with typical Hogarthian emphasis on the decline and fall from original uprightness

Many brethren of all Lodges using the Temple have contributed to the fine Museum and Library now housed in the "Sherry Room". The first recorded was in 1838 when W.Bro Eales White presented the Past Master's Apron and Jewel worn by his late father. The first Masonic Books were presented by Bro May in 1842, and the minute records his prophetic hope that they "would be a nucleus around which would be ultimately formed a Library worthy of the Lodge."

But the crowning glory of a Masonic Temple is often to be found in the ceiling. Sometimes it is the architectural design, sometimes the adornment. Standing in the Temple at Taunton Masonic Hall one cannot but be impressed with the superb illustrated symbolic G incorporated into the ceiling panel surrounded by the rays of the Sun. As the centre of a ceiling painted with stars the symbolic G is an outstanding icon for any Freemason,

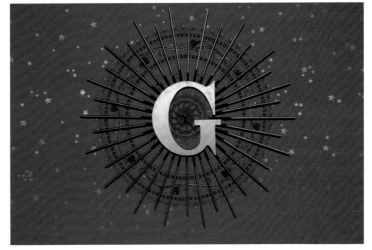

Watchet

The Masonic Hall, Watchet,TA23 0DA

Lodges Meeting in Watchet

Quantock Lodge No. 4446

Watchet Masonic Hall, the home of Quantock Lodge 4446, is situated at the junction of Doniford Road and South Road and adjoins the site of the old Court Leet Pound, where in olden times straying animals were impounded. Watchet Court Leet (an English criminal court for the punishment of small offences) continues to exist, and since Quantock Lodge was formed, many of the Lodge brethren have also been jury members of the Watchet Court Leet and this continues to be the case today. However, stray animals are no longer impounded.

Watchet Masonic Hall was consecrated by the then Provincial Grand Master, R.W.Bro Col. William Long, on the 5th April, 1923, but early Quantock Lodge minutes make no mention of the actual building of the Masonic Hall. The Building is constructed with local red sandstone, which accounts for its warm outward appearance. The cost of the building was £1,260, with the money raised partly by donations, partly by the issue of numbered Bonds in multiples of £5, a lot of money in those days, and partly by a Bank Loan. It is understood that the bank loan was made possible through the good offices of the local Bank Manager, who was one of the Quantock Lodge's founding members. As the Lodge prospered, the £5 Bonds were gradually repaid, this being effected by an annual draw to see which Brother would be repaid. It was recorded at the time that some brethren requested that their Bond numbers were left out of the draw, thereby increasing the chance of a refund to those brethren in greater need. Repayment of the Bonds was helped along by W.Bro H.S. Reed who later made a handsome donation to clear the outstanding debt, so that in 1944, the then Treasurer, W.Bro F.J. Williams, was able to report that the Lodge was free of debt.

Since the Masonic Hall was built, there has been continued ongoing maintenance. Also, there have been many improvements made to the Lodge Building: one such improvement was a new improved, long overdue, heating system installed in 1956 mainly due to the personal efforts of three brethren. A new Organ was dedicated in 1964 by the then Provincial Grand Master, R.W.Bro A. de L. Cazenove and there is mention of extensive decoration of the Lodge Building in 1972.

With the approval of the Provincial Grand Master, and by permission of the Quantock Lodge brethren, in 2000 Watchet Masonic Hall also became the home of The Millennium Lodge 352 of The Order of Women Freemasons.

Print "Dedicated to the Ancient and Honourable Fraternity of Freemasons"

Possibly one of the most interesting pieces of history in this book hangs on the walls of the Masonic Hall in Watchet! What appears to be a pen and ink portrait of HRH the Prince of Wales is in fact a written History of English Freemasonry during his tenure as the M.W The Grand Master.

Wedmore

The Masonic Hall, Church St, Wedmore BS28 4AB

Lodges Meeting in Wedmore

Alfred & Guthrum Lodge No. 4535
Sir Thomas de Cheddre Lodge No. 9188
St Cecilia Lodge No. 9341

Wedmore Chapter No. 912 (RC)

The Alfred & Guthrum Lodge was consecrated on the 9th October 1923, the ceremony taking place in the Village Institute Hall, Church Street, Wedmore, which some seven years later would be purchased by the Lodge and become its permanent home.

The first meeting place, however, consisted of rented accommodation on the premises of Mr (later Bro) W.R. Withers, a builder, in 'The Borough' in an upper room with accommodation for 40-50 brethren. "Its simple beauty of decoration and its homeliness were striking to visiting brethren, and even more especially to those who had the privilege of Initiation therein." The last time it was used 42 members and guests were present. The Lodge remained at 'The Borough' until an unexpected opportunity arose in 1929 to purchase the Village Institute Hall. This building had been erected during the 19th Century as the Village Assembly Rooms and opened with a Grand Concert on New Year's Day 1868.

The old cinema screen is still discernible behind the Senior Warden's Chair.

The new Lodge room itself, on the first floor, had formerly served as the village cinema, and the outline of the screen can still be seen on the wall behind the Senior Warden's pedestal. The dedication of the Temple, conducted by the R.W.Bro the Rev. Archdeacon Walter Farrer, PGM, took place on 28th January 1930, although the first meeting had actually taken place by Dispensation the previous November.

The Lodge rooms and ante-rooms are on the first floor, and on the ground floor there was an accountant's office, the Wedmore branch of the National Westminster Bank, and at the rear a large room which until 1966 was used as a store. This was later taken over to form a dining room and provide kitchen and bar facilities. Previous to this the members had dined at the George Hotel.

The Wedmore Cinema during the 1920s

Over the years the structure and fabric of the building have undergone many alterations including a new heating system, a stair lift, very useful for our older brethren, and also new carpets and chairs. During the 1980s Provincial Grand Lodge was looking for office accommodation. As the then Provincial Grand Secretary, W.Bro R.D. Clark, was a member of Alfred & Guthrum Lodge, and lived near Axbridge, it seemed convenient for the Province to rent two of the first floor ante-rooms for the Provincial Offices, which were opened at the beginning of 1986 and remain in use today.

Above: The cinema ticket office still exists in the small room behind the Master's Chair

Left: The All Seeing Eye above the Master's Chair

Wellington

The Masonic Hall, Mantle Street, Wellington TA21 8BZ

Lodges Meeting in Wellington

Fidelity and Sincerity Lodge No. 1966
Wellington School Lodge No. 7230

Fidelity and Sincerity Chapter 1966
Monument Mark Lodge No. 1295

Even by the more passionate members of the Wellington Lodges, the Masonic Hall on Mantle Street is rarely spoken of as being a glorious edifice. Internally however it is a different story, described by one of its prominent members as akin to a Tardis.

Once a storage facility for animal feed, fertilisers and salt, the Masonic Hall in Wellington was originally acquired by the Lodge of Fidelity and Sincerity at an annual rental of £16.10s per annum, and in 1882 was bought by the Lodge for the sum of £350.

The splendid Lodge Room is accessed via a good sized ante-room which also provides access to the dining room. One cannot help but be amazed by the size of this room, which is larger in fact than the Lodge Room itself, although from the outside this does not seem possible. The answer lies at the side of the main building where, concealed from view, there is a large 'lean-to" structure erected in 1959. The dining room has many wonderful pieces of artwork around its walls, and is in regular use, not only for the festive board, but for many social events.

The Lodge Room contains some very fine furniture. The Master's Chair, and those of the IPM, Senior and Junior Wardens each are topped with emblems of their Office and pre-date the opening of the Lodge. There is also a superb lectern in the fashion of a carved Eagle which was "The loving gift of Sarah Hart" in 1894.

Notice also the heavy maul beside the Master's pedestal. One blow from this would indeed lay one lifeless!

Wells

The Masonic Hall, West Cloister, Wells BA5 2PA

Lodges Meeting in Wells

Benevolent Lodge No. 446
Avalon Chapter 446

It is difficult to imagine a more inspiring place for Freemasons to meet than within the walls of the beautiful Cathedral at Well

The Lodge Room in the West Cloister at Wells Cathedral

In 1785 the Lodge of Unanimity 473 held its first meeting at the Swan Hotel, Sadler Street, Wells, but ceased to exist by the year 1809. This is the first record of any Lodge in Wells. In 1837 the Swan Lodge of Benevolence 653 came into existence and also held its first meeting at the Swan Hotel. A year later it transferred to the City Council Chambers where it remained for 54 years.

On 23rd December 1996 the Lodge moved to the West Cloisters of Wells Cathedral. The West Cloisters appear to have been planned by Bishop Bekynton but not completed until about 1480. It was then occupied by the Grammar School until 1870. By then it had become dilapidated and was not fully used until 1888, when the Girls High School occupied the building, remaining there until 1945 when they moved to other premises. It continued to be used for some time after this as a recorder practice room. In 1973, and until December 1996, it was used as the Cathedral Choristers practice room.

The Vicars Hall (left), where the Lodge met from 1892 until 1917, and where they now enjoy a meal after their meetings, was erected at the charge of Bishop Ralph of Shrewsbury and completed in 1348. Number 10 Cathedral Green, where Benevolent Lodge also used to meet, was used as a kitchen or food storage area to supply the Vicars Hall above.

Weston-super-Mare

The Masonic Hall, Tivoli Lane, The Boulevard, Weston-super-Mare BS23 1NZ

Lodges Meeting in Weston-super-Mare

St. Kew Lodge No. 1222
King Alfred Lodge No. 3169
Wessex Lodge No. 4093
Birnbeck Lodge No. 7160
Athelstan Lodge No. 9033
Somerset Provincial Grand Stewards Lodge No. 9189
Tivoli Lodge No. 9417

Inkerman Chapter 1222 • King Alfred Chapter 3169
Else Mark Lodge No. 102
William de Irwin Chapter No. 28 (RC) • Aisecombe Manor Chapter No. 1067 (RC)
Worlebury Preceptory of St. Dunstan No. 121 (KT)

The Foundation stone of the Masonic Hall in Weston-super-Mare was laid by W.Bro W.E. Perrett in April 1908, the stone having been given by Bro Thomas Cox, and the mortar being spread with a silver trowel given by the Masters of St. Kew and King Alfred Lodges.

Top Left: The Weston Organ op
Left: W.Bro W.E. Perrett lays the Foundation Stone
Lower Left: Entrance to the Masonic Hall
Above: The Gold Key - face & reverse views

On 1st October of the same year it was consecrated by W.Bro Wm. Long, Deputy PGM, assisted by Officers of the Provincial Grand Lodge. Bro W. Cornwell was WM of St. Kew Lodge at the time, and was presented with a gold key by the Architects with which to open the new building.

Weston-super-Mare Masonic Hall is not only a handsome building but located on an historic site as far as the town is concerned. In 1920 Wessex Lodge joined St. Kew and King Alfred Lodges in Weston, and in 1927 it was decided to sell sufficient shares and an amount of furniture to St. Kew and Wessex Lodges to equalise the interest of each Lodge in the premises. Thus was formed the Masonic Hall Co. Ltd.

Above: In the ante-room there is a striking collection of Masonic jewels. Here are displayed
'In Memoriam' the jewels of several distinguished Masons, who over the years served their Lodges so well.
Below: Left - 19th Century Sunderland Mug;   Right - Liverpool Jug

The Masonic Hall has an enviable collection of artifacts and perhaps most striking is the display of Masonic Jewels adorning the walls of the Ante Room. Here can be seen the Jewels 'In Memoriam' to the distinguished Brethren who have served their Lodges so well over many years. It equally contains several Masonic treasures, both of beauty and interest. With a wealth of symbols are an early 19th Century printed mug made in Sunderland, and a fine jug probably printed in Liverpool. Both are Masonic, made of earthenware, in good condition and worthy of close examination.

However, perhaps the most interesting Masonic object at Weston is a solid marble cube about five inches square, engraved on all six sides with a most curious set of Masonic signs, symbols and lettering, the deciphering of which would be a test for any Masonic scholar. It is said to have been produced in order to commemorate and/or record the Union of the Antients and Moderns Lodges in 1813. The texts were decoded in a Quatuor Coronati Lodge transaction in 1890. The cube is certainly rare and of great historical interest.

The magnificent furniture surrounding the Master's Chair in the Lodge Room at Weston-super-Mare

Wincanton

The Masonic Hall, Church St, Wincanton, BA9 9AA

Lodges Meeting in Wincanton

Lodge of Science No. 437

Science Mark Lodge No. 128 • Herbert Fuller RAM Lodge 128

Freemasonry in Wincanton began with a debate amongst the brethren of the Lodge of Science 437 in August 1869. The proposition was put for removal of the Lodge from its home in the Province of Dorset to Somerset. Wincanton was the town of choice for the new location as there were a significant number of brethren residing in the town.

It was agreed that the move would take place in the November of that year, and on Friday 17th December 1869 the first meeting was held in The National School Rooms on North Street.

The Lodge continued to meet at the National School Rooms until July 1871 when the Lodge moved to the Town Hall where it remained for less than a year. In June 1872 the Lodge had the opportunity to move into its present premises which were owned by Mr R.R. Hutchings, later to become W.Bro Hutchings. The premises were then known as the 'Foresters' Hall'. The Foresters held their meetings on the ground floor whilst the Lodge met upstairs which is approached by way of a stone winding stairway. The original Temple exists today and continues to be used.

Perhaps pride of place, however, goes to the Master and Senior Warden's collar jewels, which are exceptional. There can be few finer jewels not only in the Province but also the country. The Lodge of Science can be very proud of these late 18th Century jewels which are of superb design and workmanship.

The Master's Chair, strikingly impressive with its satin drapes and marble pedestal

This arrangement continued until 1931 when the Lodge was able to purchase the whole property for £200.0s.0d; the premises were renamed 'The Masonic Hall'. The premises date from the late 18th century and little is known of its original intended use. However, during the Napoleonic Wars the building was used as a silk factory.

There is a fine Temple particularly noticeable for a pair of very fine columns, topped by a superb pair of celestial and terrestrial globes, and the most unusual marble pedestals of the Master and Wardens. The Lodge possesses a fine Second Degree tracing board which includes the winding staircase shown on its banner, complete with lettered stairs, the deciphering of which is a test for any aspiring Mason, and a folding coffin, titled H.A. which would equally be a test for any Brother undertaking a Third Degree ceremony.

133

Wiveliscombe

The Masonic Hall, Station Road, Wiveliscombe, TA4 2LT

Lodge Meeting in Wiveliscombe
Loyal Vacation Lodge No. 6209

St. George at Wiveliscombe Chapter No. 1173 (RC)

Wiveliscombe is an old market town, with Masonic roots dating back to 1802 when the first Vacation Lodge was founded. Although erased in 1862 the Lodge was fortunately restored in 1945 and its several Masonic artefacts of note reflect this revived history. The fine Temple of today no doubt compares favourably with that of the early 19th Century. The present Lodge Rooms in Wiveliscombe are housed in a fine period building on the south side of the road running into the town from Taunton. The Loyal Vacation Lodge met in the Congregational Rooms for fifteen years, but the difficulties of sharing with other organisations prompted a search for new premises.

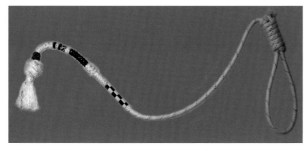

A "running noose" as a wall illustration is rare, and that at Wiveliscombe is indeed a visual and searching reminder of the First Degree ritual.

The current building, which comprised of two flats, was purchased in 1960 with the aid of loans from the members. It was converted by the voluntary labour of Lodge members to suit Masonic needs. The Service of Dedication was held on 23rd May 1961, and was conducted by the Provincial Grand Master R.W.Bro Brig. A de L. Cazenove.

Undoubtedly the main connection with earlier times remains the superb frieze over the stairs at the present Wiveliscombe Masonic Hall, which can be compared with that of the original Lodge,

which was reported as a panel in the dining room of the White Hart Inn in Wiveliscombe, although no trace of it appears to remain today

The old Volume of the Sacred Law is a superb Bible dating from 1633, graphically illustrated with graffiti as was often the case with Bibles of this vintage. It is a striking example of how old Bibles have managed to survive over generations despite misuse and neglect, and one often wonders just where it came from and what tales it could tell, especially as it dates from the pre Commonwealth period, a time of great upheaval in the area.

Above: Photograph of the panel in the Dining Room of the White Hart in Wiveliscombe which was the Lodge Room of the first Vacation Lodge.

Right: Replica of the White Hart panel in the present Masonic Hall

Yatton

The Masonic Hall, 89 High Street, Yatton BS49 4DW

Lodges Meeting in Yatton

The Lodge of Agriculture No. 1199
Gordano No. 6244
Winscombe No. 6474
Woodspring No. 8791
Yatton Lodge of Hospitality No. 9299
Sylvanus No. 9741

Wrington Vale Chapter 1199
George Norman Mark Lodge No. 967
Royal Order of Scotland
Paracelsus College (SRA)

Freemasonry first came to the Yatton district in 1867 when, encouraged by Beaufort Lodge 103 in the Province of Bristol, the Lodge of Agriculture 1199 was established. As was the general custom they initially met at an Inn, the Ship & Castle on the bridge at Congresbury.

In 1891, persuaded by W. Bro John Mountstevens and others, the Lodge decided to re-locate to the Railway Hotel & Assembly Rooms by the GWR Station at Yatton. It was said that rowdy youths tended to peer through the windows at the Ship & Castle and disrupt the Lodge proceedings. However, it is also worth noting that the Hotel and Assembly Rooms just happened to be owned by W. Bro Mountstevens!

In those days, political correctness not having been invented, hunting was the order of the day, and the Clifton Harriers were kennelled in the stables attached to the Assembly Rooms. The Provincial Grand Treasurer and Master of the Lodge in 1892 was also Chairman of the Hunt, the son of the Lodge Secretary looked after the hounds, and the farmer Brethren enjoyed gargantuan breakfasts in the Assembly Rooms, where lengthy speeches were made by such sylph-like athletes as Dr W.G. Grace.

During the 1930s the Lodge started to look for quarters of their own. Larchmount, an impressive building in the centre of Yatton had originally been a private school for girls but had become a small factory producing soaps and perfumes. On 20th March 1935 it was destroyed by fire. The Lodge of Agriculture being quick to seize an opportunity bought the burnt out shell. Yatton Masonic Hall opened less than one year later; a feat that it is unlikely could be accomplished today.

Upper: Larchmount School for Girls
Lower: Larchmount reduced to rubble

Upper: The building on fire 20th March 1935
Lower: 16th March 1936, Yatton's new Masonic Hall

137

The Masonic Hall sits in large gardens to all sides with ample parking. The lawns to the rear are often the scene for outdoor social events, and are used by the children of the Methodist Church playgroup next door in the summer months.

The building houses a large and very fine Lodge Room which is accessed by a wide dog-legged staircase, now equipped with a stairlift. On the landing can be found on display many of the Masonic treasures which have been collected over the past 140 years, most notably those that belonged to R.W.Bro Col. William Long, PGM for Somerset, and three times Worshipful Master of The Lodge of Agriculture.

On the ground floor to the left of the entrance hall is the large dining room containing the Honours Boards of the resident Lodges and the recently refurbished kitchen, the envy of many a commercial chef. There is also a comfortable and well equipped bar.

The whole premises are looked after by the resident caretaker and his wife who live in the adjoining three bedroom 'cottage' with access directly into the main building. The building is actually still owned outright by the Lodge of Agriculture, but is managed and run by the Yatton Masonic Club which comprises a proportional representation from each of the Lodges and other Orders meeting there. Needless to say, the maintenance of a building and grounds this size comes at a considerable cost, which is bourne both by the members and profit from the bar.

Above: *Unique clock designed and presented by W.Bro James Milner, Master of The Lodge of Agriculture in 1947*

Left: *A very rare RMIB Vice President's Jewel*

Below: *A fine Masonic Jug, probably Sunderland Pottery circa 1835*

Yeovil

The Masonic Hall, Hendford, BA20 1TQ

Lodges Meeting in Yeovil

Lodge of Brotherly Love No. 329
Royal Naval Lodge No. 2761
Progressive Science Lodge No. 5007
Corinthian Pillar Lodge No. 7552

Chapter of Brotherly Love 329
William de Irwin Mark Lodge No. 162
Yeovil Chapter No. 519 (RC)
Conclave of Holy Peace No. 381 (RCC) • Somerset & Bristol Sovereigns Conclave No. 486 (RCC)

Freemasonry came to Yeovil very early, the Lodge of Brotherly Love being formed when England was still at war with France, just five years after the battle of Trafalgar and five years before the battle of Waterloo.

George III was on the throne, aged 72 years, but because of his illness with porphyria his son HRH George Augustus Frederick, the Prince of Wales, and incidentally the Grand Master of the Premier Grand Lodge, was virtually acting as Regent, which he became a year later in 1811.

The Lodge was also warranted just over three years before the union of Premier and Antient Grand Lodges., Consecration of the Lodge being held on 11th August 1811, eighteen months after its first meeting.

The ceremony was advertised in the Southern Mercury, at a cost of £1, and was held at the George Inn in Martock. In 1814 the Lodge meetings moved to the White Hart Inn, also in Martock, but then transferred in 1819 to the expanding Yeovil, with the greater likelihood of attracting new members.

The first four meetings in Yeovil were held in Bro T. Cave's house and then in December 1819 at the Mermaid Inn. The Lodge moved shortly after to 'private rooms' in a building next to the Vicarage in Vicarage Street, a main thoroughfare. It stayed there for seven years and then moved to the Three Choughs Inn in March 1827 where meetings were held for the next 70 years. However, in June 1844 it became necessary for the front of the Three Choughs Inn to be rebuilt so the Lodge decided to meet on the top of the Windmill Hill, which overlooks the town centre. The brethren first walked to the Hill through a lane, and then climbed the steep side of the Hill. Fourteen brethren were present at this amazing event where the only other sounds were 'the bleating of the sheep and the songs of the birds in the trees'.

During their time at the rooms in Vicarage Street the brethren had hoped to build their own Masonic Hall. Land was acquired in 1824, and plans drawn up, but the committee was unable to raise the £760 needed, so the land was sold. Further attempts to secure a building were made in 1836 and 1887, without success, but in 1893 the energetic WM, W.Bro H. Whitby, supported by other brethren, led the efforts for land to be purchased in Hendford, which was then on the edge of Yeovil.

A request was made to Provincial Grand Lodge for a contribution of £100 but was declined! A contract was nevertheless let for the building to (Bro) Lye & Sons of Crewkerne for £950. There was little delay in building and the Masonic Hall was dedicated in November 1894 by the Rt. Hon. Viscount Dungarvan, the Provincial Grand Master, and is still the home of Yeovil Masonry.

However, by the latter part of the 20th Century pressure of numbers at the Festive Board led to calls for the dining and bar area to be extended. Discussions took several years until a decision was made in 1994 by the Masonic Hall Company to build a single-storey extension, financed by donations and loans from Lodges and brethren, and a commercial loan. It cost approximately £117,000 and was built by (W.Bro) Rogers & Son with several local brethren employed on the work. The impressive extension was opened in 1995.

The present Masonic hall, opened in 1894, possesses a very fine Lodge Room, and as one would expect there are several Masonic antiques to be seen, some of which are mentioned in the Lodges section. Others include a colour printed jug, possibly of Sunderland lustre origin from the early 19th Century, depicting anti-slavery sentiments on one side and Masonic illustrations on the other.

One of the Yeovil Globes

Another jug dating from the early 19th century is a presentation piece of unusual construction, creamware and hand painted, showing the square and compasses incorporating the number 624, The Lodge of Brotherly Love's number at the time. The inscription on the base, dated June 1821, shows that it was presented .by James Lucas, a Bristol Mason.

Part Four

CRAFT LODGES

The Masonic Lodges of the Province of Somerset

Year	PGM	No.	Lodge Name	Location	Page
1733	Pre-Province	41	Royal Cumberland	Bath	147
1764	Pre-Province	135	Perpetual Friendship	Bridgwater	164
1788	Dunckerley	261	Unanimity & Sincerity	Taunton	174
1792	Dunckerley	285	Love & Honour	N. Wootton	177
1793	Dunckerley	291	Rural Philanthropic	Burnham	182
1801	Smith-Leigh	232	Marine (Portishead)	Nailsea	168
1812	Smith-Leigh	53	Royal Sussex	Bath	159
1810	Smith-Leigh	329	Brotherly Love	Yeovil	186
1825	K K Tynte	379	Honour	Bath	191
1836	K K Tynte	437	Science	Wincanton	197
1837	K K Tynte	446	Benevolent	Wells	204
1859	K K Tynte	772	Pilgrim	Glastonbury	208
1860	G. Reg	814	Parrett & Axe	Crewkerne	210
1862	G. Reg	906	Royal Albert Edward	Bath	213
1863	G. Reg	973	Royal Somerset	Frome	219
1863	G. Reg	976	Royal Clarence	Bruton	224
1867	Adair	1197	Nyanza	Ilminster	229
1867	Adair	1199	Agriculture	Yatton	234
1868	Adair	1222	St. Kew	Weston-super-Mare	241
1869	Carnarvon	1296	Vale of Brislington	Keynsham	245
1878	Carnarvon	1750	Coleridge	Clevedon	248
1878	Carnarvon	1756	Eldon	Clevedon	252
1879	Carnarvon	1833	St. Keyna	Keynsham	255
1881	Carnarvon	1953	Prudence & Industry	Chard	258
1882	Carnarvon	1966	Fidelity & Sincerity	Wellington	263
1884	Carnarvon	2038	Portcullis	Langport	266
1891	Dungarvan	2390	Exmoor	Minehead	271
1899	Dungarvan	2761	Royal Naval (Malta)	Yeovil	273
1902		2925	Somersetshire (London)	London	277
1906	Dungarvan	3158	St. George	Taunton	282
1906	Dungarvan	3169	King Alfred	Weston-super-Mare	284
1912	Long	3573	Connaught	Midsomer Norton	286
1915	Long	3746	Somerset Masters	Various	288

The Masonic Lodges of the Province of Somerset

Year	PGM	No.	Lodge Name	Location	Page
			World War 1		
1920	Long	4093	Wessex	Weston-super-Mare	291
1920	Long	4095	St. Alphege	Bath	294
1922	Long	4399	Severn	Nailsea	297
1922	Long	4446	Quantock	Watchet	300
1922	Long	4491	Abbey	Keynsham	303
1922	Long	4494	Tyntesfield	Nailsea	305
1923	Long	4535	Alfred & Guthrum	Wedmore	308
1924	Long	4692	Admiral Blake	Bridgwater	314
1927	Farrer	4947	Tennyson	Clevedon	317
1928	Farrer	5007	Progressive Science	Yeovil	321
1930	Farrer	5221	Taunton Deane	Taunton	324
1932	Farrer	5361	St Bernard	Minehead	329
1938	Norman	5736	Uno Corde	Keynsham	330
			World War 2		
1945	Norman	6209	Loyal Vacation	Wiveliscombe	332
1946	Norman	6244	Gordano (Portishead)	Yatton	335
1947	Norman	6474	Winscombe	Yatton	337
1947	Norman	6540	St. Lukes	Bath	341
1948	Norman	6650	Southey	Clevedon	346
1948	Norman	6817	Estune	Nailsea	348
1949	Norman	6913	Priory	Keynsham	350
1949	Norman	6942	Whitchurch	Keynsham	352
1950	Norman	6988	Queen's College	Taunton	355
1952	Norman	7160	Birnbeck	Weston-super-Mare	357
1952	Norman	7230	Wellington School	Wellington	359
1953	Norman	7296	Elizabethan	Bath	363
1957	Norman	7552	Corinthian Pillar	Yeovil	367
1960		7724	Old Aluredian (London)	Taunton	368
1962	Cazenove	7824	John de Clivedon	Clevedon	371

The Masonic Lodges of the Province of Somerset

Year	PGM	No.	Lodge Name	Location	Page
1964	Cazenove	7964	Backwell	Nailsea	373
1964	Cazenove	7973	St. Dunstan	Glastonbury	375
1964	Cazenove	7994	Tynte	Bridgwater	377
1965	Cazenove	8019	Forest of Mendip	Blagdon	379
1968	Cazenove	8215	Taunton School	Taunton	382
1973	Hughes	8518	Richard Huish	Taunton	384
1974	Hughes	8633	Saltford	Keynsham	386
1975	Hughes	8654	Vivary	Taunton	388
1977	Hughes	8791	Woodspring	Yatton	390
1980	Hughes	8912	Forest of Selwood	Frome	392
1981	Kinnersley	8999	Gerard	Keynsham	394
1980	Kinnersley	9011	Wraxall	Nailsea	397
1982	Kinnersley	9033	Athelstan	Weston-super-Mare	399
1982	Kinnersley	9043	Cornucopia	Keynsham	401
1983	Kinnersley	9075	Somerset Tablers	Ilminster	403
1983	Kinnersley	9089	Showman's Guild	Clevedon	405
1985	Kinnersley	9180	Somerset Farmers	Langport	407
1986	Kinnersley	9188	Sir Thos. de Cheddre	Wedmore	408
1986	Kinnersley	9189	Som't Prov G Stewards	Weston-super-Mare	411
1986	Kinnersley	9218	Kenneth Kinnersley	Midsomer Norton	413
1987	Kinnersley	9251	Somerset Fairway	Burnham	415
1988	Kinnersley	9299	Hospitality	Yatton	416
1989	Kinnersley	9341	St Cecilia	Wedmore	418
1989	Kinnersley	9391	Emergency Services	Taunton	421
1991	Hopkins	9417	Tivoli	Weston-super-Mare	422
1999	Hopkins	9703	Olympia	Clevedon	424
2001	Hopkins	9741	Sylvanus	Yatton	427
2005	Jenkins	9801	Sir Isaac Newton	Nailsea	430

Royal Cumberland Lodge No. 41

Meets at the Masonic Hall, Old Orchard Street, Bath

Deputation dated 1733

Taken from "A Provincial Jewel 1733-2008"
by D. Mosley

Royal Cumberland Lodge No. 41 was originally known as the Lodge at the Bear Inn Bath, whose earliest recorded meeting was on 28th December 1732. That first minute finds a fully-fledged Lodge regularly forming itself, already having a Master, two Wardens and a Secretary. The fact that it was a fully furnished Lodge prompts the question, 'Was it the inaugural meeting or had the Lodge been founded earlier and the Minute Books lost?'

When considering its origins, however, we can only build a sensible picture if we look at the earlier Masonic activity in the vicinity, for its founding members seem to have been local men. It is logical to conclude, therefore, that they had been made Masons by a local Lodge and we do know that an earlier Masonic Lodge had met at the Queen's Head tavern in Bath. Indeed, this was the first Lodge to have been constituted in the provinces by Grand Lodge.

Those two great Victorian Masonic historians W.J. Hughan and R.F. Gould, researching the history of the Royal Cumberland Lodge in 1880, concluded, on circumstantial evidence, that the 'Queen's Head' Lodge had been founded in 1723. There is, however, conclusive proof that it was actively working a year later in 1724, for on 16th May that year a newspaper report tells that 'Dr J.T. Desaguliers FRS (Past Grand Master) attended a Lodge at the Queen's Head, Bath, and received several fresh members into the fraternity. The Master of the Queen's Head Lodge was Charles Beauclerk, KG, 1st Duke of St Albans, who was an illegitimate son of King Charles II by his mistress Nell Gwynne.

When looking at early 18th century Freemasonry it would be a mistake not to view it against the backcloth of the English social order at the time. It was the age of Enlightenment and yet the Country was just emerging from centuries of political/religious turmoil. Parliament and no doubt the public, and particularly the Crown, feared a Catholic resurgence led by the deposed Jacobite Stuarts, rightly so as Charles Stuart's (Bonnie Prince Charlie) defeat at Culloden was still more than a decade in the future.

France at that time was giving shelter to the Stuarts and when in 1693 the French National Grand Lodge came to write its own history and that of the Rectified Scottish Rite it had this to say (sic):

'The Rite started at the very first moments of French Masonry and at the time when

Freemasonry was introduced into our Country and perpetuated until our day, by the Rectified Scottish Rite, is indisputably connected with the passing through France of exiles, supporters of the Stuarts, who had been driven from their throne. The Rectified Scottish Rite is truly Scottish by reason of its forebears, pioneers and founders of Freemasonry in France, Catholics fighting for their King and their faith. It is this Christian aspect, which permitted certain writers, such as Gustave Bord, to affront the organised Freemasonry of 1717 on English soil, under Anderson rules, drawn up in 1723 by a Masonry of Orange lineage.'

If not a child of the Enlightenment, English Freemasonry was certainly cut from the same cloth and was proving to be attractive to men of learning and status. However, with Masonry's Catholic Jacobite antecedents, if it wasn't to be suppressed, it had to be controlled and, as clearly intimated by the opposition in France, it came to be ruled by the Crown in the form of the Royal House of Orange (Royal control has continued to the present day in the person of our own Grand Master).

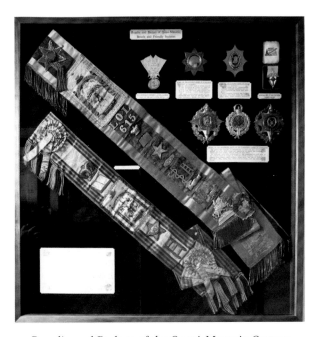

Regalia and Badges of the Quasi-Masonic Orange Order in Bath Masonic Museum

Grand Lodge and Anderson's new rules, it will be recalled, removed Christian references from the rituals and banned the discussion of religion and politics, the reason for doing so now seeming obvious. In the circumstances it is hardly surprising that we find a loyal Royal Protestant Duke leading the first Masonic Lodge formed far from London in the provinces. During the last illness of his mother in 1687 it was said that the Duke of St. Albans was about to go to Hungary and return a good Catholic. He did not, but in fact he was to be a supporter of William and Mary and the Protestant succession.

During the succeeding years the Duke had proved himself a gallant soldier in the Protestant cause and came to be highly esteemed by the King. St. Albans died in Bath on 10th May 1726 and doubtless his death caused a great hiatus in the Lodge's continuity. We don't know what happened, but clearly it struggled on for in 1729 it made a membership return to Grand Lodge showing 42 members listed, which included two Dukes, three Lords and four Baronets. Five of those listed were to become Mayors of Bath.

Grand Lodge minutes also record a subscription from it on 2nd March 1732 of one guinea for charity. Nothing is heard of it after that date and it was left out of the Engraved Lists of 1738-9 What occurred to make the Lodge fail or what happened to all its members when it failed we can only speculate, for when the 'Bear' Lodge emerged it had only thirteen members, one of whom had been on that 'Queen's Head' list.

No other Lodge of Freemasons is known to have existed in the vicinity at that time and it is reasonable to conclude that the remaining twelve members must have been made Masons at the 'Queen's Head' between 1729 and 1732. When the Secretary penned that earliest or first minute on 28th December 1732 he did not write that 'the brethren met' but that 'the Lodge met', implying by that one word that he and the brethren were members of a Lodge. Indeed, to paraphrase Bro Godfrey Day from his Lodge history of 1933, 'Like a dissolving view the picture of the 'Queen's Head' fades out and the 'Bear' appears.'

On this point Bro W.J. Songhurst in his 'Masonic Reprints' of Grand Lodge minutes reports that "..when the 'Bear at Bath' attended Grand Lodge on 29th May 1733 it was given the place of precedence due to the 'Queen's Head' Lodge, suggesting that the two Lodges were really one".

Why the Lodge ceased to work at the 'Queen's Head' we may never know. Maybe the political uncertainty of the time influenced its end. Maybe its titled leadership, who would not have permanently resided in Bath, had left the City and in the light of the uncertain times, and without patronage of a trusted leader, it may have found it too politically problematic to continue. We have no answers to those questions, but there may be a clue to its resurrection, in a most unusual and curious 'Bear' Lodge minute from it's meeting on 18th May 1733. The minute reads:

"For ye many good Offices, useful Instructions, and unnumbered Favours the Lodge have received from their worthy Brother Charles De Laboley, through his Zealous Endeavours to promote Masonry, they unanimously desire the Right Worshipful the Master to return him their Hearty Thanks in Form; which is accordingly done and a memorandum thereof ordered to be entered in the Lodge Book: which will be here by the Order of ye Worshipful Lodge in Obedience hereto most willingly done."

This was the tenth recorded meeting of the Lodge and the first and last occasion that we meet Bro Charles De Laboley in the minutes. On that night he appears to have been appointed Senior Warden and on that same night he resigned the office and the Lodge, because his private business was to take him to London permanently. It is curious behaviour to accept such a senior office knowing that you could not either fill it or remain a member of the Lodge. It only makes sense if he had been appointed to the office at the same time as the other officers, sometime before that first recorded meeting on 28th December 1732 and before he knew his business was to take him to London permanently.

What did Bro Charles do to deserve such grateful thanks? It must have been important for apart from his specific help to the Lodge the words mention his zealous endeavours to promote Masonry. Did he perhaps gather together those previous members of the 'Queen's Head' who wished the Lodge to continue, and did he also perhaps counsel that the Grand Master be petitioned so as to enable Bro Hugh Kennedy to be accepted as a Loyal, Protestant, and a Fit and Proper person to lead a Lodge.

With its founding date around 1723 the Queen's Head Lodge would have been constituted according to the Ancient Usages of Masons, and would not have a written warrant-like authorisation, but by 1732 it was a necessary prerequisite. This was doubtless inspired not by Masonic needs, but as a license or permit made necessary by the insecurities of the day to allow these 'secret' meetings to be held. For the moment we must look somewhere else for another clue.

At that time the person responsible for the major eighteenth century exploitation of 'Bath Stone' was Ralph Allen, who mined the stone at the hilltop known as Combe Down. In order to market it, he needed to move the stone down to the river Avon to be shipped, a distance of one and a half miles from the mine and a descent of 500 feet. This was achieved in 1731 by the construction of a tramway, which was one of the earliest to use flanged wheels.

The drawings of the wagons, by Charles de Laboley, appear in 'A Course of Experimental Philosophy', which was written by J.T. Desaguliers and published in 1734. It is clear, then, that both Charles de Laboley and J.T. Desaguliers knew and worked with each other, so it is not difficult to imagine that their relationship may and probably did help to rekindle the new Lodge.

There being no evidence to the contrary, it is reasonable to assume that the 'Queen's Head' Lodge ceased to work in its previous form at or about the time it sent that one guinea to Grand Lodge in March 1732, the guinea probably being the residue of money from a moribund Lodge, properly disposed of. From that point in time those brethren who wished the Lodge to continue would have had to organise themselves and find one among them who would be acceptable to higher authority as being safe and sufficiently trustworthy to hold a Lodge.

In this case it was Bro Hugh Kennedy who was chosen to be Master, and it was he who with others made the formal petition to the Grand Master to enable them to be constituted into a regular Lodge. At this date the authority was by way of a 'Deputation', in which the Grand Master deputised Bro Kennedy to act in his place and stead and constitute the brethren into a regular Lodge.

As a regularly made Freemason, having allegiance to the Grand Master and the Crown, we can be sure Bro Kennedy would not hold a Lodge or call any meeting until he knew it was acceptable for him to do so. The fact that the Lodge met at the 'Bear Inn' months before the receipt of the Deputation must mean that someone of sufficient rank and status had authorised it. In this respect Dr. Desaguliers was at hand and seems to be the most likely candidate to both authenticate the proposed Master as a person fit, proper, and politically trustworthy, and to authorise the holding of

the Lodge on 28th December 1732. It must also be a safe assumption that Bro Charles de Laboley had a hand in the matter and doubtless is the reason he gained such an accolade from the Lodge in that extraordinary minute of May 1733.

We know that in conformity with Masonic culture at the time, the Lodge celebrated both the St. John's days: St. John the Baptist in June and St. John the Evangelist in December. Up until 1818 it elected its Master on both those days. It follows that the logical day on which to resurrect the Lodge would be on one of the St. John's days; the June date being too soon whilst the Evangelist on 28th December would possibly be the earliest and most suitable date on which to restart the Lodge.

Where it all began – The Bear Inn at Bath
Reproduced by kind permission of
Bath in Time/Bath Central Library Collection

In support of 28th December 1732 being the resurrection date, it is interesting to note that the Lodge had no other business on that evening, it did not make any Masons that night nor did it pass any Masters. To clarify this last point, at that time the Lodge worked a two-degree system, of first-degree Fellowcraft and second-degree Masters, and with Dr. Desaguliers' interest and involvement we can be very sure its working would have been orthodox and regular.

Using its Deputation, the Lodge continued to meet at the Bear Inn, encouraged by Dr. Desaguliers who, on his frequent visits to the City, attended the Lodge and occupied its chair.

Until 12th December 1737, when the Angel Inn Lodge was founded in Shepton Mallet (erased January 1768), the Bear Lodge remained the only Lodge of Freemasons in the Province.

On 30th October 1738, the Lodge held an extraordinary meeting to honour the birthday of the King. The Earl of Darnley, late Grand Master, John Ward, Deputy Grand Master, and Dr. Desaguliers, Past Grand Master, attended in the company, it is believed, of the Prince of Wales, who was at the time 'taking the waters at Bath' and who had been initiated into the Craft that same year.

From 1752 to 1755, for some obscure reason extraordinary Lodges were held at the private house of a Brother instead of at the Bear Inn, and there is record in the minutes of this also occurring at the home of John Smith at Combe Hay, Bath, who was at the time Bath's Member of Parliament. John Smith was initiated at the Bear Lodge and had a meteoric rise in the Craft to become the first Provincial Grand Master for the Province of Somerset. The content of the Lodge minutes at that time is sparse but from them it is clear that he was proposed to be made a Mason on 7th October 1766, was balloted on 21st October 1766 and made a Mason that same night. Later, on St. John's Day 28th December 1767 it seems he was raised as a Master Mason and took the Master's chair that same evening, a position he held, but with many absences, until St. John's Day 24th June 1768.

He was elected Worshipful Master of the Lodge, again in 1784, 1785, 1791 and 1792. On 7th June 1768 the minutes record for the first time that he was Provincial Grand Master for Somerset. At the time he was made Provincial Grand Master there were only five Lodges meeting in the Province namely the Bear (Bath), St. George's (Taunton), Perpetual Friendship (Bridgwater), Perfect Friendship (Bath), and Virtue (Bath). It may be interesting to note that John Smith paid the Lodge three guineas to be made a Mason.

A recent parliamentary study reported that the purchasing power of one pound in 1750 would equal £118 in 1998 and using that figure in present day terms he would have paid the equivalent of £370 to be initiated; additionally he paid a further five shillings to be raised, or the equivalent of £29.50p.

As time went by a number of bye-laws were adopted until finally the book held 38. These were dictated, no doubt, from experience; bye-law 21 is a prime example for it ruled that: 'If a Brother is found distempered with drink he shall be admonished to go peaceably home, which, if he refuses, he shall be turned out and taken care of with as little disturbance as possible and fined two shillings – except the Lodge vote him excused from this fine'.

From these records it would appear that at some point in time the original two degree system changed to a three-degree system. We cannot say with certainty when the new system was adopted or how Lodges acquired their new ceremonies. Some believe that Lodges used the exposés then prevalent as a guide to ritual as practiced by others. The Lodge archives contain a copy of the exposure 'Hiram or the Grand Master Key to the Door of Both Ancient and Modern Freemasonry' printed in London in 1764.

The Lodge archive copy is very dog-eared and worn, indicating long hard use and, whilst there is no conclusive proof, it is probably the ritual practiced by the Lodge between 1764 and its amalgamation in 1785. Clearly the book had been precious to somebody and cared for as though irreplaceable, such is the manner in which a Lodge of that day might have been expected to care for its precious book of ritual. The book's cover had long since disappeared and it had been carefully recovered by a piece of vellum salvaged from a discarded indenture. Therefore one can understand why the brethren would have been agreeable to discard it when

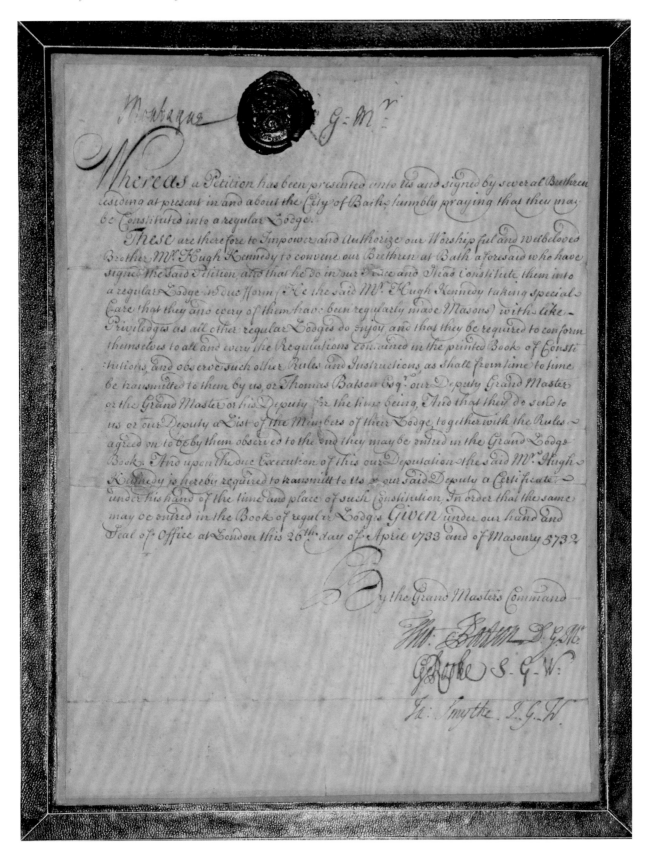

The 'Deputation' dated 26th May 1733 authorising Bro Kennedy to constitute the brethren into a Regular Lodge.

offered another ritual with a higher status such as Dunckerley's.

We now come to the adoption of the name, Royal Cumberland Lodge. In 1784 Thomas Dunckerley (then Provincial Grand Master for Somerset) constituted a new Lodge in Bath with the name of Royal Cumberland Lodge No. 458, named after the Duke of Cumberland who had been elected Grand Master in 1782. They met at the Bear Inn by a Warrant of Dispensation, and were presided over by Thomas Dunckerley, Worshipful Master (pro tem) with six members and three visitors. One candidate was initiated and passed.

On 16th December 1785, after previous negotiations between the members of the Bear Lodge and the new Royal Cumberland Lodge and, at the suggestion of the PGM Thomas Dunckerley, the old Lodge No. 39 which met at the Bear Inn, but which had no other name, resolved: 'That this Lodge in future take the name of the Royal Cumberland Lodge, retaining the Bear Lodge Number 39, and that the mode of working and the several bye-laws used and observed by the Royal Cumberland Lodge No. 458 shall be used and observed by this Lodge in future, instead of those now used, and that the following brethren of No. 458 be admitted members of this Lodge viz. Thomas West, DPGM (Somerset), Milborne West, PPGM (Canada) and nine others.'

The new members were all men of good professional repute in Bath. The Lodge, having left the Bear Inn, moved back to it and received all the Lodge property of No. 458 including the Hall Medal now attached to the Master's Square. Thomas Dunckerley was the natural son of George II and was probably the most influential Freemason in the 18th century. In 1770 he had been commissioned by the Premier Grand Lodge (the Moderns) to compile an improved ritual in all three degrees, which the records say he did to the satisfaction of the fraternity. At Royal Cumberland it is believed that he would have provided his new Lodge with his own ritual, for in an age dogged by numerous exposés it alone had the status of being authorised and recognised by Grand Lodge.

The first or original Hall Medal was struck in 1780 and was granted to 26 Lodges that made donations of 25 guineas or more towards the completion of Freemasons' Hall, and they were authorised to attach it to the Master's Square. Nine of these Lodges are now extinct and there remain thirteen in London and four in the Provinces, namely Royal Cumberland 41, Love and Honour 75 (Falmouth), Unanimity 154 (Wakefield) and Indefatigable 237 (Swansea).

Of these four Lodges, the only one possessing the original medal is the Royal Cumberland Lodge. The consolidation of the two Lodges, however, did not restore prosperity; this was largely due to the French Wars and their aftermath. During the period 1790 to 1817 the minutes of the Lodge become very irregular. Often no new Worshipful Master was elected and two brethren remained in that office for years, Bro Thomas West DPGM and Bro Charles Geary serving twelve years each.

As early as 1776 it had been proposed that the three Bath Lodges, the Bear Inn Lodge, Lodge of Perfect Friendship and Lodge of Virtue, should endeavour to set up a common meeting place. The suggestion fell through at the time but in 1817 it was revived and the Foundation Stone of a new Masonic Hall in York Street was formally laid by W.Bro Geary, Master of the Royal Cumberland Lodge, supported by the Masters of the two other Bath Lodges.

The building being completed, it was formally dedicated and opened by HRH the Duke of Sussex, GM, on 23rd September 1819. To mark the occasion a medal was struck and one of these medals is included among the treasures of the Royal Cumberland Lodge. It was soon apparent, however, that these three Lodges had undertaken more than they could manage. There was financial trouble, the building having cost three thousand pounds of which only about 500 pounds had been subscribed.

On 25th March 1823 the Shareholders assigned their interests to W.Bro Geary, a Past Master and local philanthropist. He found it necessary to close the Hall and impound the furniture in spite of appeals from the Provincial Grand Master and the Board of General Purposes. Then, after patiently waiting for payment for twenty years, in January 1843 the furniture was sold to the Loyal Lodge 251, Barnstaple, and there, for the most part, it remains. The York Street hall ultimately became the property of the Society of Friends and remains so today.

After the closing of the York Street hall the Royal Cumberland Lodge moved to the White Lion Hotel, but in 1834 in conjunction with the Royal Sussex Lodge and the Lodge of Honour took a lease from a Mr. Goodridge on the Corridor Rooms. Things were not satisfactory and again the Lodge moved, this time to W.Bro Temple's Castle Inn.

Two other Lodges met elsewhere, Royal Sussex Lodge having internal troubles during the period 1847-1854, when it was dormant, but it was revived by the efforts of W.Bro Tunstall, Past Master of the Royal Cumberland Lodge (1848), making a remarkable recovery, and, with the Royal Cumberland Lodge, took the initiative in finding the present permanent home for Freemasonry in the city. This is the building in which we find ourselves today. In 1866 it was agreed that the Royal Sussex Lodge should purchase the premises with the Royal Cumberland Lodge as tenants. Since then other Lodges and Orders have found a home here and the many extensive alterations and repairs have resulted in one of the finest temples in the country

It would take too long to say a great deal about the ritual used in the Royal Cumberland Lodge, and it has already been said that at the union of the Bear Lodge 39 and the Royal Cumberland Lodge 458 the 'Working' was provided by the PGM, Thomas Dunckerley. As far as is known, it is the same ritual used by the Lodge today. Until 2001 this ritual had not been printed, being in manuscript form only, and a special copy known as the Master's Book was the definitive version from which all others were written.

The 'Working' includes what seems to be in essence another degree; this is the ceremony of Installation which confers the rank of Installed Master. It is of course not a degree, but is worked when the Lodge is open in the third and the candidate, in this case the Master Elect, after certain questions and replies, retires to re-enter in due form. A meaningful ceremony follows with an obligation, entrustment with secrets and finally by him being installed in the Master's chair.

On 20th June 1803 Thomas West, WM of the Royal Cumberland Lodge, wrote to the Grand Secretary:

'...to request your opinion, whether we ought or ought not to work according to Finch's 'Masonic Treatise', three of our new members being very desirous of so doing; solemnly asserting, that in three very respectable Lodges in London, which they visited last winter, they all worked in that manner; and that it has become very general, in both town and country Lodges. P.S. We now work after Bro Dunckerley's method.'

The reply to the letter is not known but it is probable that the Lodge was not encouraged to follow Finch for at the time Grand Lodge held him to be persona non grata.

On entering the Bath temple one of its most eye catching items are the Royal Cumberland tracing boards. These are very large and measure three feet six inches wide by six feet five inches long. The design of tracing boards commonly seen in English Lodges is that of John Harris, whose designs were submitted to the Emulation Lodge of Improvement in a competition in 1845 and were officially adopted.

Our own boards follow Harris's design and were painted in 1852 for the Lodge by a Past Master and local artist Bro Charles Haseler; the Lodge paid him ten guineas for the job. The Lodge's original board was a table board painted with all three degrees; this was sold with the rest of the furniture in 1843 and is now the property of the Loyal Lodge 251 in Barnstaple.

It is interesting to note that in 1852 the Lodge still met in the Corridor Rooms, and our minutes tell us that when the Lodge relocated to its present home in Old Orchard Street, our landlord, the Royal Sussex Lodge 53, waived part of the rent to enable them to use some of our furniture. Today, some 145 years later, it is pleasing to say that both Lodges still use these tracing boards.

A small story associated with the Lodge well worth recording occurred in 1858, when a Past Master, Bro Fredric T.P. Wells, emigrated to South Australia. Doubting the validity of the ritual he found being used there he introduced the Royal Cumberland form of 'Working'. London was consulted on the matter and due to its resulting approval the Royal Cumberland ritual became generally adopted and came to be used by all the Lodges in the fledgling Freemasonry in the south of that far distant land. Throughout South Australia at the time it became known as the 'Somerset Ritual'. In 1879 a committee was set up to investigate the Lodge's 'Working' and as a result a form of ritual was approved; comparison with an extant ritual of 1869 shows that very little alteration was made.

On 1st January 1925 the Permanent Committee of the Lodge unanimously resolved: 'That no Brother be approved as Worshipful Master of the Lodge unless he is prepared to bind himself to carry out our ritual in accordance with the 'Master's Book', and without any variation, and that it be a recommendation to the Worshipful Master that he appoints only such officers as will agree similarly to perform.' The same ritual is used by Daughter Lodge, the Royal Albert Edward Lodge 906 and Granddaughter Lodge, St. Alphege Lodge 4095.

Installation night at the Royal Cumberland Lodge in 1880 was on the first Thursday of February. That evening a distinguished Mason was placed in the Master's chair of the Lodge. This was Dr. Henry Hopkins who was 72 years old at the time and who had become a Joining

Member of the Lodge some six years earlier. Dr. Hopkins discovered that his year of office was the centenary year of the acquisition by the Lodge of the Freemasons' Hall Medal which is affixed to the Master's Jewel.

He was privileged to have some high-ranking Masonic historians as friends who, on his behalf and in celebration of the centenary, turned their thoughts to the history and background of the Royal Cumberland Lodge. These were Bro W.J. Hughan PGD of England, Bro R.F. Gould SGD of England and Bro Gen. Albert Pike of Washington City, United States of America, and it is from their researches that the early history of the Lodge was uncovered.

The Lodge will always be grateful to Bro Hopkins because he made a full and comprehensive record of those proceedings. At this time Bro W.J. Hughan PGD of England, presented a paper to the Lodge in which he said:

'The fact of the 'Constitutions of the Freemasons' of AD 1738 containing no reference to a Lodge at Bath before the one of AD 1733 (present No. 41) seem to have led many to suppose that this Lodge was the first warranted for the city. There was however one much earlier chartered, viz the latter part of 1723 or 1724. If any list of Lodges was issued for 1724 no copy is known at the present time, but of 1725 two copies are now extant. In both of these is to be found a Lodge at the 'Queen's Head', Bath, and as it was the first warrant ever issued by the Grand Lodge of England for any part of the 'Country', Bath may rightly be termed the Premier Masonic Provincial City of England.'

If Bro Hughan is correct in his view, then by the same token Somerset may fairly be said to be the Premier Masonic Province of England. Bro Dr. Hopkins was succeeded by Bro Charles Radway as Master and it was Bro Radway who presented the Masonic Hall with William Hoare's masterpiece, the 'Pool of Bethesda'. It

hangs in the west of the temple and is today a valuable painting of National importance.

It would be surprising if a Lodge that has met continuously since the early years of the 18th century had not preserved some of its earlier ceremonial customs. The visitor to the Lodge will not be disappointed in this respect, for he will discover many practices that are considerably different to his own familiar traditions.

A very rare pierced silver jewel presented to W.Bro Radway in 1882

Among other things he will discover that the Lodge Stewards wear red aprons and collars. He will notice that, before giving his first degree salute, a Royal Cumberland Brother holds his right arm out horizontally in front of him palm down with his thumb in the form of a square. He will doubtless observe that the Director of Ceremonies, as his name implies, directs and conducts the ceremony, that both Deacons escort the candidate, and that much of the work takes place in the west where the principal VSL resides. Also that the candidate is restored to light amidst a circle of swords and, when proving themselves Fellowcraft, the brethren seem to give the signs twice but in fact don't. In the third degree the Master's candle is extinguished and a five-pointed star illuminated in the east.

The regularity of some of these customs has been questioned. Grand Lodge for example cast doubt on the Stewards red regalia but, after consideration of the historical facts, the regalia was accepted as authorised and regular.

The practice of extinguishing the Master's candle, which has been the Lodge tradition since time immemorial, has been similarly challenged but due to its age-old use was again accepted as regular. The oil and gas stars of earlier times may be viewed in the Museum at the Bath Masonic Hall.

The earlier Bright Morning Star Believed by some to be the first ever domestic gas appliance in Bath

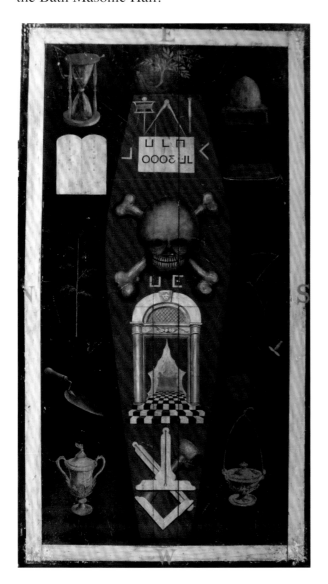

The Third Degree Tracing Board

It is believed that of all the Lodges ranged beneath the banner of the United Grand Lodge of England, Royal Cumberland Lodge is alone in this ceremonial custom. Our form of first degree salute arises from the Mason's due-guard; this was used in England before the union of 1813 and is still current Scottish practice. It may be noted that the sign used by all Freemasons when giving assent to a motion undoubtedly has a similar origin.

The Lodge has distinctive lectures in explanation of the Tracing Boards in each of the three degrees. The third degree is particularly unique, for it contains an explanation of sixteen symbols, most of which were lost to English Masonry at the union of 1813. It carries for example the only known explanation in England and Wales of the beehive symbol which, like the others, was widely used by English 18th century Masons but is unknown today.

This lecture led one current distinguished Masonic writer to say 'that nowhere had he come across anything like the sophisticated moral and ethical teachings which this lecture attaches to its symbols.' The Tracing Board also carries the symbol of the trowel; this is not described in the explanation but, uniquely, is used by the Lodge as a third degree tool.

The Lodge is very proud of all its traditions and so jealously guards them that, as mentioned, it requires a special and serious promise from each incoming Worshipful Master that he will neither deviate nor permit any deviation from these established rituals, customs and practices. It is a great responsibility upon every member of the Royal Cumberland Lodge to so labour that the genuine tenets and principles of our Order may be transmitted pure and unsullied through this Lodge from generation to generation. Long may it last.

*The magnificent Royal Cumberland Loving Cup
Presented by the Worshipful Master,
Bro Dr Henry Hopkins MA FCP
October 7th 1880*

*Bible, printed in Antwerp by Phillipe de Lens in 1565.
Presented to Royal Cumberland Lodge by Le Louis D'Argent Lodge, France*

Royal Sussex Lodge No. 53

Meets at the Masonic Hall, Old Orchard Street, Bath

Warrant dated 1812

Previous to the formation of the United Grand Lodge of England in 1813, few Lodges were named as they are today, but were distinguished by a number and place of meeting. It frequently occurred on a new Lodge being formed that instead of it receiving a number and place in the Grand Lodge Register, which it should have done, it was given the warrant of an older Lodge which had lapsed. Thus the Royal Sussex Lodge, the warrant of which is dated 23rd January, 1812, under the Atholl constitution, received the number of '49' which was that of a Lodge warranted 30th March, 1756 to meet at the King's Head, Drury Lane, London.

The first traceable meeting was held at the Bladud's Head Inn, Ladymead, in February, 1812; subsequent meetings being held in a number of other Inns in the City of Bath. At the renumbering of the Lodges in 1814, the Lodge became No. 69.

In December 1813 a letter was addressed to the brethren of the Royal Sussex Lodge which read:

"The name which I have permitted your Lodge to assume gives it an additional interest to my solicitude, and therefore requires me expressing the hope that, as it is the first in this instance, so may I trust that by your Masonic conduct you will always preserve and maintain the credit of the same, as an example to all others.

Masonry is the most sublime and perfect institution that ever was formed for the advancement and happiness and general good to mankind, teaching us the useful wise and instructive doctrines upon which alone happiness is founded, and the duties we owe to our neighbour never to injure him in any one

situation." Signed by His Royal Highness the Duke of Sussex, The Grand Master.

The Lodge Banner was presented in December 1883 by 21 Past Masters. It was restored in 1987 at a cost of £300, being fully met by donations from the brethren of the Lodge.

In May 1817 the meeting was at the Greyhound Inn, at the corner of High Street and Bridge Street, and there the Lodge was to meet for some years. The brethren about this time were evidently very enthusiastic, for in the year 1818 nine emergency meetings were held in addition to the ordinary monthly ones throughout the year, together with weekly meetings in the months of July and August. In November 1818, at the request of a majority of the brethren then present, the WM consented to a private exhibition of Masonic emblems, and the Lodge room was visited "by about 300 of the Beauty and Fashion prior to the opening of the Lodge."

Around this time it was becoming readily appreciated that the holding of Lodges in various Inns could not be altogether satisfactory, and no doubt this reason prompted the building of the first Masonic Hall in the City. The Royal Sussex Lodge did not directly participate, and its headquarters remained at the Greyhound Inn. However, in July 1826 the Lodge resolved to leave the Greyhound Inn in and to move to the Masonic Hall, York Street, at a rental of £14 pa.

The first meeting took place in September 1826, and in the February of the following year the By-Laws were agreed in open Lodge to include:

(i)   Meetings to be held at Masonic Hall, York Street.
(ii)   Scales of fines for non attendance of officers. (In December 1820 the Junior Deacon had been fined one shilling for non-attendance!)
(iii)   Profound silence to be observed in the Lodge.
(iv)   Stewards to observe the greatest economy concerning refreshments.
(v)   Visitors not to be admitted during private business etc. etc.

In March 1831 it was resolved that the WM should meet the WMs of Royal Cumberland Lodge and the Lodge of Honour and arrange more convenient days of meeting to enable members of different Lodges to visit each other. Later that month, due to the York Street Hall being advertised for sale, it was resolved to move to the White Lion Inn. 7/6d to be charged per evening and 7/6d to be spent on refreshments, including fire, etc. The first meeting took place in October 1831. Two years later, in February 1833, a letter was received from Grand Lodge changing the number from 69 to 61.

In April 1834 it was reported that a lease had been entered into with a Mr. Goodridge for the new Masonic Rooms in the Corridor, at a rental of £40 p.a., which was to be divided between the three Lodges to meet there, Royal Cumberland £12; Royal Sussex £8 and Lodge of Honour £20. Each Lodge was to pay for its own consumption of gas. By 1843, however, the three Lodges had agreed to pay £10 each. January 1855 saw the first printed Lodge summons issued.

In March 1860 the Lodge resolved "that members of Her Majesty's Services, or those in the militia or Volunteer Corps attending this Lodge in uniform be requested to leave their arms in the care of the Tyler in the ante room".

UNITED GRAND LODGE OF ANTIENT, FREE AND ACCEPTED MASONS OF ENGLAND THE Rt. HON. THE EARL OF ZETLAND THE MOST WORSHIPFUL GRAND MASTER.

"The G.L. having resolved that the number of all Lodges in the Register shall be brought forward in regular succession by filling up those numbers which have become vacant within the voluntary surrender of warrants or by the erasure of Lodges. I have the honour to inform you that your Lodge which has hitherto been known and distinguished as No. 61 will henceforth stand in the Register of G.L. as No. 53 and this latter number you are to refer to in all returns and communications addressed to the G.L."

By Order of W.Bro. Gray Clarke, Grand Secretary, Freemasons Hall, London 6th July, 1863.

In January 1864 it was resolved to commence a charity fund to relieve brethren in distress. Also that month Bro R. Pitt gave an interesting account of a visit to a Lodge in Berlin, and the fraternal manner in which he had been received. By October the following year a committee was appointed to consider the expediency of seeking fresh accommodation and in November it was resolved to build a new hall, and by the following April a number of alternative proposals were considered but rejected in favour of the purchase of the present building in Old Orchard Street. The site was originally in the orchard of a Benedictine Abbey but prior to purchase it was a Roman Catholic Chapel and from 1750 to 1805 the first Theatre Royal in the provinces.

The premises consisted of a chapel and two houses, freehold but subject to a ground rent of £47.3s which were offered by the vendors for the small sum of £150, but subject to two conditions, namely:

(i)   That the church should be allowed to retain undisturbed possession of the vaults below, with the right of access thereto by a separate entrance, and

(ii)   That the chapel itself should never be used for the purposes of amusement and entertainment permitting dancing.

The chief alterations to the chapel were the removal of the pews, which were used to provide the screens to be seen on each side in order to lessen the width of the building, and the portioning off of the space under the gallery at the west end to form an ante room.

In December 1866 the new Masonic Hall was consecrated by Bro Rev. C.R. Davy, WM. of the Royal Sussex Lodge, with full Masonic ceremony. There were 49 members and nearly 70 visitors present. Two brethren were passed to the second degree and two were raised to the third degree, after which, Bro William Gibbs was installed Worshipful Master and Bro W. Smith was re-elected Treasurer. It is of interest to note that the total expenditure on the hall and adjoining houses, which were at that time let, was £636.8s.8d.

In December 1868 Bro Stothert was installed as WM. During his year of office the minutes report that the Lodge was out of debt, and that the £636.8s.8d had been fully paid off. Sub-tenancies were offered to the Royal Cumberland Lodge 41 and its Royal Arch Chapter; the Lodge of Honour 379 and the Bladud Encampment of Knights Templar No. 1.

The minutes of February 1869 record a list of gifts from various brethren, to the estimated value of £95, towards the fitting up of the Lodge. In May the following year the Lodge building fund was first established, a wise move which was to prove of immense value in later years.

Bro Watts suggested in March 1884 that it would be advisable "that the Emulation working should be adopted in the Lodge, instead of the

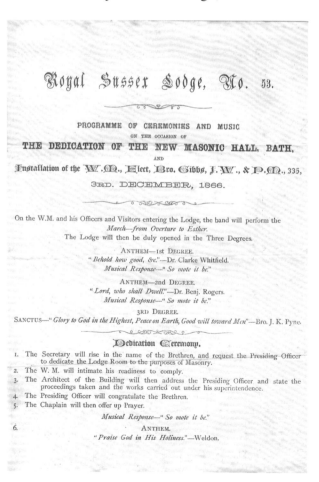

Summons for the Consecration of the new Bath Masonic Hall on 3rd December 1865

present working, which is uncertain." The WM agreed, and said that he understood that the Lodge professed to work by the Emulation. Even today, however, the brethren appreciate that small differences which have been accepted for very many years have become traditional in this Lodge and it is hoped that they will remain so.

In the Great War the Lodge saw thirteen of the brethren enlist in 1914, sadly two failed to return. The declaration of the Second World War in 1939 immediately influenced Lodge activities. Meetings were held on Saturday afternoons and the "supper" cost the sum of five shillings.

On the nights of April 25th and 26th 1942 enemy planes bombed Bath causing extensive damage to the Masonic Hall. A lot of valuable glass and china was lost through blast damage and in the confusion that followed the raids the Warrant, the Tyler's Sword, and numerous small items, including silver snuff boxes, mysteriously disappeared. Of the missing items only the Warrant has since been recovered, and that from the coal cellar of all places. In order that Lodge meetings could continue temporary repairs were effected pending the end of the war.

Thus it was that in January 1949 the Keynsham Temple became the temporary venue for meetings in order that war damage repairs could be undertaken. Because of petrol rationing transport was made available – a coach was organised to leave North Parade at 5.45 pm and returned at approximately 9.30 pm. The repairs were completed at a cost of £4,500.15s.2d and in 1950 the Lodge returned to its Old Orchard Street abode.

1956 saw the inauguration of the annual Ladies' Festival – this tradition has been continued to this day. This encounter was the first since 1818 when the exhibition of regalia was held. 1957

saw the return of petrol rationing and numerous apologies for lateness and absence were recorded in minutes of the period. The next year it was agreed that the Lodge in future would meet seven times a year instead of 8. Also, the first Almoner was appointed.

Since the war, and the loss of the Tyler's sword, holders of this office had been frustrated by having to borrow swords from other Lodges. In 1972 Bro J. Legg finally solved the problem by donating a handsome antique sword, the origin of which was contemporary with the founding of the Lodge.

In 1973 one of the brethren, W.Bro Sidney Smith, met a French Brother, Jacques Lycett, at the Bristol Aeroplane Co., which resulted in the first visit from Versailles of 'Loge la Delta 134. Fraternal visits large and small have taken place ever since, often accompanied by brethren of other lodges from Bath and the surrounding area. The R.W.Bro Kenneth Kinnersley, Provincial Grand Master for Somerset, often accompanied the brethren on these visits which were subsequently organised by Bro Robert James Davies and Jean Boissiere of the Loge La Delta. In May 1975 the Loge La Delta 134 visited again and presented the Lodge with a silver candelabrum.

W.Bro Robert James Davies organised a meeting of all lodges in the United Grand Lodge of England bearing the title of Royal Sussex to take place on 26th April 1980 at the Masonic Hall, Old Orchard Street, Bath. It is believed this was the first time such a meeting has taken place. The Royal Sussex Lodge's practice of Stewards wearing red collars was recognised by the United Grand Lodge of England in 1983. From this necessarily short history it will be seen that like many other Lodges the Royal Sussex has not been without adversities, especially in its earlier years, but while preserving a characteristic independence it has been ever ready to face up to the responsibilities which rightly fall to one of the oldest Lodges in the Province, and to work in harmonious relationship with the other Craft Lodges in Bath.

A typical example of this is the Lodge of Instruction which is run jointly for the proved benefit of the younger brethren of the Lodge of Honour and the Royal Sussex Lodge. Thereby maintaining our assurance of 1825 of co-operation in everything tending to the benefit of Masonry.

An early 19th century Battersea Enamel Jewel

Members of the Royal Sussex Lodge are rightly proud of, and give grateful thanks for the labours of those who have gone before and made it possible for us to enjoy the undoubted privilege and the joy of heritage of this wonderful Lodge.

On 10th March 2005 Royal Sussex Lodge hosted the rededication of the Masonic Temple after extensive alterations to the basement. The ceremony was presided over by the Provincial Grand Master R.W.Bro David L. Jenkins and the rest of the Provincial team. All the other Lodges in Bath were represented by their Masters, Officers and many of the Brethren.

Lodge of Perpetual Friendship No. 135

Meets at the Masonic Hall, King Square, Bridgwater

Warrant dated 1764

The Lodge of Perpetual Friendship was founded in 1757, a Mother Lodge of the Admiral Blake Lodge 4692, from which in turn the Tynte Lodge 7994 originated.

According to the United Grand Lodge of England the 250th year anniversary of the Lodge of Perpetual Friendship is 2014. Its Centenary was in 1864, its bicentenary in 1964, dating back to 1764 the year it received its Warrant from the Grand Lodge of England (the Moderns). The true birth, however, lies seven years earlier, in 1757, and it could be said to be even before this date.

The present Banner dates from 1935; regretfully earlier banners appear to be missing. The banner depicts a centenary symbol, from 1864, the Lodge's symbol of a pair of clasped hands, a dove of peace, Bridgwater Castle (the present Masonic Hall sits in the old castle moat) and, interestingly, the date AD1764, the year the warrant was granted, and AL5768, AL representing Anno Lucis (in the Year of Light). The difference is normally shown as 4000, representing the number of years once supposed to have elapsed since the beginning of the World, and Craft Masonry observes this custom today. It is confusing to find the year AL is also found by adding 4004 to the Calendar year, this being in accordance with the chronology of Archbishop Usher. Although not now used in Craft Masonry it was widely used in the 18th Century when the Lodge of Perpetual Friendship was founded.

The first minutes, which still exist today, were dated January 28th 1757. They show that six members attended the first meeting, held at the Old Angel, Bridgwater.

There were 25 meetings held in 1757. The minutes generally indicate only those members who were present, there is no record of the business transacted. From these regretfully slender entries it is almost certainly possible to declare that the Lodge had been working in some fashion before 1757, as the minutes begin with what appears to be an already settled organisation.

It is surprising that the UGLE did not accept 1757 as the date from which the Centenary could be measured, especially as the original minutes are extant. Indeed all the minutes from 1757 are extant, which is very rare for a Lodge of this age. What is probably beyond any doubt is that the Lodge has the oldest surviving Warrant in the Province, and one of the earliest in the country. The Lodge was originally numbered 326, changing its number six times, before becoming 135 in the last renumbering in 1863.

Although the Lodge was erased from the roll of Lodges in 1783, it was quickly re-instated in 1784. The practice of meeting on a Monday began in 1786. The Lodge name was agreed upon in 1774, until that time it was only known by its number.

Almost certainly the most famous member was initiated into the Lodge in 1817. This was Colonel, as he afterwards became, Charles Kemeys Kemeys Tynte. Just three years later he became Provincial Grand Master of the Province of Somerset, a post he filled for 40 years until his death in 1860. Eminent not only in the Craft he also became Grand Master of Masonic Knights Templar in England and Wales.

As one would hope such an old and distinguished Lodge as Perpetual Friendship thankfully retains possession of a number of antique Masonic pieces, in some cases specifically relevant to the Lodge. Foremost amongst the retained artefacts is a Bishops' Bible dating from 1574. Recently restored to its former glory the Bible's history is not known, not even the benefactor's name or when it was given to the Lodge.

The Lodge also possesses an 18th Century Lodge seal. A very fine object, it incorporates the Arms of the Antient Grand Lodge, although the Lodge was always, from founding in 1757, part of the Moderns Grand Lodge.

Originally such a seal was used for the issue of private Lodge certificates. The practice continued in English lodges certainly up to the year 1830, and later in outlying districts. A beautifully illustrated Lodge ballot box dated 1793 also exists, with the Perpetual Friendship name incorporated in the top.

The Lodge has a number of the original Lodge Officers' collar jewels. These include the Master's, Senior and Junior Wardens, and Treasurer's jewels. They date to circa 1770, and clearly are very rare. Also very rare is a set of collar jewels incorporating the Perpetual Friendship name, all dating to the early 19th Century and probably from Exeter. They include the jewels for the Organist, Inner Guard, Chaplain, and most peculiarly Superintendent of Works, which is not a Lodge office.

The silvered mug presented to the Lodge by W.Bro Moses Abraham in 1814 and restored in 2009.

Early in life the Lodge met at the Old Angel and Swan Inns in Bridgwater, followed by over 50 years at the Royal Clarence Hotel, finally moving in 1912 to a purpose built Masonic Hall in King's Square, which remains in use today.

Among several other old items belonging to the Lodge pride of place should perhaps go to a Master's Tressall (or Tracing) board, once again dating back to the late 18th Century.

A set of collar jewels made by Thomas Harper, the pre-eminent Masonic jewel maker in the early 19th Century, exist for the Senior Warden and Immediate Past Master, both hallmarked 1817, and for the Deacons, of the Winged Mercury type used in old lodges, both hallmarked 1807.

The first mention of a Past Masters Jewel was made at the Installation Meeting in 1873 when the new Master presented one to the IPM. In 1906 the first Ladies' Evening was held. Members paid for the dinner, the wine provided at Lodge expense, and a dispensation was granted for the brethren to appear in Masonic clothing.

During WW1 several Emergency Meetings took place, mainly to Initiate or to confer degrees on those joining the Armed Forces. In 1919 a record 25 Initiations were held. Not surprisingly this was followed by the Warranting of the Daughter Lodge, Admiral Blake, in 1924.

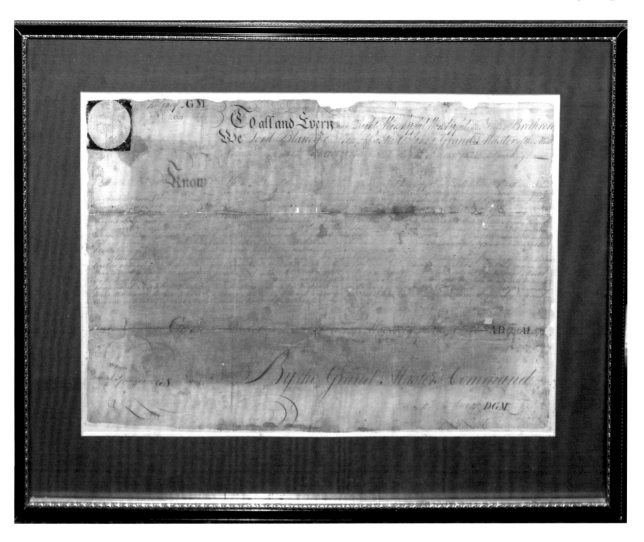

Barely legible, the Warrant of the first Lodge of Perpetual Friendship.

After 250 years of existence, and despite many life-threatening problems with finance, membership, and other adverse events, the Lodge of Perpetual Friendship continues to flourish with membership at a substantial level.

Initiations are carried out on a regular basis and there is an eager determination to face the difficulties which will undoubtedly arise in a rapidly changing 21st Century.

Lodge Marine No. 232 EC

Meets at the Masonic Hall Nailsea

Hall Stone Lodge. Constituted in Calcutta, India, in 1801

It is on record that Lodge Marine followed Lodges "True Friendship" and "Humility with Fortitude" in joining the "Atholl" Constitution. It is obvious therefore that it must have been in existence as a Lodge under the older Constitution, but of its number and position there is now no record. It has been suggested that the Lodge was an off-shoot of Lodge "Anchor and Hope". At any rate whatever the Lodge was; whether it merely had a Bengal Warrant or whether it was ever previously registered under the old English Constitution, there is no question that it seceded to the "Ancient" or "Atholl" Constitution along with the two other Lodges in Calcutta in the year 1801.

The next point of interest is why "Marine" with two other Calcutta Lodges should have seceded to the "Atholl" Constitution. It is stated that at this date (about 1800) the Provincial Grand Lodge appointed all its officers from Lodges Nos. 1 and 2, "Star in the East" and "Industry and Perseverance" respectively, which gave rise to great dissatisfaction amongst the Lodges in Calcutta, and this reason is given why Lodges "True Friendship", "Humility and Fortitude" and "Marine" broke away from the old Constitution.

At the Union in 1813 Lodge Marine had the number 410 accorded by the United Grand Lodge. Subsequently at the general renumbering of the Lodges in 1832 "Marine" became No. 282 and at the later renumbering in 1863 it became No. 232, which number it retains. For some years after the Union, and the revival of Masonry following it, there is nothing of great importance to record.

The current and original banners of Lodge Marine

Lodge "Marine" took part in several local Masonic functions, such as the laying of the Foundation Stone of St. Andrew's Church in 1815, the laying of the Foundation Stone of the new Custom House in 1819, and the laying of the Foundation Stone of St Peter's Church in 1822.

In 1827 Provincial Grand Lodge, when reporting on the state of Masonry in Bengal, referred to Lodge "Marine" as follows:

"This Lodge, as its name would imply, was originally formed of persons employed in the Marine Service of Government. The uncertainty incident to the profession to which its members belong subjects its numerical strength to repeated fluctuations, but in spite of this drawback it has maintained a character for good conduct and regularity which is highly meritorious".

We now arrive at the period of which we have Quarterly returns and other documents in the archives of District Grand Lodge. A copy of the bye-laws of the Lodge for 1837 has been found which show that a Steward was the officer whose duty consisted in keeping charge of the furniture, jewels, dresses, etc. and to maintain them in proper order. There is nothing said about his duties at the Banquet.

In the general rules for meetings we find that members omitting to send excuses for non-attendance were liable to punishment at the discretion of the Master. We also find provision against the use of bad language, which was as follows:

"Swearing and obscene conversation shall never be allowed in Lodge. Whoever is guilty thereof shall be admonished by the Master for the first offence and for every subsequent transgression shall be punished as provided for in the Chapter on Penalties".

These penalties consisted in disqualifications from Office; two to five entries in a quarter against a member resulted in him being disqualified from being Master, Warden, Deacon, or Secretary and Treasurer respectively.

We now come to the interesting subject of the admission of Indians to Freemasonry. In the records we find that in 1838 J. Peterson, then Worshipful Master of "Marine", initiated a Mohammedan; a Mogul was also admitted in the same year and an Arab in 1839. None of these brethren could speak English. These facts are interesting because in 1838 Lodge "Humility with Fortitude" had refused to admit two Mohammedan gentlemen. It appears that the question was submitted to the Grand Secretary in London, who replied that Grand Lodge made no distinction about creed or religion, and he quoted the fact of the appointment of the Ambassador from Oudh as a Past Grand Warden, and of the initiation in 1776 of the son of the Nawab of Arcot.

On the strength of this letter from the Grand Secretary there was no hesitation on the part of Lodge "Marine" which, as far I can find out, was the first Lodge in Calcutta to admit a native of India to Freemasonry. The sequel is important. The action of Lodge "Marine" was opposed by Provincial Grand Lodge which announced "that the Grand Lodge had unanimously resolved to suspend the admission of Mohammedans and Hindus into the Order of Masonry". Provincial Grand Lodge here attempted to exceed its powers, and as its resolution was totally at variance with the letter of the Grand Secretary in London before referred to it was not accepted by Lodge "Marine". Other Mohammedans were admitted later.

We now come to a period of about twelve years when internal dissensions were frequent and the fortunes of the Lodge fluctuated considerably. Several members were suspended for unmasonic conduct and amongst them were even Past Masters. On 20th December 1843 the Lodge was placed in abeyance on account of a paucity of members. This lasted until 10th June 1845, when eleven brethren got permission and re-opened the Lodge.

In 1849 another disaster occurred and the Worshipful Master (J.W. Walton) had to report that in consequence of not being able to find a Master for the Lodge it had to be placed in abeyance. For the second time therefore we find a lapse in the continuous working of the Lodge. This period of abeyance lasted from December 1849 to December 1852. After this date Lodge "Marine" was more fortunate, and we find that in 1856 it had no less than 80 members.

This popularity was maintained for several years but in 1860 further troubles began. The Worshipful Master was suspended and the Senior Warden was placed in charge, but in consequence of a 'great disturbance' which occurred at the January meeting the Warrant was suspended. An inquiry was instituted and three of the officers were suspended, but the Worshipful Master was restored to his position and the Warrant again put in force.

Still other disagreements followed and the Lodge tried to exclude V.W.Bro Thomas Jones, one of its old Masters, but the result was that no less than 42 members were suspended for libelling him. Of these, 32 expressed regret and were restored to their Masonic privileges.

Then, in 1861, charges of forgery were made against Bro W. Sier, the Secretary and Treasurer, who was suspended but later 29 members tendered their resignations with the intention of joining a Scotch Lodge. All this trouble reduced the number of members to five, and the Lodge again went into abeyance. The suspended Secretary and Treasurer did a strange action in sending the Warrant to England without the knowledge of the Worshipful Master, but the Provincial Grand Master granted a Warrant of Dispensation and a meeting was held in the next month (April 1861). This Warrant is the one under which the Lodge is working at the present time.

Despite the lack of retained minutes, although realised in the early 1900s, it is unfortunate that still we did not learn. Although United Grand Lodge retain in their Archives the Atholl Grand Lodge's copy of a Marine Lodge minutes of an Emergency Meeting of 23rd March 1812 together with some correspondence, the only Minute Books now in our possession are from 1963. However, these will cover the period relevant to relate the fall and rise of Marine and hopefully detect the special "flavour" that Marine Lodge and its visitors now enjoy.

The minutes open on the 9th September 1963, fourteen brethren in attendance, but interesting to see that the WM was W.Bro Richard Preston, and the Secretary Bro Cyril Honey, two members who contributed so much to the transfer of our Lodge to Somerset in the 1970s. The bye-laws of the Lodge held three classes of membership: Resident, i.e. residing within twenty miles of Government House, Calcutta; Sea-faring i.e. occasional attendance by naval members; and Absent, i.e. those usually transferred back to the UK by business or indeed to anywhere in the world, as our present membership list still bears witness.

Following Indian independence many members were required to leave Calcutta. This resulted in insufficient members in attendance to successfully run the Lodge and brought many "interesting" variations during the next nine years between the Summons and the minutes recording the actual work carried out. There were instances of members being 'passed on arrival in India' although not necessarily mentioned on the Summons for that Meeting, and planned ceremonies not being proceeded with as a result of 'ship not docked', or 'flooding of railway line from Dacca'.

It is recorded that the British National Anthem was always sung as opposed to the Indian National Anthem composed at the time of Independence in 1947, and that between 1972 and 1975, prior to acceptance into Somerset, the principal Toast prior to "The Queen and the Craft" at the Festive Board was "The President of India", possible unique in Somerset, this being the first Toast of all Lodges in India after 1947.

The Installation Meetings were always held in two parts, a morning session when the Lodge opened at 8am, and 'called off' at about 8.45am. The Lodge was 'called on' at 7pm. when the actual Installation Ceremony was undertaken and the Lodge closed about 9.15pm.

December 1964 saw the Installation of W.Bro Cyril Honey although he was unable to actively complete his year of office, being returned to the UK by his Company in the following May. Marine was finding it difficult enough to fill the Regular offices and thereby hold their Meetings without their WM being called home. Whilst it will have quickly been observed that the general running of the Lodge was beset with difficulties rarely experienced by "home" Lodges, Marine now moved into a period of some five years where events, and thereby given circumstances, combined to make the future of the Lodge at least uncertain, if not a fatality.

On numerous occasions no Degree was worked due to the general lack of Candidates or to the due Candidate not being present. Attendance was on average only nine to ten including visitors, sometimes less, with those in attendance often combining more than one office, e.g. Director of Ceremonies and Secretary, Inner Guard and IPM. This situation gives a fine example, in that while Candidates are important for the future of a Lodge, a good nucleus of Past Masters is essential. At some Meetings, the Candidates being absent, a rehearsal of the intended Degree was undertaken in lieu.

The first recorded suggestion of a possible move of the Lodge to England is recorded at the Meeting held on the 9th October 1967. "W.Bro L.V.C. Griffiths addressed the brethren on the advisability of taking such steps as may be necessary to ascertain from all members their views on the transfer of the Lodge to the UK, a move the W.Bro considered advisable within the next two years due to the falling active membership of the Lodge". However, it was another three years before further progress is noted when at the Meeting on 14th September 1970, the Secretary reported in the Third Rising, 'a proposed gathering of UK Absent Members at Freemasons Hall, London on 17th October 1970. The convenor is W.Bro C.S. Honey.'

Despite what was now becoming an emergency situation it was another fifteen months before the Report of that meeting was conveyed in Open Lodge in Calcutta in December 1971. To illustrate this emergency, the attendance records, including visitors, for the last four Meetings of 1971 were as follows:

13th September 1971 6 including Tyler
11th October 1971   5 including Tyler
8th November 1971   8 including Tyler
13th December 1971   6 including Tyler

It should be borne in mind that the total membership list of the Lodge at this time was over 70 but very few members were in Calcutta.

It is particularly worthy of mention at this point that the Secretary during the preceding seven years, W.Bro Dick Preston, was perhaps almost solely responsible by his efforts and diligence in keeping the Lodge together in any form at all. It is apparent from the minutes that, as so often is the case, the unsung hero of a Lodge is the Secretary whose work "behind the scenes" ensures the smooth running of the Lodge and, in our case, the very survival of Marine Lodge during this period.

The Meeting in September 1972 had again only five brethren present including Bro D Black, who was the Candidate for Raising but insufficient numbers being present, the Ceremony could not proceed and Bro Black took the minutes instead. Bro Black again served as Acting Secretary for the last Marine Lodge Meeting to be held in Calcutta on 9th October 1972. Only three Lodge members were present, plus two visitors who naturally acted in offices. The Second Rising records the following significant and historic event in the annals of Marine Lodge:

"The Dispensation from the Provincial Grand Lodge of Somerset was read, authorising the Meeting of Marine Lodge No. 232 EC at Freemasons Hall, Pier Road, Portishead, Somerset."

W.Bro R.C. White, in the Chair on behalf of the WM, and the Brethren of the Lodge expressed thanks to W.Bro Honey for the time and effort he had taken in finding a safe mooring for the Lodge after 171 years sojourn in India, and expressed the hope that Marine Lodge would grow from strength to strength in the new home by the sea.' There being no further business the Lodge was closed in peace and harmony at 7.40pm for the last time in Calcutta.

Saturday 4th November 1972, was our first meeting in Somerset, with twelve in attendance, 140% improvement on the last Meeting in Calcutta. The next distinctive date in our history consequently occurred on the 6th September 1975 when the Provincial Grand Master, R.W.Bro Lt. Col. Harry Owen Hughes, accompanied by his Deputy, the Provincial Grand Wardens, Provincial D of C and Provincial Grand Deacons attended the Lodge to officially accept Marine Lodge into the Province of Somerset. The welcome given to us by the Provincial Grand Master in his address was particularly poignant, and fitting, since he had known Marine in Calcutta during World War II when he had visited us whilst District Grand Master of Hong Kong. Having achieved this enormous step, it appeared that there was only one way to go, naturally forwards.

However, fate was to deal us a very cruel hand when less than fifteen months later, the two brethren who had most to ensure the transfer of the Lodge to Somerset, and thereby its survival, W.Bro Cyril Honey and W.Bro Dick Preston, died within eighteen days of each other, Bro Cyril on the 31st October 1976 and Bro Dick on the 17th November 1976. Marine Lodge members not only suffered grief by these partings but reeled in a state of shock (both brethren were only in their late fifties).

Gradually our day to day ties with Calcutta were being released and early 1974 saw a notice of Motion for the realisation of Lodge Marine's shares in the Calcutta Electric Supply Corporation.

From 1972 to 1986, 61 candidates were initiated and Lodge Marine's popularity flourished, meetings averaged between 60 and 70, about half being visitors. It is worthy of note that W.Bro Trevor Johnson (the then secretary, and who was to become a major player in Marine's history over the next twenty years or so), stated in 1986

"Whilst this number would at first impression appear to be good for Marine, we now look back from a position of comparative strength to realise that maybe we have made a mistake. Undoubtedly by receiving such a large number over such short a short space of time, we have been unable to give new members our sufficient time to teach and this has not been good for either Marine or Masonry, for we have with regret lost some of this large intake"

Members and visitors travelled large distances to attend Lodge Marine, this was always reflected at the festive board with the Master of the day taking wine with these brethren, to the point where it was almost obligatory to travel such distances, this is perhaps why Marine then held such a unique atmosphere.

In the later part of 2000, with the future of the Portishead temple under threat, the members of Marine voted to move yet again, this time to the Masonic centre situated at Nailsea. This was not an easy decision, but one borne out necessity. The then Secretary, W.Bro Mike James, was instrumental in the highly successful relocation of Marine. There were many happy memories of the Lodge's time at Portishead, but as Marine had proved almost 30 years earlier it was time

for a change. So on the 3rd March 2001 Lodge Marine was removed to Nailsea, in North Somerset.

A short while later Marine celebrated its Bicentenary, with the dedication of a new, very large and beautifully bound Bible. A great day in Marine's history. Over the next couple of years great sadness was again to visit Marine, with the death of several highly regarded and distinguished Marine Brethren namely W.Bros Les Jelly and Ron Gale and sadly including in 2004 the then incumbent Worshipful Master W.Bro Derek Baker.

In the years since Lodge Marine arrived from India many brethren have come and gone and many have contributed enormously to Marine's success, too many to mention from W.Bro Ted Gawronski and W.Bro Peter Strong through to W.Bro Steve Gale.

Over 200 years of history cannot possibly be covered in the space available; suffice it to say that Lodge Marine, despite all its trials and tribulations, remains greater than the sum of its parts

When it was founded Nelson hadn't yet fought at Trafalgar, Pitt the younger was Prime minister, George III was King and Britain was at war with France. Yet Lodge Marine 232 EC is still surviving, meeting four times a year, mostly on cold and wet Saturday mornings, and currently has about 40 members.

Lodge of Unanimity and Sincerity No. 261

Meets at the Masonic Hall, Taunton

Warrant dated 1788

The Lodge of Unanimity and Sincerity, for over two Centuries closely associated with the town of Taunton, appears to have actually been founded in Ilminster in 1781. The Lodge was formally constituted in 1788 as the Lodge of Unanimity and numbered 524, transferring to Taunton in 1797, and following several number changes it became 261 in 1863.

The first Minute Book starts with by laws agreed in 1788. Regretfully several early pages were removed, but the key minute was of a Special Lodge held at the George Inn, Ilminster, in 1797, when it was unanimously agreed to move the Lodge to the London Inn, later the County Hotel, in Taunton.

At early meetings in Taunton a number of Masons were 'made' and it was common practice for candidates to have been made and passed in the same evening. At the time those in trade were described as Mr and those not in trade as Gentlemen.

The minutes of June 1798 are the first to record fraternal visiting resolving that, in particular, the Lodge of Perpetual Friendship, Bridgwater, and Rural Philanthropic Lodge, Huntspill, be invited to attend. In 1799 there were 21 members, all but three resident in Taunton, comprising three gentlemen and the remainder in 'trade'.

As with many early lodges the influence of certain families was apparent and in the early 19th Century the names Jacobs and Trenchard appear, the latter to appear in Lodge records for over 150 years.

In 1807 an Initiate, one William Dight, was paid £9 for painting three floor cloths, which now adorn the North Wall of the Taunton Masonic Hall, and are so well known. The tripods supporting the rough and perfect ashlars still in use are precisely depicted in the first degree tracing board.

In 1817 at the October meeting eight gentlemen were initiated, but the WM directed the ceremony for three to be performed over again due to some inaccuracies, which was done. The following month 'the whole of the Brethren present took the Union Obligation'. This arose from the Articles of Union between the two Grand Lodges of England in 1813. In the year 1817 there is the first record of the presentation of a Past Master's jewel.

The minutes of the December 1818 Installation meeting contain for the first time the phrase 'all the brethren except Past Masters were requested to withdraw'. During this period cases of distress were not often recorded, but in 1822 the Lodge sent £2 to Bro Caines 'now confined for debt in the King's Bench'. It is clear that the Lodge also valued honour and virtue at least as well as rank and fortune, and in one ceremony they initiated a candidate 'servant of Bro Billett' together with an officer of the East India Company and a Surgeon.

In these early days a frequent visitor was Bro Dr Crucifix PGD, who subsequently became an Honorary Member of the Lodge. He was a founder of what became known as the RMBI, and the Lodge donated £50 in 1836 to help establish an 'asylum', later the RMBI. The Lodge was the first to contribute such a substantial sum, and can be said to be a true founder of the RMBI.

In 1842 the initiation of one of the Lodge's most famous, or perhaps infamous, members took place. This was William Tucker. He became Master in 1844, and again in 1846, in the meantime becoming PGM of the Province of Dorset. In 1853 he attended a Lodge meeting, acting as IPM, after being deposed as PGM of Dorset by the Grand Master. This related to his wearing a 33rd Degree robe of the Ancient and Accepted Rite (Rose Croix) over his Craft regalia as PGM at a meeting of the Provincial Grand Lodge of Dorset. He died soon after in 1855.

In 1852 Capt. Alexander William Adair became a Joining Member of the Lodge, becoming Master in 1860 and PGM of Somerset in 1864. He resigned in 1869 by reason of his military duties. As the Victorian era progressed so changes occurred. Lodge minutes became more formal and more ceremonies were held, for example, in 1876 the Installation Meeting commenced with First, Second and Third Degree

Bro Thomas Jacobs, the third Initiate of the Lodge of Unanimity and Sincerity in 1797, and destined to have a great influence on the success of the Lodge in the early 19th century and Master on nine occasions.

ceremonies before the Installation ceremony! In 1878 the acquisition of the premises in the Crescent, Taunton commenced. The new premises were dedicated in 1879, following a service, clad in Masonic clothing, at St Mary's Church. A Lodge tradition was established in 1881, the appointment of a Brother as Chaplain, who then progressed through the Wardens chairs to that of Master.

In 1916 the Lodge waived subscriptions for brethren in the service of the Crown and resolved that all members of HM Forces stationed in Taunton should be guests, a by-law not revised until 1983.

After the First World War the Masonic Hall was extended and the Lodge was presented with the Treasurer's and Secretary's collar jewels of the original St George's Lodge (1764-1783).

During this period one of the Lodge's members, Bro Hiram Hallett, offered great service to Somerset Freemasonry in general in terms of historical research, issuing a stream of papers and articles of great interest. He became a member of the illustrious Quatuor Coronati Lodge 2076 and subsequently its Master.

The Lodge's unique Tracing Boards, first painted in 1808 were renovated in 1956, and for the first time hung on the north wall of the Temple. It is recorded that the tranquility of the Lodge was disturbed more than a little.

As with many old Lodges, ritual working has undergone many changes, and although changes have been necessary in signs and the

positioning of Officers there remain areas where the ceremony differs from the more uniform workings.

A collection of early Masonic firing glasses is rare, and that at Taunton is finely engraved, including the number 327, which belonged to the Lodge of Unanimity and Sincerity between the years 1832 and 1863 before it became its existing number of 261.

The Tracing Boards were painted in 1808 as floor cloths by Bro William Dight, a "limner" (painter) initiated in 1807. For many years they continued as such, but because of wear they were enclosed in frames which in 1924 required the united efforts of two stewards to move them. Due to signs of further deterioration they were restored and mounted in their present position on the North wall of the Lodge Room in 1956.

Lodge of Love and Honour No. 285

Meets at the Crossways Hotel, North Wootton

Warrant dated 4th June, 1792

No record of how the Lodge came into being has survived, except for a letter from Thomas Dunckerley, the Provincial Grand Master, addressed to the Grand Secretary of the Premier Grand Lodge of England The letter is dated 8th August 1792. It shows the dispensation to form a Lodge in Shepton Mallet dated 4th June 1792 and this is the date on the Warrant. Dunckerley asked for the Warrant to be sent to him in Wells where he was to hold a meeting of Provincial Grand Lodge on Tuesday 21st August 1792 at the Assembly Rooms. This meeting was held under the sponsorship of the Lodge of Unanimity which met in Wells between 1785 and 1809, when it was erased.

At that Provincial Meeting there may have been some kind of a ceremony to hand over the Warrant but no record has survived. In those days there was no consecration ceremony as we know it, a new Lodge was just said to be constituted. The original Lodge banner is now in storage; the one in use today bears the coat of arms of The Grand Lodge of England. The letter of sanction for its use, issued by Grand Lodge, is framed nearby.

The first minute book of Love & Honour has a brief account of its first recorded meeting which was on Tuesday, 9th October, 1792 at the Bell Inn. Six brethren of the Lodge were present together with ten visitors. Bro Pulsford, possibly of the Lodge of Unanimity was, to quote, "called to the Chair" and two other brethren from Wells were called to take the Wardens' Chairs. Samuel Norman, the Master Designate, was taken through the ceremony of Passing the Chair, then invested and sworn in as "Right Worshipful Master, until the next St John's Day".

A Bro Bowles was sworn in as Worshipful Past Master, which may indicate that he, unlike Sam Norman, had been Master of a Lodge at some time. It is tempting to wonder if that Lodge might have been a 'Lodge of Freemasons' which met in Shepton Mallet some 25 years earlier at the Angel Inn. It held its first meeting in December 1737 and was only the third Lodge to be formed in Somerset. The Angel Inn was situated, in Shepton Mallet, near where the Lloyds TSB Bank is now.

It is interesting to note this would have been next door to the Bell Inn where Love & Honour had its first meeting. The 'Angel' Lodge was erased in 1768 and probably ceased to meet some time earlier. Love & Honour (sometimes 'Honor') continued to meet at the Bell Inn until 1819, it then moved to various venues in Shepton Mallet until it moved to Sales House in 1912. At that time it had a rental agreement and did not purchase the property until 1947, how that came about will be explained later.

As the Lodge was Constituted under the 'Moderns' Grand Lodge it originally had the number 502, and at the union of the two rival Grand Lodges, it became No. 537, then in 1832 No. 357. Finally it became No. 285 in 1863.

Past Master's Jewel pre 1815 and two Hall Stone Jewels

On the 9th July of 1863 the town of Shepton Mallet was witness to an immense number of Freemasons who had assembled for a meeting of the Somerset Provincial Grand Lodge of Freemasons, who were to meet in the Music Hall, which had been especially prepared for the occasion. A report in 'The Shepton Mallet Illustrated Magazine', states "It was a great day for the town, and had been anticipated with much eagerness and trumpeting.

The brilliant day was ushered in by bell-ringing, and the brethren of different Lodges arrived in considerable force on several morning trains". The Lodge opened at 10.30 for normal business, at the conclusion of which a procession was formed from the Music Hall to the Parish Church for Divine Worship. This

procession left at 12.15, in the following order, with Love & Honour in pride of place. As can be seen, these Lodge numbers differ from those of today:

Royal Albert Edward 1208 ~ Keynsham
Parrett and Axe 1116 ~ Crewkerne
Pilgrims 1074 ~ Glastonbury
Benevolent 653 ~Wells
Honour .528 ~ Bath
Brotherly Love 412 ~ Yeovil
Rural Philanthropic 367 ~ Highbridge
Unanimity and Sincerity 327 ~ Taunton
Perpetual Friendship 157 ~ Bridgwater
Royal Sussex .61 ~ Bath
Royal Cumberland .48 ~ Bath
Love and Honour 357 ~ Shepton Mallet
Visiting Brethren Two by Two
Provincial Lodge Officers

Thomas Harper Jewels Hallmarked from 1817

On the way to the Church it was reported, "the windows were filled, and the street, peopled by curious crowds of the uninitiated, who, however ignorant of the mysteries of the venerable Craft, testified by their presence there, and in the Church, their sincere interest in the occasion".

Following the Church service, the Banquet was supplied by Mrs. Alford at the George hotel, where 130 brethren sat down, with some disappointment being felt as all could not be accommodated in the same apartment. At the conclusion of the repast, it is reported "the cloth was removed, when the usual toasts, glees, duets, and songs appertaining to the Craft were given, and the proceedings passed off very pleasantly".

The Lodge met regularly between 1792 and 1805, then after the meeting in March 1805, and without any apparent explanation there were no more meetings recorded in the minute books until July 1813. This is, of course, the year of the amalgamation of the 'Ancient' and 'Modern' Grand Lodges, to form the United Grand Lodge of England. Could it be that during those last few years, under the 'Moderns' banner, interest in Freemasonry within Shepton Mallet waned, until its revival by the Union. We shall never know.

The design of the Temple Pillars was decided upon, and constructed by a Brother of the Lodge. The chapiters presented a problem and at this stage, either by accident or design the project came to the knowledge of a professional architect and member of the Craft who offered to design the chapiters and prepare working drawings. This was Bro Kirby, Past Master of Longleat Lodge, Warminster. These chapiters are unique in Craft Masonry and were made from specially selected and seasoned sycamore given by W.Bro Norman James. They incorporate the sacred lotus flower of Egypt. The terrestrial and celestial globes from the old pillars having been cleaned and fixed on top, the network is thrown over.

The Lodge was granted a Centenary Warrant in 1892, 100 years after it first met, but the United Grand Lodge would not authorise a Bicentenary Warrant in 1992, ruling that it could not be issued until 2012 which is 200 years from 1813. This

caused much dismay in the Province but in spite of a plea from the PGM, Grand Lodge would not budge. So, in a mood of cheerful defiance the Lodge celebrated the 200th anniversary of the first meeting of the Lodge in style with as its centrepiece a demonstration of an 18th century ceremony.

This was at the regular meeting in October 1992 which was attended by the PGM and other Officers of the Province. This was also the occasion when the new dining room was used for the first time, R.W.Bro Stanley H.A.F. Hopkins formally declaring it open.

Following the discovery of an outbreak of 'dry-rot', in 2001 the brethren decided that the time for pouring good money after bad into a building, which consumed it at an alarming rate was over. Alternative premises were secured at the Crossways Hotel in North Wootton. The last meeting at the Old Convent and Lodge

A lovely print belonging to the Lodge,
believed to be early 19th Century and of American origin

premises in Draycott road was held on the 15th May 2002. The Ceremony was the Installation of Bro Paul Davis.

The first Ceremony to take place in the new premises was on 18th September 2002. The passing of Bro Andrew Snook to the second degree was conducted by the newly Installed Master .

The highlight to the first Masonic year in the new premises was the visit of the Provincial team on the 16th April 2003 who conducted a third degree ceremony when Bro Andrew Snook was raised to the sublime degree of a Master Mason by R.W.Bro David L. Jenkins PGM assisted by his active Provincial Officers.

The Provincial Team again honoured the Lodge with a visit, on Wednesday 15th November 2006 and with W.Bro David Medlock taking the Chair. A third degree Ceremony was conducted, with Bro Tony Guidi being raised. Following the move to The Crossways the Lodge of Love & Honour 285 has gone from strength to strength, with a steady stream of Initiates.

The PGM, R.W.Bro David L. Jenkins, was kept fully occupied, with the presentation of the Lodge's second 'Acorn' award to represent the donations made towards the RMBI 2007 Festival.

Until 1870 the Lodge only had the first Tracing Board which was in need of repair. Bro Foxwell made the second and third Tracing Boards, painted them, and those same Boards are still in use today. They are fixed to the wall of the Lodge room and appear at first view to be a single board, sections being concealed behind a roller blind.

Rural Philanthropic Lodge No. 291

Meets at the Masonic Hall, Burnham on Sea

Warrant dated 1793

The Rural Philanthropic Lodge was warranted in 1793, the warrant being signed by the celebrated Thomas Dunckerley as PGM of Somerset. The first Master was John Jennings, a very vigorous Freemason in the Bridgwater area, whose headstone is still to be seen standing in West Huntspill Churchyard, albeit in a somewhat sad state.

The earliest minutes of the Lodge are under the heading Rural Lodge of Philanthropy, however, after seventeen meetings it was given its proper name the Rural Philanthropic Lodge, No. 517, and subsequently numbered 550, 367 and finally 291 in 1863. It was duly constituted, i.e. consecrated in 1795 by Thomas Dunckerley.

As with many early lodges the meetings appear to have been very frequent, many with more than one ceremony. These included the ceremony of Passing the Chair as Master of the Lodge, a means by which a Master Mason could qualify to join the Royal Arch without actually being a Master.

The minutes also indicate that the brethren were involved with absenteeism, non-Masonic conduct, indeed one Brother was excluded, and unpaid dues, and on more than one occasion a Brother had two degrees conferred upon him in one day. By 1803 the Lodge numbered seventeen members. Regretfully all Lodge minutes were lost between 1811 and 1857.

Among the Lodge treasures are a pair of very fine Deacons' jewels, made by the celebrated silversmith Thomas Harper, and presented to the Lodge by a Past Master in 1817,

The original Lodge Banner, recently discovered after many years of neglect, hidden in the boiler house!

Worcester mug with Masonic inscription

Other presentations in the mid Victorian period included a superb painting of the original Three Grand Masters and a fine pair of globes.

Other treasures include a fine Bible, with much graffiti, dating from 1628, a superb Worcester mug, circa 1810 with a printed Masonic inscription, and a fine print of the Moira apron from the early 19th Century
.

In 1902 the Lodge purchased a book, at a cost of fifteen shillings, containing the names of all the Brethren in the Province. This was compiled by the Provincial Grand Treasurer, and is probably the first Somerset Masonic reference book.

Lodge Bible, with much graffiti

During late Victorian times and well into the 20th Century Lodge work compared with today was both lengthy and arduous. Even on Installation days it was quite common for other ceremonies to be worked.

Moira apron from the early 19th Century

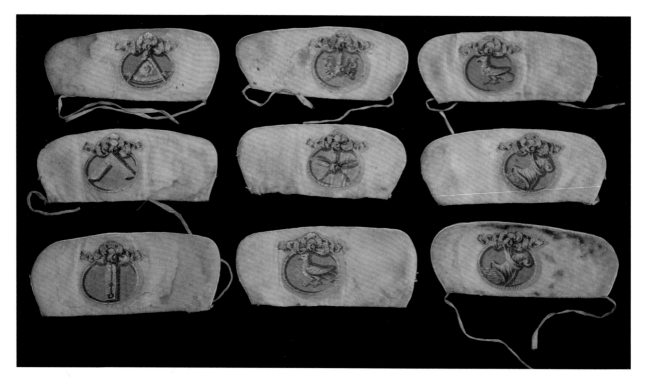

Two boxes of valuable books and papers were deposited in 1903 in a bank, never to return. The loss probably included the missing early Minute Books. In 1911 the Lodge commenced the practice of singing the Opening and Closing Odes, a practice opposed by a number of the members.

The Lodge was presented with a portrait of W.Bro John Burnett in 1916 following 60 years membership. He was a descendent of the Lodge Founder, W.Bro John Jennings, and just one member of the Burnett family who served the Lodge over 200 years. As with many lodges in existence at the time the Lodge struggled through the 1st World War, loosing at least one member to enemy action.Following a growth in membership after the War, a daughter Lodge, Alfred and Guthrum, was founded in 1923 at Wedmore, with an undertaking being given that there would be no loss of membership from 291.

In 1938 the Lodge resolved to lend the Grand Lodge museum half of the cuffs, or gauntlets, which had been exhibited by the Lodge from early times, and probably dating from the late

18th Century. These old tie on gauntlets are probably unique in the country. The gauntlets retained by the Lodge are still exhibited; those lent to Grand Lodge remain there.

Framed banner in the ante-room

184

Despite the outbreak of the 2nd World War plans for the construction of a new Masonic Hall were completed, and its dedication took place in June 1940. A number of emergency meetings were held during the War to accommodate members serving in the Forces on being posted overseas or elsewhere.

In January 1952 white gloves were introduced as part of the Masonic dress code, one Brother refused to comply and never did so during his Masonic life. Despite the age of the Lodge a Ladies' Festival was not held until 1953. Later in this decade a new organ was presented to the Lodge, and the dining room reconstructed. Until this time dining took place in local hotels.

Political correctness is not necessarily a modern phenomenon as in 1963 a check was made that Masonic music and odes did not offend the religious beliefs of members. In the same year the wearing of white gloves at funerals and the casting of acacia sprigs into the graves of deceased brethren was banned.

A fraternal visit was made in 1973 by six brethren of the Grand Lodge of Oregon, when a letter of greeting from the Grand Master of Oregon was read to the Lodge. The visitors were again welcomed in 1975, doubled in number.

On a third visit, in 1977, the WM was presented with a medallion commemorating the Bicentenary of the USA and the Masonic Brotherhood of Oregon.

In 1987 the Lodge sponsored a new Lodge, to be known as the Somerset Fairway Lodge, which was duly Consecrated in the Burnham Lodge room.

Bicentenary year came in 1993, the celebration of which was held at the Webbington Hotel, with a large attendance of over 100, including the PGM and the Grand Secretary, who presented the Bicentenary Warrant of the Lodge.

As with many old lodges Rural Philanthropic 291 has been able to survive and prosper over 200 years due to the long service undertaken by many brethren carrying out the main offices, with service of even twenty years quite common, thus ensuring there was continuity and stability during many stressful times.

Lodge of Brotherly Love No. 329

Meets at The Masonic Hall, Hendford, Yeovil.

Warrant dated 1810

The Warrant of Constitution for the Lodge of Brotherly Love was granted to seven petitioning brethren and dated 8th March 1810, which authorised the Lodge to be opened and held at the George Inn in the town of Martock. The Lodge was given the number No. 617.

Its warrant had been assigned from the Lodge of St John, 534, which had met at the sign of the Grapes in Lancaster, but it had not been in contact with or paid dues to Grand Lodge for some years and its warrant was forfeited, although the warrant was never delivered to Grand Lodge. The Lodge number, incidentally, did not become 329 until 1863 by which time it had already been changed to 624 in 1814 and 412 in 1832.

The Lodge has three Banners. The original banner is now situated behind the Worshipful Master's chair, whilst a second Banner, which was presented to the Lodge in 1896, is now situated behind the Senior Warden's chair

At the Centenary of the Masonic Hall in 1994 the Deputy Provincial Grand Master, V.W.Bro Thomas A. Hughes, dedicated a new Lodge banner that had kindly been presented to the Lodge by W.Bro Richard C. Stallard

The Lodge was formed when England was still at war with France, just five years after the Battle of Trafalgar and five years before the battle of Waterloo. George III was on the throne, aged 72 years, but because of his illness with porphyria, which caused bouts of instability, his son HRH George Augustus Frederick, the Prince of Wales, and incidentally the Grand Master of Grand Lodge, was virtually acting as Regent, which he became a year later in 1811.

The Lodge was also warranted just over three years before the union of premier Grand Lodge and the Antient Grand Lodge.

Consecration of the Lodge was held on 11th August 1811, eighteen months after its first meeting. The ceremony was advertised in the Sherborne Mercury, at a cost of £1, and was held at the George Inn at Martock with 53 brethren present, but with no Provincial Officer in attendance.

A procession was formed with members dressed in the manner of the Georgian period with badges of various design, wands, banners, Lodge jewels, and many items of Lodge furniture distributed amongst them.

Accompanied by the parish band the procession travelled down the main street and then back to the Church of All-Saints, where the bells were ringing, and the event viewed, no doubt, in some awe by the local people to whom Masonry was unknown.

In 1814 the Lodge meeting moved to the White Hart Inn, also in Martock, but then transferred in 1819 to the expanding Yeovil, with the greater likelihood of attracting new members. This was borne out by eighteen new members, who lived in Yeovil, joining the Lodge in 1819 and 1820.

The first four meetings in Yeovil were held in Bro T. Cave's house and then in December 1819 at the Mermaid Inn.

The Lodge moved shortly after to 'private rooms' in a building next to the Vicarage in Vicarage Street, a main thoroughfare. It stayed there for seven years and then moved to The Three Choughs Inn in March 1827 where meetings were held for the next 70 years.

However, in June 1844 it became necessary for the front of the Three Choughs Inn to be rebuilt so the Lodge decided to meet on the top of the Windmill Hill, which overlooked the town centre. The brethren first walked to the Hill through a lane, and then climbed the steep side of the Hill. Fourteen brethren were present at this amazing event where the only other sounds were 'the bleating of the sheep and the songs of the birds in the trees'.

During their time at the rooms in Vicarage Street the brethren had hoped to build their own premises, and land had been acquired in 1824, plans drawn up, but the committee was unable to raise the £760 needed, so the land was sold. Further attempts to secure a building were made in 1836 and 1887, without success, but in 1893 the energetic WM. Bro H. Whitby supported by other brethren, led the efforts for land to be purchased in Hendford, which was

then on the edge of Yeovil. A request was made to Provincial Grand Lodge for a contribution of £100 but was declined! However a contract for the building was let to (Bro) Lye & Sons of Crewkerne for £950. There was little delay in building and The Masonic Hall was dedicated in November 1894 by the Rt. Hon. Viscount Dungarvan, the Provincial Grand Master, and is still the home of Yeovil Masonry.

However by the latter part of the Twentieth Century pressure of numbers at the Festive Board led to calls for the dining and bar area to be extended. Discussions took several years until a decision was made in 1994 by the Masonic Hall Company to build a single-storey extension, financed by donations and loans from Lodges, brethren and a commercial loan. It cost approximately £117,000, and was built by (W.Bro) Rogers & Son with several local brethren employed on the work. The impressive extension was opened in 1995

The very fine painting of the symbol incorporated in the Lodge Banner is of interest and capable of several interpretations

The Centenary of The Lodge took place on 20th April 1910 and was marked by two days of celebration. The brethren marched in their regalia, watched by large crowds, from the High Street to St John's Church, where they held a service of thanksgiving followed by a meeting of 200 brethren in the Town Hall.

The brethren also marched in procession through the streets of Yeovil to mark the accession of King George IV in 1820, for King William in 1830 and Queen Victoria in 1837. The last public occasion of a procession was in March 1934 when the of the foundation stone of St Andrew's Church was laid by R.W.Bro The Venerable Walter Farrer, Archdeacon of Wells and Provincial Grand Master for Somerset, assisted by his Provincial Grand Officers and with many other Masons present. This created much local interest as The Western Gazette reported 'Long before it began, many townspeople had gathered at the site and every point of vantage was occupied.

In the Lodge Room the three mahogany candlesticks of the Doric, Ionic and Corinthian Orders are at the Master's and Wardens' Chairs and are indeed those carried in the procession at the Consecration in 1811. The Master's and Wardens Chairs were bought in London in 1820, but date from the eighteenth century, and their pedestals were purchased in 1884. The original Master's pedestal is now to be found in the ante-room. The hand-painted wall-lamp shades, bearing Masonic symbols, were originally used on the candles which provided the lighting in the Lodge. When the Masonic Hall was built they were placed on the east and west walls and lit by gas, which was subsequently replaced by electricity. The imposing celestial and terrestrial globes were purchased in 1860. The Secretary's table is made of old oak from the bell tower of St John's Church and presented to the Lodge in 1909, as was the pair of columns in the west. The oldest tracing board dates from 1859.

During the First World War Grand Lodge recommended that all brethren of German, Austrian, Hungarian or Turkish birth should not attend Lodge meetings for the duration of the War. Members of Brotherly Love voted to 'entirely disapprove of this recommendation'. It was, however, confirmed by Grand Lodge in June 1915. Rules of dress though were not relaxed until just before the War ended in 1918 when it was advised that evening dress would no longer be a requirement as morning dress would be quite acceptable!

During the Second World War a Government Emergency Order prohibited all meetings and the meeting in October 1939 was cancelled, but they were then resumed subject to special conditions. However, the dining hall was not available because Southern Command had requisitioned it, for which £45 per annum was paid in compensation. Some of the valuable Lodge furniture, including the three Chairs of the Worshipful Master and Wardens, was stored at the premises of Mr S. Vaux, an Antique dealer from Ilchester, whose son, William, became a very well known and respected Mason in later years.

When the Masonic Hall was first built in 1894 shares were sold in the Yeovil Masonic Hall Company. Brotherly Love subsequently bought the shares so the Hall Company was liquidated in 1902.

In October 1928, a second Lodge, Progressive Science 5007, with 30 of its 36 Founders from Brotherly Love, was consecrated and met in the Hall. In 1953 Brotherly Love invited Progressive Science to become joint participants in The Masonic Hall instead of paying rent. It was agreed to form the Masonic Hall Company that would buy the property and its contents, for a nominal sum of £2500, with each Lodge contributing half that sum.

A third Lodge, Corinthian Pillar 7552, with eleven Founders from Brotherly Love, was consecrated in November 1957. In 1985 the Royal Naval Lodge 2761, meeting until then in Malta, was considering the possibility of transferring to Yeovil and attended the December meeting in 1985. Subsequently they were received into the Province of Somerset. Both these Lodges are also shareholders in the Masonic Hall. However the first 'daughter' Lodge was that of Parrett and Axe 814, which met at Crewkerne from July 1860. Every Founder, with one exception, was a member of Brotherly Love and its first Master was one of Brotherly Love's most distinguished members, W.Bro R.J.F. Thomas, who later held the rank of Grand Chaplain of England.

The day of meeting has changed since its inception. The original By-law No.2 stated "that the Lodge do assemble on the Thursday on or before the full moon in each month" The arrangement to meet "on or before the full moon" has been continuous and is a link connecting the Lodge with early Masonry, reflecting that in its early years travel from the neighbouring towns and villages would have been by foot or by horseback and the full moon would have provided some light. The day of meeting however changed from Thursday to Tuesday from 1820 and since 1850 it has been held on a Wednesday. In 1911 however some 'emergency' meetings were held on a Sunday, which met with disapproval from the Provincial Grand Lodge.

There have been many interesting episodes in the Lodge history. A Joining Member in 1811, William Bridle, was the Governor of Ilchester Gaol, but in 1823 was prosecuted for the ill treatment of prisoners. Lodge members were most indignant and raised funds for his defence. He was later acquitted of all but one charge, but fell on hard times and received Masonic relief. In 1850 it was determined that Officers and brethren not attending to their duties or failing to advise of their non-attendance would be fined!

In 1855 a Brother was admonished for attending the Lodge in a state of inebriety for which he apologised and went on to be the Tyler for 34 years. One Brother asked for financial assistance for a friend; the Lodge replied suggesting that if he would remit the seven years of arrears of his subscription they would send half to the person concerned!

Supporting a range of Masonic and non-Masonic charities has been a theme of Freemasonry throughout the ages and indeed for Brotherly Love. In recent times the Lodge has raised over £21,000 and £31,000 for the 1993 and 2007 Festivals respectively and along with Somerset Freemasons helped raise over £50,000 for the St Margaret's Hospice that was opened in Yeovil in 2003.

Fine old Masonic aprons of handmade origin and depicting symbols not used today are unusual. Pride of place at Yeovil must go to a plain black and white apron with the emblems of mortality, i.e. skull and crossbones, in the centre. This originates from a time when all aprons were hand made, often to a Mason's own design.

It is said to have belonged to Bro Thomas Hamlyn, a physician of Martock and one of the founders of the Lodge of Brotherly Love 329. The apron certainly dates to the very early 19th Century, if not earlier. It is now carefully preserved and framed.

APRON of the LATE Bro Thomas Hamlyn Physician of Martock one of the Founders of the Lodge Brotherly Love. Presented by Miss May Stuckey-Clarke great great-Niece April 20 1910.

Lodge of Honour No. 379

Meeting at the Masonic Hall, Old Orchard Street, Bath

Warrant dated 1825

On 24th January 1825 a meeting was held at York House, Bath, attended by, amongst others, Captain Maddison, ex Royal York Lodge of Perfect Friendship, and Col. Kemeys Kemeys Tynte, who had been appointed Provincial Grand Master for Somerset in May 1820. Following the meeting a petition was sent to the PGM for onward transmission to the M.W The Grand Master requesting that a new Lodge be formed in Bath entitled "The Tynte Lodge of Honour and Independence". Of the seventeen names on the petition no less than eleven were from the Royal York Lodge.

The petition was granted by the Grand Master, but with some modifications regarding the name. The word "Tynte" was removed "for the present" because of previous unmasonic proceedings at Bath "which had unfortunately occasioned so much trouble and wasted so much time" and it was thought that it would be unwise for the PGM's name to be associated with these proceedings. Also deleted were the words "and Independence", Grand Lodge having ruled against any Lodge assuming such a title. The Warrant of the Lodge was issued on 23rd February 1825 under the designation The Lodge of Honour and assigned the number 798.

The first regular meeting took place on Monday 7th March 1825. There was no formal consecration of the Lodge which was simply opened in the First Degree. A letter from the Grand Secretary was read concerning the title. A minor, aged twenty years was balloted for, approved and initiated with the consent of his father and by Dispensation from the PGM. The Royal Sussex Lodge lent their regalia for this occasion.

The Tracing Boards were painted by Arthur Thistleton, a theatre scene painter at Drury Lane, London. They were inscribed on the reverse with "Tynte Lodge of Honour and Independence", so it would appear that they were ordered before Grand Lodge had confirmed the name. Two of these boards still remain in use today as is the VSL which was presented to the Lodge on its foundation and had been in use ever since, albeit repaired in 1936 under the direction of W.Bro A.L. Fuller.

The Lodge was greatly indebted to Col. Tynte and Capt. Maddison for its formation and successful launching, Col. Tynte presented a handsome chair for the Master, (now occupied by the IPM), and Capt. Maddison donated the jewels of the Lodge.

Another artefact dating back to these first meetings is a 'Pillars Certificate' belonging to Bro Dr. Joseph Chamberlain Buxton who had been initiated into the Lodge on 3rd May 1825, (the second working meeting of the Lodge). The certificate, which was donated as a gift in 1962 by a W.Bro George Walker, had been found wrapped round the telescope of Lord St. Vincent.

By the end of 1825 membership had risen to 40, half of whom had belonged to the Royal York Lodge. Admissions continued during 1827 and 1828 and in the following year the Lodge moved from York House to the White Lion, no reason being given. The Lodge was allocated a new number in 1833 and became No. 528. There were then 36 members and 38 transient ones. Captain Maddison became the Master and was re-elected again for the following year. The Lodge again relocated its premises, this time to the Corridor Rooms, which were leased at a rental of £40 per annum of which the Lodge of Honour paid £20, the Royal Cumberland £12 and the Royal Sussex £8. Furniture was provided at a cost of £101 of which the Lodge of Honour paid more than half.

At that time it was customary for the Lodge dinner to be provided at York House on the day following the monthly meeting. However, conditions at the Corridor Rooms were not very satisfactory; all Lodges experiencing continual interruptions from the room below. These trying conditions remained until December 1849 when a move was made to No. 3 Westgate Buildings. Captain Maddison was again elected WM in 1839 and during that year a certain William Long was initiated. It was his son, Col. William Long, who was ultimately to become PGM for Somerset.

In 1840 it was necessary for the WM, still W.Bro Maddison, to write a letter to several members of the Lodge, particularly the Officers, drawing their attention to the necessity of a more regular attendance at Lodge Meetings. This did not produce the desired effect and only five brethren, out of 32 subscribing members, attended the next meeting. A Lodge of Emergency was called for December 21st to ballot for WM and Treasurer. Nine members attended that meeting, Captain Maddison again being elected WM. Only five brethren were present in January 1842 when it was decided to have only three meetings per year and the banquet held on the same day as the meeting. In 1843 the Lodge suffered a most grievous loss in the death of Captain Maddison who, for eighteen years, had been a tower of strength and WM for no less than six of those.

Lodge records show that there were only eleven subscribing members in 1845 but nine of these were present at the Installation Meeting. Because of the small attendance at meetings, offices in the Lodge were often filled by brethren from the Royal Cumberland and Royal Sussex Lodges, the Installation of the WM being performed by the WM of the Royal Cumberland Lodge.

In 1846 W.Bro William Tucker of Bridgwater became a Joining Member. He was Provincial Grand Master for Dorset from 1846 until 1853 when he was removed from office by the Grand Master, the Earl of Zetland, for appearing at the Provincial Grand Lodge in the costume and wearing jewels of what were termed 'high degrees not sanctioned by Grand Lodge.'

1849 saw the move to Westgate Buildings and the following year brought a decided increase in numbers and interest, there being no less than thirteen meetings during that year. Dr. William Falconer became a Joining Member and Bro Charles Vigne was initiated. The following December Bro Vigne was appointed a Warden and in December 1851 became WM. Both of these brethren were responsible for ensuring a higher standard of work in the Lodge. A Lodge of Instruction was proposed, this to meet on Friday preceding the Lodge Meeting, and became the forerunner of the present day rehearsal.

In 1850 a major re-organisation of the working of the Lodge took place. The month of Installation of the WM was changed from January to December as it is today, thus there were two ceremonies that year. Also, up until then the office of Director of Ceremonies was not filled on a regular basis, and even when it was the person filling it seldom appeared on the list of brethren attending the meeting.

In 1853 the Lodge moved back to the Corridor Rooms owing to the inability of the landlord of 3, Westgate Buildings to reserve the room solely for Masonic purposes and other Masonic bodies. W.Bro Falconer was WM that year and the Lodge continued to prosper. On 9th May the Lodge opened at 3.00 pm, when two candidates were Raised. There was an adjournment till 7.00pm when there was an Initiation, followed by a Passing. The minutes state "This lengthened business was admirably performed by the WM"

In 1854 Francis Allen was WM after receiving special dispensation from the M.W Grand Master as he was already Master of the Lodge of Rectitude in Wiltshire. During his year of office W.Bro Capt. Alexander William Adair became a Joining Member and was appointed Junior Warden the following year. He became Provincial Grand Master for Somerset from 1863 to 1868. All his Regalia was presented to the Province of Somerset in May 1968 by his great grandson, who was then Deputy Grand Master, and is now exhibited on the stairs of the Masonic Hall in Bath.

In 1856 the Lodge was temporarily moved back to Westgate Buildings prior to leasing rooms at 42, Milsom Street, where W.Bro Capt. Adair was installed as Master, but was only able to attend one meeting owing to Regimental duties. In November of that year a special Dispensation was obtained to confer all three degrees on a Brother in one evening. This was another short lived change of address as in 1858, it became necessary once again to look for a fresh meeting place as the Milsom Street Rooms were required for a club.

On 27th November 1860 the Lodge suffered a great loss when the R.W PGM Col. Charles Kemeys Kemeys Tynte died. He had been a Founder Member and great supporter for 35 years.

By 1863 the Lodge was on the move again and had to return to the Corridor Rooms and became tenants of the Royal Cumberland Lodge. Owing to diminishing numbers, it was again proposed that the Warrant should be returned, but this proposal was adjourned "sine die". In December of 1863, the Lodge's number was changed to 379, the number it has retained to this day.

Conditions at the Corridor Rooms soon became as bad as ever and in 1864 a Committee of all three Lodges was set up to seek new accommodation. After considering various proposals it was agreed to obtain possession of a Roman Catholic Church and two dwelling houses in Old Orchard Street. The undertaking was vested in the hands of the Royal Sussex, the other Lodges becoming tenants. The Lodge of Honour paid an annual rent of £6.

From 1866 onwards and for some 30 years the Lodge passed through a chequered existence, sometimes reviving, sometimes failing, and constantly dependent on sister Lodges for assistance in the working. At least during that time the Lodge was free from worries of accommodation.

1875 marked the fiftieth anniversary of the constitution of the Lodge and finishes the most interesting period of its history, but it heralded yet another particularly difficult period. By 1878/9 the question of disbandment was uppermost in the mind of the Lodge. Three meetings could not be held because of lack of a quorum.

"Was it lawful to have no meetings and no election to office for one year, but pay regular dues to Grand and Provincial Lodge?" To this question the PGM gave a very definite "No". Regular meetings must be held and officers elected. W.Bro Bartrum resigned and recommended disbandment of the Lodge. However, a special meeting was called and the brethren pledged themselves to use their best endeavours to improve the working of the Lodge and increase its membership. This time it did appear to have some effect as in February 1880, four candidates were initiated at once, in March five Passed and the following month the five were Raised. An interesting note appears at the foot of a summons in 1882. "It is particularly wished that you will ask your Masonic friends to come and assist."

Within three years however things were as bad as ever, the membership having fallen to fourteen of whom more than half lived away from Bath. The bye-laws were altered to only two meetings per year, and in December 1885 the Lodge moved out of the Masonic Hall, being unable to pay the rent, and took up residence in smaller premises at 4 Church Street, Abbey Green, which the Secretary had arranged for them to occupy free of charge.

By a stroke of good fortune, in November 1886, W.Bro the Rev. J.A. Lloyd, Past Provincial Grand Chaplain of Oxfordshire and Wiltshire became a Joining Member and was elected Master the same evening. He promptly proposed four other clerics as Joining Members, another two joining shortly afterwards and in 1887, parsons occupied the chairs of IPM, SW, JW, Chaplain., DC, and JD. W.Bro Lloyd was appointed Grand Chaplain of England in 1888. By this time the premises at Abbey Green were too small and a move was made to Hetling House. This,

however, was quite unsuitable, (was it because it was also used as an Oddfellows Hall?), and a return was made to the Masonic Hall where it has been housed ever since.

On 14th April 1903 Dr. Leonard Fuller was passed to the second degree and raised on the 11th May 1903. It was not until four years later, in May, when he was Junior Warden, that Grand Lodge discovered that 28 clear days had not elapsed between passing and raising. Grand Lodge therefore insisted that he should be re-obligated, which was done at a Lodge of Emergency on 13th May 1907! He went on to become WM in 1908 and again in 1922 and 1928 and was for many years DC of the Lodge. In 1927 he missed a meeting because of the death of his wife. This was the first Lodge meeting he had missed since his initiation in March 1903. W.Bro Leonard Fuller went on to present several items of exquisitely carved furniture to the Lodge which "adds much to its dignity". A chair for the Master, a replica of that belonging to the Royal York Lodge which had been sold to Barnstaple, two chairs for the Wardens and three mahogany pedestals for the candlesticks.

During the First World War years little work was done, the office of WM being invariably filled by a Past Master. Naturally when the War was over the Lodge became more active, five brethren being initiated in 1919. As they were all desirous of being passed to the second degree, a special dispensation was obtained from the PGM (Col. Long, to confer the degree on any four of them providing the ceremony was performed twice and not more than two candidates passed at once.

The period between the wars saw many distinguished Masons rise through the ranks of the Lodge, notably Bro George Travers Biggs and Bro Harold L. Petavel, both of whom held the office of Provincial Grand Secretary for many years.

Following the outbreak of War in 1939 the Lodge Committee decided to carry on normal activities in the Lodge as far as possible except that the refreshment side would be considerably curtailed, but as there were no Bath candidates during 1940 the Lodge was pleased to assist other Lodges who had made appeals for help.

*The Master's Chair
presented by W. Bro Leonard Fuller
is an exact replica of the original
owned by Royal Cumberland Lodge
in the early 19th Century*

In December 1940 the PGM recommended that Warrants should be stored in a Bank or other safe deposit using a copy when necessary. In January 1941 it was reported that a photographic copy, endorsed by the PGM, had been placed in the frame in the Lodge and the original stored in the care of W.Bro Pictor of the Royal Sussex Lodge in the underground vaults of Bristol University, the cost borne by the Lodge.

W.Bro Leonard Fuller attended Lodge in December 1941 and saw his greatest ambition in life fulfilled when his son Herbert was installed in the Chair of King Solomon. Less than three weeks later W.Bro Leonard died. Herbert Fuller went on to give long and loyal service to the Lodge and to Masonry in general. He was appointed Provincial Grand Mark Master for Somerset in 1955, a post he was to hold until his death. This was an office his father had held from 1939 until his death in 1942, believed to be a unique occurrence. W.Bro Herbert Fuller was again WM of this Lodge in 1965, dying one day after his successor had been installed.

The 1944 meetings were largely devoted to conferring the three degrees on Cpl. Walter Pearson of the US Army. This was done at the request of a Lodge in the Province of Iowa, but when he subsequently asked for permission to become a Joining Member of the Lodge the request was refused. Apparently the Grand Lodge of Iowa did not permit its members to join any Lodge under another constitution!

May 1945 saw the end of hostilities in Europe and at the meeting that month, after an address by the Secretary, the WM, W.Bro Rev. C. Hereford Simmons, conducted a short service of thanksgiving. The following month a Thanksgiving Service for Freemasons was held in Ascension Church, Bath and a dispensation was given by the PGM for regalia to be worn inside, but not outside, the Church.

The end of 1949 saw the Lodge on the move again, albeit only for three meetings, which were held at Keynsham while war damage to the Bath Masonic Hall was repaired.

The 1950s and 60s saw a period of stability and consolidation, membership numbers remaining roughly constant at around 60, with a goodly number of eminent Masons passing through the ranks. W.Bro R.A.C. Forrester in 1967 was appointed DPGM for Wiltshire and only eighteen months later became Provincial Grand Master, and W.Bro R.A.I. Dodsworth who became Deputy Provincial Grand Mark Master.

In 1971 and 1972 the Lodge was fortunate in having two Joining Members who were also members of Grand Lodge and both gave papers when no candidate was available. In April 1971 W.Bro Dr. Geraint White-Phillips gave a lecture on "Our Ceremonies, Customs and Masonry in General". The following April W.Bro Dr. Geoffrey W.R. Bishop gave a paper on "The Past Master's Jewel".

1974 was an important year for two brethren, both celebrating 50 years in Masonry - W.Bro E.T. Symonds, (WM in 1934), and W.Bro W.A.H. Denne, (WM in 1959). Both received congratulatory telegrams from the PGM

A Special Dispensation was granted to hold the meeting on Saturday 8th March 1975 to celebrate the 150th Anniversary of the Lodge's formation. A Thanksgiving Service was held in St. John's Hospital Chapel conducted by Bro Rev. D.W. Harvey, Chaplain, and the address was given by W.Bro Rev. B.W.J. Turnock, a Past Chaplain, with Bro A. Mayland as organist. The lessons were read by the WM, W.Bro L.A. Scott-White, and the Provincial Grand Master. After tea the Lodge was opened but no ceremony was performed. Instead W.Bro. R.F. Sanders, IPM, gave a paper on the History of the Lodge.

There has always been a close liaison with the other Craft Lodges in Bath - probably never stronger than in the 1970s as shown by the joint fund-raising and social events, perhaps most notably the setting up of a block of flats for aged Freemasons and their widows. This venture was opened by Princess Barbara of Yugoslavia in April 1977 and made possible by the generosity of W.Bro Royston Tucker of the Royal Albert Edward Lodge. 1977 onwards was a busy period with regular ceremonies taking place, but unfortunately punctuated by the deaths of five respected and well loved brethren before the turn of the decade; W.Bro E. Lewton-Brain, LGR was initiated in January 1909 and became a Joining Member of the Lodge in 1959 and was the most senior veteran in the Province when he died in 1978 aged 95.

As would be expected Charity Appeals have received great support over the years, for example the Restoration of Wells Cathedral, (twice), Restoration of Bath Abbey, (three times), and more recently the Holiday Home for the Disabled in Combe Down, the Royal United Hospital appeal, Dorothy House Foundation as well as the Redevelopment Fund for the Royal Masonic Hospital, the Samaritan Fund and the setting up there of a four bedded ward to be designated "The Somerset Ward".

In writing a history of a Lodge, especially one as abridged as this one, it is not possible to include every single Brother making up the membership. Therefore only a small percentage of those brethren who have already made their mark are included. Younger brethren are already making their influence felt, and when the next chapter comes to be written they will have achieved the same degree of eminence as those mentioned here.

Lodge of Science No. 437

Meets at The Masonic Hall, Church Street, Wincanton

Warrant dated 13th August 1836

The Lodge of Science dates from 1836, and although we can only speculate, it is likely that around this time a number of brethren were probably fed up with travelling to the nearest Lodge and came up with the idea of forming a Lodge in Bourton. It is situated on the main (A303) road to London. It boasted a fine hostelry called the Red Lion Inn which was a large coaching Inn. The petitioners applied to the Province of Dorset to form the Lodge and on the 13th August 1836 the new Lodge called Lodge of Science No. 640 came into being at Bourton, meeting at The Red Lion.

There was presumably a Consecration, however, we only have the Warrant to substantiate that claim! There is no doubt that the Lodge Warrant is genuine and issued by Grand Lodge on the 13th August 1836. The Warrant states that the first Worshipful Master was a Richard Tucker, although there is no record of that first meeting. In fact the first minutes are not recorded until November 10th 1836 at Bourton and we have to assume at the Red Lion as the location is not recorded. This most assuredly is not a Consecration meeting as it clearly records an initiation, the Worshipful Master being Bro R. Tucker.

However, from that date forward every meeting is recorded or at least every meeting we know of. The meetings are haphazard and not at all regular, and the minutes are generally speaking very brief and to the point., this original laissez faire attitude causing, over a period of later years, a number of problems; even 100 years later. This first had an effect when, regretfully, probably during 1845 one of the Founders, W.Bro Tucker, died, and his family offered to the Lodge seven silver jewels to purchase.

At a meeting on March 19th 1846 there was a proposition "that a Committee of five brethren be appointed to make out and examine into the late WM's account, and that three be a quorum to act, and that they be at liberty to ask for such papers as are required of the representatives of the late Bro R. Tucker." This was carried unanimously.

There had been no hint of a problem in earlier minutes but it appears that the offer of the seven silver jewels had precipitated this enquiry. There is no record in the minutes of this matter ever being resolved, however, at the meeting of July 5th 1849 the WM informed the Lodge that a Mrs Woodgate, a daughter of Bro R. Tucker WM, had laid a claim to the Lodge jewels. It was resolved "That the Secretary write to Mrs Woodgate and explain to her that the Lodge Furniture and Jewels which belonged to the late WM Bro R. Tucker were given up by him to the Lodge in liquidation of the balance due from

Bro R. Tucker to the Lodge on the Treasurer's account." Further mention is made in respect of the jewels and furniture at a meeting in October 1849 but does not clarify the matter any further. Quite how he could give them up when the investigation commenced after his death cannot be resolved!

Unfortunately, as far as can be ascertained, the Lodge was not well run and was said to have 'imperfect minutes.' It also failed to make yearly returns to Dorset Province. Quite obviously a very dim view was taken of this by the Provincial Grand Master of Dorset. This matter, amongst others, was subject of investigation and report by the Provincial Secretary for Dorset 1867. It is very fortunate that the Lodge of Science at that time had just installed a Bro Atwell as Worshipful Master.

On Thursday 18th July 1867 a meeting was held which confirmed the new byelaws of the Lodge, however, at the same meeting the WM, Bro Atwell, regretted that he had to read a letter sent by the Provincial Grand Secretary to the Provincial Grand Master. There had been no indication of any Provincial, let alone Grand Lodge, involvement in any previous minutes but the letter makes clear that communications had taken place. The letter is long so its contents have been condensed:

Dorchester 27th June 1867: "I have the honour to report that the Lodge of Science 437 Bourton having laid a copy of its minutes before the Grand Secretary, he found some great irregularities:
First: Bro Cox having been elected Master then and there without any confirmation of minutes approved his Wardens.
Second: At an Emergency Lodge six brethren were proposed, balloted and elected.
Third: At an emergency Lodge minutes were read and confirmed.
Fourth: The bye Laws were disregarded as to the payment of joining fees and another Master

was elected.
Fifth: The Master Elect seems to have been installed by two persons one never having been himself installed."
The letter was signed by the Provincial Grand Secretary.

The PGS had been in touch with the WM who had to explain these irregularities and the Master had travelled to Dorchester to try and resolve the difficulties. Following that meeting and assurances given by Bro Atwell, Provincial Grand Lodge was persuaded that he could revive the Lodge's position. (It is fair to say that these complaints had extended over many previous years)

The PGS was able to satisfy himself with regard to the complaints that: "...the irregularities arose from the obscure and inaccurate minutes, neglecting to insert such particulars as should have appeared and also probably to some degree from over-anxiety to secure the Lodge from the inert shape into which it was fast sinking"

There is no doubt that with the steadying hand and dedication of W.Bro Atwell the Lodge of Science was revived, otherwise it could have sunk without trace! Sadly difficulties continued to occur, although this time with two of the brethren.

At a meeting on the 13th February 1873 Bro Atwell proposed with Bro Shackleton seconding 'That a committee be appointed to consider as to the brethren who have left the town and holding funds of the Lodge to write to the Grand Secretary for advice in the matter and report at the next Lodge' At the next Lodge it is merely reported that 'The Committee appointed to enquire into the late Treasurer and Secretary presented their report' So we have now identified the alleged culprits! However, at the meeting on the 10th April 1873 the full report is given and unanimously adopted by those present. It states:

'To enquire into the Lodge funds received and not paid over by the late Treasurer and Secretary and also to consider what steps should be taken in enquiring into charges of unmasonic conduct of the said members of the Lodge.

Firstly; as to the two members jointly. For a considerable time, after the meetings of the Lodge, these members were in the habit of going to an Inn and conducting themselves in such a manner as to bring disrepute in Masonry and acting altogether in direct opposition to the Ancient Charges and solemn obligations entered into by them.

Secondly; as regards the Treasurer: It appears that a sum of £38 or thereabouts has been appropriated for his own use and retained by him. That he was summarily dismissed from his situation as cashier at Messrs. Hartleys Bank has left the town and is reported to have left England.

W.Bro Atwell

Thirdly; as regards the Secretary: In October last he received from the members of this Lodge the sum of 30/- for quarterages and has not handed the amount over or in any way accounted for the same he being also 10/- in arrears in January last. That in his business transactions as an auctioneer it is charged against him that he has been employed to dispose of property for persons and has not handed over the proceeds of such sale, but used it for other purposes and also that he has given cheques in payment of sale and other matters after he knew that his account at the Bank had been closed.

For these causes the brethren have refused to meet him in Lodge and considered his conduct to be inconsistent with the principles of Masonry and tend to bring our noble order into disrepute." (Quite an understatement!)

A letter was eventually written to this Brother requesting him to pay all monies owed by him to the Lodge including a further 37/6d for fifteen chairs sold by him belonging to the Lodge! Whether or not any of the missing money was ever recovered is not recorded.

Of course all of this missing money would clearly have had a profound effect on the finances of a small Lodge and indeed at the Lodge following they have to 'Consider the desirability of raising funds to clear the Lodge of its financial difficulties' This was eventually managed by the members paying their dues in advance! This then entered into the by-laws, and as a consequence of that action members of 437 to this day pay in advance!

The original Warrant number was 640, and it has often been speculated upon by members and visitors alike as to how the number changed. The most popular theory that it changed when the Lodge moved to Wincanton in 1869 is a myth. The reason for the change is because Grand Lodge carried out a renumbering process. In Lane's History of Freemasonry the year of number change is 1863, and dates taken from the Lodge Minute Book show that the last meeting under the original Lodge number 640 is February 2nd 1864. In fact the next meeting took place over twelve months later on September 14th 1865, an emergency meeting when 'Bro Oliver Maggs was appointed to the office of WM.' Although there is no mention of any change of the Lodge number this was the first meeting held and recorded as Lodge of Science 437.

For some time membership applications had been declining from Dorset applicants, whilst at the same time a greater number of applicants were coming from the Wincanton area. This state of affairs was considered unsatisfactory by the ever-growing numbers from Wincanton who petitioned to have the Lodge removed from the Province of Dorset and relocated in the Province of Somerset.

The first of those events occurred on the evening of Monday 19th July 1869 at an Emergency Lodge in the form of a notice of proposition. Bro Atwell proposed and Bro Oborn seconded 'That in consequence of there being only one subscribing member of this Lodge now residing in Dorset and for the greater convenience of the rest of the brethren who chiefly reside in the town of Wincanton in the Province of Somerset an application be made to the PGM of Dorset and also to the PGM of Somerset for their consent to remove the Lodge to Wincanton.'

At the next Lodge on the 12th August 1869 the proposition was debated and clearly some correspondence had already taken place because the date for removal to Wincanton was set for the 1st October that year. However by the meeting of the 9th September the date had changed to November, a date to be

fixed. The most important information being that the Lodge would be held in The National School Rooms, North Street, Wincanton. The final debate on this matter was held on the 23rd September when the future location of 437 was finally sealed. The last meeting of Lodge of Science 437 in Dorset was held on the 14th October 1869 there was no Lodge in the November. Finally on Friday 17th December 1869 the first meeting was held at the National School Rooms and a letter of authorisation for the removal of the Lodge to Somerset was read!

The Dedication of the new premises took place on the 13th January 1870. This month is not without significance as it is also Installation Night and just to round things off there was an Initiation! The Deputy Provincial Grand Master for Somerset, Bro Bridges, accompanied by other Provincial Grand Lodge Officers, was in attendance. The DPGM conducted the Ceremonies of Dedication, Installation and Initiation!

The Lodge continued to meet at the National School Rooms until July 1871, when due to a change of circumstances at the School the Lodge had to move, initially to the Town Hall

The desk containing the writing test given to the Initiate

where it remained until June 1872. It was at this time that the Lodge had the opportunity to move into its present premises. At the time a Mr. R.R. Hutchings owned them. (He joined the Lodge in 1874 and subsequently became Worshipful Master). The premises were then known as the 'Foresters Hall'. The Foresters held their meetings on the ground floor whilst the Lodge met upstairs, which is approached by way of a stone winding stairway. The original Temple exists today and continues to be used.

This arrangement continued until 1931 when the Lodge was able to purchase the whole property for £200-0s-0d, and the premises were renamed 'The Masonic Hall'. The premises date from the late 18th century and little is known of its original intended use. However, during the Napoleonic Wars the building was used as a silk factory. Many Napoleonic Officer Prisoners of War were held in Wincanton and billeted locally.

As a matter of related interest some of the Napoleonic prisoners formed themselves into a French Lodge in 1806 which lasted until 1810 or thereabouts. They were known as the 'De La Paix Desiree'. The location of their Lodge has been lost in the mists of time; it is highly unlikely its meetings were held in 437 Lodge premises. There are two artefacts from the French Lodge still on display. One is a Certificate issued by that Lodge and the other which is attributed to them is a small spring loaded table which would be used during the First Degree Ceremony. The artist's work is somewhat gruesome should you ever visit and lift the table top! This table was loaned to the Province of Bristol to copy following the destruction of their Lodge premises (including a similar table) by enemy action in February 1942.

The Volume of the Sacred Law, which is still in regular use, was presented to the Lodge by the Provincial Grand Master of Dorset, William Tucker (1846-1853). He was apparently a man of great contradictions, and as such is worthy of mention. He is also of further interest because he was originally a Somerset Mason having been initiated into the Lodge of Unanimity and Sincerity 327 (renumbered 261). He was by all accounts a highly accomplished Mason with a very clear understanding of Masonry's purpose.

He was however very outspoken and tended to discuss matters at Lodges such as religion when he propounded that all religions and peoples should be included (in Masonry) which was misconstrued by some members. Sadly in 1853 he appeared at Provincial Grand Lodge in Dorset in his Craft regalia but also in the full robes of a Sovereign Grand Inspector General of the 33rd Degree, Ancient and Accepted Rite. This was obviously not very well received! As a result he regrettably bears the distinction of being the only Provincial Grand Master to have his Patent cancelled. He died only two years later in 1855.

On the 11th December 1884 a most important presentation was made to the Lodge by the Master, Bro W.N. Good, the Lodge Banner. The minutes state that it was a new banner. It is possible that this Banner originally came from another Lodge as there is an imbalance in the wording. On the 8th January 1891 a vote of thanks was made to Mrs W.N. Good for repainting and renovating the banner

The Lodge has a very unusual Director of Ceremonies' Baton, which may be unique. It was presented to the Lodge on the 10th October 1940 by W.Bro Wilson PPGSW in memory of W.Bro W.P. Hayter, PPGDC and previously a DC of the Lodge for many years. The Baton was constructed by Bro R.W. Domoney of Horsa Lodge 2208, Bournemouth, in the Province of Hampshire and the Isle of Wight. The first Lodge DC to use the baton was W.Bro H.E. Dyke. It is interesting to note that his name & Lodge number are inscribed upon the Baton. On the 9th October 1941 W.Bro Wilson gave an explanation on the symbolism of the baton. This beautiful explanation of its symbolism and meanings has only been given twice since that date.

Many of the Worshipful Masters had their portraits taken when they achieved the Chair of the Lodge. This commenced in the late 1800s and continued to be taken until about 1947. The earliest portrait is that of W.Bro Atwell who was Master in 1867. It is particularly pleasing

to have his photograph among the collection because 437 was turned around under his Mastership. Although there are many missing photographs they remain an important link with the past as are the Lodge artefacts. This practice was reintroduced a few years ago.

In 1936 the Lodge became a Centenary Lodge. This was not without its complications as there was great difficulty at that time sorting out exactly when the Lodge was founded. This was due in no small part to the 'imperfect minutes' previously mentioned. The Master for the year 1936 was Bro H.E. Dyke. As you will recall the Lodge Warrant is dated 13th August 1836 and that was the month in which the Centenary was celebrated by the Lodge. A special Lodge and a Church Service were held.

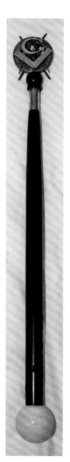 

The unique Director of Ceremonies Baton

However, it was some months later that the Centenary Warrant was applied for, and it was only then, when the minute books of 1836 were checked by Grand Lodge, that a discrepancies appeared. There were no Consecration minutes, no record anywhere, not even within the Provincial Grand Lodge of Dorset was any record to be found! In the event Grand Lodge accepted the evidence put forward, but would not accept 13th August as the date, and used 10th November 1836 instead, the date of the first recorded minutes which is why that date appears on the Centenary Warrant. In 1986 the Lodge celebrated its 150th Anniversary on the 13th August with a Church Service followed by a celebratory tea at the Lodge which echoed the 100 year celebrations.

Two Lodge brethren are particularly worthy of historical mention for the important parts they have played in the history of Freemasonry in the Province of Somerset.

The first is The Venerable Archdeacon Walter Farrer MA. He was initiated into the Lodge on 12th October 1897, passed on the 11th November and raised on the 9th December of the same year. He was elected Worshipful Master in 1906. Also in the year 1906-7 he was promoted to Provincial Grand Chaplain. He was eventually appointed Grand Chaplain of England in 1919. On the 21st October 1926 he was installed as Provincial Grand Master for Somerset until his sudden death in 1934. His regalia, which he bequeathed to the Lodge is proudly displayed..

The second came from the Dyke family, well known within Freemasonry during the middle of the 20th Century. Herbert Dyke was initiated on 8th February 1923, passed on the 8th March and raised on 13th September of the same year.

He became Worshipful Master in 1936, the same year that Provincial Grand Lodge was held in the old cinema at Wincanton and as has already be mentioned it was the Lodge Centenary year. He was promoted to Past Provincial Grand Registrar in 1947. In 1958 he was promoted to Assistant Provincial Grand Master and in 1973 to Deputy Provincial Grand Master.

Display of the Regalia of The Ven. Archdeacon Walter Farrer

Benevolent Lodge No. 446

Meets at the Masonic Hall, West Cloister, Wells

Warrant dated 1837

On 4th July 1785 the Lodge of Unanimity 473 held its first meeting at the Swan Hotel, Sadler Street, Wells. Seven members were present, three of whom were initiated. Unfortunately the Lodge had ceased to exist by the year 1809. This is the first record of any Lodge in Wells.

On 2nd March 1837 the Swan Lodge of Benevolence 653 came into existence, following a petition signed by nine brethren, one of whom, Thomas Lax, became the first Master, and on 6th April 1837 the Lodge held its first meeting at the Swan Hotel, Wells. A year later it transferred to the City Council Chambers where it remained for 54 years, changing its name firstly to the Lodge of Benevolence and finally to Benevolent Lodge. This name was sanctioned by United Grand Lodge in 1842 and its number became 446 in the general renumbering in 1863.

October, 1848, saw a Provincial Grand Lodge meeting, the PGM having taken possession of the Lodge, all paraded in full regalia to Wells Cathedral. Also in 1848 Bro Pope produced a petition for a warrant of constitution for a Lodge in Glastonbury called Pilgrims Lodge No. 1074, later 772.

In 1876 Avalon Chapter 446 was formed and in 1892 both Lodge and Chapter moved to the Vicars' Hall, Wells Cathedral, where they remained until 1917. They then transferred downstairs to No.10 Cathedral Green.

The move to the Vicars' Hall commenced a cordial relationship with Wells Cathedral which continues to this day. Whilst no longer meeting in Vicars' Hall, happily it is still used for the Festive board, giving visiting brethren a

unique opportunity to dine in such magnificent historical surroundings.

In the early 1990s the Cathedral asked if they could use the Lodge Room at 10 Cathedral Green for other purposes, and following negotiations the Lodge moved to the West Cloisters, which date from 1348, although not completed until about 1480

In 1996 the two Lodges Mendip and Benevolent moved to the West Cloisters. Whilst a little smaller than No.10 it is a superb hall and the Lodge is very appreciative of the privilege of meeting in the Cathedral.

At that time Sir Thomas de Cheddre Lodge moved to the Masonic Hall, Wedmore, and in 1999 Mendip Lodge moved to Shepton Mallet Masonic Hall.

In 1884 annual Fraternal visits were arranged with the Lodge of Love and Honour 285 and Pilgrims Lodge 772, which still continue. In 1922 Mendip Lodge 781 was formed, and in 1986 the daughter Lodge of Benevolent was created and named Sir Thomas de Cheddre 9188.

The original Lodge banner was presented in 1880. This did sterling service for over 100 years, but its condition necessitated retirement, and it is now stored in a display case. The Lodge now has a magnificent replacement banner provided by the brethren. Like many old lodges Benevolent Lodge has a number of interesting artefacts in its possession. Probably the oldest is a silver trowel presented to the lapsed Unanimity Lodge by a visiting Bro Jas. Bacon. It dates to the period 1785-1792.

It is interesting to note that at this time an Initiate wore a trowel attached to a collar during the hours of refreshment. It was also referred to in the ritual "The Trowel teaches us that nothing can be united without cement."

Many of the Lodge jewels were made by John Acklam, and bear a hallmark showing they were made in 1836. John Acklam was apprenticed

to the greatest Masonic jewel maker, Thomas Harper, and continued the business following Harper's death.

The Lodge tracing boards were presented to the Lodge in 1859, and in 2007 professionally restored to their former glory and rededicated by the Provincial team.

One of the Lodge's foremost members was Colonel Alfred Thrale Perkins. He was Master of the Benevolent Lodge on four occasions; 1875, 1876, 1878 and 1915, and presented the Lodge with a number of items, including a collecting box in 1875 which is still used at every festive board for small coins and opened annually, when the contents are given to a charity of the Master's choice

His Masonic career embraced both Somerset and Monmouthshire, and he served as Deputy Provincial Grand Master of Somerset from 1909 to 1926. On his death in 1934 his sister presented his many jewels to the Lodge, which have been cased and displayed in the Lodge Room. These include his Founder's and Past Master's jewels of the Somerset Master's Lodge, of which he was the Founding Master. Unfortunately these are now framed behind glass and permanently fixed to the wall, and could not therefore be photographed to a standard high enough for reproduction here.

Col. Alfred Thrale Perkins

Distinguished brethren of more recent years include V.W.Bro V.R. Harding who served as APGM of Somerset from 1990 to 1999, and then Deputy PGM until 2001, and currently W.Bro Chris Shrapnel has edited the Provincial year book and been involved in the development and introduction of the UGLE Adelphi computerised record system.

But undoubtedly one of the most significant members of Benevolent Lodge was the Rt Rev. George Wyndham Kennion, Bishop of Bath and Wells, Past Grand Chaplain and Provincial Grand Chaplain for Somerset.

Little is known about his Masonic Career. Indeed, the Masonic Library in London has only the barest information, but records show that Bishop Kennion joined Benevolent Lodge 446 in Wells on 7th April 1897 and resigned on 28th September 1921. Unfortunately neither

the register nor the annual returns from which it would have been compiled tell us from which Lodge he joined; the index card merely confirms his Past Rank appointment as Grand Chaplain in 1897.

The files also contain a copy of his obituary from The Times, 20th May 1922. It is very informative about his career and character; he was, apparently, the first English Bishop to become a cyclist, but it says nothing about his Freemasonry. His obituary in the Masonic press is also not forthcoming about his Masonic career.

Bishop Kennion
Reproduced by courtesy of the State Library of South Australia

George Wyndham Kennion was the son of George Kennion, M.D. and Catherine, daughter of J.F. Fordyce. He was born at Harrogate, England, on 5th September 1845 and educated at Eton College and Oriel College, Oxford University, where he graduated B.A. in 1867 and M.A. in 1871. He was ordained deacon in 1869 and priest in 1870. He was an inspector of schools 1871-3, vicar of St Paul's, Hull, in 1873, and of All Saints, Bradford, in 1876.

In 1882 he was chosen by Archbishop Tait to be the second bishop of Adelaide and was consecrated in Westminster Abbey on 30th November 1882. On 5th December he married Henrietta, daughter of Sir Charles Dalrymple Fergusson.

Kennion arrived in South Australia early in 1883, and soon realized that more churches were needed in the rapidly-growing suburbs of Adelaide and in outlying country districts. He set to work to fill this need and personally visited all the centres in the colony. During his twelve years in the Diocese many churches were built, considerable progress was made in the building of the cathedral, and the number of clergy increased from 50 to 75.

In 1894 Archibald Primrose, 5th Earl of Rosebery, called him to the Bishopric of Bath and Wells. There he found no lack of work and ruled the diocese with tact and wisdom. He had some difficulties with the extreme high church movement, but although he allowed much liberty there were limits he would not allow to be passed.

He had in early life been associated with the evangelicals, but became a moderate high churchman. He did not take a leading part in ecclesiastical affairs, but was an excellent chairman of the English committee on faith and order. He was lecturer in pastoral theology at Cambridge University in 1899, and Ramsden preacher in 1901. He suffered a serious illness at the end of 1917 and resigned his see in August 1919. He died at Ayr on 19th May 1922.

Benevolent Lodge was awarded a Centenary jewel in 1937, and the Certificate framed and mounted in the Lodge room. In recent years Initiates have had this drawn to their attention as the Warrant of the Lodge. Fortunately a sharp eyed Brother noticed and now the Warrant of 1837 is proudly pointed out.

As in all lodges the Festive Board is an important part of the Master's Installation, and a menu and summons recently found requested attendance at "Refreshment after Labour" at a cost of six shillings and six pence (33p) for a six course meal, and evening dress required. This Worshipful Master presented the Wardens' pedestals to the Lodge, which have recently been beautifully restored.

In recent years retiring Past Masters have made a presentation to the Lodge, and most notably a Master's gavel set made from timber from HMS Victory together with a certificate of authenticity, which has been framed and displayed.

After 170 years Benevolent Lodge continues to thrive and provide a welcoming fraternal life in beautiful surroundings in England's loveliest city.

George Wyndham Kennion
Commemorative plaque in Wells Cathedral

Pilgrims Lodge No. 772

Meets at the Masonic Hall, Glastonbury

Warrant dated 1859

It is believed that the name 'Pilgrims Lodge' was chosen out of recognition that over the years Glastonbury had attracted many pilgrims to see the Abbey ruins and to visit other holy sites around the area, including the Tor and Weary All Hill.

The Pilgrims Lodge 772 was consecrated on 26th July 1859 with Dr. Chas. Pope, PPGSW, as its first Master. Prior to the Consecration a letter was sent to the various local lodges in the Province inviting them to attend. This generated so much interest that a special excursion train was necessary, which called at all the principal railway stations between Bristol and Taunton from Yeovil. To this day copy of this letter remains posted into the fly leaf of the VSL in the Lodge.

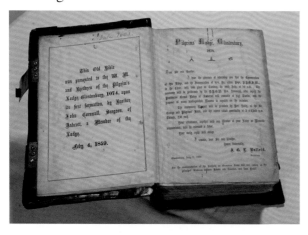

The letter dated 7th July 1859 which was sent to the various local Lodges in the Province inviting them to attend the Consecration of the Pilgrim Lodge is pasted into the fly leaf of the VSL in the Lodge.

After such a promising start it comes as something of a mystery as to why, in a relatively short space of time, acrimony amongst some of the brethren caused the Lodge to enter a period of decline, with low attendances at meetings. However, certain senior members took steps to rectify matters, and by 1864 the Lodge was again in good heart, mainly due to their collective efforts, and in particular, W.Bro Captain Bridges DPGM, PGSW.

In appreciation of this help and assistance Captain Bridges was presented with an ornate snuff box made from the wood from the roof of St Cuthbert's Church, Wells. It was presented to Bro Bridges by W.Bro C Pope of Pilgrims Lodge in May 1864. There is a plaque on the box which reads: "Originally presented to Bro Capt. Bridges DPGM PGSW in token of his zealousness in resurrecting the Pilgrims Lodge."

In March 1916 the snuff box was presented to Pilgrims Lodge by W.Bro Lt. Col. G.H.N. Bridges, Provincial Grand Deacon for Somerset, a Senior Past Master of the Lodge and nephew of the original recipient.

The Breeches Bible is now used only at the Installation Ceremony and other special occasions

An ornate tobacco box and charity box, also made from wood from the roof of St Cuthbert's Church, presented to Pilgrims Lodge in the year 1875 by W.Bro C Pope.

Perhaps the most treasured possession of the Lodge is a Breeches Bible which was presented to the brethren of the Lodge by Bro John Cornwall on its formation. Bro Cornwall was a surgeon of Ashcott, and later a member of the Lodge. He presented the Bible to the Formation Committee on 4th Feb 1859.

Pilgrims Lodge enjoys a healthy and happy relationship with other local Lodges, and it is no coincidence that the Lodge held its Festive Board at the George & Pilgrims Inn, from where visitors left not only replete with festive fare, but a little bemused by the local dialect In 1964 the first daughter Lodge of Pilgrims Lodge was formed, St Dunstan's 7973, which adopted this Saint to appear on its Banner.

Parrett and Axe Lodge No. 814

Meets at the Masonic Hall, South Street, Crewkerne

Warrant dated 1860

Prior to attempting to give an account of the history of the Parrett & Axe Lodge it is worth noting the earlier association of Masonry in Crewkerne

The Registers of Grand Lodge show that on 13th August 1807, six years before the formation of the United Grand Lodge, a warrant was issued to the Scientific Lodge No. 203 to meet at the George Hotel Inn in Crewkerne. This had been the name and number of a Lodge meeting at Shadwell-on-Thames constituted in 1766, but had ceased to exist, and the transfer of the name and number to a new Lodge was then a common practice. This number was changed to 254 in 1813, presumably on the compiling of the Register of United Grand Lodge

The first meeting of this Lodge was held on 10th September 1807, with six founder members and four initiates. The Lodge lapsed in 1827, but not without leaving tangible evidence of its existence, as can be seen today in a photograph of the Worshipful Master and his Wardens' chairs now on display in the Parrett & Axe Lodge room.

The Banner is believed to be the original one as a reference is made to it in the minutes of recent years.

On the 8th March 1810 a warrant was granted for the establishment in Martock of the Lodge of Brotherly Love with the number 617. The founders of this Lodge were all members of the Scientific Lodge, who at that time were still meeting in Crewkerne.

The original Parrett and Axe Banner

In July 1859, by which time the Lodge of Brotherly Love had transferred to Yeovil, a number of the brethren signed a petition asking that a Lodge under the name of Parrett & Axe might be located in Crewkerne, and the petition carried the recommendation of that Lodge, which had then been renumbered 412.

It seems that Grand Lodge at first raised some objections, the nature of which is not now known, but the continued efforts of the petitioners were successful, and a Warrant was issued exactly one year later for the formation of a Lodge under the title as proposed with the number 1116, and its consecration duly followed on 10th July 1860. Subsequently, in July 1863 the number was changed to the present number 814.

The first accommodation of the Lodge was at the George Hotel Inn as stated on the Warrant, where the Lodge continued to meet until 1890, when according to Lodge returns now at the County Records Office meetings were held at the Town Hall. This accommodation may have become a part of the Victoria Hall, which was first mentioned in 1899 and again in August 1918 when the lease was renewed. The move to the present premises was made in 1933, the Dedication Ceremony taking place on 19th December.

The most notable article of Lodge furniture is the hinged set of Tracing Boards which are quite unusual in both design and construction. They include the emblem of the Beehive which was discontinued around 1815, so it is likely that they were painted earlier and may have previously belonged to the Scientific Lodge as they bear the date 1809. The Lodge is fortunate in possessing the minutes from the date of its inception and whilst their perusal shows no incidents of great magnitude it is worth mentioning that meetings of Provincial Grand Lodge were held at Crewkerne on 16th May 1885 and 1st May 1924.

The first Master was the Rev R.J.F. Thomas. He was then Vicar of St Johns Parish in Yeovil, Grand Chaplain of England and Chaplain of the Lodge of Brotherly Love and was awarded the rank of Provincial Grand Chaplain in 1860. A portrait of him now hangs in the Lodge Room. The Volume of the Sacred Law which is used at all Lodge meetings was a gift from him.

When not in use, the Tracing Boards are folded away to reveal the original Lodge Number 1116.

The membership of the Lodge fluctuated greatly during the years of these records, varying from 42 in 1865, to 26 in 1874 and 35 in 1904. During that period the Budge family was closely associated with the Lodge and provided Masters for the years 1867, 1868, 1872, 1902 and 1904.

Amongst the early notable members of the Lodge was Dr William Wynn Westcott who, after studying medicine in London, came to live in Martock and was initiated into the Lodge in 1871 and installed as Master in 1877. The same year he was appointed Provincial Grand Director of Ceremonies. Also the Hon. Aubrey Herbert of Dulverton joined the Lodge in 1910, being at that time Member of Parliament for the Yeovil Division, and the following year the Rt. Hon. William John Lydson, Earl Poulet, joined the Lodge.

The Lodge prospered over the years with membership waxing and waning, especially during the war years when brethren were called to serve in the Armed Forces.

On 20th September 1960 the Lodge celebrated its centenary and to mark the occasion a paper was produced and read out giving an account of the Lodge history. Since then the Lodge has had to overcome the trauma of a burglary in January 2003 and a fire in May of the same year which resulted in the Lodge having to hold four meetings care of Prudence and Industry Lodge in Chard.

Since returning to Crewkerne in January 2004 the members of the Lodge have been able to replace the dining chairs, thanks to the efforts of brethren and their wives who organised several Sunday lunches.

In May 2005 a firing glass was presented to the Lodge. The glass has significant historical interest in that it had been presented to a Reginald Pavord, a member for 35 years and Tyler of the Parrett & Axe Lodge for a number of years. It is engraved with the original Lodge number 1116 and is now in safe keeping.

The Lodge has been presented with three acorns for its support to the 2007 Masonic Festival and after years of deliberation in December 2006 gas central heating was installed to the delight and comfort of the brethren and their guests.

As we head towards the Lodge's 125th year in 2010 the Lodge has a membership of around 60. Plans are being made to improve the fabric and facilities of the Lodge ready for the future.

The Parrett & Axe Lodge has a reputation for being a happy and welcoming one, a Lodge that should inspire members with the high traditions of the past and ensure that we continue to make good Masons of those who seek our privileges and also provide a centre of beneficial service to all those who live in our community.

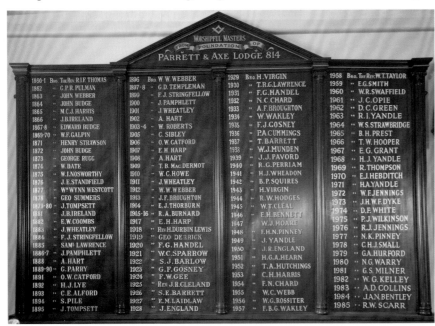

Royal Albert Edward Lodge 906

Meets at the Masonic Hall, Old Orchard Street, Bath

Warrant dated 1862

On the 25th July 1861, five Officers, one Past Master and two Master Masons, all members of the Royal Cumberland Lodge 48 (now 41), met at the Christopher Hotel in Bath to consider the desirability of establishing a Masonic Lodge in one of the villages in the neighbourhood of Bath.

Over the following months the proposal gained much support and in consequence it was proposed and seconded that a warrant be applied for to hold a Lodge at the Lamb and Lark Inn in Keynsham and that the Lodge be called the Royal Albert Edward. It was agreed that the Lodge should meet only in the summer months of June, July, August and September. A petition to this effect was drawn up by seven members of the Royal Cumberland Lodge and one member of the Royal Sussex Lodge 61 (now 53) and this was duly submitted to Grand Lodge.

A further meeting was held on the 24th February 1862, at which the petitioners were pleased to report that the Most Worshipful the Grand Master had granted the Prayer of their petition.

At the time of the petition the Province of Somerset had no Provincial Officers and was under the charge of the Grand Registrar. This was in consequence of the constitution at that time which prescribed that, if the Provincial Grand Master were to resign or die, the operation of the Provincial Grand Lodge would cease until a new Provincial Grand Master was installed and able to appoint his Officers. It was therefore the practice to place a Province affected by such circumstances under the charge of the Grand Registrar in order to reduce the inevitable disruption.

To avoid delays consequent on this situation it was agreed to apply for a dispensation to commence holding meetings of the Royal Albert Edward Lodge prior to its Consecration. This was granted under the signature of the Grand Registrar.

As a result the first meeting of the Royal Albert Edward Lodge 1208 was held at the Lamb and Lark Inn, Keynsham on 29th May 1862, recorded in the minutes as a "Lodge of Emergency". The Chair was occupied by Thomas Broadwood Moutrie of the Royal Cumberland Lodge. In response to a toast to his health he added that "When Installed as Master of the Royal Cumberland Lodge, the oldest Lodge in the Province, he thought he had obtained the summit of his ambition. He now felt he had achieved still more in being the first Master of the youngest."

This meeting included the first Initiation to be performed by the Lodge, the candidate being a Mr William Williams of 11 Lower Camden Place, Bath, aged 48 years, and who was a Professor of Music.

At this time the Consecration Ceremony, as we know it, had been developed but rarely performed and many Lodges up to the 1870s were never formally Consecrated. Nevertheless the Royal Albert Edward Lodge met six times by Dispensation until 16th October 1862, when on, 'this day at high noon the Deputy Provincial Grand Master, W.Bro Bridges, accompanied by Provincial Grand Lodge Officers, confirmed as valid and constitutional all the minutes of the Lodge held by Dispensation and consecrated the Lodge, the ceremony being most impressively performed'.

Following the Consecration W.Bro Thomas Broadwood Moutrie was formally installed as the first Worshipful Master. A contemporary account of the meeting states 'the occasion being a rare one to the brethren of this and adjacent Provinces, caused an unusually large assemblage of the members of the Craft, several of whom had attended from a considerable distance'.W.Bro Moutrie continued as Master for two years. Upon installing his successor he was invested with a Past Master's Jewel and presented with an illuminated memorial in a guilt frame.

The problems associated with holding a Lodge in the rooms of a public house must have been considerable and varied. A key figure in ensuring the smooth running of the Lodge was the Tyler. The original Bye Laws of the Royal Albert Edward Lodge included the following:

"Election of Tyler and his duties:-

The Tyler shall be elected by a show of hands on every night of Installation of the WM, or oftener if necessary, who shall be continued in office only during the pleasure of the Lodge. He shall attend upon the Secretary, deliver, or cause to be delivered, all Summonses, Notices, etc, to every member of the Lodge when required in due and proper time; to see to the proper cleansing of the room, lighting of fires, setting out of proper and necessary furniture for the business of the Lodge; to guard the door, and do such other necessary business as may be required of him, for which services he shall be paid as follows:-

For every days attendance 5/-. For every Initiation 1/-. For every Joining Member 1/-. For every Brother Passed or Raised not having been made in the Lodge 1/-. But if he shall neglect any of these duties, or the business of the Lodge becomes retarded through his negligence, he shall forfeit for every such neglect, any sum the majority of the brethren may think proper to inflict; or in case he shall neglect to attend in proper time at any meeting of the Lodge, he shall, in addition to the above-named fine, forfeit all pay and fees which would have belonged to him, unless prevented by sickness or other sufficient cause, of which he shall give due and timely notice to the WM, who shall, in such cases, provide a proper substitute, who shall receive the Tyler's fees for his services".

In 1863, due to a general renumbering of Lodges, the number of the Royal Albert Edward Lodge was changed to its present one of 906.

As originally intended, Lodge meetings were held during the months of June, July, August and September, on the second Wednesday, and at a somewhat late hour of 7.30 pm. The reason for this may well have been the lack of transport other than by horse-drawn vehicle, additionally, it was not unusual for brethren of those early days to walk considerable distances in order to attend Lodge. Despite the late start it was not unusual to work two and sometimes three degrees in one evening.

The Lodge continued to meet in Keynsham until 1867 when because of the frequent change of landlord of the Lamb and Lark and the unpleasantness to which the brethren were subjected, both in the working of the Lodge and in their personal comfort, it became imperative that other accommodation be found.

On the 14th June 1867 the first meeting of the Lodge was held at its new meeting place, the Crown and Anchor Inn at Upper Weston, Bath, were it remained for 24 successful years.

However, a meeting of Past Masters in December 1890 felt that, "from various circumstances that had arisen, the time had arrived when steps should be taken to remove the Lodge from its present location." At a Special Meeting of the Lodge, held on 19th December 1890 a Proposition was proposed by W.Bro T.B. Moutrie PM and Founder and

seconded by W.Bro C Becket PM "That it is desirable that this Lodge be removed from the Crown and Anchor Inn Weston to the Masonic Hall in the City of Bath and that negotiations be entered into to carry this into effect."

As a result members of the Lodges already meeting at the Bath Masonic Hall were balloted, the result being almost unanimously in favour (just one vote against). Provincial dispensation was duly signed on 21st February 1891 and the move from Weston was successfully achieved thanks, in part, to W.Bro I Stuckey PM who "very generously offered to provide the horses and van required for the removal of the effects to Bath".

The first meeting of the Royal Albert Edward Lodge in its new home took place on March 30th 1891 and a vote of thanks to the members of Lodge 41, 53 and 379 was recorded in the

The Crown and Anchor

minutes "expressing warm appreciation of the kindly feelings of the trustees and brethren in accepting the Lodge as co-tenants of the Masonic Hall."

The Royal Albert Edward Lodge remained a Summer Lodge until July 1906 when because of 'meagre numbers' and the realisation that it was no longer a Country Lodge, it was unanimously decided to change the meeting months to January, February, March, April, September, October and November (the Installation date had been changed to October several years earlier). Surprisingly, the low

attendances were despite the Initiation of many new members, which necessitated occasions such as in February 1904 when there were three Passings at 7pm and a further three at 8pm, or at the November 1905 meeting when there were four simultaneous Raisings. The probable record, however, was in November 1891 when the Worshipful Master performed ten Raisings, five at 5pm and a further five at 7.15pm.

Being the daughter Lodge of Royal Cumberland, and using their ritual and mode of working, it was believed that the Royal Albert Edward Lodge had also inherited their traditions

Framed photographs of the early Masters of the Albert Edward Lodge
Top centre is the first Master Thomas Moutrie 1862-1863

and privileges. Consequently, the use of the illuminated star in place of the Master's Light in the third degree was enjoyed for a period of 76 years. However, in 1938 the irregularity of its use was pointed out by Grand Lodge and although strenuous efforts were made to retain it in loyalty to Grand Lodge it was reluctantly discontinued. More recently approval was given for the Lodge Stewards to continue wearing their traditional red aprons and collars.

In 1920 a daughter Lodge, St. Alphege 4095, was consecrated. The founding Master was W.Bro William Brake, a Past Master of the Royal Albert Edward Lodge. It was originally intended that the Lodge should be called the William Long Lodge, but it eventually received its present name.

In 1940 the Lodge was asked to sponsor a Lodge of Instruction for the benefit of Freemasons among Admiralty staff evacuated from London to Bath during WW2. This was agreed and supported by Province provided that at least two Past Masters from the Royal Albert Edward be present at each meeting. The L.o.I was titled the Royal Albert Edward Lodge (Admiralty Section). In response to requests by the L.o.I dispensation was obtained for the Royal Albert Edward Lodge to hold an Emergency Meeting to discuss the formation of a new Lodge, primarily for the benefit of the Admiralty Masons, and as a result a petition was submitted to Grand Lodge. This was successful, and St Luke's Lodge 6540 was consecrated later that year. This increased the number of Bath Lodges to six.

In the late 1940s it was not unusual for 80 or more brethren to attend Regular Meetings of the Royal Albert Edward Lodge, and well over 100 at Installations.

Over the past 145 years there have been many distinguished members of the Lodge. The Lodge has been honoured five times by the Grand Lodge of England - W.Bro Edward Brake was

promoted to PAGStdB in 1931 and W.Bro W.A. Gayner, who was the charity representative of the Lodge for over 30 years, was promoted to PAGDC in 1940. The Lodge currently has two Grand Officers – W.Bro John Pearson PJGD and V.W.Bro Denis Calderley PGSwdB.

Not only has the Royal Albert Edward Lodge served the cause of Freemasonry with distinction, but its members have also made notable contributions to the civic life of the City of Bath. No less than six members of the Lodge have been called upon to serve the high office of Mayor of the City - W.Bro A.W. Wills in 1918, W.Bro L.G. Adams in 1937, Bro Edward Taylor OBE in 1946, W.Bro R.W. Pearson in 1951, Bro A.C. Knight in 1960 and W.Bro R.E. Tucker in 1961. Members of the Lodge also served this country with distinction during both World Wars, several receiving high awards.

During the history of the Royal Albert Edward Lodge there have been many occasions of note.

In May 1914 two distinguished brethren of the Royal Albert Edward Lodge were on their way to London by train and met at Bath Spa station. One was W.Bro Will Gayner (who had been Master of the Lodge in 1908) and his companion W.Bro: Edward Brake who was then the Immediate Past Master. W.Bro Gayner proudly announced that his wife had just presented him with a son and invited Edward Brake to be the boy's godfather. When asked what name had been chosen for the boy, he was told that this had not yet been decided

As soon as he reached London W.Bro Brake went to Selfridges and purchased a silver rattle for the new baby. He arranged for it to be engraved and dispatched to the baby's parents. During their return journey he explained to his friend what he had done and what he had requested to be engraved on it. On arriving home to his wife and new baby W.Bro Gayner was able to explain to his wife that a name had been chosen for the boy, for the inscription on the rattle read "Albert Edward 906". It was of course W.Bro Albert Edward Gayner PGStdB (Eddy) who had devoted so much of his time to the support of this Lodge and in developing the renowned Masonic Museum located at the Bath Masonic Hall which continues to attract much interest locally and beyond.

Ironically within a few months of W.Bro Eddie Gayner being initiated into Freemasonry in January 1942 the Masonic Hall was bombed and meetings returned, temporarily, to Keynsham but this time at the Masonic Temple and not the Lamb and Lark Inn. Special dispensation to hold the meeting in Keynsham was again obtained in September 1949 in order that the war damage be repaired.

Unusually three generations of one family served as Master of the Royal Albert Edward Lodge. W.Bro Jesse Hayward was installed in 1890, followed by his son W.Bro George Hayward in 1913 and then by his son W.Bro Jack Hayward in 1938. It was W.Bro Jack Hayward who officiated at the Centenary celebrations.

More recently the PGM, R.W.Bro David Jenkins, presented two brethren of the Lodge, who were consecutive Initiates, in December 1955 and January 1956, with 50th Anniversary Certificates. They were W.Bro John Pearson PJGD and W.Bro L.J. Cottell PPr.G.Supt. ofWks who between them and their fathers have so far contributed an astonishing 213 years of membership and service.

As with many Lodges, the membership has significantly reduced in recent years and currently stands at about 40. Nevertheless, thanks to an excellent reputation for the standard of ritual (Royal Cumberland Working) and hospitality to guests, who are always made very welcome, the Royal Albert Edward Lodge looks to the future with considerable optimism.

Sadly it has not been positively established how the Lodge came by its name. The most feasible explanation has come from W.Bro Hamill, past Librarian and Curator of the United Grand Lodge Library and Museum. He has suggested that since seven of the eight brethren who sponsored the original petition were from the Royal Cumberland Lodge, which in 1786 took its name from HRH Henry Frederick, Duke of Cumberland, Grand Master from 1813 to 1843 and the other petitioner was from the Royal Sussex Lodge, which took its name in 1818 in honour of HRH Augustus Frederick, Duke of Sussex, Grand Master 1813 - 1843, then what better than to name the Lodge "Royal Albert Edward" in honour of the Prince of Wales.

He was then 21 years old and it would be a further six years before he was Initiated into Freemasonry (in Stockholm) and thirteen years before he was Installed Grand Master at the Royal Albert Hall in front of the largest assembly of Freemasons that had ever met.

Royal Somerset Lodge No. 973

Meets at the Masonic Hall, North Parade, Frome.

Warrant dated 1863

Freemasonry had been established in Frome, before the present Warrant of the Royal Somerset Lodge was granted in 1863, a Lodge having existed prior to the year 1811. In that year it is recorded the Masons of Frome attended, as a body, the Parish Church of St. John, when a sermon was preached by the then vicar of Horningsham, the Rev. Skurry. Further evidence of Masonry in Frome prior to 1863 appears in a minute of 11th January 1917, when Bro A Duckett, on behalf of Bro Palmer, presented a framed record of music sung in the Parish Church in connection with a Provincial Grand Lodge meeting held in Frome in 1822.

Even earlier than this, there appear these extracts from the minutes of the Love and Honour Lodge, Shepton Mallet, of 11th December 1792 as follows:

"It was unanimously agreed to have a Dinner on St. John's Day the Evangelist, and the letters of invitation be sent to Masters and Officers of the Bath, Wells and Frome Lodges".

Also on 8th January 1793:

"The Quarterages was collected from the brethren present, and the Frome Lodge having made several persons who had been rejected in this Lodge, it was ordered that the RWM do state the facts to the Provincial Grand Master"

The Warrant under which the Lodge is now working was granted by the Grand Master of England, the Earl of Zetland KG, dated 11th June 1863 and constituted William Addams Grimes, Lord Edward Thynne, Malim Messiter, Augustus J. Marsh, John William Turner, George Campbell Knight, and George Hinchcliffe into

The new Banner (above) dedicated in June 1991 by R.W.Bro Stanley H.A.F. Hopkins Provincial Grand Master for Somerset replaced the Old Banner, (below) which had become somewhat worse for wear.

a Lodge of Free and Accepted Masons, under the title of the Royal Somerset Lodge 1275, to meet at the George Hotel, Frome on the Thursday nearest the full moon every month.

The first three brethren were named respectively as the Master, the Senior Warden, and the Junior Warden. The number of the Lodge was amended from 1275 to 973 in a Dispensation dated 25th July, 1863, and to meet as authorised until the consecration of the Lodge.

The first Regular Lodge meeting was held at the George Hotel on 27th August 1863, and two further meetings were held before the consecration. The sole business of the first meeting was to initiate Mark Callaghan of Frome, who was to act as Tyler or serving Brother, the ceremony being carried out by W.Bro E. Turner Payne, WM of the Royal Sussex Lodge 53 Bath and Provincial Grand Treasurer, who also passed Bro Callaghan at the second meeting. At this second meeting Lord Henry Frederick Thynne, the second son of the Third Marquis of Bath, was proposed as a candidate for initiation. He and Malcolm Magill, another candidate, were initiated on the same day as, but before, the Consecration ceremony.

The Consecration took place on Thursday 29th October 1863 at the George Hotel Frome, and the Ceremony was conducted by W.Bro Henry Bridges, PGSwdBr (England), the Deputy Provincial Grand Master of Somerset, who was supported by many Provincial Grand Lodge Officers, and a large number of other distinguished visitors.

The Lodge held its meetings for some six years at the George Hotel, when members thought it desirable to have premises of their own. They secured a lease on premises in Palmer Street, formerly used as a Museum, but now designated the Masonic Hall.

It was dedicated by the Deputy Provincial Grand Master, W.Bro Henry Bridges, on 21st October 1869, about £200 having been spent in adapting the building to its new purpose. Here Freemasonry found its home and prospered for 22 years during which time many distinguished brethren held office, and others passed the chair. Among the former were R.W.Bro Viscount Dungarvan, the then Provincial Grand Master for Somerset, and Bro Lord Henry Thynne. Among the Past Masters was Bro Lord Justice Lopes who was Worshipful Master in 1875.

As time progressed the Lodge increased in numbers and it became necessary to find even more commodious premises. For two or three years various committees appointed by the Lodge inspected sites, and many places were visited, and at last a plot of land where the present premises now stand was made available and purchased for £100 through the kind offices of W.Bro A.G. Hayman. Plans were prepared by Bro P. Edinger, the Town Surveyor, who gave his services as Honorary Architect, and supervised the work.

The contract for the work was entrusted to the local firm of Messrs. Hodder and Sons, the cost of the building, excluding certain additions which have since been made, amounting to about £1,400 which gives some idea of the change in monetary values since that time.

The Dedication of the new Masonic Hall was held on 13th October 1891 at the Annual Installation meeting. The Dedication ceremony was performed by the R.W Provincial Grand Master, Viscount Dungarvan, in the presence of W.Bro R.C. Else, the Deputy Provincial Grand Master, Col. Perkins, PGD (England), and a very large company of distinguished brethren from Somerset and the neighbouring provinces. After the Ceremony R.W.Bro Viscount Dungarvan then proceeded to lay the foundation stone. Under the foundation stone was placed a bottle containing copies of the Times, Somerset Standard, and the Somerset and Wiltshire Journal; a Roll of Members of the Lodge; a Book of Constitutions; the bye-laws Lodge; a copy of the Trust Deeds; a history of the movement with a list of Officers and Members; Silver and Bronze coins from a five-shilling piece to a farthing.

"This was done without the usual ceremonies, owing to the bad state of the weather" according to the minutes. A very eloquent oration was delivered by Bro Rev. E.J. Austin, PG Chaplain, and a handsome silver cup was presented to Bro Philip Edinger as a token of appreciation of his services in connection with the building of the new hall.

In February 1893, a resolution was passed, "that the consent and hearty recommendation of the Royal Somerset Lodge of Freemasons be hereby given to a petition about to be made for the formation of a New Chapter of Royal Arch Masons to be attached to such Lodge and that the Worshipful Master be hereby empowered and directed to sign on behalf of the Lodge a copy of the resolution to be forwarded and the Petition to the Supreme Grand Chapter". In October of that year, at the Installation Meeting, the Charter of the Dungarvan Chapter was presented to the Worshipful Master by Bro A Duckett, asking that it be hung on the walls of the Lodge, and was graciously accepted. The Dungarvan Chapter No. 973 thus came into being.

In September 1911, the Lodge was asked to support the formation of a new Lodge at Midsomer Norton, and it was resolved that the Petition be signed by the Worshipful Master and Wardens as desired. On 11th April 1912, the daughter Lodge, named the Connaught Lodge 3573, was consecrated, at which ceremony a large number of brethren from 973 were present.

In those early days the brethren must have spent long hours in the Lodge room, judging by the amount of work they carried out at some of their meetings. Here are a few examples, but there are numerous others: 3rd September 1868: three Raisings and four Passings; 1st October 1868: four Raisings and an Installation; 10th June 1890: two Initiations, four Passings and one Raising (on this occasion the Lodge opened at 6.30 p.m. and closed at 10.53 pm); 10th November 1891: The regular meeting, including five Initiations, followed the Dedication of the new Masonic Hall in North Parade.

The Lodge also experienced serious setbacks, for at a regular meeting held on 5th January 1871 only the Secretary and Tyler were present! Also in June, July and August 1888 the regular meetings were not held "there being not sufficient brethren to hold same".

A brief reference might here be made to what may be termed the Lodge Library, the first indication of which we find in 1899, when W.Bro Hayman, presented the Lodge with three volumes on Freemasonry by Gould. In May 1922, W.Bro A.M.G. Daniel, who was then Junior Deacon, presented the Lodge with five volumes on Masonry and this was immediately followed by many other such contributions, this forming the nucleus of a Lodge library, so that in June of the same year he was elected Librarian. This library which is in the robing room upstairs, we commend to the use of the younger brethren who wish to make a daily advancement in Masonic knowledge.

This history would not be complete without some reference to the Lodge of Instruction, the importance of which cannot be too strongly stressed. As far back as July 1868 it would appear that a Lodge of Instruction was mooted, and in May 1882 a further proposition that a Lodge of Instruction under Warrant of 973 be formed to meet each Monday prior to the regular meeting.

It may have been little more than a Lodge of Rehearsal as it was confined to acting Officers of the Lodge. This apparently, as a Lodge of Instruction, ceased to exist, for no early records are available, but it would appear from the minutes that various attempts were made to revive it. Eventually, in December 1921, it was proposed that the Lodge of Instruction be resuscitated, and it became the Lodge of Instruction as it exists today.

Masonry being a Universal Brotherhood, the basic principles of which are Brotherly Love,

Over the history of the Lodge there are many brethren who have distinguished themselves, and who are outstanding for the work they did in their varying capacities, and whom the Lodge will wish to remember, not least R.W.Bro the Rt. Hon.Viscount Dungarvan the son of the Earl of Cork and Orrery, whom he succeeded in June 1904. He was elected a Joining Member in October 1884 and installed as Provincial Grand Master of Somerset at Bath in May 1891, in which capacity he dedicated the new Masonic Hall in North Parade in October of the same year.

Also John Olorenshaw Lewis, author of "History of the Royal Clarence Lodge from 1790-1838". He was WM of the Royal Somerset Lodge in 1920 and was Treasurer for 21 years 1925-1946.

Time and space will not permit the recording of many others. We are proud to recall that among those who have passed beyond, there are many who have left a reputation behind them that we may do well to follow, and it should be the aim and endeavour of us all to emulate their example, that we too, it may be, in days to come "may leave behind us some footprints, however faint, upon the sands of time".

Relief and Truth, it is not only fitting but natural and essential that Charity should be an outstanding feature of the Lodge.

In the very early days following 1863 no doubt the exercise of Charity was left to the individual member, but after W.Bro John Baily was granted five guineas to entitle him to vote at the Festival of the Royal Masonic Institution for Boys, it is apparent that the interest in and support of the Charities have rapidly and financially increased. W.Bro John Baily became the first Lodge Charity Steward to be appointed. The Royal Somerset Lodge Charity Association under which we are at present working was launched in April 1936, under the guidance of W.Bros A.M.G. Daniel and G.H. Scotchman, both of whom in turn were Charity Stewards and worked very hard on behalf of the Charities and the Lodge's record at the last three festivals at which the Provincial Grand Master of Somerset has presided is something of which it is rightly proud.

Royal Clarence Lodge No. 976

Meets at The Masonic Hall Bruton

Warrant dated 1863

Bruton is a small country town with a population of about 1700 inhabitants, situated within ten miles of the eastern boundary of the County of Somerset. It is well known for its schools, which have accepted pupils from all over the country and many far off lands, some of whom have names firmly established in public and commercial life.

In the preparation of this short history of Royal Clarence Lodge facts have been gathered from the earlier writings of W.Bro E.R. Hayter, PPGReg and W.Bro R.T.A. Hughes, M.A., DPGM for Somerset from 1926 to 1936, in addition to those obtained from the Minute Books covering the past 100 years. Both of these worthy Past Masters of Royal Clarence Lodge must have spent a considerable amount of time in their search for information, for which we owe them a debt of gratitude.

The first recorded history of Freemasonry in Bruton dates from 1841, when the meeting of brethren forming the Royal Clarence Lodge, No. 695, took place at the Wellington Hotel, Bruton, which formerly stood on the site now occupied by the Library, at the junction of Patwell Street and Quaperlake Street. This first meeting was attended by Bro Merchant, WM, Bro Hill, JD, Bro Chippett, SW, Bro Goodall, IG, Bro Jones, Secretary, Bro Gale, Bro Moody, JW, Bro Griffiths, Tyler. Bro Marchant, SD.

Royal Clarence Lodge 695, Bruton, undoubtedly followed the surrender of the Warrant in 1838 of the Royal Clarence Lodge 560, formed at Frome in the year 1790, and as is shown by subsequent events the earlier history of Freemasonry in both towns had some connection with Masons brought into the area

in the course of the construction of what is generally known as the Weymouth Branch of the Great Western Railway.

This influence continued during the early life of Royal Clarence Lodge 976. In the notes compiled by the late W.Bro R.T.A. Hughes he refers to the book of Bye-laws of the first Royal Clarence Lodge of Bruton, being acquired by the courtesy of the Gooch Lodge of Swindon, 1295, together with other articles and papers of interest both to the Frome and Bruton brethren.

In the minutes dated April, 1881, it is recorded that a pair of engravings, illustrative of King Solomon's Temple, were presented by Bro John Green, Worshipful Master of Royal Sussex Lodge of Emulation 355, Swindon, as a memento of "many pleasant hours spent in Bruton."

Jewel from the first Royal Clarence Lodge, No. 560 commemorating the Initiation of Bro E. Culverhouse in 1790. Now in the collection at Frome

Soon after the formation of the present Royal Clarence Lodge the influence of the Railway staff was still very much in evidence, for in 1870 several brethren from Bristol and Bath were elected as Joining Members. All employees of GWR, they included Bro W. Thompson (late mayor of Bath) Bro Reynolds, Bro G.N. Tyrrell, Bro Hearne, Bro Simpson, Bro Graham, Bro G. Goldney, and .Bro Inskip (Bristol). From these names, seven brethren, including the W.M. Bro Thompson, took office in December, 1870.

Again, in 1933, mention is made in the minutes that "thanks were due to the Swindon Lodge" for the return of certain articles, some of which related to the Frome Lodge, and in November, 1934, a copper plate for the engraving of the Lodge certificates then issued during the life of the first Royal Clarence Lodge at Frome was presented to the W.M. of Royal Somerset Lodge 973, W.Bro A.E.V. Spill.

Returning to the first Royal Clarence Lodge 695 in Bruton, its life was of short duration and not without many difficulties. The first meetings were held at the Wellington hotel but the minutes of the 11th September, 1843, are dated at the "Lodge Room" which was in the building known as Stockwell House in the High Street, Bruton, and by 1850 it had been resolved to remove to the Sun Inn. One of the many difficulties was finding suitable Worshipful Masters and sufficient officers to form a Lodge. Bro Thomas Moody seems to have occupied the chair for some five or six years of the Lodge's existence. It appears that on November 12th, 1849, Bro John Jones was elected as W.M. but could not be induced to accept the office and Bro G. Parfitt was then elected and installed as W.M..At the next Lodge on the 26th March Bro Moody resigned and Bro Charles Pope, M.D. was elected. So the Lodge had the unusual experience of electing three Worshipful Masters in the same number of months.

Difficulties and lack of interest prevented the Lodge from meeting from the 30th April, 1850 until the 21st January, 1851, and on this last mentioned date a meeting was held attended by only one member residing in Bruton, at which Bro Marchant explained the position of affairs and it was resolved to pass the Warrant to the R.W Provincial Grand Master. So ended the short and difficult life of the first Royal Clarence Lodge 695, in Bruton, and for twelve years there was no recorded Freemasonry in Bruton.

The Warrant for Royal Clarence Lodge, No. 976, was dated 24th July, 1863 and on the 25th August, 1864, the Lodge was consecrated at the Blue Ball Hotel, Bruton, by the R.W Provincial Grand Master, Col. A.W. Adair. The first W.M. of the Lodge was W.Bro W.A. Humphries, a Past Master of Love and Honour 285, Shepton Mallet. Apparently there was a considerable amount of interest and enthusiasm in the early days for only a few weeks later, on the

4th October, 1864, the Lodge was opened at 3.30pm. and continued until 9.25 p.m. during which time there were four separate initiations and a Lecture on the First Tracing Board. Proceedings at the next Lodge on the 1st November occupied more than three hours, and on the 2nd April, 1867, the Lodge was opened at 5.30 p.m. and closed at 10.30 p.m. after six separate ceremonies had been performed and a portion of the Ancient Charges read to complete the meeting.

This enthusiasm seems to have been of short duration for only three years later, in February and March, 1870, there were insufficient brethren present to form a Lodge. It was for this reason that the brethren from Bath and Bristol were elected as Joining Members. It is also interesting to note that a dispensation was granted for Bro J.W. Parfitt to be installed in December, 1868, as he was then W.M. of the Science Lodge, 437, Bourton (now Wincanton), thus having the distinction of being W.M. of two neighbouring Lodges at the same time. December, 1877, was the occasion for another unusual practice. At this Installation meeting additional officers were appointed and invested as Assistant Senior Deacon, Assistant Junior Deacon and Assistant Inner Guard.

The Western Gazette published on the 13th September, 1878, a cutting from which is inserted in the Minute Book, gave a full account of Provincial Grand Lodge held at Bruton on the 7th September, at which the Earl of Carnarvon presided over a company of 120 in the King's School and the banquet in the National Schoolroom.

1885 witnessed a serious allegation being made in Provincial Grand Lodge by a Past Master of Royal Clarence Lodge that " at one time politics were discussed in Lodge." This suggestion created quite a stir and resulted in a searching inquiry being made, after which the allegation was withdrawn.

It is interesting to note that for more than twenty years following the Consecration of Royal Clarence Lodge the Installation ceremony was carried out by the Provincial Grand Master or his Deputy and it was not until 1903 that a reigning Master installed his successor, when it was performed by W.Bro R.T.A. Hughes.

In the minutes of the Installation meeting on the 2nd December, 1920, a newspaper cutting inserted noting the fact that in one part of the ceremony three Past Masters of the Lodge were in office, whose ages totalled the grand figure of 241 years, and each one had been initiated in the Lodge.

1922 records the move from the Blue Ball Hotel to the Wesleyan Schoolroom, and on the 7th December, the Dedication was performed by the Deputy Provincial Grand Master, Col. Thrale Perkins, CB Early in 1925 a Building Committee was formed for the purpose of providing a permanent home for the Lodge, and in October, 1932, the premises known as the Infants School in the High Street were purchased, although in the intervening years other property at West End, Bruton, had been bought and disposed of in 1929. The conversion was completed at a cost of nearly £1,500. The Deputy Provincial Grand Master, W.Bro R.T.A. Hughes, performed the Dedication on the 7th December, 1933, and so for the first time in 70 years, the Lodge met in its own premises.

Part of the collection of Masonic Jewels on display in Bruton. That on the far right was presented in 1882 by Bro Wm. Humphries, first WM of 976

Royal Clarence Lodge is justly proud of its Lodge of Instruction, and its success is reflected in the standard of work carried out in the Lodge. Not only is its usefulness in the learning and practice of the ritual accepted, but the cultivation of brotherly love, particularly with the younger Masons, is enhanced to a marked degree.

The first mention in the minutes of a Lodge of Instruction was made in 1918. Bye-laws of the proposed Lodge of Instruction were read, and it was agreed to hold the first meeting the following month. It has since gone from strength to strength and for a number of years it has not been unusual to record an attendance of some twenty members. Of its activities two are worthy of special mention. Each year it is customary to set aside one evening when all Past Masters of the Lodge are guests of the Lodge of Instruction, and secondly it provides a Past Master's Jewel for presentation at the Installation Festival of the Lodge each December.

Mention of the work for Masonic Charities which has been done in Royal Clarence Lodge could very well take up much space and time, and indeed its importance would be ample justification. The minutes of the past 100 years are studded with reference to various amounts being voted to the Charities, contributions being made by individual members, and some serving as Stewards at the Festivals. It was gratifying to learn in December 1962 that Royal Clarence Lodge was a Patron Lodge of the Royal Masonic Hospital.

For the 165th Anniversary Festival on the 5th June, 1963, over which the Provincial Grand Master for Somerset presided, the record of the effort by the Royal Clarence Lodge with its 82 members was most pleasing. The figure of £3,461 was the second highest total in the Province and provided the highest average for the individual member. This achievement was undoubtedly responsible for the Lodge being accorded an honour not previously recorded in its long history, namely, the attendance at the Installation Festival in December, 1963, of the R.W Provincial Grand Master, the Deputy Provincial Grand Master and the Assistant Provincial Grand Master, with a record gathering of 124 members and visitors.

By the hands of such distinguished brethren as W.Bro Hayter and W.Bro R.T.A. Hughes the qualities and achievements of many members of Royal Clarence Lodge have been recorded, but as we turn the pages of history at the close of the first 100 years certain names will serve to inspire those who follow and who will take upon themselves the responsibility and good management to ensure success for the Lodge in future years. In this short history one can only find space for a few names.

W.Bro R.T.A. Hughes, who was a Master Mason of Love & Honour 285, Shepton Mallet, becoming a Joining Member of Royal Clarence Lodge on the 4th January, 1894. He was W.M. in December, 1902, and again in December, 1905. From 1909 to 1926 he was regularly appointed the Director of Ceremonies, when he reluctantly declined to accept the Office owing to his work in the Province, for in 1924 he became Editor of the "Somerset Freemasons' Calendar," and in 1926 he received the honour of being appointed Deputy Provincial Grand Master. He loved what is known as the traditional working of the Lodge, which he had spared every effort to preserve, and to this end spent some years perfecting his notes until the final copy, consisting of some 120 pages, was approved in 1935. Towards the end of that year his health deteriorated, and he died on the 11th January, 1936.

On the 4th May, 1939, a memorial in the Lodge to perpetuate his memory was unveiled, and in February, 1942, W.Bro F.E. Nutt, Deputy Provincial Grand Master for Somerset, at his Installation for the second year in succession as

Master of the Somerset Masters' Lodge, read a paper consisting of extracts from the notes compiled by W.Bro R.T.A. Hughes. Much of his work has been preserved to this day, particularly the Installation Ceremony as now used in Royal Clarence Lodge.

W.Bro J. Stuart Jones, a grandson of John Jones, a founder member of the original and also the present Royal Clarence Lodge, was initiated on the 3rd March, 1898, became W.M. on the 1st December, 1904, and completed more than 60 years as a member of the Lodge. His many years of loyal service will be remembered for his outstanding efforts to see Royal Clarence Lodge established in its own premises. Having given up the Treasurer's Office in November, 1932, he concentrated on the building programme as soon as the Infants' School in the High Street was purchased.

As one enters the Dining Hall adjoining the Lodge our thoughts turn to the memory of the late W.Bro W. Viney, who, amongst his many acts of generosity, was mainly responsible for the cost of the building conversion. To him much credit must be given for many gifts to Charities and the Masonic Hospital.

The Somerset Farmers' Lodge 9180, which was sponsored by Royal Clarence Lodge, was consecrated in April 1986, and took up residence at Bruton. Plans were subsequently drawn and approved by the Local Planning Authority to extend the Lodge in order to have a purpose built dining hall. Two motorised wheelbarrows were purchased to move rubble up the path and building materials down. Work started in 1989 and was completed by the brethren of the two Lodges, who showed they could also be operative masons. The new larger dining room enabled the Lodge to hold its Installation and Charity nights on the premises, also other social functions. The hoped for growth of the Farmers' Lodge with candidates and brethren from Dorset did not materialise,

and after a survey of possible relocation sites a democratic ballot proved in favour of St Mary's Chapel, Langport. The Farmers' Lodge moved in September 2003.

Royal Cyrus Chapter 285 and the Lodge of Love and Honour 285, finding the financial drain of looking after an ageing listed building too much, moved away from Shepton Mallet. Royal Cyrus Chapter relocated to Bruton in 2002.

In 2002, when Freemasonry and the Community week was held, Royal Clarence Lodge was fortunate to have left to it, by a local Freemason, a legacy which was to provide benefits to the local youth. During the week the youth organisations put on a display of their activities in the dining room, which resulted in them being presented with new sports equipment or other equipment according to their needs and a payment of £35,000 towards the rebuilding of the sports hall on the playing field and £12,000 for refurbishment of the Scout Hall.

The Lodge is due to celebrate its 150th Year in 2013.

Nyanza Lodge No. 1197

Meets at the Masonic Hall, Court Barton, Ilminster

Warrant dated 1867

The Lodge of Unanimity 524 was instituted at Ilminster in 1788, the first meeting being held at The Swan Inn, Ditton Street. From 1792-1797 the Lodge moved to the George Hotel, after which owing to the lack of support it was decided to move to the London Hotel, East Street, Taunton.

In October 1867 Nyanza Lodge was instituted with sixteen members and met in the Commercial School Rooms, there present premises, for just over a year. The Dispensation was dated 24th December 1867 and the first meeting was held on Friday, 27th December at 9am, when five candidates were proposed for Initiation and four Masons as Joining Members. On 6th January 1868 the five were initiated and the four Joining Members approved and admitted.

The Consecration and Installation of the first WM John Knott, was on Friday, 10th January 1868. The brethren attended a banquet at 3pm, in their Masonic clothing, at the Crown Inn. We are told that all ended in harmony and goodwill. On 14th January, four days after the Consecration and Installation Meeting, another meeting was held at which 50 brethren attended, of whom 32 sat down to an extensive banquet. The cost for the banquet was the equivalent of 35p per person and the wine bill exceeded that for the food!

The Lodge was named Nyanza after Lake Victoria Nyanza in honour of the local explorer, Captain John Hanning Speke, who had discovered the source of the River Nile on 3rd August 1858. Four years prior to the formation of the Lodge Speke died in a shooting accident and was buried in Dowlish Wake Church. His funeral was attended by David Livingstone.

The banner depicts the source of the River Nile where it flows out of Lake Victoria Nyanza

It appears that neither Captain Speke nor any members of his family had any connection with the Lodge. The word Nyanza derives its name from the Sukuma, a Bantu speaking tribe living on the Tanzanian shore of Lake Victoria. To them it means a large mass of water.

A letter dated 31st March 1868 was received from Grand Lodge severely reprimanding the members of Nyanza Lodge for holding meetings on 27th December and 6th January, before the Lodge was consecrated, and contrary to the Book of Constitutions.

The Grand Master, on this occasion, decided to deal leniently with the matter as there was no doubt that the members of the Lodge had been misled by the Provincial Grand Secretary who had obtained the Dispensation.

After the first year of meeting the Lodge transferred to the Royal George Assembly Rooms but this proved unsatisfactory as the Lodge furniture was being continually damaged. Subsequent meetings were held in a secure room at The George Hotel at the cost of £4 per year. In April 1884 a resolution was passed to move to a room in North Street (the building no longer exists) but it took a further 21 months, until February 1886, for the lease to be agreed and the new premises occupied.

On 12th April 1870 W.Bro Knott, the Secretary, received a copy of the Warrant issued to Ilminster in 1788 from the W.M. of the Taunton Lodge. It was agreed that an engraving of it on parchment should be made and Bro Bragge's offer to carry out the work was gratefully accepted. It was framed and hangs on the wall to the right of the WM's chair. It was originally issued by Thomas Dunckerley, a natural son the George II, then Provincial Grand Master for Somerset, and is in the full wording of the Grand Lodge model. The name is given as Unanimity and Sincerity 261 Taunton. A letter of thanks for the copy was sent to the W.M. of the Taunton Lodge.

On 1st March 1892 the W.M. Elect, Bro Stringfellow, gave the banner. It can be seen that it depicts the source of the River Nile where it flows out of Lake Victoria Nyanza and where early on the morning of 30th July 1858 Speke first saw the blue waters. He was greatly impressed and added "the pleasure of the view vanished in the presence of those more intense and exciting emotions which were called up by the consideration of the commercial and geographical importance of the prospect before me".

This land, for centuries, had tantalised the curiosity of the civilised world, and of all the mysteries which the Earth had kept from the inquisitiveness of man none had been so engrossing or fired his imagination as the

mystery which shrouded the interior of Africa. So the name of the Lodge indicates the survival of man in fulfilling his treasured ambition.

The present premises were purchased for £150 on 13th May 1913 and another £110 was spent on alterations; the return move being completed in September of that year. The purchase and alteration work was achieved from Lodge funds and loans free of interest from some members.

To mark the Jubilee of the Lodge in May 1917 £105 was raised by subscription to purchase votes in the three Masonic Charities. An excellent amount considering that only four years previously the Lodge Rooms were purchased and considering that the average Alms at the monthly meetings were the equivalent of 60p between approximately 35 members.

To commemorate the end of the First World War, the junior members presented the Lodge, in March 1919, with a pair of oak pillars surmounted by celestial and terrestrial globes. In accepting them the Worshipful Master said "They will stand for ever as a handsome ornament of our Lodge and a reminder of the critical period of history through which our country had so victoriously passed"

The Master's Chair
Beautifully carved with much imagery
of African influence

Provincial Grand Lodge was held in the boys' gymnasium and adjoining rooms of Ilminster Grammar School on 24th May 1928. The excellent arrangements were greatly appreciated by all the visitors and no doubt partially due to the Headmaster being a member of Nyanza Lodge.

The Second World War having started, it was agreed at an emergency meeting in February 1940 to let the Lodge as an Evacuee School, and in September it was temporarily closed. Meetings were held in June, July and August instead of November, December and January. A dispensation was granted on 28th May 1940 and the Lodge opened again in February 1941

and continued to meet all through the War. Great credit must be given to the Tyler, Bro Paull, and his helpers for their work during that trying period in transforming the Lodge from a classroom to a Lodge Temple for each meeting. Masonic degrees were regularly performed and the work did not suffer during the period of hostilities. Naturally, owing to food rationing, after-lodge activities were curtailed but on a few occasions the wives of some to the brethren saw to it that there was a little refreshment. The Master in charge of the Evacuee School wrote a very appreciative letter of thanks for the use of the premises and wished the Lodge success and prosperity for the future. Framed and hanging in the Lodge is a letter signed by all 32 girls who attended.

After the Lodge meeting of 8th May 1945, the brethren went upstairs to listen to a broadcast from the King to his people. It began, "Today we give thanks for a great deliverance" and ended "In the hour of danger we humbly committed our cause into the hand of God and He has been our strength and shield. Let us thank Him for His mercies, and in the hour of victory, commit ourselves and our new task to the guidance of that strong hand." A thanksgiving service to mark the conclusion of hostilities was held under the auspices of Nyanza on Sunday, 16th December. The organist was W.Bro Sharpe, the address was given by W.Bro Ford, PG Chaplain and the benediction by the Lodge Chaplain, Bro Rev. Hickman. It was very well attended and the sincerity and inspiring nature of the service no doubt remained for a long time as a pleasing memory to those who attended.

A letter dated 9th January 1951, addressed to the Trustees of the Masonic Lodge, Ilminster, read: "Notice is hereby given that the building known as the Masonic Lodge, Court Barton, Ilminster, has been included in the list of buildings of historic interest in that area, compiled by the Minister of Town and Country Planning on 23rd September 1950".

The Ilminster set of Tracing Boards, hand painted and presented in 1867, the year Nyanza Lodge 1197 was formed.

The boards, although naïve, are of great interest in terms of the design and layout, and a welcome change to the formalised boards of modern times. That for the third Degree is particularly striking, and would certainly impact on any Candidate.

During the war the Standard Telephone and Cable Company set up a factory in Ilminster and a numbers of their employees were Lodge members. In the early 1960s the workforce was transferred to Paignton and in 1963 four Nyanza members were founders of Quest Lodge 7883. Nyanza Lodge presented them with a Bible and the fraternal contact still remains strong.

The Centenary of the Lodge was celebrated with due ceremony on 10th January 1968. The Centenary Warrant was presented by the Provincial Grand Master, supported by the Provincial Team.

Two school friends who became auctioneers and Masons, but in different Lodges, arranged in June 1977, by special dispensation, a biannual meeting. This is known as the Minster Meeting and first met in Axminster. This made it possible for the members of Nyanza Lodge and the Lodge of Virtue and Honour 494 of Axminster in Devon to meet. For the remainder of the year their meetings are held on the same day thereby precluding any visiting. In 1985 Beaminster Manor Lodge 1367 in Dorset was invited to join. Since then three Lodges from three adjacent provinces have met every two years, whilst rotating the location, and usually three PGMs attend; a unique Masonic meeting.

A daughter Lodge, the Somerset Tablers Lodge 9075, and the second in Ilminster, was Consecrated in April 1983

Whilst the name of every Past Master is individually recorded on a shield and displayed on the walls of the Lodge, the practice of presenting Past Master jewels only commenced in 1958.

In this brief history very little mention has been made of the provision of regalia, furniture, artefacts, organs etc which have either been purchased or donated since the Lodge's formation. The generosity and foresight of our predecessors as well as the historical and monetary value of these items is greatly appreciated.

Whereas it can be invidious to compare the old with the new, some of the ways in which Masonry has changed to move with the times can make interesting reading. When, in 1992, Grand Lodge met at Earls Court to celebrate the 275th anniversary of English Freemasonry it also heralded the real beginning of openness. Like many other Lodges, Nyanza has embraced this policy to involve their wives, family and the public, particularly at its summer events. In 1969 a Christmas carol evening was held, with family and friends, in the Lodge Room; this is now a popular and ongoing occasion. The Lodge byelaws had to be changed to allow the original carols to be sung!

Charity money is raised at the annual summer garden party, when friends and family are present. The money given at these local events is distributed locally to non-Masonic charities. Presentations, with photographs, are often made in the Lodge Room. In 1974, however, an application by the Lodge to give money to local non-Masonic charities was refused by Grand Lodge!

Let us consider ourselves as custodians of a great heritage and endeavour to pass to our successors an even greater one.

The Lodge of Agriculture No. 1199

Meets at the Masonic Hall, High Street, Yatton

Warrant dated 1st November 1867

The Lodge of Agriculture was formed under a Warrant dated 1st November 1867, of Thomas Dundas, Earl of Zetland, Baron Dundas of Aske in the County of York, the Most Worshipful the Grand Master of the Most Ancient and Honourable Fraternity of Free and Accepted Masons of England.

The Founding Members of the Lodge, with perhaps one exception, were all members of Lodges in the Province of Bristol and it therefore seems probable that in the early days of the Lodge Bristol Working may have been adopted. There is in fact some evidence of this, as the minutes of the meeting held on 12th June 1871 record that Bro Dr W. Benham, PM of the Beaufort Lodge No. 103 in the Province of Bristol, was present and having regard to his proficiency in working the Ritual, the WM invited him to take the Chair and conduct a 3rd Degree Ceremony. The other offices were filled by the regular officers of the Lodge, who must therefore have known the Bristol ritual. At this period it was, however, not unusual for the DPGM to attend and conduct the ceremony of Installation of the Worshipful Master, so Bristol ritual would not have been used on those occasions. On 15th March 1880 the Lodge resolved that the London Ritual be adopted. When the subsequent change to Emulation working was made is not clear.

The Founder members were W.Bro James Roger Bramble, Bro John Hurd, Bro William Partridge, Bro Thomas W. Hardwick, and Bro Gilbert P. Montague Blackburn, all of the Beaufort Lodge, 103, Province of Bristol; Bro Alfred Wm. Stiff, Royal Sussex Lodge of Hospitality, 187, Province of Bristol, and Bro Henry Belcher, (Lodge unknown).

It was, therefore, to brethren of the neighbouring Province of Bristol that the Lodge owes its existence, but it is known that of the Founding Members, four at least lived locally, W.Bro Bramble at Yatton, Bro Stiff at Cleeve, Bro Partridge in Congresbury and Bro Hurd in Yatton.

It is hardly surprising then that Beaufort is widely regarded as the Mother Lodge. Indeed, the earliest surviving menu card, from 1868, records "The Fraternal visit of our Mother Lodge, the Beaufort Lodge 103". (One shilling and nine pence for four courses!) The Mother Lodge, however, for reasons no longer clear, is actually Rural Philanthropic, 291.

The first meeting place of the Lodge was at the "Ship and Castle Inn" at Congresbury and it is interesting, and perhaps somewhat surprising, to find that the first Masonic Lodge to be formed in the north west corner of the County should be in the small village of Congresbury. The nearest Somerset Lodges to Congresbury were then at Wells and Highbridge.

The first meeting of the Lodge was held on 11th December 1867, when the Chair was taken by the Master Elect, W.Bro J.R. Bramble, and six candidates were proposed for initiation.

The first was the Rev. Wm. Hunt, Vicar of Congresbury, the second James Mountstevens, who later became the proprietor of the Railway Hotel, Yatton, to which the Lodge subsequently moved, and the third Henry Shiner. Three further meetings were held, all by dispensation, before the Consecration Meeting, eight candidates, including two serving brethren, being initiated. The Consecration was held on Tuesday 14th January 1868 at, to quote the letters of invitation, "1.30 p.m. precisely".

The ceremony was performed by R.W.Bro Col. Alexander William Adair, Provincial Grand Master, assisted by W.Bro Capt. Henry Bridges, Deputy Provincial Grand Master and other officers of the Provincial Grand Lodge. W.Bro J.R. Bramble was then installed as Worshipful Master and he invested his Officers. It is interesting to note that of the Officers five had only been initiated during the previous month. A banquet was held after the ceremony, but unfortunately no menu card has been preserved. The invitations disclose, however, that the cost to the brethren was 4s.0d. each.

W.Bro Bramble was at the time of the Constitution of the Lodge only 26 years of age and had already occupied the Chair of the oldest Lodge in the Province of Bristol, the Beaufort Lodge. He was later the first Master of the St. Vincent Lodge 1404 in that Province. In 1909 he was appointed Provincial Grand Master of the Province of Bristol and in Grand Lodge he held the rank of Past Grand Deacon.

Quart cider mug believed to have been presented by W.Bro Bramble

It was to be only seven months before the first daughter Lodge of 1199 came into being; St Kew Lodge 1222, on 7th July 1868 in Weston-super-Mare.

The early minutes of the Lodge are notable for their brevity, one page frequently being sufficient to record the proceedings at a meeting. It is not surprising therefore to read that at the meeting held on 14th December 1868 it is recorded that "Bro Wm. Long was duly balloted for and accepted". This simple statement recorded the admission to the Lodge as a Joining Member of one who later became not only a great figure in Somerset Masonry, but also a distinguished public figure in the north western part of the County.

He was initiated in 1866 in the Morning Star Lodge 552 Lucknow in the District of East India and passed and raised in the Royal Sussex Lodge 52 in Bath. He occupied the Chair of 1199 in 1874, 1880 and again in 1918, the year in which he attained the distinction of 50 years as a member of the Lodge.

He was also the first Master of the Coleridge Lodge 1750, Clevedon, when it was formed in 1878. W.Bro Col. Long also had a distinguished career as an Officer of the Provincial Grand Lodge of Somerset becoming Deputy

Provincial Grand Master in 1902 and installed as Provincial Grand Master in 1909, a position he occupied until his death in May 1926.

In Grand Lodge he was a Past Grand Deacon. The gavel now used by the Master of 1199 is a constant reminder of R.W.Bro Long, as it was presented to him at an Especial Provincial Grand Lodge Meeting, held on 30th July 1909, on the occasion of the laying of the foundation stone of the church of St Mary at Washford by the Provincial Grand Master.

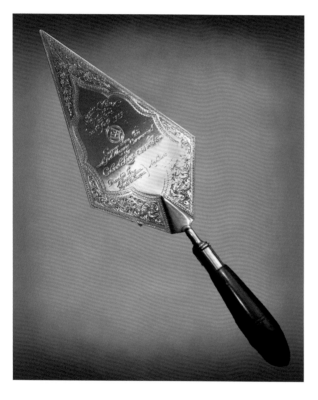

Trowel used by R.W.Bro Wm. Long at the laying of the foundation stone of the Church of St Mary, Washford

In 1913 the RMBI presented a unique illuminated book to R.W.Bro Long to mark "His great kindness in presiding at the Anniversary Festival of the Institute" when £13,167.9s.6d was raised; over £1M today, quite remarkable. The book is one of the proudest possessions of the Lodge.

At the meeting held on 9th August 1869, W.Bro C.L.F. Edwards was elected as a Joining Member. He was to have a considerable influence on Freemasonry, both in the Lodge of Agriculture and in the Province of Somerset generally,

Bro Edwards was initiated in the Apollo University Lodge, 357, Province of Oxfordshire on 27th April 1869. He first reached the Chair in the Lodge of Agriculture in 1875 and again filled that office in 1876 and 1892. He was Treasurer of the Lodge from 1878 to 1891 and from 1894 to his death in February 1924, a total of 43 years. He also was elected to the Chair of his Mother Lodge and, in its inaugural year of 1878, to that of the Coleridge Lodge, Clevedon, this being the second daughter Lodge of 1199

In the Province he was appointed Junior Grand Deacon in 1876, Senior Grand Warden in 1883 and was Provincial Grand Treasurer from 1885 until his death. In Grand Lodge he was appointed Senior Grand Deacon in 1898. Amongst his services to Somerset Masonry probably one of the most important and enduring was the production of the Provincial Handbook. He was responsible for the initial publication in 1882 and continued as its editor until his death. W.Bro Edwards also took an active and prominent part in public affairs in the County.

On 18th February 1878 the Lodge approved a Petition to the M.W The Grand Master for the formation of a Lodge at Clevedon, to be known as the Coleridge Lodge. This was the first Lodge to be formed at Clevedon and from it has descended the other three Lodges now meeting at Clevedon, as well as the Tyntesfield, Estune and Backwell Lodges meeting at Nailsea. It seems somewhat surprising that Freemasonry at both Weston-super-Mare and Clevedon originated at a Lodge located in the small village of Congresbury, the population of which in 1870 was less than 1,200 persons.

It appears that in the early days of the Lodge it was not the practice for the brethren to partake of refreshments after each Lodge meeting, but by 1886 it had become customary to hold quarterly suppers. However, at the August meeting of that year it was decided to discontinue the quarterly suppers, but to continue to hold the annual dinner in September as before. This annual dinner was additional to the Installation Banquet. It was also decided that at his Installation Banquet the Master should provide oysters and stout for the brethren and that the remainder of the refreshments be provided at the expense of the Lodge. How long that resolution remained effective history does not relate.

In 1891 the first steps were taken for the removal of the Lodge from Congresbury to Yatton and at the October meeting that year it was resolved after full discussion "that the Lodge be removed from Congresbury to the Assembly Rooms, Railway Hotel, Yatton" eighteen members voting for the motion, one against with two abstentions.

Perish the thought that this decision may have been influenced by the fact that Bro Mountstevens was the proprietor of the Railway Hotel. More likely it was because it had become the sport of several disgruntled gentlemen, whose applications for membership had been rejected, to quietly row their boats along the River Yeo to a point where they could peer in through the Lodge window and disrupt proceedings!

The first Lodge meeting at the Assembly Rooms Yatton, was held on 1st February 1892 and was an Emergency Meeting. It was followed on 15th February by the Regular Meeting at which Bro C.L.F. Edwards was installed as Worshipful Master of the Lodge for the third time.

After his installation he asked the Lodge to accept the gift of a Lodge Banner. This banner, which remained in use until 1929, had fallen

into disrepair, but when the Lodge removed to its present premises in 1936 was restored and framed through the generosity of the late W.Bro W.H. Hardwell. It now adorns the staircase leading to the Lodge Room.

In August 1914 the First World War commenced. Fourteen brethren served in HM Forces. Three made the supreme sacrifice: W.Bro E.H. Openshaw, Bro Capt. F.P. Wheeldon and W.Bro H.R. Miles. At the unveiling of the Lodge's War Memorial, the Worshipful Master proclaimed "Should the Lodge ever forget such sacrifice as this, so shall it forfeit the stature of its soul"

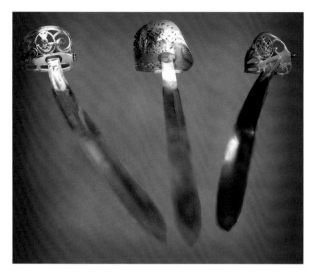

The Swords of W.Bro Lt. Col. E.H. Openshaw PPJGW; Master of the Lodge of Agriculture in 1903 who died in action in Mesopotamia on 23rd July 1917. They were presented to the Lodge by his son, Bro Group Capt. E.R. Openshaw DFC on 19th May 1947

From the beginning of the century until the end of WW1 the membership of 1199 had only increased from 56 in 1900 to 66 in 1918. By 1924, however, the membership had risen to 79. The steady rise in membership may well have been a contributory cause of a resolution passed on 16th June 1924, that a committee be appointed to consider and report on the advisability of the Lodge finding premises of its own. Although this decision had no immediate result it led to a building fund being established in 1926, to which voluntary contributions were made by the brethren.

In 1935 the Lodge took its most momentous decision since its formation in 1867, when at a Special Meeting held on 4th June 1935, the removal to the present premises, then known as Larchmount Hall, was agreed. At the time the building was a shell, the interior having been gutted by fire.

The planning of the reconstruction of the interior of the building was placed in the hand of W.Bro P.B. Rigg and the handsome and spacious Lodge Room is a proof of his architectural skill.

The Dedication Ceremony of the new Lodge Room was conducted by the PGM, Brig. Gen. C.L. Norman, and took place on 16th March 1936.

The outbreak of the Second World War in September 1939 soon had an effect on Lodge meetings. Apart from difficulties of travelling caused by petrol rationing, many brethren found it difficult, if not impossible, to attend Lodge regularly due to either National Service or the greater calls made on them by their normal occupations.

In September 1940 the Military Authorities took possession of the ground floor of the Lodge premises and remained in occupation for the remainder of the war. Lodge meetings continued to be held, but there could obviously be no period of refreshment.

The "blackout" and enemy air activity at night caused alterations to the day of meeting. Commencing in November 1940 the meetings were held on Saturday afternoons. In 1942 a further change was made and no meetings were held in the months of December, January and February, but in substitution thereof the Lodge met in June, July and August.

Two notable additions to the amenities of the Lodge Room were the organ, for which the brethren subscribed at the conclusion of World War II, and the unique clock designed and presented to the Lodge by W.Bro James Milner at the termination of his year of office as Master in 1947.

The year 1945, after the return to peacetime conditions and during the Mastership of that most eloquent of after-dinner speakers the late W.Bro Charles Porter, saw the institution of what is now called "Farmers' night". The originators were brethren of the farming fraternity, prominent amongst whom were Bros G.H. Collins, C.J. Cook and W.W. Keel, who, as they had not taken office in the Lodge, felt they owed some services to the brethren. Accordingly they offered to entertain the members and their guests to supper at the December Lodge meeting on the condition that following supper a collection be taken, the proceeds of which should be devoted to charity.

This invitation was most cordially accepted by the brethren and "Farmer's Night" has since become an annual event. In 64 years to December 2009 the Masonic Charities have benefited to a total of nearly £45000 from collections made on these occasions. It has become the tradition now for the Master and his Officers to vacate their Offices on "Farmers' Night", the various chairs being filled by the farming brethren.

To this day, at the age of 96 years, the 'Father of the Lodge' W.Bro Henry Collins, PJGD, son of Bro G.H. Collins, stands up at the Festive Board to sing solo 'The Farmer's Boy', to the delight of everyone, and something the visitors never forget. If you find yourself invited to Farmers' Night you're in for a night to remember.

The year 1947 was notable for the Consecration of the Lodge's third daughter Lodge, a petition for the formation of the Winscombe Lodge being signed at the meeting held on 17th February of that year and the Consecration Ceremony taking place on 4th June 1947.

The Lodge meeting held on 18th October 1954 was one that no doubt lived in the memories

Pages from the unique illuminated book presented by the RMBI in 1913 to R.W.Bro Col. William Long, Provincial Grand Master for Somerset, and three times Master of the Lodge of Agriculture.

of those brethren who attended, as the Lodge was honoured by a visit of the R.W.Bro Maj. Gen. Sir Allan Adair, Assistant Grand Master, who took part in the ceremony that evening. It is of interest to note that Sir Allan was a great-grandson of R.W.Bro Col. A.W Adair, who in his capacity as Provincial Grand Master Consecrated the Lodge in 1868.

In 1977 the Lodge extended its family even further with the Consecration of its fourth daughter Lodge, Woodspring Lodge 8791, and then in 1988 the fifth, and to date last, Yatton Lodge of Hospitality. 9299 Nobody can say that 1199 has not done its best to promulgate Freemasonry in Somerset.

Space does not permit tribute to be paid to all the brethren of the past who did so much for the good of Freemasonry in general and the Lodge of Agriculture in particular. However, recognition must be given to those brethren who have more recently risen to eminence in the Province, in particular, W.Bro Terence E. Hart.

W.Bro Terry was Master of the Lodge in 1982, was appointed Provincial Junior Grand Warden in 1994, and served as Assistant PGM from 2002 to 2006. He was also a most able Provincial Grand Secretary between 1998 and 2001, being appointed PSGD in 2003. W.Bro Terry was also the Chairman of the 2007 RMBI Festival. He continues to support the Lodge in every department and is one of the mainstays of the Lodge of Instruction.

The Lodge is truly proud of its continuing ability to attract and retain new members, and to have all the progressive offices filled by Master Masons. Indeed, not for over 90 years has a Past Master of the Lodge been installed in the Chair.

There is likewise a strong tradition of fathers introducing their sons into the Lodge, and in April 2009, the newly installed Master, W.Bro Bob Woolley initiated his son Christopher. Also present on that night were six other fathers with their sons, all members of 1199.

R.W.Bro Stanley H.A.F. Hopkins, PPGM for Somerset, who took part in the ceremony, said that to have seven Lewises and their fathers as members, let alone present at the same meeting was probably unique in the Province.

Members of the Lodge of Agriculture today look back with great pride at the distinguished record of the Lodge during its first 140 years.

The best tribute which they, and those who come after them can offer to the memory of those brethren who laid so solid a foundation is to ensure that, when the landmark of the next 100 years is reached, the reputation of the Lodge of Agriculture stands just as proudly in the Province.

Right: Specially commissioned Jewel presented by the Lodge to R.W.Bro Col. William Long.

St. Kew Lodge No. 1222

Meets at the Masonic Hall Weston-super-Mare

Warrant dated 1868

In the story of Weston-super-Mare there is an old and oft repeated tradition that the adjoining village of Kewstoke was named after St. Kew. He, it was said, was a hermit who lived in a cell, the ruins of which can still be traced, in a ravine climbed by a long flight of stone steps leading from Kewstoke Church to the top of Worle Hill. The ravine is known as "The Pass of St. Kew" or Monks Steps.

The St. Kew Lodge was consecrated in the year 1868, when Weston-super-Mare was a small town of some 10,000 inhabitants; it is the first daughter Lodge of the Lodge of Agriculture, 1199. Of the seven Petitioners for the Lodge four were Bristol Freemasons and from the first nine officers invested no less than six were members of Bristol Lodges. The petition was granted, and on 7th July 1868 the Warrant of Constitution was granted by Grand Lodge and signed and sealed. The said Lodge to meet at the Royal Assembly Rooms on the first Wednesday of every month.

Francis George Irwin was named as the first Master, with George Boland Munbee as Senior Warden and Thomas Clarke Junior Warden. A set of By-laws was drawn up and approved by the PGM for Somerset Col. A. W. Adair fixing the Initiation fee at five guineas, members' subscriptions at 7s.6d per quarter, with a joining fee of one guinea

After February 1869 the Lodge met in new rooms called the Carnarvon Hall in the York Hotel at a rent of £20 p.a, but by December of the same year the brethren were already discussing the possibility of acquiring premises to be the property of St. Kew Lodge.

In June 1871 the lease of the Carnarvon Hall was due to expire and the Lodge was unwilling to pay an increase in rent. It therefore took up a lease on the old Town Hall in Plough Court and on 3rd July 1872 the Lodge was consecrated by the DPGM. Five years later, however, it was resolved to give up the Town Hall and returned to the York Hotel.

On November 5th 1879 it was agreed to purchase a Lodge Banner, and the Lodge worked under that banner for the next 121 years. On 23rd February 1880 an Emergency Meeting of the Lodge was held to consider the advisability of building a new Masonic Hall. Bro W.H. Wooler produced plans of a building at an estimated cost of £1600 and it was agreed that it was desirable to proceed. Thus was launched the scheme for the erection of the Masonic Hall in the Boulevard.

The first regular meeting of the Lodge was held there on 5th October 1881. V.W.Bro R.C. Else, DPGM of Somerset accepted the gavel from W.Bro W.E. Perrett and performed the ceremony of dedication.

The imposing building was used continuously for the next 28 years during which time, in 1904, it was thought justified to form a second Craft Lodge, and in 1906 the King Alfred Lodge 3169 was born. Now that two Lodges were occupying the building, even one that was especially built for Masonic purposes, the majority of the brethren now considered it necessary to secure larger premises.

A very fine cigar humidor presented to the Lodge by W.Bro W.E. Perrett, PM, PPGDC on 1st January 1894

In 1907 there was much discussion about the erection of a new and enlarged Masonic Hall. Little time was lost and the Boulevard building was sold to the Weston-super-Mare and District Constitutional Club Ltd for £4000. The Lodge was closed for the last time on 2nd June 1908 by W.Bro Perrett, this being deemed appropriate as it was he who had first opened it.

Superb ram's horn ink pot and stand presented in 1885 to the WM of St. Kew on the occasion of his wedding

In April 1908 the Foundation Stone of the New Masonic Centre was laid by W.Bro Perrett, and on 1st October 1908 the new Masonic Centre was consecrated, the door being ceremoniously opened with a golden key.

During the Great War the Lodge met, but with depleted numbers. Thoughts of a Jubilee Celebration in 1918 were abandoned owing to the prevailing circumstances. With the return of men to civilian service there was a decided increase in interest in Masonic membership such that it was decided that a further Lodge in Weston-super-Mare was necessary and accordingly a Petition to form the Wessex Lodge was signed by the Master and Wardens on 2nd December 1919. By the end of 1920 St Kew had 131 members.

One of the Lodge's most remarkable characters, W. Bro Henry Butt, spear-headed the campaign to raise £50,000 for a new Weston Hospital. Within two years he had raised £40,000 including £1000 from the three local Lodges so that one of the wards could be named "The Masonic Ward". The Foundation Stone of the hospital was laid on 11th November 1926 when a special meeting of Provincial Grand Lodge was convened and proceeded in formal procession to the Boulevard where the Provincial Grand Master, R.W.Bro The Venerable Walter Farrer laid the stone with full Masonic ceremony.

W.Bro W.E. Perrett

who was on fire watch prevented destruction by fire. His courageous action saved not only the building but all of the Lodge's minute books and artefacts.

W.Bro Robert Henry Coate Butt died, aged 84, on 7th November 1944. He was one of the most notable members of St Kew, born at Langport and educated at Queen's College, Taunton, Initiated into St Kew in 1886 and Master in 1901. He was renowned as a great benefactor of the Town whose crowning work was probably the Hospital mentioned previously. He also gave the site for the Winter Gardens. Bro Butt was a County Councillor, Town Councillor, first Charter Mayor and first Freeman of the new Borough.

In 1951, St Kew sponsored the creation of the 4th Weston Lodge, Birnbeck which was consecrated on 11th June 1952. At the November 1954 meeting a "handsome new volume of the Sacred Law" was presented by W.Bro S. Betts.

W.Bro Butt became President of the Hospital and W.Bro Ernest Baker the Honorary Secretary. The occasion was attended by 226 Freemasons. The stone is still in existence at the former hospital entrance.

Having not celebrated the 50th Anniversary in 1918, steps were taken to mark the Diamond Jubilee in 1929 when the Provincial Grand Master attended the October meeting.

In keeping with the edict from Grand Lodge meetings were temporarily suspended in the autumn of 1939, but having been quickly restarted continued throughout the war despite the constraints of blackout and rationing, and more particularly, a number of air-raids on the town. During raids on 28th & 29th June 1942 high explosive and incendiary bombs fell around the Masonic building. The Temple and adjoining buildings were damaged but the quick action of the Tyler, Bro H.A. Freeman

A collection of the Masonic Jewels of W.Bro W.E. Perrett

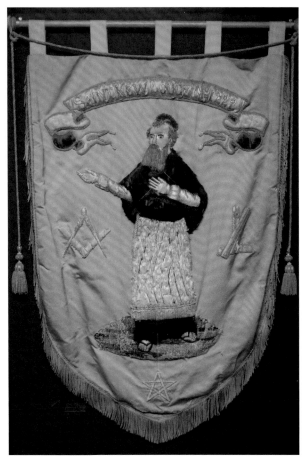

The original Lodge Banner from 1879

In 1963 rising costs were causing concern to the Caterers who sought a significant increase in prices. These were held to be unacceptable and it was agreed to set up a "Catering Establishment", employ a cook and "washer-up", and the Stewards would serve at table. A Catering Fund was created to set up the new arrangements which were reported in 1968 to be working well such that a good meal was served at a moderate charge. Lodge attendance had increased and the Stewards "without exception" were thoroughly enjoying their new role.

The Centenary Festival of the Lodge was held on 9th July 1968. The R.W Provincial Grand Master, Brig. A. de L. Cazenove presided over the afternoon meeting at which the Centenary Warrant was read by the Provincial Grand Secretary W.Bro D.B. Durie and the Provincial Grand Chaplain, W.Bro the Rev. John T. George, Rector of Backwell, delivered an Oration. A short history was presented by W.Bro C D Curtis based on his published Centenary History. The meeting was followed by a Service of Thanksgiving at the Parish Church of St John the Baptist lead by the Rector W.Bro Rev. B. Turnock PPrGChaplain. The Celebrations concluded with a Grand Banquet at the Grand Atlantic Hotel attended by some 120 brethren. In proposing the Toast to St Kew Lodge the Provincial Grand Master hoped that it would continue to maintain the great traditions of Freemasonry in the next 100 years and more.

In 1998 it was decided that a new Lodge Banner was needed, which would allow the original one to retire to a well earned rest and is now on show in the anti-room in a specially designed showcase. On Tuesday 4th January 2000, R.W.Bro, Stanley H.A.F. Hopkins, the Provincial Grand Master for Somerset, assisted by members of the Somerset Provincial Team and the Master of St. Kew, W.Bro Pat Morrisey dedicated the new Banner which is based on the original design and was made by Mrs. Joan Lake of Weston-super-Mare, whose husband Tony is now an Officer of the Lodge.

Vale of Brislington Lodge No. 1296

Meets at the Masonic Hall, Keynsham

Warrant dated 1869

The proposal for the Petition to found the Vale of Brislington Lodge was made in the Royal Albert Edward Lodge Number 906. This Lodge then met at the Crown and Anchor Inn, Bath, and was itself only ten years old.

The relevant extract from the minutes of that Lodge for November 3rd 1869 reads: "Bro P.M. Scott read a communication from some brethren desirous of forming a Lodge at Brislington and asking the recommendation of this Lodge. Bro P.M. Moreton proposed and Bro Hill seconded that it be signed by the Worshipful Master and Officers of Royal Albert Edward Lodge. Motion carried." The Petitioners' Warrant was granted on November 12th 1869. The stage was now set for the first meeting and Consecration of the Vale of Brislington Lodge. A copy of the first summons is pasted in the first minute book.

The Vale of Brislington Lodge was formed as a Vacation Lodge and met on the third Friday in May, June, July and August at 5pm. Bro E.T. Inskip purchased the furniture of the Loyal Vacation Lodge 67 in Wiveliscombe to equip the Lodge room at the White Hart Inn. This Lodge had ceased to exist in 1861 and returned its Warrant in May 1862.

The ritual was the one used in Bristol in 1870. The first Worshipful Master, the Senior Warden and three brethren were from Beaufort Lodge 103 in Bristol and were in the habit of using the Bristol ritual. As the petition was regularly supported and recommended by the Provincial Grand Master for Somerset there was obviously no objection raised to the use of the Bristol ritual in a Somerset Lodge.

The first initiate was C.H. Dowson, Surgeon. He became Worshipful Master in 1874 and was subsequently Treasurer for several years. The second initiate was J. Coles, a Sergeant Major in the Royal Engineers. He was the first Tyler. In September 1879 William Miller, Coachman, was initiated as a Serving Brother. He was then in the service of Dr. Samuel Bryant, the Lodge's first Worshipful Master. He remained Tyler until 1913 when his son, Arthur Miller, Carriage Proprietor, was initiated and followed his father as Tyler. He remained in the service of the Lodge until March 1951 when he retired at the age of 70. In June 1884 Bro Walsh appeared at the Lodge meeting and asked if W.Bro Pierrepont Harris, who had initiated him in April 1883, would perform the Passing ceremony on him. This apparently was duly performed by W.Bro Harris and the rest of the Lodge business was then carried out. It speaks volumes for the adaptability of W.Bro Harris who must have performed the ceremony at a moment's notice.

Several times during the early years of the Lodge the meeting day was changed. At first the Lodge met on the first Friday in May, June, July and August. In 1871 the day was changed to the second Friday. In 1891 it was altered to the fourth Wednesday. It was again moved in 1895 to the fourth Friday, where it has remained ever since. In the formative years the attendances were naturally somewhat smaller than today. It would appear that an average of 10-12 members, with some 6-8 visitors, was usual for ordinary meetings. The minutes of the July meeting in 1871 read "There were not sufficient members present to form a quorum."

As the first Worshipful Master, Samuel Bryant, was a doctor it is not surprising to find that the first candidate was also a doctor. Early Joining Members were mainly doctors, solicitors and members of other professions. Many of the names were of men very well known in their day in the business and professional life of Bristol. Two early members of the Lodge, W.Bro J.R. Bramble and W.Bro W.A.F. Powell, became Provincial Grand Masters for Bristol, whilst W.Bro G.W. Pierrepont Harris became Deputy Provincial Grand Master of Bristol.

The first suggestions for a Jubilee celebration were made at a Lodge finance meeting in June 1915. The minute reads "Bro E. Spear, IPM, proposed and Bro F.S. Bolt PM, seconded, that the Secretary should point out to the Provincial Grand Master the fact that the Jubilee of the Lodge would occur in 1919 and that it would be very nice if we asked that Provincial Grand Lodge should visit us during that year instead of in the year 1917 and to leave the Provincial Grand Master to decide whether a change in the year shall, or shall not, be made".

A special Jubilee medal was to be struck which every subscribing member of the Lodge at the date of the Jubilee would be entitled to wear. Dispensation for this jewel was to be obtained from Grand Lodge.

New collars were to be presented to the Lodge by the respective officers serving at the Jubilee meeting. The total cost of the history and the jewel was not to exceed two guineas per member.

It is noticeable on reading through the minutes, and noting the list of candidates, that through the years it has been a Lodge with strong family ties. There have been several father and son members. Cousins, uncles and brothers-in-law have been common throughout the years. The strongest link traceable is that of the Chandler family. In 1890 W.Bro W.R. Chandler became a Joining Member and was organist for several years. His son, Gilbert Lionel Chandler was initiated and passed in 1901. He was then raised in Powell Lodge as he was going to South Africa for health reasons. He was a member of the Lodge for nearly 40 years. Two of his sons and his son-in-law were initiated into the Lodge and also occupied the Chair. A more tenuous link is that of the first initiate into the Lodge, Dr. Dowson, who was W.R. Chandler's family doctor.

The biggest change the Lodge experienced was the removal from the White Hart Hotel to the Masonic Hall at Keynsham in 1953. After 83 years it was a considerable undertaking and caused much sadness and regret at the time. Only £20 a year was paid as rent for the whole of the middle storey of the Hotel which was used about five times a year. The rest of the time the rooms were not in use. However, in 1950 there was a new landlord of the Hotel, who quite reasonably needed more living accommodation as he had young children.

At the time the Masonic Hall at Keynsham was very much under-utilised and was very pleased to welcome a new Lodge into its ready-made Lodge Room and modern accommodation. Another attraction was that the Lodge was able to meet under the same roof as its daughter Lodge, St. Keyna. This move enabled a change from four regular meetings and a couple of very cold emergency meetings annually to ten meetings. At the White Hart the Lodge only met in the summer as there was no heating in the Lodge room in the winter.

The change in the size of the Lodge Room was a challenge in that it now enabled the Lodge to give full value to the beauty of the Bristol Ritual where the floor work was enhanced by the space available. From 1953 onwards the quality of the ceremonial has been improving year by year and is a great attraction, not only to the visiting brethren, but to the Lodge members themselves.

The atmosphere of friendliness in the Lodge has often been remarked upon by visitors and has always been most apparent. Some of this doubtless can be attributed to the 80 years of meeting at the White Hart Hotel where the Lodge Room was very small, not much larger than two rooms in a large house knocked into one. The changing accommodation was little larger than a large passage. The only seating space was the top of the Lodge chest of miscellaneous articles. The result was that everyone pushed everyone else and the larger frames usually won! Even the Provincial Grand Master was jostled on his visits. Hence it was impossible to be other than friendly! Very fortunately, the spirit has continued until the present day.

During the period following the Centenary, the Lodge has prospered and become even more popular to visit by the brethren from the surrounding area. The standard of work in the Temple has been incredibly high under successive Masters. The interest of the Past Masters in the Lodge has been exemplified by their very good attendance at Committee meetings and ceremonies. The officers and brethren attend in goodly numbers and bring their Masonic friends with them. The future appears to be well assured for the next few years at least, and hopefully, for the next 100 years.

Coleridge Lodge No 1750

Meets at the Masonic Hall Clevedon

Warrant dated 1878

Freemasonry came to Clevedon in 1878 when the Coleridge Lodge was formed by brethren from the Lodge of Agriculture at Yatton and the Beaufort Lodge in Bristol. The idea was driven mainly by Col. William Long who was for many years Chairman of the Clevedon Urban District Council. Col. Long later became Provincial Grand Master for Somerset, Grand Superintendent and Provincial Grand Master in the Mark Degree and was the first Master of the Coleridge Lodge.

The Founders chose the name Coleridge in recognition of a slightly dubious connection that Clevedon has with the poet Samuel Taylor Coleridge, who actually spent his honeymoon in Clevedon. The idea that Clevedon had been an inspiration for literary figures was obviously encouraged by the Victorian Town Elders, due to the growing popularity of the time for taking holidays at the seaside. The idea of naming the Lodge Coleridge was, however, an inspirational decision as others followed this trend and there are now several Lodges in Clevedon named after other literary figures, for example Tennyson, Southey, Thackeray & Hallam, most of whom have a traceable connection with Clevedon.

The first meeting and consecration of the Coleridge Lodge, on the 17th August 1878, was held at a now demolished house, Sandringham House on Clevedon sea front, with the Consecration Dinner being held at The Royal Hotel which was situated on land were the Catholic Church of the Immaculate Conception was later built. Meetings continued in various locations within the town, the Regent Hotel in Hill Road, Clevedon and later the Public Hall in Clevedon, which is actually situated next door to the present Clevedon Masonic Hall.

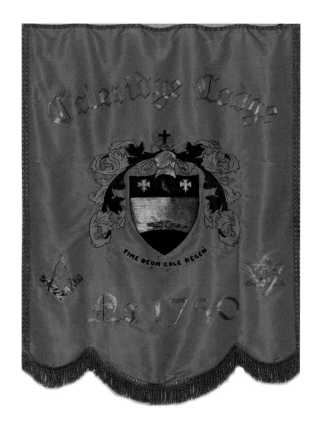

The Lodge and Freemasonry in Clevedon continued to grow with the opening of a Royal Arch Chapter, Adair 1750, in 1888 and brethren numbers grew towards the end of the 19th and early 20th Century up until the outbreak of the 1st World War. Coleridge Lodge continued to meet during the war although several members were away on active service and it was difficult to Officer the Lodge.

No member of the Coleridge Lodge died during the First World War, although Bro A.W. Strange, who had served every office within the Coleridge Lodge up to and including Senior Warden, died as a result of illness that he contracted while serving in the Far East.

Coleridge Lodge always wanted a permanent home even from its early days. In the mid 1800s a wing had been built onto the Public Hall in Albert Road, the Coleridge Lodge had never met in this wing as the Local Board occupied it. However, when the local Town Council was formed, from the Local Board, it moved to larger premises and the wing became unused. This part of the Public Hall was therefore offered to Coleridge Lodge, who purchased it in 1923.

The actual wing consisted of two rooms, one on the Ground Floor, and one on the 1st Floor plus a small plot of land at the rear of about the same size. There was, however, no access between the two floors as entrance to the whole wing was originally gained from the main building. The purchase price was £750 all of which was raised by various methods by the brethren of Coleridge Lodge, although mainly by a subscription of bonds at £250 each from nineteen members all of whom were made Trustees of the Clevedon Masonic Hall. The total also paid for the work on the extension and its furnishing. It is interesting to note that none of the Bonds were repaid, each being turned into a donation.

One of the Coleridge Lodge members was W.Bro Col Sydney Keen, who ran the local brick works, and he donated sufficient bricks to double the size of the building, this donation was subject to the proviso that every Brother of Coleridge Lodge should contribute something. The new wing meant that there would be a front door and entrance hall on the end of the building complete with a staircase to the first floor, a toilet on the ground floor and a committee room on the first floor. The Coleridge Lodge accepted the tender from Mr W. Carey of Portishead for the work for the sum of £1,784.

The first meeting of Coleridge Lodge that was held in the new Clevedon Masonic Hall was the Installation Meeting on Wednesday 14th January 1925. The Clevedon Masonic Hall is still fully owned by Coleridge Lodge although these days it is leased to Clevedon Masonic Club which is fully responsible for the day to day running.

The Coleridge Lodge uses Emulation Workings but has several unique additions, one being that the Master, assisted by his Wardens, presents the Working Tools in all degrees; the only Lodge within the Province to do this. The Lodge also uses the additional explanation of the Apron in the first Degree.

Mark Masonry came to Clevedon with Hallam Lodge 730 being consecrated 1921. In 1922 a Petition was presented to the Coleridge Lodge for the formation of a new Lodge at Nailsea to be called the Tyntesfield Lodge and the Lodge was duly consecrated on the 20th March 1923. The Golden Jubilee of the Coleridge Lodge was celebrated during 1928 not only with a banquet but also mainly with the Petition to form a new Lodge within the Clevedon Masonic Hall. The Tennyson Lodge was consecrated on the 18th April 1928 four months short of the actual 50th Anniversary. An interesting minute on the 14th March 1934 proposed that a Ladies' Night should be arranged and the Lodge agreed this proposition.

The Coleridge Lodge met throughout the 2nd World War although the minutes state that the Warrant of the Lodge had been deposited in a bank for safety. During hostilities the Clevedon Masonic Hall was used as a linen supply store run by Lady Teignmouth, Lord Teignmouth was a member of Tennyson Lodge. During the Second World War two members of the Lodge paid the ultimate price, Bro F.J. Berry and Bro Chaffe were both killed in action. It was also during the Second World War that the Coleridge Lodge started Past Masters Evenings, this being forced upon the Lodge by the regular Officers being away on War Service. This custom continues to the present day.

Coleridge Lodge and Tennyson Lodge brethren, as a thanksgiving for the end of the Second World War, presented the pipe organ to the Trustees of the building. This organ was rebuilt and placed in its present position in 2000 to mark the Millennium. At a Coleridge Lodge meeting held in June 2000, when all the Lodges in Clevedon were invited to attend, the Organ was re-dedicated by the Provincial Grand Master R.W.Bro Stanley Hopkins. This Coleridge Craft Lodge Meeting was also attended by E Comp Denis Calderley, Grand Superintendent in and over the Province of Somerset for the Royal Arch, and R.W.Bro Tony Hick, Provincial Grand Mark Master. This was probably the only occasion where the wearing of Royal Arch and Mark Regalia was authorised by the Provincial Grand Master in a Craft Lodge at Clevedon.

Samuel Taylor Coleridge
This portrait of the inspiration for the Lodge's name is by Peter Vandyke
Reproduced by kind permission of The National Portrait Gallery

On the 11th February 1948, 70 years after the Consecration of the Coleridge Lodge, another Petition was presented this time for another Lodge within the Clevedon Masonic Hall, the Southey Lodge 6650. A further Petition was presented on the 8th November 1961 for the founding of The John de Clivedon Lodge 7824. The Coleridge Lodge continued to flourish during the 1950s, 1960s and 1970s. Numbers at regular meeting were rarely below 70 and the Installation Meetings were so over subscribed that the Installation Dinners were held at the nearby newly-opened Princes Hall, dining numbers regularly being in excess of 120.

The Coleridge Lodge first had a Banner in 1880, but by the early 1960s the Banner was looking a little tired. Mrs Lillian Clist, the wife of W.Bro Leslie Clist, offered to produce for the Lodge a new Banner. This was presented to the Lodge in May 1964 and dedicated by the Provincial Grand Master R.W.Bro A. de L. Cazenove. The Lodge, however, felt that some sort of appreciation should be given to Mrs Clist and it was decided that the Lodge would hold a Christmas celebration in December 1964. This started the Lodge's Christmas Carol Celebration, which is now held every year.

Charity has always played a big part within Coleridge Lodge and the Lodge has supported the various Festivals that have been sponsored by Provincial Grand Lodge. Following the Girls, Festival in 1973 the Lodge was presented with a Commemorative Jewel for contributing the second highest amount from within the Province of Somerset.

The Centenary of the Coleridge Lodge was celebrated during the summer of 1978 when a Thanksgiving Service was held at St Mary's Church in Clevedon. All members of the Coleridge Lodge were invited together with their families and this was followed by tea in the adjoining Church Hall. The actual Centenary Meeting of the Coleridge Lodge was held on Thursday 17th August 1978 at the Clevedon Masonic Hall with 140 brethren attending and the Centenary Banquet was held at the Princes Hall. At this time the Coleridge Lodge had 109 Subscribing Members, who were not only spread around the United Kingdom, but also around the world, with one member running a tea plantation in Ceylon (Sri Lanka) and one member being the Harbour Master at Freemantle, the port for Perth in Western Australia; truly Freemasonry Universal.

On the night of the 27th December 1991 the Clevedon Masonic Hall was broken into and the bar lost all its stock of spirits, wine and cigarettes. Whilst it was covered by insurance, the thieves also took away a safe that contained the records and minute books of Coleridge Lodge. Appeals were made in the press, and after a few days a lady who had been walking her dog besides the river bank on Kenn Moor reported to the Police that there was the safe lying on its side in the water. The safe was recovered, but; its back had been removed and all of the records were saturated. These were dried out professionally and the minutes were rebound. However, about ten years were missing, and some are today unreadable.

The 125th Anniversary of the Coleridge Lodge was celebrated in 2003 with a visit by the Provincial Grand Master, R.W.Bro David L. Jenkins, and W.Bro Peter Osborne presented new gavels to the Lodge on this occasion.

Virtually all of the furniture and artefacts within the building belong to the Coleridge Lodge, and most appear in an inventory of Lodge furniture dated 1880 and were obviously in use prior to the move to the Clevedon Masonic Hall. They include the Master's and Wardens' Chairs, the Pillars and the Tracing Boards; these form the whole history of the Lodge although through the years they have been added to. The seats in the Lodge Room were purchased by a member at an auction at the Embassy Cinema in Queens Road, Bristol. They were refurbished and presented to the building in about 1960; previously to this chairs were used. The Lodge was also presented with two heavy cast iron Deacons' wand stands by W.Bro Cecil Forbes, who was a Scottish Freemason. The stands had previously been used in a Scottish Lodge which had ceased to function.

During its 130 years of existence the Coleridge Lodge has always played an active part within the Province and Freemasonry in general. Several members have been honoured as Grand Officers and also with high ranking and active Provincial Offices. Others have carried on from their Initiation in Coleridge Lodge and have carried the Masonic message to the far-flung corners of the World. The Coleridge Lodge, therefore, continues to flourish, although like many lodges membership numbers are not what they were 50 years ago.

Eldon Lodge No. 1755

Meets at the Masonic Hall, Albert Road, Clevedon

Warrant dated 1878

Eldon Lodge 1755 first saw the light of day on the petition of one W.Bro Robert Compton, Past Master of Royal Clarence Lodge 68 in the Province of Bristol, and other brethren residing in Portishead. The town being in Somerset it was necessary to obtain support from this Province and that was duly provided by a recommendation from St. Kew Lodge 1222 at the request of W.Bro V.H. Scott, (on behalf of W.Bro Compton), a member of that Lodge and a Past Master of the Colston Lodge 610, Bristol

The senior Founder of the Lodge was W.Bro Charles Fisher, an interesting personality, nephew and heir to W.Bro John Fisher, a wealthy Bristol wine merchant. Charles Fisher carried on the wine business and built Eldon Villa, described as a beautiful residence with a fine garden and picturesque tower. From this tower in ignorance, and mistaken loyalty, he flew the White Ensign (the premier British maritime flag flown by all Her Majesty's ships) until an irate captain in the Royal Navy called upon him and ordered him to take it down without a moment's delay!

W.Bro Charles Fisher is reputed to have befriended Prince Louis Napoleon, later to become Emperor Napoleon III of France, and to have lent him money. Be that as it may, the Emperor gave Charles a portrait of himself which was hung on the grand staircase of Eldon Villa.

W.Bro Charles Fisher financed the founding of the Lodge and as a compliment to him it was agreed that the Lodge should take its title from the name of his home. Subsequently he was elected as the first treasurer of the Lodge.

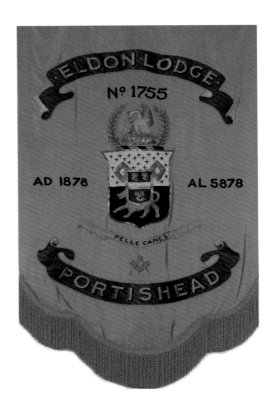

The Consecration of this Lodge took place at the Royal Hotel, Portishead, on 3rd September, 1878. The ceremony was performed in the most solemn and impressive manner by the Deputy Provincial Grand Master, V.W.Bro R.C. Else. He was assisted by the Officers of the Provincial Grand Lodge of Somerset, and the meeting was attended by brethren from Somerset and neighbouring Provinces. The Lodge having been constituted, the Consecrating Officer installed W.Bro Charles E. Daniel as Worshipful Master who proceeded to appoint his officers for the ensuing year. The first regular meeting of the Eldon Lodge took place on the 14th September, 1878, the second Saturday of the month and meetings are still held on that particular day of the month.

A minute dated 11th January, 1879 reads:-

'The Worshipful Master generously offered to present the Lodge with a banner.' The announcement was received with applause by the brethren and thankfully accepted.

Some discussion took place as to what the motto should be, and it was proposed by W.Bro Compton and seconded by W.Bro Hardwick, SW, that the Arms of the Worshipful Master, W.Bro Charles E. Daniel, being the first Master of the Lodge, be the emblem or device of the Eldon Lodge banner. Carried unanimously and by acclamation.

Eldon Lodge continued to meet at the Royal Hotel until 1911 when the Lodge entered into an agreement with the Great Western Railway to lease the Pier Station, now no longer in use, for the sum of £30 per annum and also to be responsible for any repairs or alterations.

However, in June 1933, due to the foresight of some of the members, the premises were purchased outright for the sum of £800. Here, with the exceptions of the war years 1939-1945, the brethren continued to meet until a combination of local development, the lack of adequate parking facilities and problems with local utilities, caused the brethren to reluctantly agree to vacate the premises and transfer to the Masonic Hall at Clevedon, here to remain until such time as a suitable new building became available in Portishead.

During the War years, with brethren being in the armed forces or on other war work, the rationing of petrol, transport problems, blackout restrictions and catering difficulties it became necessary to alter the arrangements for meetings. In 1939 and 1940 some meetings were cancelled while the Installation of W.Bro E.C. Harvey in 1940 was held, by dispensation and by the courtesy of the Vale of Brislington Lodge 1296, at the White Hart Hotel, Brislington.

From 13th June 1942 until 9th June, 1945 when a return was made to Portishead, the Lodge met at the Albert Hall, Dowry Square, Hotwells, Bristol by dispensation from the Provincial Grand Masters of Bristol and Somerset, with W.Bro G.E. Denman actually being installed in 1944 at the Victoria Rooms, Bristol, again by dispensation. It is reported that in those days the festive board consisted of weak tea and biscuits!

Eldon has always been considered 'a maritime Lodge', having had among its members many master mariners, pilots and boatmen. Indeed, such brethren are still numbered among the members, albeit some of them are now retired. It has been reported that some skippers, passing the Lodge, either inbound to the docks or making their way seaward, and knowing that the Lodge was meeting would give three blasts on the siren. An outward sign of this relationship is the display of the White and Red ensigns on the dining table in front of the Worshipful Master at the festive board.

One such member worthy of note was W.Bro. T.G.H. Hunt who completed 50 years in Masonry in the Centenary year. W.Bro Tom was a Master Mariner who, in his career, had spent time 'before the mast' under sail. He was a real 'character' and would entertain the brethren with tales of his experiences, more often than not, out East. He 'got the book out' whenever he could on his voyages, very often while 'hove to' in Lady Bay awaiting tide and pilot. He put off taking office until he retired at 65 and eventually became an exemplary Worshipful Master.

The Lodge, of course, not only had connections with the sea through its members but also through both of its Portishead locations, the Royal Hotel and the old Pier railway station, both of which were within a cable's length of the shore, albeit in the opposite direction to the shifting sands of the sea.

There was a disadvantage in this, however, in the days before accurate radar and pollution control when dense fog would sometimes descend on Lodge and sea and the local fog-horn would come into operation. While not completely drowning the words of the participants in the Lodge it was enough to disrupt proceedings more than a little, particularly when the first blast occurred unexpectedly. The maritime connection is important to Eldon Lodge and it is to be hoped that it will not be long before the Lodge is once more situated close to the sea.

A proposal was made by the brethren in 1905 to form a Royal Arch Chapter at Portishead but it was over four years before Eldon Chapter was eventually consecrated on 16th April, 1910. In September 1921 the brethren of Eldon Lodge took the first steps toward forming a new Lodge at Portishead leading to the consecration on 27th May, 1922, of its first daughter Lodge, the Severn Lodge 4399. In 1924 the Warrant of Eldon Mark Lodge 807 was issued, the Founders being mostly Eldon and Severn brethren who were members of the Lyegrove Mark Lodge 218 or Canynge Mark Lodge

In 1946, under the sponsorship of Eldon, the second daughter Lodge, the Gordano Lodge 6244 was consecrated on 5th October and the third, the Olympian Lodge 9703, in 1999.

Over the years many fraternal visits have been made and received by a variety of lodges, but the only regular and reciprocal ones still going strong are those with St. Alphege Lodge 4095 in Bath. Their first recorded visit to Portishead was on 11th July, 1925, and long may they continue.

Like a number of other lodges in the Province Eldon Lodge does not necessarily adhere rigidly to Emulation Working. Many of the differences, albeit slight, originated many years ago and have been passed on by word of mouth from generation to generation.

However, at rehearsals, differences of opinion were sometimes aired, so it was decided, eventually, to commit an agreed version to print with the result that in 1999 " Eldon Practice in Emulation Working" rolled off the press. A unique piece of ritual included in this booklet is the description of the Eldon Cable-Tow which had its origins in Royal Navy tradition.

It was brought to Eldon by a Joining Member of the Lodge, Bro R. Derrick, a one-time serving officer in the RN, whose Royal Marine Lodge regularly used it in their ceremonies. This description is delivered to every candidate once he has been raised, using as an example such a cable-tow fashioned by Bro Derrick himself and presented to the Lodge. A copy of the Eldon Practice booklet is presented to every new member. It is much cherished in the Lodge, great care being taken to see that it is adhered to. Vive la Deference!

St Keyna Lodge No. 1833

Meets at the Masonic Hall, Bath Road, Keynsham.

Warrant dated 1879

St Keyna Lodge was formed in 1879 following a petition to Grand Lodge by ten brethren, eight of whom were living in Keynsham and two in Bristol, probably early in 1879. The Petition was recommended by the Master and Wardens of the Vale of Brislington Lodge 1296 and the warrant creating the Lodge was dated 9th June 1879. The Founders of the Lodge were nine of the petitioners and ten additional brethren. Although these brethren were in Lodges mainly in Bristol and Bath, some were from as far away as Birmingham and Poole, and some were under the Scottish Constitution.

How did these brethren come together to form St Keyna Lodge? This may be explained by their possibly being members of a `club' in Bristol or they were frequent visitors to the `White Hart' at Brislington where the Vale of Brislington Lodge met as a Summer Lodge in its early days. We shall never know for certain where the original inspiration came from to create St Keyna Lodge, but it is generally thought that W.Bros Thomas and Crisp of the Vale of Brislington Lodge had a lot to do with it.

Twelve years before St Keyna Lodge was formed Freemasonry had already started to spread out of Bristol. In 1867 seven Bristol Masons, six of whom were members of Beaufort Lodge, petitioned to form the Lodge of Agriculture 1199 in what is now North Somerset. Two years later another group of Masons, again mainly from Bristol, founded the Vale of Brislington Lodge which was to become St Kenya's mother Lodge. The Vale of Brislington's petition was recommended by Royal Albert Edward Lodge 906, thus becoming the "grandparent in direct line" of St Keyna.

The Lodge name was chosen to link the Lodge to the town. The derivation of the name `Keynsham' is thought to be either from 'Keyne's Ham' (Ham being a Saxon word for settlement) or alternatively 'Keyne's Hamm' - Hamm meaning a low-lying meadow.

There is a charming legend which purports to derive Keyne from St Keyna, an early Christian Saint of that name. According to the story, Keyna was a virgin who lived in these parts in the 5th century A.D. She was the daughter of Braganus, a Prince of Brecknock in Wales. She had many admirers but having taken a vow of perpetual virginity she refused them and became known as `Keyn-Wyryf or Keyna the Virgin'.

She left Wales to find a deserted place to indulge her religious devotions. Her travels took her to a wooded place in North-East Somerset.

She obtained permission to stay there but was warned that the place "so swarmed with serpents that neither man nor beast could live there". She firmly believed that she would be able to drive the venomous brood out of the country. By her prayers all the serpents were turned to stone and to this day the stones in and around Keynsham resemble the windings of serpents. The Crest of the Lodge depicts St. Keyna with one of her "venomous brood".

The ceremony of Consecration took place in the Masonic Hall at the 'Lamb and Lark' Keynsham, a George's Public House, on Tuesday, the 5th August 1879 at 2.30 p.m. The Ceremony and Installation was performed by W.Bro R.C. Else, DPGM and Officers of the Provincial Grand Lodge of Somerset by command of the Pro. Grand Master, the Rt. Hon. The Earl of Carnarvon. The banquet followed at 4.30 p.m. costing six shillings (30p), exclusive of wine!

The first Master was W.Bro R.W. Thomas of the Vale of Brislington Lodge. He was a member of Cambrian Lodge, 364 Neath, and held the rank of Past Provincial Grand Pursuivant. He was a surgeon and on moving to Keynsham he joined the Vale of Brislington Lodge in August 1877. The second Master was W.Bro Nathaniel Crisp, another member of the medical profession living at Keynsham. Initiated in Holyhead, he joined the Vale of Brislington Lodge on the same day as W.Bro Thomas. Two other founders also became Masters; W.Bro Wm. Roberts (Moira) in 1882 and W.Bro A.G. Williams (Colston) in 1883. The first Initiate was Bro G. O'Connor-Parnell, and St Keyna being a new Lodge he made rapid progress, and was Master in 1884; only five years, which even in those days was very fast.

The Lodge Banner was made by the wife of W.Bro Parnell (the first initiate), and the design was left entirely up to her. Her husband had received a Provincial collar from the PGM, the Earl of Carnarvon, and she thought it

Printed boards listing the names and years of Past Masters are common in Masonic Halls, but occasionally one which is particularly pleasing and of note stands out, and such a one can be seen at Keynsham, that of the St.. Keyna Lodge 1833.

appropriate to incorporate the Arms of the Earl into the design, which she did. Also there are three lions rampant, two compasses and squares and another Masonic emblem. Also included is a serpent stone being a reminder of the legend of St Keyna. Beneath is an inscription in Old French - UNG JE SERVIRAI (one will I serve). After 60 years of use the banner required repair. This was done in 1956 by Mrs Parnell's daughters.

St. Keyna Lodge held it's regular meetings at the 'Lamb and Lark' at Keynsham for 60 years, together with Carnarvon Mark Lodge and Irwin Lodge of Royal Ark Mariners. As far back as the years following the First World War there were shortcomings in the facilities at the 'Lamb and Lark'. The roof of the building leaked whilst the nearby stables did not improve the 'atmosphere'!! However, the main problem was that the membership had increased beyond the capacity of the room.

Just before the Second World War land was bought on the main Bath Road in Keynsham and the present Masonic Hall erected there during 1939/40. This was due to the inspiration and foresight of the St Keyna Lodge brethren and the considerable financial backing of St Keyna Lodge which made construction possible.

The present site was not the first to be considered. Two cottages and ground attached at the High Street, Keynsham, were considered in 1920 but after several meetings the project was dropped. In 1923 a discussion was held on the purchase of a house at Keynsham for conversion into a Masonic Hall and club, but this was abandoned because of the cost of conversion. Also in 1923 there is reference to a site at Burnett Lane, Keynsham, but nothing came of it. Initial enquiries were made to see if the existing temple (Lamb and Lark) could be enlarged.

Early in 1924 a site at Priory Road was bought for £200. That project was abandoned but the land was not sold until 1942 to J.S. Fry and Sons for £200. Suggestions to enlarge the Lodge room at the Lamb and Lark were made in 1923 and revived in 1927. The idea was favourably received with the cost of £2,000 to be recouped by an annual rent to be paid to George's Bristol Brewery, who owned the Lamb and Lark. The new room was opened by the PGM, R.W.Bro The Venerable Archdeacon Walter Farrer, M.A. on the 21st November 1927. However, satisfaction with the new arrangements were short lived, particularly with regard to catering.

In 1933 the purchase of 'The Lido' in Brislington was considered but after lengthy discussions was also turned down.

Following all these disappointments it was decided in 1935 that a definite decision must be taken by the whole Lodge, presumably for a building to be erected on land at Chandos Road, Keynsham, owned by St Keyna Lodge and at an estimated cost of £4,600. St Keyna would provide £2000, Abbey £300, Carnarvon Mark, St Keyna Chapter and Irwin R.A.M. each £100, leaving £2000 to be raised. The proposal to go ahead was approved by ballot of 51 to 3. Much effort was put into the design and a two storey building was agreed upon. This was put out to tender and the lowest amounted to £8,000, way over budget! The scheme was eventually abandoned.

In March 1939 a site on the Bath Road became available and this was purchased for £400. Due to the eminent possibility of war no time could be lost. New plans were prepared and a contract for the building estimated to cost something over £5,000 was given to Bro Sperring, of Saltford, a builder. Work started on 1st September 1939 and the temple was completed one year later.

St Keyna Lodge gave the fixtures and fittings, and the organ (valued at £1432), £3,000 from Lodge resources and in all a total of £5,282. Abbey Lodge gave £300, Carnarvon Mark Lodge £25 and St Keyna Chapter £50. The total bill amounted to £7266.

The building was first used on 26th August 1940 for a Lodge committee meeting and the first ceremony took place on Saturday afternoon, 14th September 1940. Bros B.W. Stacey and Gordon Bennett (still a Lodge member in 2007) were the initiates. Because of the war the Consecration Ceremony was held over until 22nd June 1946.

A point of interest is that in 1953 the Vale of Brislington Lodge left the 'White Hart' Brislington and met at the Masonic Hall, Keynsham. Thus 'mother" and 'daughter' came together for the first time since 1870.

Originally the Lodge Meetings were held on the third Monday in alternate months starting from July, the Installation being in May. Six candidates a year were being admitted, two at a time with emergency meetings being called if necessary. By the 1960s the number of candidates was down to four and with the Installation on the third Friday of June no emergency meetings were required. In 1965, until the present day, the Installation meeting is held in January with initially eight regular meetings and now only six each year.

It must be noted that the Vale of Brislington Lodge uses `Bristol Working'. The first Master came from Beaufort Lodge, Bristol, so did his Senior Warden and there were four other Bristol brethren. Understandably they would use a ritual familiar to them. The Vale of Brislington Lodge is the 'mother' Lodge of St Keyna, so as a dutiful 'daughter' St Keyna followed her `mother'. Consequently St Keyna Lodge has always used 'Bristol Working'. Over time slight differences have occurred, so perhaps we should really call it the 'St Keyna Working' based on Bristol Working.

Over the years St Kenya Lodge has been prolific in sponsoring 'daughter' Lodges. In 1922 the Abbey Lodge 4491 was founded through the efforts of St Keyna brethren and uses 'Bristol Working'. In 1949 the Priory Lodge 6913 was formed by St Keyna but was asked to practice the Emulation Ritual in line with most other Lodges formed and meeting in the Province of Somerset. In 1974 St Keyna was asked to sponsor the Saltford Lodge 8633, again to be an Emulation Working Lodge. In 1981 the Gerard Lodge 8999 was sponsored, another Emulation Working Lodge.

Prudence and Industry Lodge No. 1953

Meets at the Masonic Hall, Chard

Warrant dated 1881

The first Lodge of Prudence and Industry was constituted under a Warrant issued by the Provincial Grand Lodge of Somerset on 25th March 1799 and numbered 579. The warrant was signed by John Smith-Leigh, Provincial Grand Master for Somerset; Charles Phillpott, Deputy Provincial Grand Master and William Meyler, Provincial Grand Secretary. All the Petitioners had been members of the Lodge of Unanimity and Sincerity 433 meeting at Taunton.

At the Union of the Grand Lodges in 1814 the number was changed to 598 under which the Lodge met for the first time on 27th July 1814 and continued to meet until December 1831 when the warrant was surrendered to the Grand Master HRH the Duke of Sussex to be cancelled.

To understand the background to the present Lodge in Chard it is necessary to look back to the formation of the original Lodge in 1799. It seems probable that the early Lodge 579 was formed in 1799 because Unanimity Lodge, Ilminster had recently moved to Taunton as Unanimity and Sincerity under the Master, Charles Marsh. Even though meeting dates were arranged nearest to the 'full moon', the thought of travelling by horse at night, and not on roads as we know them today, it is not surprising that some members living on the Devon coast at Beer found the extra journey to Taunton too difficult and so, under a Master resident in Chard, founded the Lodge of Prudence and Industry 579.

Charting the early history for the Lodge is difficult as there are no minutes available before 1803; the book commencing in that year says that they were destroyed. Also, in 1807, the minutes record that the Secretary "shamefully left" and left no record of membership. During the period of the original Prudence and Industry Lodge there are estimated to have been 181 members. A third of these were not registered at Grand Lodge mainly because 'subscribing membership' at the time required an additional proposal and ballot, and without this they were not included in returns to Grand Lodge.

During its early existence the Lodge met at various locations in Chard, from 1799 to 1801 at the George Inn, 1801 to 1808 at the Red Lion, 1808 to 1816 at the Angel Inn, and 1816 to 1831 at the Freemasons' Hall. Both of the original Lodges at Chard and Axminster were erased by Grand Lodge in 1830.

From the very incomplete records which exist in the archives of Grand Lodge it would seem that 'inaccurate minutes' and 'bad returns' may have contributed to the downfall of Lodge 598. The period from 1831 until Lodge 1953 came into being has no direct Masonic record.

Bro Sumner Toms

A warrant from Grand Lodge dated 23rd November 1881 signalled the return of the Prudence and Industry Lodge to Chard with the number 1953 and named Bro Sumner Toms as Master, Bro Curteis Norwood was Senior Warden, and Bro Frederick Bath as Junior Warden.

On the 19th April 1882 the Deputy Provincial Grand Master, W.Bro R.C. Else, accompanied by six officers of Provincial Grand Lodge, and before an assembly of 79 brethren, consecrated the Lodge and installed Bro S. Toms as the first Worshipful Master. The Lodge of Instruction was started in September 1882 to meet monthly on the second Wednesday. In fact more than five meetings in any year were never achieved and the Lodge apparently ceased in 1888 for twenty years. Much of the remaining history of the Lodge is contained in the nine minute books, the first covering the years 1882 to 1903:

Though a committee examined alternatives over several months in 1895-6 the Lodge met in the George Hotel until Bro Toms built the new Lodge "over the stables at the rear of the George Hotel". The first meeting was held there in September 1897. No re-consecration was judged to be necessary by Provincial Grand Lodge.

Efforts to learn more of the Freemasons' Hall in Chard have led nowhere, which is a great pity as some knowledge of who owned the property, its exact location etc, could perhaps provide clues which would enable the wanderings of some of the artefacts to be traced.

An example is an entry in the minutes of a Lodge of Emergency held on 18th August 1913, "That it is desirable to make an effort to secure the return of three chairs to this Lodge Buildings and that a Committee be appointed to meet representatives of the Town Council and learn definitely upon what terms the Council would be prepared to transfer the three chairs to the Lodge".

How the Corporation came to be in possession of the chairs, which are admitted to be the property of the old Prudence and Industry Lodge, remains a mystery, but the outcome of the sub-committee meeting with the Corporation resulted in the Lodge buying back the chairs for £12, which subsequently purchased a set of chairs for use in the Town Hall by Magistrates and the Council. Following a refurbishment of the Guildhall they were no longer required. The Council retained the carved 'Carver' and one each of the others was given to the Chard Museum and the Lodge.

In September 2004 a remarkable coincidence saw the return of one of the original three chairs given to the Guildhall in 1913. W.Bro Page was informed that several old chairs were being disposed of on the refurbishment of the Guildhall and made due enquiries only to find that these were the chairs purchased by the Lodge in order for the originals to be returned. He was able to successfully negotiate the return of one of them to the Lodge where it is now the ADC's chair, the other two being preserved for posterity, one in the Guildhall and the other in Chard Museum.

The Masonic career of Bro Toms had progressed over the years and he was very much the driving force in the Lodge in its early days. He was a partner in the local brewing business of Messrs. Mitchell, Toms and Company, and we find both surnames appearing constantly in the proceedings of the Lodge.

Initially attendances were small and in keeping with the limited membership even as few as eight or ten during the earliest years, with very few visitors and these were most usually at Installation Meetings. By approximately 1900 attendances were reaching the twenties, and at about this time the numbers of visitors, increased significantly. There were some set backs to attendances during the First World War, but there was a rapid improvement afterwards. Fraternal visits with the De La Pole Lodge in Seaton were started by W.Bro Toms, who became a Joining Member at Seaton. The first was when he became Master of De La Pole in 1900, and they have been an annual fixture ever since.

Around this time the call on Lodge charitable funds records contributions to "Our Brothers Bed in the Home for the Dying at Clapham", and purchases of votes for the Royal Masonic Institutions. Not all demands on the Lodge charity funds could be met, and a number are recorded as being "allowed to lie on the table". Between 1882 and 1903 there are only four references in the minutes giving any financial figures, September and October 1885, February 1886 and May 1900. It may be worth noting that the cost of initially furnishing the Lodge is recorded as £76.12s.6d, and it was not until the third year that the Lodge was out of debt, the Bank having charged £3.7s.2d. during the period. Subscriptions were £1.1s.0d. p.a.; Initiation fee £5.5s.0d; Joining fee £2.2s.0d. and a year's rent for the Lodge was £10.

The appearance of the Lodge during this period must have changed considerably, the first item being the purchase of two large columns in 1909. A committee deliberated on this for almost twelve months and evidently arranged to view samples at the manufacturers, Bro H.T. Lamb, Clerkenwell, before ordering them in January 1910 at a cost of £14-£21. In 1915 an inventory of the furniture of the Lodge and ante-room was read to the Lodge and the insurance value increased from £150 to £240.

In September 1911 it was voted that smoking in the Lodge room be discontinued; this was a very early success for the anti-smoking lobby! Nevertheless in June 1915 improvements to the Lodge ventilation were discussed, but alas all three alternative schemes prepared (the most expensive costing £10) were "postponed to a future date" on the WM's casting vote.

The first proposal to hold a Ladies' Night was in 1913. This was overtaken by the events of the Great War but no doubt contributed to the brethren and the ladies arranging major entertainment for wounded soldiers in the hospital in Chard in 1917 and 1918. A newspaper cutting attached to the minutes details the 1918 entertainment for 120 including a dinner, whist drive and concert by professional and amateur artists, all at a cost of £14.3s.3d. The first formal Ladies' Night consisting of a dinner and whist drive was held in 1921.

In 1922 the Lodge was re-carpeted at a cost of £20.10s.0d; it is assumed that this included the chequered carpet. Worthy of note is that in 2006 much of the debate at the Past Masters Committee meetings was about the poor condition of the chequered carpet, as several attempts had been made to 'nail down' the curling edges to avoid trips and falls. They did not deliberate for long on replacing it; the decision being taken to proceed, ensuring that it was laid for the 125th anniversary meeting. The cost of the carpet was £5,478!

Between 1935 and 1949 the general impression is that records are now of meetings much nearer to those seen today, and of course are within the memory of current members who attended. This period brought significant change; the installation of electricity to the Lodge in 1935 which had been rejected in 1923!

During the period of the 1939-45 War it is recorded that evacuated and English and American service visitors attended the Lodge, and letters of thanks for hospitality noted. In the manner of the period W.Bro Major Nicholls presented a gavel made from part of an aircraft which crashed in Nottingham (presumably an enemy one). Grand Lodge had appealed for jewels to be given for the War effort and the collections of W.Bro Dymonds and W.Bro Bailey Toms were to be checked for value. The result of this is not recorded.

By now contributions to the Masonic charities were a regular feature of the minutes, and the allocation of alms from the Installation Meeting was changed from Chard Hospital to being regularly given to the Royal Masonic Hospital from 1937 onwards. One unusual item was a gift to the Somerset Agriculture Disaster Fund in 1947 following the serious weather conditions of that winter.

As a result of expenditure on repairs in 1959 the committee recommended that the subscription should be raised to three guineas, of which ten shillings per member should be allocated to a sinking fund. Notice of motion was not given until April 1960 and the figure eventually agreed at the October meeting was three pounds ten shillings.

Bro F.C. Harris was initiated in December 1966 and elected Tyler in 1967. He continued to serve the Lodge until illness prevented him attending in 2004. He was promoted PPrAGPurs in 1998 and presented with Provincial Grand Lodge clothing with thanks from the Lodge. Bro Fred was made an Honorary Member

The Original Lodge Banner

of the Lodge in February 2004 in recognition of his many dedicated years service. It is worth recording that Bro Harris had also acted as caretaker for many years and had been present at just about every meeting. Sadly he passed to the Grand Lodge above in July 2005. He had been Tyler of the Lodge for 38 years.

The minutes from 1965 to 1977 indicated a complicated period with much recorded of discussions over the lease of the Lodge premises, including a special meeting by dispensation. Serious thought had to be given to the purchase of alternative premises and a temporary move to Ilminster or Crewkerne.

Eventually an extended lease was arranged which led to additional work to the structure, and a programme of decorating work carried out by volunteers within the Lodge. During this period there were more lectures than previously, being given by both Lodge members as well as others, including special ones arranged by the Province.

Also during the period covered by this minute book many improvements were made to the Lodge premises, and a building fund was established to finance much of the on-going work. A "Lodge of Improvement" was formed whereby Lodge member volunteers met to decorate and carry out improvement works to both the changing rooms and the ante-room. This initiative was led in the main by Bros. Cavill, Penfold and Barnes.

Prudence and Industry Lodge was proud at the time of its Centenary to have numbered a Provincial Grand Master, a Deputy Provincial Grand Master and an Assistant Provincial Grand Master amongst its members.

A Banner Dedication ceremony was carried out by the Provincial Grand Master and his team on the 27th October 2000. The original banner was bought in 1887 at a cost of £10. The new one was £885, the cost being met entirely from the legacy of Mrs Emily Pace, whose husband Bro Charles Pace was a Joining Member of the Lodge and a Masonic Veteran. He was initiated in Canada in 1934. The Oration for the Banner was given by W.Bro T.M. Isherword, PG Chaplain. Plans were made to encase the original banner to preserve it, but unfortunately it was lost in the post and despite efforts to ascertain its whereabouts, it appears no longer to exist.

Lodge of Fidelity and Sincerity No. 1966

Meets at the Masonic Hall, Mantle Street, Wellington

Warrant dated 1882

The first records of a Lodge in Wellington date back to 1804 and refer to a Lodge called Liberty & Sincerity No 300. The first minute book is in the Library and Museum at Grand Lodge. The number was changed to 382 in 1814 after which it had a short life, being erased in 1828.

The Lodge as we know it today was consecrated at the Wellington Town Hall on 13th June 1882 by the Deputy Provincial Grand Master for Somerset W.Bro R.C. Else, the Lodge having been sponsored by the Lodge of Unanimity and Sincerity 261 of Taunton. At the consecration there were 114 Freemasons present who had travelled from all parts of the Province and included some from Devon and one from New York.

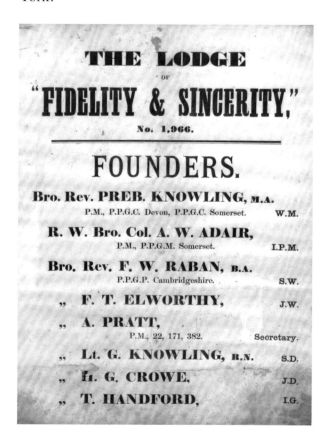

THE LODGE

OF

"FIDELITY & SINCERITY,"

No. 1,966.

FOUNDERS.

Bro. Rev. PREB. KNOWLING, M.A.
P.M., P.P.G.C. Devon, P.P.G.C. Somerset.   W.M.

R. W. Bro. Col. A. W. ADAIR,
P.M., P.P.G.M. Somerset.   I.P.M.

Bro. Rev. F. W. RABAN, B.A.
P.P.G.P. Cambridgeshire.   S.W.

„ F. T. ELWORTHY,   J.W.

„ A. PRATT,
P.M., 22, 171, 382.   Secretary.

„ Lt. G. KNOWLING, R.N.   S.D.

„ H. G. CROWE,   J.D.

„ T. HANDFORD,   I.G.

The summons convening the meeting was printed by " The Freemason" printing works, opposite Freemasons Hall in Great Queen Street, London.

There were eight Founder Members who set up the Lodge and the first WM was Rev. Preb. George Knowling, the Vicar of the parish of Wellington, and also a Prebendary or Canon of Wells Cathedral.

A banquet was held at the Squirrel Hotel, Wellington when the menu included a selection of the following: Mock Turtle or Green Pea Soup, Round of Beef, Baron of Lamb, Savoury Brawn, Pigeon Pie, Thatched Pie, Lobster in Aspic followed by Tipsy cake, Raspberry Tart and many more mouth watering choices.

The Lodge intended to hold its regular meetings at the White Hart public house, but the landlady had other ideas and refused to allow the Lodge furnishings to be moved there. Only ten days after the Consecration meeting an emergency meeting was held at the Vicarage at Wellington, primarily for the consideration of the meeting place problem but also to discuss the eligibility of one of the candidates for initiation, because it transpired that he had lost his right arm in an accident.

The problem was passed to the PGM (The 4th Earl of Carnarvon) for his advice but he, having had no similar case during his Masonic experience, wrote to the Grand Secretary seeking the views of Grand Lodge. The matter was considered by the Board of General Purposes who felt it was impossible to lay down a hard and fast rule in such circumstances but considered that a candidate would be eligible for election who, although not perfect in their limbs, were sufficiently so to comply with and go through the various ceremonies required for each degree.

The problem of a meeting place was resolved by the renting of premises off Mantle Street, which were formally a repository for animal feeding stuffs, fertilisers and salt, at a rent of £16.10s per annum and the building was called "The Masonic Hall". The term of the lease was 21 years, however, in 1884 the owner agreed to sell the premises to the Lodge for the sum of £350. The legal expenses amounted to £13.19s.6d.

The first regular meeting was held on 10th July 1882 when there were seven brethren present. The Lodge then proceeded to initiate four candidates. On 11th June 1883 Francis William Raban was installed as WM and the brethren agreed that a Founders Jewel (to the value of two guineas) be presented to the Installing Master, W.Bro Knowling.

The Founders

The first record of a Lodge of Instruction is in the minutes for July 1884 and it is noted that the subscription would 2s.6d. p.a.

In March 1885 it was proposed that the future dress of the brethren should be evening dress viz: knee breeches, silk stockings, and low shoes, this was carried by eight votes to four, but the minute is struck through with a note in the margin saying, " this proposition being irregular was ordered to be cancelled ".

A special meeting was held at the Masonic Hall, Wellington, on 10th September 1888 at 11.30 am for the purpose of assisting at the ceremony of laying the foundation stone of the new church at All Saints, Rockwell Green. The stone would be laid by R.W.Bro Brig. Gen. A.W. Adair PPGM Somerset at the invitation of the Deputy Grand Master. The meeting was duly held and the brethren of Fidelity & Sincerity held their meeting in the evening.

An attempt to alter the date of the meetings of the Lodge from Mondays to Tuesdays was rejected in October 1888. In 1892 the Provincial Grand Lodge of Somerset held their annual provincial meeting at Wellington by invitation of the Lodge. In 1896 the number of meetings was reduced from twelve to nine a year.

In 1903 W.Bro Bowyer died and in October 1904 the Church Council of All Saints wrote stating that it was proposing to erect a stained glass window to his memory and inviting the Lodge to contribute, which they did with the sum of £20, sufficient for the provision of a light. The window was unveiled at a service on Easter Sunday 1905 by W.Bro Elworthy.

During 1910 there were again discussions about the number of meetings held in a year and it was finally decided in February 1911 to hold the regular meetings from September to May inclusive with the installation of the new W. M. in the month of October each year. Ballots to be held in September for the relevant officers. This pattern has remained in force ever since.

Following the onset of the Second World War the military authorities requisitioned the Lodge ante-rooms in May 1941 for use as an officer's mess, and the occupation lasted until 1945. In May 1946 new seating was introduced into the Lodge in the form of pews removed from the Parish Church and a sum of £3 was sent to the vicar as a token of acknowledgement. February and March 1949 saw a movement by the junior brethren towards rehearsing ceremonies at meetings additional to the main rehearsals, which are held on the first Monday of each month while the Lodge is in session.

In May 1952 the Lodge agreed to sponsor the proposed Wellington School (Somerset) Lodge and a petition was sought. The Lodge was consecrated on 10th January 1953 in the Great Hall of the school. The School Lodge have subsequently used the Wellington Masonic Hall for their meetings. The original rent paid by the School Lodge to the Lodge was £1.5s.0d.

The School Lodge presented a new carpet to the Lodge in 1959 and in November of that year a scheme to purchase and erect a hut (from the Taunton Red Cross) to form a Dining Room was approved.

Below: A most interesting print combining The Lord's Prayer with many of the more familiar Masonic symbols hangs outside the door of the Lodge Room

Portcullis Lodge No. 2038

Meets at St Mary's Chapel, The Hill, Langport

Warrant dated 1884

Minutes of Nyanza Lodge 1197 record that on 22nd May 1883 there was a request that the Lodge support the formation of a new Lodge at Langport. However, in December of that year a formal motion was deferred as there were not enough members present. The motion was eventually carried the following month.

The Warrant was granted on the 14th March 1884. A meeting place had been arranged at the Langport Arms Hotel owned by Bro Barling of Nyanza Lodge and a founder of Portcullis Lodge. The Consecration Ceremony took place on Tuesday 24th June 1884, at 12.30 pm in Langport Town Hall and was conducted by the Deputy Provincial Grand Master, VW.Bro R.C. Else, on behalf of the R.W PGM the Rt. Hon. the Earl of Carnarvon.

The local Railway Companies (GWR, LSWR, and SDJR) had made special arrangements for brethren travelling to the meeting by train, the only alternative at the time being to travel by horse or on foot. There appears to have been no formal connection between the Lodge and any railway company, however the ancient minutes record that at various times there were station masters and railway employees who were members of the Lodge. No doubt they used their influence!

115 brethren attended, a remarkable number by the standards of the age, including five official representatives of Provincial Grand Lodge. Also present were representatives from fourteen Somerset Lodges, including Royal Cumberland, Royal Sussex Lodge and of course Nyanza, together with 35 brethren from neighbouring Provinces. The first Worshipful Master was W.Bro John Hughes.

After the formal business some 90 of the brethren dined at the Langport Arms Hotel, the banquet commencing at 3.30 pm. The tickets cost 3s.6d each, including waiters but excluding wines! After the Banquet the sum of five guineas was subscribed to the Masonic Boys School.

The first regular meeting of the Lodge was held sixteen days later, on Thursday 10th July, 1884 at the Langport Arms Hotel, which was to be the meeting place for the next seven years. As no Secretary had yet been appointed the minutes of the Consecration meeting were not read. Four Joining Members were elected: W.Bro W.J. Nosworthy, of Lodge of Brotherly Love, 329, described as a "Professor of Music"; it was he who had acted as Organist at the Consecration, and who made a substantial contribution to the musical life of the Lodge; Bro Edward Western, of St. Kew Lodge, a schoolmaster at Langport Grammar School, who became the fourth Master of the Lodge; Bro Alfred Reynolds of All Souls Lodge of Weymouth, also a Schoolmaster, who became the first Secretary and later the third Master of the Lodge; and Bro. T.D. Berry of the Lodge of Regularity in London, described as an Architect and Surveyor residing in Wandsworth.

Immediately on election Bro Alfred Reynolds was appointed Secretary. Three Candidates for Initiation were proposed, and a special meeting was arranged, to be held the following week, to draw up a code of Bye-Laws.

No record seems to have been kept of the special meeting, but at the next Regular meeting, on 14th August, the first Bye-Laws were read and confirmed. These original Bye-Laws are still in the Lodge's possession, hand written in a fine copperplate hand, and complete with annotations by the Provincial Grand Secretary and the Grand Secretary. The first annual subscription was fixed at one guinea; the Initiation Fee at six Guineas and the Joining Fee at one Guinea. The Bye-Laws also included a number of features which are interesting to compare with modern Bye-Laws:

A Brother proposing a Candidate for Initiation or Joining had to pay the sum of one Guinea by way of "Caution Money", which sum was to be set against the respective fees if the Candidate was initiated or joined, refunded if the candidate was to be rejected on ballot, but forfeited if the Candidate, once elected, failed to present himself for Initiation within six months. Marginal notes by both the Prov. Grand Secretary and the Grand Secretary add the words, "except for a reason acceptable to the Brethren"; the G.S. adding, by way of explanation, "He may have broken his leg." The Tyler's fee was fixed at 2s.6d. plus one shilling if there was an Initiation, Passing or

Raising. This was a sizeable sum of money in those days when an agricultural labourer could expect to earn about ten shillings per week. However, if he failed to inform any Brother correctly of the Degree in which the Lodge was open, or improperly reported a visiting Brother before admitting him, he was to forfeit his fee; a penalty indeed!

If at the end of the year the Treasurer's accounts were to show a deficiency that sum had to be made good by an equal levy on the whole of the membership, the amount of which was to be shown on the summons for the February meeting, and payable forthwith.

The meeting date was fixed on the second Thursday in every month (the meeting date on the warrant was the first Thursday on or after the full moon), and the Installation meeting was to be in February, provisions which remain unchanged to the present day, however, it should be noted that there was no "summer break" in those days.

In the early years dress at Lodge meetings was extremely formal. This continued for many years: Dinner Jackets were regularly worn at meetings until the middle 1960s, not disappearing completely until the early 1970s.

Also in those early years full Festive Boards were only taken after Installation meetings and Initiations; after other meetings the brethren took light refreshment in the ante-room. The Lodge only started taking full meals after every meeting after the Second World War.

From 1888 to 1895 it was the custom to precede the Installation by a Raising, the marathon meetings starting at 12.30 pm, followed by a Banquet at 3.30 pm. One cannot help wondering how they managed to get through both ceremonies in three hours, particularly bearing in mind that they almost certainly used the "old" long Inner Working at that time.

In April 1888 'Fees of Honour for Officers' were introduced at the rate of £1 for the Worshipful Master, 10s.0d. for the Wardens, and 5s.0d. for the Deacons and Inner Guard. In 1984 these rates remain unaltered even though prices have increased considerably.

By April 1891 the Lodge is recorded as considering the possibility of using the Hanging Chapel as a Lodge Room. If it were to be used alterations would be necessary, and it was agreed to discuss the matter with the freehold owners, the Langport Town Trust.

The chance of using this beautiful Medieval Chapel must have seemed a heaven-sent opportunity at the time. It possessed greater character, and conveniently situated for the

town. The lack of space, which is proving so much of a problem in the present day, is unlikely to have been a great consideration at a time when average attendances were around twelve at ordinary meetings, rising to about double that at Installations.

Finally, in October 1891, it was unanimously resolved to hold Lodge meetings at the Hanging Chapel with effect from the next meeting. Permission was sought and obtained from Provincial Grand Lodge and Grand Lodge; and the first meeting at the Hanging Chapel was held on 12th November, 1891, and was, appropriately enough, an Initiation.

The WM's Gavel was given to the Lodge by W.Bro Samuel Herbert Knight, a corn merchant and baker, who was initiated into the Portcullis Lodge on 10th December 1891. The head is made up of four different types of wood; Acacia, Oak, Balsam and Olive, and there is a small silver plate on each piece of wood denoting the type of wood. "Jerusalem" is inscribed on the Gavel and there is an engraved silver collar around the handle stating: "This Gavel was used by the presiding WM at Jerusalem April 1902. Presented by W.Bro S.H. Knight to Lodge Portcullis No 2038 as a memento of his visit to the Royal Solomon Lodge No 293, Jerusalem, Palestine Oct. 1902"

There is no mention of the Senior and Junior Wardens' Gavels. However, "Jerusalem" is inscribed on both of them, and both are made,, to the same pattern as the Master's gavel, and also from four different types of wood: Locust Wood, Oak, Balsam (from Jordan) and Olive Wood, so it is assumed they were presented at the same time.

In June 1909 it was proposed that a Lodge of Instruction be formed, and in February 1910 the Portcullis Lodge of Instruction met for the first time.

In recognition of the hardship being suffered by Lodge members serving with the Armed Services in the Great War it was agreed in April 1915 that they should be made Honorary Members of the Lodge for the duration of the War. However, the following month, in compliance with a direction from Grand Lodge, the resolution was rescinded. The following December the Lodge decided to send a Christmas card, and a tin of cigarettes to each member of the Lodge serving in the Forces.

The Golden Jubilee meeting of the Lodge was held at Langport Town Hall on Tuesday, 26th June 1934. The R.W Provincial Grand Master, the Ven. Archdeacon Walter Farrer M.A. was present, and the meeting was attended by 27 members and 40 visitors from nineteen Lodges. The Ceremony consisted mainly of the Raising to the Third Degree of Bro I.T. Warren, in which the Working Tools were presented by the Provincial Grand Master.

After a congratulatory address by the Provincial Grand Master the Lodge was closed, and during the Closing Ode the alms were collected, amounting to £3.0s.6d, over £150 current value, which were donated to the Samaritan Fund of the Royal Masonic Hospital. After the meeting the brethren enjoyed an eight course banquet consisting of: Hors d'oeuvre, Soup, Fish, Entree, Roast Meat, Sweet, Savoury, Dessert and Coffee!

In 1945 a new "Portcullis" Lodge 6085 was consecrated in London and following a chance meeting in the Royal Masonic Hospital between W.Bro Tom Lewis, the DC of that Lodge, and W.Bro H.C. Clarke, of Benevolence Lodge 1168 meeting at Sherborne, a frequent visitor to Portcullis Lodge, Langport, W.Bro Lewis wrote a letter to the Worshipful Master of Portcullis Lodge, Langport. As a result of this letter, on 25th October 1946, the Worshipful Master, W.Bro J.T. Prideaux, accompanied by W.Bro H.J. Denman, the Secretary, paid the first

official visit to Portcullis Lodge 6085, London, and in May 1949 W.Bro E.C.T. Humberstone (WM 6085) together with his Senior Warden, Secretary and Assistant Director of Ceremonies paid a return visit to Langport, thus initiating an exchange of visits which has continued to this day.

In May 1948 the members of Portcullis Lodge Langport presented a water colour of the Hanging Chapel to Portcullis Lodge, London, this being received by W.Bro Clifford Evans, and thereafter being passed to successive Masters of that Lodge on Installation. The following May the members of Portcullis Lodge, London presented a "Broken Column" charity box to Portcullis Lodge, Langport, which remains in use to this day.

In October 1954 Portcullis Lodge, Langport presented a VSL Marker to Portcullis Lodge, London, on the occasion of their annual visit and in 1957 it was decided to confer Honorary Membership of the Lodge on the Worshipful Master of Portcullis Lodge, London, during the year of his Mastership.

In the late 1960s it was becoming apparent that extensive repairs would soon be necessary, particularly to the roof. A new lease was agreed with the Langport Parish Council, who had by then taken over the rights and liabilities of the Langport Town Trust, and the work was financed by grants from Somerset County Council and Langport Rural District Council. The former entailed a lengthy correspondence between the Secretary of the Lodge, the late W.Bro A Rothwell, and himself as Clerk to Langport RDC.!

In February 1970 the Installation of W.Bro W.H.R. Lovesay was held at the Langport Arms Hotel in an effort to accommodate the overcrowding problem and avoid excluding Portcullis's own members. Later that year, and up to May 1971, all meetings were held at the Langport Arms while renovations were being carried out.

In September 1971 the Lodge returned to the Hanging Chapel, when the Lodge Room was re-dedicated, and the new organ dedicated by the R.W Provincial Grand Master, Lt. Col. Harry Owen Hughes, accompanied by the Deputy PGM, V.W.Bro H. Frampton, and the Assistant PGM, W.Bro H.E. Dyke

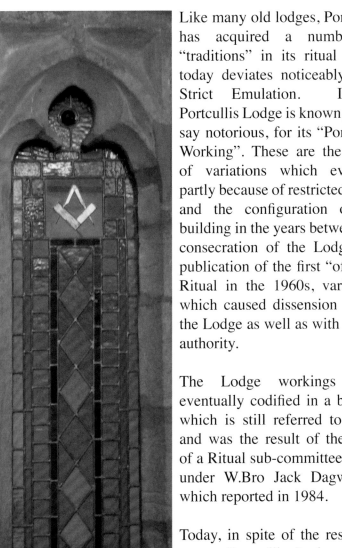

Portcullis Lodge celebrated its centenary in 1984 with a meeting in Huish Episcopi School and a banquet at the Langport Arms. Possibly the most notable of the Centenary functions was a Barbecue organised by Bro J. H. (Toby) Cobden, and attended by over 300 people. The other functions included a car treasure hunt, a Mad Hatters' party, a Greek evening, and a country evening

Like many old lodges, Portcullis has acquired a number of "traditions" in its ritual which today deviates noticeably from Strict Emulation. Indeed, Portcullis Lodge is known, not to say notorious, for its "Portcullis Working". These are the result of variations which evolved, partly because of restricted space and the configuration of the building in the years between the consecration of the Lodge and publication of the first "official" Ritual in the 1960s, variations which caused dissension within the Lodge as well as with higher authority.

The Lodge workings were eventually codified in a booklet which is still referred to today and was the result of the work of a Ritual sub-committee set up under W.Bro Jack Dagworthy, which reported in 1984.

Today, in spite of the restricted space, Portcullis Lodge boasts one of the highest subscribing memberships in the Province; happily they don't all turn up at once! The Lodge has a programme of ceremonies planned well into the future, and visitors are most heartily welcomed at ceremonies and to the festive board, still held in the Langport Arms. Visitors, Masonic or not, are very welcome to visit the Lodge building by appointment, and are invited to contact the Lodge Secretary, who will be pleased to make the necessary arrangements.

Exmoor Lodge No. 2390

Meets at the Masonic Hall, Minehead

Warrant dated 1891

The Lodge was consecrated on 26th May 1891. It met in the Minehead Public Hall, or Town Hall as it was sometimes called, where the present hospital is located.

After a few years friction between the landlord and the Lodge led to Mr Luttrell, who owned most of the town, providing a piece of land in Bancks Street and suggesting the Lodge erect their own building. The Bancks Street building was opened on 18th June 1893.

The money was raised by setting up a limited company and selling shares to the members. This company still exists today and is responsible for the building. Over the years they have faced many challenges. In 1922 the Temple was proving too small and the members embarked on a scheme to enlarge the building and construct a new Temple at the rear. This was opened on 20th September 1923.

In the early days most of the members were drawn from the Lodge of Unanimity and Sincerity 261. It was the practice of business and professional men who worked in Taunton to travel to the more pleasant surroundings of the coast from their homes particularly during the summer months and rent or buy accommodation in the grand villas that were being built.

It was to accommodate this summer migration and the need for a more convenient Masonic Lodge during the summer that the Lodge was started, and in the early days it was a Summer Lodge, meeting in May, June, July, August and September. In 1893 the months of January and March were added, probably a reflection of the increasing number of local members joining the Lodge.

It was the development of the Minehead to Taunton railway that made this summer migration possible, and an interesting insight into the standing of Masonry in the community is that on some occasions, when a number of Taunton Masons were to travel to Minehead, the summons carried a note that a concessionary fare was obtainable on production of a Provincial Lodge card.

The first Master of the Lodge was W.Bro F.T. Elworthy. This was the third Lodge in which he became Master. He was promoted to Grand Lodge in 1904.

The principal source of detail for a Lodge history are the minute books. One wishes that more detail was provided into the background of some of the more tantalising entries.

One of the modern hand carved plaques of great charm, appropriately depicting a fine stag,

What, for instance, caused the Lodge to provide a new ballot box with three holes; Yes, No and Neutral?

There have been moments of great excitement and emotion too, none less so than at the outbreak of the 1914-1918 war, when the Lodge found itself with a German member, who just before the outbreak of war had returned to Germany and was openly accused of being a spy; which he certainly was not. Much intemperate and even vitriolic discussion ensued on how the Lodge was to deal with the situation.

There have been other examples where the Lodge narrowly avoided financial catastrophe such as when it received a bill from an American Lodge for the funeral expenses of an

Exmoor member who had died in America and the Standing Committee resolved to send it to his mother, fortunately soon reversed.

On a brighter note, the Lodge has sponsored two other Lodges, Quantock Lodge in March 1919 and another Minehead Lodge, St Bernard in 1932. The need for another Minehead Lodge was becoming critical due to the long waiting list. They say that rules are made to be broken, and so it was that in 1931 Exmoor passed a resolution stating that no more than six candidates were to be initiated in one year and immediately had to break it in order that the Master could initiate his own brother!

Building developments have continued over the years, usually financed by generous donations from the all the brethren. A few years ago it was discovered that lack of building maintenance meant that the Lodge Room ceiling was in an imminent state of collapse and a major fund raising programme followed. Thankfully the repairs were effected before any catastrophe could ensue.

Recent developments to bring the building up to standard have included new fire exits, a chair lift and a new kitchen with quality fittings and more space.

Royal Naval Lodge No. 2761 EC

Meets at the Masonic Hall Yeovil

**Warrant dated 1899, Constituted in Malta
Transferred to Province of Somerset 2nd January 1987**

In its early life the Royal Naval Lodge 2761 was not in Somerset, in fact it did not meet in this Province until 1985, so perhaps one might think that it is a fairly new Lodge. Not at all; it began life over 100 years ago when Queen Victoria was still on the throne.

The history of 2761 is essentially tied up with the Royal Navy proper, and in its early days, the old British Empire. The history of the Lodge is so different from the others in the Province that it is quite unique. To begin at the beginning we must look back to the latter days of the 19th Century, when the Country still basked in the glories of Admiral Nelson, and the Royal Navy was so large that it had bases in many parts of the world. The main Mediterranean base was in the Island of Malta where the Grand Harbour of Valletta, the capital city, could hold a fleet of ships.

Freemasonry had been active in Malta since the 18th Century and in the 1800s developed and thrived. The main reason for the enthusiasm and expansion was the presence of the Navy and the Island's large Army garrison and support.

Many naval members were spread amongst the five Lodges of the English Constitution (EC) already in existence on the island, which had allegiance to the United Grand Lodge of England (UGLE). There were also other Lodges of Scottish and Irish Constitutions, but it was natural for these seafaring men want a Lodge more dedicated to the traditions of the Royal Navy.

Thus it was that the Royal Naval Lodge 2761 came into existence.

The Royal Naval Lodge banner (1993) showing the Naval Crown, RN fouled anchor badge and "Maltese" Cross under the All Seeing Eye.

The Warrant of the Lodge specified the original meeting place to be 27 Strada Stretta (Straight Street). That street was known to many as "the Gut", a place of end! It has been firmly established at 6 and 7 Marsamxett (pronounced: Marsamshett) Street since 1908 and this remains the current home of Freemasonry (English Constitution) in Malta.

Another peculiarity about the Warrant was that because of time and distance it could take weeks for mail to arrive by "picket" boat or fast sloop,

273

so the District Grand Master, then General Sir John Owen KCB, issued a Provisional Warrant, which is proudly displayed at the meetings in our Yeovil, Somerset home, alongside the regular Warrant from the UGLE and our 1999 Centenary Warrant.

The first By-laws stated the Lodge was formed "especially for brethren of the Naval Services, namely those of or above the rank of Chief Petty Officer or equivalent". There have been many changes since then, but the spirit of the definition remains the same; good men and true who you would be happy to call "shipmate".

In 1899 Deputy Inspector General James Martin DSO RN was installed as the first Master, with Lieutenant Henry Brocklebank RN as Senior Warden and Mr Frederick Hannaford RN as Junior Warden. In those days medical men bore no naval ranks and a Deputy Inspector General was like a Surgeon Commander of today, with staff duties to inspect the ships and crew.

The Senior Warden's Masonic career moved onwards and upwards, in 1938 Henry Brocklebank becoming Deputy PGM for Dorset and Senior Grand Deacon of the UGLE. Mr Frederick Hannaford became Master in 1900, moved on, but was back in Malta as WM again in 1904. His title "Mr" was that of a Warrant Officer. Such titles were lost to the Navy in the 1950s but are now, happily, back in being. (Here it may be appropriate to state how the Navy worked so as to understand the comparatively short spells some of the members stayed in Malta).

It was usual for any appointment or draft to last for two to three years, so Officers and ratings ("other ranks" for non-RNers) were appointed to a specific ship for that time and a new appointment or draft would be issued on completion. That was peace-time working.

In the early years of the 20th Century the only significant Naval action in the Mediterranean was in 1915 in support of the Gallipoli campaign in Turkey. The Navy endured great difficulty in performing this role as the warships were "sitting ducks" for the enemy shore batteries along the narrow Bosphorus straights. The Fleet returned. Malta hospitals cared for the wounded and the dockyard cared for the ships.

In 1915, with the Fleet away, there was little work in Lodge, only four initiations, when in the years 1914 and 1916 there had been thirteen each year.

Valetta Harbour 1896 – the Fleet firing a Royal Birthday Salute

The activity in Lodge was quite phenomenal in the years 1911 to 1921 with 145 initiates for the Lodge and numerous Passings and Raisings. One might question how the workload could be managed, but then it is frequently written that the Lodge "divided"; that is to say a second team, PM and "stand-in" Officers acted for the WM in another room conducting one or more ceremonies. The District Grand Master was very generous in granting permission to hold twelve emergency meetings during the ten years. However, during the Lodge's life in Malta it is often written "No ceremony, Fleet at Sea".

The administrative workload was heavy and constant. Bro Budgen was Secretary from 1899 to 1925, although other names appear as Secretary. He carried out the work and progressed to the chair in 1908. The Lodge was so pleased with his untiring work that he was presented with a special gold jewel to mark his efforts and this "Budgen" jewel is now held by the Lodge Secretary.

Events in the 1920s and 1930s seem to follow the established pattern of the peace-time Navy, but 1939 heralded the Second World War. About this time a young qualified Pharmacist called James Skipp was appointed to Malta and was making his way in a blacked out train to Gourock in Scotland. There he embarked on a troop ship sailing in convoy to South Africa, changed to another "luxury" liner and sailed up the East coast to Egypt, then from 1st class to "freight" he was placed on a draughty old Dakota aircraft and flown to Malta.

The weather was so bad that they overflew the small island and had to turn back to find it. Landing at the much-bombed RAF Luqa Jim was met by RN car only to have the driver stop en route to RN Hospital Bighi and run off! When he returned some time later he said to his bemused passenger, "Air raid, Sehib (Sir), had to take shelter".

Jim arrived, and as Senior Pharmacist did great work in Malta, and followed the fleet to Sicily and Italy supplying their medical needs. Such is the story, in brief, of our much-revered "Father of the Lodge", who was initiated in the Crypt of St Paul's Anglican cathedral as the Lodge Rooms had suffered bomb damage. Jim is now in his nineties and still active.

There are many hair-raising stories of Naval life during the War years, but suffice it to say that the Lodge continued working, with the help of the Royal Engineers of course. In Post War years the Lodge continued to flourish and it is noted that Gerald Bryant, Master in 1962 and Cyril Jones Master in 1966, both from Bath, played a significant part in establishing the Lodge in Somerset.

The closure of HM Dockyard and service airfields was part of the armed-forces "run-down" in the 50s, 60s and 70s. The number of Navy and Army members dwindled until it was impossible to run the Lodges effectively. Some Lodges were repatriated, and after much deliberation Yeovil was chosen for the new home of Royal Naval Lodge 2761 EC.

"Successful Integration
In 1986 all the WMs of the Yeovil Lodges were members of 2761. Left to Right, Richard Stallard, 329 Norman Richardson MBE, 5007, John Rawlins, 7552, and John Marshall in the chair of 2761

Much background work and dispensations from Somerset and Malta allowed Royal Naval Lodge to meet in Yeovil in 1985 when "Jack" Warner flew to UK to install his successor, Gerald Bryant. The very experienced Cyril Jones became Secretary and a number of original members returned to take up the offices with local Past Masters filling in any gaps. At that time there were eight Stewards, all Past Masters! So began the second part of the life and times of the Royal Naval Lodge

For two years 2761 met by dispensations as an overseas Lodge until in 1987 the Lodge was officially welcomed into the Province of Somerset at a ceremony in Yeovil, which included the PGM, his Provincial "team" and Masonic dignitaries from the Group of Lodges, Malta, (no longer a "District" due to the reductions).

The Lodge had been quickly and successfully integrated into the Yeovil Masonic centre, many of the new "recruits" being members of the other local Lodges. In those early days in Yeovil there were many visitors, perhaps to see this "strange bunch", and to listen to the Secretary, who always had a batch of Registration forms to read for Initiates and Joining Members, and so the Lodge survived and thrived.

When the Lodge left Malta its membership totalled over 200, it was indeed the strongest Lodge in the District. The "overseas" annual subscription then was nominal, but in the Lodge's new home increases were necessary. Although a number of members were lost in the change the membership became the highest in the Province. Inevitably numbers settled to a good figure and remain comfortable, albeit that there are still many members in more than one Lodge.

Norman Nuttall was initiated in Malta in 1963 and has remained a loyal member. When he left the Royal Navy he took up the post of Grand Tyler. This involved management of the Grand Lodge building and Tyler to Grand Lodge; a caring and dignified role. In 1993 he presented a beautiful Banner to the Lodge It was the third banner in the Lodge's history, the first in 1900 cost fifteen shillings, (a month's pay for a CPO or junior officer), and it was badly damaged by the voracious Maltese moths, the second by Secretary, John Bryden, was of man-made (moth-proof) materials in 1981.

In 1993 the new Banner was dedicated by the Provincial Team, all three Banners were paraded and John Rawlins wrote a lecture on their history and meaning. That lecture was given again in Malta, when the second banner was paraded and presented back to the Malta Masons in 1999 as part of the Centenary celebrations. These went on all year as the members enjoyed the special Festive Board in Yeovil, a trip to Malta (dinners at the Phoenicia Hotel and Masonic Hall) and a visit to old HMS Warrior, Portsmouth; dinner on the Gun-deck!

Now, in the 21st Century, we continue our Somerset journey with great pride in our Lodge and our Province, maybe we will celebrate 110 or 125 years of our history soon with another trip to Malta- our old home.

The Future; a message for the 21st Century from Gerald Bryant: "Royal Naval Lodge is in good heart. The members pride themselves on the standard of Lodge work and the hospitality extended to all. We are proud of our Malta heritage and look forward to the future with confidence. We will continue to pipe 'Hands to Dinner' and have rum on the dinner table!"

The Somersetshire Lodge No. 2925 (London)

Meets at Mark Mason's Hall, 86 St. James St., London SW1

Warrant dated 1902

On 14th June 1902 a few prominent business men with Somersetshire connections, residing in London, had the commendable idea of regular fraternal gatherings and submitted a petition to Grand Lodge requesting the formation of a new Lodge to be called The Somersetshire Lodge.

The petition was recommended by Gresham Lodge 869 which at that time met at The Great House, Cheshunt, Hertfordshire. There were twenty petitioners, headed by R.W.Bro Viscount Dungarvan, (later the Rt. Hon. The Earl of Cork and Orrery), Provincial Grand Master for Somerset and member of Royal Somerset Lodge 973.

The warrant was granted on 25th June 1902 by the MW Grand Master, the Duke of Connaught and Strathearn, and signed by the Grand Secretary, V.W.Bro E. Letchworth (later to become Sir Edward).

The Somersetshire Lodge was duly consecrated at the Trocadero Restaurant, Piccadilly, London, on 28th July 1902. The consecration and dedication of the Lodge was performed by V.W.Bro E. Letchworth and continued to install R.W.Bro Viscount Dungarvan as the first Worshipful Master. At the Lodge Dinner on 12th October 1902 a 'fine antique Charity Collection Box' was presented to the Lodge by the ensuing Master, W.Bro T. Whitemore Chant. It is a treasured possession and still continues to be used at every meeting.

The Warrant of the Lodge was damaged by water whilst in a deed box in a bank for safe keeping. However, as it was still readable and so as to maintain tradition, it was resolved to continue using it.

On 15th June 1903 it was agreed to adopt the Alfred Jewel as the design for the Lodge breast jewel and crest. It is a replica of the original jewel dating back to 891, and was found in 1693 at Newton Park, north of the site of Athelney Abbey in Somerset.

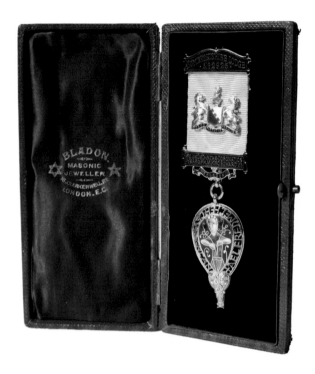

In 1698 it was in the possession of Colonel Nathanial Palmer of Fairfield, Somerset, and later his son in 1718 donated it to the Ashmolean Museum, Oxford, (named after Bro Elias Ashmole FRS, initiated in 1646) where the original remains on display. The inscription running around the frame, ' Aelfred mec heht gewyrcan' translates to 'Alfred had me made' and is generally acknowledged to refer to King Alfred the Great who died in 899.

Another historic day was made on 10th October 1904 by two Founder Members. The first Lodge banner was a gift from W.Bro Sholto Hare, and W.Bro Henry Newlands presented an antique porcelain Loving Cup depicting scenes of Taunton. The latter was almost totally smashed when the Lodge moved to Freemasons' Hall in 1984 due to the closure of Piccadilly Hotel,

which had been the base since April 1951. The Cup was finally restored to its former glory in 2004 by John Farmer of Whitchurch and now rests adjacent to the Tynte Cup (this was presented to the Provincial Grand Master of Somerset in 1836 by the Brethren of the Province) in the Museum at Grand Lodge.

Four members of the Lodge, namely W.Bros T.W. Chant, T.C. Goodman, Sholto Hare and J.C. Jones, were Founder Members of Somerset Masters' Lodge 3746, which was consecrated on 22nd April 1915 in the Assembly Rooms, Bath. In the same year, another member, W.Bro H.A. Badman became a Joining Member. The By-Laws of this new Lodge quote, "This Lodge is founded for the association of Brethren who have been, or are members, of Lodges in the Province of Somerset and of The Somersetshire Lodge 2925 being Installed Masters".

In 1920 the Lodge became a Founder Member of the Freemasons' Hospital and Nursing Home established in Fulham Road, which was later to become The Royal Masonic Hospital, re-located at Ravenscourt Park. Subsequent donations by the Lodge and its members contributed to the present Grand Lodge Headquarters in Great Queen Street, built as a memorial to those who made the supreme sacrifice in the 1914-18 war. In 1931 to commemorate this the Lodge received the Hall Stone collarette and jewel with which each Master is invested on his Installation.

Until 1933 advancement in Masonic knowledge was made by brethren in their own separate ways, but in that year a Lodge of Instruction was formed and accommodation was found at Scotch House, Melford Street, Strand.

Being proud of its County origins the Lodge was privileged to sponsor a daughter Lodge, the Old Tauntonian Lodge 5735. A Petition recommending the formation was signed in March 1938 and the Lodge was consecrated in

July 1938. A motion was passed in November 1938 "That the Master and Secretary for the time in being of The Old Tauntonian Lodge 5735 be elected Honorary Members of the Lodge".

In January 1939 this was reciprocated by making the Master and Secretary of 2925 for the time in being Honorary Members of the Old Tauntonian Lodge. Many years later in 1968 the Taunton School Lodge 8215 was consecrated, which is regarded as the Granddaughter Lodge of 2925.

During both periods of war regular meetings continued to take place, mostly by Dispensation, but at different venues, dependent upon the availability of suitable premises not affected by war damage. The formal full 'white tie' dress of past years at Lodge meetings had of necessity changed during the Second World War and a more casual attire had appeared in the Craft. Dinner suits were occasionally worn at Installations, or special occasions, and the dark lounge suit and black tie remains the order of today.

At this point it may be appropriate to mention a further possible connection with the Province of Hertfordshire, in addition to that of the sponsoring Lodge. On 12th February 1912, W.Bro T. W. Chant Initiated his second son Maurice G. Chant into the Lodge. In 1940 he became Master of Hertfordshire Masters Lodge 4090 and at some later date was appointed Assistant Provincial Grand Master of Hertfordshire.

At the Jubilee Anniversary and Installation of W.Bro J.D.T. James held on 27th October 1952 92 members and guests met to celebrate the 50th meeting of the Lodge. The original banner had been destroyed by enemy action during air raids in London and a new banner had been made. It was dedicated at this Jubilee Meeting by R.W.Bro Brig. Gen. C.L. Norman DSO, MVO, DL, PGM for Somerset, assisted by R.W.Bro H. Frampton, MC, Deputy Provincial Grand Master. The R.W.Bro Rev. J. Moffett, Provincial Grand Master of Hertfordshire, acted as Chaplain. All three were granted Honorary Membership of the Lodge.

As the next few decades rolled on the membership continued to be fairly static around 40. Fortunately the number of Initiates and Joining Members allowed the Lodge to remain active and progress.

Upon completing his term as Worshipful Master in October 1972 W.Bro George Stephenson presented the Lodge with three silver goblets to be used by the three principal officers at the festive board. At the same meeting R.W.Bro Lt. Col. Owen Hughes, Provincial Grand Master for Somerset, was a visitor and elected an Honorary Member of the Lodge.

On 24th October 1977 the Lodge celebrated its 75th Anniversary and invested W.Bro R.E. Collins, PAGStdB, as Worshipful Master. At that time he had served continually as Secretary for 23 years.

A welcomed visitor in November 1982 was R.W.Bro Kenneth Kinnersley, Provincial Grand Master for Somerset, who became an Honorary Member.

Due to the closure on 11th July 1984 and after 33 years meeting at the Piccadilly Hotel the Lodge had to quickly relocate and Freemasons' Hall was the only available accommodation. Perhaps the spaciousness of this venue didn't suit the brethren, so on 25th February 1991, by Dispensation, a move was made to Shuttleworth's Restaurant in the Aldwych. During these years the Lodge of Instruction had found it necessary to change venues numerous times for varying reasons and in 1984 moved to The Rugby Club, in Hallam Street, W1.

Appreciating the support from the Province, R.W.Bro Stanley Hopkins, Provincial Grand Master for Somerset was elected an Honorary Member on 8th May 1991, becoming a Joining Member on 17th May 2001.

In March 1994, without any warning, Shuttleworth's suddenly closed and we were 'out on the street'. The Lodge became nomadic, meeting by Dispensations at The Duke of York HQ Club, Chelsea; Blakemore Hotel, Bayswater; Great Eastern Hotel, Liverpool Street; Freemasons' Hall; and finally Mark Mason's Hall, 86 St. James's Street, London, which became the Lodge's permanent home in September 1996.

It was whilst the Lodge regalia was stored at the Great Eastern Hotel it suddenly appeared for sale at Camden Market. Apparently a member of the Craft, browsing for Masonic regalia, became so suspicious to find so many items for sale from one particular Lodge that he checked to ascertain if the Lodge had in fact ceased. He promptly contacted Grand Lodge which confirmed that the Lodge was indeed still active. The Brother then contacted the Lodge Secretary who established with the hotel that

the storage box had in fact been broken into. He immediately prompted a police investigation, which succeeded in recovering the majority of the possessions. Apparently the guilty party was traced and convicted.

The rising costs imposed by The Rugby Club forced the Lodge of Instruction to vacate to Mark Mason's Hall in March 1997. The next seven years saw attendance gradually diminish as the majority of members either worked or resided in the provinces. Therefore, due to higher transport costs travelling into London for weekly meetings and the lateness of the hour returning home, it was decided not to continue with any further meetings after May 2004.

In May 1998 due to the hard work of the Charity Steward and the generosity of the brethren, the Lodge was awarded a silver collar jewel for its donation to the New Masonic Samaritan Fund.

The Installation meeting on 5th December 2001 became a landmark in the history of the Lodge when R.W.Bro Stanley Hopkins, Provincial Grand Master for Somerset was installed as the 100th Master of the Lodge. His leadership and popularity cemented the bond between the Province and the Lodge even further. By invitation and with enthusiastic support from the Provincial Officers an annual visit has been made in most of the years since. Their eagerness to participate in the ceremonies added to the enjoyment of all.

The Centenary meeting was a great celebration held at Mark Masons' Hall, on 30th October 2002. The R.W Assistant Grand Master, David Kenneth Williamson was principal guest and a total of 188 sat down to dinner. To mark the occasion the Lodge purchased a silver Loving Cup, suitably engraved to commemorate its Consecration. This is charged with brandy and Somerset Cider and is circulated with traditional ceremony at the festive board after the Installation of a new Master.

Donations were made to the four major Masonic charities to achieve Grand Patron status. The festive board was 'white table' as Mr. Laurence Brady was an invited guest to receive a donation of £3000 in aid of Cancer Research.

R.W.Bro David L. Jenkins, on behalf of the Provincial Grand Lodge of Somerset, presented the Master with a wine decanter and three goblets, made in Bristol Blue glass, engraved in gold, indicating the presentation and the anniversary.

In appreciation of the flourishing and continued support from the Province, R.W.Bro David L. Jenkins was elected Honorary Member on 23rd September 2002.

The Lodge is a Founder of the Metropolitan Grand Lodge of London and numerous brethren attended the Inauguration Ceremony at the Royal Albert Hall on 1st October 2003. It is considered a privilege for the Master and Secretary to be invited to the Provincial Annual General Meeting and to be acknowledged as guests of the Province.

From twenty Founding Members a further 226 brethren have contributed to its continued progress. Honours have been awarded as follows:

Eleven to Grand Rank
Five to Senior London Grand Rank
39 to London Grand Rank
21 to Honorary Member

It is gratifying that the foresight and commitment of our forbears have truly realised their objective. Their courage and determination to extend beyond their native territory has greatly contributed in promoting the tenets of our Order within the universal framework of communicating happiness and harmony.

Lodge of St George No. 3158

Meets at the Masonic Hall Taunton

Warrant dated 30th April 1906

The Lodge of St George is the second oldest in Taunton, it may have held the honour of being the oldest, but for history, as the first Lodge formed in Taunton in 1764 was called 'St George's Lodge No 315' but this Lodge surrendered its warrant in 1783. The Lodge of Unanimity and Sincerity 261 (date of Warrant 1788) now holds that honour, and remained the only Taunton Lodge until the members were of a mind to create a second Lodge in the town in 1906 and so the Lodge of St George 3158 became the daughter Lodge of the Lodge of Unanimity and Sincerity 261.

The date of the Warrant from the United Grand Lodge of England is 16th March 1906 and the consecration ceremony took place in the 'London Hotel Assembly Rooms' on Monday the 30th April 1906, the hotel later being known as 'The County Hotel'. The then Provincial Grand Master for Somerset, R.W.Bro the Rt. Hon. The Earl of Cork and Orrery officiated and W.Bro G.H. Kite (Past Master of 261) was installed as the first Worshipful Master.

All of the other Offices were filled by members from Lodge 261 as that was the sponsoring Lodge. Anyone reading this who is familiar with the recent history of the County Town will recognise the names of some of those early Officers and Past Worshipful Masters. To name but a few there were C.W. Stansell, Master in 1913, A.E. Goodman (1915), A.C. Mole (1917), P.J. Barnicott (1924) and W.B. Clatworthy (1931).

In 1945 the brethren of the Lodge of St George formed a Lodge at Wiveliscombe, the Loyal Vacation Lodge 6209, and so its own daughter Lodge was born.

Visiting brethren to the Lodge will notice that the practise is not to 'square' the Lodge during the perambulations. This is not sloppiness on the part of the current members but a continuation of a 'Tradition' of the Lodge, although the reason for not doing so has been lost in the passage of time.

Some say it was because the Lodge was made up of mainly 'businessmen' and therefore Company owners who were, after an active and busy day, anxious to complete the Ceremony as soon as possible and have more time to relax and take part in the Festive Board.

However, as most Lodges were made up of business people in those days it seems unlikely that it is this that made the difference. Nevertheless, that is the Tradition, and hopefully, a Tradition that will be maintained.

This scene is set in November 1942, right in the middle of the Second World War, and it is interesting to note that the Lodge was still meeting on a regular basis, and that the present 'Father' of the Lodge was Initiated into the Lodge: R.H. (Peter) May was at the time serving as a fighter pilot in the RAF, and stationed at West Malling in Kent. His father had proposed him into the Lodge, but as Peter recalls it was difficult in those days to get from Kent to Somerset for the evening ceremony, and be back in time for duty the next day.

After some discussion with his Commanding Officer, however, it was determined that he would do a 'test flight' with one of the new 'Spitfire' aeroplanes. So it was that Peter was able to fly himself to Taunton, landing at the local airfield at Culmhead, which at that time was being operated by a Polish Squadron. Having got himself to the airfield Peter hitched a lift into the town where he was met by his father, Initiated into Freemasonry, and then promptly made his way back to his base in Kent the next day. Peter says that in wartime one could get away with that sort of stunt!

W.Bro Peter soon became friends with many of the 'Founders' of the Lodge and progressed through all of the Offices on the way to the Chair which he attained in 1956, the 50th Anniversary year of its founding!

An interesting story told by Peter concerns a Bro Sam Shattock who had been trained in 'Hotel Work' at the County Hotel, the former London Assembly Rooms, and became a serving member of the Lodge in 1907. Bro Sam was eventually appointed as 'Tyler' to all of the Taunton Lodges. He was also the caretaker and with the assistance of his wife did all of the catering. Bro Sam remained as Tyler for a number of years and was eventually awarded 'Provincial Honours'; one of a select few to have been so rewarded without ever having served in any other office.

There have been very many interesting and colourful characters who have been members of the Lodge, and we are sure that they would have been proud of the 'Centenary Celebrations' which took place during 2006. The date of 30th April in 2006 fell on a Sunday, and a Celebration Luncheon was held at the Castle Hotel, attended by members, partners, friends and the widows of previous Lodge brethren.

At the regular Lodge meeting on the first Monday in October 2006 a more formal ceremony took place when the Provincial Grand Master for Somerset, R.W.Bro David L. Jenkins, presented the 'Centenary Certificate' to the Worshipful Master W.Bro Terrance R. Leach. As well as being honoured by the presence of the Provincial Grand Master for Somerset there were a further twenty members of the Provincial Team, complete with choir, taking part in the ceremony, and together with visiting brethren from other Lodges both the Temple and Festive Board were filled to capacity. The success of the evening was in no doubt due to the hard work of the committee formed to arrange both the Luncheon and the Presentation, and the current members feel that they paid due honour to all of those brethren who have gone before, and like to think that they live up to their Lodge motto "Faithful and True."

King Alfred Lodge No. 3169

Meets at the Masonic Hall, Weston-super-Mare

Warrant dated 1906

It was in 1904, when Bro R.E.M. Lawrence was in the chair of St. Kew Lodge 1222, that a suggestion was made by the brethren that the time had arrived when the number of suitable applicants to join the Craft justified the formation of a second Lodge in Weston-super-Mare. The proposal was debated at their June Lodge meeting and, unusually, it was resolved that the whole Lodge be formed into a Committee to debate the matter. This was to be done during the recess period between the June and October Lodge meetings, the outcome of this debate being that if one sixth of the members of the Lodge were in favour of a new Lodge then they would do everything possible to assist in the formation.

At the meeting of St Kew Lodge on 3rd April 1906 the matter of forming a second Craft Lodge in Weston-super-Mare was put to the members. The minutes of the meeting report that the proposition was carried. W.Bro J. Cooper then proposed, seconded by W.Bro F.T. Perrett, "that a Committee be appointed by the Lodge to arrange terms with the Founders of the new Lodge for the rent of the hall, furniture and regalia". The minute continues "The Worshipful Master and Wardens then signed the Petition for a new Lodge to be called the King Alfred Lodge".

The choice of 'King Alfred' was felt to be a highly appropriate one. As King of Kent and Wessex in AD 871-901 Alfred fought for many years against the marauding Danes, and two Somerset Villages, Athelney and Wedmore, then on islands in undrained marshes, figured prominently in his campaigns.

The Banner now used by the Lodge dates from 1952 and was made by the 'Art College' at Weston-super-Mare under the direction of Mrs D.M. Hislop and the supervision of W.Bro F.C. Horstmann. It replaced the original which after 50 years of use was showing signs of wear. It depicts King Alfred in the same posture as the famous statue by Hamo Thorneycroft RA erected at Winchester. There is no reference in the minutes as to who designed the original Banner, but comparing the design with the black and white image reproduced in the 1956 Jubilee book by W.Bro L.E. Snelgrove it appears to be an almost exact replica of the original.

The Warrant of the Lodge was issued by Grand Lodge, and on Monday June 18th, 1906, at 12.30 p.m., the Consecration Ceremony took

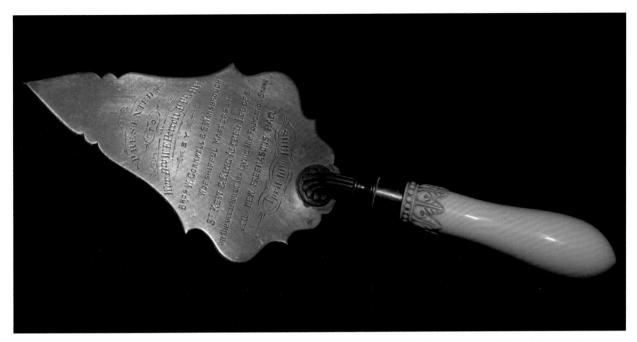

The Trowel used by W.Bro W.E. Perrett to lay the Foundation Stone of the Weston-super-Mare Masonic Hall.
Presented by the Masters of St. Kew and King Alfred Lodges

place in the Assembly Rooms. There were some 200 brethren at the Consecration including the Provincial Grand Master for Somerset and his Deputy.

Immediately after the Consecration ceremony a meeting of the King Alfred Lodge was held and the Worshipful Master designate, W.Bro William Charles Thomas, PPGDC, was installed in the Chair of King Solomon. The ceremony was performed by the Right Worshipful Provincial Grand Master in due and ancient form. After some formal business, and the closing of the Lodge, a large number of the brethren repaired to the Victoria Hall where a banquet was served. The cost was 3s.6d. per head.

In 2006 King Alfred Lodge celebrated its centenary which it did by holding a special centenary meeting followed by a lunch with ladies and guests present. The Right Worshipful Provincial Grand Master for Somerset, David. L. Jenkins, presided over the meeting which had been opened by one of the senior Past Masters of the Lodge, W.Bro Peter Kimmins.

After much pomp and ceremony the Centenary Warrant was read and presented to the Worshipful Master, W.Bro Chris Avery.

The King Alfred Lodge has had 100 years of continuous working and has continued to promote Masonry in Weston-super-Mare. It uses 'Emulation' working with a few variations, one of which being the singing of chants whilst the candidates are perambulated in the various degrees.

Replica of 9th Century King Alfred's Jewel

Connaught Lodge No. 3573

Meeting at the Masonic Hall, Redfield Road, Midsomer Norton, Bath

Warrant dated 10th January 1912

The Lodge Banner is the Knight of the Garter Arms of His Royal Highness, Arthur, Duke of Connaught, after whom the Lodge is named. The Duke, a son of Queen Victoria, was Grand Master from 1901-1939.

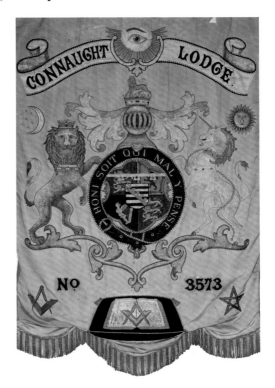

The Banner contains the Order of the Garter motto, "Honi soit qui mal y pense". (Old French for, "shame upon him who thinks evil of it"). The rest of the Banner depicts the basic Masonic imagery, the all-seeing eye, sun and moon, square and compasses, five-pointed star of fellowship and the VSL.

The Connaught Lodge 3573, which was consecrated in 1912, meets as it always has done at the Masonic Hall in Midsomer Norton. The provision of a suitable meeting place in the town was one of the first items to be considered by the brethren concerned, when in June 1910 the formation of a Lodge was first proposed.

Perhaps one of the most notable dates in the history of the Lodge was Wednesday November 16th 1938. On this occasion the Chaplain, W.Bro W.R. Edwards, stood in the Lodge Room and proposed a 25 year old ironmonger as a Candidate for Initiation. This was seconded by W.Bro H.C. Taylor on behalf of W.Bro C.E. Shepherd, who was unavoidably absent. The ballot took place on December 21st 1938, and although it is not recorded as such it is assumed that it proved pure, as the Worshipful Master, W.Bro F.F. Shearn, declared him duly elected. The candidate's name was Kenneth Casswell Kinnersley.

Minutes of the next regular meeting record that " Mr Kenneth Casswell Kinnersley, a poor candidate in a state of darkness was admitted,

properly prepared, and having answered the requisite questions satisfactorily, was initiated an Entered Apprentice by the Worshipful Master." Bro Kinnersley was Passed on February 15th 1939, and Raised on March 15th 1939. This was the start of a remarkable Masonic career leading all the way to the role of Provincial Grand Master from 1981 to 1991.

It was also the start of a great fraternal partnership, because the first Lodge Officer Mr Kinnersley saw that evening was Tyler, Bro Jack Mills, who 60 years later was at his post, still the holder of that office to receive R.W.Bro Kinnersley. Incidentally, Bro Jack Mills was Tyler continuously from 1936 until his death in 1999, which is believed to be the longest term of regular office in English Masonic history.

Another member of that august assembly from 1938 present that night was W.Bro Leslie Shearn. These three eminent brethren shared 190 years of Freemasonry between them, and the Lodge is justly proud of them.

During the First World War the Lodge suffered a single casualty, Lance Corporal Percy Blinman of the Gloucestershire Regiment, who is listed on the Masonic Roll of Honour. The membership register at Freemasons' Hall records Percy Blinman as 'missing presumed dead, sometime between 1916 and 1918'. However, the War Graves Commission records the date of his death as 23rd July 1916. He lies interred in Pozieres British Cemetery, Ovillers-La Boisselle, France.

In 1939 the ground floor of the Masonic Hall was requisitioned by the War Office and a company of Welsh Guards was stationed there. The normal Masonic calendar was disrupted during the War, but during this time, not to be done out of 'doing their bit for King and Country', Connaught Lodge brethren voted to use its funds to buy a Spitfire for the RAF!

However, Grand Lodge advised on 15th October 1940 that:
"whilst it is within the competence of a Lodge to dispose of its funds as may be deemed advisable by a majority of its members, I do not think it wise that a contribution should be made for buying a Spitfire. I agree that the intention is a laudable one, but it must be remembered that it cannot in any sense of the word be deemed Charity".
YS&F Grand Secretary.

It just so happens that about this time a German plane came down at Hayden near Radstock, and Bro Leslie Shearn thought it a jolly good idea to take possession of it, his intention being to charge people to come and view it, and donate these entrance fees towards buying that Spitfire. Accordingly he sent some of his employees to the site, loaded it on his lorry and brought it back to his backyard in High Street, Midsomer Norton. Later that evening he received a momentous shock when the Royal Navy arrived, severely admonished him, and removed his prize. It's always been tough being a Mason!

It appears that Bro Shearn is not alone in suffering a little embarrassment, as the Lodge minutes of 20th September 2000 record: 'Worthy of note is the dignified manner in which the Assistant Director of Ceremonies, W.Bro Bill Moore, remained steadfast whilst assisting in the presentation of the Working Tools, even though his personal comforts were slowly deserting him. As his trousers gradually slipped to his ankles, like the trouper he was, he remained focused on his duty. In death too he was a faithful and true Brother, bequeathing £10,000 to the Lodge

Connaught Lodge celebrates its Centenary in 2012, and the membership feel it can do so with immense justification. It has always been a fiercely proud, traditionally purist, and extremely generous Lodge, as has been demonstrated throughout its history by its members.

Part of R.W.Bro Kenneth Kinnersley's PGM Regalia on display in Midsomer Norton Masonic Hall

Somerset Masters' Lodge No. 3746

The Lodge meets at Bath, and various venues within the Province.

Warrant dated 1915

The Somerset Masters' Lodge is unique within the Province as being primarily one for Installed Masters. From this it follows that no new Masons are initiated in the Lodge, although Master Masons are welcome as guests and are eligible for membership of the Correspondence Circle.

The Somerset Masters' Lodge provides a Province-wide base for social and fraternal contacts between brethren beyond the bounds of their "home" Lodges, and as a forum for research and discussion hopes to maintain lively interest in matters Masonic, at a time, perhaps, when the responsibility of the Masters' Chair has been lifted. The objects of the Lodge are succinctly summarised in the Provincial Masonic Reference Book, as follows:

"To provide a centre and a bond of union for Masonic students and to attract and interest brethren by means of papers on the history, antiquities and symbols of the Order".

An examination of the first Minute Book of the Lodge shows that its creation was first mooted in the year of 1914, when in March, a notice of its proposal was circulated, inviting installed Masters of the Province to sign the petition to Grand Lodge, for a Warrant. The invitation specifies costs of half a guinea as annual subscription, and one guinea each for founder member status and founder's jewel. It is to be supposed that many have wondered why a new Masonic Lodge was being proposed in that inauspicious year which saw the start of the greatest conflict known to us; that of the Great War in Europe. Later that year, on 14th September, a further letter was circulated

seeking the payment of fees for the advancement of the work to be done but postponing the consecration "on account of the war".

After Consecration, at the first regular meeting of the Lodge, at Weston-super-Mare on 5th July 1915 the Worshipful Master had a first, sad duty to perform by reading the following communication from Grand Lodge:

"That in order to prevent the peace and harmony of the Craft being disturbed that all brethren of German, Austrian, Hungarian or Turkish birth should not, during the continuance of the war, attend any meetings of Grand Lodge, of Provincial Grand Lodge or District Grand Lodge, or of a private Masonic Lodge, or any other Masonic meeting, and that such brethren be, and they are hereby required by Grand Lodge to abstain from such attendance". The writing and the announcement of such a measure must have been a bitter task for all Masons!

There were, however, happier times. The Lodge was consecrated at a meeting in the famous Assembly Rooms in Bath, on 22nd April 1915 at 3pm, in a ceremony performed by V.W.Bro Sir Edward Letchworth, Grand Secretary, and the Master Designate W.Bro Col. Alfred Thrale Perkins.

In view of much modern talk of "secrecy and openness" it is interesting to note that local newspapers reported the proceedings in some detail, including the names of all 126 Founders of the Lodge. The Bath and Wilts Chronicle tells us that the venue was adorned with splendid floral arrangements by Messrs. Cooling and Son, while draperies and carpets were supplied by Powell and Powell. Matters were concluded by the installation of the Master and his officers. An important event, as the press acknowledged.

Further reference to the inconvenience of war was made in 1916, with the unusual occurrence of two consecutive meetings being held in the same place. Not all, however, was "doom and gloom" and on that same occasion 20th October 1916 the Lodge was honoured by a lecture from the Librarian of Grand Lodge, visiting Bath. This present year, 2007, the Lodge was similarly favoured by a visit from Mrs. Diane Clements, Director of the Library and Museum of Freemasonry who spoke of her fascinating historical case study "Charity Begins at Home, on donations to non-Masonic causes."

The local press continued to take an interest in the affairs of the Lodge, so that we find in the local newspaper a detailed report of the meeting of 28th June 1920 at Glastonbury, under a sub-heading of "Unique event in town's history". The report included a quite full account of the lecture delivered by W.Bro Bligh-Bond concerning the modern diminution of spirituality in labour, a Masonic idea he wished to see restored.

The Great War was now over, and happier times were in the ascendancy. One such must have been the visit on 5th July 1923 of the internationally renowned Quatuor Coronati Lodge during their summer outing to Bath.

On 5th July 1923, during a visit by the Lodge of Quatuor Coronati, members of the Bath Lodges presented a demonstration of the workings of a Lodge of the "Antients" performed in period dress. A photograph of those brethren was presented to the Somerset Masters' Lodge by the retired Keeper of Archives W.Bro A.E. Gayner, whose own father is among those depicted.

On this occasion members of the Bath Lodges presented a demonstration of the workings of a Lodge of the "Antients", performed in period dress.

Once the Somerset Masters' Lodge set out upon its course it seems to have taken the bit between its teeth and kept going through peace and strife; even through the conflagration of the Second World War. Meetings continued to be held, papers delivered and heard. Many speakers of note favoured the Lodge with their deliberations, including a number of Prestonian lecturers, as visitors to the assemblies have been much in evidence. One such noted scholar was W.Bro Hiram Hallett, himself a member of the Lodge, as well as being Master of the Quatuor Coronati Lodge. The membership of the Lodge has also been graced by the addition of a goodly number of our Provincial Grand Masters, as well as their Deputy and Assistant Grand Masters.

There is, in the possession of the Keeper of Archives, a printed catalogue listing the titles of lectures given from 1915 to 1989. What a fascinating menu it offers. There are talks on well known buildings such as Bristol Cathedral, Solomon's Temple, and Solomon's stables. There are accounts of monastic and religious houses, like the abbey at Bruton, as well as histories of Masonic heroes, holders of the Victoria Cross.

The growth and development of Grand Lodge, as well as that of several private Lodges is scrutinised, as well as the Lodge Rooms where they are situated. A lecture on the Masonic Lodges of Bath, by W.Bro G. Norman, involves an account of changing urban geography of great interest to Bathonians, as it tells of building and streets in constant change, and Lodges moving from place to place. One meeting place, the White Hart, we are told, was demolished by the Second Somerset Militia when in Bath for training! The same author tells us, in 1923,

that the formation in 1920 of St Alphege Lodge "was deemed necessary to relieve the pressure on No. 906." No lack of initiates in those days it seems.

As might be expected, Masonic rituals, symbolism, dress and teachings are also subject to examination. Neither did our forebears confine their deliberations to factual matters, for we find among the lectures some which are speculative, and even exhortational. Thus we find, in October of 1923 a reminder from a writer of great repute, W.Bro the Rev. W. Covey Crump, that Masonry is a system of morality, which sends men into the world to "shape their lives and characters in accordance with the lessons learnt in the Lodge." Here is a veritable feast of knowledge and inspiration, and all has been recorded in the Transactions of the Lodge, where it can be seen by all of us today. Copies of the Transactions are regularly sent to Masonic bodies across the land, and indeed to overseas Lodge libraries as far away as Australia, New Zealand and the USA. In addition to the catalogued years the Lodge holds copies of the Transactions for years up until 2004.

Where then does the Lodge stand today? Not, one hopes, as merely a repository of the past. Not that alone! One of the original objects of the Somerset Masters' Lodge, nearly a century ago now, was to encourage brethren to think about the Craft, discuss, debate and propagate. Here are tasks redolent of the charge to "make a daily advancement in Masonic knowledge" and to "afford instruction to the brethren." It is, would we see it as such, a call to educate both ourselves and others, and chimes well with the present day thinking at Provincial level. The Lodge, through its collection of past Transactions, can offer a reservoir of information and inspiration, and by means of its meetings and future publications the opportunity for brethren to exercise "such of the liberal arts and sciences as are within the compass of their attainments".

Wessex Lodge No. 4093

Meets at the Masonic Hall, Weston-super-Mare

Warrant dated 1920

Whilst Clevedon has its Poet's Lodges, Weston has its Saxon ones. Athelstan, King Alfred and indeed Wessex itself preserves the memories of the Land of the Angles: Engleland! Weston Masons are indeed 'Da Engliscan Gesidas'

With the ending of the Great War of 1914 and two Lodges already formed in Weston-super-Mare, it was considered that, with the increase of those who sought to enter Freemasonry, it had become desirable for a third Lodge to be formed in the town. There was no lack of enthusiasm amongst the members of St Kew and King Alfred who were prepared to sponsor and become founders of the new Lodge.

The proposal of the Petitioners received the sanction of Provincial Grand Lodge and Grand Lodge, and was duly granted a Warrant by the Most Worshipful The Grand Master The Duke of Connaught and Strathearn KG under the title of "Wessex Lodge 4093" dated the 17th February 1920 and the Consecration date was fixed for Tuesday the 1st June 1920 at 12.30 pm. There were 59 founders, of these 33 were members of St Kew Lodge 1222 and nineteen of King Alfred Lodge 3169 and included many well known personalities in the town at the time.

The Consecration ceremony was to have been performed by the Provincial Grand Master, R.W.Bro Col. William Long, assisted by the Deputy Provincial Grand Master, W.Bro Colonel A Thrale Perkins, but unfortunately both were absent owing to indisposition. The responsibility for carrying out the Consecration was entrusted to W.Bro Charles Curd, who had been appointed an Assistant Grand Director of Ceremonies in Grand Lodge.

Among the items of business prior to closing the Lodge were proposals, duly seconded, for the election of two candidates for Initiation, each being a Lewis, together with three Joining Members and an Honorary Member, namely the Officiating Officer who had ably conducted the Consecration ceremony that afternoon. Many gifts were presented to the Lodge which included a Lodge Banner by W.Bro F.W. Day. The first Initiate of the Lodge, Bro Percy Blackmore was installed as Worshipful Master in April 1928.

All Lodges were obliged to contend with difficulties with the outbreak of war in September 1939. Wessex Lodge resumed its meetings on 27th October 1939, but many of its members had joined either the Armed

Forces and had temporarily left the district, whilst others had joined the Home Guard, Fire Service, etc. A total of 56 brethren of the Lodge were engaged in Service during the 1939-1945 War period. Despite this, some 40 members attended the October 1939 meeting; naturally the festive board was minimal.

Further disruption of Masonic activities in Weston-super-Mare occurred in June and July 1942 owing to enemy action throughout the town. The Masonic Hall however escaped damage through the swift action of the Tyler, who was carrying out his duties as an ARP warden, protecting the temple during air raid warnings and attacks.

The 25th Anniversary Meeting of the Lodge took place on 28th September 1945 when 64 Officers and brethren were present and 49 visiting brethren. A souvenir Summons and brochure was issued for this occasion along with a group photograph of the Officers of the Lodge. In 1950 an annual fraternal visit was established between the Wessex Lodge and Winscombe Lodge 6474 in Yatton

Wessex Lodge is particularly proud of its support for the Masonic Charities. In 1953 the Anniversary Festival of the Royal Masonic Benevolent Institution under the Presidency of the Provincial Grand Master R.W.Bro Brig. Gen. C.L. Norman the impressive sum of £50,000 was presented. Of this sum £1,000 was from the 82 brethren of Wessex Lodge, 50 of whom who became Stewards of the Festival. This splendid total demonstrated the value of the Covenant scheme introduced in 1947, and also enabled the Lodge to qualify as a Patron Lodge of the Institution.

In 1957 the Provincial Grand Master dedicated a new Lodge Banner to replace the original one presented when the Lodge was consecrated. The new Banner was greatly admired being hand embroidered on silk, the cost being £70.

In 1963 the Festival was the 165th Anniversary of the Royal Masonic Institution for Boys, over which our own Provincial Grand Master presided. The total amount subscribed by the Province was £98,153, the Wessex Lodge contribution amounting to £2,200.

Framed Apron belonging to Wessex Lodge
On display in the Weston-super-Mare Masonic Hall

The Golden Jubilee festival was held on 5th June 1970 at 6pm at which W.Bro Arthur Smart was the last surviving Officer from that year, being initiated on the 28th December 1962 at the age of 42 years. The Festival Banquet was attended by 100 brethren and served by the brethren of the St Kew Lodge. During the intervals the brethren were entertained to most enjoyable musical items by various artistes.

On Friday 23rd June 1995 the Lodge celebrated the 75th Anniversary of its consecration when the Provincial Grand Master and the Provincial team attended. There followed a Third Degree ceremony to raise Bro Peter Hodder. A formal presentation of a collarette and jewel to be worn by future Masters was made. Special Anniversary glasses were presented to the dignitaries to celebrate the occasion.

In the millennium year, the Lodge received from Germany many brethren from the Hildesheim Lodge, the twin town of Weston-super-Mare who enacted an Initiation Ceremony of the Grand Lodge of the Ancient Free and Accepted Masons of Germany. The ceremony had been translated by their Worshipful Master Egon Perkuhn who accepted the gavel from the Worshipful Master and firstly welcomed and escorted the principal guest, the Assistant Provincial Grand Master W.Bro David Lloyd Jenkins into the temple in due form.

All Officers and brethren wore black bows and top hats. The ceremony was very different and memorable from that of the English constitution, and showed what a united Brotherhood we belong to.

27th April 2001 witnessed the finest gathering of eminent visiting Masons in the Wessex Lodge history. It reads:

The Provincial Grand Master of Somerset
    R.W.Bro Stanley H.A.F. Hopkins
The Deputy Provincial Grand Master of
    Somerset V.W.Bro J. Peter Layzell
The Assistant Provincial Grand Master of
    Somerset W.Bro David Lloyd Jenkins
        The Provincial Grand Master of
            South Africa North
    The Deputy Provincial Grand Master of
            South Africa North
The Past Deputy Provincial Grand Master of
            South Africa North
Two Assistant Provincial Grand Masters of
            South Africa North
        Nine Grand Officers and
Eight Active Provincial Grand Officers

Under the direction of the Provincial Grand Director of Ceremonies, W.Bro Terry Stephens, the salutations were an Olympic marathon for all the members, but what a fantastic experience of our Craft.

On 26th September 2003 the Province gave special dispensation to initiate Bro Graham Roberts, a Lewis who was just nineteen years of age. In 2009 Bro Graham became the Senior Warden of the Lodge, a fantastic advert for Freemasonry in the Province.

Since 2002 Wessex Lodge has held Trafalgar Night Dinners as its main Charity event. 2005 marked the 200th Anniversary of the battle with 350 people attending a grand dinner at the Winter Gardens. The proceeds raised along with gift aid donations from the brethren over a six year period has enabled the Lodge to achieve a 5th Acorn Award for the RMBI Festival representing £600 per Brother.

The Lodge is now much smaller with just 42 members, but it is very strong, with an average age of only 42 years. The next major event will be the 2020 centenary year when all look forward to another fantastic celebration.

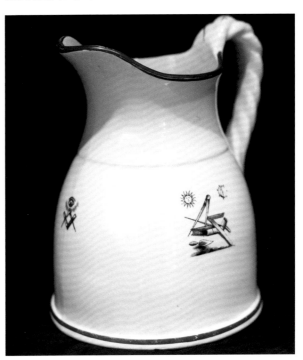

St. Alphege Lodge No. 4095

Meets at the Masonic Hall, Bath

Warrant dated 1920

The establishment of another new Lodge in Bath was first considered on 14th November 1919 when the name proposed was "The William Long Lodge". Grand Lodge however would not sanction a new Lodge named after a living person and it was therefore agreed to name the Lodge "St. Alphege" But why St. Alphege?

Alphege was born in Weston, near Bath, of a noble family, but in early life gave up everything to devote himself to his faith. Having assumed the monastic habit in the monastery of Deerhurst, Alphege came to the City of Bath in 973 where he became an anchorite and ultimately Abbot of the Abbey there, distinguishing himself by his piety and the austerity of his life, and reforming the Abbey along the lines of Benedictine Rule. Later in 984 through Dunstan's influence he moved to the important See of Winchester as Bishop.

While Bishop of Winchester, he was largely responsible for the building of a large organ that was audible over a mile away from the Cathedral and said to require more than 24 men to operate. He also built and enlarged the city's churches. After a Viking raid in 994, a peace treaty was arranged with Olaf Tryggvason in which not only Danegeld was paid to Olaf, (the Danegeld "Dane gold" was an English tribute raised to pay off Viking raiders to save the land from being ravaged), but Olaf was converted to Christianity. There are indications that Alphege had a hand in negotiating the treaty, and it is certain that it was Alphege that confirmed Olaf in his new faith. Unfortunately the words of Kipling in his poem "Dane Geld" were to ultimately ring true. " Once you have paid him the Danegeld you never get rid of the Dane."

In 1006, at the age of 52 Alphege succeeded Aelfric as Archbishop of Canterbury. While at Canterbury, he furthered the cult of Saint Dunstan, as well as introducing new practices into the liturgy. He also brought Saint Swithun's head with him as a relic! At the sack of Canterbury by the Danes in 1011, Alphege was captured and kept in prison for seven months. Refusing to allow a ransom to be paid, he was put to death on 19th April 1012 by stone and axe at Greenwich, reputedly on the present site of St Alphege's Church.

St. Alphege Lodge was Consecrated at the Masonic Hall, Bath, on 6th September, 1920 by the R.W.Bro Col. William Long, CMG, PGM. He was assisted by W.Bro Col. A. Thrale Perkins, CB, PGD, DPGM. The Consecrating Officer said one of the four Lodges in Bath had become unduly large, and a number of brethren had petitioned the Grand Master, His Royal Highness the Duke of Connaught, who had graciously acceded to their request to issue a Warrant for the new Lodge. There were 50 founder members and it was agreed that the Ritual should be that used by both the Royal Cumberland and the Royal Albert Edward Lodges.

A report of the Consecration appeared in the 'Bath Herald' of 7th September 1920, written by Bro Herbert Staines of the Royal Albert Edward Lodge, 906, and one of the Founder Members. The report stated that in the course of the consecration ceremony the Provincial Grand Master had referred to the City of Bath as one of the keenest places in Masonry that he knew.

On 3rd March 1928, the Banner of the Lodge was dedicated by the R.W Provincial Grand Master for Somerset, the Venerable Walter Farrer, Archdeacon of Wells. Thus although consecrated in September, 1920, it had no Banner for eight years. The design of the Banner shows a full length figure of St. Alphege together with

Carvings on the pillars of the Church of Our Lady and St. Alphege, Bath , by William Drinkwater Gough,.

Top: Alphege confirms Olaf at Andover.
Middle: Alphege refuses to allow a ransom to be paid.
Bottom: Alphege is carried back to Canterbury

implements and emblems of his martyrdom. It was designed by Bros. A.J. Taylor and A. C. Fare and the embroidery was by a Miss Hyatt, of Limpley Stoke. The Latin inscription on the border "Pax Vobiscum Frates Aelfheah Bathon Sum" translates as "Peace be with you brethren, I am Alphege of Bath"

During the Second World War the Masonic Hall at Bath, was badly damaged during air raids, and meetings were held at Keynsham for a short period. Thankfully all Lodge records and property were preserved. During the air raids on Bath two members, Bros W. McDougall and C. D. James were killed while on duty with the Civil Defence. Bro F. R. Elliot of the Royal Navy lost his life at sea.

In April 1948, within the space of twelve days, the Lodge lost W.Bros W.T. Ellery and W.A. Gayner who had been respectively Secretary and Treasurer of the Lodge since its Foundation. The Worshipful Master, W.Bro T.C.W. Inskip paid tribute to the high standard of their work and efficiency, which would set a pattern for every Brother of the Lodge.

The Masonic Year for the Lodge starts with Installation in April with a break in the summer months to continue in October through each of the winter months to March the following year. Meetings are held on the first Saturday of theses months. Fraternal visits have been held with the Eldon Lodge in Clevedon, and previously in Portishead, for a number of years and long may they continue. St Alphege Lodge also holds a number of social events during the year including the Ladies' Festival, which during the few past years has been held in Bournemouth, an annual Carol Service and family Barbecue.

Since its consecration in 1920 St. Alphege Lodge has played a very small, but we trust important part in promoting the good of Freemasonry and may we continue to preserve our Order and strive to set a standard, which will be an example to others and a credit to ourselves from generation to generation.

Perhaps the most striking and ornately carved Honours Board in the Province that of St Alphege Lodge in Bath Masonic Hall

Severn Lodge No. 4399

Meets at the Masonic Hall, Nailsea

Warrant dated 1922

Severn Lodge is the elder daughter of Eldon Lodge and elder sister Lodge of Gordano Lodge, and more recently the Olympian Lodge. The first suggestion for a new Lodge at Portishead was made to the WM of Eldon Lodge W.Bro Pugh Williams by junior members of the Lodge who were prompted by the fact that Eldon had grown to almost 170 members with increasing numbers of candidates coming forward. This of course may have also caused frustration to younger members as such large numbers would have affected progression.

There were a number of suggestions for the name of the Lodge and the original petition requested the name 'William Rice' a founder of Eldon Lodge but this name was not approved and the PGM suggested 'Severn'.

Accordingly on the 24th August 1921 a meeting was held at 10 Orchard Street, Bristol for those brethren who wished to become founder members. W.Bro Pugh Williams was elected Master Elect and it was agreed that any Brother taking office in the new Lodge would relinquish any office he may have held in Eldon Lodge in order to give the younger brethren there, a better opportunity for advancement. It was settled that the regular meetings of the Lodge be held on the fourth Saturday in January, March, May, July, September and November with Installation being in May. The only variation to those original dates being May, now on the third Saturday to avoid a Bank Holiday.

The Lodge Banner, which forms the centre piece of the current banner, bears the family crest of the then PGM, R.W.Bro Col. William Long, late of the 4th Somerset light infantry, and is

that of the Longs of Rood Ashton, Wiltshire, given by King Henry VIII to Henry Long. The Latin motto, which is also that of the Long family, translates as 'pious yet courageous'. The Banner was worked by the wife of the first SW designate Bro Compton West and was incorporated into the current banner in 1997, as part of the 75th Anniversary celebrations, and to record the Lodge's move to Nailsea in 1994.

Severn Lodge was consecrated on Saturday afternoon of the 27th May 1922, by the R.W PGM Col. William Long, assisted by the DPGM Col. A. Thrale Perkins. W.Bro William Pugh Williams IPM of Eldon Lodge was installed as 1st Master, Bro J. Compton West as SW and our own W.Bro Fred Webb's great uncle, Bro Jim Tucker as JW.

Initiation fees in 1922 were fifteen guineas, joining fees five guineas, rejoining fees two guineas and annual subscriptions 30 shillings. Note that Severn Lodge paid rental, inclusive of heating, lighting and use of regalia of £30 per annum. During the first year of the Lodge, six candidates were initiated, passed and raised, nine more were initiated and passed and a further eleven were initiated.

To achieve this, three extra emergency meetings were held plus double initiations and second degrees followed by a double third in the same meeting! In the second year eight brethren were initiated, nine passed and ten raised, involving five emergency meetings. Current officers note how easy we have it now. During the following years up until the second world war a minimum of four candidates were initiated passed and raised every year.

In the early war years meetings were intermittent. In the 1942/43 Masonic year, due in some measure to travel restrictions, Eldon and Severn Lodges decided to hold their meetings at the Albert Hall, Dowry Square, Bristol and from 1942 there were still four candidates initiated in each of the war years. The Installation meetings for 1943, 1944 and 1945 were all held, by dispensation, at the Victoria Rooms, Bristol, with the consent of the R.W PGM of Bristol. In July 1945 the re introduction of the 2.30pm train service from Bristol to Portishead made it possible to resume meetings at the Portishead Masonic Hall.

Over the following years the Lodge generally settled into the pattern of having two candidates each year which allowed for two first degree meetings, a double second, two third degree meetings, plus Installation. This filled the six meetings of the Masonic year and allowed for candidates to generally be initiated, passed and raised by the same Master.

In the 1950s the now Famous Severn Anthem was first sung at the festive board by W.Bro James Knapp. It is noted that as he had blatantly plagiarised the tune of 'Sussex by the Sea', he was a little concerned as one of the guests was the Colonel of the Sussex Regiment! However the Colonel enjoyed the performance and it has been sung ever since.

April 1963 was the first occasion of a fraternal visit to Severn Lodge 5583 in Stourport, in the Province of Worcestershire when the visiting WM and his Wardens were invited to close the Lodge, thus beginning a tradition which still continues today.

1972 saw the 50th anniversary of the consecration of the Lodge and the Installation meeting of W.Bro H.W.T. Giles as Master, was attended by R.W.Bro Lt. Col. Harry Owen Hughes PGM, V.W.Bro Henry Frampton, DPGM and W.Bro H.E. Dyke Asst. PGM. On the 16th of June a service of commemoration was held in the Lord Mayors Chapel in Bristol. During these first 50 years there had been 133 candidates and 59 Joining Members, with 299 regular meetings and 39 emergency meetings. The average attendance at Lodge over the 50 years had been 69.

In the 1980s W.Bro Ron Bawn's brother Reg was then located in Devon and became WM of Prudence Lodge No 1550 in Plymouth, Province of Devonshire and suggested that a Fraternal visit should be organised. W.Bro Ron as Secretary organised the Severn brethren and visits began which have continued each year since, with Prudence last being here in July.

Also in the 1980s W.Bro Gordon Budge travelled to Germany as a guest of Bro Hans Fuhres for his 60th Birthday party. Gordon and his wife had met and befriended Hans in 1946 when German prisoners of war had been allowed out of their camp to attend church services and mix with the local people and later in the 1950s Gordon had been present at Hans' initiation into Freemasonry in Germany. During that visit when Hans had also invited members of his Lodge to his Birthday celebrations, Gordon met W.Bro Eddie Brum and invited his Lodge to visit Severn as his guests.

This they subsequently did and another very special part of Severn's history was established with Fraternal visits between Post Nubila Phoebus Lodge No. 900 under the United Grand Lodge of Germany and Severn having taken place almost every year since. Recently Severn Lodges visited Aschaffenberg when they witnessed W.Bro Eddie being invested as District Grand Master.

One of the most significant events in the later years was the move to Nailsea which was prompted by the increasing difficulties being experienced by many of the elder brethren in negotiating what was known as 'cardiac' hill. So with much sadness in leaving our home at Portishead the Lodge was welcomed to Nailsea in 1994.

1997 saw the Lodge achieve it's 75th Anniversary and the Installation meeting was attended by V.W.Bro Vernon Harding, who was then Asst. PGM. The Menu's and proceedings replicated as far as practical those of the 50th Anniversary, and the new Lodge Banner was rededicated. Unfortunately, when it came to arrange a service of commemoration, as had been held for the 50th, Bristol City Council refused the use of the Lord Mayors Chapel. However the Dean of Bristol was pleased to allow the service to be held in the Lady Chapel of Bristol Cathedral to lead the service. R.W.Bro Stanley Hopkins as PGM in 1997 read the lesson originally read by the R.W PGM in 1972, likewise the WM read the same lesson as was read by the W.Bro Giles, WM in 1922.

As with many Lodges suitable candidates have become scarcer in the last few years, but Severn Lodge has managed at least one candidate each year. It has been interesting to note that most of the recent and candidates have been of the younger variety.

Group Photograph of the Severn Lodge Founder Members in June 1922

Quantock Lodge No. 4446

Meets at the Masonic Hall Watchet

Warrant dated 1922

The first Worshipful Master of Quantock Lodge was the then Vicar of Watchet, W.Bro Rev. T. Hawkes, PProv Grand Chaplain. However, Lodge minutes record that at the Installation Ceremony, a 'Deputy' Worshipful Master, W.Bro Westacott was also appointed, which surely was an unusual practice, if not an irregular one by present day standards. However, it would seem that W.Bro Westacott's appointment was justified in that the Reverend Gentlemen did not attend any Lodge Meetings during his year of Office. Later records show that W.Bro Reverend T. Hawkes left Watchet during his Master's Year having accepted a living in another part of the country.

During the Second World War, Watchet Masonic Hall and Quantock Lodge were able to provide a truly Masonic welcome to those visiting brethren to the area stationed at the near-by camps. These visitors came from all parts of the UK, the USA and also, what we used to call in those days, the "British Empire"!

One Australian visitor, when responding to the Visitors' Toast, told a story which he vouched for as being true and had occurred in his own Lodge "down under". A Candidate was asked in the North East Corner the usual question "Have you anything to give...etc?" and when the Deacon was slow to prompt, the Candidate replied "I have not anything on me at present but put me down for a few dollars", or was it still pounds in those days? Anyway, the Candidate had evidently been properly prepared.

It is recorded that in 1946 the Lodge was presented with a Charity Box in the form of a Broken Column which is still used today and

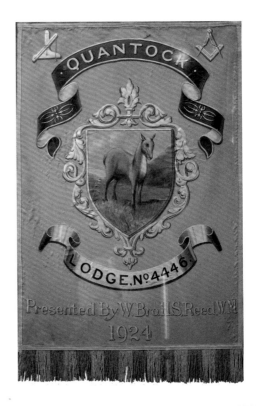

in 1947, Quantock Lodge's First Master, W.Bro Rev. T. Hawkes paid a surprise visit to the Lodge after an absence of 24 years!

The 50th Anniversary of the Lodge and the Masonic Hall was celebrated in the presence of the then R.W PGM Lt. Col. Harry Owen Hughes and the Assistant Grand Master W.Bro H.E. Dyke, and because the Lodge building was too small, the Festive Board was held at the Benares Hotel in Minehead.

In October 1977 when W.Bro Robin Bex was installed as Master, W.Bro Robin's Father, W.Bro Leslie Bex, a former Master of the Lodge, and a superb craftsman in wood, presented a new Gavel to the Lodge which W.Bro Leslie had made from acacia wood and suitably inscribed

Founder's and Past Master's Jewels

In 1981 a new carpet for the Lodge Room was acquired to replace the original carpet purchased in 1923. By this time the old carpet was so frayed that it would have given the Health and Safety Executive a heart attack. During W.Bro Steve Groves's year as WM (1982/1983), the dining room floor was replaced. Previously there had been bare floor boards badly stained by drink and food. Also in 1983 (again masterminded by the late W.Bro Jack Cozens) the fire escape from the Temple was completed, and in 1984, a programme of building maintenance work was undertaken by the Lodge brethren themselves.

During the late W.Bro Vivian Howells' Master's Year (1984/1985) the Dining Room Tables were replaced. The old trestle tables were sold for £100 – nowadays no doubt these trestle tables would not be out of place on the "Antiques Roadshow". The Dining Room chairs were replaced in 1988.

In 1977, committee records show that Watchet Masonic Hall bar prices were very low. Gin and whisky; 20p a double, and no wonder the brethren could not afford to go home.

During the summer of 1979, the late W.Bro Hurley and his Son in Law decorated the Main Hall, stairs and what was the then main kitchen. The late W.Bro Ken Oakey was instrumental in setting-up the "Building Fund", which continues in existence today, this being a fund of money set aside not only to maintain the Building but also with capital improvements to the Building in mind.

Repairs during that year, masterminded by the late W.Bro Jack Cozens cost £1800. In July 1980 damp proofing was undertaken, but this proved to be unsatisfactory so that further work was necessary ten years later! Also, by the summer of 1980, W.Bro Jack gathered together enough materials for the new bar and this was built, decorated and christened by Bro Malcolm Bale, W.Bro Mike Nicholas, W.Bro Ted Dudderidge and the late W.Bro Jim Hurley.

W.Bro Ted Duddridge (Master 1985/1986) made two Bench Seats for the Past Masters to sit on, and in December 1985 Quantock Lodge held its first Carol Service, which has now become an annual event. Roof repairs costing nearly £2000 were undertaken during 1986, and the kneeling mat in front of the pedestal was professionally restored, and two Quantock Lodge brethren redecorated the dining room, hall and stairs.

In December 1987 the Masonic Hall was burgled on two occasions, when all beer and spirits were taken plus the ceremonial sword. The drink was missed immediately, but it took a little longer to realize that the sword had also been stolen. The loss of the alcoholic beverages was instrumental in the installation of a burglar alarm and other security measures. During 1988, a velvet cushion for the WM's pedestal was given to the Lodge by Mrs. Ivy Slade in memory of her late Husband.

In August 1990, when a firm was employed to deal with woodworm in the roof timbers, it was found that the roof was infested with dry rot. An estimate for the necessary repairs was accepted in the sum of £6620 plus VAT, and as this did not include any redecorations, the redecorations and a good deal of the work in connection with the dry rot was undertaken by the brethren themselves. During 1996 the new gas central heating system was installed.

Since then there was the massive undertaking of a new kitchen and bar area, the project being made financially feasible, in that one of the Lodge Wardens was employed by an Industrial Kitchen Fitting Company, and with the co-operation of his employers, the measurements of the kitchen which had been constructed for display at an exhibition, were found conveniently to match the requirements of the Watchet Masonic Hall. Again, much money was saved by Lodge members volunteering to undertake building work themselves.

Over the years, thanks to the generosity of many brethren, much has been achieved. Looking to the future, active consideration is currently being given to perhaps extending the Lodge Building, both upstairs and downstairs, improving access for the disabled (perhaps a lift), and also upgrading the Lodge toilets.

The Abbey Lodge No. 4491

Meets at The Masonic Hall, Bath Road Keynsham

Warrant dated 1923

In 1922 the Past Masters of St Keyna Lodge 1833 considered that, as their Lodge had more than 100 members, it should petition to form a new Lodge. The suggestion by W.Bro George Booth that this new Lodge should be called 'The Abbey' was accepted. This recognized the fact that Keynsham Abbey had been one of the largest and most important religious establishments in the Kingdom in the 14th and 15th centuries. The names of the first Officers were approved and the Petition signed by seventeen brethren at the regular meeting of the St Keyna Lodge on 17th July 1922. Five of those seventeen brethren went on to become Master of the new Lodge.

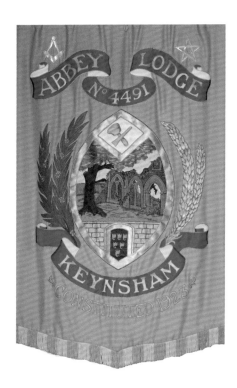

At a Founders meeting held on 20th November 1922 the seven names on the warrant were agreed. The meetings of the Lodge were to be held on the first Friday of the month. The Founders were invited to contribute £1 each towards initial expenses. The initiation fee was to be ten guineas, with the joining fee three guineas and the subscription fee two guineas annually. The Founders each gave a further £2, which included subscriptions to the end of the year. To put these sums into context, at that time an unskilled workman could expect to receive £150 per annum or less, a skilled craftsman £200 to £300 and for a professional person £500 would be a good salary. Medals were presented to the Founders early in 1924.

The PGS wrote on 28th February 1923 that the Warrant had been received and that arrangements could proceed for the Consecration. The Worshipful Master Designate asked the brethren of St Keyna Lodge for, and was granted, free of charge the use of the furnishings and regalia until the 1st January 1924.

The Consecration ceremony, on Friday 6th July 1923 at 2.30 pm, was performed by the Provincial Grand Master, R.W.Bro Colonel William Long, CMG, assisted by W.Bro Colonel A Thrale Perkins, CB, PGD, DPGM and the officers of the Provincial Grand Lodge of Somerset. The oration on the Nature and Principles of the Institution was given by the Provincial Grand Chaplain W.Bro T. Bulloch. The Abbey Lodge 4491 was then duly constituted and the new Master installed in the 'Emulation' manner to which the officers of Provincial Grand Lodge were accustomed. Officers were appointed to their respective duties and candidates and Joining Members duly proposed and seconded for the coming year. The principal Provincial Grand Lodge Officers were presented with suitably engraved silver ashtrays as mementoes of the occasion and the Lodge closed in harmony and with prayer.

The first regular meeting was held on Friday 5th October 1923 at 18:00. The first candidates for initiation were Wallace Edgar Wiltshire and Haydn Charles Morgan who became Master in 1931. Three of the four Joining Members, H.T. Parks (1928), A Martin (1929), H.J. Chidgey (1930) became Masters.

In the early days many candidates were forthcoming and double candidate ceremonies were the order of the day; a procedure which was soon discontinued in favour of the single candidate ceremony now used. From its consecration until moving into the present, purpose built Masonic Hall in 1940 the Lodge held its meetings at the Lamb and Lark Hotel, Keynsham followed by supper at the Wingrove Hotel which involved a walk along the High Street. Both these hotels have long since been demolished. Committee meetings and rehearsals were held at Orchard Street, Bath. The first Ladies' Night was held at Fortes, Clifton in November 1925; tickets 7/6 each (37.5 pence!).

The Abbey Lodge Banner shows an oval panel in which is a representation of a ruined abbey in the form of a part demolished Gothic door and window in front of which is a stretch of greensward with an oak tree standing in it. On the left-hand side of the panel are two sprigs of acacia and on the right hand side two ears of corn. Masonic symbols are included and the whole is completed by the original arms of the de Clares, Earls of Gloucester, six gold clarions or trumpets on a red ground. These are appropriate because their arms were adopted by Keynsham Abbey from its founder and patron William, Earl of Gloucester.

In 1981 it became clear that a new banner was needed. Accordingly, a new one was produced by a Miss Christine Burton of Nether Stowey, at a cost of £250. The new banner was presented to the Lodge at a wine and cheese party held on Easter Saturday in 1983 and dedicated at the July 1983 meeting by the Provincial Grand Master for Somerset R.W.Bro K.C. Kinnersley. Following the dedication, a 17th Century Masonic Working was performed by the Sutton Players (from the West Midlands). 1983 was our 60th year of existence - our Diamond Jubilee

In September 1978, W.Bro Peter Timney, after discussions with the Past Masters, made an approach to Grand Lodge for permission to make contact with a French Lodge. After consultation with Grand Lodge, R.W.Bro S.T.L Humbert, Provincial Grand Master of Neustrie and a party of French Masons, including W.Bro J. Muchard, Worshipful Master of Guillaume le Conquerant Lodge, 176, paid a visit to Abbey Lodge. In a reciprocal visit, twelve members of Abbey Lodge visited Guillaume le Conquerant Lodge, and in April 1979 a twinning ceremony between our two Lodges took place.

The Provincial Grand Master of Neustrie conferred Provincial Grand Rank on W.Bro P. Timney and Honorary Membership of the Guillaume le Conquerant Lodge on the Worshipful Master, the Senior and Junior Wardens of Abbey Lodge, who wear this jewel during their time in office.

Members and visitors alike have questioned the origin of the unique mixture of "Bristol" and Emulation workings used by the Lodge. The use of the 'Bristol' working for our regular meetings arises from the fact that our grandmother Lodge, Vale of Brislington Lodge 1296 and our mother Lodge, St. Keyna Lodge 1833 were founded largely by Bristol Masons, who brought a form of that ritual with them. The use of the Emulation working in our installation meetings derives from the consecration of the Lodge, when our first Master was installed, in this manner, by the officers of the Provincial Grand Lodge of Somerset.

Tyntesfield Lodge No. 4494

Warrant dated 1922

The origin of the Lodge name is the name of the residence of Lord Wraxall, but at the time of the formation of the Lodge, Col. G. Gibbs was owner and Lord of the Manor, and it was he who gave his consent for the Lodge to take the name "Tyntesfield" and to use the Coat of Arms on the Lodge Summons and the Lodge Banner.

The Tyntesfield Lodge 4494, was founded by the brethren of Coleridge Lodge 1750 and the Lodge of Agriculture 1199. On the 9th September the Master of Coleridge W.Bro H. G. Hedges, presented the Petition for a new Lodge to be called Tyntesfield and to be founded in Nailsea. It was duly Consecrated on 20th March 1923 by the Provincial Grand Master for Somerset R.W.Bro Col. William Long CMG. Apologies were received from W.Bro The Bishop of Bristol and R.W.Bro Col. George Gibbs, Provincial Grand Master for the Province of Bristol in whose honour the new Lodge had been named.

The first Banner obviously stood up well to the early years of its existence because it was not until the early seventies that the Lodge committee decided it needed to undergo renovation. Bro Donald West, who served for many years as Tyntesfield Chief Steward, undertook to get this work done at his own expense. However, a straightforward renovation was not possible and the only parts of the old banner suitable for use in the new were the cords and tassels. A further 23 years passed before the Lodge committee decided to commission this new hand-made Banner which was almost two years in the making. It bears the arms of "Gibbs of Tyntesfield in the County of Somerset and Clyst St. George in the County of Devon" and "Gibbs of Clifton Hampden, Oxfordshire".

The original Banner was presented to the Lodge by Bro Lt. Col. W.O. Gibbs, of Barrow Court, who had been appointed first Chaplain of the Lodge. The motto Tenox Propositi, translates to "Firm of purpose"

Tyntesfield Lodge considers this a very apt motto, as between 1923 and 1939 much progress was made by the Lodge with the purchase of the original building by the Founder Members and the raising of cash by gifts and loans to adapt the building to provide a Temple and dining hall as well as the provision of Temple furniture. This was done mainly by the efforts of the Founder Members and first Officers of Tyntesfield Lodge.

The original Masonic Hall consisted mainly of a single storey building attached to a small cottage. In late 1934 it was decided to extend the building and consequently a ceremony for the laying of the Foundation Stone of the new work was held on 21st March 1935 with the Deputy Provincial Grand Master of Somerset, W.Bro Rowland T. A. Hughes PGD attended by Provincial Grand Wardens, and assisted by the Worshipful Master, Past Masters and Officers of the Tyntesfield Lodge. The alterations and enlargement were completed during the closed season of 1935 and in October of that year, R.W PGM for Somerset, Brig. Gen. C.L. Norman, DSO, and MVOAL (PSGD) was cordially invited to visit Tyntesfield Lodge for the purpose of its re-Consecration. This Ceremony took place on 11th December 1935 in accordance with the new Ritual, specially composed for the purpose and used for the first time.

In September 1940, the Lodge premises, with the exception of the Temple and a small Masters room, were requisitioned by the War Office and were continually occupied by them until March 1945. The Ceremonies in the Temple continued, but no after the meeting refreshment or fellowship was possible. After the War, the Lodge re-occupied the whole premises and by 1947 membership had risen to 88.

A minute entry of 5th November 1935 records the transfer of the Title Deeds of the building to Somerset Provincial Masonic Trust Ltd. In 1963 the Tyntesfield Lodge passed ownership of the Masonic Hall to the newly formed Nailsea Masonic Hall Company.

In 2002 Tyntesfield House was purchased by the National Trust after seeking support from the public to add to its own funds to meet the huge purchase cost involved and much needed renovation. A visit by the Worshipful Master and senior brethren of the Lodge identified a motto above the door of the House which after translation is now used by all Ruling Masters of Tyntesfield when opening the Lodge: "Peace to those who enter, Health to those who depart".

The Founders

Oration by W.Bro J.S. Anderson.
Provincial Grand Chaplain
at the Banner Dedication
5th September 1995

"The Clarion call on the bugle, the pounding of the drum and the flag flying high have proved to be heart-stirring events in the recent times. The VE day celebrations produced a large number of banners representing all branches of HM Forces. The Trooping of the Colour earlier in the year received universal acclaim and gave the flag a truly central part in the proceedings, whilst the Royal Tournament gave the present-day Forces an opportunity to present their flags.

On the heals of this, the opening and closing ceremonies of the World Games at Gothenburg showed us the National flags of so many countries amidst great excitement. Mid-August produced the VJ Day celebrations and a huge parade which contained the greatest number of flags seen in human memory: the flag is a feature deeply etched in the national consciousness.

Banners have been used these many years in the Craft and it is perhaps entirely appropriate that we examine how the banner came to be significant in furniture of a Lodge. Any such line of enquiry should, quite naturally begin with the word itself: in this case a word first used, as far as scholarship perceives, in the thirteenth century. The henchmen of William the Conqueror, Duke of Normandy, are very likely to have brought the word over, although the origins of the word ban from which Banner is derived, are partly Middle English and partly Germanic. It has nothing to do with our word meaning 'prohibit', but seems to have indicated a summons to arms, or a proclamation.

From the earliest times and long before the first use of the word 'banner', families, tribes, armies and nations have been called to arms by decorated standards or flags which have been prominently displayed with many differing effects and, perhaps, intentions all seemingly connected in some way with war or territorial ambition. How interesting it is that the diametrically opposite notion obtains in the heart of the Freemason who would have brotherly love, relief and truth, service to God and neighbour at the forefront of his thinking, But in this brief review we can seek to understand the reasons for displaying banners in Masonic terms so that we learn more of our duties to God, to one another and to our Lodge.

As a rallying point, the banner is as important to a Mason as it was to the Norman Knight, the gunner at Waterloo, the infantryman at El Alamein or the veteran in Hyde Park. The Banner has always identified those who gather beneath it, whether such identification be directed towards friend or foe, it declares to the world who we are and whom we serve. Whilst it may have induced fear into the hearts of an enemy, in Masonic terms, we would declare our adherence to the Craft and allegiance to our Lodge and look for respect in return. To all those in allegiance with us serves now, as always, to give security and comfort.

Beneath such a banner we seek fraternity and community of interests. It offers the opportunity to bathe in the Masonic tradition and to follow it and in so doing as a member of a Lodge, we very properly develop pride in our banner as a symbol of our beliefs, our honour, our fellowship and our loyalty. Thus the banner enables us to rise above ourselves and render superior service. It is a powerful enabling factor. It represents us."

Alfred and Guthrum Lodge No. 4535

Meets at the Masonic Hall, Church Street, Wedmore

Warrant Granted 1923

"King Guthrum came to Aelfred, at Aller, which is near Athelney, where the King stood sponsor to him at Baptism, and the ceremony of the removal of the Baptismal fillet took place at Wedmore."- Saxon Chronicle for the year 878

Prior to 1906, when W.Bro W.E. Bracey was initiated into the Rural Philanthropic Lodge 291, Highbridge, Freemasonry was represented in Wedmore by only E.H. Smith, Headmaster of Wedmore Council School. Shortly afterwards, W.G. Burrough was initiated into St Kew, Weston-super-Mare, but later, probably because of travelling difficulties, lost interest for a period. However, when Bro Bracey returned from service in Gallipoli and Mesopotamia and was elected Master of Rural Philanthropic in 1917-18, Bro W.G. Burrough then joined the Highbridge Lodge.

These two, together with several brethren of the Lodge of Agriculture 1199, meeting in Yatton, who came from the Cheddar district felt the need for a Lodge nearer their homes. Thus it was that W.Bro Bracey was asked to investigate the possibilities of one being formed in Wedmore.

However, many difficulties were to be encountered, the most significant being that the brethren from Wedmore had played a prominent part in the affairs of Rural Philanthropic Lodge, and their absence would be a serious loss to that Lodge. Another being the rather "insular" character of Somerset Freemasonry at that time and that certain prominent members of the Provincial Grand Lodge felt very strongly that their consent had to be obtained before any changes in their respective "areas" could be contemplated.

These difficulties proved the downfall of the scheme for a Lodge at Wedmore, though the main reasons given, to quote W.Bro Bracey were "that Wedmore could not support a Lodge, and that in any case nobody outside could ever visit such an isolated place". The result was that, "although I had the promise of all the necessary furniture and the plans for the construction of a small Lodge room in 'The Borough', the scheme was turned down".

Fortunately it only lay dormant, and in 1922 W.Bro Bracey tried again, this time obtaining enthusiastic support from influential members of Rural Philanthropic Lodge 291 and from Benevolent Lodge 446, meeting at Wells. From these came the founders of the Albert and Guthrum Lodge.

The Lodge was consecrated on the 9th October 1923, the ceremony taking place in the Village Institute Hall, Church Street, Wedmore, which some seven years later would be purchased by the Lodge and become its permanent home. The Lodge Banner was presented in October 1925 by the wives and two sisters of the brethren, a list of names of the Donors being recorded in the Minute Book. The Lodge was named Alfred and Guthrum after King Alfred and the Danish King Guthrum who met at Wedmore in AD878 to negotiate a peace treaty.

The first meeting place consisted of rented accommodation on the premises of Mr (later Bro) W.R. Withers, a builder, in 'The Borough' in an upper room with accommodation for 40-50 brethren. "Its simple beauty of decoration and its homeliness were striking to visiting brethren, and even more especially to those who had the privilege of Initiation therein." The last time it was used 42 members and guests were present.

Over 100 brethren attended the Consecration Ceremony which was conducted by R.W.Bro Col. William Long, the Provincial Grand Master of Somerset, assisted by the R.W Deputy Provincial Grand Master of Somerset, Col. A Thrale Perkins and officers of the Provincial Grand Lodge. This was to be the last Masonic act of R.W.Bro Long's career, as he died soon afterwards. At the meeting W.Bro W.E. Bracey was installed as the First Master and Bros W.G. Burrough and H.A. Wall as Senior and Junior Wardens respectively.

A minute of the meeting of December 1924 W.Bro C.A. Ogilvie proposed that the IPM should be asked to present a portrait of himself, and that the Founders should also be asked to do the same so that the Masters of the Lodge should be perpetuated, a practice which continues to this day. The Lodge remained at The Borough until an unexpected opportunity arose in 1929 to purchase the Village Institute Hall.

The Original Lodge Room

This building had been erected towards the end of the 19th Century as the Village Assembly Rooms and opened with a Grand Concert on New Year's Day 1868. Recalling the events surrounding the acquisition, W.Bro Bracey writes, "The purchase of the Village Institute was effected by telephone when WGB and I were talking and the owner rang up and said he did not wish to sell for any industrial purposes and would sell it to us for the reserve price. So we bought it first and asked the Lodge after!"

As a result the minutes of the Regular Lodge meeting of 8th October 1929 record: "The Lodge Committee informed the brethren that W.Bro Burrough had purchased the Wedmore Village Institute premises and had offered the same to the Lodge at the sum of £735, such sum being £700 purchase money of premises, £12 12s.0d Auction and Contract fees paid, £7.8s.0d Stamp Duty etc, and £15 for 40 chairs all curtains and they recommended the brethren to purchase same on these terms." The brethren unanimously agreed.

To this sum of £735 had to be added £165 for work to be carried out and for the termination of the Lease of the "present premises". The £900 subsequently became £940. It appears that some compensation also had to be paid to the owner of the former meeting place for premature termination of the Lease. The "Plan" for paying for the new premises is outlined in the Resolutions:

"That the sum of £900 required be found by the brethren, free of interest, and be repaid by two sums of £5 each and every Lodge night the receivers to be ascertained by means of a ballot. That the Lodge shall pay the sum of £45 a year by instalments of £5.12s.6d every Lodge night. That all brethren be earnestly requested to subscribe 2s.6d a Lodge night to the Tontine (a form of lifetime annuity) to assist in discharging the loan. And that the Asst. Secretary, Bro H.F. Hibberd be appointed to run the Tontine and

that a Promissory Note for each unit of £5 be prepared, stamped and numbered and issued in exchange for each £5 subscribed."

Fifty brethren and one lady, in memory of her father, subscribed the money and a Tontine was formed, the debt being duly cleared during 1938.

The first Meeting, by Dispensation, in the new Temple was the Installation of 1929. Again by Dispensation, the December 1929 meeting was also held in the newly acquired Hall, and on January 14th 1930 a Special Lodge Meeting unanimously passed the following Resolution, notice of which had been previously given:

"That the Lodge be moved from the premises in the Borough and permanently established in the new premises in Church Street".

The Dedication of the new Temple took place at a Special Meeting on 28th January 1930. The Ceremony was conducted by the R.W PGM the Ven. Archdeacon Walter Farrer MA supported by the PG Wardens, Chaplain, Treasurer and Director of Ceremonies. Present were 47 brethren of the Lodge and 21 visitors. In the minutes the Secretary described the ceremony as "simple, yet beautiful and impressive".

Thus, only six years after its formation, the Lodge was in possession of premises sound in construction, convenient in position and with accommodation which in the future would be adapted for a variety Masonic purposes. The new Lodge room itself, on the first floor, had formerly served as the village cinema and the outline of the screen can still be seen on the wall behind the Senior Warden's pedestal.

At the meeting of the Lodge held on 12th February 1935 a double first ceremony was undertaken when H.J. Hatch and L.C. Hatch were initiated into Freemasonry. Herbert Hatch is now the longest serving Mason in Somerset, at the same meeting the Master, who was the local doctor, was called away on urgent business but later returned to carry out a 2nd Degree Ceremony.

The year 1936-37 was marked with sadness. At the supper after the Lodge of April 1937 the health of the WM was proposed and received in the usual manner. Before the Master (W.Bro H.W. Jay) could respond he was taken ill and died early next morning.

Although the Lodge room continued to be used during the 1939-45 war, permission was given for one of the anterooms to be used as a First Aid point and another room by evacuated mothers during the daytime, and one by the Women's First Aid Party for sleeping accommodation. Under the date 10th October 1939 the Secretary recorded in the minute Book: "On this date the ordinary Regular October Meeting should have been held but in accordance with orders received from the Grand Secretary and the Provincial Grand Secretary the meeting was not held. The following is an extract from the notice from the Grand Secretary dated 4th September

"Having regard to the Emergency Orders of HM Government I am to inform you that, until further notice, all Masonic Meetings should be suspended".

Thus at the November meeting it was necessary to elect the WM for the coming year, and to install him at the same Lodge Meeting. After the restrictions on holding Lodge Meetings was lifted, in February 1940 there occurred a most severe frost, and in the absence of fires, radiators and pipes cracked. The Senior Trustee (W.Bro Bracey) with his customary foresight gave orders for the pipes etc, to be taken out to avoid damage to the Lodge furniture. From then on until December 1941 the Lodge was heated by a few oil stoves. Various methods of heating were considered and ultimately it was decided to continue with a hot water supply system.

Again W.Bro Bracey came to the rescue, purchasing privately a quantity of the necessary piping which happened to become available. Under the personal attention of the Tyler, a new heating system came into being at a cost of £165. As the surplus funds of the Lodge had previously been invested in War Bonds, the Lodge asked its bankers to make the necessary financial accommodation for a few months, when it anticipated that the Annual Subscriptions would defray the cost of the installation.

At a later date the Lodge decided that, during the War, all brethren who might be evacuated from their homes to this district should, if they so desired, be admitted as Honorary Members of Alfred and Guthrum. This resolution was interpreted to include brethren in HM Services stationed in the area.

In November 1940 the Senior Warden of Alfred and Guthrum Lodge was W.Bro H. Frampton, who was at that time also the Master of the Mother Lodge, Rural Philanthropic. As he was not allowed to undertake the Mastership of two Craft Lodges at the same time, W.Bro W.E. Comer continued in office for a second year. At the end of the year in which W.Bro H. Frampton occupied the Chair, Bro M. Pulliblank was chosen as Master Elect. Unfortunately the latter was taken ill and was unable to be present at the meeting in November and December 1942 and W.Bro Frampton continued as Master until November 1943.

It was fortunate that the Lodge was able to meet regularly and enthusiastically during the war years, and that no damage was caused to the premises, and in October 1945 it was possible to restore the GL Warrant from the place of safety to which it had been removed.

The Lodge rooms and ante-rooms are on the first floor, and on the ground floor there was an Accountant's office, the Wedmore branch of the National Westminster Bank, and at the rear a large room which until 1966 was used as a store. When the tenant vacated this, the opportunity was taken to alter and improve it to form a dining room and provide kitchen and bar facilities. Previous to this the members of the Lodge had dined at the George Hotel.

Many have been the gifts to the Lodge, the three splendid pedestals, the kneeling stools, and the screen behind the Master's chair, all made of old English oak, and the canopies over the principal chairs.

Here it is fitting to pay tribute to our late Bro W.R. Withers, through whose craftsmanship so much dignity and beauty have been added to the Temple. It should be known that he journeyed up the Masonic ladder as far as the Office of Senior Deacon and then preferred to serve his Lodge in the more humble capacity of Tyler.

Alas, after the presentation of his gift of the Screen behind the Master's Chair, a gift which completed the decoration of the Temple, only once more was he to attend the Lodge before being suddenly called to the Grand Lodge above. The minutes of January 1937 record: "Bro Dunning spoke of the unfailing devotion to the Lodge ever since he (Bro Withers) was initiated, and of his labour of love of Masonry and demonstrating the wisdom of the brethren who proposed his Initiation as our serving Brother".

From the formation of the Lodge, many brethren have contributed gifts which have made the Temple one which evokes the admiration of visiting brethren. The Lodge has been fortunate over the years in having amongst its members skilled woodworking craftsman who have provided some beautiful furnishings not only for Wedmore but for other lodges in the Province. Special mention must be made of W.Bro H.J. Hatch, Somerset's longest serving

Mason, whose skills are admired throughout the Province. On the Secretary's table lies a small manuscript book prepared by one of the brethren. In it are recorded, with the names of the donors, all the gifts to the Lodge. Among the many interesting items of furniture in the Lodge are a stool used at the Coronation of our present Monarch, a large gong, stand and hammer particularly useful in the third degree ceremony and last but not least the Tyler's sword presented to the Lodge by the parents of an officer killed on the Somme during the First World War.

An important part of a Masonic ceremony is music and we are fortunate to have a fine organ installed in 1955 at a cost of £700 from a bequest by W.Bro W.F. Bracey, PAGDC, who had done so much in the formation of the Lodge, purchase of the premises and in many other ways. This replaced the original one dating from 1923.

Until a Rose Croix Chapter was formed in Wedmore in 1982 the Alfred & Guthrum Lodge was the only Masonic body using the Masonic Hall, but in October 1986 the Temple was used for the consecration of the Sir Thomas de Cheddre Lodge 9188, who then met at Wells, returning to meet permanently at Wedmore in 1997. In 1989 St Cecilia Lodge 9341, 'The Singing Lodge' was formed and now also meets on a regular basis at Wedmore.

It is thought fitting to mention the close connection which has existed between the Lodge and Sexey's School at Blackford. W.Bro E.H. Smith the esteemed Headmaster of the school for many years was our first IPM and one of the Founders. His successor as Headmaster, W.Bro L. Abram was also one of our Founders, our first Organist and Master in 1928. His claim, in his after dinner speeches, was that he was the first of the Blackford Dynasty and as a result of his Mastership occurring between that of two vicars, his reign suffered from an "Ecclesiastical draught".

When W.Bro Evans was initiated, passed and raised, with him for the same ceremonies was another Sexey's master, Bro L.C.H. Passmore, who although by 1947 had left the school to teach elsewhere still retained his membership of the Lodge. The Governors of the school have been represented by many brethren, many of the school's " Old Boys" have joined the Lodge and some have attained the Chair.

Admiral Blake Lodge No. 4692

Meets at the Masonic Hall, King Square, Bridgwater

Warrant dated 1924

On 24th February 1924 at a meeting of the Perpetual Friendship Lodge of Instruction, Bro A.E. Coles announced that he proposed to discuss with the brethren the desirability of forming a new Craft Lodge in Bridgwater, this being deemed desirable owing to the vastly increased numbers in Perpetual Friendship, and difficulty of progressing with the Initiation of suitable candidates.

On 8th April 1924, Bros Coles and Brooks called upon the DPGM V.W.Bro Col. Thrale-Perkins and asked for his advice, and having heard all the circumstances he expressed the view that the time was most opportune to proceed with the formation of a new Lodge. The petition to Grand Lodge was accepted on 14th November 1924 with the provision that, unless there was a good reason to do otherwise, the Warrant would be drawn in the name of Admiral Blake, and not Robert Blake as proposed. We can be grateful to Grand Lodge for their sense of history.

Robert Blake (1598-1657) was a hero of the Roundheads through his dogged defence of Lyme and Taunton during the Great Civil War. After the civil war he was well known in England as a statesman and soldier, but it was his later naval career that gave him the fame he deserved. He was born in 1598 in the house which is now the Admiral Blake Museum, and records show that he was christened in St Mary's Church on September 27th 1598. Educated at Bridgwater Free Grammar School and recommended for a university education, in 1614, at the age of 16, Blake went up to Oxford and enrolled at St Albans Hall. Two years later he moved to Wadham College and graduated with a BA degree in 1618. In 1640 he was elected as a Member of Parliament, to what

was to become known as The Short Parliament. He failed to be re-elected to Parliament in November of the same year.

He was appointed General at Sea (a rank corresponding to Admiral) in 1649 under the Commonwealth and is regarded as second only to Nelson in British naval history, often being referred to as the "Father of the Royal Navy". He is also well known for defeating the Dutch Admiral Tromp who had sailed down the Channel, boasting that he would sweep the sea of every English ship! Suffering from old wounds Robert Blake died at 10am on the 7th August 1657 as his ship The George entered Plymouth sound. He received a State Funeral and was buried in Westminster Abbey on the 4th September 1657.

The driving force of the new Lodge was Bro A.E. Coles and he was elected Master of the Lodge in 1926, and it is interesting to note that not only did he initiate his own son Frances, passed and raised him, he also installed him in the Master's Chair in 1936. During the first year of the Lodge, on the 28th April 1925 to be precise, a young man in Wincanton took unto himself a bride and in the fullness of time he was to become the Deputy Provincial Grand Master of Somerset. His name was V.W.Bro H.E. Dyke, and as his pre-arranged wedding plans clashed with the Lodge meeting evening which is the fourth Tuesday of the month, it was agreed that the April Lodge meeting would be moved to accommodate the happy event, and as a result of this alteration the Lodge 50th Jubilee meeting was also moved to ensure the exact date for the anniversary was observed.

In 1930 the original byelaws were temporarily amended to allow a December meeting to be moved to the third Tuesday of the month. This was repeated in 1976 when the byelaws were again amended to ensure permanent dispensation to accommodate the Christmas holiday period. A few months later at the March 1931 meeting, the Lodge decided not to purchase a letter written by Robert Blake after the Battle of the Naseby. The sum involved was only £7.10s, a fact regretted by the Lodge ever since.

Marble "Ten Commandments" Tablets
Bridgwater Masonic Hall

The meeting on the 28th January 1936 coincided with the funeral of HM King George V and on instructions of Grand Lodge only the minutes of the last meeting were read and confirmed and the Lodge was closed after a brief tribute to the late King.

In September 1939 on the outbreak of hostilities a letter was received from Provincial Grand Lodge instructing the Lodge to state and explain the break in the continuity of the regular meeting prohibited by the Government emergency regulations. The subsequent relaxation of these regulations came too late to save the meeting, but it is with great relief that the Lodge progressed quietly through the war years, except that in 1943 the Provincial Grand Master suspended a Brother from all Masonic privileges on the grounds of his membership of another organisation.

Lodge tranquillity was sadly shattered in 1950, when a candidate properly prepared was admitted to the Lodge but refused on the grounds of conscience to take the obligation. He withdrew, and the Lodge was closed immediately. The Provincial Grand Master demanded a full report saying the incident was entirely outside his experience, and possibly that of the Grand Lodge. His enquiries exonerated those concerned from blame but the incident reinforced the cardinal rule of exercising the greatest of care in selecting all candidates.

In 1951 another incident not without its humour occurred, when Bro Dawson having been initiated on the 27th November 1951 was passed to the Second Degree at the December meeting. This meeting was brought forward to the 15th December, and Grand Lodge were very quick to pick up this breach of the Book of the Constitutions from the returns and the ceremony had to be retaken in December 1952. Bro Dawson then had the unique experience of being passed and raised on the same evening.

On the 24th September 1963 the Worshipful Master announced he was sponsoring a new Lodge in Bridgwater, and in the course of time he signed the petition to Grand Lodge and thus our daughter Lodge, Tynte Lodge 7994 was born.

The Provincial Grand Master at a simple service of dedication presented a new Lodge Banner to the Lodge in 1968, and in 1970 a Brother anonymously presented a new organ to the Lodge. In 1975 the Lodge made the highest individual Lodge contribution to the Masonic Hospital Appeal. Throughout the eighties the Lodge continued to support the Royal Masonic Hospital and regular donations were made. This tradition of supporting local causes has continued to the present day, with frequent donations being made to St Margaret's Hospice, the Provincial Benevolent Fund and many local charities including Penrose School, the Special Needs Action Group, St John Ambulance and Brainwave.

W.Bro Ray Jenkins was elected as Worshipful Master on the 23rd March 1977. W.Bro Ray was the first (and only) alumnus of the Masonic Boys School.

Throughout the history of the Admiral Blake Lodge there has been a strong tendency to patronage by Lewises, that is those candidates who are sons of Freemasons. Examples of this are the Waterton, Washer, Bedford, Dunn and Forkin families, leading right up to the present Worshipful Master Steve Dare and Grand Lodge officer W.Bro Michael Waddleton, both of whom were proposed by their respective fathers.

In 1991 a Brother for use at his ceremony presented the Lodge with a Hindu Holy Book and in 1999 the ladies were invited into the Lodge for the first time. They attended a lecture by the Bridgwater Blake Museum curator posing as Admiral Blake's brother in full period costume to celebrate the 400th anniversary of the birth of Robert Blake. The close contact with the Admiral Blake Museum has continued with the Lodge receiving a book on the "History of Admiral Blake" from the curator of the museum in 2000. A link had previously been established with the senior member of the Blake family who now resides in South Petherton. This had been done at the time of the Lodge's Golden Jubilee, which was held in 1975 under the stewardship of W.Bro Charles Langdon who remains an active member of the Lodge although now in his nineties. It was attended by 44 guests, which included the Provincial Grand Master of Somerset and his full Provincial Team.

Over the years several brethren have received a 50 year certificate. In 2003 Bro G. Tottle was presented his at his home in Dorset, and more recently in 2006 W.Bro R. Bedford LGR received his in London.

In September of each year the Showman's Guild Lodge attend the Lodge for their fraternal visit. This coincides with the annual Bridgwater Fair and in 2000 the Showman's Guild presented a plaque to the Admiral Blake Lodge to commemorate their Millennium year visit. In recent years the Lodge has received several very interesting lectures, they include the "Origins of Freemasonry", "The Masonic Organist", "Famous Masons" and the "Temples of Jerusalem".

2002 saw the Admiral Blake Lodge entering cyber-space. The Lodge debated and voted on the proposal to participate in the Provincial Grand Lodge website. A potted history of the Lodge was compiled and forwarded to the Provincial Web Editor and the Lodge web page was launched. The Lodge also participates annually in the National Heritage Day when the Lodge is opened to the general public, as it did in the "Freemasonry in the Community" initiative.

Tennyson Lodge No. 4947

Meets at the Masonic Hall Clevedon

Warrant dated 1927

This brief history is indebted to the work of W.Bro A.E. Gray PPrSGD and the late W.Bro R.F. Marks PPrJGW, who produced Lodge histories to celebrate the 75th and 50th Anniversaries of Tennyson Lodge respectively..

In the mid nineteen twenties, the interest in Freemasonry in Clevedon was such that certain prominent brethren in the town decided the time was ripe to establish a second Lodge. Minutes of the Coleridge Lodge 1750 reveal that on Sept. 8th 1926, W.Bro Keen proposed that a daughter Lodge be formed. He pointed out that Coleridge Lodge had members residing over a very wide area and suggested that a new Lodge, principally for local residents, would be welcome. He suggested the name "Tennyson" as a suitable title.

Due enquiries having been made and support obtained, the Tennyson Lodge 4947 was consecrated on 18th April 1928 in the presence of the Provincial Grand Master, R.W.Bro the Ven. Archdeacon Farrer MA, the deputy PGM R.T. Hughes MA and 84 brethren. Colonel S. Keen DSO was installed as the first Master. Hence the Tennyson Lodge was the second of the three Craft Lodges in the town to be named after poets associated with the area.

In accordance with the original intentions of the founders, a byelaw was introduced restricting membership only to those who lived within a five mile radius of the town – a decision which was to have unfortunate consequences some years later. A study of the honours board shows that in its earlier years the Lodge was well supported by local shopkeepers, businessmen and prominent residents from within the town.

In 1932, the need was felt for a Lodge Banner bearing the Tennyson Coat of Arms. Enquiries were made regarding a painted type, but this was not pursued. Then a local lady, a Mrs. Wilkes, offered to make a hand embroidered one, all she asked was that the Lodge pay for the materials. This was accordingly done and a banner produced. A fund had been set up to cover costs, which was so well supported that an "At Home" was arranged to formally thank and pay Mrs. Wilkes for her efforts. She was presented with a cheque to the value of £13.11s.5d for a coat, inside a handbag costing 15s.6d (77-1/2p).

From its Consecration the Lodge had met on a Wednesday evening, probably as Wednesday was the customary early closing day in the town. In the early 1930s, with the growth of the town, larger stores reducing the number of shopkeepers and tradesmen, and residents commuting out of the area to work, it was felt that a Friday evening would be more suitable. Grand Lodge was consequently petitioned, and Lodge meetings moved to a Friday. This has since remained the case, apart for the period between October 1940 to 1943. Following the end of the 'phoney war', ceremonies were often interrupted when air raid sirens caused the immediate withdrawal of many brethren to their duty posts. Consequently meetings were temporarily moved to a Saturday afternoon

It could be said that the original Founders showed much foresight in establishing the Lodge, and planning when best to hold it. They also paid close attention to the minutiae of running a Craft Lodge. In the Lodge minutes of October 1932, it is recorded that the WM had noticed certain members were attending minus gloves.

It was proposed that the Lodge should purchase several pairs and hire them out at a cost of 1/- per pair, per ceremony (9d. to the Benevolent Fund, 3d. for laundering!) In 1933, a member (Bro Gillmore) presented the Lodge with a clock for the dining room, in his words "To assist the WM to regulate the hours of refreshment". Some time later another minute records that permission had been granted to other Lodges using the room also to use the clock.

As social patterns changed over the years it became clear that the early limit on membership within a five mile radius was unsuitable for the Lodge. This was made abundantly clear in 1964, when a Mr. Lionel Webb was proposed for membership by his father, Bro Len Webb. Unfortunately Lionel lived too far afield, and would not be eligible for admission. Tennyson Lodge's loss was, however, Coleridge's gain, for Lionel was proposed for membership there and went on to become the W.Bro Lionel Webb PPrJGW well known in the Craft and Chapter

within the Province. By the time Lionel's father had reached the chair in 1969 the distance limit had been removed, and W.Bro Len was able to initiate his other son Colin into Tennyson Lodge as his first candidate on 23rd January 1970.

It has been said, very unfairly, that if there is a long way to do a ceremony, Tennyson Lodge will use it. Since it's inception, our Lodge has prided itself in emphasising the variety, beauty and meaning of our ritual, as a means of educating both candidate and brethren alike. The workings that are used are Emulation, with alterations and additions introduced by one of the founders, and second WM, W.Bro R.S. Renton MD, PAGDC. Great pride is taken in this work, particularly in the Installation Ceremony.

Although none of the extended work is original to this Lodge and has been adapted from work performed elsewhere, the manner in which it has been brought together has produced a most distinctive and beautiful ceremony. In an age where everything has to be made smaller, and even national events reduced to sound bites, there ought to be room for workings which prompt brethren to look further into the origins and meanings of our Masonic traditions. The founders of Tennyson Lodge recognised this need; the present day Lodge members continue to try to provide for it in their ceremonies, and impart a daily increase in Masonic knowledge.

Although the Lodge was named after Alfred Lord Tennyson, there was no connection with any of the poet's works for many years within the Lodge. This was to change in 1984 on the death of W.Bro R.D. Cousins, when his son-in-law W.Bro Bill Elliot requested that Tennyson's moving poem, "Crossing the Bar" be read whilst the brethren stood to order in respect of departed merit. brethren were so moved by the poem's deep significance that its beautiful words have been read on all such occasions since.

Alfred Lord Tennyson
Photo by London Stereoscopic & Photographic reproduced
by kind permission of The National Portrait Gallery

Crossing the Bar

Sunset and evening star,
And one clear call for me!
And may there be no moaning of the bar,
When I put out to sea,

But such a tide as moving seems asleep,
Too full for sound and foam,
When that which drew from out the boundless deep
Turns again home.

Twilight and evening bell,
And after that the dark!
And may there be no sadness of farewell,
When I embark;

For tho' from out our bourne of Time and Place
The flood may bear me far,
I hope to see my Pilot face to face
When I have crost the bar.

It was W.Bro Reginald Cousins who introduced the first Lodge Ladies' Night in November 1945. This was held at the Walton Park Hotel in the town, and became a regular event. The venue altered on several occasions, latterly moving to the Grand Atlantic in Weston-super-Mare. In 1993 W.Bro R.D. Poynton, on his second time as Master, introduced the first Ladies' Weekend which was held at Torquay. This idea has since been adopted by other Masters, seeing the event held in Barnstaple and Torquay, as well as more local evenings at Shapwick, Cadbury Country Club and the Walton Park.

In 1997 the ladies were invited to attend a Lodge evening for the first time and were entertained with a short lecture on famous Freemasons whilst the Lodge was called off. This proved most successful, and other similar evenings have since taken place. In order to make the evening more comfortable, the Lodge is opened and closed by the officers in the ante room, whilst ladies assemble in the main Lodge room. In 2003 the Lodge held its first White Table evening for non-masons, which yielded one candidate for the Lodge.

Charities have always been of paramount importance to the Lodge, be they local or national. In 1952 the Tennyson Benevolent Fund was established as a Trust so as to obtain the benefit of tax relief offered for covenanted income. Since the establishment of the Charity Chest Scheme by the Grand Charity this Benevolent Fund no longer retains the majority of the monies collected by the Lodge. Consequently in 2000 it was decided that the fund's Trustees should take on the role of an advisory group and make recommendations for the best use of the Lodge's charitable resources in general.

The trustees now meet twice a year and produce a report so that every member of the Lodge is kept abreast of the state of its charitable accounts. The Trustees act in the capacity of an advisory group, and provide a valuable means of bringing particular worthy causes to the attention of the Lodge. Brethren are encouraged to inform them of, in particular, local charitable causes which merit the Lodge's attention and assistance.

The Lodge first appointed a Charity Steward in 1977, and since then the office has been filled by a series of most capable brethren in the persons of W.Bro George Pritchard (1977-1992), W.Bro Sydney Hodge (1992-1995), W.Bro Robert Plumley (1995-2000) and Bro Alan Douglas (since 2000). The tireless effort and careful planning of these brethren has ensured that the Lodge has been able to support the Festival Scheme very ably.

Since its consecration, five members of the Lodge have received Grand Honours. W.Bros R.S. Renton PAGDC in 1943, Preb. J.H. Hugh PAGChap in 1962, A.E. Butler PAGDC in 1959 and PJGD in 1973, G. Collins PAGDC in 1979, and R.D. Poynton PAGDC in 2004.

When the Founders chose the name of Tennyson, one can but wonder if they had in mind the Latin motto of the Tennyson family, namely "Respiciens, Prospiciens", which appears on the Lodge banner. This translates as "looking backwards, looking forwards". Intentional or not, this can be said to have been the course adopted by the brethren of the Lodge over the years. Tennyson is proud of its origins, its ceremonies, and its particular traditions, and tries as much as possible to keep faith with the spirit in which it was founded.

At the same time the Lodge has been only too aware of the need to look to the future and keep abreast of change, and is proud of its involvement in the Freemasonry in the Community project, the Provincial Information Group, the Mentoring Scheme, and the more open approach which the Craft has adopted over the past two decades. May these principles be continued within this Lodge throughout the years ahead.

Lodge Progressive Science No. 5007

Meets at The Masonic Hall, Hendford, Yeovil

Warrant dated 1st February 1928

Following a visit to Brotherly Love Lodge 329 in 1925 the Deputy Provincial Grand Master W.Bro Col. Alfred Thrale Perkins commented regarding the growth of the Lodge, pointing out that Yeovil was one of the few towns in the Province that showed an increase in population and that the Lodge having such a large membership, over 100 in 1924, it was obvious that there was little prospect for the most zealous Freemasons of ever attaining their laudable ambition and urged the need for calling another Lodge into existence.

During 1926 the matter was taken seriously in hand. Towards the end of the year a large percentage of the Past Masters of Brotherly Love Lodge 329 agreed to become Founders of the new Lodge and on the 4th March 1927 at a meeting held at the Westminster Bank it was unanimously decided to proceed with the formation of the new Lodge. As to the name of the Lodge, both 'Wyndham' and 'St Ivel' were rejected in favour of 'Progressive Science'.

The day of the meeting as previously selected was approved, as was the choice of W.Bro Swaffield to be the first Master a Joining Member of Lodge 329, Past Master of Lodge of Unity, Wareham, and PPGSW, of the Province of Dorset.

In November 1927 the signed Petition with all cleared certificates complete was sent to the Provincial Grand Secretary and at a meeting of the Founders at the Masonic Hall on the 9th February 1928 a communication was read announcing that The Most Worshipful Grand Master had granted the Petition and that the warrant was dated 1st February 1928.

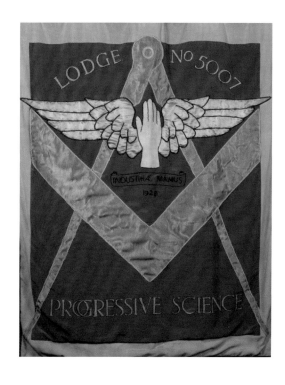

Bro G.J.M. Mitchell undertook the task to prepare a Lodge Badge, creating a design which incorporated a glove and a pair of wings depicting Glove making and Aircraft Manufacture, the two principle industries of the Yeovil area with the motto Industrie Manus.

The Consecration was fixed for Tuesday, 2nd October Provincial Grand Lodge was held in the Masonic Hall. The Provincial Grand Master, R.W.Bro the Ven. Archdeacon Walter Farrer, MA, was the Consecrating Officer and the Ceremony was solemnly and impressively performed. The silver Consecrating Vessels were kindly lent, the flagon for the wine and pattens for the corn and salt, by Bro The Rev. J.E.S. Harrison, Vicar of the Parish Church and the flagon for the oil by Bro The Rev. Maxwell Fisher, Vicar of Holy Trinity, the later also supplying the Censer for incense used during the Ceremony. Lodge Progressive Science 5007 had arrived!

There follow a few notable extracts from our minutes along with one or two handed down stories, to be believed because as Freemasons we could not possibly exaggerate:

On the 4th February 1930 a Chippendale Chair was presented to the Lodge by W.Bro R.J. Norton PPAGDC for the use of the Director of Ceremonies and most comfortable it is.

A combined Lodge of Emergency and Sorrow was held by Lodges 329 and 5007 on the 23rd December 1930 when the Lodge was opened in the three degrees, proceeded in procession to the residence of the deceased and thence preceded the cortege to the cemetery, returning to the Temple to close the Lodge.

On the 6th October 1931 Alms collected at the Installation Ceremony were sent to the Samaritan Fund for the first time. This has been a feature at each successive Installation Ceremony and still continues today.

At an ordinary meeting in November 1932 the candidate was so overcome by emotion that he 'lapsed into unconsciousness immediately following his Obligation, but recovered following the use of restoratives, the ceremony continued but the giving of the Charge was deferred'.

An Especial Provincial Grand Lodge of Somerset was held on the 8th March 1934 at the site of St. Andrew's Church, Preston Grove, Yeovil, under the Banners of Lodges 329 and 5007 for the purpose of laying the Foundation Stone of the new Church with Masonic Ceremonial.

Elegant, perfectly proportioned and beautifully carved
The Master's Chair in Yeovil

The ceremony was performed by the Provincial Grand Master for Somerset R.W.Bro the Ven. Walter Farrer, Archdeacon of Wells, assisted by Officers of Provincial Grand Lodge and Officers of Lodges 329 and 5007.

The new Church of St. Andrew's is a daughter of the ancient Parish Church of Yeovil, St John Baptist, the Vicar at that time being the Rev. J.E.S. Harrison M.A., Chaplain of Lodge 5007. The architect of the new Church was W.Bro John Petter, Worshipful Master of Lodge Progressive Science 5007.

On the 23rd May 1935 the Assembly Rooms, Princes Street, Yeovil was converted into a Masonic Lodge under the United Banners of Lodges 329 and 5007 to host the Provincial Grand Lodge of Somerset on the occasion of the Installation of W.Bro Brig. Gen. Claude Lumsden Norman, DSO, MVO, PGD, formerly Deputy District Grand Master of the Punjab, as Right Worshipful Grand Master for the Province of Somerset.

The impressive ceremony was performed by the most Worshipful Pro Grand Master, The Rt Hon., the Lord Ampthill GCSI, GCIE.

The Installation of Bro John Robert Seward, the first initiate of the Lodge to occupy the Chair of King Solomon, was marked by a gift of a Silver Tankard presented to the Lodge by the 'Initiates since its inauguration'. This Silver Tankard has every subsequent Master's signature engraved on it and is still used by the Worshipful Master at the Festive Board.

The Volume of the Sacred Law and the Silver Square and Compasses which were presented to the Lodge by W.Bro J.R. Seward PPGDC on the 6th September 1949 are still in use today at every ceremony.

At the meeting held on the 4th February 1947 the Director of Ceremonies reported that a Brother was improperly dressed - it transpiring that the Brother's house had been burgled and the thief had cut the tassels from his apron. Under these circumstances he was allowed to remain in the Lodge. This meeting was also the first conducted by the Past Masters of the Lodge, a practice which still continues annually.

In April 1949 the first meeting of the Lodge of Instruction took place, it continues today as a major part of the Masonic Year and every May a Lodge of Instruction Festival is held. The Senior Deacon of the Lodge takes the chair and performs a demonstration ceremony with non Past Master members of the Lodge of Instruction filling all the offices. This is followed by a Festive Board, usually fish and chips, with all the correct procedures being observed.

Whilst this brief history of Lodge Progressive Science relates how the Lodge arrived at this stage, members believe that the best is yet to come and that they brethren feel privileged to be members of Freemasonry in general and brethren of 5007 in particular.

Taunton Deane Lodge No. 5221

Meets at the Masonic Hall Taunton

Warrant dated 1930

In February 1930, W.Bro H.S.W. Stone, who was then WM of Lodge Unanimity and Sincerity No. 261, called a meeting of the Past Masters of that Lodge and of the Lodge of St. George No. 3158, to discuss the desirability of supporting the founding of another Lodge in Taunton.

They concluded that a new Lodge was indeed desirable, and that they would advise their Lodges to support a petition to the M.W the Grand Master asking him to sanction its founding .The Founders asked W.Bro C.L. Norman to be Master Designate, who named Bro R.J.L. Stenlake and Bro E. Young as his Wardens.

The New Taunton Deane Lodge was consecrated on 1st October 1930 by the R.W.Bro the Venerable Archdeacon Farrer, MA, PG Chaplain (England) and PGM for Somerset assisted by Officers of Provincial Grand Lodge. W.Bro Brig. Gen. C.L. Norman, DSO, MVO, SGD (Eng.) Past Deputy District GM (Punjab) was installed as WM and on this occasion was permitted the honour of wearing his chain of office as SGD, to which office he had just been appointed. The customary addresses to the WM, the Wardens and the brethren were given by the Deputy PGM.

The List of Founders and subsequent WMs of the Lodge is inscribed on a board in the lobby of the Masonic Hall. This board was presented by Bro Stenlake. The Lodge received many presents from Founders and Friends. The Banner and Badge of the Lodge were designed by W.Bro Stone and Bro R.D. Burt and the actual needlework on the Banner was carried out under the direct supervision of Bro Burt.

The Tracing Boards were presented by W.Bro Dr. A.J.H. Iles, the mahogany pedestals by W.Bro W. G. Potter and Bro H.F. Potter. W.Bro P.J. Barnicott gave a kneeling stool, W.Bro S. Goodman a set of Anthem cards and Bro Hamlin slippers for the Candidates. Bro H. E. Knott set the Guest's Song and that for Absent Brethren to music.

The Lodge used much of the furniture of Lodge Unanimity and Sincerity and the carpet belonging to the Lodge of St. George.The Mother Lodge, Unanimity and Sincerity also allowed the use of its crockery and cutlery for the proceedings after Lodge. Later, the Lodge was able to repay this last kindness by making a contribution to the cost of these articles and still later a group of brethren headed by Bro J.E. Ridal presented to the Masonic Hall four dozen full sets of cutlery. Taunton Deane Lodge certainly had a good beginning.

On 5th March 1931, W.Bro Norman installed his successor Bro Stenlake. As a memento of his Mastership, he presented to the Lodge these ivory gavels for the use of the WM and Wardens. Four years later he was appointed PGM for Somerset, being installed at Yeovil on 23rd May by the M.W.Bro Lord Ampthill, Pro Grand Master.

The appointment naturally involved a considerable increase in Masonic duties which prevented a regular attendance at Lodge, but R.W.Bro Norman generally managed one attendance during the year, and on 5th March 1936 Bro E.D.S. Pean, Master Elect, and was honoured by being installed as Master of the Lodge by R.W.Bro Norman.

With the outbreak of war many arrangements altered rapidly, there was even the possibility of the Lodge closing down. The Masonic Hall was requisitioned for war purposes and only the Temple was left to the brethren. It looked at first as though the activities of the Lodge would be somewhat restricted to formal meetings. But under the Temple is a cellar which had been used as a store room. The Trustees had this cellar cleaned and tidied so that after Lodge Meetings the brethren could repair downstairs to partake of light refreshment. It was, of course, a stand up snack, and perhaps the more enjoyable for that, as brethren were free to mingle as they pleased.

In 1945 Taunton Deane Lodge had what is possibly a unique occurrence. The Grand Master of Ohio, U.S.A. had preferred a request to our M.W the Grand Master that Lt. T.R. Jones of the U.S. Army in England might be initiated in an English Lodge. Passing down through the proper channels the request came to Taunton Deane Lodge, and at an emergency Lodge in November, Lt. Jones was initiated by W.Bro S.S. Orchard, acting WM, in the unavoidable absence of the WM W.Bro.A.P. Stoner.

During the war, owing to the impossibility of obtaining Masonic jewels, only token presentations were made to the retiring Masters. Similarly, the array of photographs of Past Masters was not kept up to date. After the war, in W.Bro Blandford's year of office, it was decided to purchase Past Masters' jewels for those Worshipful Brethren to whom only token presentations had been made.

To lighten the charge on the Lodge, the Founders gave up their Founder's jewels as the badges on them were the same as the badges required to make up the PM's jewel. At the same time, the collection of photographs of PMs was brought up to date. Here, also to lighten the cost, the frames were presented by W.Bro W. S. Stansell. The collection now hangs in the supper room.

1955 brought the celebration of the 25th year in the life of the Lodge. There are several members who had special reason to remember this year. Amongst them was W.Bro W. B. Clatworthy who received the collar of PGStdBr. Another was W.Bro Orchard who joined the ranks of Masonic veterans having been initiated in March 1905, and still another was W.Bro S.W. Shepherd who had been elected Mayor of Taunton.

The Ceremony to mark the 25th anniversary took place on 6th October 1955 at the Masonic Hall. The Provincial Grand Master the R.W.Bro Brig. Gen. C.L. Norman attended, supported by the Deputy Provincial Grand Master V.W.Bro H. Frampton and the Assistant Provincial Grand Master W.Bro G.H. Harrison. The WM W.Bro L.J. Hockey invited the PGM to occupy the Chair of King Solomon to conduct the Ceremony of the Passing to the Second Degree of Bro J.G. Kennedy, which he accepted, and was assisted by the Founder Members W.Bro R.J.L. Stenlake as SW, W.Bro S. Goodman as JW, and W.Bro G.O. Boundy as IG.

A silver salver inscribed with facsimiles of the signatures of members of the Lodge was presented to the PGM who expressed his deep appreciation for the gift. 25 years later, at the meeting held in November 1980 the salver was officially returned to the Lodge for safe keeping by the daughter of Brig. Gen. Norman.

The Regular Meeting of the Lodge on 6th November, 1958 marked the occasion when the PGM made a presentation to the Lodge of his personal sword. The sword was handed down to the PGM by his father, Field Marshall Sir Henry Norman, also a member of the Craft. The PGM had carried the sword since his early days as a Subaltern and it is now carried on all appropriate occasions in Lodge proceedings. The Lodge is indebted to W.Bro W.S. Stansell who donated the glazed case in which the sword is kept.

The ceremony on the 2nd November, 1961 will always be remembered by those who were fortunate enough to attend. The Lodge was honoured by the presence of the Provincial Grand Master R.W.Bro Brig. A. de L. Cazenove, the Deputy Provincial Grand Master V.W.Bro H. Frampton and the Assistant Provincial Grand Master W.Bro H.E. Dyke. The Provincial Grand Master then called upon V.W.Bro H. Frampton who gave an address to the brethren on the outstanding events under Brig. Gen. Norman's leadership and concluded by expressing to R.W.Bro Brig. Gen. Norman the gratitude of the whole Province.

Following the address, the Provincial Grand Master then formally invested R.W.Bro Brig. Gen. C.L. Norman with the Full Dress Regalia of a Past Provincial Grand Master. The Regalia had been purchased by donations made by all Lodges in the Province, most of which were represented at the Meeting

On the 5th November, 1964 the Past Masters of the Lodge made a presentation to the Lodge of an Ivory Gavel for use by the JW. The gavel, suitably inscribed was similar to those donated by the R.W.Bro Brig. Gen. Norman which were carved from ivory brought back by General Norman from India during his period of military service there.

At the Regular Meeting of the Lodge on 6th April, 1967, members learned with deep regret of the death of R.W.Bro Brig. Gen. Norman, PPGM, Founder Member and first Worshipful Master of Taunton Deane Lodge. The brethren stood in silence as a tribute and in memory of this very distinguished Mason. During the next decade the Lodge continued to prosper, although not without the loss to Grand Lodge above of some of it's much loved Brethren.

For many years the functions of the Masonic Hall had been in the hands a Management Committee. In 1978 this Committee discussed the need for a revision of the Rules under which it operated. All the Taunton Lodges were consulted, and it was decided to draw up a new Constitution and By-laws for a Club to be known as Taunton Masonic Club. The new Constitution and By-laws were approved and ratified by Taunton Deane on 5th October 1978 resulting in an improved organisation for the benefit of everyone.

The Ceremony on Thursday 2nd October 1980 was a celebration of the 50th Anniversary of the Lodge; 114 brethren attended including 64 guests. The Ceremony was honoured by the presence of the PGM, R.W.Bro Lt. Col. H. Owen Hughes OBE who paraded in accompanied by PSGW, PJGW and other distinguished brethren. The minutes of the first meeting of the Lodge held in 1930 were read. The Master, W.Bro K. Farrell then offered the gavel to W.Bro W.B. Clatworthy a founding member of the Lodge who conducted the ceremony of passing.

It was at the meeting in March 1981 that the Silver Salver presented to R.W.Bro Brig. Gen. C.L. Norman was used for the first time to collect the alms bags in the temple, a tradition that has continued to this day. W.Bro Kinnersley PGM designate attended the meeting to inaugurate a special display panel containing various memorabilia and certificates of R.W.Bro Norman. The display was paid for by members of the Lodge and has permanent place in the sherry room.

At the April ceremony in 1985 the Provincial Grand Master, R.W.Bro Kenneth C. Kinnersley took the chair and with his Provincial Team undertook a 3rd Degree ceremony, a unique occasion in Taunton Deane Lodge history. A 50th Anniversary Certificate was presented to W.Bro C. G. Toy who had just been promoted to PPSGD. The Provincial Grand Master closed the Lodge from the Third Degree straight to the First, after which he give an explanation to the brethren on how this conformed to strict Emulation Working.

During the November meeting it was announced that Bro N.G. Oram, Tyler of the Lodge and Caretaker of the Temple, would shortly retire. The Past Masters decided that in future the position of Tyler would become a progressive office.

December 1986 brought a milestone to Taunton Deane, the Lodge initiated its 100th member into Freemasonry, Bro T.J. Cramp. To commemorate his Initiation he was presented with a Bible which had been handed down to the Lodge by the family of the late W.Bro R.M. Hewlett.

At the installation ceremony in March 1989 for Bro J. Cozens, the new Master, presented to the Installing Master, W.Bro Richard Went the Past Masters Jewel from his father W.Bro John Went; this was the first time in the Lodge's history that this had happened.

At the installation ceremony in March 1991 of Bro M. Blackwell it was announced that W.Bro T.A. Hughes PSGD, Deputy PGM would be appointed Past Grand Sword Bearer, a rank entitling him to be addressed in future as Very Worshipful Brother. That same year the Master set up a Lodge Fund to raise money for the restoration of the Lodge Banner which needed urgent repairs. The monies required amounted to £500.

During the installation of the new Master Bro P.B. Read, the Lodge received its new Banner after having been completely refurbished. A rededication ceremony took place in December 1992 with the Provincial Grand Master R.W.Bro Stanley H.A.F. Hopkins and the Provincial Team.

The new Banner was paraded into the Lodge by the Provincial Grand Director of Ceremonies. An oration was given by the Provincial Chaplain reminding brethren that the Banner had originally been designed by W.Bro Stone and Bro Burt, some 60 years earlier and not surprisingly need refurbishment, but that much of the original fabric and needlework was saved and used in the new Banner.

March of 1993 saw the installation of the new Master, Bro D.C. Hughes, a presentation of a Bible and part of the ceremony being undertaken by his father V.W.Bro T.A. Hughes yet another first for Taunton Deane Lodge. A new Bible Dedication was held in the temple in April 1996. The Bible was a gift to the Lodge by W.Bro C. Bacon, with V.W.Bro T.A. Hughes taking the chair, the Master his Wardens and Deacons formed an escort to parade the new Bible into the Lodge. Afterwards, W.Bro B.R. Hearle gave a very informative lecture on the explanation of the Provincial Grand Master Apron which once belonged to Brig. Gen. Claude L. Norman. The Apron can be found today displayed in the sherry room.

At the April 1997 meeting Bro B.J. Renwick became both an Honorary Member and the Lodge Organist. Bro Barry's music has brought much joy to the Lodge and greatly enhanced its ceremonies.

At the installation ceremony of March 1999, Bro G.D. Snook became the 70th and last Master of the Lodge in the second millennium but the first in the third. The Lodge was honoured by a visit in the same year from W.Bro John Upward the Provincial Grand Charity Steward for Somerset. He gave a most interesting talk to the brethren on the different charities that Freemasonry supports and in particular the launch of the 2007 Festival for the Royal Masonic Benevolent Institute. The new Masonic year for the Lodge got off to a flying start with donations towards the RMBI 2007 Festival totalling £5000 enabling the Lodge to achieve its first Acorn from the Province.

The Acorn was presented to the Lodge at the February 2004 meeting where W.Bro Ray Guthrie Assistant Provincial Grand Master gave an explanation of the four Masonic Charities, before presenting the Worshipful Master and Charity Steward with the Banner and the Acorn.

The second Acorn was presented in the December by the Provincial Grand Master R.W.Bro David Lloyd Jenkins after a further £4000 had been donated. At the ceremony the Worshipful Master W.Bro S. C French offered the Gavel to the P. G. M. Upon taking the chair the PGM informed the brethren that the Province had already raised over £1,500,000 and was on course to meets its £2,000,000 target.

Saint Bernard Lodge No. 5361

Meets at the Masonic Hall Minehead

Warrant dated 1932

The Exmoor Lodge 2390, founded in 1891, was the original Craft Lodge in Minehead. The seeds of thought for the forming of a second Lodge were sown by the R.W Provincial Grand Master, the Venerable Walter Farrer, in 1931. He was at an Exmoor Lodge Installation meeting and remarked that as that Lodge had a membership of 129 there was room for another Lodge in the town. Acting on the suggestion Bro C.T. Gibbs, a member of Exmoor Lodge, successfully obtained 25 prospective Founder Members all but one being members of the Exmoor Lodge. The necessary authorisation was forthcoming and the new Lodge 5361 was consecrated on Wednesday 20th July 1932. The Consecration was performed by R.W Provincial Grand Master for Somerset, the Venerable Walter Farrer, MA, PG Chaplain, Archdeacon of Wells and assisted by the DPGM of Somerset, W.Bro R.C.A. Hughes, MA, PGD

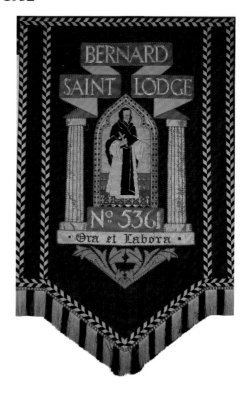

The name of the Lodge was suggested by Bro Gibbs. He was Headmaster of the newly built Minehead Grammar School and being a very noteworthy historian was very interested in the background of the 15th Century Cleeve Abbey at Washford near Minehead. The Abbey was of the Cistercian Order and its teachings and charitable principles were influenced by a highly renowned monk named St Bernard of Clairvaux. The name St Bernard was eventually agreed and the motto of the Abbey – "Ora et Labora" (Pray and Work) was also adopted by the Lodge.

A Lodge Banner was designed featuring the figure of St Bernard in his monk's habit. After local approval it was submitted to Grand Lodge and, after some comments, it was eventually authorised.

It was decided to meet mainly in the summer months to cater for holiday visitors. Minehead in those days was more of a Victorian type resort. Suggestions to change to winter months have failed. An unusual feature was introduced at Installation ceremonies and still continues today. Seven roses are placed by the Master's and Warden's pedestals, Red for the Master, Pink for the Senior Warden and White for the Junior Warden.

The first Master of the St Bernard Lodge was W.Bro H. Harrison who had twice been Master of the Exmoor Lodge; Bro C.T. Gibbs was invested as the Senior Warden. The Treasurer appointed was Bro J. (Jack) Webber who was the father of J.J. (Jim) Webber. The latter was Initiated into the St Bernard Lodge in 1943 and later became well known in the Mark degree as its Provincial Grand Master for Somerset.

After a slow start the Lodge got well established following the 1939-1945 conflict and went from strength to strength.

In 1982 the Lodge celebrated its 50th Anniversary by obtaining permission to hold a Masonic ceremony in the refectory at Cleeve Abbey. It was well attended and was followed by a dinner at Chapel Cleeve where the original Cleeve Abbey was once sited.

2007 marks the 75th Anniversary and it was hoped to yet again hold a ceremony at the Abbey, but the charge from English Heritage was prohibitive. 2007 also saw a celebration for the Master of the Lodge, W.Bro L.W. (Bill) Shorey who occupied the Chair for the second time at 90 years of age.

One of the modern hand carved plaques on display in the Hall shows the insignia of the St. Bernard Lodge 5361 a figure of the Saint and the motto of the Lodge "Ora et Labora" (Pray and Work).

Lodge Uno Corde No. 5736

Meets at the Masonic Hall Keynsham

Warrant dated 1938

In the early months of the year 1938, a group of Freemasons who were Past Masters and brethren of various Lodges in London and the Home Counties, decided they would like to form their own Lodge. From that moment in time, Lodge Uno Corde was conceived and, soon after, was born. Lodge Uno Corde 5736 was consecrated on 24th June 1938, at Freemason's Hall, Great Queen Street, London WC2.

Why the Name 'Lodge Uno Corde'?

The initial meetings to discuss the forming of the new Lodge were mostly held in the front parlour of Bro W.H.D. Crick's house at 15 Milton Road, Hanwell, Middlesex. At one of the initial meetings at Milton Road, one of the Founders happened to say how wonderful it was that they all seemed to be of one accord in their decisions

regarding the formation of the new Lodge. This was immediately taken up by another of the Founders, who suggested using those words as the name of the Lodge. Further discussion followed and it was eventually agreed to use the Latin translation 'of one accord' which was Uno Corde, and the Lodge was named 'Lodge Uno Corde' (Lodge Of One Accord). Having completed their discussion regarding the Lodge itself, the next important item was the formation of a Lodge of Instruction.

It was agreed that Lodge of Instruction meetings would initially be held at 15 Milton Road and that it would be known as the Milton Lodge of Instruction 5736. There was a report that during one of the LoI meetings the head of the gavel came off and hit against the wall, just missing a large mirror. It was seen as a token of good luck for the future of the Lodge that the mirror was not broken. Meetings of the LoI were later held in a room above a tavern in the City of London, a very popular venue and well supported!

The Founders must have been personal friends of some very senior Grand Officers. There is frequent mention in the early minutes of visits by the Assistant Grand Master, R.W.Bro Brig. Gen. W.H. Darrell, and in March 1939 the Grand Chaplain, V.W.Bro Rev. the Rt. Hon Lord Blythswood presented the Lodge with an engraved glass Toasting Cup.

Lodge meetings were initially held at the Leicester Corner Restaurant in Leicester Square, London but "Enemy Action" destroyed that venue, along with the Lodge collars and jewels, in April 1941. The Lodge then moved to Freemason's Hall where it prospered and the 50th Anniversary meeting in 1988 was well attended.

By the year 2000 however, numbers had fallen, and a brief recovery following the admission of some keen young members was reversed when three of them went to work abroad. The Past

Masters kept it going for a while but in 2002 decided to hand in the Warrant.

W.Bro Brian Ruse had moved to Somerset in 1979 and of course joined in local Freemasonry. He mentioned the imminent closure of his Mother Lodge to a Grand Officer and news of this reached the Assistant PGM, W.Bro Terry Hart who suggested that Brian contact a group of brethren in Keynsham who were hoping to form a Saturday daylight Lodge.

Meetings were arranged and agreement reached that Lodge Uno Corde be moved to Keynsham. To facilitate this W.Bro Brian Ruse was elected WM (for the third time), and installed in September 2002 at which meeting several brethren from Keynsham were proposed as Joining Members.

The Lodge was formally welcomed into Somerset on 1st March 2003 by the Provincial Grand Master, R.W.Bro David L. Jenkins, and the Provincial Team (Note was made that this was appropriately St David's day).

The Lodge meets on Saturday mornings, and whilst the brethren meet upstairs their ladies are entertained by a speaker downstairs. The brethren and their ladies then lunch together and many friendships have developed over the past few years from this happy arrangement.

The Lodge Banner now in use was presented by W.Bro Gerry Carter. He commissioned it from the Royal School of Needlework, and it has been a prized asset of the Lodge since its dedication at a special meeting on 8th June 1963. Sadly, Gerry died in 1990 but all are sure that he would be pleased to know that the Lodge has survived and his banner will be displayed at Keynsham for many years to come.

Loyal Vacation Lodge No. 6209

Meets at The Masonic Hall, Wiveliscombe

Warrant dated 7th November, 1945

Two Banners adorn the east wall of the Temple at Wiveliscombe. One is of painted silk, and originates from the early nineteenth century. The other, bearing the motto 'Resurgam', belongs to the mid-twentieth century. Between them, they summarise the history of the Loyal Vacation Lodge.

The pictorial on the early Banner is based on the arms of the Mason's Company of London, granted in 1472, and displays the name 'Loyal Vacation' together with two beavers as supporters. These creatures, until the Union of the two Grand Lodges in 1813, were often used to depict operative masons and builders. After that date, the practice of including them on Masonic furniture was discontinued. It can be assumed therefore that the early banner pre-dated, or coincided with, the formation of the United Grand Lodge of England.

The first Lodge was formed at Wiveliscombe in 1802. It was granted the name of the erased Vacation Lodge 55, formerly of Covent Garden, which had been constituted in 1737 and named

'Vacation Lodge' in 1779. It had no Warrant to pass to its successor. Grand Lodge, accordingly, issued a Warrant of Confirmation to the Loyal Vacation Lodge 64, in 1837. The Lodge had twice been re-numbered; it had been designated 76 in 1814, and 67 in 1832.

The first Master of the revived Vacation Lodge, in 1802, was Charles Marsh, known as 'Saddler'. He must have been highly skilled in Masonic ritual being Master of several other Lodges in Somerset. These included Unanimity and Sincerity 261 at Taunton in 1797, Liberty and Sincerity at Wellington in 1804, and Brotherly Love at Martock in 1810. It is to be hoped that Bro Marsh's skills as a saddle-maker enabled him to enjoy a degree of equestrian comfort during his journeys between the Lodges. He died in 1819 and is buried at Wiveliscombe.

It is probable that the word 'Loyal' was added to the Lodge's name, shortly before or very soon after 1813, to mark the great service provided by one of its members, Dr Henry Sully, to the Duke of Cumberland. The Duke was a Prince of the Royal blood and a Freemason. He had been placed in command of troops in the South West District in 1803 and was based at Bristol. Dr Sully successfully treated this eminent personage for cataracts. The Duke never forgot this service and, on accession to the throne of Hanover in 1837, he appointed the good doctor Honorary Physician to the Hanoverian Court.

Others well known in Wiveliscombe became members of the Loyal Vacation Lodge. Not least among them was William Hancock, founder of the town's brewery in 1807, which by 1875 was reported by Kelly's Directory to be 'the largest in the West Country'.In 1827 the same Wm. Hancock was a principal organiser of the ceremony during which the foundation stone of St Andrew's Church, Wiveliscombe, was laid. The Taunton Courier reported that 'it was intended that the stone should be laid in full Masonic order'. The report of the event also informs us that of the 43 ranks that made up the procession from the town square to the church, 28 were occupied by the Masons.

Dr Henry Sully of Wiveliscombe
Deputy PGM of Somerset, 1817-1820
Surgeon Extraordinary to HM The Duke of Hanover.

The ivory Gavel with which the foundation stone was laid subsequently graced the Master's pedestal in Freemasons Hall, at the White Hart Hotel, Wiveliscombe, and, with other Lodge furniture, was taken to Dulverton when the Loyal Vacation Lodge moved there in 1854.

The first Loyal Vacation Lodge surrendered its Warrant in 1862, and the original Banner, in the course of time, passed into the hands of the Vale of Brislington Lodge. The Gavel was returned, in 1870, to the family of Col. C.K.K. Tynte who, as the PGM of Somerset in 1827 had originally presented it to the Wiveliscombe Lodge.

Today's Loyal Vacation Lodge was granted its Warrant in 1945 and received the number 6209. It was consecrated on 3rd January 1946 by the Provincial Grand Master R.W.Bro Brig. Gen. C.L. Norman DSO, SGD. W.Bro W.R. Ford was installed as the first Master of the Lodge.

During the time of scarcity after the War, Masonic furniture was almost impossible to obtain. W.Bro J. Duncan, who had done more than anyone to bring the present Lodge into existence, prepared drawings of Pedestals and Working Tools, among other necessary items, which were then fabricated by local craftsmen. The first carpet was of white squares painted onto redundant blackout material.

The Lodge met in the Congregational Rooms for fifteen years, but the difficulties of sharing with other organisations prompted a search for new premises. A property in Church Street was eventually purchased, in 1960, with the aid of loans from the members. The building, which comprised of two flats, was, by the voluntary labour of Lodge members, quickly converted to suit Masonic needs. The Service of Dedication was held on 23rd May 1961, and was conducted by the Provincial Grand Master R.W.Bro Brig. A. de L. Cazenove.

W.Bro J. Duncan had, a few years earlier, presented the Lodge with a Banner depicting a Phoenix rising over the word 'Resurgam', and this was dedicated at the same time as the new Temple. The original nineteenth century Banner had been restored to Wiveliscombe by the kind offices of the Vale of Brislington Lodge, and the Tynte family had generously allowed the historic gavel to be returned to Loyal Vacation Lodge in 1950.

The three principal items of Lodge furniture were now in place. Over the intervening years, in which the Lodge has prospered, they have been cherished as reminders of the long history of Masonry in Wiveliscombe.

Right:
A very fine Masonic print from the early years of the first Loyal Vacation Lodge.
This print is also very rare, and of great interest to any Freemason, depicting a large range of pre-Union symbols

Gordano Lodge 6244

Meets at the Masonic Hall, Yatton

Warrant dated 1946

The Lodge Banner contains several items of Masonic furniture; in particular the pillars on a chequered pavement, all surmounted by the All Seeing Eye. The centre panel between the pillars shows the connection between the Lodge and its surrounding area. In the foreground is the Griffin of Somerset, a mark of respect to the County and Province of Somerset and sign of allegiance despite recent local government boundary changes. Behind the Griffin, the scene shows The Bristol Channel, with the local hills (The Long Ashton Ridge) beyond. By the waters edge can be seen a structure signifying the Portishead Temple, the Temple by the Sea.

The Temple itself was originally built as a broad gauge railway station for Brunel, being the terminus of his railway line from London where passengers could embark onto his steam ships en route to America, using the adjacent Portishead Pier. History shows that this scheme was not entirely successful, and the building was purchased from the Great Western Railway by Eldon Lodge in 1933 for £800.

Gordano Lodge was consecrated immediately after the end of the Second World War, on 5th October 1946 in the `Temple by the Sea' in Portishead. The Lodge is the second daughter of Eldon Lodge 1755, the elder daughter being Severn Lodge 4399.

Eldon Lodge was formed in 1878 by Bristol Masons who, amongst other reasons, were apparently looking to form a Saturday Lodge, but could not gain permission within the Province of Bristol for Saturday meetings. Hence the move into the Province of Somerset. Eldon Lodge flourished in Portishead, to such an extent that in 1921 they formed their first daughter Lodge, Severn, also meeting on Saturdays. By 1946, not only was there the end of the war to celebrate, but Masonry had grown more popular, and Gordano Lodge was created. Part of the desire to form this new Lodge was that many members did not wish to meet on a Saturday, but instead wished to meet on a weeknight. A full circle had been made.

Over the years, there have been a great number of Masons of character in the Lodge. The first Master was W.Bro John Sargent, a Past Master of Eldon Lodge, and part of the driving force to form the new Lodge. The working within the Lodge is strongly based on the influence of the Eldon Masons such as him; these workings being a cross between Emulation and Eldon working, which itself is strongly influenced by Bristol working.

Probably the Masons who mostly set the distinctive character of the Lodge were W.Bro Ivor Richards, a fearsome Director of Ceremonies who controlled and guided the Lodge for many years, with the Secretary W.Bro Harold Amor, a local shopkeeper, and the stabilising hand of the Treasurer, W.Bro Hugh Vowles, another local shopkeeper. These traditions were then reinforced by two other towers of strength, W.Bro Crandon Gerrish and W.Bro Les Jelley. All these Masons are greatly missed.

From its beginnings, Gordano Lodge was a local Lodge for local people. There was an agreement with both Eldon and Severn Lodges that Gordano Lodge would only take its membership from brethren with a strong connection with the Gordano Valley. The rule normally applied was that all members either lived or worked in the Gordano Valley, anywhere from Abbots Leigh to East Clevedon.

Membership grew rapidly, reaching about 110 in the late 1970s. The membership waiting list exceeded three years, and the nine appointed Stewards of the Lodge worked hard during after meetings coping with large attendances. There were no waitresses in those days!

Meetings were held under W.Bro Jack Barker to form a new daughter Lodge for Gordano Lodge. When W.Bro Jack moved away, the idea was dropped. After then, there was a steady fall in membership, to such an extent that during the 1990s permission was sought and gained to drop the Gordano Valley rule. However, despite this change of rule, most members still have their roots in the Gordano Valley.

In the spring of 2004, problems with the Portishead Masonic Hall caused it to be closed at short notice. All the Lodges and Chapters meeting there moved down the coast to the Clevedon Temple, with the exception of Gordano Lodge.

Gordano Lodge considered it important that a Masonic presence be maintained in Portishead whilst a new temple was found or built within the town. The Lodge moved to a local licensed club, Clarence House, and started practising Masonry in a way which would have been more familiar 200 years ago. The ballroom of the club was transformed into a Lodge Room with travelling lightweight equipment and after the meeting, the Lodge room was stripped and set up for dining.

Unfortunately, after two years, there was no sign of there being a new Portishead Masonic Hall. The decision was therefore reluctantly made to move the Lodge out of Portishead into a normal purpose built Masonic Building. The Hall at Clevedon was, by now, full to bursting, and the brethren voted to move to Yatton Masonic Hall. The first meeting was held here in October 2006, and the Lodge has now settled in nicely, with a great many new friendships having been forged.

Although the Yatton Masonic Hall and all its facilities are wonderful, and the members of the other Lodges meeting there have been truly welcoming, some of the present members of Gordano Lodge still have their hearts in the Gordano Valley, and hope that, one day, it may be possible to return.

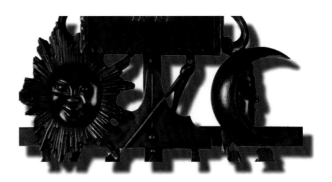

Winscombe Lodge No. 6474

Meets at the Masonic Hall, Yatton

Warrant dated 1947

The original idea of forming a new Lodge, which subsequently, became Winscombe Lodge, was conceived by Bro George Hawkins of Shipham, in the autumn of 1946. Bro Hawkins was, at the time, Senior Deacon of Wessex Lodge, 4093 and also a Subscribing Member of The Lodge of Agriculture, 1199.

At his suggestion a meeting took place at the Sidcot Hotel, Winscombe on the afternoon of Saturday 7th December 1946. 24 brethren attended to discuss his idea, thirteen of whom were members of The Lodge of Agriculture, four of Wessex Lodge and the remainder from other Lodges in Somerset and other Provinces. These included Alfred & Guthrum Lodge, 4535 and Rural Philanthropic Lodge, 291.

W.Bro Tom Locke, a Past Master of both The Lodge of Agriculture and Tyntesfield Lodge, was elected Chairman of the Meeting and it was unanimously agreed to petition Grand Lodge for the formation of the new Lodge, ideally to meet in Winscombe. Several further meetings were held, both formal and informal, culminating with a meeting, again at the Sidcot Hotel, on the 1st of February, 1947, when the Petition to Grand Lodge was completed and signed by all present. It was at this meeting that it was agreed to adopt the name "Winscombe Lodge".

W.Bro Tom Locke was Elected Master Designate of the new Lodge by secret ballot (stated in the minutes of the meeting to have been unanimous!!), W.Bro W.S. Perry, a Winscombe Bank Manager was Elected Treasurer Designate and Bro James Baines was Elected Secretary Designate. All three Officers were members of The Lodge of Agriculture.

With the support of The Lodge of Agriculture and of the Provincial Grand Master, the Petition was then presented to Grand Lodge. Much credit must also be given to Bro G. Hawkins, W.Bro F.J. Mabbett, a Winscombe farmer and W.Bro R.H. Kinsey a Winscombe Draper and Outfitter for all the work they did in the formation of the new Lodge.

A major topic for discussion was the proposed meeting place for the new Lodge, which the Founders thought should be in Winscombe. One vacant building was found within hours of the first meeting of the 7th December. After a survey had been carried out and a detailed study of the financial implication undertaken, it was reluctantly decided that in the rather austere post war economic conditions the proposition was not viable.

Shortly after the Consecration Meeting one of the Founders very generously gave to the Lodge a plot of land in Winscombe which it was felt would make an ideal site for a new Temple. Some years passed during which great efforts were made to raise funds with a view to fulfilling the ambition which this gift had made possible. Unfortunately, once again building costs and the very likely rising maintenance costs outstripped the funds available and ultimately the land was given back to the original donor. Some say that an opportunity was lost whilst others feel the decision, in light of the events which have happened, was a wise one.

By modern standards the figures appear insignificant but, in real terms, very large sums of money would have been required, and such money was simply not available at that time. Thus a Building Fund was set up with a view to purchasing a building at the earliest possible moment, but, unfortunately, inflation continued to outpace their aspirations and those ambitions have never been realised.

Other possible meeting places in or near Winscombe were considered but none were thought suitable, and ultimately an agreement was reached with The Lodge of Agriculture to meet at the Masonic Temple in Yatton, at a rent of £40 per annum. This arrangement continues to this day - but not at the same rent!

The foresight of the Founders was, however, fully vindicated when the original Building Fund, together with the accrued interest, was loaned to the Combined Lodges meeting at Yatton in 1993 to modernise the Yatton Temple and this loan formed a substantial part of the contribution made by Winscombe Lodge and its members to the cost of these works.

The first Lodge Dues were set at an annual Subscription of three Guineas (for the benefit of younger readers, a Guinea is the equivalent of £1:05p) an Initiation Fee of fifteen Guineas, and a Joining Fee of five Guineas. The Founder's Fee was set at five Guineas payable immediately and a further five Guineas as payable later. Dinner following the Consecration Ceremony cost eight shillings and sixpence (43p). These Fees may appear modest now, but they were substantial in the context of the time.

The Ceremony of Consecration took place on the 4th June, 1947 and was conducted by the Provincial Grand Master, R.W.Bro Brig. Gen. Claude Lumsden Norman, DSO, MVO, DL, assisted by his Deputy, V.W.Bro H. Frampton, W.Bro F.E.J. Hill, Preb. J.E. Pugh, W.Bro H.G. Travers-Biggs, Provincial Grand Secretary and W.Bro L.H. Buchan, Provincial Grand Director of Ceremonies. W.Bro Tom Locke was installed as the first Worshipful Master.

The first Regular Meeting of the Lodge was held on Wednesday, 8th October, 1947. The Candidate for Initiation that evening was Bro E.B. Card, the son of W.Bro Burnett Hugh Card, a Founder Member. At the invitation of the Worshipful Master, the Ceremony was conducted by W.Bro Burnett Card. W.Bro Edwin Card was Installed as Worshipful Master on the 12th October, 1955. As well, therefore, as being the first Initiate, he was also the first Initiate of this Lodge to be Installed as the Worshipful Master.

By virtue of the enthusiasm and industry of the Founders the Lodge grew steadily and by the end of W.Bro Locke's year of Office he had Initiated four Candidates and received into the Lodge eight Joining Members, so that, by October, 1948 there were 40 Subscribing Members.

Steady growth continued for the next three years and, by October, 1951 there were 45 Subscribing Members and a considerable waiting list of Candidates for Initiation. For this reason it was decided, at the Regular Meeting held on the 9th of April, 1951, to hold an additional Regular

Meeting in September of each year. As a result of the additional September Meeting the Lodge continued to grow so that, despite the death of five Founder Members by October, 1955, the number of Subscribing Members had risen to 55. However, in 2002 the Lodge voted to revert to the original October to May meetings and the additional September meeting was discontinued.

During 1954 a difference of opinion arose as to the precise form of Ceremony being practiced by the Lodge. Apparently music was being used during part of the Ceremonies which, in the opinion of some members was not strictly in accordance with Emulation Ritual. These differences were resolved at a Regular Meeting held on the 8th of December, 1954 when, upon the Proposition of W.Bro Tom Locke, Seconded by W.Bro Norman Wills, it was resolved without dissent that "Winscombe Lodge should strictly adhere to Emulation Working." Visitors may notice, however, that "Winscombe Workings" of which the Lodge is very proud change at least one sentence in every ceremony! Not quite "strictly adhering to Emulation Working as resolved in 1954.

In the early 1950s the family of the late Dr. Openshaw of Cheddar, a Past Master of the Lodge (1960), presented the Lodge with a Royal Air Force Sword and Scabbard. Sadly, in September, 1981, this sword "disappeared" from the Lodge premises in mysterious circumstances. Despite exhaustive enquiries the sword was never recovered.

In September, 1989, Bro Peter Gibson very kindly presented to the Lodge a replacement sword which had originally belonged to his late uncle, W.Bro Owen Kean who was an Officer in the First World War and a Provincial Grand Officer in the Province of Berkshire. Bro Gibson had the sword suitably engraved and presented it to the Lodge so that "Winscombe Lodge was not "guarded by 'borrowed Arms'",

as he put it at the presentation. It is this sword which is now presented to the Tyler at each Installation Ceremony. Bro Peter Gibson was later appointed Chaplain of the Lodge, a post he held until his untimely passing to The Grand Lodge Above in 1999.

On the 28th May, 1997, the Deputy Provincial Grand Master, V.W.Bro Roger D. Clark, accompanied by the Worshipful Master, W.Bro R.J. Rees, the Lodge Secretary, W.Bro Ben White and Lodge Almoner, W.Bro G.T. Hutchings, visited W.Bro Kelvyn King at his home to honour the 76th Anniversary of his Initiation into Freemasonry and also to celebrate his 100th birthday on August 23rd 1997.

The Deputy Provincial Grand Master presented a Certificate to mark the occasion, and W.Bro Rees presented a gift on behalf of Winscombe Lodge. W.Bro King also received congratulatory letters form Provincial Grand Lodge and Grand Lodge, both of which were given to him by the Deputy Provincial Grand Master. He also received a letter of congratulations from the Grand Secretary on behalf of the Grand Master, and a free pipe from Dunhill's! He passed away just before his 103rd birthday.

The standard of the working of the Ritual set by the Founders, particularly the Directors of Ceremonies and their Assistants, was always

Members of Winscombe Lodge at the 60th Anniversary meeting on 9th May 2007.

a feature of Winscombe Lodge, of which its members were justly proud. The Lodge continues to strive to maintain this to this day in honour of the Founders of the Lodge.

At the 530th meeting of Winscombe Lodge held on Wednesday 9th May 2007 the Provincial Grand Master, R.W.Bro David L. Jenkins and the Provincial Team conducted a 3rd Degree Ceremony and raised Bro Christopher Gardner to the Sublime Degree of a Master Mason. This was a celebration of the 60th anniversary of the Lodge. Mrs. Margaret Bradley, the 2007/8

Worshipful Master's Wife, also baked a splendid 50th Anniversary cake for the occasion, which the brethren who attended thoroughly enjoyed

Some ten years earlier at an Extraordinary Meeting of the Lodge, held by Dispensation on the 4th June 1997, the Lodge was "Called Off" to enable Mrs. Monica White to be escorted into the Lodge to formally present her very generous gift of a new banner. It was gratefully accepted and, as a token of appreciation, the Worshipful Master, W.Bro R.J. Rees, presented Mrs. White with a gift from the Lodge.

St Lukes Lodge No. 6540

Meets at the Masonic Hall, Old Orchard Street, Bath

Warrant dated 1947

In 1939 there were five Craft Lodges meeting in Bath; Royal Cumberland 41, Royal Sussex 53, Lodge of Honour 379, Royal Albert Edward 906 and St. Alphege 4095. The Chaplain of Lodge of Honour was Bro the Reverend W. Hopkins, the Vicar of St. Lukes Church in Wellsway.

Within a month of the Admiralty moving to Bath, on 17th October in fact, he invited Admiralty Masons to an informal meeting in the St. Lukes Church Hall in order that local Masons could meet and welcome the evacuees and Admiralty staff could meet and discuss how best to continue their Masonic lives whilst living in Bath. Present were representatives of Royal Cumberland, Lodge of Honour and Royal Albert Edward together with seventeen Admiralty brethren from fourteen different Lodges. It is interesting to note that the meeting was chaired by a Past Master of the Royal Albert Edward Lodge. This was the Lodge which later sponsored St. Lukes.

An informal approach was made to the Provincial Grand Master and indeed to the Grand Secretary, with a view to forming an Admiralty Lodge, but the suggestion did not meet with favour as it was said, quite rightly, that the Government had promised that all evacuated staff would return to London after the war, when any such Lodge would inevitably lapse. What is more, no-one at that time expected the war to last very long.

On the 19th March 1947 the Royal Albert Edward Lodge 906 Lodge of Instruction (Admiralty Section) convened a meeting at the Beau Nash Rooms to consider the formation of a new Lodge "Primarily for the Admiralty staff in Bath". W.Bro F.S.J. Boots, PPJGD (Hampshire and the Isle of Wight) and Preceptor of the

Lodge of Instruction took the chair and present were 30 members (from twenty lodges) and three visitors. The proposal was now possible because the Government had announced that certain departments of the Admiralty were to remain permanently in Bath. A number of names for the Lodge were suggested: NAVIS, St. Lukes, Anchorite, Anchorian Sulis and Vanguard were the most promising. Vanguard was suggested as various prospective members had been involved in designing the Royal Navy's new and last battleship of that name.

The Committee, after considerable discussion decided on Vanguard but this was reversed at a Founders meeting and St. Lukes was finally chosen. This of course was in recognition of the help received from the start from St. Lukes Church, St. Luke also being the Patron Saint of sailors.

One of the most important items to be decided was which ritual should be adopted. As has been mentioned before the new Lodge would have members from many lodges using many rituals. For some unknown reason Nigerian ritual was used for this occasion until superseded by Emulation when first printed in 1969.

A crest had to be designed, and with so many draughtsmen available this was no problem. The one agreed at a meeting of the Founders on 26th August 1947 was primarily the work of W.Bro Boots. As presented for Grand Lodge approval, a line separated the ship from the square and compasses. This was not acceptable to Grand Lodge; a rope was substituted for the line and this was agreed, having nautical connections.

Regalia proved a minor problem as not only did it take twelve months to obtain delivery due to war-time shortage of materials, but clothing coupons were needed. Royal Albert Edward offered their collars on loan but the Master's collar was peculiar to them and the Stewards' collars were red. W.Bro Boots offered his Past Master's collar for use by the Master and the Lodge of Instruction found six old collars for the Stewards. Each officer designate offered to purchase his own collar and jewel for presentation to the Lodge when they could be obtained and various brethren gave the necessary clothing coupons. The jewels were all engraved with the donor's name and are still in use.

A choir for the Consecration ceremony, which was to include three anthems, was provided from Lodge members and trained by Bro Arthur Metherall who was organist and choirmaster of Oldfield Park Methodist Church. Several members had been members of church choirs prior to evacuation, and the choir became known as the St. Lukes Singers and carried on for several years, mainly providing music at lodge suppers. Bro Lloyd Webb of Royal Albert Edward Lodge, a local nurseryman, offered to provide floral decorations free of charge for the Consecration ceremony and continued to render the same kindness for Installation meetings until his death.

Minutes of 28th October 1947 record that a letter of greeting had been received from W.Bro T.A. Wright of the Lodge Pacific 490 of Melbourne, Australia, stating that 32 food parcels were being sent for the Founders, also a tinned ham and a Christmas cake. These were surely most acceptable as it must be remembered that some war-time food rationing went on for several years, into the 1950s in fact.

It was a long time since there had been a Consecration of a new Lodge in Bath (St. Alphege in 1920) so there was considerable Masonic interest. 223 brethren signed the attendance register and there may well have been more. Because the numbers were too large for the Masonic Hall it was decided to book the Pump Room, which meant of course, arranging for Lodge furniture, carpet, organ and so on to be found and moved in.

All of the portable items were found by our good sponsors, the Royal Albert Edward Lodge 906. On the day W.Bro Freddie Boots was his usual bluff self. "Who are you?" he is reported to have said to the Provincial Senior Grand Warden, W.Bro Henry Frampton (who subsequently became the Deputy Provincial Grand Master and the holder of the Order of Service to Masonry). He also refused to admit one visitor who arrived straight from the golf course dressed in "plus fours". "Not in that pantomime outfit" he said.

The Banquet was held in Fortt's Dining Rooms in Milsom Street at a cost of One Guinea (£1.05) per head including wine. Dues were set at £2.10.0 per annum. In 1950 a sum of up to £30 was approved to provide a 'plain' Honours Board.

Presumably because of the evident success of the new Lodge, the PGM suggested that membership should be restricted to 80 members. On 19th May of that year the Lodge Banner was dedicated by W.Bro Dr F.A. Pollard, PPG Chap. The Oration was written by Bro F.V. Materaley, the banner was given by W.Bro F.S.J. Boots and was made by his daughter Marjorie to a design by Bro F.W. Coles.

In 1951 Bro Lemmon, serving as Manager of Gibraltar Dockyard, offered to present a set of Gavels and a Broken Column. He also offered to send a set of wands, from Gibraltar. During this year many complaints were made that the cost of the meal at the Festive Board was too high at three shillings and sixpence. Indeed, in January 1960, because of the continuing high cost of dining, consideration was given by St. Lukes to obtaining a fish supper from 'Fishy Evans', the local fish and chip shop, but this was not acceptable to the members.

The beautiful and ornate sword and Scabbard of St Lukes Lodge

By 1953, in view of the large number of candidates waiting for entry into St. Lukes it was decided to form a Daughter Lodge, the Elizabethan Lodge 7296, which was Consecrated on 11th November. The St. Lukes Singers provided the music and this time the ceremony was conducted in the Masonic Hall. In order to accommodate the numbers invited, scaffolding was erected above the side panelling in the Temple and seats placed thereon in a sort of gallery. In December the Lodge became a Patron of the Royal Masonic Benevolent Institution. That year saw the Province of Somerset as sponsors of the Festival for the Benevolent Institution. St. Lukes contributed £1,000 towards the total of £129,000 collected.

In 1955, W.Bro Wilkinson, whose wife sang professionally under the name of Jeanne Galbraith, quite unknown to him was engaged to sing at the Festive Board after his Installation. His surprise and pleasure can well be imagined. It should be noted that with true Masonic spirit Bro Longshurst stood down for one year in order that Bro Wilkinson could become Master before leaving Bath for a tour of duty in Singapore.

An anonymous Brother offered to present a book of St. Lukes ritual to every candidate. This was accepted with thanks and continued until the Brothers death when he left a sum of money in his will so that the arrangement could continue for ever. After his death it became known that the generous donor was Bro "Ernie" Merritt, the long serving Almoner of the Lodge. Bro Merritt did not pass through the Chair of the Lodge, but because of his exceptional services he was honoured by the granting of Provincial rank in 1968 as Past Assistant Grand Director of Ceremonies.

In January 1958 there were still ten on the waiting list for Initiation; at this time the Lodge only accepted two candidates per annum. On May 16th it was decided to delete the September and May meetings and replace then by November and February, so that meetings became monthly from October to April. It was also decided to change the month for Installation from January, when the weather was often bad to October. As a result of this W.Bro Fricker continued as Worshipful Master until October, a period of

21 months. During this period V.W.Bro J.M. Richardson MA BD, Past Grand Chaplain of the Grand Lodge of England a former Moderator of the Church of Scotland honoured St. Luke's by becoming a Joining Member on moving to Bath. He was St. Lukes first Grand Officer other than Honorary Members.

In 1959 Bro E.E. Merrett presented a silver cigarette box, at the March meeting, for use at the Festive Board. In later years, as smoking became less popular it became used in Lodge meetings for ballot balls. The following year he presented a splendid set of silver Working Tools to the Lodge

A ship's bell was presented by Bro Lemmon in 1960 for use at the Festive Board for the Absent Brethren toast. At 9.30 the hands of the clock are almost at right angles and so form a square. Three bells are struck; three bells is the first watch, which is Naval parlance for 9.30 p.m. The bell is supported on a wooden gantry and the whole is a miniature copy of the bell of HMS Howe and its support as it stands in the High Kirk of St. Giles in Edinburgh. The first bell used by the Lodge had consisted of an empty brass 4.5 inch shell case supported on a framework made of boiler tubes. This was given by Bro A.E.A. Robertson who was working in the Armament Supply Department of the Admiralty at the time.

In 1961 Bro Haywood was the first Initiate of St. Luke's to become the Worshipful Master. When the Japanese attacked Pearl Harbour and brought America into the war, W.Bro Oldreive was working for the Admiralty in Hong Kong dockyard. As is well known, the Japanese quickly captured Hong Kong and Singapore and Bro Oldreive became a Prisoner of War, but not before he had taken down the Union Flag from the dockyard mast to prevent it being captured. He hid it in his pillow and kept it with him, and there is remained throughout the war. When, in due course, the Japanese retreated it was quickly run up the mast again to welcome the rescuing troops, much to their surprise.

1968 saw St Luke's 21st year, and on 15th November a celebration meeting was held in the presence of the Deputy Provincial Grand Master V.W.Bro Henry Frampton MC PGSwdB and many other Provincial Officers. Also present were the Master and Wardens of the Mother Lodge, Daughter Lodge, the Master of St. Lukes Lodge Ipswich 225, and representatives of St. Lukes Camborne 5371 and St. Lukes Liverpool 6006.

In 1974 membership of the Lodge peaked at 104. It dropped a little until 1984 when it began to decline steadily. Many reasons have been offered; the continual reductions in Admiralty staff since the end of the war, the ageing of the population especially in Bath, which is becoming a retirement city, the increasing cost largely due to the expense of the rather special Masonic building, public criticism of Freemasonry and so on.

It was decided in 1976 to set up a separate Memorial Fund to cover bequests and memorial collections to commence with those of Bro E.E. Merritt and W.Bro Max Robinson. It was agreed that the capital should remain intact, only interesting being expended on appropriate occasions. The Brethren's names would therefore be permanently remembered

In 1978 the Provincial Grand Master set up an investigation into the variations in ritual which pertained within the Province. After explaining the origins of the Lodge's numerous variations he agreed that St Lukes should carry on as before, as a special case.

For a number of years in the 1980s the Lodge had as a Joining Member Bro Eddie Murray. He had gone off to join the French Foreign Legion in 1937 for a half-penny a day leaving in 1945 after war service with a clutch of medals including the Croix de Guerre. He then joined the Metropolitan Police and in 1950 became the personal bodyguard of Sir Winston Churchill until Churchill died in 1965. Sir Winston had once been an active Mason but lapsed when other duties became rather pressing.

In October 1983, Mrs Joyce Candy made a short visit to the Festive Board to present three silver candlesticks to the Lodge in memory of her late husband, W.Bro Donald Candy, a most active and enthusiastic member. They are used at the Festive Board and lit for the Absent Brethren toast.

On November 20th 1987, which was the nearest meeting to the actual Consecration date a re-enactment of the Consecration ceremony was presented by various Past Masters. The Lodge was honoured by the present of the Provincial Grand Master R.W.Bro K.C. Kinnersley and the Provincial Grand Director of Ceremonies W.Bro T.A. Hughes, SGD. Also present were representatives of our Mother Lodge and Daughter Lodges and those of St. Lukes

Lodge Ipswich. The remaining three Founders, W.Bros J.E. Barrett, E. Binstead and Bro C. Matthews and three Originals, W.Bros E.G. Longhurst, C.T. Wilkinson and V.W.D. Fricker also attended.

A choir was recruited to provide music, one member, W.Bro J.E. Barrett having been in the original choir. Wherever possible the officers taking part were in their actual Provincial rank and for the first time in many years all officers wore the Gauntlets appropriate to their rank. W.Bro V.W.D. Fricker acted as Consecrating Officer, learned the whole ceremony and was word perfect. W.Bro David George produced a facsimile of the 1947 Programme which was indistinguishable from the original and a copy was given to all those present.

In 1991 the Lodge was especially proud of its Master as for several years W.Bro Edbrook's sight had been steadily deteriorating as he progressed through the various offices, and it was very sad that he was unable to see his Lodge from the Master's chair, although no visitor would ever have known.

'In February 2004 a new Lodge Banner was dedicated, The original was small, and produced from limited materials in the years following WW2. The new Banner was hand made by R.W.Bro Peter A. Marsh PGM of Gloucestershire who attended the dedication ceremony which was carried out by V.W.Bro Peter Layzell DPGM and members of the Provincial Team'

The winds of political change have over recent years had a marked affect upon the Lodge, probably starting as far back as 1960 when the Admiralty began to group together several of its departments. Then again later, the Royal Navy, the Army and the Royal Air Force were combined into the mammoth Ministry of Defence and moves started to bring the civilians of the Army and RAF Departments to

Bath to link up with the Navy Dept. (Formerly Admiralty). For various reasons this came to nothing. An impressive purpose-built new office block has been opened to the north of Bristol, and it seems that most of the Ministry staff is likely to leave Bath for Bristol. Indeed they have started to do so, and thus the reason for starting St. Lukes back in the 1940s is in the process of fading away, and although there have been over the years, notable "non-Admiralty" recruits, unless more of these are forthcoming the future will be uncertain.

But to finish on a lighter note, it is perhaps worth remembering one of the characters who graced St Lukes Lodge proceedings in the past. During the 1950s, the paid steward of the Masonic Hall was a Bro Shepherd who liked to be known as "Nutty" because, he said, he had a large head. One of his duties was to act as Tyler for all the Lodges. Bro Shepherd had the habit of leaving the door unattended when he thought he wasn't required in order to get the bar ready. This practice caused some problems, and complaints. Additionally, he seemed unable to knock on the door in an even fashion, varying from the inaudible to deafening thunder.

Being an ex Chief Petty Officer Telegrapher, Royal Navy, he overcame the two problems by making an electro-magnetic door knocker with an operating push both outside and inside the door. This enabled him to give consistent knocks when he was there and permitted the IG to give the Tyler's answering knocks when he was missing.

For added efficiency he placed an indicating light box near the IG's chair saying "Tyler on duty" or "Building secure, Tyler attending the bar". When Nutty departed so did the phantom Tyler of Bath.

Southey Lodge No. 6650

Meets at the Masonic Hall, Clevedon

Warrant dated 1948

During the nineteenth century Clevedon became known as the "Poets Town" and the Masonic Brethren named their Lodges accordingly. The Past Masters of Coleridge, 1750 and Tennyson 4947 decided in July 1947 that a new Lodge was necessary, and proposed the founding of "Wordsworth" Lodge, although the name was changed to "Southey" Lodge some two weeks later. Robert Southey being a Bristolian and brother in law to Coleridge probably influenced this change of mind.

Born in Bristol in 1774 Southey went to Westminster School from which he was expelled for editing a magazine entitled the 'Flagellant'. He then went on to study at Balliol College, Oxford where he became friendly with Coleridge and together they

established their Pantisocratic Society (all equal and all rule).In 1795 he married Edith Fricker who was the elder sister of Coleridge's wife Sara. Southey settled in the Lake District and became one of the Lake Poets, a collective term for Wordsworth, Coleridge and Southey who all lived there in the early 1800s where the landscape provided them with inspiration for their poetry, especially so for Wordsworth. In 1813 Southey became Poet Laureate.

Six Founders' meetings up to June 1948 established the Lodge in the aftermath of the war and the ten guineas paid by each of the 30 Founders was quickly absorbed, clothing coupons were then collected to provide collars and gauntlets!

Consecrated on 16th June 1948 a full day was planned with lunch at 12.30, the Consecration at 2.30 and a festive board at 6.30 with tea served halfway through the ceremony! At the Consecration meeting the Provincial Chaplain, W.Bro Charles Porter impressed upon the Founders that " good beginnings were essential, but they were only beginnings. The essence of vitality was continuance, a much more difficult state"

Robert Southey
Potrait bt Edward Nash reproduced by kind permission of
The National Portrait Gallery

In its relatively short history life has not always run smoothly, paper shortages after the war meant no Books of Constitutions, rationing prevented white gloves being worn until 1952, a particularly bad "pea souper" cancelled a meeting in 1953 after only three members could attend. Even worse, a visitor sadly passed away in the temple in 1955. The Lodge even took charity to the limit with a collection in 1976 amounting to £8.06 and four Green Shield stamps!

The Southey Lodge
Founder's Jewel

Arguably the Lodge's proudest moment was as the sponsoring Lodge of the Showmen's Guild Lodge 9089 in 1982. Many Showmen have given great service to the Lodge and the membership is proud of its association with them.

With its 60th anniversary in 2008 the Lodge is lucky to have a strong link with its Founders in its long serving stalwart W.Bro Bob Cole whose Father, Grandfather and Uncle were all Founders. The Lodge hopes that after 60 years its Founders see a strong, happy and flourishing Lodge, proud of its heritage and roots.

Estune Lodge No. 6817

Meets at the Masonic Hall, Nailsea

Warrant dated 1949

In 1946 the inhabitants of this country, who for a period of six years had been subjected to an almost intolerable burden of stress, and at times calamity, were endeavouring to return to some normality. Many, each in his own way, sought a haven or a refuge in which life could be rebuilt and those moral values, which had become so eroded, regained and strengthened. It was under such conditions that requests for admission into our Order rose at an abnormal rate, and means had to be sought to ease the strain on the already long list of candidates waiting.

Long Ashton, a village of antiquity and almost wholly residential, was at this time expanding rapidly. Among many of the inhabitants were members of our Fraternity, some of whom belong to Tyntesfield Lodge. Foremost among those not members of Tyntesfield were W.Bro John Randell of Rural Philanthropic Lodge at Burnham, W.Bro M.C. O'Conner of Bengal, Bro Ladbrook Hurley, Bro Robert Brown, Bro A.E. Morrish and others. The Long Ashton residents who were members of Tyntesfield were W.Bro H.E. Horler, Bros W.D. and A.V. Mereweather, Bro H. Patch and Bro R.L. Singer.

These brethren, realising the need and also the desire for a new Lodge which would be representative of the members of our Order living in Long Ashton, decided to call a meeting of those interested. With this objective in mind they invited W.Bro W.J. Mullings the Secretary, W.Bro G. Foster and Bro T.A. Gane, all of Tyntesfield, to consider the formation of a new Lodge. The stage was set.

There followed twelve pre-formative, or pre-natal meetings commencing on 12th March 1948.

The essentials of the Lodge Banner represent the Lodge of Ashton Court over the oak tree which was mentioned in the Domesday Book as growing in the grounds.

On October 5th 1948 there occurred a most important event in the history of Estune Lodge. Tyntesfield Lodge, upon a proposition by W.Bro W.J. Mullings, seconded by Bro W.D. Mereweather, agreed that a Petition be forwarded to Grand Lodge, that a Warrant be granted to form a Daughter Lodge to be named Estune Lodge, which was the ancient name for Long Ashton. This new Lodge was to meet at the Nailsea Masonic Hall.

After following the proper procedure and channels the Warrant was granted and Estune Lodge 6817 was registered. The Consecration Ceremony was held on 19th May 1949 by the R.W Provincial Grand Master for Somerset, Brig. Gen. Claude Lumsden Norman, assisted by all the Provincial Grand Lodge Officers. The Provincial Grand Pursuivant was a founder member of Estune and also the Director of Ceremonies who carried the petition in our Mother Lodge when it was presented for signatures. The Consecration completed, the Worshipful Master W.Bro W.J. Mullings P.M. 4494 was installed, the Officers were invested and Estune Lodge No 6817 was born.

The family tree is impressive stretching back to 1793, with the Grandmother Lodge being Coleridge, 1750 Great Grandmother Lodge the Lodge of Agriculture 1199, and our Great, Great Grandmother Lodge Rural Philanthropic 291. There is now also a Daughter Lodge, the Sir Isaac Newton Lodge 9801, consecrated on 8th October 2005, and with whom a very strong relationship has been forged. This Lodge was formed following a perceived need for a daylight Lodge in the area.

The Lodge Jubilee meeting and celebrations took place on 19th May 1999 under the Mastership of W.Bro B. Fowkes. The Lodge was honoured with the presence of the Provincial Grand Master R.W.Bro S.H.A.F. Hopkins supported by Grand officers V.W.Bro T. Hughes, W.Bro T. Hart and W.Bro C Edwards with W.Bro J.W. Wyatt as Provincial ADC. W.Bro Dick Pearce read the minutes of the first regular meeting held on 20th September 1949 and one of the Lodge widows, Mrs Doris Little, presented a Pedestal Cloth in memory of her late husband W.Bro Peter. Finally V.W.Bro Tom Hughes presented a Masonic Bible to the Worshipful Master.

W.Bro L. Williams presented to the Lodge encapsulated grains of corn which were scattered in May 1949 by the then Provincial Grand Master R.W.Bro Brig. Gen. Claude Lumsden Norman. These grains had been collected and passed to W.Bro Williams by W.Bro E. Hobbs for safe keeping.

Over the years the Lodge has prospered under the guidance of teams of very good committed officers who came to Estune both as Initiates or Joining Members. During these years there have also been many sad, traumatic and joyful occasions all of which the Lodge has taken in its stride. But the Lodge prides itself on having a reputation for being a very friendly, warm and welcoming Lodge, maintaining Lodge traditions whilst accommodating new ideas and technical advances.

Estune enjoys the company of many visitors and meets the needs of Grand and Provincial Lodge charities without neglecting the many local charities with which the Lodge is involved. A great deal of money has been raised and donated to the Masonic Hall Company which boasts being one of the best Masonic centres in Somerset for its facilities.

The foundations of Estune Lodge were laid by men who could truly be called "wonderful Masons". Regrettably most have now gone to the Grand Lodge Above which places the onus on their successors to carry on the great work they initiated. A steady flow of candidates and Joining Members shows that it is a happy Lodge, proud to introduce newcomers to the Estune fraternity.

Priory Lodge No. 6913

Meets at the Masonic Hall Keynsham

Warrant dated 1949

In 1948 Keynsham Masonic Hall already provided a home for two Craft Lodges, but with the village of Keynsham expanding rapidly into a small town, and a suburb of Bristol, it was thought that the time had come for the founding of a new Lodge, as both the existing ones had a large membership, and offered limited facilities for new candidates, or advancement.

W.Bro Wilfred Milton, who was a Past Master of St Keyna Lodge, and Founder Member of Abbey Lodge, approached a number of brethren whom he thought would be interested, and managed to collect sufficient names to press forward with the proposition.

The R.W Provincial Grand Master Brig. Gen. C.L. Norman gave his blessing to the new Lodge, but insisted that they must practice 'Emulation' working when the Lodge eventually became effective. Thereupon a number of Founder Members withdrew their names, saying that unfortunately they were not conversant with 'Emulation' ritual, as the existing Keynsham Lodges both used 'Bristol' working. Undeterred by this hiccup, W.Bro Milton pressed on and managed to find twenty brethren who agreed to form the new Lodge. Two names were put forward for the new Lodge, Buckingham and Priory; Grand Lodge nominated Priory to be adopted.

One of the original Founders who had expressed great interest in the new Lodge was W.Bro W. Aston, who resided in Saltford and was a Past Master of the Lodge of Sincerity 292, and had a good knowledge of 'Emulation' working. He was invited to become the very first Worshipful Master of the Lodge, and accepted the honour. A Founders' meeting was held at the Masonic

Hall, Keynsham on the 26th August 1949. W.Bro W.H. Patterson was appointed Secretary, and W.Bro G.O. Wiltshire, Treasurer. It was resolved that all present and past Officers would not be eligible for Office, except those appointed to the Principal Offices.

The petition for a Warrant to form a Lodge was sponsored by the Master, Wardens, and Brethren of St. Keyna Lodge 1833 in September 1949.

The Lodge was duly Consecrated on Friday 28th October 1949 by the R.W Provincial Grand Master assisted by seven Provincial Grand Officers and in the presence of 72 brethren visitors and new members. W.Bro Aston was then Installed as the new WM The Warrant of the Lodge was signed by the Most Worshipful the Grand Master the Duke of Devonshire, and now hangs proudly in Keynsham Masonic Hall.

The first regular meeting of the Lodge was held on Friday 11th November 1949, and Bro H.C. Wilkins was balloted for and accepted as a Joining Member, and two candidates for initiation were also balloted for. One of these W.Bro H.J. Burrow (still a member) celebrated his 50 years in Masonry, and was presented with his certificate to mark this occasion by R.W.Bro Stanley H.A.F. Hopkins, Provincial Grand Master for Somerset in December 1999. W.Bro Burrow eventually became Treasurer of Priory Lodge, and WM in December 1967. It is interesting to note that eighteen of the Founder Members held Office in the first year.

1951 saw the creation of a Benevolent Trust Fund in support of the established Masonic Charities. 1956 was a busy and satisfying year. In March came the Presentation and Dedication of a Lodge Banner by the R.W Provincial Grand Master Brig. Gen. C.L. Norman. This was followed by a presentation of 'Founders Jewels'. Also, in October, a Lodge Meeting was convened by dispensation for the special purpose of the Dedication of a new organ by the R.W Provincial Grand Master, Brig. A. de L. Cazenove. The organ is still in use.

Again in the same year, the Treasurer and Founder Member W.Bro G.O. Wiltshire MBE was honoured by Grand Lodge with a collar of Past Grand Standard Bearer.

The Lodge was further honoured in 2001 with the promotion to Assistant Provincial Grand Master of W.Bro Raymond Guthrie and he was further honoured in 2002 with the Grand Rank of Past Senior Grand Deacon.

During the past 57 years the Lodge has enjoyed the essence of Freemasonry, Brotherly Love, Relief, and Truth, it has seen the joys and sorrows like many other Lodges in the Province, and continues to find suitable candidates whenever possible, so as we advance into the 21st Century, it is hoped that the future and prosperity of the Lodge is left in their capable hands so that Priory Lodge will continue to flourish during the next 50 years.

Whitchurch Lodge No. 6942

Meets at the Masonic Hall Keynsham

Warrant dated 1949

As Britain was struggling with post-war reconstruction in the late 1940s, the thoughts of certain well known local characters of Whitchurch Village turned towards the promotion of Freemasonry in the area. Thus it was at a meeting held on 22nd March 1949 at "Wentworth" on Wells Road in Whitchurch, the home of Bro Dr Joe Smith, that the seeds were sown that would grow into Whitchurch Lodge.

At that time there existed between the village and the City of Bristol considerable green space, and this Somerset village had retained a character quite distinct from that of its larger neighbour. This was recognised in the intentions of the Founders of the Lodge who proposed that all members should be residents of the village. The intention became a reality as the village grocer, the doctor and the chemist all became members.

W.Bro J. Barwick PPJGD of Connaught Lodge 3573 agreed to be the first Master, but he unfortunately died in September 1963. Bro J.G. Nash of Eldon Lodge, 1755 engaged the assistance of W.Bro G. Travers Biggs who promised his help and guidance in the new venture. Bro Nash agreed to be the first Secretary. Bro George Cole donated a family Bible to be used by the new Lodge, and the Reverend G. Boniface of the Zion Congregational Church at Whitchurch agreed to allow the new Whitchurch Lodge to meet at the Church Schoolrooms.

Many exploratory meetings took place, not only at the schoolrooms but at the Doctors surgery, the 'Little Thatch' public house, 'Cross Hills' on Hursley Hill, 'Chota Castle', Frome Masonic Hall and the Grosvenor Hotel in Bristol. It was finally concluded that a sum of £350 would be

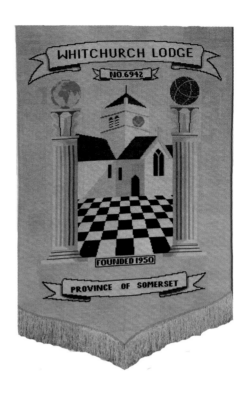

needed to fund the new Lodge and the Founders were asked to contribute £10.10s.0d each. Connaught Lodge 3573 agreed unanimously to support the Petition for the new Warrant and they offered the use of their Lodge for the Consecration Ceremony.

The first year Officers agreed to purchase their own collars and jewels for £3.4s.6d (£3.22p) and to donate them to the Lodge. The Worshipful Master's, Senior Warden's and Junior Warden's gauntlets were purchased by the Lodge at a cost of £5.12s.6d per pair. The initiation fee was £21, the joining fee £5.5s.0d and the annual subscription was £2.2s.0d.

The first rehearsal was held on 22nd November 1949, and February 1950 was to see the Consecration, but this was deferred to March because of the bad weather.

Unfortunately the Connaught Lodge room was not big enough for the Consecration Ceremony, so it was decided to hold it at the Royal Somerset Lodge room at Frome on Saturday 18th March 1950. The Consecrating Officer was the R.W.Bro Brig. Gen. Claude Lumsden Norman, DSO, MVO, DL, PSGD of England, the Provincial Grand Master. There were 31 Founders and first Officers present, together with guests.

In October 1951 the Worshipful Master and brethren of Royal Somerset Lodge presented a square and compasses to the Lodge and in November of the same year an Organ was presented to Lodge by Bro A.E. Mickleburgh.

Unfortunately, in April 1952, because of a change in church policy, the Lodge was asked to look for other accommodation. The use of Connaught Lodge room was offered and so was the new Masonic Hall at Keynsham. Both were carefully considered and Keynsham was the venue of choice. Thus it was that in September 1952 Whitchurch Lodge started meeting in Keynsham for the grand sum of £35 annually to cover nine meetings and nine rehearsals.

In 1954 concern was expressed that the rule regarding prospective candidates having to live in Whitchurch, and at a special Committee meeting held at the Black Lion Public House, Whitchurch on 14th September a 'full and frank discussion took place'.

Bro J.E. Smith, the Senior Warden proposed that the original rule be rescinded and replaced with the 'locality of Whitchurch' and left to the judgement of the Committee. This was seconded by Bro C.P. Reeves and duly carried by five votes to two.

By the year 1962 Whitchurch Lodge still did not have an Honours Board, so after much discussion it was decided to have one constructed. Young Bro Tom Pow offered to

letter the board, but as nobody had seen his work he was asked to prepare a sample, and providing it was satisfactory he would be entrusted with the task. The sample proved most satisfactory and the work was completed, the Worshipful Master commenting that he had not seen better on any other Masonic Board. Apparently Tom Pow still has the sample. The original Board was replaced during the Hall redecorations in 1981, but it is still in use today by one of the side degrees at Keynsham. In 1965, the ever active Bro Pow made a fine set of working tools for the Lodge, which we are still using today.

In December 1964 it was decided that the widows of Whitchurch Lodge should each receive a Christmas gift. A total of £5 was spent that year, and the tradition is still carried on albeit at 21st century values.

Until 1969 it had been a tradition in the Lodge that, after his year in office, the Immediate Past Master took on the position of Director of Ceremonies. However, in that year the tradition was changed. The Master elect appointed W.Bro Dansy Rogers as Director of Ceremonies. There was furore at the Past Masters meeting at the Grosvenor Hotel, with talk of resignations! There was a good reason for the appointment; W.Bro Rogers was a great ritualist. He was also a Taxi driver, and during his time waiting for fares he would read his ritual. W.Bro Rogers went on to have a fearsome reputation as Director of Ceremonies and used a three-line whip to keep up the ceremonial standard.

For a long time an informal weekly 'class' was held at the home of W.Bro Eric Daniels (Danny), in Dene Road. For about ten years Danny, in close collaboration with his Assistant Director of Ceremonies, W.Bro George Wookey ensured that the ritual was preserved in unblemished condition. It was not unknown for George, a hard working farmer, to attend rehearsal straight from the farm, bringing the savour of the countryside with him.

He was one of a distinguished roll of Directors of Ceremonies who have served the Lodge amongst them W.Bros Tom Pow, Ted Fleetwood, Wallace Chapman and Les Pearce (Bonnie). W.Bro Bonnie was awarded the high office of Provincial Grand Senior Warden in 1993 and established long lasting bonds between Whitchurch Lodge and numerous other Lodges throughout Somerset.

From time to time various professions have been well represented in the Lodge. A strong band of railwaymen belonged at one time and a splendid number of their colleagues attended the meeting in 1999 at which W.Bro Stan Tinklin celebrated his 75th birthday. Schoolmasters were much in evidence at one period and to those that knew them the names of W.Bros Jim Pugh, Tom Price, Stan Bick and Bro Vincent Davies will recall fond memories. Many Police Officers have found good companionship and recreation within the Lodge

The 'catchment area' of the Lodge now extends well beyond the village of Whitchurch. The area of south-east Bristol is still represented in our address list and a sizeable intake from north-east Somerset has always featured significantly. One very active member, Charity Steward W.Bro Colin Pitman is rumoured to have kept the Severn Bridges solvent with his frequent journeys to and from Chepstow.

Much individual talent has been devoted to the affairs of the Lodge. W.Bro Fred Shapperd took up organ music as a retirement activity and soon became skilled enough to take on the office of organist, at a time when we were in need. He was succeeded by the legendary Bro Jack Mills, who was still playing in his nineties.

Whitchurch has always enjoyed good relations with the other Lodges meeting at Keynsham. This was drawn upon in 1975 on the foundation of Saltford Lodge.

The founder members were in the main experienced in "Bristol" working, but Provincial Grand Lodge required conformity with Emulation ritual. Thus there was a need for an unofficial first Immediate Past Master to provide some guidance during the initial year of operation. W.Bro Bill Cox, being in the chair of Whitchurch Lodge at the time undertook this task and supported the brethren in their laudable undertaking.

As no Lodge history would be properly complete without a summary of its vital statistics, there are a few fact and figures that may be of interest. Since 1950 the Lodge has attracted 159 members from all walks of life, have had approximately 450 Lodge meeting, 300 committee meetings, consumed approximately 3.5 tons of potatoes, 1.75 tons of meat and drunk 4000 gallons of beer, some drinking more than others!

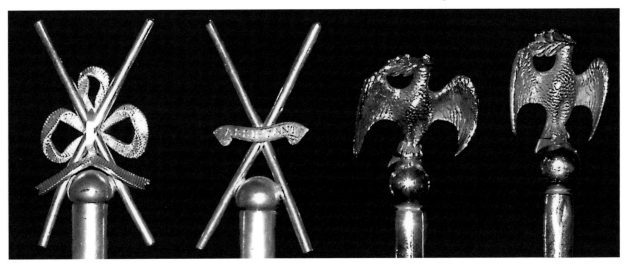

Queen's College Taunton Lodge No. 6988

Meets at the Masonic Hall, The Crescent, Taunton

Warrant dated 1950

Queen's College, Taunton Lodge 6988 was consecrated on 8th July 1950 and came into being as a result of the enthusiasm of a number of English and Welsh Old Boys of the School who were Masons. The prime instigator was Bro C.E. Coggan. The Lodge was sponsored by the Lodge of Unanimity and Sincerity 261, meeting in Taunton.

The Consecration Ceremony was carried out by the Provincial Grand Master for Somerset, R.W.Bro Brig. Gen. C. Lumsden Norman and took place in the Masonic Hall in Taunton. The first Master was R.W.Bro Dr. E.L. Bunting, the Provincial Grand Master for Worcestershire. The Founders established that the Lodge should work the Oxford ritual and that the Installation Ceremony should be an extended working.

The first Joining Members were Bros R.C. Carr and J.F. Tigg. The first initiates were H. J. Cannon and Rev. R.H. Foster, both of whom had been pupils and masters at the School. "Dapper" Cannon featured on the television programme, "This is your Life", having been a master at the School all his working life. Rev. Rod Foster was Chaplain at the School for a number of years. Many other initiates quickly followed and the Lodge became very healthy. After three or four years meeting at the Masonic Hall in Taunton, it was suggested that the Lodge might in future meet at the School. To this end, W.Bro Coggan and two other members met the Headmaster, Bro S.J. Haynes, and obtained permission to meet in the then Library. Application was made to the Provincial Secretary, the room duly inspected, and meetings were held at the School from 1955 until 2002 when the Lodge reverted to holding its meetings at the Masonic Hall in Taunton.

The Lodge has been privileged over the years to have had many eminent Brethren from Somerset and other Provinces as members, including four Provincial Grand Masters; Dr. E.L. Bunting, PGM for Worcestershire, Sir Arthur Reed, PGM of Devon, J.H. Vivian, District Grand Master for Transvaal R.W.Bro K.C. Kinnersley, PGM for Somerset (1981-1990). The Lodge has also had as members the late Laurie Francis, DPGM of Cornwall, G. Blampied, DPGM of Guernsey and Alderney, R.B. Whittingham, Assistant PGM of South Wales (Eastern Division) and D.B. Durie, Assistant PGM of Somerset. These brethren have all made a tremendous contribution to the Lodge in establishing its traditions and standards.

Bro Sidney Haynes, Headmaster of the School for over twenty years was initiated into the Lodge in July 1957. He has been a regular attendee ever since and is a great contributor to the jollity of the Festive Board when he proposes the toast to the School and often reminds certain members of their misdemeanours and academic prowess, or not, as pupils at the School. Bro Sidney received Provincial Honours in 2002 and was presented with a Provincial Golden Certificate to celebrate his 50 years as a Freemason on 12th May 2007 by R.W.Bro Stanley Hopkins, Past Provincial Grand Master for Somerset. In May 1980, W.Bro K.C. Kinnersley, who joined in January 1958 and was Master in 1968, was appointed and installed as PGM for Somerset in 1981, an office he held until 1990. In April 1984, his son, W.Bro Mike Kinnersley, was installed as Master of the Lodge.

The Lodge is a member of the Federation of Schools Lodges and has hosted the Annual Festival on two occasions, in 1967 and 2000. Several members of the Lodge have held senior positions in the Federation, including R.W.Bro Ken Kinnersley who was President, W.Bro Ralph Fielding who was Secretary and later Chairman and W.Bro Peter Whittingham who has recently been Chairman. The Lodge celebrated its Silver Jubilee Meeting on 12th July 1975. The Master that year was W.Bro Mike Fielding, son of the then Secretary, W.Bro Ralph Fielding, a founder member, and Master in 1955. This meeting was attended by R.W.Bro Lt. Col. Harry O. Hughes, the PGM for Somerset. After the Lodge meeting, the brethren were joined by their ladies and dined in the School Dining Room. The Golden Jubilee Meeting was celebrated on 8th July 2000 (50 years to the day after the Consecration of the Lodge). A brief history of the Lodge was written for this meeting.

As mentioned earlier, the Founders decreed that the Lodge should work the Oxford Ritual. After some twenty years, and with Masters from all over the country having worked different rituals, the working at Queens became somewhat distorted. Different portions of different rituals were gradually being introduced. W.Bro David Durie, the then Director of Ceremonies, suggested that the ritual, as being used in the

Lodge, should be recorded and committed to print. W.Bro Jack Tigg started by taking copious notes of the various (and varied) ceremonies. These were passed to W.Bro Peter Whittingham who produced the "Queen's Working" which could be described as a hybrid Oxford ritual. It is often the subject of comment and jocularity amongst visitors at the Festive Board! The Lodge currently has nearly 60 members who are either former pupils or members of staff. In 2006, the Lodge approved an extension to the eligibility for membership which is now open to former pupils, their fathers, sons or such other direct relatives as may be approved by the Lodge Committee, current and former members of staff and current and former Governors. Indeed the Lodge has had ten home-grown Lewis's in its history

The Installation Meeting of the Lodge is held in March and the Ladies' Festival currently follows the October meeting. A group of Lodge members and their ladies travelled to Portugal in September 2005 for a fraternal visit to Lancaster Lodge 9413, the mother Lodge of the Secretary, W.Bro David Sargison. Members demonstrated the Queen's extended versions of the three Apron presentations and afterwards fully participated in the Ladies' Night festivities. In 2006, a visit was arranged to St Mary's, Isles of Scilly, where members and their ladies were looked after in superb fashion by the 2009 Master, Bro Robert Francis who runs a hotel on the island. Queen's connections know no boundaries!

The Lodge publicises its activities in the OQs website Newsletter, and maintains regular contact with the School, holding at least one social function there each year. The current Headmaster generously hosted a splendid lunch for Lodge members and their guests in May 2007. The Headmaster also supports efforts made each year to explain Freemasonry to a group of 6th formers in an informal presentation followed by supper.

Birnbeck Lodge No. 7160

Meets at the Masonic Hall Weston-super-Mare

Warrant dated 1952

Birnbeck Lodge was formed just over 50 years ago with the aim of satisfying the needs of those members of the Craft working out of town, or with other commitments, to get to Lodge on time (our start time remains 7.00 p.m.). Over the intervening years few changes have been made, the principal one being the change to Emulation ritual whereas initially Nigerian working was used.

The history of the Lodge from 1952 to 1977 was recorded in the book, "The Foundation of Birnbeck Lodge" written by W.Bro Edward Turner, MBE, P.Pr.G.Supt.Wks. a founder member of the Lodge. From this we discover that W.Bro Cecil Haskins, a past Master of Wessex Lodge, enlisted the aid of three Grand Officers together with six Past Masters from each of the three local Lodges to serve on a committee in early 1951. Such was the beginning of the Lodge which was successfully formed and consecrated on the 11th June 1952.

By 1954 a Banner had been designed by W.Bro F.C. Horstmann which depicts Birnbeck Island as it was many years ago, deserted with the exception of its lone fishermen's hut and showing the fishing nets strung out on posts between the shore and the island. The banner was made by ladies from the School of Science and Art and was dedicated on 20th April 1955.

In early 1965 members of Birnbeck Lodge were instrumental in the formation of The Forest of Mendip Lodge and are pleased to be acknowledged as their "Mother" Lodge. The Founders, were they alive today could ask the question, "What has changed since we established Birnbeck all those years ago?"

What a pleasure to be able to say, not a great deal, for the Lodge has drifted little from those original ideas, concepts and principles laid down in 1952. One is sure that they would be most happy with the way in which The Lodge has continued over these years; and what was laid down by them has proved to be a most firm and secure foundation on which to build "Birnbeck" as we know it today.

Lodge still start at 7.00pm, delegates parts of the ceremony, has progressive offices, doesn't hold raffles and has an excellent festive board, and as Past Masters take their share of floor work during the year no "Past Masters" evenings are thought necessary.

357

A unique "Hospitality" fund was initiated on the foundation of the Lodge whereby members pay a nominal annual amount and as a result are able to invite visitors from afar (15 miles distant) at no extra cost to themselves. Permanent visitors are expected to be paid for!

Meetings are held from September to May on the 3rd Wednesday of each month, with Class of Instruction on the 1st Monday of each month at 7.30 p.m. The Installation is held on the third Wednesday in September at 5.30 p.m., (tea and biscuits at 4.30), hopefully having given the Master Elect the whole summer to "smooth and prepare" his ceremony.

Unfortunately all of the Founders are now deceased, the last active Founder being W.Bro Gerald Wadham, Worshipful Master in 1953 and who remained a true "character" to the very end, entertaining all by his special replies to the Founders Toast at meetings he was able to attend. Just one of his many memorable achievements was in visiting all the 57 or was it 58 Lodges in Somerset during his year in office on a motorcycle and sidecar despite the vagaries of the English weather.

The commitment of the Officers to their task is something of which the Lodge is justifiably proud, for they too wish to emulate, no pun intended, the success and dedication of their predecessors.

Mention should be made of the worthy Stewards who fill their office so ably with their work on the "floor" and ability to stand in for other office should the need arise, combining this with their sterling work at the Festive Board. Birnbeck is now the sole Lodge in Weston-super-Mare where the Stewards are accustomed and pleased to wait on table. Long may this continue to be the custom, for it is one of the many ways we all get to know our fellow brethren as well as sealing that bond of friendship experienced by true Freemasons.

The Charity Stewards, both long serving (and suffering), have done an excellent job over the years. Amongst the many achievements of which Birnbeck can be extremely proud is its contribution to charity. Charitable donations are not usually made public, but over the years, the Lodge has, through dedication, produced excellent results within the Province of Somerset, a remarkable achievement and all the result of dogged and determined Charity Stewards combined with the efforts of generous brethren.

What of today's "Birnbeck"? It is much the same as it was and hopefully always will be. The standards are high, its members enthusiastic and eager to progress. The memories of those who have gone before, together with their achievements, maintain that firm foundation of which "Birnbeck" can be justly proud.

The Birnbeck Cup

Wellington School, Somerset, Lodge No. 7230

Meets at the Masonic Hall, Wellington

Warrant dated 1952

W.Bro Henry Collins, at 97 years old, and still attending Lodge, is the only surviving Lodge Founder. He recalls "In 1950 W.Bro George Hawkins called to see me to say that he had been talking to W.Bro Eric Smith about the possibility of forming a School Lodge. They had agreed to make a few enquiries of people they knew who might be interested. My first thought was that it would be difficult to maintain sufficient membership as the eligible candidates would be so scattered, but in the end I decided to give it my support."

"Our first small meeting was at Bro Frank Matthews' house at Stonegallows, Taunton. There were five of us; W.Bros Smith, Hawkins, Hoyles, Bro Matthews and myself. We discussed the prospects of finding enough people interested. Bro Matthews said he had contacted someone in Bridgwater and another in Devon and was quite hopeful of their support. We had another meeting a few weeks later when there were nine people present and several more pledged their support. The outcome of that meeting was a decision that we should form a School Lodge without delay."

W.Bro Henry just before his 96th birthday.
Sharing a joke, and a dram,
with R.W.Bro Stanley H.A.F. Hopkins PPGM

"The next meeting was held at School, in Northside, when sixteen Founders were present and it was decided to ask Grand Lodge to issue a Warrant for the foundation of the Wellington School, Somerset Lodge. We then had a discussion about the Ceremony; some of the Past Masters suggested small variations which they used in their Lodges but it was decided to keep things simple and the ceremony decided upon was the one we have used from the beginning. The final pre-Consecration meeting was also held in Northside when arrangements were made for the Great Day"

Frank Matthews, who was at School from 1921 to 1928 was a key figure in establishing the Lodge. A Local Authority Valuer by profession, he was initiated into St Oswald Lodge 1124 in Oswestry, Shropshire. On returning to Taunton he became a Joining Member and later a Master

359

of the Lodge of St George. He was a member of the National Trust and in 1950, while visiting Montacute House, he met another Old Boy who was also a Mason.

They discussed the idea of forming a School Lodge, and from those meetings Frank worked very hard contacting eighteen other Old Boy Masons. Twelve were Past Masters and six Master Masons and they became our Founder Members, and today we still have W.Bro Henry Collins as a 'Grand Original'. Frank was appointed as the first Secretary, and became Worshipful Master in 1968. He also served as Treasurer and as Asst. DC. To him, and the National Trust, the Lodge owes a great deal.

The Consecration was quickly followed by the First Regular Meeting on the 2nd February 1953, when J.A. Morgan Ayliffe David was the first Initiate. Thirteen further brethren were balloted as Joining Members, among them W.Bro David Morgan who completed 32 years as Organist, W.Bro Norman Holbrow who keeps in touch from his home in Bermuda and the late W.Bro John Cooper, sometime DPGM for Dorset. On the 18th April the brethren resolved that an application should be made for the Lodge's membership of the Federation of School Lodges.

In 1955 the Founders and Past Masters Board was purchased for £35.10s.0d (£35.50), and Working Tools were presented by W.Bro V. Walters and Square and Compass by Bro D. Hill. October 1963 saw Bro Frank Courtenay Matthews, who had been a prime mover in the creation of the Lodge, installed in the Chair by W.Bro J. Cooper.

At the 1967 April meeting a Notice of Motion was given "That this Lodge shall give the Lodge Committee authority to consider the purchase of a Lodge Banner and, provided satisfactory arrangements can be made, to proceed with the purchase of such a banner up to a limit of £60". Twelve months later, on April 20th 1968, R.W.Bro Brig. A. de L. Cazenove, Provincial Grand Master for Somerset, lead the Ceremony of the Presentation and Dedication of the Lodge Banner. Present were 43 visitors including W.Bro W.A. Kneel, DPGM for Devonshire, later to become Provincial Grand Master for Devonshire, and W.Bro R.D. Clark who later became VW.Bro Deputy Provincial Grand Master for Somerset. In December 1981 an extra meeting was held by Special Dispensation at which W.Bro. J. Cooper gave his Prestonian Lecture, entitled "Robert Freke Gould, Masonic Historian".

The Lodge never lost sight of it's commitment to its Mother Lodge, and in October 1982 a letter was received from the Lodge of Fidelity and Sincerity expressing their brethren's thanks for a donation of £250 towards the new lighting in the Temple; it concluded "Over the years, the School Lodge has been extremely generous to us. We are most appreciative of this and Fidelity and Sincerity is grateful for having such a caring daughter".

Known to generations of schoolboys as 'Nic', Bert Nicol was the great link between the School and Lodge in its early days. He was a member of the Teaching staff from 1930 to 1966, teaching Maths and Physics; Housemaster of

'Hardwick' and then of 'Willows' and Second Master from 1946 to 1961. Somehow he also found time to coach and referee rugby, run the School Shop and act as Secretary of the Old Boys' Association (now the WSA).

In his spare time Bert was a Mason, a member of the Sun Lodge 106, meeting in Exmouth where he was initiated in 1937. It was very appropriate that he should be a Founder Member of our School Lodge, and at the first installation he was appointed Senior Deacon. He then became the fourth Worshipful Master in 1955 and in due time was honoured by the Province of Somerset as Provincial Senior Grand Warden. He made a tremendous contribution to the Lodge by being its longest serving Secretary, completing no less than 21 years in that office. During that time he either proposed, or seconded, many of our members. He knew them all; they must have been good pupils! When he retired as Secretary the brethren presented him with a carriage clock, a token of appreciation from all the members for the many hours he had spent to the benefit of the Lodge.

W.Bro Harold Ludicke, 'Ludi', as he was affectionately known to everyone, became a Joining Member from the 'Men of Sussex Lodge' 3712 in December 1964. He rose through the ranks and became Worshipful Master in 1977, and was subsequently honoured with appointment to PPrJGD in Somerset. He had a German father and an English mother who had the good sense to send him to Wellington School. The then Headmaster, George Corner, had a great interest in engineering and this kindled a burning fire in 'Ludi'. He became a most respected Chartered Engineer, FIMechE., FIMarE, with his own practice working in the UK and Germany. He eventually retired in his eighties! He was a Past President of the OBA (now WSA) from 1967 to 1969 and attended every Reunion. This enthusiasm was extended to the Lodge, travelling down from London for each meeting, often with guests from the Men

W Bro Harold Ludicke

of Sussex. Sadly he was called to the Grand Lodge Above in 1993. His wife remained in contact with the Lodge, and when she passed away we were delighted and surprised with a most generous bequest to used as a fitting memorial to "Ludi".

Charitable giving has always been a proud tradition among the brethren of the Lodge, and throughout its history funds have been generously donated to both Masonic and non-Masonic causes. At an Emergency Meeting held in March 1990 the William Cobbett team gave a demonstration of an 18th Century Initiation working, which proved most instructive and amusing. The team were dressed in authentic clothing of the period. The alms collected by the team, in their hats, amounted to £236.45p, which together with funds raised at the Festive Board produced a total of £905.52p towards the 1993 Festival appeal

At the February 1993 meeting a letter from the Royal Masonic Benevolent Institution was read expressing sincere gratitude for an exceptionally large bequest from the estate of our late Brother, W.Bro H.S. Hoyles, and in May was another milestone in the Lodge's history was reached; the Eighth Anniversary of the Masonic Trust for Girls and Boys was held at Shepton Mallet with the Lodge contributing £13,000 to the Appeal; some £265 per member. In February 2002 the Treasurer reported that in the past year our Benevolent Fund had received £3,800 in Bank Covenants from members, and that raffles organised by W.Bro A.H. Baker had raised £780. In September W.Bros Trump and Tokelove visited the School and presented the Chairman of the School Appeal, Lt. Col. John Moore OBE, Old Boy and Olympian, with our cheque for £500 towards the Princess Royal Sports Complex.

1995 will be remembered for our first, and continuing, very happy joint Ladies' Night with Kings College's 'Old Aluredian Lodge'. Also in 1955 the By-Laws amended to formally recognise that present and past members of the School staff could become members of the Lodge. In October W.Bro K. Trump and B. Tokelove attended the Federation of School Lodges Annual Meeting, while their wives enjoyed a festive dinner and 'Murder Mystery' evening; "The girls were late returning".

In November a Masonic Visit to the Lodges meeting in Majorca arranged by our Bro P. Howard-Baker, as a member of the Lodge of Good Intention, took place and was much enjoyed. The Grand Master of Spain appeared impressed by the English brethren; we were very impressed by him.

Sadly, on 20th February 2002 W.Bro Michael Hoare was called to the Grand Lodge Above following an illness which he fought with great courage. Mike left a sum of money with which the Lodge obtained a fine cabinet for it's Tracing Boards, made by W.Bro T. Wood of Lodge of St George 3158, who also made the Honours Boards Another member, Bro Jonathan Horler made a generous donation in memory of his mother, who was a Lady Mason. There cannot be many Lodges which have Furniture dedicated to a Lady Mason!

October 2002 saw the start of the Lodge's 50th Anniversary Year. In January 2003, by Dispensation, the Lodge returned to the Great Hall at school where it was a delight to welcome the Provincial Grand Master R.W.Bro David L. Jenkins, and many visitors, at a special ceremony, followed by a very fine festive board prepared by the school catering staff. At the culmination the brethren looked forward to the next 50 years with as much zeal and enthusiasm as has been witnessed during the past half century.

In December 2003 the Lodge welcomed "back to school" W.Bro Michael Hitt PGStdB as a Joining Member, and at the February meeting in 2007 was very pleased to see him presented with his 50th Anniversary Certificate by Assistant PGM., W.Bro Stuart Hadler. 2007 also saw the culmination of the Provincial Appeal for the Royal Masonic Benevolent Institution. The Lodge was delighted to receive five acorns, representing about £700 a Brother. Not bad considering we it meets only four times a year, and almost 50% of members live outside the Province.

The Taunton Deane School Lodges hold a joint annual reception for Sixth Form pupils at their respective schools. These are well attended by boys, and girls. As a result in 2008 the Lodge introduced its first eighteen year old Initiate, who has a keen interest in Masonry.

Elizabethan Lodge No. 7296

Meets at the Masonic Hall, Old Orchard Street, Bath

Warrant dated 1953

The year had seen the Coronation, the formal recognition of the Queen's accession, and this had prompted the naming of the new Lodge. The accession of the new Queen had encouraged the press to publish gushing columns heralding the new era and this new "golden age". This in turn inspired the Lodge Founders to produce a Lodge motto "Epocarus Doratum". It was intended to mean "Golden Age" but it does not seem to have any basis in Latin. It might have some affinity with the Greek lexicon and be considered old Greek, epocarus meaning epoch, era or season and doratum indicating gold or gilded.

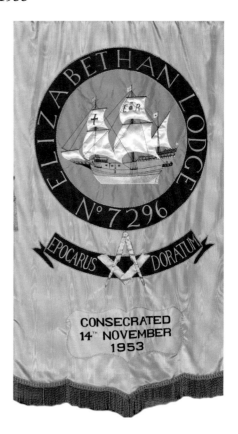

At a meeting of the Reference Committee of St Luke's Lodge 6540 on 20th January 1953 it was recorded that "W.Bro Robertson said they were proposing to form a new Lodge and asked the members of the Reference Committee whether they would be prepared to support the application. It was proposed by W.Bro F.C. Ladd and seconded by W.Bro B.H. Basham that the Lodge be asked to support the application, as a daughter Lodge of St Luke's. Carried unanimously."

At the regular meeting in March 1953 notice of motion was given: "That a Petition for the formation of a new daughter Lodge be considered at the next regular meeting", and the summons for the April 1953 meeting contained the proposal to form the new Lodge. The proposer and seconder of the motion, W.Bros Robertson and Pugsley were both Founder Members of the new Lodge and both played active roles in the early years. The founders chose "The Golden Hind", the ship captained by Sir Francis Drake during the reign of the first Queen Elizabeth, for the design of the crest.

W.Bro Prince was to become the first Master, and the meeting to consecrate the Lodge took place at 3.10 p.m. on Saturday 14th November 1953. The chair was taken by the Provincial Grand Master, R.W.Bro Brig Gen. Claude Lumsden Norman, DSO, MVO, DL. St Luke's Lodge provided support at the meeting; the brochure produced for the meeting describes the musical programme as being under the direction of W.Bro Basham, MBE, of St Luke's Lodge, with Bro T. Francis Pope, tenor and the St Luke's Quartet.

The attendance was so large that additional seating had to be provided on three rows of scaffolding erected above the oak panelling in the north-east and south-east parts of the Temple; arranged by Bro R.G. Roberts.

Besides the eight consecrating officers, there were present at the meeting eleven assisting Provincial Officers, 21 Founders and 150 visitors. The Lodge was closed at 5.34 p.m. and 167 brethren adjourned to the Festive Board at Fortt's Restaurant in Milsom Street.

It is, perhaps, appropriate to mention here W.Bro Arthur Prince, the Founding Master. He was 78 years old at the date of consecration of the Lodge and was a retired shopkeeper in the city. He was a member of St. Alphege Lodge 4095 in Bath and had been that Lodge's Worshipful Master in 1934. He held the rank of Past Provincial Assistant Grand Director of Ceremonies in the Province of Somerset. In February 1961 his resignation from the Lodge was reported, only for the resignation to be withdrawn at the following meeting. The Reference Committee minutes record some forthright views of W.Bro Prince on various topics. He died in January 1963.

Lodge records show there were six Founder Past Masters, one Original Joining Past Master, sixteen Founder Members and nine Original Joining Members. Of the last nine, two were members of lodges under the Grand Lodge of Scotland, two were members of Australian Grand Lodges and there was one each from the Grand Lodges of Ireland and New York. The average age of the Founder Past Masters was 60; that of the other Founders as 49. Of the Founding Past Masters, four had been Masters of other Bath Lodges.

The Founders of the Lodge were, necessarily, all Joining Members. At the first regular meeting in December 1953 seven Joining Members were accepted and, in January 1954, Bro Eric Naylor, currently the "doyen" of the Lodge, was accepted as a Joining Member. Joining members continued to come forward so that, in December 1955, the Reference Committee was concerned about the numbers and it was suggested that a limit of one Joining Member

The Loving Cup
Inscribed to the memory of W.Bro Neate

each year be imposed; it was finally agreed to place a limit of two Joining Members each year.

A number of brethren have received recognition of 50 or more years in Freemasonry. The most notable, certainly in length of years, was Bro William Neate, who had been initiated in St. Clair Lodge 2074 in Portsmouth in November 1923. He was one of the Founder Members of Elizabethan Lodge in 1953 and remained a member until his death in March 1997 at the age of 100.

He had been a Mason for 73 years and, in November 1993, the Worshipful Master, W.Bro K. Strange, together with the Assistant Provincial Grand Master, W.Bro Arthur Forse, and others attended on him at his home to present him with the Provincial Grand Master's 70 year certificate.

In March 1955 the offer of a grandfather clock was made by Mrs Cheeseman, the widow of W.Bro Herbert Cheeseman, who had been one of the Founder Past Masters; he had died in February 1954. It was accepted with grateful thanks, and today stands in the anteroom.

Throughout it's history the Lodge has benefited by a number of legacies. The most significant was that of Bro William Neate. To acknowledge his generosity, a loving cup was purchased and suitably inscribed, and a toast to the memory of W.Bro Neate is proposed at Installation meetings, when the cup is passed among those present at the Festive Board.

By tradition, the Lodge worked the Nigerian Ritual. However, in October 1970 the Secretary reported that he had endeavoured to obtain further copies of that ritual but it was out of print. Instead he obtained books retailing the Emulation Ritual, and this ritual has been the basis of the Lodge's working ever since.

It has been the practice to present each Master with a Past Master's jewel on relinquishing the Master's chair. These jewels contain the Lodge crest in enamel and, being unique to the Lodge, are expensive to manufacture. Interestingly, the first Master expressed his disapproval of the custom of presenting such jewels but he was overruled. The first jewels were stated to be likely to cost between £7 and £8 each and approval was given to buy three. These were not ready for the Installation Meeting in 1954 so jewels were presented to the first two Masters at the Installation meeting in 1955.

In October 1973 the idea was put forward that the 21st anniversary of the Lodge's formation, which was due to occur in November 1974, should be celebrated, and in January 1974 it was confirmed that sufficient interest had been expressed to make a celebration worthwhile; an organising committee was formed. The meeting in November 1974 was attended by the Provincial Grand Master, R.W.Bro Lt. Col. Harry Owen Hughes, and his Deputy and Assistant Grand Masters, along with other distinguished brethren. The Secretary read the names of 22 brethren who had died since the Lodge's consecration, and the Secretary to the Founders gave a comprehensive account of the

events leading to the Lodge's formation. 87 brethren attended the evening.

In 1960 it was decided to receive in rotation the Masters and Wardens of the other Bath Lodges. Lodge minutes record Masters and Wardens being admitted and welcomed, although the custom of inviting Wardens was soon restricted to those Lodges which in return also invited Wardens. The present custom of the Worshipful Masters of the other six Bath Lodges attending each Lodge meeting as guests is well established. The "Silent Six" are so described because they are not called on to speak, particularly at the Festive Board.

The honours board, with an elaborate and detailed carving of the Lodge crest, is sited on a wall of the anteroom and is very visible to anyone entering the Temple. It is an impressive piece of work and much admired, but it cannot be denied that it had a long gestation period. The acquisition of an honours board was first raised in December 1954, when it was estimated that the board would cost £60. A Reference Committee member then said he thought he had sufficient Japanese Oak for a board and would be pleased to arrange for the board to be made and presented to the Lodge. The Reference Committee, at first dubious, finally agreed. The donor requested anonymity.

The design was discussed and approved in 1955 but it was not until 1960 that the Secretary was able to report that the board had been delivered and affixed to the wall. It seems that it had been placed in position on the morning of a Lodge meeting, but in the evening, concern was expressed not only by Lodge members, but also by the Hall Trustees; the design and colour were completely out of keeping with the boards of other Bath Lodges and it was taken down the following day. Despite efforts to modify the board, it had to be acknowledged that it was fundamentally wrong in its proportions and it was agreed to construct a new board.

Sensibly, the approval of the Hall Management Committee was sought before construction began, and in December 1961 the new board was completed and in position at a cost of £160.

The first mention of a Lodge Banner occurs in the minutes of the Reference Committee meeting of February 1956 when it was decided to defer consideration of the matter for the time being. The subject was next raised in November of that year, and again it was decided to defer the matter, with the expense involved cited as the reason. Two years passed before the topic was again raised, when, in November 1958, it was yet again decided to defer any action. However, at that meeting, a comment was recorded that the Lodge was poorly furnished without a banner. And so the matter continued to be deferred until the approach of the celebration of the Lodges 25th year.

Accordingly, in 1977, it was agreed at the March Reference Committee meeting to open a "Lodge Banner Fund" and a sub-committee was formed. In March 1978 the final design was approved and was commissioned to be made by Mrs Burton of Nether Stowey in Somerset who had worked for the regalia manufacturer Toye, Kenning and Spencer in the company's London workshop. She had also been commissioned, with five other ladies, to make the Queen's wedding dress in 1948.

As early as 1954 the Reference Committee was considering the need for brethren to have the opportunity to learn ritual, and it was decided to recommend to brethren the St Luke's Lodge of Instruction, which met at Smith's Rooms in Westgate Buildings. Subsequently, the Secretary reported that he had arranged for a Class of Instruction to be held at Smith's Rooms each month from September to June and in 1958 the Secretary announced the formation of a regular Lodge of Instruction, to be held in the Masonic Hall from September to May on the second Thursday. Provincial approval of the formation of the Lodge of Instruction was reported in January 1959. The Lodge of Instruction meets monthly on nine occasions though the year and allows brethren to practice ritual in different offices.

At the December 1960 meeting the Worshipful Master expressed his regret that due to the flooding of the Masonic Hall it was not possible to arrange for the customary refreshments to be provided after the meeting. The basement had been flooded to a depth of almost five feet. By the following Friday the whole of the South part of the city was completely flooded. In spite of the difficulties, 53 brethren attended the meeting.

The future of any organisation depends on the strength of its support; strength in numbers and strength of commitment. A keen nucleus of new members currently exists within the Lodge, and the necessary commitment looks likely to ensure a successful future. It is tempting to think that, despite the various difficulties which have attended the Lodge's first 50 years, the Founders would nod their approval of the way in which problems have been tackled and resolved, and the manner in which the Lodge has lived its first half century.

Corinthian Pillar Lodge No. 7552

Meet at the Masonic Hall, Yeovil

Warranted dated 1957

In the period leading up to the formation of the Corinthian Pillar Lodge, Yeovil was increasing in population. The two Craft Lodges already established there, Brotherly Love 329 and Progressive Science 5007, were likewise enjoying great numerical strength, as was the Craft as a whole. Thus it was that a Foundation Committee was formed on 25th March 1957 to consider the possibility of forming a new Lodge.

A minimum of twenty Founder Members would be required to ensure the success of establishing a new Lodge, and each Founder would contribute £10.10s.0d each. The Masonic Hall would charge a rent to include use of the Ornaments and Furniture, but Jewels, Collars, etc, would be purchased at an expected cost of £100.

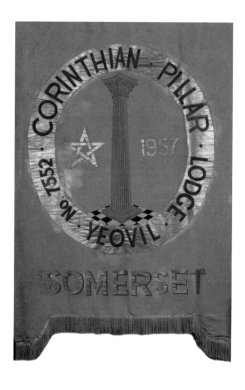

During the following weeks the Lodges of Brotherly Love and Progressive Science were informed of the request to form a new Lodge which received their support and a petition was duly endorsed and submitted to Grand Lodge for approval with Brotherly Love being the sponsoring Lodge. The name of Corinthian Pillar was suggested by W.Bro Langler and proposed by W.Bro H. Haynes and seconded by W.Bro R.H. Giles. There was a ballot for the Worshipful Master at a meeting held on 14th June 1957 and W.Bro H. Haynes was duly elected. At the same time the officers were elected and approval of the By-Laws was made. It was also agreed that acceptance of an office would be limited to five consecutive years, a term still applied today. Corinthian Pillar Lodge 7552 was consecrated on 8th November 1957 and named after the ornate architectural pillar denoting Beauty.

The Provincial Grand Master for Somerset, R.W.Bro Brig. Gen. Claude Lumsden Norman DSO, MVO, DL, assisted by fifteen Provincial Grand Lodge Officers carried out the ceremony and installed W.Bro H. Haynes as WM who then appointed and invested his officers. At this time there were 28 Founder members and a total of 97 attended the Consecration meeting which was followed by dinner at the nearby Manor Hotel at a cost of 12/6d per head.

The Lodge continued to grow and on 21st October 1960 the Deputy Provincial Grand Master in Charge, W.Bro Henry Frampton MC, PGD presented and Dedicated the Lodge Banner

There are no Founders left but each year at the Past Masters Festival in December a tribute is made to them.

Old Aluredian Lodge No. 7724

Meets at the Masonic Hall Taunton

Warrant dated 1960
Transferred to the Province of Somerset on 9th June 1976

The Lodge is one of the smallest in the Province, with a membership varying between 18 and 32 members, but has been active throughout its history and will achieve its 50th Anniversary in 2010. At its Regular Meetings visitors usually outnumber members, sometimes by two to one, despite meeting on Saturdays, and it has a well deserved reputation for hospitality and friendliness. Nevertheless it has attracted a steady trickle of candidates over the years and rarely has received lectures or worked ceremonies. Although open to members who are not Old Boys of Kings College (Old Aluredians) it has retained the unique character and atmosphere of a school Lodge and been well supported since the transfer of the Warrant to this Province in 1976. However the relationship of the Lodge with the school continues and since 1990 members of the Lodge have attended the Remembrance Sunday chapel service at the College.

It is reputed that Bishop Fox (1448-1528), whose portrait hangs in Kings College, founded a grammar school in 1522 within the precincts of his Castle of Taunton with a shield with the Pelican over the school door. The crest of Kings College incorporated on the Lodge banner is the Pelican in its Piety feeding its young with its own blood, the symbol of Christ the Redeemer, with the Latin motto Fortis et Fidelis (Brave and Faithful). It is also the crest of Corpus Christi College Oxford, Bishop Fox's major foundation.

By 1870 larger premises were required and the site of the present Kings College on the old Taunton Race Course in South Road had been acquired and the present building erected

for the contract sum of £11,285, under the Headmastership of the Rev. William Tuckwell, a Freemason and pioneer of science teaching who erected what is believed to be the first ever school science laboratory. Religious and Masonic ceremonies were observed at the laying of the foundation stone by Lady Taunton in 1868.

In 1880 the school was sold to Canon Nathaniel Woodard who founded "King Alfred's College" (now simply "Kings College") and became part of the Woodard Corporation, which he had established in 1848 as a result of noticing that the Church was providing education for the poorer families, the wealthy had private tutors, but the middle classes were being neglected. He established schools with a strong religious ethos that addressed the needs of the whole child; mental, physical and spiritual.

He believed strongly that education is best delivered in a supportive community where every child is valued and encouraged, a pioneering tradition which has continued in Kings College to this day and is reflected in the character of the Lodge. From the original ten schools he founded between 1848 and 1891 there are now 23 owned and, with the affiliated schools, together educating 27,000 pupils a year.

The Old Aluredian Lodge has seven sister Woodard School Lodges, namely the Ardingly College Lodge 4410, The Old Lancing College Lodge 4660, The Hurst Johnian Lodge 4937, The Old Ellesmerian Lodge 5368, The Old Denstonian Lodge 5490, The Old Worksopian Lodge 6963 and the Old Bloxhamist Lodge 7725. There is also a Woodard Schools Holy Royal Arch Chapter and a Woodard Chapter Rose Croix, both meeting at 10 Duke Street St James in London.

The Lodge was "founded primarily for the consideration of Old Boys of Kings College Taunton" according to its original Bylaws and was Consecrated on 6th October 1960 at Freemasons Hall Great Queen Street London WC2 by R.W.Bro Maj. Gen. Sir Allan Adair Assistant Grand Master. The Lodge was sponsored by Ardingly College Lodge, 4410, a Sister Woodard School Lodge.

The Ceremonial Music at the Consecration was under the direction of W.Bro Dr. Norman F. Smith, DM, PGD and the Glee Singers led the singing. Noteworthy were the Address to the Brethren on the motive of the Meeting and the Oration by the Chaplain. The Ceremony was described as beautiful, extraordinarily well conducted, and memorable. The Working Tools of a Master Mason were presented to the WM by the R.W.Bro The Assistant Grand Master who also gave the Address to the Master. The Address to the Wardens was given by W.Bro Sir Victor E. Groom and that to The Brethren by

W.Bro P. de L. Cazenove, PGDC. The meeting was attended by fourteen of the Founders and 69 visitors who included representatives of Sister Woodard School and other School Lodges namely Ardingly College Lodge 4410, Old Lancing Lodge 4660, Old Denstonian Lodge 5490, Old Tauntonian Lodge 5735, Old Ellesmerian Lodge 5368, Hurst Johnian Lodge 4937, Queens College Taunton Lodge 6988, Wellington School Lodge 7230 and Old Wellingtonian Lodge 5570.

The First Master W.Bro Arthur C. Robinson PPGD (Cornwall) was a Solicitor and Secretary and Treasurer of the Royal Masonic Hospital Fund Cornwall and a most experienced Mason as was the first SW W.Bro Richard H.S. Ashton LGR also a Solicitor and prominent London Mason and for many years the Secretary of The Incorporated Society of Musicians Lodge 2881. The first JW Bro Walter Long was Chairman of the Old Aluredian Club and the moving spirit in the birth of the Lodge being "possessed of boundless enthusiasm energy and zeal."

The ensuing Regular Meetings of the Lodge were held at No.4 Whitehall Court London SW1 on the 4th Fridays of January, September (Installations), and November and Dinner was taken in the Carrington Dining Room at Whitehall Court. The Regular Meetings held on the Friday preceding Whit Monday were held by Dispensations of the M.W Grand Master and the Provincial Grand Master for Somerset at the Masonic Hall, 20 The Crescent, Taunton, after which Supper was taken in the Library of Kings College Taunton in the early years, but subsequently at number 20, The Crescent.

During the early years of the Lodge many great honours were bestowed on its members, most notably in 1961 when Bro J.T.S. Hutchins, a Steward, of the Lodge was installed as Lord Mayor of the City of Winchester one of the oldest mayoralties in England; and in 1962 Geoffrey Rippon M.P., the then Secretary's son and an Old Aluredian, was appointed as first Minister of Public Buildings and Works and duly sworn in as a Privy Councillor

In 1967 due to the cost of dining in London the Bylaws of the Lodge were amended and Regular Meetings thereafter were held at The Dominions Hotel Lancaster Gate W2 where dinner was taken after the meeting, except for the May meetings which continued to be held by Dispensations in Taunton. A Dispensation was granted in 1971 for the Lodge to hold its Regular Meetings at the Windsor Hotel Lancaster Gate while the Dominions Hotel was in the course of refurbishment, which became the permanent venue after an alteration of the Bylaws at the 50th Regular Meeting.

At the 51st Regular Meeting held on 9th February 1973 it was unanimously agreed that in future the Fathers (being Freemasons) of Old Boys and present pupils of Kings College Taunton be accepted as Joining Members of the Lodge, and in the following years several such fathers of members of the Lodge have become Joining Members. At this time several Dispensations were sought and given for Regular Meetings to be held in Taunton.

In 1976 the Lodge resolved to move its regular place of meeting from the Windsor Hotel Lancaster Gate London to the Masonic Hall Taunton in the Province of Somerset, and to change the dates of its meetings to the 2nd Saturday in March, September and November and the Friday preceding the 2nd Saturday in June which was duly effected and the Warrant transferred from London to the Province of Somerset. The Lodge met by dispensation in Taunton on Saturday September 11th 1976 and has done so ever since. The Regular Meeting held on 11th December 1976 was attended by the R.W.Bro Lt. Col. H. Owen Hughes OBE, ED Provincial Grand Master to welcome the Lodge to his Province. By chance he had been present at its Consecration while home on leave

from Hong Kong and South China where he had been District Grand Master.

In 1977 W.Bro A.C. Robinson was promoted to the rank of PJGD and in 1982 he was made an Honorary Member of the Lodge as a mark of appreciation for his long and devoted service. He had held office of Secretary of the Lodge since 1963 having been the Founding WM. Also in 1982 W.Bro H.W. Culverwell was invested as Provincial Grand Organist and at the 100th Regular Meeting held on Saturday March 9th, R.W.Bro K.C. Kinnersley, PGM, honoured the Lodge with his presence.

The Silver Jubilee Meeting was held on Saturday 9th November 1985 which was attended by 23 members and 41 visitors including V.W.Bro G.A. Parrott PGSwdB Deputy PGM W.Bro S.H.A.F. Hopkins SGD Asst PGM and the Provincial Team who dedicated the Lodge Banner.

In 1987 W.Bro A.T.W. Robins succeeded W.Bro Larcombe as Secretary, and in 1990 he undertook a sponsored walk from Yeovil to Weymouth and cycled back, raising £350 for the 1993 Festival. In 1991 he walked from Yeovil to Westminster and raised another £610 for the Festival. The Lodge's contribution to the 1993 Festival totalled £9,043. Another notable fund-raising accolade goes to W.Bro J.A.G. Norman the Treasurer who in 2005 undertook a sponsored cycle ride over 1084 miles in twenty days, raising over £5,000 for the Children's Hospice S.W.

The 150th Regular Meeting was held on Saturday 13th September 1997 and was attended by V.W.Bro Roger D. Clark, PGSwdB, Deputy Provincial Grand Master and an Honorary Member of the Lodge, who at the regular meeting in May 1992 presented a portrait of the Grand Master, HRH The Duke of Kent to the Taunton Masonic Hall on behalf of the school Lodges of Taunton

At an Emergency Meeting held on 12th January 2002, in the presence of the PGM R.W.Bro Stanley H.A.F. Hopkins, together with twenty members and 63 visitors, the Rev. Canon S.F. Bloxam Rose OA, Senior Chaplain of Millfield School was initiated.

At the Regular Meeting held on 9th November 2002 he was passed to the Second Degree by the WM and Officers of the Millfield School Lodge, and raised in March 2003 in the presence of V.W.Bro the Rev. Canon Neil Collings PGC.

In October 2003 W.Bro P.E. Smith the last surviving Founder was presented with a 50th Anniversary Certificate at the Installation Meeting of his mother Lodge, Fidelity and Sincerity 1966 at Wellington. W.Bro Smith was a retired solicitor and SW Somerset Coroner. Also, in his younger days, he had played rugby for the County of Somerset.

At the Installation Meeting on 9th September 2006 the Lodge was presented with its 4th Acorn Achievement Award for its contribution exceeding £14,000 to the 2007 Festival which was a considerable achievement for such a small Lodge whose members almost all belonged to other Lodges as well, and whose target had been £8,000.

John de Clivedon Lodge No. 7824

Meets at the Masonic Hall, Clevedon.

Warrant dated 1962

In the early 1960s a group of brethren, mainly from Coleridge Lodge 1750 discussed the idea of starting a new Lodge.

The country was now rapidly recovering from the deprivations of the Second World War and so the concept of a Dining Lodge in Clevedon was formed. Before the Second World War it was traditional for members attending Lodge meetings to wear dinner jackets. The new Lodge was to be the first in the area to revive this tradition, and was to concentrate its efforts on fine wining and dining.

The idea was to have a Lodge where the ceremony, whilst maintaining all the important elements of Masonic ritual was to be kept as simple as possible in the Lodge Room, but which would concentrate its main efforts at the festive board, and so Nigerian workings were chosen.

Thus John de Clivedon Lodge was formed in the minds of the Founders with Coleridge Lodge 1750 being the sponsoring Lodge and eight of its members being founders.

The Ceremony of Consecration took place on Monday, 30th April 1962 and was conducted by the Provincial Grand Master for Somerset, R.W.Bro Brig. A. de L. Cazenove, together with the officers of the Provincial Team. W.Bro L.V.W. Storey, PPrJGD was installed as the first Worshipful Master with Bro E.N. Park as Senior Warden and Bro R.P. Bowyer as Junior Warden. After the ceremony the brethren retired to a very fine festive board indeed.

A frequently asked question by visitors and new members is who was John de Clivedon? Recently discovered information by W.Bro A.A.R. Wilkinson, PM, gives an insight into the history of this 14th century Knight:

One of the people who had great influence in Clevedon in the Middle Ages was Sir John de Clivedon. It is known that from the year 1291, when the Parish Church broke away from the rule of the Augustinian Canons of Bristol, much building work took place. This was the period when the old Norman South Transept was pulled down and the present one, dedicated to St. Thomas the Martyr, was built on a considerably larger scale. A moving spirit in this and other developments was Sir John de Clivedon.

Although there may have been a house on the site of Clevedon Court from Norman times, it was Sir John who erected the most ancient parts of the present building during the reign of Edward II (1307-27). He is also known to have been one of the Knights at the Stepney Tournament (1308).

The first recorded reference to the Chapel of St. Thomas the Martyr occurs in Sir John's will, dated 9th August 1336, in which he directed that he should be buried in that Chapel of the Church of St. Andrew. The St. Thomas referred to would undoubtedly be Thomas a Becket, the influential Archbishop who had been murdered in Canterbury Cathedral in 1170.

Other details of Sir John's will are of interest. He left a silk cope to the High Altar of the Church and to St. Thomas's Altar a set of vestments and a silver chalice. To Thomas, the perpetual Vicar of Clevedon, he left a horse with full armour, which was to go before his body on the day of his burial, or twenty marks, whichever the Vicar might prefer. He also left the rest of his vestments to the Chapel of St. Peter in his Manor of Clevedon Court. That chapel still exists within Clevedon Court, and was only rediscovered in modern times.

John de Clivedon Lodge jealously guards the tradition of the past. The five course Festive Board is still a splendid and enjoyable completion to a good ceremony upstairs. Pre-dinner sherry, wine on the table and port or whisky with the cheese and biscuits is still as it was originally intended. One thing has however changed as a concession to modern accepted principles. Havana cigars are no longer given to every Brother at the end of the meal.

Backwell Lodge No. 7964

Meets at the Masonic Hall Nailsea

Warrant dated 1964

The village of Backwell in 1964 was rapidly becoming an area much sought after by the citizens of Bristol as a village with both serenity and beauty in which they could spend their home lives. So a number of Backwell residents including Ted Udall and Mike Bond assisted by semi-Backwellians such as Roy Ware and the Rev. John George and imports from all over Scotland and England decided to form a Lodge based on the village.

A number of names for the Lodge were suggested including Rodney the name of a famous Admiral who once resided in Backwell. However it was decided that as all the steering committee were Backwellians why complicate matters and "Backwell" it became.

Under the sponsorship of the Tyntesfield Lodge 4494, Backwell Lodge was founded on 24th April 1964 with W.Bro John Terrett as first Master. W.Bro Leonard Williams as Senior Warden, Bro The Rev John George was the Lodge's first Chaplain.

In the early days of the Lodge a number of candidates were proposed, and many of these were residents of Bristol. All were refused membership as at this time only candidates from Backwell or neighbouring parishes were accepted. However those who were accepted received the Entered Apprentice song at the Festive Board, this being introduced by Bro Austin Shock. Backwell was the first Lodge in the area to do this, many other Lodges following their lead. The first person to be entertained in this way was W.Bro Ray Wade, son-in-law of our Founding Master. Bro Wade became the Lodge's 11th Master in 1974.

The Backwell Lodge of Instruction came into being in April 1976. From the beginning it was innovative in that the members could occupy any of the offices, including the Worshipful Master, and was the making of many of the future Officers and Masters of the Lodge.

The first Preceptor was W.Bro Gerry Pitchers followed in 1977 by the ever-willing W.Bro Ray Wade. It was also agreed that the Lodge of Instruction should host an annual meeting in October, this eventually took the form of a demonstration night with a ceremony being performed by brethren of the Lodge of Instruction. On more than one notable occasion the "candidate" has been the Provincial Grand Master, invited for that purpose.

In 1981 a Daughter Lodge, Wraxall was formed with Backwell donating the past Masters collar.

In 1985 the Worshipful Master Bro Richard Farmer heard a rumour that, if invited, the Provincial Grand Lodge Team would be pleased to visit a Lodge and perform a ceremony. An invitation was made and the team performed the ceremony of Raising for Bro Derek Abbas on the 21st March 1986. The first time the Provincial Team had done such a thing. These days the Team visits Lodges on a frequent basis, but Backwell was the first.

The first 25 years being the most exciting part of the Lodge's history, the subsequent period has been one of gentle involvement. A notable event occurred in April 1990 when W.Bro Richard Farmer was appointed Lodge D.C. The traditions and rituals which the Lodge holds dear are embodied in W.Bro Richard.

Also for a Lodge of small membership we have been honoured by the Province and Grand Lodge in no small measure, notably W.Bro Rev. John George as Provincial Chaplain. Our first candidate, W.Bro Ray Wade as Provincial Standard Bearer, later to be promoted to Past Provincial Grand Registrar, and then to Past Provincial Junior Warden. The aforementioned W.Bro R. Farmer became Provincial Deputy Grand Director of Ceremonies and then Past Provincial Junior Grand Warden. W.Bro Terry Stevens was appointed Provincial Grand Director of Ceremonies and then to the Grand Rank of Past Assistant Grand Director of Ceremonies. W.Bro Graham Bowerman to Provincial Grand Secretary, and also to Past Assistant Grand Director of Ceremonies, and finally in 2008 W.Bro Paul Bond to Provincial Senior Grand Deacon.

The Lodge has always had a strong family feel about it, with many young men following their fathers or fathers in law into the Lodge. Most notable of these being the late W.Bro Mark Brown who was the Lodge D.C. at the time of his early and tragic death. W.Bro Mark had been honoured by the Province with the rank of Provincial Assistant Grand Director of Ceremonies and was destined for many high honours in the future. His father, W.Bro Reg Brown had served the Province as both a Steward and Sword Bearer being the Provincial Charity Representative for the north of the Province. In 2008 W. Bro Reg was promoted to Past Provincial Junior Grand Warden.

Also worthy of a mention is W.Bro Alan Peters, the only Founder Member of the Lodge still active, all the other surviving Founders being Honorary Members, who was first given the Provincial rank of Deputy Director of Ceremonies later promoted to Past Provincial Junior Grand Warden and then to Provincial Senior Grand Warden in 1997, subsequently achieving the Grand Rank of Past Assistant Grand Director of Ceremonies.

His son, W.Bro John Peters who served as Provincial Junior Grand Deacon, then as Past Provincial Junior Grand Warden, also served as Provincial Senior Grand Warden in 2007 thus making these two brethren the only father and son in the history of the Province to both hold this high office. A great honour for Backwell Lodge.

The Lodge although not large in numbers is always at the forefront of Provincial affairs. It was the first Lodge in the Province to reach its target for the 2007 Festival, as well as being the highest per capita contributor. The Lodge is without doubt living up to the high standards set by its Founders

St. Dunstan's Lodge No. 7973

Meets at the Masonic Hall, Hanover Square, Glastonbury

Warrant dated 1st June 1964

St. Dunstan, the greatest Saxon saint, was born in Baltonsborough, outside Glastonbury, in 909AD. He was a talented musician, illuminator, designer and metal worker who was destined to become a great monastic leader. Many believe it was St. Dunstan who devised the monarch's consecration ceremony on which coronations right down to the present day are based. The great man was reputed to have been an alchemist who could turn mercury into gold. He also had a special way of controlling the devil.

It was said that the devil was always making playful attempts to topple St. Dunstan from the straight and narrow, and favoured the guise of a seductive maiden or starving beggar. However St. Dunstan did not stand for such nonsense. Using red hot tongs, he tweaked the devil's nose, causing him to howl and flee in terror.

In the early 1960s, W.Bro Norman James, a well known local businessman and a Past Master of The Pilgrims Lodge 772 was concerned at the length of time it was taking for would be members to be initiated and he therefore got together a committee to consider a second Lodge in Glastonbury.

The principle members of that committee in addition to Norman James were Dr. Ainsworth, George Bullied (local solicitor), Reg Green (retailer), all were Past Masters of The Pilgrims Lodge and George Murdoch, Past Master of Loyal Vacation Lodge 6209, All were in full agreement to form a second Lodge, but there was some dissent from Pilgrims members and only after a full committee meeting in which the Worshipful Master Wyatt Snell gave his casting vote in favour, was the new Lodge approved.

The question of a name for the new Lodge received a lot of attention. Various names were put forward, St. John's, St. Benedict's, St. Crispin, Arimathea and one or two other Christian names. But it was George Murdoch in his own style, who stated what the name of the new Lodge would be and that he would not expect any dissent from the committee.

We have to remember he said that Glastonbury is the holiest part of England in as much as it was the cradle of Christianity in our country. It was in the town that Joseph of Arimathea built the first wattle church and that in the village of Baltonsborough nearby a child was born in 909 who later became Archbishop of Canterbury. The name of that man was St. Dunstan and that will be the name of the new Lodge. George received his wish; there was no dissent from the committee.

St. Dunstan's Lodge was consecrated on the 1st June 1964 and the first Master was W.Bro Norman James, the working tools and regalia were given to the Lodge by the thirteen Founder Members.

The first meeting was held on the 7th July 1964 and was a double Initiation ceremony; nine Joining Members of the Lodge were also welcomed on that evening. During the next three years in order to clear the back log of would-be members, and to build up Lodge membership, a total of nineteen new members were Initiated, Passed and Raised by using double ceremonies for all degrees. Even on some occasions having a double ceremony in one degree followed by a second double ceremony in another degree on the same evening. This situation created a very strong Masonic bond and sincere friendship between the "twin" candidates which has in many cases lasted a lifetime.

Over the years the Lodge has had many characters, one of which, very sadly, was recently lost in W.Bro Arthur Edwards. Arthur gave a presentation at the 40th Anniversary meeting of the Lodge on the subject of Lodge characters. Many of them are remembered, in his words:

"The late W.Bro Norman James for the number of medals he wore on his regalia, more medals than Idi Amin."

"The late W.Bro George Murdoch, the last of the Founder Members, who at his home in Taunton had a photograph in full Highland Dress, which made Braveheart look like a cissy."

"The late W.Bro Alan Barnett, who was the first Initiate into the Lodge and the first to be Worshipful Master."

"W.Bro Ron Lukins, who at 91 years old is still a very active member and Lodge Chaplain. When he was Director of Ceremonies he was known to correct a mistake made by a Deacon with an "accidental" crack of his wand on their ankle."

"Bro Arthur Moss, one of the first Joining Members and who has been a Mason now for 53 years."

"The late W.Bro "Ginger" Harris, a legend in his own time. A local Policeman who controlled the rough element with his own form of justice. "I will only hit you once". All his ceremonies were carried out in the Ginger Harris workings, and know one ever argued."

"The late Bro David Garn who loved a Third Degree Ceremony so that he could have a snooze. He always had a Brother on each side of him in case he snored."

"W.Bro Trevor Holman, whose rich velvet tones in voice and song are well known to all."

"The late W.Bro Stanley Durston, "Mayor of Sharpham." Stan drove an expensive 4x4 Range Rover, which was often referred to by the brethren as "Stan's tractor"."

"The late W.Bro Ray Chiffers, local Farmer and a big man, in stature and character and a popular responder to the "Visitors Toast.". He was one of the "three Rays", who succeeded each other into the Masters chair. W.Bro Ray Chiffers 1989, W.Bro Ray Southam 1990 and W.Bro Ray Burridge 1991.

And many more; too many to mention.

The Lodge has organised a number of successful gentleman's evenings, from which it has without any pressure had many new members come forward. It is also very active in supporting, both local and Masonic charities. St. Dunstan's is fortunate to be a very popular Lodge with the number of visitors it receives and it looks to go from strength to strength in the future.

Tynte Lodge No. 7994

Meets at the Masonic Hall, Bridgwater

Warrant dated 1964

Tynte Lodge 7994 was founded and consecrated in 1964. It is a Daughter Lodge of the Admiral Blake Lodge 4692, and the Granddaughter Lodge of the Lodge of Perpetual Friendship, 135. All three Lodges meet in Bridgwater. Tynte is a well known and respected Somerset name, and the main family had its roots in Wraxall, near Nailsea. The Parish history of Wraxall mentions a John Tynte in 1410. By the late 18th Century the Tynte family had intermarried with the wealthy Halswell and Kemeys families, thus securing valuable estates in Somerset and South Wales.

The splendid Past Master's Jewel displaying the Arms of the Kemeys-Tynte family

The first Tynte to be associated with Somerset Masonry was Sir Charles Kemeys Tynte who was initiated into Freemasonry in 1767 at a Lodge meeting in the Bear Inn, Bath, now the Royal Cumberland Lodge 41. His descendent, Charles Kemeys Kemeys-Tynte, was initiated into the Lodge of Perpetual Friendship in 1817. A few months later he assisted the Provincial Grand Master R.W.Bro Arthur Chichester to initiate his son Charles John Kemeys into the same Lodge. In 1839 a Grandson was also initiated. All three had distinguished Masonic careers.

In 1820 Charles Kemeys Kemeys-Tynte became Provincial Grand Master for Somerset after only three years in Masonry and served in that office until 1860. Colonel Tynte, as he was known from his command of the West

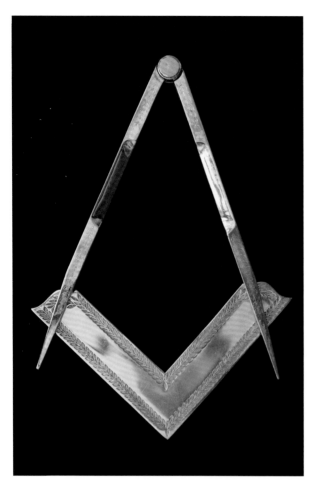

Above: Beautifully Engraved Silver Square & Compass
Below: Silver Square - both presented to the Lodge by
Charles John Halswell Kemeys-Tynte

Somerset Yeomanry, was also, apart from a few years, a continuous Liberal MP for Bridgwater from 1820 to 1860.

Almost totally blind for the last ten years of his life he was a greatly loved and respected figure throughout Somerset and, in particular Bridgwater.

In 1915 the family of Kemeys-Tynte was able to revert to the Barony of Wharton and it was the 9th Baron who readily gave his permission to use the family name for Tynte Lodge and to the reproduction of their Arms for the stationery and the Banner. The Lodge Banner was presented and dedicated in 1978. It bears the Arms of the Tynte family, which date back to the 16th century and shows, amongst other things, six crosses and a lion couchant.

The Founders of the Tynte Lodge chose very wisely when they petitioned for a new Lodge as the devotion to duty. The years of service to the community at large by the Tynte family, and its descendants, is obvious to all, and is a fitting name for all Somerset Masons to revere and admire.

Forest of Mendip Lodge No. 8019

Meets at the Masonic Hall, Rickford, Blagdon

Warrant dated 1965

The Forest of Mendip Lodge was formed in 1965 and its successful creation was largely the work of W.Bro Reg Young with the support of fourteen other brethren who, like him, all became Founder Members.

Reg Young was the musical director of the Blagdon Carol Party which used to tour the village and surrounding countryside before Christmas, dressed in Dickensian Costume. In February 1962 at their Annual Dinner at the Star Hotel Wells, Reg was approached by several male members of the Carol Party who suggested that it would be a good idea to form a Masonic Lodge in Blagdon. He pointed out that if it was such a good idea why did they not do something about it! They explained that they were young and inexperienced Masons and thought it would be more appropriate for him to get things started.

He decided that the embryo Lodge would need to find a regular meeting place and it happened that three months later he was having his hair trimmed by Mr R.C. Sampson, a local oracle, and inquired whether the Baptists were still using the hall at Rickford. He was delighted to learn that they had vacated the premises a month earlier.

Reg rang Sir John Wills the same day and an appointment was made for the following day. Sir John was willing for the proposed Lodge to have the use of the Hall and very relieved that the premises were likely to be occupied. So, having secured the premises, W.Bro Reg Young's next move was to visit the Provincial Grand Master for Somerset, the R.W.Bro Brig. Cazenove.

At first the Provincial Grand Master seemed very doubtful whether there was sufficient terrain to draw on; but he was reminded that there were no Lodges in all the Chew Valley nor any between Nailsea and Keynsham. Eventually he gave the project his blessing. W.Bro Young then proceeded to lobby his Masonic friends and eventually fifteen Masons were pleased to become Founders.

The records show that twelve meetings were held and that there were many changes to the personnel. Some of the most eager opted out when an estimated figure of £2,300 was mooted as being the realistic cost in total for starting and equipping the new Lodge; remember this was the early 1960s.

On the 21st March 1962, the Founders unanimously agreed to proceed with the formation of a Lodge and on 19th September 1962 this was confirmed and W.Bro Young was nominated as Master Elect. Meanwhile the Founders, in negotiation with Sir John Wills, proposed that they should carry out the necessary repairs to the building. This did not meet with Sir John's wishes, instead he generously offered £500 towards the repairs, to be repaid as rental over ten years. The Lodge has continued to pay for the upkeep and repair of the building and in return they have paid a modest annual rental.

The Founders had unanimously agreed that the title of the Lodge should be "Rock of Ages" which was thought to be appropriate since the premises would be only a few hundred yards from the well known landmark. However, the Provincial Grand Master would not give his approval. He argued that this could have only a Christian connotation and as the Constitution accepted all creeds who believed in an Almighty Being the name was not acceptable, he suggested the Lodge should be called "Forest of Mendip", a name which found favour with all the Founders.

The next task was to find a Lodge to sponsor the petition and as W.Bro Young was well-known to the members of Birnbeck Lodge at Weston-super-Mare, where he had been organist for a number of years, they readily agreed to act as sponsors. On 15th December 1964 the Founders attended a regular meeting of Birnbeck Lodge when the Petition was

duly endorsed. In March 1965 the furniture and regalia was delivered and five rehearsals were held in preparation for the Consecration.

This ceremony was held at four o'clock on Tuesday 25th May 1965 and was carried out by the then Provincial Grand Master the R.W.Bro Brig. A de Lerisson Cazenove, assisted by the Deputy Provincial Grand Master V.W.Bro Henry Frampton and members of Provincial Grand Lodge. In replying to the Master's toast on that occasion W.Bro Reg expressed his thanks to all his fellow Founders and paid particular tribute to the encouragement and very active assistance he had received from the Treasurer, W.Bro Percy Moore.

Forest of Mendip Lodge has a great deal for which to thank W.Bro Reg Young. Not only was

he a Founder and the first Worshipful Master, he also served as Organist from 1966 until the year prior to his death in 1984 in his 101st year. It is fitting that his portrait hangs in the Lodge in recognition of this service.

Attendance at the early meetings of the Lodge stretched the accommodation to its limit owing to the large number of visiting brethren. One frequent visitor was Bro Bill Whalley (now Worshipful Brother) who early in 1965 was approached with the suggestion that, in his professional capacity, he would be aware when demolitions were being carried out in Bristol, and that he may be able to assist the Lodge to increase its accommodation by installing a spiral staircase to the balcony. A few months later he informed the Lodge that he had obtained one and that it would give him much pleasure to present it to the Lodge. It was fitted the following September under the guidance of W.Bro Norman Minto; it fitted perfectly and, incidentally, consists of fifteen steps.

On Friday 24th April 1981 the Presentation and Dedication of the Lodge Banner took place; the ceremony being performed by V.W.Bro Herbert E. Dyke, the Deputy Provincial Grand Master-in-charge. The Banner was very kindly presented by Bro Fred Rainey.

On 25th May 1990 the Lodge celebrated its Silver Jubilee and the meeting was attended by the Provincial Grand Master the R.W.Bro Stanley H.A.F. Hopkins together with nineteen Past Masters, sixteen members and 39 other visitors. Over the years the Lodge has regularly attracted many visiting brethren no doubt largely due to its attractive and unique premises.

When the Lodge was formed, after each meeting it was customary to adjourn to the upper floor of the Seymour Arms for the "Festive Board"; then for a number of years these meals were provided in Burrington Village Hall. In more recent years brethren have gathered for their meal in the Blagdon Club, and until very recently in the magnificent surroundings of Combe Lodge, once the stately residence of the Wills family. Unfortunately, owing to a change in management at Combe Lodge, Forest of Mendip now dines at the Burrington Inn.

In addition to making their contribution to the Grand Charity, the Forest of Mendip Lodge regularly donates to local worthy causes. Recipients over recent years include Blagdon mini-bus appeal; Blagdon Playground equipment; St Peter's Hospice; CLIC; and the Children's Hospice South West.

Since its consecration in 1965, 65 men have been initiated into Freemasonry in the Forest of Mendip Lodge and 64 brethren have joined from other Lodges and contrary to original predications, members are drawn from a wide area. Although almost half come from the Chew Valley, others come regularly from such places as Weston-super-Mare, Bridgwater, Bristol, Portishead and the Forest of Dean. A few have moved to other parts of the country too far away to attend meetings but still keep in touch.

The wide variety of occupations from which they come provides for a great breadth of experience. The Lodge has welcomed as members Newsagents, Farmers, Sales Executives, Builders, Local Authority Officers, Hauliers, Solicitors, Vicars, Police Officers, Heating Engineers, Motor Mechanics, Civil Servants, Postmasters, Electric Engineers, and Sawyer and a Carpenter to name but a few.

On 4th June 1995, conforming to the principle of more openness about Freemasons' activities, the Lodge held its first Open Day. Members of the public were invited to visit the Masonic Hall Rickford and given the opportunity to ask questions about Freemasonry. The event proved to be a considerable success and the Lodge is considering planning to repeat the event.

Taunton School Lodge No. 8215

Meets at the Masonic Hall, The Crescent, Taunton

Warrant dated 1968

Taunton School Lodge was consecrated on 22nd July 1968 in the tranquil beauty of the School Chapel by the then Provincial Grand Master, R.W.Bro Brig. Cazenove. As a result, it made Taunton unique among the great Public Schools in that it could boast two Lodges and a Royal Arch Chapter bearing its name. The Old Tauntonian Lodge 5735 was not able to act as sponsor for its new sister Lodge as it met in London, but Queen's College Lodge were happy to sign the petition.

At that time the OT Lodge had 78 members, a full programme of work, a waiting list of over two years for would-be Initiates and a daunting 20+ years progression to the Chair. W.Bro Jim Redgrove PJGD Assistant PGM (Surrey), the Secretary of the OT Lodge, suggested that the new Lodge would widen the opportunity for OTs to enjoy "... that finest of all Old School activities ... and that the new bridge over the River Severn might bring Welsh OT Masons within the Somerset sphere of influence". Both prophecies proved true.

The first Master was a distinguished Taunton Mason, W.Bro John Went PAGDC. The first Initiate was Roger Jago, a medical student at St Thomas' Hospital Medical School, and on the same evening Jack Dean, a stalwart of Starkey Knight and Ford's Brewery was also entrusted with the secrets of an Entered Apprentice Freemason.

Four of the Founders were Grand Officers and two others were later appointed to Grand rank, as have two Joining Member and three Initiates. Of the latter, V.W.Bro Dr Roger Jago P.G.Swd.B., P.M. was installed Grand Superintendent in and over Hampshire and Isle

of Wight in July 2001 and R.W.Bro David L. Jenkins P.M. was installed as Provincial Grand Master of Somerset in April 2002. Not a bad record for a small Lodge

There are two Old Tauntonians of particular note. The first was W.Bro Professor Sir Geoffrey Organe MA, MD, FRCS, FFARCS, FFARACS(Hon), FFARCSI(Hon), PSGD. Sir Geoffrey was one of the great pioneers of British Anaesthesia and was appointed as London University's foundation Professor of that speciality at the Westminster Hospital Medical School. As an interesting aside, the Lodge's first Initiate was examined by Sir Geoffrey when he obtained his FFARCS in 1975. The second was R.W.Bro Colonel Myrddin Jones OBE, TD, DL, a Past Master of the OT Lodge and the Provincial Grand Master for Monmouthshire, who was elected an Honorary Member in 1993.

For King and Country

On 7th November 1942 the 10th Battalion Somerset Light Infantry, commanded by Lt. Col. K.G.G. Denny, was rebadged as the 7th (Light Infantry) Battalion of the Parachute Regiment. Despite wastage caused by some soldiers not wishing to undertake parachute training (at that time in its infancy in the British Army) and others, including the CO, failing the necessary medical, 70% of the original strength survived the turnover. By the time the Battalion went into action on D-day it was commanded by Lt. Col. R. Geoffrey Pine Coffin MC, known affectionately by his soldiers as "Wooden-box"!

At 00.50 hrs on D-day the Battalion parachuted into Normandy with the task of securing and holding the area surrounding the bridges across the Caen Canal and Rover Orme at Bénouville and Ranville (now known as Pegasus and Horsa bridges respectively). Some 70 soldiers of the 2nd Bn the Oxford and Buckinghamshire Light Infantry, under the command of Major John Howard, had already landed alongside the bridges by Horsa Glider at 00.10 hrs and taken the German guards by surprise.

The airborne forces were due to be relieved at 11.00 hrs by No. 2 Commando Brigade, under Brig. Lord Lovat DSO, MC The Commandos were the first soldiers ashore on Sword Beech. Despite all the usual problems of command and control inherent in air-borne soldiering the bridges were taken intact and the sea-borne force eventually marched across them led by Lord Lovat's Piper at 14.00 hrs.

Two 7th (L.I.) Para soldiers involved that day were later to become prominent Somerset Masons – Capt. Jim J. Webber, 2i/c of A Coy; and Capt. John D. Went, Admin Capt. of HQ Coy. A Coy held the forward easterly flank against determined German counter-attacks for most of D-day and all its officers were wounded in the process.

The Company Commander, Major J. Nigel Taylor, remained notionally in control from his stretcher, but active command was exercised by Capt. Jim Webber, despite himself having received a gun-shot wound to the chest. Both were casevacced and survived their injuries. John Went served throughout the War relatively unscathed and was later promoted to the rank of Major. Among the many decorations gazetted after that momentous day was a DSO for Lt. Col. Pine-Coffin and MCs for Major Taylor and Capt. Webber.

Bros Webber and Went both had distinguished Masonic careers and achieved Grand rank in the UGLE The former was also the Provincial Grand Master for Somerset in the Mark Degree.

Richard Huish Lodge No. 8518

Meets at the Masonic Hall, Taunton

Warrant dated 1973

Consecrated on 1st September 1973, the Richard Huish Lodge took its name from the former grammar school in Taunton. Like the school the Lodge has been somewhat itinerant, meeting at Wellington (where it was consecrated), Wiveliscombe, back to Wellington, and finally to the Masonic Hall in Taunton.

The minutes of Committee Meetings from 1972 and 1973 reveal that there was a certain reluctance for yet another Taunton-based Lodge, with a number of Masons worried that members would simply be drawn from other Lodges across the area. However, it seems that they need not have worried, for many of the Richard Huish Lodge members are now also Joining Members of other local Lodges.

Supported in the Petition to Grand Lodge by Wellington School, Somerset Lodge 7230, the Founders worked tirelessly until in April 1973 approval was received from Great Queen Street for the new Lodge to be formed. The first Worshipful Master was Rolf Junker, a formidable sports master at the School, who had a variety of ways of ensuring that pupils took part in "games" despite forgotten kit.

Rolf was a Dane by birth, and had during the war served with distinction in the Resistance, was captured and imprisoned by the Nazis, and later honoured by his country. Rolf was followed as Worshipful Master by nearly all of the Founders, though sadly all but five have now passed to the Grand Lodge above. Many were past teachers at the School. The consecration ceremony was conducted by R.W.Bro Lt. Col. H. Owen Hughes OBE, the then Provincial Grand Master, supported by the full Provincial

The Banner bears the School crest and motto
"Spe Certa Quid Melius"
"What better than sure hope"

Grand Lodge team, and attended by 99 other brethren, which would have been quite a crush for the Temple at Wellington! The ceremony was reported to be "superlative" and the guests were entertained "in a most hospitable manner" with Roast Sirloin of Beef at the Festive Board. The initial annual subscription to the Lodge was £4, the Initiation Fee £20, and fees for Joining Members £10. Oh happy days!

The first few meetings understandably were Initiation Ceremonies; and 41 members have been initiated Entered Apprentices since. The September of 1984 was a milestone in the Lodge's history, for that meeting saw the first progression of a Richard Huish Initiate, John Villis, to the Chair of King Solomon. Many have since followed.

John and Martin Howe, and hope that before too long their names will also appear on our role of Past Masters.

Various pieces of Lodge furniture were donated by a number of the Founding Members. Of special mention is the Lodge banner, donated by the late W.Bro Ron Merrett, Worshipful Master in 1977/78 and a past Headmaster of the School. It bears the School crest and motto, "Spe Certa Quid Melius - what better than sure hope", both taken from the family insignia of Sir Richard Huish, founder of the Taunton Great School in 1554, later to form the basis of Huish's School for Boys in 1874. The Bible was donated by our fraternal sponsors, Wellington School, Somerset Lodge, 7230.

As a School Lodge, Richard Huish membership has traditionally been restricted to past pupils, teachers, Governors, and staff of the School, although this has lately been extended to include relatives.

These constraints on membership and the fact that the Lodge meets only four times in the year means that membership has remained fairly low. However, despite this the Richard Huish has a strong reputation as a friendly, happy, and welcoming Lodge with a high proportion of guests at every meeting.

RICHARD HUISH
DIED 1615

Like many School Lodges, Richard Huish has seen a number of blood brothers pass through its ranks. Some are with the Lodge still, but a number are sadly missed. Included in the number are Ken and Hubert Webber (Founders), Sam and Dougie Baker, Denny and Alan Calvert (Founders), and Alan and Mike Davey. Also there are two "Father and Son" combinations; Eric and Michael Saffin, and

Saltford Lodge No. 8633

Meets at the Masonic Hall Keynsham

Warrant dated 1974

Early in 1971 the Master of St. Keyna Lodge 1833, W.Bro L.E. Burden with a few other members of that Lodge, and of Priory Lodge 6913, decided it was high time a new Lodge was formed in Keynsham. At that time there were already five Lodges meeting in Keynsham but these, because of their origins, had always drawn their membership primarily from Bristol and South Gloucestershire, and only occasionally from Keynsham itself. It was hoped that a new Lodge would, in the course of time, have a more local flavour.

Further justification for having another Lodge was that many Masons from other parts of the country were living in the Saltford and Keynsham area and were wanting a Masonic home. They had been accustomed to one or other form of Emulation working, and the Bristol ritual used some of the Keynsham Lodges was apparently not particularly to their liking. Altogether it was felt the time for a new Lodge was ripe.

On the 13th May 1971 the Secretary wrote to the Provincial Grand Secretary asking for any guidance supplementary to the Book of Constitution in forming a new Lodge. Thus it was that W.Bro R.E.F. Smith, PPSGD (Som), Secretary of St. Keyna Lodge was asked to attend a meeting called for 24th May 1971 to help the prospective founders of a new Lodge to attain their objective

At the Provincial Grand Lodge Meeting in Bath on 20th May 1971 R.W.Bro Lt. Col. Harry Owen Hughes, PGM, announced with pleasure that brethren in the Keynsham area consider there is a need for a new Lodge, and on 17th

July 1971 the Provincial Grand Secretary offered every assistance and guidance as necessary and required. Provisional decisions relating to the place and times of meeting, fees and subscriptions etc, were reached and the Secretary was asked to write to the Secretary of the Masonic Hall Company, Keynsham for that Company's requirements to provide all the necessary facilities for the new Lodge.

The principal officers were appointed, and establishment costs, which Ritual to use, the fees and subscriptions to be charged, the framing of byelaws etc were all discussed. It was also decided St. Keyna Lodge should be asked to sponsor the project. By this time over £500 had been subscribed by various founders. So far so good, but difficulties were soon to loom on the horizon!

Thus followed a period of argument and acrimony, which is well enough documented, but cannot be entered upon here. Suffice it to say that the difficulties appeared to arise out of the fears that the formation of a new Lodge would have a deleterious affect on the other Keynsham Lodges. Indeed so entrenched became the positions of the various parties that nine months later The Provincial Grand Master found it necessary to write a letter stating "I want to see another Lodge in Keynsham, but it must start with the goodwill of the brethren".

The Provincial Grand Secretary had in the meantime written to all the Keynsham Lodges for their views and in June 1972 the R.W PGM indicated that although he felt there could well be a need for a new Lodge the presentation of a petition should be deferred until it could come forward with spontaneity.

In June 1972 a request was made to the PGM to receive a deputation from the founders of the new Lodge and it was arranged that they should visit the him at his home at Compton Dundon. It transpired from the meeting that the PGM was satisfied a new Lodge in Keynsham was desirable. He also stated he would like to see some of the objectors so that they could state their case against a new Lodge. This resulted in the PGM writing once more to the Founders saying "bide your time" and expressing his disappointment. And bide their time they did, as there seemed no let up in the disagreements. By this time we were into 1974, and the leading founders were despondent. It was feared the project would die, but at last the light suddenly broke.

As a result of a chance conversation at a meeting of the Forest of Mendip Lodge it was agreed in due course that Forest of Mendip would sponsor the petition for a new Lodge in Keynsham.

The Provincial Grand Secretary being satisfied with this new approach gave the Province's full approval to proceed, and on Friday 27th September 1974 in the presence of the Provincial Grand Master formal support for a petition for the Saltford Lodge was approved unanimously by the members of Forest of Mendip Lodge.

However, the difficulties were not yet over. The Keynsham Masonic Hall company wrote on 21st December 1974 that approval would not be given for the Saltford Lodge to meet at the Keynsham Masonic Hall, a worrying development, only resolved by the intervention of The Province. The Hall Company management recanted and gave the formal approval to Saltford Lodge to meet in the Keynsham Masonic Hall. The many arrangements for the Consecration were made without a hitch, and the Consecration took place on 7th April 1975.

Since then Saltford Lodge 8633 has gone ahead successfully. The membership is growing steadily and most of the early objectors now visit us, and the past troubles seem to have been forgotten. Much of the success of Saltford Lodge since its consecration has been due to the work of the founders particularly W.Bro W.E. Thomas and W.Bro Roy Britton, but the younger members too are doing their part in making Saltford Lodge a useful and very satisfactory member of the Keynsham Group of Lodges.

Vivary Lodge No. 8654

Meets at the Masonic Hall, The Crescent, Taunton

Warrant dated 1975

The first meeting of brethren interested in the formation of a new Lodge in Taunton was held on 23rd July 1974 under the Chairmanship of W.Bro Dr K.C. Bailey PAGDC. Deliberations continued for more than a year during which time the Lodge's name was decided on 24th February 1975 and the formation was formally sponsored by the Lodge of St George 3158, on 3rd March 1975.

The Consecration took place on 17th October 1975 at the Masonic Hall, The Crescent, Taunton by the Provincial Grand Master R.W.Bro Lt. Col. Harry Owen Hughes, aided by fifteen members of the Provincial team. As part of the Consecration ceremony the Provincial Grand Chaplain gave an inspiring Oration on the Nature and Principles of the Institution. At the conclusion of the Consecration the First Master was installed and he then appointed and invested the first Officers. After the meeting there followed the Consecration Dinner. The usual toasts were proposed with responses by the PGM, the Worshipful Master and R.W.Bro W.A. Kneel, Provincial Grand Master for Devonshire, on behalf of the guests.

The collars and jewels of the various offices were donated by the First Officers, the gavels and the Master's square and compasses were donated by various members of the Lodge and the Ballot Box was presented by W.Bro W.A. Bird PrSGW, a Consecrating Officer. The Banner was presented by W.Bro Dr K.C. Bailey PAGDC and dedicated by the Provincial Grand Master on 15th April 1977. Other items of furniture and regalia have been donated subsequently by, and in memory of, various brethren of the Lodge.

The Lodge has continued to meet at the Masonic Hall, Taunton since its Consecration. At the second meeting held on 21st November 1975 the Consecrating Officers were elected Honorary Members, seventeen brethren were elected as Joining Members and the Chaplain, ADC and Stewards were also appointed.

At that same meeting Mr J.A. O'Connell, who died some years ago, was Initiated. Mr T.J. Case was Initiated at the third meeting on 19th December 1975 and later became the first Initiate of the Lodge to attain the Chair of King Solomon on 17th October 1986. The third candidate was Mr I.G. Roberts who was Initiated on 16th January 1976 and who was subsequently installed as Master by W.Bro Case 16th October 1987. Sadly, W.Bro Case died shortly afterwards.

On 19th March 1982 a "Festive Meeting of Founders and Consecrating Officers was held when the First Officers and Consecrating Officers were invited to perform a Raising Ceremony.

All the Past Masters of the Lodge have given great service served both Freemasonry in general and Vivary Lodge in particular. Many have subsequently received Provincial Honours and several Grand Lodge honours, but unfortunately some have now passed to the Grand Lodge above. In addition, many other brethren have given great service, and whilst it is not possible to recognise them all individually here, there were three in particular whose contributions have been of the greatest significance.

Even before the Consecration, W.Bro B.C. Turner PGStdB played an important role; W.Bro Bryon participated in the formation of the Lodge, was responsible for the production of the Lodge emblem, was a Founder Member; was Master in 1978/79 and became Secretary in October 1982 until September 1998. W.Bro N.W. Tucker has been the Treasurer since October 1978, with a short respite between October 1982 and October 1985 while he progressed to the Master's Chair, and Organist Bro A.J. Betty, has enhanced our ceremonies with his music since October 1980. Enviable records indeed.

Vivary Lodge has also fulfilled its commitments in the cause of charity having contributed £13,500 to the 1983 RMBI Festival and £20,000 to the MTGB Festival in 1993. It is interesting to note that the subscription in 1975/76 was £17.50 and £4.00 for Country Members, yet there was a financial surplus for that first year of £624.57.

Vivary Lodge also supported the Provincial 2007 Festival in aid of the RMBI, contributing over £33,000 in total. It has also supported a number of local non-Masonic causes which include the new Children's Hospice at Wraxall, the Conquest Centre of Disabled Riders at Bishops Lydeard, the Selworthy Special School in Taunton and SURE towards the provision of a radiotherapy treatment centre at Taunton's Musgrove Park Hospital.

The Vivary Lodge of Instruction, which has played an important part in the history of the Lodge, held its first meeting on 23rd November 1983 with W.Bro P. Palmer, the first Preceptor, in the Chair, W.Bro B.C. Turner as Senior Warden and Bro I.G. Roberts as Junior Warden. It has met consistently since then imparting Masonic knowledge to the brethren, providing them with the opportunity to gain experience in the various offices, and of performing work of the floor of the Lodge. (The ranks quoted above are those applicable at the time.)

Vivary Lodge has also played an important part in the Masonic life of Taunton and in the Province of Somerset during the last 25 years, and continues to do so. In writing this history and in looking around the Masonic Hall one becomes only too aware that the same names appear time and time again. Much is owed to them all, past and present, a great debt of gratitude. It is hoped that in reading it you will too perhaps be inspired to make your contribution for the benefit of Freemasonry, present and future.

Vivary was formed to provide a Masonic "home" for brethren coming to Taunton and the surrounding area usually either to work or to retire. The Lodge gained a number of its members from the UK Hydrographic Office and, prior to its closure, the Culmhead Radio Station and it still performs that function. Indeed we recently received an enquiry from a Brother from Brazil who is working in Taunton. The 25th Anniversary of the Consecration of the Lodge was celebrated in style at its Installation Meeting in October 2000.

Woodspring Lodge No. 8791

Meets at the Masonic Hall, Yatton

Warrant dated 1977

The concept of the formation of the Woodspring Lodge originated when a number of Councillors of the then Woodspring District Council wished to form a Lodge. The membership of the proposed Lodge never was intended to be restricted in any way to members of that Council, and now in fact the Woodspring District Council is no longer in existence, having been superseded by the North Somerset District Council.

With the support and sponsorship of the Lodge of Agriculture No. 1199, now of course our "Mother Lodge", the Lodge was duly formed at the Masonic Hall in Yatton, and was Consecrated in October 1977 by The Provincial Grand Master for Somerset, R.W.Bro Lt. Col. Harry Owen Hughes, OBE ED accompanied by fifteen Provincial Officers and 104 Visiting members, together with 29 Founder Members, making a grand total of 147 in the Lodge.

It is interesting to note, that the name "Woodspring" emanated from the Woodspring Priory, a church steeped in tradition, a pictorial representation of which being the focal point of the Lodge Emblem, and the Lodge Motto, 'ESSE QUAM VIDERI' translated as 'TO BE AS ONE SEEMS' was a natural and appropriate choice.

The Ceremony of Presentation of the new Lodge Banner was carried out on the 15th of May 1981, by V.W.Bro H.E. Dyke JP, PGSuptWks, Deputy Provincial Grand Master in Charge, and the 'Ceremony for the Dedication of the Lodge Bible' was carried out by R.W.Bro David L. Jenkins, Provincial Grand Master for Somerset, on the 15th November 2002.

There is indeed a fascinating history behind the Woodspring Priory:

It was, in the 12th century, a manor owned by one of the Knights allegedly responsible for the murder of Thomas a Becket, prior to passing by marriage into the de Courtenay family and the Chapel there was dedicated to, (as a penance?), St Thomas, the Martyr of Canterbury. By 1225 the de Courtenays had given the property to the Augustinian Canons of Bristol.

Following the Dissolution of the Monasteries it became secularised in 1536, part becoming a residence.

Nowadays, it is owned by the National Trust, is frequently visited by tourists, and has become a popular choice for holiday lettings, administered by the Landmark Trust.

The Lodge became a reality following meetings in the Town Hall, between District Councillors W.Bro Bill Cox, now sadly no longer with us, and W. Bro Horace Ashman, the Chairman of Housing at the time, and some two years later, Chairman of the District Council.

W.Bro Horace was the first Worshipful Master of the Woodspring Lodge and still regularly attends. Indeed the Lodge was fortunate to have a number of Founder Members active in the Lodge at the time of the anniversary, namely W. Bro Tony Wilkinson, W. Bro Brian Cox, Bro Ken Cordery, Bro David Cox and W. Bro Tom Ward, now an Honorary Member in recognition of the hard work he carried out on behalf of the Lodge, together with those who joined the Lodge during it's first year. These include W.Bro Brian Gilson, who now holds Grand Rank, W.Bro Graham Sharp, and the very first Initiate, W.Bro Tony Snook. Many of them are still actively involved in the Lodge.

The Lodge is very proud to have had as its first Joining member the V.W.Bro Rt. Rev Sir Roger P. Wilson, KCVO, PG Chaplain, known to all affectionately, as 'Bishop Roger'. He had a most distinguished career, being first appointed Bishop of Wakefield and subsequently Bishop of Chichester, during which period he was appointed Clerk to the Closet, a spiritual advisor to the Sovereign. He was appointed Grand Chaplain of the United Grand Lodge of England in 1957. He had been initiated into the Salopian Lodge 262 in 1932 and installed as Master of the Richard Linnecar Lodge in 1956 prior to becoming the first Joining member of the Woodspring Lodge in 1977, where he became Chaplain from 1978 until 1989. At the time of his death in 2002, he had been a Freemason for almost 70 years.

Today, Woodspring is a very progressive and thriving Lodge. Many new and younger members have joined, and are encouraged to take active parts in the Ceremonies, which they do so very well. This participation continues as they progress through the various Offices, and this bodes well for the future of the Lodge.

The Festive Boards take place in a most convivial atmosphere, are always well supported by a large number of visitors, thus helping to ensure that the Lodge continues to prosper. In addition, many enjoyable and imaginative Social Events, again all well supported, are held throughout each year and the proceeds dedicated to Charity.

Founders and members active in 1977, and who are still active in 2007:
Founding Master
W.Bro Horace J. Ashman
in The Chair
Standing, left to right
Bro Ken Cordery MBE
W.Bro Brian Gilson PAGDC
W.Bro Tony Wilkinson PPSGW
W.Bro Brian Cox PPJGW
W.Bro Tony Snook PPJGW

Forest of Selwood Lodge No. 8912

Meets at the Masonic Hall, Frome

Warrant dated 1980

Selwood ("sallow wood") is the Anglo Saxon name for a forest. To the Britons, Selwood's Celtic name was "Coit Maur" both mean the Great Wood or "big forest". Its name is recorded in Anglo Saxon around 894 as Seluudu, which is perhaps also Sealhwudu, or"Sallow wood". An Anglo-Saxon period document states for it a Latin name Silva Magna

The Saxon occupation of Frome (From) is the earliest of which there is evidence, the settlement being due to the foundation of a monastery by Aldhelm in 705. A witenagemot was held here in 934, The name witenagemot derives from the Old English for "meeting of wise men" (witan, wise man or counsellor; gemot, assembly).

The reasoning behind establishing a new Lodge in Frome was that the Royal Somerset Lodge, 973 had a large membership and offered restricted opportunity for new candidates or advancement.

W.Bro Jim Dore the subscribing Secretary, together with Frank Mounty and C.H. Evemy, being Past Masters, approached a number of brethren of Royal Somerset, and other Lodges, whom they thought would be interested and were willing to act as Founder Members. W.Bros E. Naylor, J. Padwick, D. Wright, and Bob Morgan were amongst those founder members, and are still regular attendees today.

The Provincial Grand Master for Somerset at that time R.W.Bro Lt. Col. H. Owen Hughes OBE ED gave his blessing for the founding of the new Lodge. The Petition for a Warrant to form the Lodge was sponsored by the Master, Wardens and Brethren of Royal Somerset

on the 10th May 1979 and the Lodge was duly consecrated on 20th March 1980, by the Provincial Grand Master for Somerset assisted by all his Officers and in the presence of 100 brethren.

The Most Worshipful the Pro Grand Master Earl Cadogan signed the Lodge Warrant.

At the Lodge Consecration, the Provincial Grand Chaplain W.Bro Rev W.T.R. Daven-Morris in his Oration referred to "the name of the Lodge having been well chosen".

"The timber from 'Selwood Forest' which covered some 20,000 acres, extended from what we now call Braydon Forest, near Cricklade in the very north of Wiltshire to Blackmoor Vale in north Dorset, and straddled the Wiltshire/

Somerset border in between. Like other Forests, the Oaks and other Timber were used for many great works of Charity They were dragged out of the woods on the order of the Lord of the Manor for the Building and repair of religious houses and hospitals set aside for the care of the sick and the homeless"

"The Forest of Selwood Lodge symbolises charity and loving kindness, a warm flame for the cold, food for the hungry, shelter for the homeless, love, charity and brotherhood offered in good measure, shaken down and running over and given to all men everywhere"

He ended his Oration with "May the Great Architect endue the Officers and Brethren of the Forest of Selwood Lodge with the wisdom and strength essential to it proving to the world the happy and beneficial effects of our ancient order"

The trust shown by our founding members has been justified as The Forest of Selwood Lodge continues to prosper and endure more than 27 years after the issue of its charter.

Today it draws its members from far and wide, having members who were initiated in Scotland, Wales, and the City of London amongst its brethren. Recently the 35th Initiate took his place in the Lodge

When you hear the shout "Timber" at a roll call of Lodges at Provincial Grand Lodge you will know we are in and are about the Forest.

No matter where your home, if the opportunity to visit The Forest of Selwood Lodge should presents itself, you can be certain that you will be offered a warm sincere and hearty welcome, an excellent Festive Board and equal hospitality.

The Officers and Brethren of the Lodge adhere to the Masonic principle of being happy and promoting happiness. They support charities both outside of Freemasonry and within it and have achieved the Fifth Acorn for the RMBI Somerset appeal.

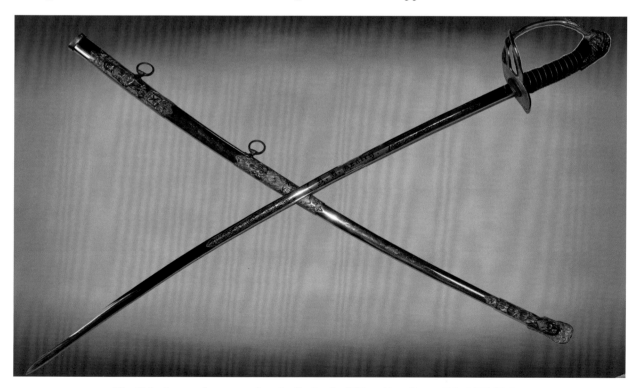

The Tyler's sword presented to the Lodge by W.Bro Alex Carter PPrJGW SLGR,
A genuine Officers Dress Sword Circa 1895 from the USA, with etched designs to the Blade

Gerard Lodge No. 8999

Meets at the Masonic Hall, Keynsham

Warrant dated 1981

The creation of Gerard Lodge 8999 was due to the long connections with the St. John Ambulance of W.Bro Lennard E. Burden and of his family since 1900. It was in 1971, as Worshipful Master of St. Keyna, that his first attempt to form the Lodge was made but the time was not right and the ambition was not realised until ten years later.

The name Gerard was taken from the Blessed Gerard, Founder of the pilgrim's hospice in Jerusalem from which the Order of St. John evolved.

Gerard was conceived as a Saturday daylight Lodge to convene at lunchtime work a ceremony, followed by a high tea and continue into the evening with a dinner dance with the ladies. All undertaken in evening dress. The Lodge would meet in September, December and March with the Installation in June.

21 brethren from various lodges in and around Somerset, several with associations with the St John Ambulance, agreed to become Founders. The Petition was presented to St. Keyna Lodge 1833 at their regular meeting on 13th April 1981. The brethren unanimously approved and recommended it for the favourable consideration of the Most Worshipful Grand Master. It is worth noting that other Lodges outside Keynsham had also offered to sponsor the new Lodge.

Gerard Lodge was consecrated on 19th September 1981 by the R.W Provincial Grand Master Kenneth Caswell Kinnersley supported by the Provincial Team. The Banner was also dedicated on that day. All the Founders received a Jewel to commemorate the occasion.

The Lodge Banner incorporates the eight pointed cross of Amalfi, a pilgrim's stave and a motto "Summo Ducente Deo", the later chosen by W.Bro Burden while he was designing the Banner and Badge. The Latin words mean "Under the Guidance or Leadership of God". This he felt very appropriate due to pilgrims making their pilgrimages under God's leadership and the Masonic Order meets under God's guidance.

The white represents Purity, red the Blood of Life and black, Death. The cross, which is also used by the Order of St. John, was originally used by the merchants of Amalfi on the products they sold. The merchants financed the hospice and the monks wore the cross on their cloaks in order to recognise one another. The stave was used by pilgrims to help them on their way and also as a means of protection while on pilgrimage to Jerusalem.

It was unanimously agreed by the Founders that the Consecrating Officers and also the Past PGM R.W.Bro Lt. Col. H. Owen Hughes be made Honorary Members. All the Founders gave a collar and collar jewel to the Lodge; these were engraved with their names. Various items were also given by other members. Mrs. D Burden made and gave to the Lodge, the Bible Cushion with front drop, the Lodge Banner and the Alms Bags. A number of firing glass were given by Prior Walter Lodge 8687 of London.

W.Bro Burden appointed W.Bro Les Atthews as first Senior Warden and W.Bro Ray Lord as the first Junior Warden. Each followed on as Worshipful Master. Les Atthews later becoming Director of Ceremonies and Preceptor of the Lodge of Instruction establishing a solid practice of the Emulation Ritual which has enabled Gerard to achieve and maintain a high standard of ceremony ever since.

W.Bro Ray Lord, a member of Lodge of Harmony and Concord 8106, at Stapleton, regularly travelled to meetings from Nigeria where he worked and was a member of St George's Lodge 3065. Ray had the especial pleasure of initiating his son David in 1983. Sadly, perhaps as a result of work pressures, Ray died suddenly and prematurely a year or two later.

The first joint Initiates on 5th December 1981 were Leslie Webber and a certain Stuart Hadler. Both held senior roles in the St John Ambulance and thus helped develop the link with that Organisation. A further ten or so St John members were Initiates or Joining Members over the following years.

Gerard Lodge set out with a distinctive social programme that served it well for its first ten years. However with a growing number of brethren living at a distance and others with young families, the Saturday evening event proved difficult to sustain. Ladies' Nights were

however a highlight of the year as were other events such as Valentine's evenings, barbecues and car rallies. These have always been well organised and successful, in large measure due to the flair and enthusiasm of the youngest Founder, Bro Denis Bradbeer, WM in 1987 and our longest serving Secretary.

One of our Founders was W.Bro Edward (Ted) Fowler a Past Master of St Keyna 1833 and WM of Gerard Lodge in 1984. W.Bro Ted is fondly remembered for his dedication, enthusiasm and support as well as for his lively dancing with his sister Rose at all of our social functions. Ted was always available to provide wise counsel and guidance to both the Lodge and individuals. W.Bro Ted completed his 60 years in Masonry in 2008 the year in which he reached his 100th birthday and passed to the Grand Lodge Above.

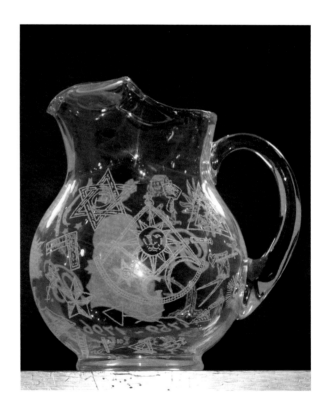

Engraved glass is not uncommon, but a water jug at Keynsham Masonic Hall could almost be said to be the most engraved of all in its depiction of Masonic symbols, and well worthy of close study.

Gerard Lodge has always been a generous supporter of Masonic and other charities becoming a Patron of the RMBI in 1983, of the RMTGB in 1993 and the recipient of five acorns for its support of the 2007 Festival in support of the RMBI.

Over the years experience showed that four meetings were not sufficient and following several years in which Emergency Meetings were required an additional February meeting was regularised. Despite this it proved difficult to Initiate and attract sufficient Joining Members to keep pace with losses and numbers declined from their peak of around 45 in the early 1990s to no more than eighteen some ten years later. Despite this the Lodge persevered, determined to reach its 25th Anniversary. Numbers have slowly increased so that by 2009 the Lodge has over 25 members and visitors comment positively on the friendly welcome and atmosphere that prevails.

Many of our members travel a distance to our meetings. Very few are local residents. Mention must be made of Bro David Causon, Initiated in 1985. A former fireman, David moved to Cornwall. Nevertheless he has been Lodge Tyler for over fifteen years, rarely missing a meeting and for which he was appointed PPrGTyler in 2002.

Many other brethren have given sterling service to the Lodge in various offices and over an extended periods of time. Gerard Lodge is extremely grateful for their dedication without which it would have struggled to survive. In particular, as Treasurer, Bro Herbert Bourns FRCS, and W.Bro David Kingscott; as Secretary, W.Bros Eric Crabtree, W.Bro Denis Bradbeer and W.Bro Bob Stanley; and as DC, W.Bro Derek Wall, W.Bro Stuart Hadler and W.Bro David Sage. In common with many other Keynsham Lodges and Chapters we have also to thank W.Bro Dick Honeywell, WM 1998 & 2003, for his long service as our Organist.

Gerard Lodge is particularly proud that one of its first Initiates W.Bro C A Stuart Hadler. Stuart having been appointed an Assistant Provincial Grand Director of Ceremonies in 1995 later became Provincial Grand Director of Ceremonies, then an Assistant Provincial Grand Master in 2006 and will become Deputy Provincial Grand Master of Somerset in 2010.

The March meeting in 1999 was honoured with a visit from the R.W.Bro Stanley Hopkins, Provincial Grand Master who with the assistance of the Provincial Team conducted a Third Degree Ceremony. To added delight the visiting Deputy Provincial Grand Director of Ceremonies W.Bro Tony Helliker of Athelstan Lodge 9033 successfully delivered the Keynsham version of the Third Degree Traditional History explaining the most unusual and treasured wall plaques featured in the Keynsham Hall section of this book.

2006 marked the 25th year of the Lodge and W.Bro Lennard E. Burden, the founding Master, was again installed as Master of the Lodge. In December 2006 the Provincial Team visited lead by the Provincial Grand Master for Somerset R.W.Bro David Lloyd Jenkins. The PGM accepted the Gavel and took the Chair to dedicate the Lodge Bible which had somehow escaped Dedication in the previous 25 years! The Lodge Banner was renovated for the occasion by Mrs. Diana Burden who had made it at the Lodge's inception.

In recent years Gerard Lodge has sought to strengthen its ties with members of St John who are also members of the Fraternity. They are regularly invited to our meetings, wear their uniform if they wish and, we hope, enjoy the opportunity of sharing the double bond of Masonry and St John membership. We thank our Founders for their foresight in establishing Gerard Lodge and hope that we shall carry the Gerard Banner forward for many years to come in fulfillment of their vision.

Wraxall Lodge No. 9011

Warrant dated 1980

Prior to the full concept of a banner, complete with crest and motif, it was necessary to consider presenting the new Lodge in a truly representative and local manner. The development of the crest is perhaps the most interesting, since many designs were produced and discarded before the present one finally obtained Grand Lodge approval. The crest was developed from part of the design of one of the stained glass windows in Wraxall Church.

This proved to be related to the Wraxall family and consequently permission had to be obtained from the late Lord Wraxall of Tyntesfield before it could be used.

To this end, a group of committee members met Lord Wraxall and invited him to become the Lodge's first Initiate; knowing that his father had been a Provincial Grand Master for Bristol This he promised to bear in mind, but in view of his heavy commitments as County Commissioner for the Scouts at the time, he felt unable to make that commitment.

The designs of both the crest and Lodge Banner were produced by W.Bro Bill Jefford and Mrs Marion Jefford, who also made the Banner. The Lodge motto, 'E Pluribus Unum',which comes from the stained glass window in Wraxall Church literally translated means 'Out of Many, One'. It is a quite simple one, but decisive in its intent.

At the time of considering the formation of the Lodge there were only three Craft Lodges meeting at Nailsea. Each having healthy waiting lists, which meant that those aspiring to progress towards the Master's Chair could not hope to do so for ten years or more.

Of the Nailsea Lodges, Backwell Lodge appeared to attract most visitors, possibly because it met on Fridays, and it was a group of those visitors that floated the idea of forming a new Lodge. These aspiring brethren, with the support of a number of Backwell Masons, formed the nucleus of the 'formation committee' of Wraxall Lodge.

A number of prospective Founders and Joining Members also belonged to Lodges outside the Province and often a long way from where they currently lived, and hence were very keen to form a new Lodge nearer to their homes.

Of the original Founding Members, eight were professional Senior Local Government Officers (Engineers, Education Officers, Architects, Planners etc) of the then Avon County Council, and were in regular contact on a daily basis.

Recognising this collective professional expertise and background, along with their Masonic experience, it followed that the formation and future planning of a new Lodge was well within their grasp. Thus, it was essentially this group which took the lead in 'setting up' Wraxall Lodge, to fully meet what was considered to be an essential additional need. In choosing the name "Wraxall" for the Lodge the connections between Lord Wraxall of Tyntesfield and Freemasonry were once again forged together.

The committee was formed, and from the outset W.Bro Dr John Taylor was a leading member of the team. W.Bro Hugh Evans was chosen as Master Designate. He was a senior member of Backwell Lodge and, as this was to be the sponsoring Lodge, it was felt only fit and proper to have a distinguished member of the Mother Lodge as the first WM.

By the time of the consecration of the Wraxall Lodge there was a waiting list of prospective candidates for initiation. Incidentally, the cost of the Consecration Banquet was a modest, by today's standards, £7.50 per head, including wine. From the first notions of the desire to create a new Lodge, some two years of hard work was required by the Founding Committee, including designing a suitable motif for the Lodge Banner, along with an appropriate logo, before Grand Lodge approval. To these Founders and committee members, the Lodge owes a deep debt of gratitude for their tenacity and strength of purpose.

From the outset, the ritual followed has been strict emulation working, under the Emulation Lodge of Improvement Rules. Dress is standard attire, being dinner jacket, dark suit or morning dress with white gloves. Each year, in October, the Past Masters of and in the Lodge, take over from the regular Officers and put on the 'The Past Master's Night'.

As is current practice in many Lodges, much of the work of the Worshipful Master is now delegated to former Officers of the Lodge, along with some presentation parts to the more junior members. By this means a wider interest is maintained, along with competence in depth throughout the Lodge.

Having now been in existence for just over 25 years, the Lodge has moved into the phase of having the sons and grandsons of Founders entering the ranks of their distinguished predecessors. In particular, W.Bro Bob Swift is the son of W.Bro Brian Swift and along with his son, Bro M.G. Swift, maintains this family continuity. Likewise, there is Bro P.J. Taylor following in the footsteps of his father, W.Bro Dr John Taylor, and W.Bro J.N. Peters following on after his father, W.Bro A.J.N. Peters.

Decorum within the Lodge is of a high order, and a very happy social atmosphere pervades the regular meetings. This naturally spills over to the Festive Board where visitors are always most warmly welcomed. Also, by virtue of having held 'Open Evenings', when interested prospective members are invited to the meet Lodge members, and enjoy the Festive Board (without Masonic Toasting), a steady flow of Initiates has been maintained.

Thus the Lodge remains in a very active and healthy state, both numerically and financially, and the future looks bright.

Athelstan Lodge No. 9033

Warrant dated 1982

In 1979, at King Alfred Lodges' Installation Festive Board, the diners were so numerous that the ante room was laid with extra tables to accommodate the attending brethren. Observing the crush, the Assistant Provincial Grand Master suggested there was room for another Lodge in Weston. Little did the Assistant PGM realise that those casual comments would set in motion a chain of events that culminated in the consecration of Athelstan Lodge 9033, warranted on September 3rd 1982.

Thus began three years of preparation and negotiation, mostly by enthusiastic King Alfred members looking to the future of Masonry in Weston-Super-Mare, while St Kew as the senior Weston Lodge, became the sponsor. Of its founding members, Athelstan is currently privileged to count W.Bros L.V. Crews, P.T. Kimmins and A.J. Bowen as surviving Honorary Members.

The new Lodge was named Athelstan after the ninth century grandson of King Alfred who, as King, was credited with granting Royal Charter to York Rite Masonry that established trade rules and charges that obligated a mason's loyalty to God and his Master.

With variety and character in mind, the twenty Founding Members adopted Taylor's Workings knowing there to be few other Lodges in the West Country practising such ritual. The first Officers each donated their respective collars and jewels and Bro Wilf Lyons donated the Lodge Banner depicting Athelstan as he is represented in Cambridge's Corpus Christi College, presenting a book to St Cuthbert. Miniature tools and furniture were constructed

by Bro Alf Bowen for the Classes of Instruction which were held four times a month in the Windsor Castle pub in a secure upstairs room.

The Installation of Athelstan's first Worshipful Master, C.J. Frazer was successful even in the face of the unfamiliar Taylor's Workings. After two meetings however, the solid start of the Lodge was to be in peril with the untimely and sad death of its Master.

Resourcefulness and determination rescued the situation by calling upon W.Bro P. Kimmins to occupy the Chair of King Solomon for the remaining part of the year. However, the difficulties of the formative year of the Lodge resulted in the laying of a solid foundation on which to build a successful future.

Unfortunately, the death of W.Bro Frazer was not the only misfortune to challenge the resources of the Lodge. Regrettably in 1990, two days prior to installing the Master Elect, Bro Dickie Garland, the Worshipful Master, W.Bro Hicks, suffered serious health problems, and as Installing Master was unable to undertake the ceremony. Consequently W.Bro Bill Jackson acted as the Installing Master at exceptionally short notice.

W.Bro Bill delivered a ceremony that engendered positive remarks from the Provincial visitors, and was later recommended for the Grand Lodge honour of PAGDC, which he bears with great pride.

Other notable events have been happier ones. Athelstan has seen four of its members propose their sons as Lewises; W.Bros R.B. Elliot, R. Garland, T.J. Rhodes and A.C. Helliker having all occupied the Chair of King Solomon for the Initiation of their own sons.

The Assistant Secretary, J. Burtenshaw, though never having been installed as Master, was honoured with Provincial Grand Rank of PPrAsstGStdB for his services to Freemasonry, and Founder Member Alf Bowen emulated W.Bro Brian West's achievement when, like W.Bro West, he was presented with a certificate marking his 60 years in Masonry. More recently, in the 2006/7 Masonic year, the Lodge was honoured with three Provincial promotions.

A brief examination of some of the members' achievements outside Freemasonry highlights the quality and contributions to society by Athelstan members. W.Bro Chas. Heard served as 2005/6 Mayor of Weston-Super-Mare, Bro Burtenshaw was honoured by the English Table Tennis Association Ltd for 56 years voluntary work, and W.Bro Hall served as a representative of the World Council of Churches in the Middle East.

Visiting is an important activity, and the Lodge is very successful at attracting large numbers of guests as can be gauged, amongst other things, by observing the Lodge's £580 washing up bill for 2004/5! Athelstan's fraternal visiting is geographically wide, and the annual visits to and from Bristol's Temple Lodge 6673 are enthusiastically welcomed. From further afield, W.Bro Sam Boyd has welcomed visitors from the Province of Ulster, while in 2002 seven Athelstan members were warmly received as they made a fraternal visit to the 100th anniversary of New York's Athelstane Lodge.

A most memorable event in 2003 was W.Bro T.L.B. Horner's Installation when the Lodge played host to three Provincial Grand Masters. In addition to our own PGM for Somerset, W.Bro Horner's brother, PPGM for Invernesshire, accompanied by the PGM for Invernesshire also attended.

Charitable giving is a role which Athelstan has embraced whole-heartedly, and as early as 1993 the Lodge donated £25,000 to the Royal Masonic Trust for Girls and Boys. W.Bro Sam Boyd worked tirelessly as Lodge Charity Steward from 1997, achieving most impressive results. Fund-raising for the 2007 RMBI Festival was spectacular, but not to the exclusion of local charities. Indeed, Athelstan is proud of the healthy donations it has made to other good causes which include Prostate Cancer Research at Bristol's Southmead Centre, the Poppy Day Appeal, Weston Bar Code Youth Cafe, The Town Mayor's Charity, Weston Super Kids Appeal and SANDS. Income for these charities has raised through the generosity of Athelstan members and their guests who have attended an imaginative range of social events.

The immediate future promises to hold good for Athelstan as it plans to mark its 25th anniversary by restoring the Masonic Centre's Master's pedestal having achieved its RMBI target.

During the ensuing years of Athelstan's active life, the Lodge has continued to meet nine times a year. The progression of future officers looks secure for several years hence, having annually initiated at least two Entered Apprentices for the last several years.

A policy decision was taken at the outset that the ritual book should not be used in Lodge and to this it has remained faithful to this day. Thus the Lodge and its members work hard to achieve a standard of ritual that any lodge would be proud of without losing that essential quality of fraternal enjoyment that all Lodges strive for.

This account is by no means complete and is not a chronological record; it attempts to be factually accurate but hopes to provide a flavour of Athelstan's life-blood by conveying the enthusiasm with which the Lodge is blessed.

It does not recount instances such as the 'gentle' corrections of the DC or the differences that will inevitably occur in any Lodge where passions have run high and prompted resignations. Neither does it itemise the tireless work of individual officers and brethren. Athelstan works well as a team where each member contributes in a manner that delivers as a whole; together these make up the product that is far greater than the sum of its parts.

Cornucopia Lodge No. 9043

Meets at the Masonic Hall, Keynsham

Warrant dated 1982

It must have been sometime in 1978 that three members of Prior Lodge 6913, suggested that there were enough Freemasons in the Bristol Fruit Market to start a Lodge. With this in mind W.Bro Ray Wade invited W.Bro Ron Wilmott (a member of Priory) and his wife Joan to an evening meal to discuss the possibilities.

Once the meal was over and wives off to watch TV they got down to business. They made a list of known Masons within the fruit market and when this was broadened to include retailers and fruit and vegetable merchants in the vicinity, i.e. Stroud, Gloucester, Bradford-on-Avon, Taunton and Newport, 50 Masons had been identified.

It was decided to hold a general meeting in the boardroom of the Wholesale Fruit Market to test the water. The response was overwhelming

and at that meeting a secretary (Bro E. New), a treasurer (W.Bro Wade) and the first Worshipful Master (W.Bro R. Wilmott) were elected. W.Bro Ron Wilmott had recently vacated the office of Master at Priory. Thus Priory became the Mother Lodge.

It had already been decided that the Lodge would be called "Cornucopia" after the Horn of Plenty, with fruit and vegetables to be prominent in the Banner design.

The centre of the Banner depicts Coopers Hall in Old King Street, Bristol. This building contained the auction rooms which had been used for many years for the sale of produce imported from Spain and South America which was landed at Bristol and Avonmouth docks.

The Cornucopia is prominent in the design of the Banner, as is the consecration date 1982 and the motto 'Uberrime Fides" which translates, "my word is my bond". The reason being that the fruit trade traditionally traded by word of mouth and once this had been given one would not dream of backing out.

A 'round robin' of £25 per head secured enough funds for the Banner which was designed by W.Bro R.E. Wade and made by Carol Eastwood in embroidery, gold thread and appliqué.

The Consecration date had been set for 12th September 1982, and Banner having been completed, the Lodge enjoyed the unique situation of the Banner being dedicated and the Lodge consecrated on the same day by the Provincial Grand Master R.W.Bro Kenneth Kinnersley, and the Provincial Team.

Now the question of a venue.

During the following months meetings were held and the two options of Keynsham and Nailsea resulted. Keynsham won by a short head as there was strong support from the Wiltshire lads. This was carried by majority vote.

Over the next months the groundwork went on. The Lodge had chosen an excellent Secretary and, with the help of the Provincial Office things gradually took shape. It was decided to hold four meetings a year, September (Installation), December, March and June. The meetings had to avoid bank holidays and times of the year when business commitments were at their greatest. Tuesdays were to be the meeting days to avoid weekend high trading levels.

Members who had "volunteered" to hold office each purchased and donated the collar and jewel of their office which were suitably inscribed. In the meantime the Lodge byelaws were formulated. Also the subscription fee, initiation fees, Joining Members' fees and any other rules agreed.

All the Founding Members wore a Founder's Jewel, having been designed and produced for the event. This design was incorporated into the Master's jewel.

It was agreed that the Lodge would conduct its ceremonies using the 1969 Nigerian Workings. This was chosen as the Lodge had amongst its members many who were already using Bristol, Wiltshire and Somerset workings, and it was felt that if they adhered to the Nigerian Workings there would be no excuse for variation.

The first candidate was Bro Harvey Piper a former pupil of the Masonic School in London who spent two years as Worshipful Master of the Lodge. W.Bro T.W. Rogers and W.Bro E.W.J. Mills have also served as Worshipful Master on two occasions.

Since 1982 the Lodge has progressed steadily. Sadly it has suffered more than its fair share of senior brethren passing to the Grand Lodge above which, in relatively a small Lodge such as this can have a disastrous effect. However, the Lodge has weathered the storm and now has a steady flow of new candidates and Joining Members.

The year 2002 saw W.Bro E.W. Cannon becoming the first member of the Lodge to receive an active rank in the Province as a Provincial Grand Steward. He was promoted to Provincial Deputy Grand Director of Ceremonies in April 2008. W.Bro R.S. Holley and P.S. Brown have achieved active rank in Wiltshire whilst W.Bro E.W.J. Mills and G.M. Smith have achieved active rank in Gloucestershire.

Through the efforts of the present and past Charity Stewards, W.Bro T.W. Rogers, W.Bro M.A. Wake and now Bro D.A. Watts (and of course the brethren!) The Lodge succeeded in achieving its 5th Acorn as well as being able to support a wide range of other charities.

Recently a small innovation in our Ceremony resulted in the Candidate, at his Initiation being taken to stand in front of the Banner. The Banner is then described to him. This is to ensure the reasons and guidelines, which were laid down all those years ago, will not be forgotten with the passing of time. It also highlights the loyalty he owes to the Lodge.

Visitors to the Lodge will enjoy a rare and perhaps unique treat at the Festive Board which, will not be explained here for fear of spoiling the surprise for first timers. Suffice it to say it was the brainchild of one of the Founders, is musical, a little whimsical, and very sincere.

Somerset Tablers Lodge No. 9075

Meets at the Masonic Hall, Court Barton, Ilminster

Warrant dated 1983

The Lodge was consecrated on 28th April, 1983 under the sponsorship of Nyanza Lodge 1197 following a meeting within Nyanza Lodge of Masonic Round Tablers and ex-Round Tablers.

The idea of a Round Table Lodge had been originally promoted by W.Bro Stuart Shepherd, a Past Master of Nyanza Lodge, and also Past National President of the Round Table movement in the British Isles, having visited several other Round Table Lodges throughout the United Kingdom during his period of office within the movement.

The Founder members were W.Bros Shepherd, Pedder, Price, Harris, Edwards, Tremaine and Kallender and Bros Browning, Poole, Adams, Cannings, Blackwell, Paul, Hearle, Chapman, Berry, Layzell, Irish and Mellor.

The Consecration Ceremony was held at The Shrubbery Hotel, Ilminster under the direction of the Provincial Grand Master, the R.W.Bro Kenneth C. Kinnersley and the Installing Master, W.Bro Stanley H.A.F. Hopkins, Assistant Provincial Grand Master Designate, together with the rest of the Provincial Team. The ceremony was attended by 115 visiting brethren representing 48 Lodges from eleven Provinces and including eight Round Table Lodges. The Provincial Grand Chaplain, Rev. G.E. Mullard delivered the Oration in which he referred to the Round Table movement and the similarity of its' objectives to Masonry. "Service and Fellowship".

The Round Table motto "Adopt, Adapt and Improve" is incorporated in the Lodge Festive Board Toasts. All members of the Lodge are, or have been, members of the Round Table movement and the Tablers Lodge is a valuable and warm extension of Round Table Fellowship throughout the Province and beyond.

Elected Honorary Members at the first meeting were R.W.Bro Kenneth C. Kinnersley PGM and W.Bro Stanley H.A.F. Hopkins, APGM Designate, and at the subsequent 2nd meeting of the Lodge W.Bro Newton Pitcher, Secretary of Nyanza Lodge 1197. 17 further Joining Members were elected at the 2nd meeting of the Lodge bringing the initial membership up to 38 including Honorary members. The Lodge has now grown to a total membership of 55.

During its 25 year life Round Table Lodge has received strong recognition from the Province with the award of several active collars, perhaps most notably that of J. Peter Layzell, DPGM, as well as many Past Provincial Collars and promotions. The Lodge is still Mother Lodge to barely half the current membership, but is proud to make both continued and regular charitable donations to Masonic and non-Masonic charities.

It continues to attract a steady flow of Initiates and prides itself in providing a popular "extension" to the Round Table movement and the continuance and fostering of fellowship amongst like-minded men throughout the whole of the Province and its surrounding areas.

Showmen's Guild Lodge No. 9089

Meets at the Masonic Hall, Clevedon

Warrant dated 8th June 1983

The Showmen's Guild Lodge was consecrated on the 17th of November 1983. The Lodge takes its name from the Showmen's Guild of Great Britain, which is the governing body of the Fairground industry of which the members of the Lodge are all associated.

The Lodge was formed at the suggestion of Bro R.G. Henderson "for members of the Showmen's Guild of Great Britain in order that they may further their knowledge of the Craft".

There were many Showmen's Guild members who were members of various Lodges throughout the country, but from the very seasonal nature of the fairground business they were finding it very hard to make full attendance of their respective Lodges and therefore to progress through the offices. Thus it was decided to form a Lodge which could accommodate and fit in with the needs of Showmen, and the idea of the Showmen's Guild Lodge was formed.

The founders came from far and wide but there were several who were members, and indeed some Past Masters of the Southey Lodge 6650 which met at Clevedon. It was decided to approach Southey to see if they would sponsor the new Lodge, which they thankfully agreed to do, and it is fair to say that without their help and assistance, the Showmen's Guild Lodge would have struggled to get off the ground. Strong ties with Southey Lodge remain to this day and long may they continue.

The Showmen will always be grateful to such people as W.Bros Fred Matthews, Roy Stephens, John Norris, Burt Bult and Bob Cole to name but a few.

The founders decided that the Lodge should meet four times a year. On the third Thursday in the months of November, December, January and February as this is the close season for the Showmen's business, and that Clevedon should be their home, for which permission was subsequently granted.

Everything was now in place. The first Worshipful Master was to be W. Bro Len Harvey who was himself a Past Master of Southey Lodge, with Bro R.R.C. Henderson as Senior Warden and W. Bro A.R. Jenkins as Junior Warden.

Finally the big day arrived. The 17th of November 1983 and in front of a packed Lodge Room at Clevedon, the Provincial

*Almost certainly not a Masonic artifact, but a
fitting addition to the treasures to be found in
the Clevedon Masonic Hall*

*Founder's Jewel, beautifully enamelled
depicting the Fairground Roundabout*

Team headed by the Provincial Grand Master for Somerset the R.W.Bro Kenneth Casswell Kinnersley performed the Consecration which was followed by a lavish Festive Board at the Walton Park Hotel in Clevedon. It was a very successful evening and a good time was had by all.

The following month of December saw the first ever degree ceremony to be performed by the new Showmen's Guild Lodge. It was of course a First Degree Ceremony, the first Initiate being Bro E.A. Henderson, the son of Bro R.G. Henderson starting a long and proud tradition of Father and Sons and indeed Grandsons within the Lodge. Unfortunately by this time Bro R.G. Henderson was suffering ill health and was unable to progress through the offices and was subsequently confined to a wheelchair. Despite this, he was very proud in 1991 to receive the honour of Past Assistant provincial Director of Ceremonies for his services to Freemasonry.

Thursday 20th November 1986 saw a momentous occasion for the Lodge with the Presentation and Dedication of a splendid and colourful new Banner depicting a traditional fairground roundabout which is a proud symbol of the Showman's heritage

As The Showmen's Guild Lodge only meets four times a year it remains a relatively small Lodge but is now well established within the Province and is extremely proud of its reputation as a friendly, happy and welcoming Lodge and from the foundations laid by its Founders back in 1983 long may it continue.

Somerset Farmers' Lodge No. 9180

Meets at St. Mary's Chapel, Langport

Warrant dated 1985

In 1985 W.Bro Stanley Hopkins, APGM formed a Steering Committee with W.Bro Tom Clothier as secretary, W.Bro M.G. Vearncombe as treasurer plus several other like minded committee members. The Masonic Hall at Bruton was chosen as the venue and Royal Clarence Lodge 976 was the sponsoring Lodge. It was decided that the Lodge would use strict Emulation working. The opening hymn would be 'We plough the fields and scatter' and the first Chaplain W.Bro B. Maidment wrote the closing hymn and the Tyler's Toast both based on an agricultural theme.

The Lodge was consecrated on 12th April 1986 at Bruton Masonic Hall. R.W.Bro K.C. Kinnersley PGM was the Consecrating Officer assisted by V.W.Bro G.A. Parrott DPGM, and W.Bro S.H.A.F. Hopkins, APGM. W.Bro R.M. Morrison PSGW, W.Bro A.T. Holman PJGW and other officers of Provincial Grand Lodge. 145 members and visiting brethren witnessed The Somerset Farmers' Lodge being consecrated according to ancient usage using corn from a Bruton farm, wine from Bruton vineyard, oil from Somerset rape and salt.

W.Bro Stanley Hopkins was installed as the first Master of the Lodge who then invested W.Bro Stuart Parry as IPM. The Worshipful Master then invested the first officers of the Lodge. The Festive Board was held in the Assembly Hall at Ansford School where the brethren ate Somerset roast beef carved at the table by the Stewards and other brethren. W.Bro Joe Laver was the first Director of Ceremonies and set the standard and the way 9180 interpreted Emulation Working, which has remained relatively unaltered during the twenty years of our existence.

For several years the Lodge was very popular with attendances averaging over 60 and sometimes 100 brethren. However by the middle 1990s few candidates came forward for Initiation, and by 2003 it was decided to move the meeting place to a more central part of Somerset. Langport was chosen and since 22nd September 2003 the Lodge has met at St Mary's Chapel with the Festive Board at the Langport Arms Hotel. Since then the Lodge has attracted a number of new members.

The brethren are very grateful for the help received from Portcullis Lodge 2038, for being hosts to the Lodge. Through the generosity of some of their brethren the opportunity was taken to add various pieces of equipment, like the Working Tools etc, so that the Lodge now owns most of its own furniture.

At the first regular meeting in September 1986 there were 28 members. In November 2006 the Lodge membership stood at 47 brethren including three Honorary members, two of whom were consecrating officers and one member balloted for in October 2006. Membership now stands at 34. The Lodge has six Grand Officers as members including a Past PGM and a Past DPGM.

In September 2006 a Lodge of Instruction was started which should help the newer brethren. November is set aside as Charity night at the Festive Board and the Lodge has a reputation for its Hog Roasts with stalls and raffles for charity and in 2006 qualified for its Fifth Acorn award for the Provincial 2007 Festival.

> "*Let the Wealthy and Great,*
> *Roll in splendour and state*
> *I envy them not I declare it.*
> *I eat my own ham,*
> *My own chickens and lamb,*
> *I shear my own fleece and I wear it.*
> *I have woods, I have bowers,*
> *I have lawns I have flowers,*
> *The lark is my morning alarmer,*
> *So jolly boys now,*
> *Here's God Speed the Plough*
> *Long life & success to the Farmer*"

Sir Thomas de Cheddre Lodge No. 9188

Meets at the Masonic Hall Wedmore

Warrant dated 1986

Initial soundings taken regarding the formation of a new Lodge were taken at an Alfred and Guthrum, 4535 Festive Board in December 1983. These met with some enthusiasm, soon to be dampened by adverse reactions from some senior A&G members.

There was however sufficient interest from within A&G, members of other Somerset Lodges and members of Lodges from other Provinces who had relocated to the Cheddar Valley area. The first Meeting of potential founders met in Cheddar on 17th April 1984 in the "Den" of St. Andrew's rectory under the Chairmanship of W.Bro Reginald Ferm.

Following that initial Meeting the Secretary of A&G was formally approached to see if the Lodge would sponsor a new Lodge. The response at that time was not favourable. Application was the made to other local Lodges culminating in a formal approach being made to Benevolent Lodge 446, Wells who subsequently became "Mum", and with the full support of the Province the formalities commenced.

Having been agreed by the forming committee, and submitted to Province, the name of the Sir Thomas de Cheddre Lodge was approved by the PGM and confirmed in a letter from the Prov. Grand Secretary in November 1985, but stipulated that the permission for the use of the name had to be obtained from the family. Also, consent to use the Coat of Arms in our badge, as included in various designs drawn up by W.Bro Denis Underhill, had to be sought.

Clearance of the Lodge Name was obtained and use of the Arms of Sir Thomas was accepted by the College of Arms providing we did not say it was our Coat of Arms. The result can be seen in our Banner today. The Banner, dedicated on 4th March 1997, was the generous gift of W.Bro Stephen Wilkinson, the then Worshipful Master, and reflects many hours of dedicated work by his wife Sally.

The Sponsoring Lodge, Benevolent Lodge 446 approved formal application in Open Lodge on 5th December 1985. There were 21 petitioners, all of whom went on to become Founder Members. A letter was received from United Grand Lodge dated 18th February 1986 agreeing to the formation of the new Lodge.

Although it was the intention for the new Lodge to meet at the Lodge Room of Benevolent Lodge in the Cathedral Green , Wells, Alfred and Guthrum Lodge then offered the use of its larger Wedmore Temple for the Consecration of the Lodge, to be held on Monday 6th October 1986.

Following a buffet lunch on that day, provided by the Founder's wives, the Consecration of the Lodge was conducted by the Provincial Grand Master R.W.Bro Kenneth C. Kinnersley at 3pm. W.Bro Reginald Ferm was the first Master, appointing W.Bros Barry Pardue and Ronald Smith as his Senior and Junior Wardens. Gifts to the Lodge of equipment had previously been made by the Founders. The Consecration Dinner was held at the Swan Hotel, Wedmore.

Honorary Membership of the Lodge was conferred upon:-
R.W.Bro Kenneth Casswell Kinnersley, PGM.
V.W.Bro Gilbert A Parrott, DPGM.
W.Bro M.G. Harkom, Prov. SGW
W.Bro J.B. Dalziel, Prov JGW
W.Bro. Rev. D.S. Bennett, Prov Grand Chaplain
W.Bro R.D. Clark, Prov Grand Secretary
W.Bro T.A. Hughes, Prov Grand DC

Since the Lodge was sponsored by Benevolent Lodge No. 446 and its Consecration was held in the Lodge Room of Alfred and Guthrum Lodge No. 4535 the Masters of those two Lodges acted as Senior and Junior Wardens for the first Installation Meeting of 9188. At future Installation Meetings this became the custom of the Lodge in grateful thanks to those two Lodges for what they had done.

Meetings of Sir Thomas de Cheddre No 9188 commenced at 10 Cathedral Green, Wells, Somerset on 3rd November 1986 at 6.30pm. The Lodge remained based there until February 1997 when in response to the Wells Cathedral authorities, after much debate, an invitation from Alfred and Guthrum and with the blessing of "Mum", the Lodge relocated to Wedmore.

From those early days the Lodge has effectively doubled in membership and continues to meet at the Wedmore Masonic Hall on the second Thursday of the months October through to and including May.

On those occasions its own numbers are added to by the many welcome visitors who find the warmth and friendship of our Meetings and Festive Board a pleasure. Often referred to as a most "Friendly Lodge", visitors do return.

The Lodge is also well known for its social events to involve our ladies on more than just the traditional Ladies' Festivals. The first Lodge barbeque was held at the home of W.Bro Schofield in the summer of 1987, and continued there virtually unbroken for some fifteen years when it became the tradition of the current WM to host the events. Ladies' Festivals are celebrated locally or with weekends away, Christmas lunches and Scottish Nights have also been long runners.

Railway trips, skittles nights and numerous other events have added to the host of socials generating a spirit of friendship between members and guests. Not forgetting the associated and enjoyable fund raising to the benefit of both Masonic and non Masonic charities.

Cheddre is the way maps recorded the spelling of the village of Cheddar until as late as the 1700s. Sir Thomas de Cheddre was the last male heir of the De Cheddre family which for several generations had important associations with both the City of Bristol and the village of Cheddar.

Thomas was the son of Robert & Joan de Cheddre. His mother was an heiress of the Hanam family which had a small manor in Cheddar, later known as Manor Farm in Station Road. He was born in 1382 and died in 1443. He was buried in the canopy tomb in the chancel of Cheddar Church of which he and other members of the family were benefactors. The tomb has a fine brass of a knight in armour, and the family Coat of Arms is Sable, Chevron ermine between three scallop shells argent.

Thomas married Isabel Scobahull of Cornwall. By the marriage there were two children. Isabella, who married Sir John Newton of Court de Wyke, Yatton, Somerset (see tomb in Yatton Church) and Joan, who married Sir John de Lisle who was subsequently killed in battle. She was buried in Wells Cathedral. The widow of Thomas de Cheddre, was buried in Cheddar Church in 1474, beside the canopy tomb and is commemorated with a fine brass and inscription.

Although little is known about the life of Sir Thomas de Cheddre other members of his family had played an important part in the life of Bristol. His father Robert, was a burgess and represented the Shire in Parliament in 1421 and 1426; His uncle Richard was Member of Parliament in 1407, 1413, 1417 and was a knight. His grandfather, Robert de Cheddre was a Mayor of Bristol in 1360 and 1362 and an M.P. in 1369.

Somerset Provincial Grand Stewards Lodge No. 9189

Warrant dated 1986

It was in June 1985 that V.W.Bro Gilbert Parrott Deputy Provincial Grand Master of Somerset suggested to the Provincial Grand Master, R.W.Bro Kenneth C. Kinnersley, that there were sufficient brethren holding or who had held the rank of Provincial Grand Steward to form a Stewards Lodge. The Provincial Grand Master authorised W.Bro Maurice Rich to write to all qualifying brethren to ascertain the interest in forming such a Lodge. The response was very encouraging with 25 brethren expressing an interest in attending the first steering committee meeting.

On the 28th September 1985 the first steering committee meeting was held chaired by the Deputy Provincial Grand Master V.W.Bro Gilbert Parrott. It was stated that the Provincial Grand Master and his colleagues were wholeheartedly in favour of the new Lodge, which was seen as an extension of Freemasonry in the Province in general, and also an active arm of possible support in the administration and organisation of the Province. It was agreed that membership should also be extended to include Royal Arch Chapter and Mark Stewards. A visit was made to the Sussex Provincial Grand Stewards Lodge, founded in 1967 to review and discuss their organisation and activities and a report delivered back to the steering committee.

The second steering committee meeting was held on 30th November 1985. It was agreed that the Lodge would be known as Somerset Provincial Grand Stewards Lodge. W.Bro M. Rich was elected Secretary, W.Bro Rendall Treasurer, and the first Officers of the Lodge were agreed, each of whom purchased and donated the collar and jewel of their office.

The sponsoring Lodge would be St Kew Lodge 1222, and the Consecration would be at the Masonic Temple at Weston-super-Mare. The Lodge would meet three times a year on the 3rd Saturday of the months of October, February and May. It would be a morning meeting followed by lunch. It was agreed that ceremonies would be conducted in accordance with 1980 6th Edition Emulation Working and any variation strictly controlled, and only permitted with the approval of the brethren in open Lodge assembled.

The third steering committee meeting was held on 22nd February 1986 when it was advised that the Petition had been accepted by Grand Lodge and the number in the Register of the United Grand Lodge of England was 9189.

The Banner, which had been designed by W.Bro B.W.J. Cox, featuring the cornucopia, the stewards' badge, the motto "We Serve", and the consecration date 5986 was approved.

The Consecration of the Lodge by the Provincial Grand Master R.W.Bro Kenneth C. Kinnersley and his Provincial Team took place on the 18th October 1986. There were 26 Petitioners present and 34 Lodges were represented. W.Bro T.A. Hughes PAGDC was the Provincial Director of Ceremonies. The Rev. D.S. Bennett Provincial Grand Chaplain gave the Oration. On conclusion of the Consecrating Ceremony W.Bro Stanley H.A.F. Hopkins PSGD Assistant Grand Master took the chair as Installing Master and V.W.Bro Gilbert A Parrott JP PGSwdB; Deputy Provincial Grand Master was installed as Master of the Lodge. W.Bro W.S. Stansell was invested as IPM. The first Joining member of the Lodge was R.W.Bro Sir Lionel Brett P. Dist GM Nigeria

At the first Regular Meeting of the Lodge, on 21st February 1987, the Lodge Banner, the cost of which had been donated by an anonymous member, was dedicated by the Provincial Grand Master R.W.Bro Kenneth C. Kinnersley and his Team. The ladies were invited to dine at the Festive Board, which subsequently became the tradition for the Lodge.

Since 1986 the Lodge has held a steady membership with Joining Members from the Craft, the Holy Royal Arch and the Mark. Meetings are now held at the Temple at Weston-super-Mare where the Lodge was consecrated, but in the earlier years the Lodge moved around the Province and meetings were held in other temples including Yeovil, Keynsham and Bridgwater.

A decision was taken to try a number of other venues to find a location which reflected the spread of the membership throughout the Province. At a meeting in Yeovil it was decided to return to Weston-super-Mare which was considered the most suitable, and the Lodge has since acquired shares in the Weston-super-Mare Masonic Hall Company entitling two members to be appointed to the Board of Directors.

The Lodge decided to adopt red collars, red aprons for the Master and Wardens, and red cuffs for the Master in keeping with the practise adopted by all other Provincial Grand Stewards Lodges. The change was formally carried out by R.W.Bro David Jenkins, Provincial Grand Master who placed the new collar on each of the Officers in turn. An engraved Stewards red Bible frontispiece is used in the Lodge.

Members assist the Province by undertaking duties at the Annual Meeting and other special occasions. The Lodge is pleased to perform a Second Degree ceremony or a Third Degree ceremony on behalf of other Lodges in the Province. In the absence of a ceremony members receive an interesting talk or lecture,

A number of Provinces have Provincial Grand Stewards Lodges and fraternal contact is maintained by exchange visits, usually the Master and Secretary, to the Provinces of Berkshire, Dorset, Gloucestershire, Hampshire, Surrey, Warwickshire and Worcestershire. Whilst all of our members are members of other lodges within the Province of Somerset the Lodge has been able to make substantial contributions to Masonic Charities and other local deserving causes.

Kenneth Kinnersley Lodge No. 9218

Meets at the Masonic Hall, Midsomer Norton

Warrant dated 12th November 1986

Being a relatively 'young' Lodge, much of it's history naturally revolves around its illustrious Founder R.W.Bro Kenneth Casswell Kinnersley, Provincial Grand Master for Somerset, and affectionately known as 'KK'.

In early 1985, as part of its desire to see Freemasonry expand, the Province of Somerset was actively looking to open new Lodges. Many existing Lodges were keen to sponsor a new Lodge but it was decided to offer the honour to Connaught Lodge, the Provincial Grand Master's Mother Lodge in his home town. After much debate and discussion Connaught Lodge was pleased to accept the offer, although at that time a few members felt that the population, and hence potential candidates, might not be sufficient to support a second Craft Lodge in the town. Fortunately, these fears proved unfounded an the two Lodges have thrived and continue to work in harmony.

The then Deputy PGM, V.W.Bro Gilbert Parrott, petitioned the Grand Lodge of England for permission to name a new Lodge after the incumbent PGM. To his surprise, and delight, this request was granted, as it was indeed a very rare occurrence for a Lodge to be named after someone living, a great honour indeed.

After several months of feverish activity by the then Secretary, W.Bro R.N. Filsell, the Treasurer W.Bro F.W. Pillinger, and others, the date was set for the consecration of Kenneth Kinnersley Lodge. It was to be Saturday 11th April 1987.

It soon became apparent that as so many Masons wished to attend the Consecration that the Midsomer Norton Hall would not be able to cope. Hence the ceremony was held at

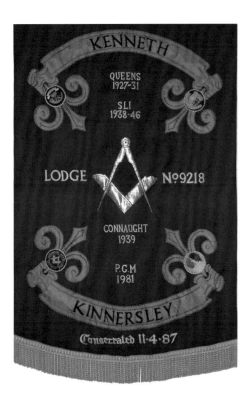

'KK' designed and commissioned the Lodge banner which depicts his time as a pupil at Queen's College Taunton, his period spent as a Captain with the Somerset Light Infantry, his Initiation into Connaught Lodge in 1939 and his time as Provincial Grand Master of Somerset. He and W.Bro John Legg also donated the honours board, which still hangs in the Lodge Room

Keynsham, presided over by V.W.Bro Gilbert Parrott, Deputy Provincial Grand Master for Somerset. The Provincial Grand Masters for both Bristol and Monmouthshire were also in attendance. There were approximately 126 brethren present to witness the Consecration and the Installation of R.W.Bro Kenneth Casswell Kinnersley as the first and Founding Master of the Lodge.

The Rough and Perfect Ashlars of the Kenneth Kinnersley Lodge
The Rough Ashlar shows the KK Crest emerging, at the hands of the more experienced Craftsman

Connaught Lodge kindly allowed their new daughter Lodge to make full use of the fixtures, fittings and regalia of the Temple. The Founder Members and Officers of the Lodge were encouraged to purchase their collars, which was duly done, and each was suitably engraved.

The first regular meeting of the Lodge was held on the second Tuesday of September 1987 when Mark Griffiths, a solicitor from Bristol, was initiated. Mark has since gone on to become Master of the Lodge, Director of Ceremonies and has been promoted to Provincial Grand Rank.

The Lodge is particularly proud of its two Ashlars, which stand in the NE and SE corners of the Lodge. They were commissioned by W.Bro J. Legg in remembrance of our Founder, R.W.Bro Kenneth Kinnersley and were made by W.Bro Alwyn Leek of the Royal Sussex Lodge, No. 53, in Bath. The Lodge is also pleased to own a Masonic Library for the benefit of all the brethren, which was generously donated by W.Bro Alex Parkin.

The Kenneth Kinnersley Lodge continues to thrive and is a fitting memorial to a much loved and respected Provincial Grand Master.

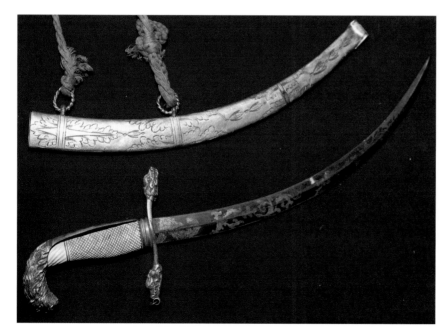

Left: The very ornate and most unusual poignard of the Kenneth Kinnersley Lodge

Somerset Fairway Lodge No. 9251

Warrant dated 1987

Somerset Fairway Lodge is relatively new, having been consecrated in November 1987. It was originally formed to oversee the matches and competitions organised by Somerset Masonic Golfing Society.

In February 1987, the then Secretary of the SMGS, one David L. Jenkins, circulated an idea to all members of the Society with a view to forming a 'Golfing Lodge'.

It was originally proposed to have just two meetings, in June and September, meeting at various locations around the Province with the Installation meeting at Burnham-on-Sea in November. Lodge meetings were to be held at 11.00 a.m. followed by a golf competition in the afternoon. Such was the success that when the Lodge was formed a third meeting in April was soon added.

Members and guests now tend to play golf in the early afternoon followed by a Lodge meeting at a convenient Masonic Hall.

The Lodge was sponsored by Rural Philanthropic Lodge No. 291 and the Consecration Ceremony took place at Burnham-on-Sea on Wednesday 4th November 1987. The ceremony was conducted by R.W.Bro K.C. Kinnersley, Provincial Grand Master assisted by V.W.Bro G.A. Parrott JP, Deputy PGM and W.Bro Stanley H.A.F. Hopkins, Asst.PGM.

There were twenty Founder Members in attendance together with 22 Consecrating Officers and 37 visitors. W.Bro A.J. Rees, PPrJGW was installed as the first Master of the Lodge with Roger Clark and David Jenkins

as Senior and Junior Wardens respectively. An Oration suitable for the occasion was delivered by the Provincial Grand Chaplain, Rev. Preb. Clive Moore.

The Lodge continues to meet in accordance with the original intentions of the Founders and usually Initiates one Candidate each year and there are currently 59 subscribing members.

Many of the golf competitions are open to any Somerset Mason, not just Fairway Lodge members. Matches also take place each year against the Provinces of Monmouthshire, Bristol, Gloucestershire, Wiltshire, Devon, Dorset and Cornwall

Yatton Lodge of Hospitality No. 9299

Meets at the Masonic Hall, Yatton

Warrant dated 1988

The Lodge was created for two reasons. Firstly, in order to bring together the brethren of Somerset with their Fraternal colleagues from over the great Gorge in the City of Bristol. The basic design of the Banner is the Clifton Suspension Bridge, 'bridging the gap' as it were. The second reason was to enable brethren to enjoy the facilities of a Dining Lodge, the standards of catering being generally somewhat rudimentary in the 1980s.

A steering committee was established, largely from Backwell, Wraxall and Agriculture Lodges, and on Friday 17th February 1989 R.W.Bro Kenneth Kinnersley and his team Consecrated the Lodge, as a daughter of the Lodge of Agriculture 1199.

This proved to be a gastronomic marathon which started at Lunch (12.15pm) and concluded with Dinner at 6.30 pm (with Venison as main course.) An attempt was made, with some degree of success, at emptying the Common Market surplus Wine Lake.

On Tuesday 30th October 1990 the new Provincial Grand Master R.W.Bro Stanley Hopkins & his team dedicated the Banner, and the Lodge was able to proceed with colours flying. Among the early driving force were a range of notable brethren, with our Founding Grand Officer W.Bro Fred Mountsey as IPM, W.Bro Alan Peters as WM. On our 10th Anniversary, in February 1999, R.W.Bro Stanley Hopkins and his team again visited us, this time to Dedicate a Bible. Bro Keith Gardner delivered a 'Decadal Dissertation' (posh words for a history) and all retired for a traditional Steak & Kidney Pie dinner.

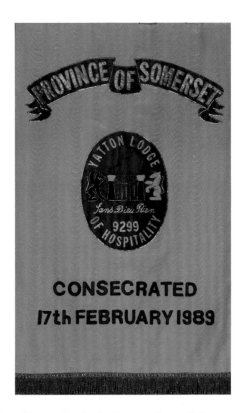

Early officers included a number of future stars. W.Bro Alan Peters became Pr SGW, a post in which he has been followed by his son John who also served 9299 as WM and an impressive DC. Terry Hart succeeded Alan into the Chair and then became Secretary, a post which he vacated to become Provincial Grand Secretary. His successor, Graham Bowerman, again a Past Master of the Lodge, served as Lodge Secretary until he too became Provincial Grand Secretary on Terry Hart's elevation to Assistant Grand Master of the Province. W.Bros A.J. Peters, Bowerman and Hart are all now Grand Officers and one of the Joining Members, W.Bro Arnie Mason, WM for 2008 our 20th year, brought the honour with him. To suitably celebrate the Millennium, in January 2000, the SW and Master Elect, Fred Abernethy was the first of the Lodge's Initiates to achieve the Chair.

Sadly the Lodge lost its Founding Grand Officer W.Bro F. Mountsey (IPM) a well loved and enthusiastic supporter of the Lodge. Also their organist W.Bro Garth Kew, PPrJGW & PPrGOrganist (Bristol). Others of course have passed on over the last twenty years but perhaps the biggest shock was to lose the three musketeers, John Shermon, Julian Rose and Brian Tulk, all Founder members, all Wraxall brethren, all the closest of friends and all far too young.

It will be realized that meeting only four times a year it is only possible to progress one Initiate per year. Even so, time is found for other activities. Among other excellent evenings, on 31st March 1995 the Lodge was honoured to receive the Prestonian Lecture on Sport & Freemasonry from W.Bro John Webb. The main theme, however, may well be 'that Profit & Pleasure may be the result'. The choice of Yatton and its splendid kitchens proved a good one as it had always employed the finest of chefs, who in turn produced the finest of food.

Hospitality being the name, the Lodge was one of the first to annually extend this to the ladies at the Festive Board after a Lodge Meeting, and to take them on Ladies' Weekends instead of the normal local hotel Ladies' Nights, which were becoming passé; happy week-ends were spent in a wide range of environments such as the New Forest, Saunton Sands and Richmond.

The 'Profit & Pleasure' theme was pursued even further when all flew off to Monte Carlo, courtesy of Mr John's Tours. Now, W.Bro John Peters being a somewhat wily fellow; he chartered the 'dog-end' of an Air Canada flight from Montreal to Nice, via London. All the Canadians got off in London and all enjoyed the benefit of a cheap and nigh-on empty plane. The brethren stayed in an excellent hotel in the Marina, with a Memorial Rose Garden to Princess Grace, they dined well, made further inroads into the surplus wine lake, and satisfied at least the 'Pleasure' part of the scheme. Unfortunately, in the 'Profit' aspect, visits to the Casino were not so productive but you can't win 'em all! With rental cars the revellers 'did' the Grand Prix circuit and ventured forth to Grasse, Sospel and other gems in the foothills behind the Riviera.

The serious 'excuse' for being there at all was a Fraternal Visit to the Pillars of Hercules Lodge 4626 (EC) which met in the Library Rooms of St Paul's Church in the Avenue de Grande-Bretagne. Although an English Constitution Lodge, there were a number of French names on the officers list and we were graced with the presence of the Provincial Grand Master for Provence. The cuisine was, needless to say, fit for such a French soirée. Mr John's Tours however did not stop there; Christmas shopping by luxury 'Pullman' type coach in Le Touquet, again with compatible attacks on French victuals, cosmetic stores and a 'booze-only' Tesco!

The Lodge held its 20th Installation in January 2008, when Provincial Assistant Grand Secretary Steve Merryweather (WM) installed W.Bro Arnie Mason PAGStdB (SW) in the chair of King Solomon. The early traditions seem to survive yet.

St Cecilia Lodge No. 9341

Meets at the Masonic Hall, Wedmore

Warrant dated 1989

The man that hath no music in himself and is not moved by the concord of sweet sounds is fit for treasons, stratagems and spoils. The motions of his spirit are dull as night and his affections dark as Erebus. Let no such man be trusted, - mark the music, AUGETE ET CONSERVATIVE HARMONIUM.

So quoted, in March 1992, upon the occasion of the Lodge's Banner Dedication. Awed though we might be, by the reality and power of those words, we must immediately become aware, that in time, we are ahead of ourselves; for our brief though much illuminated history begins some four years earlier, with a casual conversation at a festive board.

Here W.Bro Max Harkcom, speaking with a small group of Masons, including the then Provincial Grand Master the R.W.Bro Kenneth Kinnersley, suggested that it might be a useful idea to have a Lodge whose purpose was to carry music throughout the Province. Such was the enthusiasm to this idea that in a very short space of time musicians throughout the area were joining together to form a steering committee to resolve the technicalities of establishing such a Lodge. Which essentially, it was decided must augment the rich prose of emulation ritual with appropriately supporting music.

Exploration within the pages of this volume and in the published histories of Freemasonry will prove that music has a long association with the Craft in general, and many composers, such as Mozart, have been inspired by it. More intimately, each of us will be able to cite the use of opening odes and musical entertainments at festive boards.

Yet, never before in the history of the Province, and only rarely in Grand Lodge, has music been used as a pivotal part of the ceremony. Thus the committee had a difficult task, if it was to blend into the traditional texts, music that would both amplify and enlighten their recital. That this has been achieved in such a unique way is not only a credit too, but also a display of the Masonic and artistic skills of our Founders.

Thus on Saturday 21st October 1989 the Lodge duly assembled at the Masonic Hall, Wedmore, for its Consecration. In addition to the presiding, Provincial Grand Master for Somerset, there was present on that day, the Provincial Grand Masters for Monmouthshire and Gloucestershire, the Deputy and Assistant Provincial Grand Masters of Somerset with the remainder of the Provincial Team and an additional 61 other Grand Lodge Officers, Provincial Officers and Brethren.

The Ceremony began with the first rendition of 'In this Lodge of St Cecilia', whilst the other music used on that occasion included 'Lead Me Lord (S.S. Wesley)', 'Behold How Good And Joyful A Thing It Is'. Then as the corn, wine and oil, was used to anoint the proceedings, the assembled choir sang When Once Of Old In Israel, (tune: Gonfalon Royal; P.C. Buck.) followed by the dedicating anthem 'O How Amiable Are Thy Dwellings'. It is worth repeating that according to several there present, this was so beautifully sung as to leave a lasting impression, indeed, an impression preserved unto this day.

Many of the pieces that were sung on that first ceremony were to become fixed in the Lodge's catalogue of music and continue to be regularly used. Amongst that number was the poignant and heart given rendition of 'I Will Lift Up Mine Eyes Unto The Hills' as Max Harkcom, the Master Elect was settled into the chair of King Solomon".

Space does not permit to single out any other person present on that occasion, with the exception of W. Bro Steve Jones who was invested as Treasurer of the Lodge, a post he was to hold until the writing of this account, noteworthy as the longest single continuous service in the same post, for any officer to date. Though as you would expect, many of the other Founder Members, then invested, have also given continuous service in support of the Lodge's daily business and indeed the majority of them have had the honour to serve in progression and attain the chair of King Solomon in their own right.

Thus as the Lodge steadily matured, so we arrive once more at the Banner Dedication of March 1992, here as premised above, we heard the Provincial Grand Chaplain in his address, as he told of St Cecilia the Patron Saint of music and reflected upon the nomadic state of the Lodge, as it travelled around the four quarters of the Province, in fulfilment of its duties and ceremonies.

In particular he picked on the symbolism of the Banner itself, pointing out to those present, that the harp of gold, placed as it was on the background of sky blue is representative of heavenly music. He then focussed on the legend inscribed on the post of the harp, which also concludes the verse above and which might be translated as 'Swell and maintain the harmony'.

From its very first season the Lodge has indeed fulfilled this promise, building firm on its foundations or should I say stave, attending special memorial services, and other events like bible and organ dedications. Additionally it regularly assists at the biannual Church Service at Wells Cathedral as well at other eminent anniversaries. To sustain the brethren in these duties, they have many friends and invited guests and of course the mainstay of our Masonic lives, our ladies, to assist in both leading and supporting roles.

Over the years not only have the members of St. Cecilia become known for their musical ability, but also for the research they carry out into ancient rites and ceremonies. The results of such labours are included in its performance catalogue and such dramatic presentations include a step-by-step explanation of the salient parts of the Ceremony of Initiation (in dramatic form), based upon an ancient ritual and the demonstration of the Ancient Masonic Ritual and Ceremony of The Laying of a Foundation Stone, as last practiced in the Province, at the building of St Andrew's Church, Yeovil. The Bible Dedication, held in March 1994, has become a template, which has since been re-enacted at various locations.

As with all societies or groups; when reviewing their historical fortunes, there must inevitably be times of feast. Similarly there are contrasting periods of difficulty and famine.

Such a trial came for us with the turning years of the millennium. To fulfil the nomadic aims of the Lodge, the brethren were often asked to travel the length and breadth of the county on a regular basis, which sometimes conflicted heavily with other areas of commitment. This inevitably created a fluctuation in attendance amongst the participating membership.

The Lodge Committee, with increasing concern, felt that the reputation of the Lodge was being damaged, by an unfortunate succession of poor attendances. At a special meeting, which by coincidence was the 50th meeting of the Lodge, they sought to resolve the problem. An active discussion took place with many ideas being mentioned, but the sticking point seemed to centre on the conflict of attendance, the need to retain the existing format of ceremonies, coupled with the sometimes-difficult winter travelling and above all an aging membership.

Consequently it was resolved that for the present, the Lodge should suspend its nomadic existence and centralise all regular meetings at Wedmore; thereby, reserving the travelling for the more special occasions and duties. Such accommodation has proved beneficial to the membership and in recent years the Lodge has welcomed good levels of initiates and Joining Members, so that once again the choir can be heard in its former four-part splendour.

Despite any difficulty, one aspect of this Lodge that has always been assured, is that wherever it might be found within the Province, visitors have always been certain of a warm welcome, and are commonly heard to remark most favourably on their first sampling of the unique and enjoyable experience. One to be found not only on the floor of the Lodge itself, but also, it is not unknown for them to be overawed and agog at the melodic experience of the festive board itself. Here music is used as a vehicle to enhance the atmosphere of comradeship and well-being.

The delights of the 'Graces' and the uniquely performed visitors toast, remains with them as a lasting and favourable impression of a wonderful evening, for although St Cecilia is but a young Lodge in time, it already has some wonderful traditions, which include not just the music but extends to many small touches such as the superbly illuminated menus and programmes, produced by our secretary, for the installation evening.

St Cecilia though young in years, has matured with a reputation for excellence that can stand proud amongst this company of distinguished veterans.

Emergency Services Lodge No. 9391

Meets at the Masonic Hall, Taunton

Warrant dated 1989

Bearing mind that the Lodge was only consecrated in 1990, that history is not long, and antiques and artifacts are in very short supply.

In February 1989, W.Bro Jerry Heyes, a serving police officer, was being installed in the chair of Tynte Lodge. Amongst the many guests and members present that night were a number of police, fire and ambulance officers, both serving and retired, amongst whom were W.Bro Eddie Owens and W.Bro Ron Nurcombe.

Talking amongst themselves, the idea came to mind to form a new Lodge, one that was to be open to members of the three emergency services, or to those who at some time previously had some sort of connection with any of the emergency services. Both the aforementioned brethren were members of Unanimity & Sincerity Lodge No 261, and that Lodge was approached with a view to sponsoring the new Lodge.

Consequently, on 13th September 1990, the Emergency Services Lodge No. 9391 was Consecrated, and now meets regularly at the Taunton Masonic Temple four times a year.

A great deal of thought went into the motif of the banner. In the centre is the eight-pointed star coloured silver, which is the basis of the badges of the police, fire and ambulance services. In the centre of this is the Somerset Wyvern in red to represent the fire service, the circular green background to represent the ambulance service, all of which is surrounded by a dark blue border representing the police force.

This border bears the title 'Emergency Services Lodge No. 9391'. On one side of the star is a pillar in the Ionic style denoting wisdom, whilst the other pillar is in the Corinthian style denoting beauty. Under the star is the motto of the Lodge, 'Semper Paratus' – 'Always Ready'.

The Banner was dedicated on 27th January 1994 by the Provincial Grand Chaplain, W.Bro A.D. Parker, who also dedicated the Lodge Bible.

Unlike many other older Lodges, Emergency Services has the distinction of having most of its Founding Members not only alive and active, but still regularly taking part in the ceremonies. The Lodge now has a growing core of brethren who regard Emergency Services as their Mother Lodge.

The Tivoli Lodge No. 9417

Meets at the Masonic Hall Weston-super-Mare

Warrant dated 1991

The Provincial Grand Master for Somerset, The R.W.Bro Stanley H.A.F. Hopkins consecrated the Tivoli Lodge, No. 9417 on Saturday 28th September 1991, assisted by members of the Provincial Team. It is the newest Lodge in Weston-super-Mare, and was sponsored by the St Kew Lodge, the oldest in the town. It was the brainchild of three Weston Masons, namely W.Bros Maurice Rich (first Master, now deceased), Brian A.R. Jones, currently the Lodge Secretary, and Bro Russell Bacon, also now deceased, who wanted to involve the ladies more fully into Masonic happenings besides the usual Ladies' Evening once a year, and the occasional Charity event. Thus it became the 2nd Lodge in Somerset to meet on a Saturday morning and invite the ladies to the Festive Board.

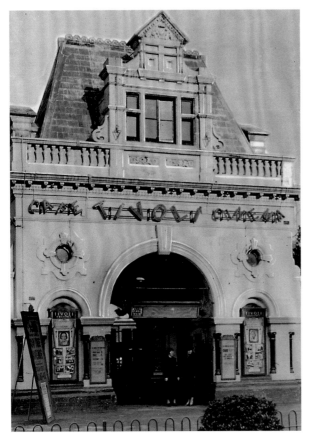

The Lodge was named after the Tivoli Theatre which was destroyed, along with many other buildings during the bombing raids on the weekend of 28th and 29th June 1942. It stood adjacent to the Weston Masonic Centre which, due to the prompt action of the Firewatcher, survived with only minor damage.

The Lodge Banner, which was presented and dedicated in May 1992 depicts the Tivoli building as it was immediately before its destruction. The building represented on the Banner, is in fact the 'Triumphant Arch' entrance to the cinema, whilst the masks of joy and sorrow within the entrance gateway represents its theatrical history. The arch was joined to the theatre by a conservatory type approach complete with grape vines.

Left: The Tivoli Theatre in 1938 after its refurbishment.
Reproduced by kind permission of North Somerset Library Service

*This old photo on the Lodge wall shows the Tivoli
on the morning immediately after the bombing,
with fire hoses in position and water from
the fire fighting still on the ground.*

The local newspaper stated at the time that firemen used water pumped from the sea half a mile away and also from rhynes the same distance in the opposite direction. The Weston Masonic Hall was immediately behind the theatre and was saved from destruction by incendiary bombs through the roof by the quick action of Bro Freeman, the resident Firewatcher. The Masonic Hall was partly occupied as a canteen by the Royal Air Force during the war, which would account for the RAF vehicle alongside the Tivoli arch in the newspaper photograph. The destroyed auditorium can just be seen in the left background.

The Tivoli building was built in the late 19th Century and was first called the Victoria Hall, (from which later the nearby and newly created Victoria Bowling Club took its name) and during the first decade of the new Century, was developed as the Summer and Winter Gardens. Down through the years it became Shanly's Victoria Skating Rink, Albany Ward's Palace of Varieties, The Palace Theatre and finally, The Tivoli.

It had been a concert hall, a theatre, an opera house, a cycle track and a roller skating rink and staged, Pantomimes, Carnivals, Balls and Exhibitions. In 1928 it became a cinema complete with afternoon tea and waitress service and was the first of Weston's four picture houses to show a "talkie".

In 1938 it was completely refurbished and advertised as the last word in air-conditioned luxury. "You'll always be cool at the Tivoli"! Only one piece of the original building appears to have survived, that being a finial from the top of one of the wrought and cast iron gates that stood at the entrance.

49 years later it was presented to the Lodge by one of the brethren who had, as a boy 'collected' it as a souvenir the day after the air raid, and had used it as a doorstop ever since! To prevent this last surviving memory of the Tivoli being lost and forgotten, it was fashioned into a gavel-block, and has been used by each successive Worshipful Master at every Festive Board since the Consecration of the Lodge.

*All that now remains of the Tivoli Theatre;
The Gavel Block*

Olympian Lodge No. 9703

Meets at the Masonic Hall, Nailsea

Warrant dated 1999

Olympian Lodge was proud to be the first Masonic Lodge formed in England (and perhaps elsewhere) in the new millennium, being consecrated on the 8th January 2000. The idea for a Masonic Lodge where "sporting" Freemasons from different Provinces could meet and promote Freemasonry as well as raising money for charity, had often been talked about, but only became a serious proposition in the latter part of the 1990s. The fact that the idea for the new Lodge finally came to fruition was largely due to the efforts of a small group of Masons who had always been closely involved in sport, the most active of whom were W.Bros Arnie Mason, John Massey, and John Peters, who subsequently became the founding Worshipful Master, Secretary and Director of Ceremonies respectively.

After several meetings and much hard work, the steering committee was able to produce some concrete proposals for the new Lodge. Of all the issues considered perhaps the easiest decision was what to name the new Lodge. There was only ever one realistic option for a Sportsmans Lodge, it had to be Olympian. W.Bro Terry Hart, PAsstPrGM, was at that time the Provincial Grand Secretary for Somerset and was instrumental in the development of the idea; without his enthusiastic support and expert guidance it is doubtful if the new Lodge could have become a reality.

Soon many other Masons with sporting links came forward to support the project and it did not take long to find the founding members necessary to sign the Petition to form the new Lodge. By the time of the Consecration, the founders numbered 40 and came predominantly

from the three local Provinces; Somerset, Bristol and Gloucestershire. The Petition was supported by Eldon Lodge 1755, which then became the sponsoring and Mother Lodge, and from which came eight of the founding members including the founding Worshipful Master.

The Consecration Ceremony was held at the Portishead Masonic Centre and was conducted by the then Provincial Grand Master for Somerset, R.W.Bro Stanley Hopkins, who was assisted by the Somerset Provincial Team, which included all the senior officers in the Province. Over 90 Masons including the Provincial Grand Masters for Bristol and Gloucestershire, together with the senior officers from both those Provinces attended the Ceremony.

The three Provincial Grand Masters and all the Provincial Consecrating Team were made Honorary Members of the Lodge at that meeting. Lord Swansea PPrGM (South Wales Eastern Division) attended and was also made an Honorary Member in recognition of his sporting achievements and the fact that he had given considerable support to the new Lodge being named Olympian as there was some opposition to that name at Grand Lodge. Lord Swansea himself was an international marksman and captained the Great Britain and Welsh shooting teams many times, winning a gold medal at the 1966 Commonwealth Games and Silver in 1982; he remained our most illustrious sporting member until his death in 2005.

Eldon Lodge met at Portishead and it was decided that Olympian should also meet there. The installation meeting would be held in February with subsequent meetings in June, September and November, which would allow one Candidate to be initiated, passed and raised by each Master. The Installation meeting was originally held on a Saturday afternoon, but it was soon realised that this was, not surprisingly, causing problems as clashes with sporting fixtures were inevitable. The Installation was therefore moved to a Friday evening in keeping with the other meetings, and the second Friday in the designated months is now the norm.

The ceremony to dedicate the Lodge Banner was held on 21st September 2001 presided, over by R.W.Bro Stanley H.A.F. Hopkins.

On 20th September 2002 the new Provincial Grand Master, R.W.Bro David L. Jenkins presided at the Dedication of the Lodge Bible, which was presented to the Lodge by the then Senior Warden W.Bro Ray Firks. Indeed, much of the regalia and furniture needed to equip the Lodge was donated by individual founding members.

All the founding Officers purchased their collars, and the Master and Wardens also provided their respective aprons; all of these items being equipped with a brass plate bearing the name of the donor. The wands, which were made by Bro Bob Williams who became Master in 2005, were donated by the Founding Deacons. The Tyler's sword was donated by W.Bro David Williams, the founding Treasurer, who also donated a magnificent honours board in memory of his late wife.

The first Initiation Ceremony took place on 9th June 2000 when Bro Brian "Dolly" Vowles was welcomed into the Lodge. Brian was an ideal first Candidate as he was a very well known local sportsman excelling at rugby, cricket and football. Since that first Initiation five other sportsmen have been initiated and approximately 25 others have become Joining Members. The membership currently stands at 66 including Honorary Members and most sports are represented including rugby, football, cricket, hockey, bowls, golf, rowing, sailing, riding and several others which are less well known.

The objectives of the Lodge are the same as any other Masonic Lodge but members are expected to be active, or have been active, in a recognised sport regulated by a national governing body. The meetings are always well attended and although not strictly a dining Lodge, high quality Festive Boards are arranged and the atmosphere is always convivial.

Emulation ritual is performed with some slight variations copied from the Mother Lodge, which gives added interest to the ceremonies and even more to the rehearsals! One particular innovation was the introduction of the "Ceremony of the Lights" which, it was felt, was particularly appropriate to a Lodge with a sporting pedigree. For those who haven't seen this take place, a flame, very much in the tradition of an Olympic torch, is paraded into the Lodge and used to light the Master's and Wardens' candles during the singing of the Opening Ode. It is left lit during the meeting and is paraded out at the end of the meeting at the head of the column.

Another "Olympianism" was the introduction of a referees whistle to call the brethren to order at the festive board. Initially the whistle was used throughout the evening, however this proved a bit too much even for hardened sportsmen to tolerate so the practise has been relegated to the start and end of proceedings, still causing much amusement to visitors.

As well as supporting Masonic charities, it was decided, at the inception of the Lodge, that the main thrust of the fund-raising activities would be directed towards supporting non-Masonic sporting charities, particularly those providing facilities for the disabled or disadvantaged. In the first six years of the Lodge's existence approximately £11,000 has been raised and distributed to disabled sportsmen and women who have included cricketers, rugby players, horse riders, swimmers and sailors.

Portishead Masonic Centre closed at the end of the 2004 Masonic season and Olympian had the honour of holding the last ever meeting in that building on the 11th of June. The meeting was very well attended and the Provincial Grand Master for Somerset, and most of the other senior members of the Province were present, together with members from Eldon and Gordano Lodges who also met at Portishead. A fine Festive Board was held and the old building closed in considerable style but with much sadness.

Lighting the 'Olympian Torch'

Olympian Lodge then transferred to Clevedon where a very warm welcome was extended by the Clevedon brethren, however increasing attendances at the meetings meant the facilities were soon outgrown and the Lodge has now moved to Nailsea, although it is hoped to return to Portishead when a new Masonic Centre is opened in the town.

Freemasonry and sport have much in common, a sense of team spirit, brotherhood, fair play and camaraderie. It is a testament to both institutions that a new Lodge that combines so much that is to be applauded in life has, in such a short time, become a great success.

The Lodge motto "Brotherhood Through Sport" says it all, and long may it continue.

Sylvanus Lodge No. 9741

Meets at the Masonic Hall Yatton
& peripatetically throughout the Western Provinces

Warrant dated 2001

The suggestion for a Hunting Lodge was first made in the mid 1990s by Colonel 'John' Speller, past (Hunt) Master of the Shrivenham Beagles, and now a PM of Old Exonian Lodge in Devon and of the Victoria Rifles Lodge in London. Several years later John Appleby and Joe Doyle, both Gloucestershire Masons, together with Anthony Burnett Brown, a Grand Officer from Wiltshire, all of whom hunted with the Wick Beagles, raised the subject again. There was general interest and agreement but the problem was how and where to start the process.

Bro Keith Gardner, a Somerset Mason and Master of the Clifton Foot Beagles had been party to both the Devon and the Gloucestershire discussions. In February 2000 he raised the matter with R.W.Bro Stanley Hopkins, (PGM for Somerset) who was hunting with the Clifton in Co. Cork, where he had property.

Certain parameters were indicated by the PGM, notably that in the current political atmosphere it would be wise to widen the cover to include all Country Sports; he would also require a Founder's List of some 35 plus Masons. The suggestion that it should be a West Country Lodge to encompass at least the four Provinces of the original promoters was accepted, with, at the PGM's suggestion, Somerset as its 'home' Province.

In March 2000 Bro Gardner wrote formally to W.Bro Terry Hart, then Provincial Grand Secretary for Somerset, with the proposition that a letter be sent to as many potential Founders as the 'proto-Steering Committee' knew personally. The Committee had by now

The Silk Banner from China.
The Boar's Head is the symbol of Hospitality
Dedicated 13th March 2004

grown to seven with the welcome addition of David Hobbs PAGDC, Master of the Wilts & Infantry Beagles, and Michael Hickmott PM (Old Exonian) and MFH of the Mid Devon Foxhounds. After further discussion with the PrGSec a meeting of the Committee was held over dinner at the Castle Hotel Taunton on 25th May 2000. The results were minuted and communicated to the PrGSec.

On 1st June 2000 Bro Gardner wrote to the Secretary of the Yatton Lodge of Hospitality, W.Bro Graham Bowerman, asking if that Lodge would agree to act as Sponsor. Agreement was received on 10th July 2000. By 8th September Gardner was able to write to the PrG Sec advising him that there were now over 50

Masons interested in becoming Founder Members, and suggesting a formal meeting with the Steering Committee.

Accordingly on Tuesday 3rd October 2000 a meeting was held in Wedmore at the Offices of the Provincial Grand Lodge of Somerset and the Committee received the Petition with permission to proceed. Following this meeting Col Speller retired from the Committee due to advancing years, and his place was taken by the JW designate, Andy Tarr, a 'gun'. Provincial Grand Treasurer for Somerset, Tony Norman, (Chairman of the Ilminster Beagles) agreed to become Lodge Treasurer and joined the Committee.

A Roman British intaglio of Sylvanus

By the turn of the New Year of 2001, some 58 Founders and six Joining Members had expressed interest; the Petition was placed before the Sponsoring Lodge's Installation meeting on Friday 26th January 2001. It required 122 supporting Clearance Certificates. W.Bro D.P.S. Hobbs presented the Petition which was accepted and signed by the WM, the SW & JW of 9299. The Provincial Grand Master for Somerset being present he also signed them. The signed Petition was subsequently passed with all Clearance Certificates for Founders to UGLE via the Prov. Grand Sec. Approval was received from UGLE on 29th March 2001 via PrGSec, with a Consecration date of Friday 5th October 2001 at Yatton. The Lodge was allocated No 9741. The name Sylvanus was chosen as 'the God of the Woods', a hunting deity of Rome. The II Legion Augusta, based at Exeter had an officers 'Lodge' dedicated to it.

In April 2001 approval was received for the Lodge Badge design; a Gold Elliptical belt bearing the inscription SYLVANUS LODGE 9741; VIVE la CHASSE. Within, a field of Provincial Blue bearing a gold Boar's Head to represent both Sylvanus domain (beasts of the wild woods) and the Hospitality of the festive board, and our Mother Lodge.

By the end of April, three petitioners saw fit not to proceed; these were Bros Dr. K. Collins, D. Date & R.Y. Edwards. Several Joining member applicants did not pursue the matter further for various reasons. Unfortunately R.W.Bro Stanley Hopkins was not permitted by Grand Lodge to be a Founder Member if he also intended to Consecrate the Lodge; he opted for the Consecration and so became our first and senior IJM, and Chaplain Designate.

On 30th June 2001, 41 members gathered at Yatton for an informal run-through of the Consecration Installation proceedings, and to have a social gathering (with 23 ladies), at a buffet lunch. The membership comprised:

Founders 56; and Immediate Joining Members 6, drawn from the following geographical areas:-
North Somerset 16; Somerset 14; Wiltshire 13; South Gloucestershire. 11; Gloucestershire 5; Devon 2, and from Bristol 1.

Their sporting affiliations being:
Beagles: Wick 9, Clifton 3, Marlborough 1, Ilminster 1, Chilmark 1, Wilts 1.
Foxhounds: Avon Vale 1, Taunton Vale 1, Berkeley 1, Beaufort 1, Mid Devon 1.
Staghounds: Quantock 2, Devon & Somerset 1;
Shooting: 15;
Fishing: 3,
Friends: 20

By the Consecration on 5th October 2001 the Founders List stood at 56 with six IJMs including the PPrGM. Of the Provincial team eight were granted Honorary Membership. The Consecration was a fine event and the Banquet afterwards even finer; the venison was provided by Bro Bill Winn and a Boars Head was paraded to the singing of the Boar's Head Carol.

The Lodge Banner and Bible were consecrated in March 2004, the Banner having been made in China of silk and gold, and the Bible presented by W.Bro Roger Hale, it having been presented to his father many years ago.

Since then the Lodges activities have been performed in the Provinces of Devon, Gloucestershire and Wiltshire, with the Installation meeting in Somerset. Lectures have been given on Sporting Masons each year, and after Lodge, visits with the ladies are made to local places of interest, including Tiverton Castle, the Gin distillery at Plymouth, and during W.Bro John Apppleby's Mastership the group returned to his Gloucestershire home for a fine summer garden party, with swimming, jazz and an excellent tea. Teams from the Lodge have competed in Clay pigeon shoots both at national and local level.

Three ladies lunches have been held each winter at Yatton, one for St Hubert (Patron Saint of Hunting), a 'Scottish Meal' and a St George's Lunch. Charity events such as the soirées at Lacock Abbey have been successful, thanks to Anthony and Petronella Burnett-Brown.

In the first six years three candidates have been initiated and passed to Lodges in their own Provinces for Passing and Raising. The first Initiation was memorable, as the minutes record:-

"It may be worth recording that this, our first Initiation Meeting, seemed fraught with pitfalls. The weather was absolutely atrocious with torrential rainstorms affecting travel from all points. The Senior Warden gave notice of absence due to farming difficulties on Exmoor; the Inner Guard was ill in Surrey. Two brethren had parents die; the ADC had been rushed into hospital and the Asst Secretary's car had broken down. With a Rehearsal at 4pm the WM arrived at 5.30 pm and with the Ceremony due to start at 6pm there was no Candidate!

After waiting twenty minutes he arrived with his Proposer at 6.40pm. Add to this the fact that there was no Organist and had to resort to a floppy-disc that did not know the Opening and Closing Odes and it certainly proved to be a Ceremony to remember."

It should not go unmentioned that the Lodge lost the Founder IPM., W.Bro Anthony Burnett-Brown PJGD, host at our Lacock Abbey fund raising soirées, due to cancer, and Bro Mike 'the Crisp' Bailey who surprised everyone by bequeathing the sum of £5,000 to the Lodge which paid for the Banner (dedicated to his memory) and to various Charities.

Sir Isaac Newton Lodge No. 9801

Meets at the Masonic Hall, Nailsea

Warrant dated 2005

Sir Isaac Newton Lodge was consecrated on Saturday, 8th October 2005 by the Provincial Grand Master, R.W.Bro David Lloyd Jenkins at the Nailsea Masonic Centre as the 88th Lodge in the Province, and also as the first "midweek-daylight" Lodge in Somerset.

Whilst there is no evidence that Sir Isaac Newton was ever a Freemason he certainly consorted with the Masonic members of the Royal Society, of which he was a Fellow and long-time President. He was however the greatest English mathematician of his generation. He laid the foundation for differential and integral calculus. His work on optics and gravitation make him one of the greatest scientists the world has known and one of the foremost scientific intellects of all time.

Being a new Lodge in the second year of existence there is little history – in the normal sense of the word - to relate. There is, however a considerable "pre-history" of the Lodge in its formation period, which was an invigorating and rewarding Masonic experience for all concerned; and which has set the tone for the on-going life of the Lodge.

The idea of a "midweek-daylight" Lodge had been in mind for some time, but it was not until the spring of 2004 when W.Bros Frank Clarke and Neil Sims took the opportunity to discuss the possibility at a friend's birthday party (her husband is now a member of the Lodge) that the idea started to take concrete shape. They soon found seven other brethren of the same mind and the project started to gain enough momentum to justify the formation of a Steering Committee, the first meeting of which was held on 24th June 2004 in the conservatory at the home of

W.Bro Frank Clarke. The Steering Committee was soon augmented by the Provincial Grand Secretary and Director of Ceremonies and comprised:

W.Bro Frank Clarke, PrGChaplain, Chairman
W.Bro Neil Sims, PPrGReg, Vice Chairman
W.Bro John Merritt PPrGSofWks.,Treasurer;
Bro Tony Sims, PPrGStdB., Secretary
W.Bro Graham Bell, PPrAGDC;
W.Bro Lennie Ball, PM 4491
W.Bro Colin Basson, PPrJGW;
W.Bro Brian Hughes, PPrGSwdB
W.Bro Bernard Thompson, PPrSGD;
W.Bro Graham Bowerman, PrGSec
W.Bro Stuart Hadler, PrGDC

The Steering Committee set out the objectives and aspirations of the proposed Lodge and submitted their ideas to the Provincial Grand

Master. It was on 16th August 2004 that they received his formal approval "for the formation of the Lodge to be progressed", accompanied by a blank Petition form. The hard work over the next few months was done with great enthusiasm and cooperation until the final signatures of the 37 Founders were added to the Petition at the first social gathering of the proposed Lodge at the Long Ashton British Legion Club on 26th November 2004. In addition, the initial list of officers was also finalized and W.Bro Neil Sims presented us with his advanced ideas for our Founders Jewel and Banner.

A number of the Founders were members of Estune Lodge No 6817, who became our sponsoring (or Mother) Lodge. The formal sponsorship became effective at the regular meeting of Estune Lodge on 18th January 2005 when the petition, placed formally on a silver platter, was presented to the Lodge. The Petition was read in full to the members by W.Bro Frank Clarke prior to a ballot. The ballot being unanimously in approval of the sponsorship, the Petition was signed by the Worshipful Master (W.Bro Philip Mills)) and his Wardens, and handed over to the Provincial Grand Secretary, who had witnessed the whole of the proceedings. The almost-complete Petition was presented the next day by the Provincial Grand Secretary to the Provincial Grand Master, who added his signature. The Petition was finally complete and sent that same day to the Grand Lodge in London for checking and presentation to the Grand Master.

It was a happy day when news was received from the Grand Lodge in a letter dated 17th March 2005, advising us that the Most Worshipful The Grand Master "had been pleased to accede to the prayer of the Petition" for the formation of the new Lodge.

Most importantly, a Warrant had been issued, under the name of the "Sir Isaac Newton Lodge" with the number "9801" allocated. The next

Grand Lodge Communication, together with the July edition (issue 14) of MQ magazine recorded the issue date of the Warrant as 8th March 2005.

The Provincial Grand Master offered the Petitioners the date of Saturday, 8th October 2005 as the date for Consecration and first Installation ceremonies at Nailsea. We accepted the date with enthusiasm. Now the work really started, and what we had done this point paled a little in comparison with what lay ahead. The Masonic virtues of harmony and cooperation were displayed in their fullest energy as we prepared for the "big day". The scope of work undertaken by the Steering Committee in particular, and the Founders in general, is too wide to mention specifically; but included rehearsals, invitations, seating, Provincial contacts, Jewel design and procurement, regalia etc. Our secretary, in addition to all his other work, kept a record for posterity. Finally, on 8th October 2005, the Founders, the Brethren of the Provincial Team and the St Cecilia Choir started to arrive at Nailsea soon after 8am from all over the Province for an early start to the two rehearsals that had been designed and choreographed with such exactitude and skill by the Provincial DC. During the wonderful Consecration ceremony by the Provincial Grand Master (his first Consecration) all the Founder members moved onto the Lodge floor three times, in three different formations, so that exactitude was an inescapable requirement; and our rehearsals (not to mention the preparation of the Provincial DC) paid off handsomely. Amongst many notable aspects of the Ceremony was the use and symbolism of the Corn, Wine, Oil and Salt poured by the Provincial Grand Master onto the Lodge Board, and the reading in full of the Warrant prior to its delivery into the hands of the Lodge.

After a short break the first Installation Ceremony was conducted by V.W.Bro Peter Layzell, the Deputy Provincial Grand Master when W.Bros Frank Clarke, Neil Sims and Graham Bell were Installed into the three principal offices. A full team of Founder Officers was appointed and invested, including no less than seven Stewards. The full Provincial Team with their ritual, and the St Cecilia Choir with their moving and outstanding music, enhanced the whole proceedings so that those present witnessed a day never to be forgotten. We retired downstairs for a splendid Festive Board and the 110 diners (the maximum we could fit into the Lodge room for the occasion) enjoyed the festivities around circular tables with the Provincial Rulers and Officers spread evenly around the dining tables, to enjoy the fellowship of the day with the Founders and their guests in a truly fraternal manner.

Recent History

In the two year life of the Lodge following the Consecration, we have Initiated and progressed three candidates (one Passing and one Raising were done by our Mother Lodge), and at our first "in-house" Installation, W.Bro Frank Clarke Installed the Founder Senior Warden, W.Bro Neil Sims as our second Master. He in turn Installed W.Bro Graham Bell, our Founder Junior Warden as our third Master; who enjoyed an active year with a full round of ceremonies. We have a good line of succession, including two Master Masons holding office on the Lodge floor and progressing to the Chair. There is no shortage of brethren to participate in our ceremonies. Despite our short viable life we have been awarded an Acorn for our contribution to the 2007 Festival. Ladies are invited to join us at our Festive Boards (except for Installations and Initiations) and they respond with great alacrity so that we often test the skill of the chef and staff at the Nailsea Masonic Centre by seating up to 120 for lunch – and they have never failed to rise to the challenge! We arrange other social events with our ladies which are always well supported. Our numbers have grown from 37 to the mid-

50s, including a number whose Masonic life has been revitalized by our daylight approach. We look to the future with keen enthusiasm.

The Name of the Lodge

9801 is the third English Lodge to be named after Sir Isaac Newton whose intellect was said to "soar like an eagle" over his contemporaries. His treatise "Optiks" gave mankind it's first understanding of daylight; deemed very appropriate for a daylight-meeting Lodge. Sir Isaac Newton is also indelibly associated with apples, one of the undying symbols of Somerset, which we believe is also very appropriate. A more closely Masonic connection is contained in the quotation found on our summons, where his belief in an "Almighty Architect" is clearly stated.

Objectives of the Founders

The Lodge was founded to be a "working" Lodge to harmonize with the changes in Freemasonry in recent years with a relaxed and open attitude, combined with excellence of Ceremonial and a succession of candidates in a "midweek-daylight" format, the first such Lodge in the Province. We enjoy, as anticipated, an excellent Masonic day together, with lunch rather than dinner and if desired, can be home before it's dark, even in January! Involvement in the ceremonies by a wide number of brethren was planned to create satisfaction and an enlivenment of Masonic life for many. The involvement of our ladies and families at some Festive Boards and at other social events acts as a binding agent as we believe Masons should be an active ingredient in their community. Whilst practising the normal Emulation ritual, we already have our own new "traditions" whilst ensuring we honour our Mother Lodge and the Province; and at the same time offering a new and invigorating fraternal dimension to Masonry in the Province of Somerset.

Part Five

OTHER MASONIC ORDERS

The Holy Royal Arch

The origins of the Order are inextricably linked with the very earliest development of Freemasonry and elements of the Royal Arch ritual are to be found in the Third Degree worked during the first half of the eighteenth century. References to the Holy Royal Arch first appear in print following a public procession in Ireland in 1743 and are again in the minute book of a Lodge in York in the same year.

The first record of admission to the mysteries of the degree appears in the minute book of a Lodge in Fredericksburg, Virginia, in 1757.

A desire to continue working the Holy Royal Arch Degree was one of the elements that caused the rift in English Freemasonry during this period. Those in authority in the Grand Lodge formed in 1717 were refining the manner in which Freemasonry was practiced into three distinct degrees. They cast adrift the elements of the ritual that now form the Royal Arch ceremony and which did not fit this new pattern. The adherents of the Ancient Grand Lodge founded in 1751 as a reaction to this and other changes continued to confer the Holy Royal Arch Degree in their Lodges as the culmination of the Masonic journey.

Every Master Mason in Somerset will be aware of the Supreme Order of the Holy Royal Arch through the activities of a Chapter representative in his Craft Lodge and a notice printed at least annually on his Lodge Summons. Exaltation into its mysteries assists the Master Mason to gain a higher understanding of our mortal existence, to symbolically pass beyond the mysterious vale and complete the journey that began at his initiation.

The Degree not only possesses an impressive and beautiful ceremony but is characterised by both the dignity and conviviality at the heart of English Freemasonry.

While the Premier Grand Lodge or Moderns banned the working of the degree in their Lodges, it supported the formation of a separate authority to govern the fledgling order. In 1766 the Charter of Compact was signed forming the Royal Chapter of the Royal Arch Chapter of Jerusalem, the predecessor of today's Supreme Grand Chapter which has authority over the Order in England and Wales.

This bitter rift between the two Grand Lodges was eventually overcome with their amalgamation and the formation of the United Grand Lodge of England in 1813. This new authority declared that the Royal Arch Degree could only be conferred in a Chapter, but at the same time emphasised its close bond with the Craft. Each Chapter was ordered to attach themselves to a Craft Lodge and was recorded under the same number, those which failed to comply with this directive ceased to exist.

This explanation of the origins of the Holy Royal Arch gives an indication of its close relationship with the Craft. The Most Worshipful the Grand Master, His Royal Highness the, Duke of Kent is also the First Grand Principle of the Degree and for many years the Executive Officers of Grand Lodge carried the corresponding responsibilities in Supreme Grand Chapter. It was only with the increased organisational demands of the late twentieth century that this changed.

The Holy Royal Arch hold a unique position in being the only Masonic body recognised with the Craft, as part of Pure Ancient Freemasonry. The Preliminary Declaration to our Book of Constitutions it is explicitly states that 'By the Solemn Act of Union between the two Grand Lodges of England in December 1821, it was declared and pronounced that pure and ancient Masonry consists of three degrees and no more viz., those of the Entered Apprentice, the Fellow Craft an the Master Mason including the Supreme Order of the Holy Royal Arch.'

The Legend of the Degree is set during the period following the end of the reign of King Solomon when the Temple at Jerusalem had been destroyed and the tribes taken into captivity. The candidate for exaltation into the degree symbolically returns to Jerusalem after his release from captivity to assist in rebuilding the Temple.

Together with two other workmen, he is sent to prepare the ground for the foundations of the second temple and makes a discovery that leads to his exaltation into the secrets of the Degree. The explanation of the signs, regalia and furniture of the Chapter reveals an illuminating insight into mans relationship to God. The Royal Arch regalia consists of an apron, a sash and a distinctive breast jewel.

Set of three Principals' Jewels made by Thomas Harper 1818

Exaltation into a Chapter of the Holy Royal Arch is available to any Brother who has been raised to the sublime degree of Master Masons for at least four weeks. Recent changes have provided an opportunity for every Exaltee to advance through the Offices of the Chapter if desired, because advancement to Third Principal is no longer restricted to those who have been Worshipful Masters of a Craft Lodge.

Royal Arch Masonry has been worked in Somerset since the eighteen century. Royal Cumberland Chapter No. 41 meeting at Bath and the Vale of Jehoshaphat No 291 meeting at Highbridge were firmly establish long before the constitution of Supreme Grand Chapter in 1817.

Thomas Dunckerley, whose Masonic authority spread across the western half of Southern England, was the first of three Grand Superintendents appointed in Somerset before the Provincial Grand Chapter was formally constituted in 1880.

At each stage of Freemasonry's development there has been a need for more sophisticated organisational methods and with 26 Chapters now meeting in seventeen different locations throughout the Province their need are well served by an efficient and vibrant Provincial Grand Chapter.

Charity is of course the cornerstone of the Masonic Order and until recently, with a few exceptions; the majority of Royal Arch Companions supported appeals from their Craft Lodges and confined their charitable donations in the Chapter to the Alms collection at the end of each.

A need for change was recognised and social events to raise charitable funds are becoming more common. During the 2007 Festival Appeal the Right Worshipful Grand Master presented the Provincial Grand Chapter of Somerset with an Acorn banner to acknowledge the generous donations made by the Companions.

A Provincial Charity Steward has now been appointed and each Chapter now has a Charity Steward to coordinate the distribution of these funds. A scheme to make an annual donation to a charitable cause selected from propositions made by each of the Chapters.

The Provincial Grand Chapter of Somerset, like all other Provinces, is presided over by the Most Excellent Grand Superintendent and it is he who appoints a Deputy Grand Superintend together with his Second and Third Provincial Grand Principles, who together with the administrative Officers form the Provincial Executive. In addition to their administrative duties the Officers of the Provincial Grand Chapter of Somerset provide support, encouragement and assistance to each of the Chapters. Throughout its history the Province has been particularly fortunate to have had Grand Superintendents who have dedicated themselves to maintain the vibrancy of this beautiful degree.

To those members of the Craft who are not yet Companions of the Holy Royal Arch I invite them to come and join us, you will derive from the Order a high level of enjoyment. You will find true companionship together with good fun and you will be made most welcome. By joining the Holy Royal Arch you will complete your personal journey through Pure and Antient Freemasonry. We look forward to welcoming you.

Grand Lodge of Mark Master Masons of England and Wales and its Districts and Lodges Overseas

You may ask, "Why should a Master Mason become a Mark Master Mason"?

You have passed through the three ceremonies from Apprentice, (the rough ashlar) Fellowcraft, (learning the trade) to Master Mason. To quote the Tools you all received at your Raising, "We are not all operative Masons, but rather free and accepted or speculative". Speculative being the point, in other words, rough, uneven, approximate, all these are speculative.

To learn the basic history of your Masonry and to gain a further knowledge about the very building-blocks on which all is built, consider Mark Masonry.

A Master Mason is Advanced into Mark Masonry and receives the title of Mark Man. During the ceremony his own personal MARK is selected for him enabling him to indent his work. When he eventually becomes a Mark Master, his labour can then be recognised by that mark and his wages given for patient industry and merit. This personal mark is written after his name when visiting a Lodge or communicating with a fellow Mark Mason. A happy but serious Degree not to be missed.

Charities, both Masonic and non-Masonic are at the very heart of Mark Masonry. These range from the personal choices of each Lodge Master, to that of the Provincial Grand Master, The R.W.Bro David Nelson himself.

A perfect example of the latter is the Provincial Grand Master's Endoscope Appeal. In 2004, The Mark Benevolent Fund donated £2 million to help in the fight against prostate cancer. In Somerset, £100,000 of this money was used to purchase a 'Brachytherapy' Cancer treatment unit which was presented to the Bath Royal United Hospital by the PGM accompanied by many of his Mark Men; to complement this new equipment, the Endoscope Appeal was started.

Despite the many calls for charitable response over the following three years, the Mark Masons of Somerset raised £25,000 which was presented by R.W.Bro Nelson to the Hospital early in 2007.

Another very popular Mark Charity collector is the SAMMs (Somerset Ancient Mark Masters) Demonstration Team. Dressed in 18th Century costume and working 18th Century ritual, these valiant men travel far and wide, (including foreign climes) carrying the Somerset Banner and with the assistance of much ale, (compulsory in those earlier days) demonstrate the ceremony. Many well known faces can, at times, be recognised under the powdered wigs! They have their own charity account with which they give generously to many charities.

The Province also has a 'Travelling Keystone' which was introduced in December 1989 by the then Worshipful Master of the Somerdale Lodge, No. 1608 David Brian Nelson. On that occasion the heavy marble Keystone was presented to the W. Master of the Exmoor Lodge, No. 697 with the request that it be delivered by the Master supported by his brethren to a named Lodge at some distance away. This ensured that Mark Masons visited lodges they may otherwise not have attended, allowing them to experience that special friendship that exists between Mark Masons. Money raised on the evening was given to the host Lodge's Charity Account. After twenty years, the Keystone is still journeying around the Province, making new friends and meeting old ones, long may this continue!

For more information visit our website: www.somersetmarkmason.co.uk.

The Most Worshipful Grand Master, HRH Prince Michael of Kent
with the Somerset Ancient Mark Masters (SAMMs) Demonstration Team

The Ancient and Honourable Fraternity of Royal Ark Mariners

The Ancient and Honourable Fraternity of Royal Ark Mariners, more commonly known as RAM or Mariners, has been under the jurisdiction of the Grand Lodge of Mark Master Masons since 1871 and is governed by the Grand Masters Royal Ark Council. Lodges are attached or moored to Mark Lodges assuming their Lodge number.

The Province of Somerset has had a long association with Royal Ark Mariners, early records in Bath indicate that the Degree was being worked from the 18th Century, "1790, William Boyce took all the degrees of ye Red Cross also Royal Ark Mariner".

This quote was taken from the minutes of the Knights Templar Camp of Antiquity No. 1 at Bath and shows that the degree was known before that time. It can be seen that the West Country played an important part in the creation of the early ceremonial.

One of the first established RAM Lodge meeting in Somerset is Irwin No. 119 at Keynsham, which is one of the Oldest Royal Ark Mariners Lodges in the country. The warrant is dated 1873 and therefore has a unique position in the formation and progress of this wonderful ceremony we all enjoy so much;

There are now eleven Royal Ark Mariner Lodges in the Province. The Degree has a "Travelling Ark" similar to the "Mark Travelling Keystone". As with the Keystone, the Ark travels around the Province from Lodge to Lodge bringing Mariners together in friendship and fellowship.

The Degree is over 200 years old and, as its name suggests, has a nautical flavour to it. The Degree portrays the life and work of the Patriarch Noah. It exemplifies the five cardinal virtues of watchfulness, discretion, brotherly love, truth and charity. Legend states that Noah built the wooden Ark for the preservation of his family and all the living creatures of the then known earth; happily it was built in time to preserve mankind from perishing in the 'Great Flood'.

Perhaps it was the combined skills of the ancient boat builders constructing every wooden support, arch or former required for shaping, confining and holding steady the great stone blocks, walls and ceilings created by the stone masons. Time sealed them together, thus forming the great cathedrals we are privileged to enjoy and marvel at to this day, and today we remember Noah and his Ark in our Royal Ark Mariner ceremony.

For more information visit our website:
www.somersetmarkmason.co.uk

The Ancient and Accepted Rite
(Rose Croix)

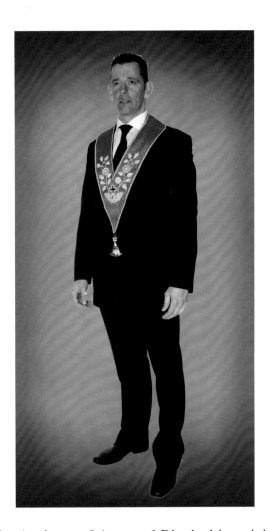

The Ancient and Accepted Rite had its origins in France in the 1750s. Taken to the West Indies by Stephen Morin, the Rite was extended to 33 degrees by Henry Francken and taken to the United States of America.

The Ancient and Accepted Rite came to this Country in 1845 when the Supreme Council for England was constituted under a Patent granted to Dr. Robert Thomas Crucefix by the Supreme Council of the Northern Jurisdiction of the United States of America.

The History of the Order in Somerset was said to begin in 1852 with the granting of a warrant for the founding of St. Peter and St. Paul Chapter No. 6 to meet in the City of Bath.

Charles John Vigne, a resident of that City, and the first Most Wise Sovereign (MWS) of the Chapter was to become a member of considerable influence in the Order, not only in Somerset but also in the affairs of Supreme Council. Under his guidance the Alfred No. 13, Antiquity No. 95, and William de Irwin No. 28 Chapters were warranted. It was no doubt a great disappointment to him when first Antiquity was suspended, and then, by the declining fortunes of William de Irwin ultimately led to the Chapter's warrant being surrendered.

At the time that William de Irwin was warranted in 1870, Somerset had more Chapters than any other County in England and Wales, including the City of London. There followed a period when, apart from the reinstatement of Antiquity and William de Irwin Chapters, there was no development in the County until 1955, a period during which time Supreme Council warranted 286 Chapters in England and Wales, and many more overseas in Crown Dependencies.

The District system of devolved government under the direction of a Deputy Inspector General, was introduced in 1873. The Chapters at Bath, Taunton, and Weston-super-Mare, along with those at Exeter, Plymouth, and Newport, Monmouthshire, were formed into the South-Western District, under the direction of Lt. Gen. H.E. Doherty, a Past Sovereign, of St. Peter and St. Paul Chapter. Even by present day standards of travel, it would be quite a task for an Inspector General to become familiar with and regularly visit all the Chapters in a 'Four County District'.

The District had a succession of four District Inspectors General before 1909 when re-structuring was carried out by SC, which resulted in the removal of the South Wales Chapters leaving Somerset, Devonshire and Cornwall as they were.

The first Grand Inspector General (a new form of title introduced at the turn of the century), resigned after two years. The appointment of a successor, Major George Davie, marked the beginning of a continuity of leadership that, apart from a short period, was to last for over 40 years. His reign was followed by that of Brigadier General C. L. Norman, for a term of 24 years.

His acceptance was no doubt welcomed by members of Supreme Council. If so their satisfaction was to be short lived. Four years after taking Office, Norman offered his resignation! The Grand Secretary General was promptly instructed to write: "....to beg you to remain as GIG anyhow for the present." The letter continued:

"They desired me to point out to you that, as you have attended all the Chapters so frequently during the last four years, it would not be necessary for you to get round your District more than once every three or four years taking only two or three each year as it may best suit your convenience taking your own time about it"

The content and tone of the letter clearly highlights the concern of SC at yet again having to face a management crisis.

Norman withdrew his resignation, combining his duties as Inspector General with that of Provincial Grand Master. However, he was obviously uneasy at the size of the District. Being only too pleased to oblige, SC once again introduced a re-structuring, this time removing Devon and Cornwall as one entity, and merging Wiltshire with Somerset.

It is interesting to note, that at the time, there were no Chapters in Wiltshire, nor for that matter at any time during Norman's tenure of office.

Bearing in mind that support for expansion should originate from a local source it can be argued that the membership at that time regarded their position as 'innovative and exclusive'. It is also worth considering that throughout the period under review, social conditions in the country encouraged differences in status, outlook, wealth, and occupation, factors that may well, have influenced thoughts of potential development.

To some extent this attitude may have prevailed amongst the Provincial Grand Masters of that time. From Adair in 1864 to Cazenove in 1961, all seven were members of the Order. Three were at various times members of Supreme Council, and one, as previously mentioned, combined the Offices of IG and PGM for eighteen years.

If there had been any enthusiasm amongst the membership for development, support from the Craft would surely have been forthcoming. Whatever the answer, be it poor management, be it elitism, the fifties saw a renaissance that was to lead progressively to the present structure of the District of Somerset.

Since 1953, when George Travers Biggs was appointed Inspector General, and under his direction the first Chapter for 85 years was Consecrated in Somerset, Estune Chapter No. 485 was warranted, there has been a steady and regular increase in the number of Chapters consecrated throughout the Province.

It can be seen that Somerset played a significant part in the development of the Ancient and Accepted Rite in Somerset, with many members holding office in the Supreme Council. Over the past few years St Peter and St Paul Chapter No. 6, which meets in Bath, have established a connection with Chapters No. 2 and 4, whose warrants were all issued on the same day in 1852, now regularly visit each other, somewhat easier now than it would have been possible 150 years ago.

To celebrate the millennium, Norman Wilkins the District Recorder wrote A History of the Ancient and Accepted Rite in Somerset, with material drawn from the various Chapters minutes. The book was published in 2000 and covers all the Chapters consecrated up to that year. Copies are currently still available from the District Recorder.

The Rose Croix is unlike any other Masonic degree as the candidate usually has to visit various rooms in the course of the ritual.

In England the first three degrees are not worked, the three degrees of Craft Masonry being regarded as equivalents. The fourth to seventeenth degrees are conferred by name, at the conclusion the candidate is told that the degree forms a fitting prelude to the principles of Christianity represented in the eighteenth degree (Rose Croix) which is worked in full.

The ritual teaches that salvation is only possible by following the principles of Christianity and the Candidate is invested with a rose pink collar, beautifully embroidered from which hangs the jewel of the degree.

Promotion to the thirtieth degree is conferred after a member has been Most Wise Sovereign of his chapter and been recommended by his Chapter for promotion. There is further promotion to the 31st, and 32nd degree, but this is very strictly limited.

Regalia for the 30th degree wear a heavily embroidered black sash together with a collarette on which is suspended a black eagle, the 31st has a white watered silk trimmed with gold and heavily embroidered accompanied by white collarette with a black eagle suspended. The 32nd degree members wear a black watered silk collar and a red silk collarette, with eagle.

The 33rd degree is only conferred when an Inspector General is created, and wears a white silk sash, a silver chain and eagle and a black cap.

Knights Templar

The full title of the Order is 'The United Religious, Military and Masonic Orders of the Temple and of St John of Jerusalem, Palestine, Rhodes and Malta in England and Wales and its Provinces Overseas'.

The Order is administered from Mark Masons' Hall, 86 St James's Street, London SW1A 1PL. As with other Orders it is headed by a Grand Master and is referred to as 'Great Priory'.

All candidates enter as Pilgrims and advance through the ceremony to Knighthood. On being installed every Knight is invested with the full Regalia. After being installed as a

Knight Templar he automatically furthers his knowledge of the Order by becoming a Knight of Malta. This Order traces the history of the Knights of Malta throughout the Mediterranean over a period of some 400 years. Regalia for Knights of Malta is not initially compulsory.

The Order officially supports one Charity, namely the St John of Jerusalem Eye Hospital, based in Jerusalem. This hospital provides ophthalmic care of high quality and relevance to people of the Holy Land irrespective of race, creed, social class or ability to pay. The support of the Knights Templar contributes to the general upkeep of the hospital as well as to the salaries of the medical staff.

You must be a Master Mason and a Royal Arch Companion and profess the Trinitarian Christian faith as the ceremony of Installation of a Knight, and all meetings, are conducted on the Gospel of St John Chapter 1 and the Precepts of the Order are founded on the book of Ephesians Chapter 6.

The military order of Knights Templar was founded in 1118, at the time of the Crusades. Their vocation was to defend Pilgrims travelling to the Holy Land from attacks of the Saracens. Knights took vows of poverty, chastity and obedience and were quartered in Jerusalem, believed to be on the site of King Solomon's Temple, from which their name was derived.

Over a period of time the Order became wealthy and its riches excited the greed of King Phillip of France who instructed Pope Clement V to summon the Grand Master of the Order before him. Accordingly the Grand Master,

Jacques de Molay, travelled from Cyprus and in 1340 he, together with 140 fellow Templars, was imprisoned. They were all subsequently executed with the Grand Master being burnt at the stake. The Order was falsely charged with the vilest of crimes, its property confiscated and distributed to the Hospitallers who had been bitter enemies of the Templars in Palestine.

The Province of Somerset was constituted in 1846 and is the second oldest Province in the Constitution of England, Wales and its Provinces Overseas. Earlier Templar activity in Somerset has been confirmed by Warrants issued in the 1790s to Encampments in Bath and Bridgwater.

During this period the Province had been named the Provincial Grand Conclave of Somerset, the Provincial Priory of Somerset, of Somerset and Monmouth, of Somerset Monmouth and South Wales and from 1953 Somerset once again. During the past 57 years the Province has been served by five Provincial Priors. The current Prior is Right Eminent Knight Barry Desmond Burridge who succeeded Right Eminent Knight Michael Veric Walsingham, Knight Commander of the United Orders, in 2006.

The Province comprises eleven Preceptories each meeting three or four times a year. Details and locations of each are contained in this booklet. The Somerset Reference Book contains all contact details for anyone seeking further information. The annual meeting of Provincial Priory is held on the second Monday in September during which Provincial Appointments and Promotions are conferred. The meeting is followed by lunch. Distinguished Knights throughout England and Wales are welcomed on these occasions and in 2009 guests included the Most Eminent and Supreme Grand Master of New South Wales and the Australian Capital Territories.

The Province also has the benefit of a thriving Preceptory of Improvement. This provides an excellent opportunity for Knights, yet to be installed in their respective Chairs, to be instructed, under the direction of qualified Preceptors, on both ceremonial and sword drill. Meetings are very enjoyable and very informal with only a sword and belt necessary

So why Join KT? Right Eminent Knight Barry Desmond Burridge, Provincial Prior for Somerset will tell you in his own words:

"As a young Freemason I was given the sound advice to think very carefully before accepting. Invitations to join other Orders and Degrees. Too many would lead to a dilution of both enjoyment and commitment. As a mature Mason I have joined more but nowhere near the number of invitations I have received".

"Why then Knights Templar? History and romance probably played a part but, more importantly, it was because I am very proud of my Freemasonry and Christian Faith both of which seem under continuous pressure in today's society."

"I knew, from the evening of my installation, I had made the correct decision. The ceremony is the most sincere, moving and complete I have been privileged to be part of. It encompasses all the disciplines, standards and beliefs that have formulated my life. Since that evening I have enjoyed the companionship of so many like-minded people from across the world."

"As a bond of friendship and as a bond of our Christian Faith at 5pm on Christmas Day every year individual Knights give a toast and remember Brother Knights everywhere."

"I look forward to the time when I welcome you into our wonderful Order and the Province of Somerset should you decide it is right for you."

In the minutes of the Lodge of Perpetual Friendship, meeting in Bridgwater, and founded in 1757, there is an entry for February 3rd 1819 of a Lodge of Emergency called to consider the propriety of painting the Lodge room at an estimate of £20. It was agreed to accept the estimate and to divide the expenses as follows: The Lodge to pay £6 and provide the paint, the Royal Arch Chapter to pay £10, and the Conclave £4.

The Conclave referred to is that of the Knights Templar, which met at the Lamb Inn, and the Lodge of Perpetual Friendship fortunately still retains and exhibits a number of shields belonging to this body, of which there appear to be no records extant. At the time it was apparently the custom for each new Conclave ruler to provide a shield with a relevant coat of arms. The shields are of hand painted metal and most are named; S. Croker, Col. Tynte, W. Stradling, Thomas Symes, Thomas Inman, J. Francis, and G.N. Lunn, and some dated. All those named were members of the Lodge of Perpetual Friendship. Colonel Tynte, Provincial Grand Master of Somerset from 1820 to 1860, later became a leading Knights Templar figure in the Country.

Holy Royal Arch Knight Templar Priests

The Holy Royal Arch Knight Templar Priests or Order of Holy Wisdom dates back to the late 1700s when the Irish Early Grand Encampment of Knights Templar and various Craft Lodges got together to confer this degree. From 1812 there was in Newcastle-on-Tyne a Council of Knights Grand Cross of the Holy Temple of Jerusalem which included Knight Templar Priests among its degrees.

From 1895 the Order prospered and in 1924 the present ruling body, Grand College, was formed in Newcastle-on-Tyne. It subsequently moved to York where it remains today. The Order is world wide with around 212 Tabernacles. It is presided over by a Grand High Priest and he is assisted by a Deputy Grand High Priest and an Assistant Grand High Priest. The Order is divided into Districts, each under the control of a Grand Superintendent. It is a Christian Order and gatherings are called Tabernacles. There are 32 degrees, the first 31 being conferred in name only in a short but impressive part of the ceremony.

The last degree is the one that is worked as the ceremony and consists mainly of readings from the Old and New Testaments while the Candidate is conducted around seven Pillars which are formed in a triangle. Each Pillar has a word referring to the Lamb of God who opened the seven seals revealing the various spirits of God.

The Symbol of the Order is an equilateral Triangle on which are inscribed certain letters alluding to the secrets of the Order.

The Master of the Tabernacle is called the High Priest. Under him are seven Pillars and a Conductor (equivalent to a Deacon). Regalia consists of a Knight Templar white tunic, with a red cross, and a plain white mantle. Knight Priests wear a mitre with a cross on the front and High Priests wear a taller mitre with a Patriarchal cross.

There are no Provincial Ranks but Grand Rank is generally conferred two years after going through the Chair. To qualify for membership one must be a subscribing Installed Master in the Craft, a subscribing Royal Arch Mason and a subscribing Knight Templar.

There are two Tabernacles in Somerset, King Ina which was formed in 1925 and King Edgar which was formed in 1965. Total membership is some 72. They are under the control of the Grand Superintendent for the South West.

Members see this Order as a logical extension to their Knights Templar membership, seeking further light and development of moral character.

The Masonic and Military Order of the Red Cross of Constantine and The Orders of the Holy Sepulchre and of St. John the Evangelist

Division of Somerset and Bristol

The Jewel of the Order

As with all Masonic Degrees and Orders, the precise dates and origins of this Order is difficult to determine accurately, but there is evidence of workings identifiable with the current rituals existing in the late 1700s.

The Grand Imperial Conclave of the Order, which is based at Mark Masons' Hall, St. James's Street, London, traces its succession of Grand Sovereigns back to 1868 and controls over 280 Conclaves in England and Wales, Benelux, South Africa, New Zealand, Jamaica and the Far East. It has contributed to the foundation of Sovereign Councils in other countries of Europe, Australia and North America.

The Order is organised into Divisions, each under the direction of an Intendant-General, there being 27 covering England and Wales and others spread widely overseas. Entry is open to Craft and Royal Arch Masons, who profess the Christian Trinitarian Faith.

The roll of conclaves lists the consecration, in 1868, of the Rose and Lily Conclave No. 10, meeting at Weston-super-Mare. This was followed in 1869 by the William de Irwin Conclave, No. 17, meeting in Bristol. Both were removed from the roll in 1923, but by that time the William de Irwin Conclave No. 162 had been constituted in Bath. This was the sole conclave in the Provinces of Somerset, Bristol, Dorset, Devon and Cornwall until the first Devonshire conclave was consecrated in 1966.

Rapid expansion in the western counties was to follow and the Division covering the Craft Province of Somerset is now that of Somerset and Bristol, comprising seven conclaves, as listed in the Provincial Year Book.

The events on which the traditional history of the Order is based took place early in the Fourth Century A.D. and were to have a profound effect on the history of Europe, and, indeed, the world, to the present day. In the year 306, the death of the Roman Emperor Constantius occurred whilst he was stationed at York. His son, Flavius Valerius Constantinus (Constantine) was thereupon proclaimed Caesar by the legions at York. However, the proclamation was opposed by competing claimants and Constantine, aware of disputes and treachery by his rivals remaining in Rome, was eventually compelled to return from his Western Province.

After a successful advance through Lombardy and cities of northern Italy, he faced the final stage of his entry into Rome itself and prepared for battle with a much larger pagan army under Maxentius at the Milvian Bridge, near Rome in 312. The traditional legend of his conversion to the Christian faith concerns the events prior to that battle. It is said that, during the progress of his campaign, Constantine was inspired by a Divine vision which led him to a decisive victory.

Constantine entered Rome in triumph on 29th October, 312, to the acclaim of the populace and Senate, and the triumphal arch raised three years later to commemorate this victory remains one of the landmarks of the city. His legacy to the Empire is distinguished by a series of acts bringing justice and enlightenment. His service to the Christian Faith started with the granting of toleration of Christianity in 313. Later, he directed that a Council of Bishops be convened; the result was the definition of the Nicene Creed in 325. In the latter days of his life he received baptism by the hand of Eusebius, Bishop of Nicomedia.

The Order of the Red Cross of Constantine represents a figurative pilgrimage by the candidate and celebrates the conversion of the Emperor and his subsequent achievements and is a fitting foundation for the Appendant Orders. As a Knight of the Holy Sepulchre, the candidate is instructed in the work of Constantine and his mother, St. Helena, in searching for the sacred sites associated with the passion of Our Lord and securing their protection.

It is customary for conferment of this Order to be followed immediately by that of Knight of St. John the Evangelist. Here, the candidate learns of a fruitless attempt by a later emperor to revert to paganism and makes a discovery leading to a striking interpretation of Craft and Royal Arch Masonry in a Christian context. Eventually, having progressed through the

various offices in his conclave, a Knight of the Order is eligible, subject to election by the members, to progress to the grade of Priest-Mason, as Viceroy of his conclave, and finally to Prince-Mason, when elected as Sovereign.

The Christian nature of the Order reinforces the work of many members who are involved in community service through their churches or independently, whilst the military aspect is reflected strongly in the enactment of the rituals.

The regalia consists of a sash and two jewels, with certain officers carrying swords. Charity is a high priority and the Grand Sovereign's Millennium Fund is targeted specifically towards the needs of children, the children's hospice at Charlton Farm, Wraxall, having been a recent beneficiary. The Division of Somerset and Bristol always gives support to the charitable work of the Craft.

The Order is recommended to all Christian Royal Arch Masons who are interested in expanding their knowledge and participating in ceremonies of great beauty and meaning.

It contains much to interest and involve the Mason of mature outlook, but not necessarily mature years, and offers a warm welcome to every Brother who seeks the fellowship and opportunities for learning which membership promises.

Royal and Select Masters

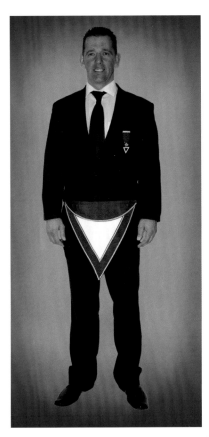

Nearly 200 years ago the degrees of Royal Master and Select Master appeared; travelling Masonic lecturers throughout the East were conferring them upon Masons, while engaging in instructing in Craft (Lodge) and Capitular (Chapter) degrees. Even one Supreme Council of the Scottish Rite included the degree of Select Master as one of its "detached" degrees. But, these beautiful degrees were not to remain detached for any length of time.

The state of Connecticut bore the first Grand Council in 1819. In Virginia and West Virginia the degrees developed in the Chapter of Royal Arch Masons where they still remain. In the 1870s a General Grand Council was formed for the United States of America.

Today this Grand Council numbers most of the Grand Councils in the United States, as well as the western section of Canada.

The Grand Council of Royal and Select Masters of England and Wales and Districts and Councils overseas was formally constituted in 1873 by four Councils chartered just two years earlier by the Grand Council of New York. They organized themselves into a sovereign body under the patronage of the Rev Canon G. R. Portal, Past Grand Master of the Grand Lodge of Mark Master Masons, who was installed as the Grand Master of the Order.

The degrees in this group are frequently referred to as 'Cryptic Degrees' two of which refer to a crypt. The degrees are the essential link between the degrees of Master Mason and Royal Arch Mason.

There are over 240 Councils under the Grand Council, administered from Mark Masons' Hall. The Statutory qualifications for membership are those of Mark Master Mason and Royal Arch Mason.

This Grand Council had its vicissitudes but continues to prosper and today has many Councils overseas which are controlled by District Grand Councils. It is somewhat surprising to note that to many, these ceremonies constitute nothing more than interesting side degrees or a random collection of unrelated incidents in the story of King Solomon's Temple, but to the serious and understanding Masonic student, they prove to be the essential link between the degrees of Master Mason and Royal Arch Mason.

The business of private councils is transacted in the degree of Select Master. Lodges of Most Excellent Master, Councils of Royal Masters and Councils of Super-Excellent Masters are opened only to admit candidates.

Select Master

Supposedly held in the secret vault which has been constructed beneath the temple consisting of several arches, into one of which the secrets were deposited and later discovered. The legend is similar to that of one of the degrees of the A and A Rite, and relates how a well known mason employed by King Solomon accidentally intruded into this crypt when King Solomon and Hiram, King of Tyre, were present.

The intruder was subsequently pardoned, but the Outer Guard who should have prevented his entry, was punished in his place.

Royal Master

This degree is set in time just prior to the completion and dedication of the first temple; it highlights the completed vessels pertaining to the House of the Lord and refers to a certain Fellowcraft making diligent enquiry of HA as to when he might receive the secrets of a MM. The subsequent deeply moving discourse by our Grand Master on the subject of death is one of the most enthralling pieces of ritual in Freemasonry. It also shows how the secrets came to be deposited in the crypt where they are subsequently found.

Most Excellent Master

Deals with the completion and dedication of the first Temple; it celebrates the completion of the whole edifice and mentions the installation of the Ark of the Covenant in the Most Holy Place. It constitutes a fitting ceremonial and dramatic preface to the Cryptic degrees.

Super Excellent Master

The legend around which this degree is built brings the story of the first Temple down to the time of its imminent destruction and refers to the siege of Jerusalem by the troops of the enraged Nebuchadnezzar, following the rebellion of the Tributary Jewish king, Zedekiah.

Regalia

On completion of the first Cryptic Degree of Select Master, a Companion is invested with the jewel of the Order, which consists of a skeleton equilateral triangle of white enamel, surmounted by a gold Imperial Crown suspended from a crimson ribbon. When he has passed through the remaining three Degrees, he is entitled to wear the triangular apron, which is of white kid with a border of crimson silk edged with gold braid.

At the end of August 2009, the District had 130 subscribing members spread over the five Councils, however several members hold multiple memberships giving a unique membership of 103.

Further information on the Order in Somerset is given on the website: www.somerset-wilts-rsm.org.uk.

The Order of the Allied Masonic Degrees

This précis has been written with acknowledgement of extracts from 'Freemasonry Today' issues 21 & 25

The Jewels of the Order

The Order of the Allied Masonic Degrees was established in 1879 although the degrees it works are much older and date before the establishment of United Grand Lodge. Before then the vast majority of 'side' degrees came under the control of the 'Antients' who entitled Craft Lodges to work any Masonic degree they had knowledge and members available who could work it. The focus of United Grand Lodge was towards the three Craft degrees and the Holy Royal Arch with no real interest outside and as a consequence there were a whole raft of separate and unattached orders working throughout the country.

The Order of the Allied Masonic Degrees was created with the agreement of United Grand Lodge with the charge that no new body purporting to be a Masonic body could be established without the consent of the governing bodies of the Knights Templar, the Ancient and Accepted Rite, the Mark Masters, the Red Cross of Constantine, the Royal and Select Masters, and that any new body established with such consent would be under the direction of the Grand Council of Order of the Allied Masonic Degrees

Originally the Order encompassed the Orders of Secret Monitor and the Knight Templar Priest. In 1925 the Knight Templar Priest degrees were given back to Grand College in Newcastle and in 1931 the degree of Secret Monitor was given independence.

Today the Order works five orders, St Lawrence the Martyr, Red Cross of Babylon, Knights of Constantinople, Grand Tilers of Solomon and Grand High Priest.

All of these orders predate Craft, Holy Royal Arch and Mark Master working as we now know them, and much in what is worked today have their origins in these degrees.

Membership of the Order requires that the candidate be a Companion of the Holy Royal Arch and a Mark Master Mason and is open to all faiths. The candidate is first admitted into the degree of St Lawrence the Martyr and the other four in any order. Having taken all five degrees the candidate is entitled to wear a jewel for each degree but nowadays a single composite jewel is worn. There is no other regalia other than collars signifying District or Grand rank. Councils are opened and closed in the order of St Lawrence the Martyr and in which all administrative business is conducted

The Allied Masonic Degrees Combined Jewel

St Lawrence the Martyr

What is really important about St Lawrence the Martyr is its possible link with our operative predecessors. Some form of this degree has been worked in England for over 200 years, principally in Yorkshire and Lancashire. While claims made by some that it has medieval origins are currently unsubstantiated, it may well be that the present version is a perpetuation of an operative degree. Moreover, the ritual suggests that the secrets of the degree, as featured in the opening of the Lodge, would have been of use by Operative Masons in proving themselves as they travelled around, distinguishing them from the increasing number of Speculative Freemasons. If so, this makes the degree of considerable historical importance as a link with our operative past and worth preserving for that alone.

Grand Tilers of Solomon

The full title of this degree is Grand Tilers of Solomon, or Masons Elect of Twenty-Seven. The provenance of the degree is clearly established from the USA, hence the American spelling of Tyler. It did not join the Allied Degrees until 1893. It is very similar in character to the Select Master degree of the Cryptic series and relates the legend of the accidental intrusion of a Mason into the Secret Vault beneath the Temple. The central characters represent Solomon, Hiram and Hiram Abif. This degree also has much in common with the degree of Intimate Secretary, the 6° of the Ancient and Accepted Rite.

Knights of Constantinople

The Knights of Constantinople is a genuine side-degree in that it was originally conferred by one Brother taking another aside, probably after a meeting in another degree. Its origin is uncertain, but the emphasis in its ritual on the equality of all men before God suggests an origin in the North of England, before it appeared in America, via Scotland, where it was being worked by 1830.

The Red Cross of Babylon

The ceremony is of a most profound and mystical nature consisting of three parts. It commences in a Royal Arch Council in Jerusalem where the Prelate presides over readings from the Book of Ezra and concludes at the Tribunal in Babylon of the Persian King Darius I. These two major scenes are linked by a short but important episode where the candidate is actually required to cross the bridge over a figurative river - either the Jordan or the Euphrates. This imagery of 'crossing the bridge' is a traditional feature to be found in all major religions of the world - the link between what man perceives and that which is beyond his perception. There is evidence that several Lodges in the late 1700s worked a knightly grade of 'passing the bridge'. This appears to have had a similar content to the degree of 'Knight of the Eagle' a degree later known as 'Knight of the Sword' and then as 'Knight of the Red Cross of Palestine'. The Red Cross of Babylon is similar in some respects to the 15th, 16th and 17th degrees of the Ancient & Accepted Rite, which also do not include the Holy Royal Arch.

The Holy Order of Grand High Priest

The ceremony is undoubtedly very old and is asserted to be an amalgamation of two separate degrees derived from the 'High Grades', which were invented on the Continent during the mid-eighteenth century. This particular French version found its way to Ireland where by 1780 it had become widespread. From there, it was carried to Scotland and to certain 'Antient' Lodges in the North-West of England where brethren were admitted under the authority of their Craft warrant. In addition, a similar but different version was transmitted to Newcastle around this time and was conferred as a Priesthood of the Holy Royal Arch Knight Templar Priests, a tradition that has been observed without interruption since 1810. The Order has an affinity with the Holy Royal Arch ritual but has a narrative that predates it.

The Allied Masonic Degrees and Bath

The Order of the Allied Masonic Degrees is represented by the Frederick Lace Council No 55, which meets three times a year on the third Tuesday in May and the third Monday in September and December, December being the installation meeting. The Council was consecrated in September 1948 and named after Frederick Lace, who was a prominent Mason in Bath and a surgeon. The Frederick Lace Council is part of the Severn District with seven other Councils – five in South Wales and two in Somerset – Nailsea and Taunton. The order is administered, like many other orders, from Mark Masons Hall.

The Order of the Secret Monitor
or Brotherhood of David and Jonathan

The Order of the Secret Monitor is Dutch in origin and was brought to England by Dr Zacharie on his return to this country after the American Civil War in about 1875. The Grand Council was formed in 1887.

The early years of the Order in this country were somewhat complicated, as the Grand Council of the Allied Masonic Degrees was also empowered to confer the degree.

In 1931, however, C.W. Napier-Clavering, who headed up both the Allied Masonic Degrees and this Order, arranged that the AMD gave up all rights to the Degree. Even today, however, a demonstration of the degree as originally performed is available to be given by the Allied Order to any Conclave which wishes to see it. The Order consists of three degrees, the First being that of Secret Monitor. This graphically describes how Jonathan warned David (in a secret manner, hence the name of the Order) not to return to King Saul's household. It is taken from the first book of Samuel. The lesson in the degree is the importance of friendship and fidelity.

The Second Degree is the Prince's Degree and tells how David received into his band a fugitive from a massacre carried out at the order of Saul. Also from the first book of Samuel, this degree again stresses the importance of friendship and fidelity.

The Third Degree is the Supreme Ruler's Degree and consists of the Installation ceremony of the Conclave. It is somewhat unique as, in addition to the Installation of the new Supreme Ruler by his predecessor, there is a ceremony of Commissioning.

This is carried out by a Grand Officer (usually the senior of those present) and gives rank and status throughout the Order. The new Supreme Ruler duly is presented with a Certificate from Grand Conclave to this effect.

The regalia for members is quite simple, consisting of a jewel suspended from a ribbon, different for each of the first two degrees. There is also a distinctive tie. The officers of the Conclave, Provincial and Grand Officers wear sashes of different colours.

In addition, the Supreme Ruler wears a robe and a collarette with a jewel suspended from it. The Grand Supreme Ruler, the Deputy Grand Supreme Ruler and Provincial Grand Supreme Ruler and his Deputy, on appropriate occasions wear robes, collarettes, chains and carry a baton. On less formal occasions they wear sashes rather than robes.

The Province of Somerset was Constituted on 30th October 2006, following the partitioning of the former Western Counties Province. At that time there were three Conclaves in the Province meeting at Keynsham, Taunton and Glastonbury. In 2008 a new Conclave was Consecrated at Nailsea. There are currently 94 subscribing members in the Province.

The Provincial Grand Conclave has an Annual Meeting in July of each year and recently an appeal fund has been set up to raise funds for a worthy local charity which will be presented at a future Provincial Meeting. At a local level, the Conclaves actively support their community by making appropriate charitable donations.

Members consider the Order as probably the most caring of all Masonic Orders, with each Conclave having four officers called Visiting Deacons, each of whom has responsibility for a quarter of the members of the Conclave.

Their duties consist 'of affording assistance and support to a Brother in time of sorrow or distress and to search out and warn him if he be exposed to danger, secret or apparent'. In practice, each Visiting Deacon must contact his members between each meeting, personally, by telephone or letter to find out if all is well, and if they are able to attend the next meeting.

At each meeting of the Conclave a roll-call of members is held and the Deacons report on their contact with the absentees, the reason for their absence and if they are in need of any help or assistance.

The order, which is an extremely happy and friendly one, is open to any Master Mason of good standing and the office of Supreme Ruler can be reached without having to have been through the chair of a Craft Lodge.

Societas Rosicruciana In Anglia
Paracelsus College

The college was consecrated at Taunton on March 3rd 1982 and remained there until the 9th of November 1996. The membership had changed from mainly Founders from Fevon to a majority of Fratres from the Somerset area, the Masonic Hall in Yatton was thus more central.

It now meets three times annually on the third Saturday in March, and June and the 4th Saturday in September and is a member of the Province of the South Western Counties, this consists of five colleges.

The Provinces are under the overall ruling of a High Council and Supreme Magus, the London HQ contains an extensive library from which books may be borrowed for further study.

With the exception of a personal breast jewel, regalia is supplied for all officers. Once a member passes the Chair of Celebrant he purchases a full length dark crimson robe to indicate he is now considered a teacher of the more junior members.

Rosicrucianism began in the early 17th century with three manifestos published during the period of the Reformation which was followed by the counter reformation.

On the continent of Europe this was at the time of the religious Thirty Years War and the English Civil War. Then, as now, religion was a cloak for political ambition but there was also an underlying struggle between forces who sought to control the way faith might be expressed and practised .

The author of the manifestos was a German Lutheran who displayed marked hostility to the Church of Rome as an institution but who advocated love to one's neighbour and a pious form of Christian life. At the centre of the manifestos is the person and the teaching of Jesus Christ. Thus we come to the first requirement of the Rosicrucian-he must be a believing and a practising Christian, this is an absolute necessity.

There were other basic rules for the subsequent fraternities which initially arose from people whose thoughts were as expressed in the manifestos. Paraphrased, the essentials of the true Rosicrucian are profession of the Trinitarian Christian faith, commitment to freely attend to the sick and study of the hidden mysteries of nature.

The healing of the sick now concerns the body, mind and spirit and study may include that of the universe and the spiritual world. Charitable contributions are left to the individual member's conscience and practice.

An extract from the first of several grades of membership states our aim as " to afford mutual aid and encouragement in working out the great problems of life and in searching out the secrets of nature, to facilitate the system of philosophy founded on the kabbalah and to investigate the meaning and symbolism of all that remains of the wisdom, art and literature of the ancient world"

One other essential in the UK and Ireland is that the candidate must be a Freemason.

The Royal Order of Scotland

The Royal Order of Scotland is governed by the Grand Lodge which directs operations from its prestigious headquarters at St. John Street, Edinburgh, a building that embodies the Chapel of St. John, and is believed to be the oldest purpose-built Masonic Lodge room in the world.

The Royal Order of Scotland occupies a unique position within Freemasonry and can rightfully claim to be a truly international Masonic body, controlling in excess of 90 Provincial Grand Lodges situated in 25 different countries across the globe. In addition, it is the only 'working' Grand Lodge in the world, admitting and promoting candidates into the two constituent degrees, as well as dealing with all administrative matters pertaining to the Order.

It can also claim to be senior to all other Masonic systems with the exception of the Craft, as authentic documentary proof exists in its archives indicating that the Order was active as early as 1741. This was substantiated in the form of a Patent of Appointment, dated 22nd July 1750, granted in London to a William Mitchell, empowering him to erect a Provincial Grand Lodge in The Hague, Holland, which was endorsed by the Provincial Grand Master of South Britain.

It appears that Mitchell later established a Province of the Order at Edinburgh and over the intervening fourteen-year period certain Scottish brethren were selected for admission, culminating in the erection of a Grand Lodge and Grand Chapter in 1767, when a new set of Laws for the government of the Order was prepared. It was at this meeting that the King of Scots was first specifically designated as Grand Master, the title of 'Royal Order of Scotland' was adopted, and the date of the annual meeting changed to the 4th July.

The 'Bruce' tradition was also embraced, and a new designation of Deputy Grand Master and Governor was instituted for the leader of the Order.

The Royal Order of Scotland exercises rule over two degrees: the candidate is first 'advanced' in a Chapter of 'The Heredom of Kilwinning', then subsequently 'promoted' to 'The Knighthood of the Rosy Cross' in Grand Lodge or its Provincial equivalent.

The Heredom of Kilwinning

This degree is traditionally associated with King David I of Scotland (1084-1153) and is of particular interest to students of Craft symbolism, as an extensive series of lectures meticulously examines the teachings of the Craft Degrees from a religious standpoint, as well as making many references to other degrees within Freemasonry, but with the difference that the symbolism employed moves from the Old Testament to the New Testament.

The candidate is admitted into the Chapter in the guise of a Master Mason and, after a long, perilous and mystical journey through deserts and over mountain tops, sustained by the source of the water of life, he finds himself in a visionary city under Divine rule where he is ultimately successful in identifying the 'Lost Word'.

The Knight of the Rosy Cross

The institution of this degree by King Robert the Bruce (1274-1329) following the Battle of Bannockburn is purely legendary and the conflict itself does not feature in the ritual but, as its name implies, the legend refers to a theme similarly found in the 18th degree of the Ancient and Accepted Rite.

Armed with sword and trowel, the aspirant knight kneels within a circle of assembled knights to take his obligation, after which the accolade is ceremonially bestowed by the Deputy Grand Master & Governor, or the Provincial Grand Master.

The statutory qualification for admission into the Royal Order of Scotland is that of being a Master Mason of five years standing. Membership is very highly prized among Freemasons worldwide and is a distinction granted by invitation only.

At the meetings of Grand Lodge and every Provincial Grand Lodge a vacant seat is permanently reserved for the Grand Master (the King of Scots) with the emblems of regality being placed in readiness upon his throne while the Banner of the Order reinforces the patriotic message of this unique brotherhood. Each member enjoys the privilege of individual recognition by the conferral of a descriptive 'characteristic', which is indicative of his calling, his personal qualities or his achievements.

The distinction is ratified when he is ennobled as a member of this genuine Order of Masonic knighthood, which is said to mirror the ancient ceremony of the Order of St. Andrew of the Thistle, originally attributed to Robert the Bruce.

There is little doubt that within the Royal Order of Scotland an ambiance exists which is seldom encountered within the confines of many other Orders. It is appropriately described as 'the highest and most sublime degree of Masonry' as its essence, symbolism and procedure, elevates Freemasonry from a simple system of morality based upon religion into the realms of true Christian Perfection, affording the vision of a divine church – not of this world, but of the mystical Kingdom of the Lord.

The Provincial Grand Lodge of the South Western Counties of England [Gloucestershire, Bristol, Somersetshire, Devonshire, and Cornwall)

Consecrated at the Masonic Hall, Bath on Friday, 15th October 1920 by the Deputy Grand Governor, R.W.Bro Col. The Rt. Hon. Earl of Kintore, and many of the most senior members of the Order. The consecration was followed by Luncheon priced at 4/- [20p] and tea after the Ceremony at 1/- [5p]. At this meeting ten brethren were advanced and promoted. From these early beginnings the Province has prospered and grown in membership.

Over the past 89 years it has been served by most of the distinguished brethren of the five Counties: To day, under the leadership of R.W.Bro Michael J. Flynn, JP, it continues to flourish strongly enjoying a membership of some 130 brethren who meet twice a year at Exmouth, in Devonshire in April and Nailsea in Somersetshire in October.

The Provincial Grand Lodge of Somerset

The Fingle Glen Hotel in Tedburn St Mary Devon was the venue on the 4th March 2009 for a unique event in British Freemasonry when a party of Grand Officers from The Royal Order of Scotland travelled from Edinburgh to perform a joint consecration of two new Provincial Grand Lodges of the Order, Cornwall and Somerset.

At the Consecration in March there were 27 Founders drawn from the Provincial Grand Lodges of SW Counties, Devon & Cornwall, Gloucestershire, South Wales, South Midlands and the Cotswolds, by the end of 2009 the membership stood at 56. The Provincial Grand Lodge of Somerset holds its meetings at the Masonic Hall Yatton on the 1st Monday in March and November and at other dates by direction of the Provincial Grand Master

The Worshipful Society of Free Masons Rough Masons, Wallers, Slaters, Paviors, Plaisterers and Bricklayers (The Operatives)

The Jewel of the Order

The Society is now approaching its centenary in 2013 and expects to total nearly 100 Assemblages by that date. It had no regular headquarters for many years and this resulted in much history being lost. It is now up to date with a website at www.operatives.org.uk and much information can there be found. Wherever possible all communications are made via the world-wide web.

Since 1913 the Society has been organized on a national basis. We are members of the Province of Western Counties and South Wales. The names of all Assemblages reflect existing or former stone quarries or significant man-made structures. Spelling of some of the words used reflects much earlier usage. The officer who would be called the DC in other Lodges is called the Super-Intendent and Ancient is "Antient".

The Assemblage was constituted on 30th March 2006, and meets at the Burnham-on Sea Masonic Hall three times annually on the first fifth Tuesday January to May, the third Tuesday in June and the first fifth Tuesday in September to November.

At its start the Society's founders were a small group of like-minded Masons, most of whom were members of the fast-disappearing Guild of Operative Masons. Several origins are put forward for the origins of Freemasonry and the claim of the early Guilds of stonemasons would seem to have as legitimate claim as any others. These founders were concerned that what was still known of the practices and usages of the Guilds was in need of preservation and the Society was formed for that purpose.

The Society feels that large numbers of members are not always advantageous. Far better to bring into your midst those whose ideas and Masonic interests you can be assured. The Society avoids uncertainty by stipulating that all candidates must already be members of Craft, Royal Arch and Mark Masonry so they will know what they are getting into and have already demonstrated their commitment to the Masonic idea.

Unlike many other Orders in Freemasonry there is recognition that age alone does not prevent any member from progressing to the highest of seven grades. Provided any of its VI degree grade of 90 years or more are still active and attending their Assemblages they can still be awarded the highest honour of VII degree

Honoris Causa. At every level members receive documentary proof in the form of Certificates personally signed by each of the three Grand Master Masons.

The Society appoints no "Past" ranks, once retired from office members return to work and dine "in the quarries". We have a seven grade system of progression, most business is conducted in a single Assemblage of Lodges IV degree to I degree. The layout varies with each grade worked and it is probably true to say that the amount of equipment used to carry out Operatives ceremonies is in excess of that required by most other Orders of Freemasonry. Moreover, it is of full size i.e. it is big enough to be used in the construction of actual buildings.

The Super-Intendent's (DC) bench is large, on and around which are placed a large variety of ashlars, mauls, plumb lines, floorcloths, gauges and tools.

On the other hand, the regalia worn by the Operatives is comparatively simple, Indentured Apprentices wear just a loose blue cord around their necks from which the suspend the "jewel" of their rank as they progress. Those of Vo and above wear their "jewels" from a light blue collarette; most of these are made of iron or are silver coloured, those of Grade VII are gold coloured.

The gauges used are worthy of special mention. These large wooden frames - similar in design to the jewels of the various grades are used by the Wardens and Super-Intendent to symbolically "test" a candidate to show he is fitted to form part of the "Temple of God". It is considered important and it should be noted that among the aims of all Operatives is self improvement. Thus, a candidate - a rough and unpolished ashlar-may arrive at such perfection that he will be fitted to form a perfect ashlar in Thy Eternal Temple (part of the initiation prayer).

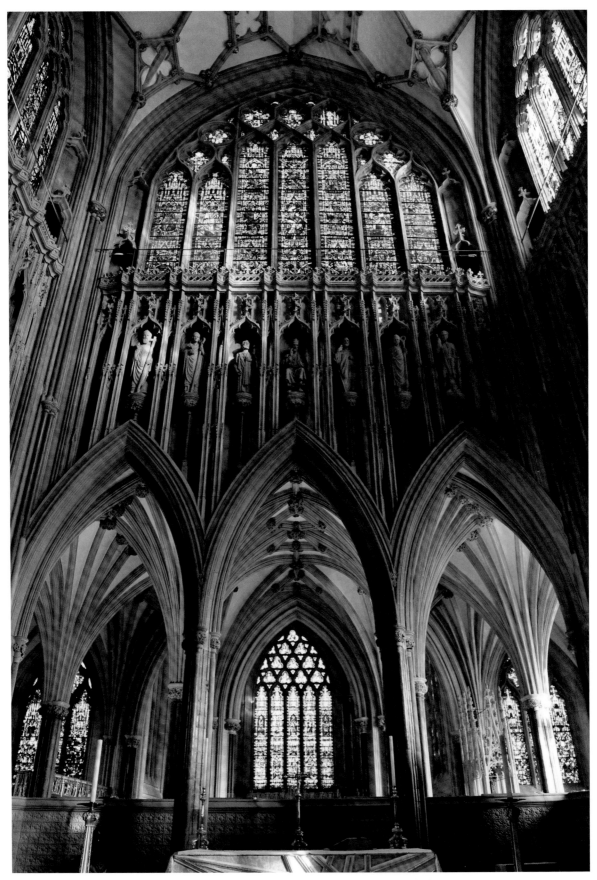

Oh Wonderful Masons - The Altar, Wells Cathedral

Part Six

APPENDICES

The Masonic Widows Association

Eileen Jackson, Chairlady of the North Somerset Branch

1996 the Provincial Grand Lodge of Somerset established a Masonic Widows Association within Somerset, and in total eleven Branches were formed. The Association is indebted to the late John Upward who, as Provincial Grand Charity Steward at the time, took so much effort and trouble in setting up the Branches over a two year period.

The Branches were to include widows of former members of all Craft Lodges and Side Degrees of the individual areas, and also to include any other Masonic widows living within that area.

The MWA has its rules and constitution, and each Branch has a liaison officer and committee, which usually comprises of up to ten members with four officers, namely chairlady, vice chair, secretary and treasurer.

The Association aims to provide an organisation that affords friendship for widows of Freemasons and to provide comfort and companionship to members if in distress. In addition the aim is to provide a programme of speakers, demonstrations and social activities throughout the year.

Each branch has its own individuality and is responsible for the running of its own group independently of the Masons. The Masons of the Province do however support the Association at all times, particularly with annual contributions to running costs and by attending social functions, for which we are extremely grateful, especially for their thoughts and support at Christmas.

The MWA has adopted the broken column as its 'Badge', which identifies the wearer as a Masonic Widow. The broken column brooch or 'Masonic Widow's Pin' was created as an emblem to symbolise the Masons' continued concern and honour for the widow of a Brother Mason. It is an emblem which is worn with pride on all appropriate occasions, especially when travelling, so that the wearer may be recognised, greeted and assisted when necessary by Masonic friends throughout the world.

The brooch was first used in the American Civil War by the ladies of Freemasons who were at war. As many did not return, the ladies continued to wear the brooch, and it was gradually accepted throughout the United States of America and Canada. Its use was first introduced into Britain by a member of the Earl of Chester Lodge No. 1565 and is now having wide acceptance across the country.

The millennium year was a special time for all members of the MWA, and to mark this important occasion the North Somerset Branch invited all the branches in Somerset to join them for a celebration lunch. Such occasions afford the opportunity to meet socially and to exchange views and ideas. Annual meetings are also held with fellow groups from Bristol, Gloucestershire, Wiltshire and Somerset. In addition, North Somerset has close links with groups in Birmingham, Rugby, Devon and Cornwall.

These links have also extended to trips away, including many wonderful holidays together as a group both in the UK and abroad; memories of Switzerland, Germany, Italy and Ireland to name but a few will remain, especially with those widows who would not have ventured there on their own.

Always of concern are those less fortunate than ourselves, and as such a good deal of money is raised for charity, and there is a good welfare service for members who are sick, disabled or need help in any way, not forgetting those who can no longer attend our regular monthly meetings.

The aim of the MWA for the future is to strengthen the ties of friendship both near and far, to continue with and to improve the ongoing commitment to welfare work, and in the wider world to continue to work and raise money for charity.

This will stimulate and give the widows the opportunity to 'forget for a while' their own needs and give them gladness and happiness in helping others. Forming a Masonic Widows Association is one of the best gifts given to the widows by the Masons. It gives us the opportunity to meet other ladies in the similar situation of widowhood, regarded as the most devastating time in their lives when they feel alone and isolated having lost their "soul mate".

It is a gift which for which I personally am most grateful; it has made provision for a new and full life, albeit a very different one.

The Pendant and Brooch of the Masonic Widows Association

The London Grand Rank Association

Somerset Group

The Association was formed by London Masons who were governed by the Assistant Grand Master and who had been appointed to London Grand Rank or promoted to Senior London Grand Rank. There are no past ranks in London as in the Provinces. London Grand Rank Officers are put forward for appointment by each respective London Lodge on an annual basis, which is quite restrictive.

The Association conforms to the normal practise of the London Grand Rank Association except that the Somerset Group does have a greater number of guests and ladies at its meetings, which do tend to be Social.

To be a full member of the Association, including Somerset, the member must be a life member of the Association. However any Master Mason may join, by becoming what is known as a Bulletin Member as outlined in the Group's by-Laws. These members however do not have voting rights within the Association.

At the present date there are some 40 active members within the Association who travel from all parts of the South West; not for every meeting but in general for at least three meetings a year.

Although not great in numbers, members do manage to give a Christmas gift to each of the group's widows, and have made donations to the Children's Hospice South West and to the Pro Grand Masters Discretionary Fund, which has been donated to the RCFDM Patient Welfare Fund for Soldiers, Sailors, and Airmen and Women who have been wounded and passed through that organisation. Charitable donations are also given to guest speakers' charity funds.

The Association's role in the community is to foster good relations and understanding between all Freemasons of whatever standing and through them good relationships with non-Masonic guests.

Eligible Provincial Craft Masons should consider becoming members in order to broaden their outlook with the London Masons, and to reach a common understanding that the differences between London and the Provinces are insignificant in respect of the working within lodges. We all work to be common brothers in trust, love of life, liberty and understanding between all men and women of every nation.

The Somerset Group was set up specifically to give the London Grand Rank Masons who have in general retired, or are working in the South West, a local meeting place to socialise, even if they are not in any Somerset or Provincial Lodge

The Somerset Group of the London Grand Rank Association came into being on the 8th of November 1984 when a group of London Grand Rank Freemasons met at the Shrubbery Hotel in Ilminster Somerset and formed the 1st committee. These were the founding members of the group which also came under auspices of the London Grand Rank Association at Great Queen Street London. The Right Worshipful Provincial Grand Master of Somerset and the Most Excellent Grand Superintendent for the Province of Somerset are invited to become Honorary Members during their term of office.

It must be stated at this point that the Association is not a Lodge as such and members do not wear regalia at their meetings.

Also within the group are London Grand Rank Masons who live in Dorset and join in the Somerset Group as Somerset members did with the Devon Fraternity. This makes for quite a large contingent and members endeavour to support charities within their area as well as Somerset and Devon.

Prior to the formation of the Somerset London Grand Rank, members either attended the London Quarterly meetings or visited the Devon Fraternity, where they were well received.

Eventually the cost of travel either to Exeter for the Devon meetings or to London was becoming expensive and time consuming. It must also be remembered that the majority of the members are retired and on fixed incomes, although Returns of the group are also made to the London office for inclusion in the Quarterly Meetings which either the Secretary or a designated member should attend

The Group still meets four times a year at its original meeting place, the Shrubbery Hotel in Ilminster. The members meet, have Coffee and biscuits, renew old friendships and make new ones. They have a talk of any one of numerous subjects, after which they have lunch. The meetings are well attended by members, wives and guests.

At least once a year the Group endeavours to make the meeting purely Masonic, when a Masonic Lecture./ Talk is given. At these meetings non-Masons and wives are not invited.

The average attendance at the Group's meetings is some 40 members and guests, rising to 60 to 70 for the December meeting.

The Somerset Masonic Bowling Association

Meets at the Shepton Mallet Bowling Club

The inaugural meeting of the Somerset Masonic Bowling Association was held at the Morlands Sports Club now called Wyrral Park in Glastonbury on June 18th 1952.

W.Bro Procter under the Presidency of R.W.Bro Brigadier General C.L. Norman called the meeting. At that meeting W.Bro Procter was elected Chairman of the Club with Bro Siddle as the first Honorary Secretary. The first game of bowls was held at the Clevedon Club Pavilion on the 23rd August 1952. Lodges from the South of the Province competed against Lodges from the North but regrettably no record of the score could be found!

The AGM that followed in Frome in May 1953, set the subscriptions at 5/- (25p) per annum and a joining fee of half a guinea (52.5p.) The present subscriptions in 2010 has risen to £10 per annum.

In the early days it was decided by the Club committee to limit the activities of the Association to organising competitions between its members, to be run as the Middleton Cup. 1953 saw the club membership rise to 60 members. In 1958 the Club minutes record the first time that the ladies were thanked for providing refreshments. They do of course continue to provide refreshments for which the Club remains extremely grateful.

1962 saw the introduction of area representatives, which has not changed to this day. The names and contact telephone numbers are published in the Provincial Year Book. Following the death of the founding Secretary the Club decided to expand its activities and in 1969 coach travel was introduced and matches were arranged against the Provinces of Cornwall, Hampshire, Gloucestershire, Wiltshire, Worcester and Wales.

The Association Chairman, W.Bro Norman Warry seen here sitting in the Bowling Wheelchair with members looking on (W.Bro Michael Adams to the right)

These Club activities continued in a similar manner until 2002 when W.Bro Norman Warry was elected Chairman and W.Bro Michael Adams Honorary Secretary.

The internal matches no longer occur but a varied programme of matches are now arranged between various Provincial Clubs (on approximately a fortnightly basis) throughout the bowling season with visits to Wiltshire, Cardiff, Gloucester, Portsmouth, Berkshire and Bristol. All home fixtures are now held at the Shepton Mallet Bowling Club venue. Under the guidance of the Tour manager W.Bro Michael Adams the Club has now visited Bournemouth, Tenerife, Cyprus and The Isle of Wight.

Although not set up to support charitable organizations the SMBA has always given freely to Charities from its inception. The first donation was 60 guineas (£63) made in 1958 to the Mark Master Masons Festival. Donations were made to various Masonic causes and during the present Festival (2007) the SMBA donated in the region of £4,000 which enabled the Provincial Grand Master R.W.Bro David L. Jenkins to present the Association with an Acorn badge.

The latest acquisition, a Bowling Wheelchair, was bought by the Association in 2008, it is permanently held at Shepton Mallet and is available for any player to use at that venue. It has already been used by a member of the Association after not being able to play Bowls for a number of years.

In recent years the Associations activities have been extend to include matches between the Craft and Mark Master Masons, both outdoors and indoors, with two games every year played indoors between the Craft, captained by the Provincial Grand Master R.W.Bro David L. Jenkins, and the Bowling Association.

The Association has had great success in these matches, prompting the Provincial Grand Master to suggest that the equivalent to a Bowls Lodge of Instruction should be arranged for the Craft team.

The SMBA is open to all brethren in the Province of Somerset, young and old. The area representative's details can be found in the Provincial Year Book.

Thomas Harper - who was he?

Reproduced with grateful thanks to W.Bro F. Austin of the Thomas Harper Lodge

Scholars will find references to R.W.Bro Thomas Harper in both the Antient and Modern Grand Lodge Records and also in the writings of many Masonic authors. His Masonic activities spanned a period of more than 70 years, the importance of which can only be briefly illustrated.

He was born of humble parents and sadly nothing is known of them or his upbringing, although we are aware of ongoing research. Thomas Harper was initiated in 1761 into Lodge No. 24 which at that time met at the Bush Inn, Marsh Street, Bristol. A few years later he was in Charlestown, South Carolina and was the first Junior Warden of Lodge No. 190.

There is also mention that he was involved in the Holy Royal Arch in this same period of the 1770s. He was a most influential member of the Grand Master's Lodge No. 1 on the Atholl Register, now No. 1 on the Register of the United Grand Lodge of England. He was honoured in September 1785, at the age 50, as a Grand Lodge Officer under the Atholl Society, being made Junior Grand Warden. He became Master of this Lodge in 1793 and in 1794 was elected Treasurer, holding office with distinction for 35 years.

He was actively involved in other Lodges including Globe Lodge, now No. 23, under the banner of the Moderns' Grand Lodge. He served as Master in 1793 and acted as Grand Steward in 1796. He joined the Lodge of Antiquity in 1792, now Lodge No. 2, and from 1797 until 1801 was Treasurer. He had a long association with Nine Muses Lodge, now No. 235, first joining in 1800 and served as Secretary in 1801, when his very good friend Chevalier Bartholomew Ruspini was Master

(the Founder of the RMIG). He was expelled by the Moderns' Grand Lodge in 1803 from all lodges under their control, however this was removed in 1810. He immediately rejoined Nine Muses Lodge and in 1814 was elected Deputy Master

This foundation provided a wealth of knowledge and experience as well as a solid schooling for what was to come. There can be no doubt he was a skilful mediator and when W.Bro William Dickey, Deputy Grand Master, died suddenly in 1801, he was hurriedly thrust into the appointment of Deputy Grand Master.

Thoughts in the Masonic world and in the mind of W.Bro Harper turned to a single Masonic authority. It was commonly known that he shared the same aspirations as his late friend W.Bro Lawrence Dermott, who been Grand Secretary and Deputy Grand Master until 1797. Dermott had openly recognised the need for universal agreement between Masons of all denominations with an adherence to the ancient Laws, if the Order were to survive.

Thomas Harper served Craft Masonry with distinction, honour, energy and dedication and from a position of considerable knowledge and authority he worked to that end. He was one of the assessors who prepared the Articles of Union and subsequently became one of its signatories in 1813.

It is recorded in the minute book of the Antient Grand Lodge that, at an especial Grand Lodge of the Most Antient and Honourable Fraternity of Free and Accepted Masons according to the Old Institutions, held on Thursday 23rd December 1813, the R.W.Bro Thomas Harper DGM in the chair, the Duke of Sussex, Grand Master of the other (Modern) Grand Lodge being present as a visitor, it was Resolved Unanimously that the cordial thanks of this Grand Lodge be given the R.W.Bro Thomas Harper for his indefatigable, zealous and honourable conduct during a period of more than 28 years that he had been an Officer of this Grand Lodge but more especially for his unwearied attention for the last thirteen years in the discharge of the arduous and important duties of Deputy Grand Master.

That the members of this Grand Lodge were led to the performance of this duty peculiarly gratifying to them from the high sense they entertain of the purity of the principles from which he has acted, from their unqualified admiration of the talents and eloquence which he has constantly displayed on their behalf and from the pleasing anticipation of those happy and glorious consequences which his exertions have so eminently contributed to produce. A resounding tribute indeed.

After the Union Thomas Harper was elected annually to the Board of General Purposes or to the Board of Finance and frequently presided over the Lodge of Benevolence until 1831. He passed to the Grand Lodge above on the 25th April 1832 at the age of 96.

In business Thomas Harper was a very successful silversmith, first registering his mark at Goldsmiths Hall on May 27th 1790. The mark consists of T.H. in a plain oblong. A version of this hallmark is now owned by Thomas Harper Lodge whose motto is Scientia Ditat means Knowledge Enriches, it being used on silver objects of virtue sponsored by the Lodge for charitable purposes. It is known that Thomas Harper was in practice whilst in America. The South Carolina Gazette in January 1773, carried an advert describing him as a working jeweller and goldsmith.

To the immense pleasure of all Masonic jewel collectors many of his jewels survive and are much sought after

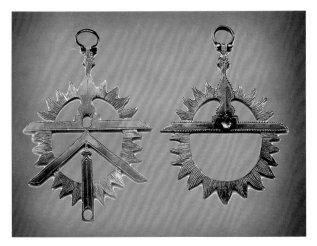

The Long Closing

Brethren, you are now about to quit this safe retreat of peace and friendship and to mix again with the busy world. Amidst all its cares and employments, forget not those sacred duties which have been so frequently inculcated, and so strongly recommended in your Lodges. Be ye therefore discreet, prudent and temperate. Remember that at this pedestal you have solemnly and voluntarily vowed to relieve and befriend with unhesitating cordiality, every Brother who might need your assistance.

Remember too, that you have promised to remind him in the most gentle manner of his failings and to aid and vindicate his character whenever wrongfully traduced. To suggest the most candid, the most palliating and the most favourable circumstances, even when his conduct is justly liable to reprehension and blame. Thus shall the world see how dearly Freemasons love each other. But, my Brethren, you are expected to extend these noble and generous statements still further. Let me impress upon your minds and may it be instilled into your hearts, that every Brother has a just claim on your kind offices.

I therefore trust that you will be good to all; more particularly do I recommend to your care, the Household of the Faithful. That by diligence and fidelity in the duties of your respective vocations, by liberal benevolence and diffusive charity, by constancy and sincerity in your friendships and a uniformly kind, just, amiable and virtuous deportment, you will prove to the world the happy and beneficial effects of our Ancient and Honourable Institution.

Let it not be said that you laboured in vain nor wasted your strength for naught, for your work is before the Lord and your recompense is with God. Finally Brethren, be of one mind; live in peace and may the God of love and mercy delight to dwell among you and bless you forever more.

Amen, Amen, So Mote it be. So say we all in Charity.